PERPLEXING PLOTS

FILM AND CULTURE

FILM AND CULTURE

A series of Columbia University Press

Edited by John Belton

For a complete list of titles, see page 493

PERPLEXING PLOTS

*Popular Storytelling and
the Poetics of Murder*

DAVID BORDWELL

Columbia University Press
New York

Columbia University Press
Publishers Since 1893
New York   Chichester, West Sussex
cup.columbia.edu

Library of Congress Cataloging-in-Publication Data
Names: Bordwell, David, author.
Title: Perplexing plots : popular storytelling and the poetics of murder /
    David Bordwell.
Description: New York : Columbia University Press, 2022. | Series: Film and
    culture series | Includes index.
Identifiers: LCCN 2022008825 | ISBN 9780231206587 (hardback) |
    ISBN 9780231206594 (trade paperback) | ISBN 9780231556552 (ebook)
Subjects: LCSH: Detective and mystery stories, American—History and
    criticism. | American literature—20th century—History and criticism. |
    Narration (Rhetoric)—History—20th century. | Popular culture—United
    States—History—20th century. | Detective and mystery
    stories—Authorship. | Motion picture authorship. | Motion picture
    plays—Technique. | United States—Civilization—20th century.
Classification: LCC PS374.D4 B67 2022 | DDC 813/.087209—dc23/eng/20220525
LC record available at https://lccn.loc.gov/2022008825

Cover design: Elliott S. Cairns
Cover image: 20th Century Fox/Photofest

For James Naremore
Man of letters and
man of the cinema ॐ

There are thirty-two ways to write a story, and I've used every one, but there is only one plot—things are not as they seem.

—Jim Thompson

CONTENTS

ACKNOWLEDGMENTS

This book goes back sixty years in my life. In high school I started reading mysteries, modernist fiction, and literary criticism while I was also getting interested in film. College and graduate school intensified my curiosity about all of the above. A full list of debts would go on for a very long time. Here are the prime ones.

Claude Held, eminent bookseller of Buffalo, kindly filled orders sent in cash, sometimes coins, from a fourteen-year-old. I still have the books he mailed to our farm. I also owe a debt to my teachers, particularly Fred Silva and Pat Ward of the State University of New York at Albany and Angelo Bertocci of the University of Iowa.

As usual, I'm grateful to my stimulating colleagues in the University of Wisconsin–Madison Department of Communication Arts: Ben Brewster, Kelley Conway, Erik Gunneson, Meg Hamel, Jim Healy, Michele Hilmes, Eric Hoyt, Vance Kepley, Lea Jacobs, Mike King, J. J. Murphy, Ben Reiser, James Runde, and Ben Singer. Hours of talk with Jeff Smith, fellow mystery addict and connoisseur of popular fiction generally, improved this book immeasurably.

On other campuses, I benefited from audiences responding to ideas I tried out in lectures. So thanks to Dan Morgan and colleagues and students at the University of Chicago, to Sean O'Sullivan and colleagues and students at the Ohio State University, and to members of the Society for Cognitive Studies of the Moving Image at our 2019 conference at the University of Hamburg.

As usual, archives have given me more than I can properly acknowledge. At the Wisconsin Center for Film and Theater Research, Mary Huelsback and Amanda Smith were ever ready to answer my questions and find obscure material. At George Eastman House, old friends Paolo Cherchi Usai and Jared Case of the Moving Image department helped me view *The Gangsters and the Girl*, a real discovery conserved by the late James Card. Thanks as well to Stéphanie Cudré-Mauroux of the Archives Littéraires Suisse for assistance with Patricia Highsmith's collection.

At the Library of Congress John W. Kluge Center, I benefited enormously from holding the Chair of Modern Culture in early 2017. I enjoyed my time with other fellows and Ted Widmer, the director, as well as Mary Lou Reker, Dan Turello, Travis Hensley, and Emily Coccia. Ensconced in the Motion Picture, Broadcasting, and Recorded Sound Division, watching movies by the hour, I was helped at every turn by Greg Lukow, Mike Mashon, Karen Fishman, Alan Gevinson, Dorinda Hartmann (supreme Nero Wolfe expert), Zoran Sinobad, Josie Walters-Johnston, and Rosemary Hanes.

My debt to the Kinematek of Belgium, under both Gabrielle Claes and Nicola Mazzanti, remains overwhelming. Through the decades its lively staff have made working there a profound pleasure. In Antwerp, I developed some of the book's ideas in lectures at the Summer Film College. Thanks as ever to Bart Versteirt, Tom Paulus, Anke Brouwers, Steven Jacobs, David Vandenbossche, Stef Franck, Cristina Álvarez López, Adrian Martin, and all the other cinephiles who make this annual gathering delightful.

For permission to reproduce published material, I'm grateful to Sarah Baxter of the Society of Authors, Denis Kitchen, and Carl E. Gropper of Will Eisner Studios, Inc.

Brian Boyd, Peter Brooks, Charlie Keil, William Luhr, Jason Mittell, Geoffrey O'Brien, and Amanda Shubert offered detailed suggestions on specific chapters, and Malcolm Turvey provided acute commentary on the first half of the book. In addition, I much appreciate information, advice, and support provided by Adam Burr, Charles Barr, Maria Belodubrovskaya, Guy Borlée, Tim Brayton, Peter Cowie, Jim Danky, Gian Luca Farinelli, Kaitlin Fyfe, Sidney Gottlieb, Sabine Gross, Mike Grost, Tom Gunning, Gregory Hartig, Scott Higgins, Glenn Kenny, Richard Koszarski, Casey Long, Paul McEwan, John McCartney, Michaela Mikalauski, Mark Minnett, Richard Neupert, David Pierce, Prednisone, Phil Rosen, Murray Smith, Kat Spring, Janet Staiger, Geoffrey Warda, Sarah Weinman, and Joseph Wiesenfarth.

Two pen pals have had their own parts to play. Martin Edwards, supreme expert on the history of mystery, kindly shared early access to his extraordinary *The Life of Crime: Unravelling the Mysteries of Fiction's Favourite Genre* (2022). Meir Sternberg's *Expositional Modes and Temporal Ordering in Fiction* (1978) and his magisterial articles on narrative poetics have shaped my research for decades. Correspondence with him has been one of the great pleasures of my academic life.

Going beyond the call of friendship, Jim Naremore read the entire manuscript. Twice. He offered the best thing a writer can get: generous encouragement laced with precise criticism.

Series editor John Belton, another old friend, vigorously supported the book and drew on his deep knowledge of film history to help sharpen my case. Philip Leventhal, senior editor, handled this project with a care and dispatch rare in publishing. Thanks as well to Monique Briones. Columbia University Press should be proud of them all.

My sisters Diane Verma and Darlene Bordwell, two tough femme fatales, grew up loving mysteries as much as I did. (Special thanks to Diane for steering me to Laura Lippman.) My wife Kristin Thompson enjoys mysteries too. Although she supported this project with love and good humor, she must at times have wanted the author to finally close the damn case.

* * *

Madison, Wisconsin
Spring 2022
Portions of chapters 8, 9, and 11 have appeared on www.davidbordwell.net, but they have been revised and updated for publication here.

PERPLEXING
PLOTS

INTRODUCTION

Mass Art as Experimental Storytelling

It's not a trick; it's flair.

—Jonathan Gash

"**A**hhh!"
        It was Friday, October 14, 1994, and my first encounter with *Pulp Fiction* was coming to a close. The two hitmen were relaxing in a diner discussing the virtues of pork products. One went to the toilet; one remained behind (fig. 0.1). Suddenly the scene exploded (fig. 0.2).

Abruptly the audience (me too) realized that the meandering story lines we'd been tracking were knit into an earlier scene. The collective *Ahhh* came because we had seen the beginning of that scene about two hours ago (fig. 0.3). We had totally forgotten about it.

Why had we forgotten? Openings should be memorable. But the scene was fairly brief; it came before the credits; it wasn't alluded to again; the hitmen weren't shown as being present; and we had a lot to keep track of in what followed. So we had the pleasure of finishing off a form that had been left suspended. The movie had a better memory of itself than we did.

Since that Friday night, I've become more aware of how popular cinema has found ways to engage us in nonlinear storytelling. Time juggling and shifting viewpoints and replayed scenes have long been associated with literary

0.1 *Pulp Fiction*: While Vincent goes to the toilet, Jules broods on his decision to quit the criminal life.

0.2 Abruptly, Pumpkin and Honey Bunny leap out of their booth and launch the robbery.

0.3 At the end of the prologue, *Pulp Fiction* freezes the frame on Honey Bunny screeching out orders, leaving the action suspended.

modernism and the avant-garde. When such formal strategies show up in popular media, they're usually treated as being pilfered from highbrow sources. Sometimes that's the case, but just as often we find that mass-market narratives have tried in their own ways to push storytelling off the linear path for several centuries. One task of this book is to show that writers and filmmakers haven't shrunk from the search for unpredictable ways to satisfy our narrative appetites.

Satisfaction is essential. Popular narrative won't aim at the severity, the downright difficulty, that we associate with High Modernism. Hollywood doesn't have a Woolf or a Faulkner, but neither does most of literature. Much of what we find among "ambitious" literature and drama reveals efforts to stretch boundaries, play with conventions, and revise traditional devices in ways that yield new but not thoroughly disorienting pleasures.

I think that was part of what audiences admired in *Pulp Fiction*. Apart from the clever dialogue, the shocking situations (all that heroin, all that blood), and the self-conscious pop-culture citations, there was an effort to surprise us through formal ingenuity. Start with the replayed diner scene. A simple readjustment does the trick. Pull something out of the climax, slide it to the beginning of the movie, and just let it sit there for a couple of hours. The pleasure is that of a piece clicking into place: the pleasure of artistic form, with the audience given a burst of insight into how the contraption worked. The *Ahhh* was in part a recognition that we were abruptly completing the movie's shape, collaborating with the filmmakers in refocusing the experience.

This book is about how that process works—about how storytellers in the twentieth and twenty-first centuries have coaxed audiences into collaborating with them in filling out form in unusual ways. I hope to show how stories at all levels of appeal have prompted readers and viewers to acquire skills in grappling with narrative innovations. One genre in particular devotes itself almost wholly to cultivating an appreciation of formal artifice. That genre rests on the promise of murder.

An Age of Complex Narratives

Pulp Fiction's suspension of the diner opening wasn't the only thing that could flummox viewers. The film's labeled chapters introduce us to a batch of characters whose relations are revealed only gradually.

A more linear and omniscient version of the story action would start with the two hitmen, Jules and Vincent. They kill nearly all the preppy punks who have stolen Marcellus Wallace's briefcase. After Vincent accidentally shoots their captive Marvin, they clean their car at Jimmie and Bonnie's home. Then they visit the diner and interrupt the holdup launched by Pumpkin and Honey

Bunny. The following night, Vincent takes Marcellus's wife Mia out to dinner and saves her from a heroin overdose. On a later night, Butch Coolidge flees the prizefight he was to have thrown for Marcellus. The next day, returning to get his watch from his apartment, Butch finds Vincent there. He shoots Vincent and flees but then runs into Marcellus. Both men are captured by the sadistic Zed and Maynard. Butch manages to rescue Marcellus and earn his forgiveness for not throwing the fight. Butch and his girlfriend Fabienne leave town.

This story world presents a fairly dispersed social network, sixteen people connected by love, acquaintance, work, or mere accident. But the screenplay by Quentin Tarantino and Roger Avary complicates our access to that world. Chapter titles tag each episode, although not always at the beginning. There's no clearly defined single protagonist; each chapter attaches us to a different character or pairing of characters. In addition, the plot we encounter scrambles the order of events; for instance, scenes showing Vincent alive follow the scene in which he's killed. Thanks to time juggling, portions of incidents—the killing of the preppies, the opening dialogue of Honey Bunny and Pumpkin—are replayed.

For all its novelty, the film draws on techniques of storytelling that have been around for millennia. The choices are basic. One protagonist, two, or several? What story world do the characters inhabit? (Here, the petty underworld; disorganized crime, we might say.) These are choices about the "what" of our tale.

But there's also the "how" of storytelling: How shall we order the story events in the plot we put before our audience? How shall they be narrated? How shall we segment the plot into parts (scenes, chapters, time periods)? At the most fine-grained level, how shall we handle style—the use of language in prose, the panoply of techniques of the theater, the images and sounds of film? On top of this, how self-conscious should we make the narration? Should we, as *Pulp Fiction* does, tease the audience to assemble the story parts, to play the game of form with some awareness?

Every filmmaker has to decide on all these matters. Tarantino's choices revealed an array of options that other filmmakers took up. *The Usual Suspects* (1995), *The Matrix* (1999), *Memento* (2000), *Adaptation* (2002), *Primer* (2004), and many other films of the 1990s and 2000s signaled a trend of "new narrative complexity" in American cinema. They had counterparts elsewhere, as in *Chungking Express* (1994) and *Run Lola Run* (1998). Nonlinearity became a badge of honor; viewpoint breakdowns were welcomed; twists came to be expected. Form, people started to say, was the new content.[1]

These films and others changed what storytellers thought a movie (or TV show or comic book or novel) might be. By 2010 Linda Aronson's plump manual, *The 21st Century Screenplay*, could lay out a dizzying menu of narrative options.[2] Beyond "conventional narrative structure" the book distinguishes among parallel narratives, tandem narratives, multiple-protagonist narratives, double-journey narratives, flashback narratives, consecutive story narratives, and fractured tandem narratives.

Aronson's categories can be contested, but her effort marks an important historical change. Although many eras hosted a wide range of narrative strategies, the very idea of mounting such a baroque taxonomy seemed to have been demanded by the sheer diversity of recent developments. What made her book possible was the dazzling range of storytelling possibilities that became prominent in mainstream American cinema.

High, Low, Middle, and Everything in Between

These options weren't absolutely new. Every fresh wrinkle has precedents. The fronting of the Pumpkin/Honey Bunny dialogue looks less unusual when we recall Philip Macdonald's novel *The Rynox Mystery* (1933), which begins with an epilogue and ends with a prologue, or Richard Hull's *Last First* (1947), which presents the book's last chapter at the beginning. The fracturing of viewpoint, the replay of key events, the shuffling of temporal order, and the deployment of flashbacks all have precedents in films, plays, and novels, particularly in stories of mystery and crime. Just as Tarantino's *Reservoir Dogs* drew on the heist novel *Clean Break* (1955) and the movie *The Killing* (1955), so *Pulp Fiction* owes a debt to the hard-boiled experiments of Richard Stark.

In an earlier book I traced some cinematic sources. *The Way Hollywood Tells It* argued that the innovations of the 1990s were a crystallization of possibilities that had been floated throughout American studio filmmaking.[3] I suggested in passing that the 1940s was another such era of coalescence. Eventually I devoted another book, *Reinventing Hollywood*, to making the case for the breadth of storytelling experiments in that era.[4]

While writing the 1940s book, I started to realize that I was tracking an energy that rippled far beyond cinema. There was a vein of intriguing narrative experiment surging through other mass media. The overall effect was to create a tradition that informed popular culture in ways I hadn't seen acknowledged.

I use the term "popular narrative" to refer to stories that belong to "mass art." This is the name Noël Carroll assigns to a cultural production that is created for large audiences, usually by mechanical reproduction, and that exhibits a high degree of accessibility.[5] It is "exoteric" storytelling, as opposed to the "esoteric" modes we find in avant-garde literature, film, theater, and kindred media.

In the twentieth century, a long-entrenched story posited esoteric storytelling, most evident in High Modernism of the 1920s, as the cutting edge of literary value. The ambitious work, seeking to expose new aspects of the world and complex states of mind, needed techniques more complex than traditional methods. The thousands of other novels, short stories, and plays were genre pieces, mass literature, or "lowbrow" art. In cinema, it's the split between art-house films and multiplex fare: *Three Colors: Blue* (1993) versus *Jaws* (1975). The distinction encouraged critics to divide their labor. If they paused to examine an exoteric novel or play or film, they usually focused on its social significance, as a reflection of cultural attitudes or anxieties. Form and style went unexamined or were ritually denounced as pat formulas.

"They wanted literature to be difficult," complained J. B. Priestley of the interwar modernists.[6] Some will reply that popular writers want literature to be too easy. The disparity goes back very far and was spelled out in responses to nineteenth-century British sensation literature; call it the Collins test. An anonymous reviewer wrote this of *The Woman in White*: "Mr. Wilkie Collins is an admirable story-teller, though he is not a great novelist. His plots are framed with artistic ingenuity—he unfolds them bit by bit, clearly and with great care—and each chapter is a most skillful sequel to the chapter before. . . . The fascination which he exercises over the mind of his reader consists in this—that he is a good constructor."[7] This distinction between artist and mere storyteller, the serious book and the page turner, true artistry and facile ingenuity would haunt critical commentary ever after.

Yet it's not hard to find examples that fall in between. For example, admirers of reflexive form, or stories that self-consciously point to their own artifice, might look to André Gide's *Counterfeiters* (1925), an account (among other things) of a young man's efforts to write a novel that may be the one we are reading. But we can find something similar in Arnold Gingrich's *Cast Down the Laurel* (1935). Part 1 consists of a dossier of background material a writer has supplied to his friend. Part 2 consists of the friend's finished novella. In Part 3, the first author criticizes the use the novelist has made of his notes.

Cut-rate Gide, some might say. And bargain-basement Pirandello might be the accusation slung at *All Star Cast*, a 1936 novel by Naomi Royde Smith. The entire action takes place during the performance of a play: The viewpoint is that of a critic in the audience, but the scenes are rendered as if in a novel. We remain attached to the critic during the intermissions, when he grabs a drink and chats with other playgoers. The novel ends with him, exulting in his first chance to publish a review, reflecting on whether criticism can do justice to the thrill of the stage. The publisher announced that *All Star Cast* was a novel "in a new form."[8]

These works are, we might say today, quirky. They require a little getting used to, and they call attention to their mildly daring forms. But they aren't formidable. Their path between hard and easy is usually characterized as middlebrow. For some purposes, this concept can be helpful, but for my purposes here, it's too confining.

For one thing, the idea of middlebrow emerged most fully in Anglo-American mass culture debates of the 1940s. (I trace some implications of that in chapter 3.) The broader application of the term has increasingly seemed problematic. The more we explore the actual output of storytelling in all dimensions—high, low, middle—the less helpful the three-bin model seems. For one thing, the middlebrow is rather hard to define in terms of narrative form. It's more plausible as a description of audience appeal and the forces that shape taste cultures.[9] One scholar, for instance, has defined "the feminine middlebrow novel" as addressed to a middle-class woman reader.[10] Worthwhile research into the middlebrow register has studied the rise of the Modern Library, the Book-of-the-Month Club, literary magazines, quality paperbacks, the British Broadcasting Corporation, and other institutions of distribution and "aspirational" marketing.[11]

Part of the problem is our tendency to think with vivid prototypes. The monumental cultural status of Ulysses, The Waves, and The Sound and the Fury can lead us to elevate only one model of modernism. But after reading dozens of novels and plays from the 1900s through the 1930s, I confess that I am unable to draw firm lines with less forbidding texts. Is the "human fugue" of Aldous Huxley's Point Counter Point (1928) middlebrow? Sensed as modern, if not modernist, at the time, it certainly affords us the comfort of satire.

Staying with literature, how about Evelyn Waugh or Kay Boyle or even F. Scott Fitzgerald, whose Great Gatsby (1925) is far less fragmentary on the surface than This Side of Paradise (1920), with its embedded playscript? What of The Grapes of Wrath (1939), the best-seller that deploys John Dos Passos's montage principles in less abrasive ways? Or is perhaps Dos Passos's U.S.A. trilogy itself a doorstop-sized lump of middlebrow? Djuna Barnes's Nightwood (1936) is a modernist classic, but it seems to me to be closer to The Good Soldier (1915) than to Ulysses. The clipped diction and opaque psychology of Henry Green's Party Going (1939) are a little forbidding, but the novel's action can be grasped as a revision of the converging-fates network of Grand Hotel (1929).

In short, avowedly modernist works are often more dependent on mainstream appeals than we notice. Inversely, some exoteric works possess more intricacy and imagination, not to mention delight, than we find in "difficult" but pedestrian modernist clones. As Carroll puts it, not wholly as a wisecrack, what's so great about difficulty in itself?[12]

The problem is even more acute if we want to understand cinema. Mainstream films are made for a larger audience than all but the biggest-selling novel can hope for, so we should expect that novels considered middlebrow such as The Magnificent Ambersons (1942) and The Godfather (1969) can yield accomplished movies. And when we get to the pulpy fictions behind Pulp Fiction, when we look closely at Clean Break and the Stark novels, we realize that fascinating storytelling strategies are at work there too.

I should admit that I succumbed to a version of the three-bin model in my 1940s book, invoking an idea of "middlebrow modernism" prevalent in the mass media from the 1920s on. It was useful for characterizing certain works, but now I find it lacking in the nuances I want to pursue here. A better model for *Perplexing Plots*, I came to realize, was supplied by the film critics I wrote about in *The Rhapsodes: How 1940s Critics Changed American Film Culture* (2016).

In the midst of the high-and-low debates, these writers largely sidestepped the problems of defining mass culture and high art. Through unusually close attention to the films' look and sound, their plots and performances, the critics could reveal the skill and power of Hollywood cinema. James Agee could show the achievement of Chaplin in *Monsieur Verdoux* (1947) without worrying whether Chaplin had declined from being a popular artist to one straining for something higher. Otis Ferguson on *The Little Foxes* (1941) and Manny Farber on John Huston's films exposed undisclosed nuances of form, style, and theme in the Hollywood product. In a series of dazzling readings, Parker Tyler, a homegrown Surrealist, played with the high/low/middlebrow distinction by showing that studio cinema harbored aesthetic resources of a wildness not easily available to avant-garde work. These critics, committed to finding artistry in popular forms, left it to the reader to decide what label to apply, if any. Why should we feel any more constrained by the lumpy categories that have hung on for eighty years?

For such reasons, drawing a bright line between popular narrative and its Other(s) isn't as useful for my purposes as analyzing congruence and difference along particular dimensions. The task calls to mind Ludwig Wittgenstein's famous effort to specify the concept of "game": "a complicated network of similarities overlapping and criss-crossing."[13] We can trace threads of this network, find nodes and knots, tease out fine-grained differences. Those analytical discoveries, not gross categorization, can yield the subtlety we should seek. Studying popular narrative through the varying demands of immediate problems and long-range traditions should lead us to expect a lot of blurred boundaries between the esoteric and the exoteric. For the sake of clarity, I employ the modernist label when sketching patterns of change, but I try to sustain a sense of affinities and creative choices that make such a label provisional or partial. Everything may not be a mash-up, but as the web slogan suggests, there are a great many crossovers.

Welcome to the Variorum

Let's assume, then, that many stories in all media are unusual but not intimidating, "challenging" but still "accessible." To clarify the situation, we can ask, "Through what storytelling strategies do all narratives elicit understanding?" In other words, what can make stories difficult?

I'll assume that one prototypical plot presents characters with traits, dispositions, bodies, and other equipment. The characters formulate goals and plans, and they encounter obstacles and conflicts in the course of their efforts. Other characters serve as adversaries, onlookers, judges, helpers, or meddlers. The plot resolves into a fairly stable situation but not necessarily a happy ending. By default, the incidents proceed in chronological (linear) order, and the presentation of the whole narrative, in prose or pictures or audiovisual media, coaxes us to infer a coherent plot, transmitted reliably. Phases of the action are broken into well-defined portions (a novel's paragraphs and chapters, a play's acts, a film's sequences).

The result is what we might call the easiest narrative. It's an ideal type, not a primal source. A great many narratives across the world conform to its principles, and it's by no stretch lacking in power. Turning against the critical traditions that favor roundabout storytelling, Meir Sternberg has shown that this model of narrative offers abundant opportunities for rich, complex experiences.[14] For my purposes, this norm serves as a convenient point of reference for tracing creative options open to storytellers.[15]

Of course easiest narratives aren't all that common, especially in an age of complex storytelling. All the parameters I've mentioned are manipulated by many of the stories we encounter.[16] We can meet characters whose goals are obscure, whose plans are ineffectual, and who shrink from conflict and turn into their own worst enemy. The plot may end ambiguously, and we may be denied information about why things turned out that way. Scenes can be juggled out of order, presented from different viewpoints, or floated as imaginary or hypothetical. Some of these options are common enough to constitute a menu of alternatives, at least for some periods or genres. And those in turn can be rejigged to become more or less difficult.

It's essential to acknowledge that popular narrative has its own experimental wing that is not beholden to modernism. When we find some novelty in an exoteric narrative, especially one labeled middlebrow, we usually think we're seeing techniques swiped from the avant-garde but also dumbed down. *Cast Down the Laurel* and *All-Star Cast*, published in the 1930s, seem to exemplify a calculated repurposing of 1920s modernist techniques for easy assimilation. But I argue that if we attend to technique we find innovations in genre fiction that constitute fresh strategies for making stories—strategies built on the conventions of the genre.

Just as the modernist was pushed to challenge the public, exoteric art has its own pressures toward novelty. Like the avant-garde, our mass-market storytellers have always played with form, and they have been keenly aware of the power of structure and style. The evidence is in the works, as well as in testimony from the creators. Genre artists are often more probing and precise about technique than are academic commentators. Dorothy Sayers, Patricia Highsmith, and

Raymond Chandler are acute analysts of their craft. Their comments point us directly toward an approach that treats storytellers as posing problems shaped by immediate purposes, weighing means against ends, and finding pragmatic solutions that can be points of departure for other artisans. Thus does a drive to novelty fuel a broader tradition.

This book is about how that tradition has changed in Anglo-American popular storytelling in the twentieth century. To keep things manageable, I look at the three broad strategies I've mentioned in regard to *Pulp Fiction*: the temporal structuring of the plot, the use of point of view, and the segmentation of the narrative into more or less explicit parts. How are the incidents arranged—chronologically or not? How is story information transmitted (or withheld) via narration?[17] How does the film or play or novel articulate its parts to present a sharply contoured pattern?[18] Examining these matters of form and style can help explain how storytellers delineate character, build conflict, and arouse our emotions. Broaching them explicitly will expose, I hope, not only some basic resources of all storytelling but some distinctive menus of options favored in certain genres, periods, or places.

By focusing on craft options, we'll find support for the idea floated by many scholars in recent years that what was called modernism borrows at least as much from popular forms as exoteric storytelling takes from prestige narrative. I argue that some modernist innovations in literature, such as nonlinear plotting or dispersal of viewpoint, rework conventions already abroad in mass-audience fiction. To understand the array of narrative options open to creators, we must consider that storytelling at all levels of access, from esoteric to exoteric, relies on techniques of form and style that are revised to yield new experiences. Some have argued that Ezra Pound's command for modern writers to "Make It New" presupposes that the "it" is nothing less than tradition.[19]

When revisions of tradition proliferate, they create what I call a *variorum*, a sort of menu of favored and less-common options. If the easiest narrative operates as a default, the sanctioned alternatives fan out into a variorum. Linda Aronson's *21st-Century Screenplay* is in effect an account of the contemporary screenplay variorum. The variants we find will, inevitably, explore the possibilities of linearity, viewpoint, and other craft strategies charted long ago by academic thinkers and self-aware practitioners.

Popular narrative can innovate on several fronts. Most of the variety in both exoteric and esoteric storytelling probably comes from devising fresh themes, subjects, and story worlds. The narrative artist can treat a subject of current concern, for example, illegal immigration in the United States, or a fresh theme, such as the tensions of racial identity, or an unfamiliar setting, such as an immigration post on the Southwest U.S. border. The storyteller will be alert for what's sometimes called the zeitgeist: ideas and images floating through the culture. These can become material for plots and characterization. For *Loves Music,*

Loves to Dance (1991), Mary Higgins Clark realized that a social trend, personal ads seeking romance, could be the basis of a serial-killer plot.[20]

Such new material is often enough to sustain a story on its own. The popular storyteller can use familiar norms of technique to throw the new material into relief. We "read past" conventions of structure and style to the characters, settings, and ideas that seem fresh. For example, Nella Larsen's *Passing* (1929) focuses on a woman reflecting on whether a fascinating, manipulative friend is loyal to her. This situation gains new force by activating conflicts specific to a community in which some Black women must choose whether to pass for white.

Inversely, the more esoteric work can use subjects, themes, and new story worlds to reward us for grappling with more difficult devices. Would Joseph Conrad's experiments in time jumping and viewpoint have found a wide readership if they weren't presenting seafaring adventures set in exotic locations? It's probably not accidental that the "art films" of the 1950s and 1960s such as *Hiroshima mon amour*, *L'Avventura*, and *À Bout de souffle* flaunted sexuality while exploring unusual formal strategies. Which impulse was the alibi for the other? My concern is mostly with technique, but throughout what follows I try to show how that interacts with subject matter, themes, and story worlds to seize audiences.

Clearly, technical innovations can come from within popular storytelling—the variorum supplied by the medium or adjacent popular media. Alternatively, we expect that popular storytellers will sometimes innovate by adapting techniques from "higher" arts, particularly those identified with modernism or the avant-garde. Those techniques, we say, will be made "accessible." Part of my task is to show some concrete ways in which that happens. But we'll also find that creators of those more prestigious stories are borrowing from popular sources as well. It's all a big swap meet, resulting in a vast number of hybrids and crossovers as narrative artists seize on and reshape whatever they find to fulfill their purposes.

Weren't We Always Smart?

All that from the side of the storyteller. What about the reader or spectator? The rise of complex stories raises the obvious question of how we learned to understand and enjoy them.

Steven Johnson has argued that popular culture became "smarter" after the 1970s, as exemplified in the difference between *All in the Family* and *The Simpsons*.[21] Several factors enabled audiences to keep up with the new narrative demands. There was a rise in IQ scores, a new intellectual flexibility born of computer games such as Tetris, and a sense that the old popular culture of TV sitcoms and ordinary movies no longer offered much intellectual challenge. Johnson points to other conditions as well, such as an escalation effect provided by the internet, which coaxed consumers to dig deeper into the music and stories they loved.

I find a lot to agree with in Johnson's case, but historical evidence suggests that we've managed tricky story techniques in many genres for a long time. In the film *Memento* (2000), Johnson finds a "blisteringly complex narrative," presumably not just because it's a mystery but because it presents story events in reverse order. Yet as early as 1914, a drama critic asked why no writers had pursued the possibility of telling a story backward.[22] A little later, several writers did. Zoë Akins's play *The Varying Shore* (1921) begins with the death of a woman and moves back through her life, ending with her at age seventeen. The chapters of Rex Stout's novel *Seed on the Wind* (1930) follow reverse order in telling of a woman who wants to bear children outside marriage. In 1934 W. R. Burnett published the novel *Goodbye to the Past*, and George S. Kaufman and Moss Hart staged their play *Merrily We Roll Along*. Both depended on 3-2-1 chronologies.

The evidence is overpowering that at least since the nineteenth century large segments of Western audiences could track fairly complex narratives of many sorts. Maybe long before: Icelandic sagas offer vast genealogies and intricately braided plots akin to what's on display in *The Lord of the Rings*.[23] In any case, in chapter 1, I show that a good deal of early twentieth-century storytelling has offered the kind of challenges to easy, linear presentation that Johnson finds in recent years. If we look just at the examples I've mentioned, we have to conclude that some authors in all registers and at many times have made demands not alien to what we find in Indie Cinema and Peak TV. Yes, people nowadays have learned to cope with complex narratives. My claim is that across history they've done that before, again and again—provided that certain conditions are met.

What conditions? The story I'd tell, in brief, would go like this.

A storytelling innovation typically must be balanced by cues for comprehension. The avant-garde artist deprives us of a lot of those cues, but the exoteric artist can't afford to do so. Christopher Nolan speaks for this breed when he says that his first feature, *Following* (1998), "had structural complexity that they could understand."[24]

To give viewers that understanding, novelty needs a strong dose of familiarity. We know that mass-market storytelling must be accessible to broad audiences. One task I undertake here is to show some principles of narrative that can ease audiences' engagement. I want to "operationalize" accessibility, to show how concrete technical options, in particular historical circumstances, have made stories user-friendly.

Access doesn't equal mechanical predictability. No form is utterly a formula; every story has to be minimally different from others. A mass market in narrative demands novelty, the variorum I mentioned. To generate that variety, and in response to the pressures of a given task, the storyteller takes from tradition a *schema*, a pattern of action or presentation, and revises it in certain ways.

This way of explaining stability and change is pretty common in the arts. Charles Rosen notes that Haydn, Mozart, and Beethoven recast the cadences of Baroque music by inserting new material that strengthened the process of key modulation.[25] Ernst H. Gombrich, from whom I borrow the term *schema*, shows that pictorial patterns serve as inherited points of departure in visual art, with the revisions of these schemas yielding stylistic differences.[26] The "type-scenes" analyzed by biblical scholars, such as the betrothal, and the folktale formulas studied by anthropologists, such as the three-wishes tale, function as recurring patterns that get reworked for the purposes of a particular story.[27] Schemas include but aren't limited to what we usually call influences. Influences tend to be one-off inputs, but schemas form a body of options felt as part of tradition.[28]

Most storytellers are content to replicate their schemas with minimal alteration. If the storyteller wants to revise a schema more drastically, other schemas need to be left untouched. For instance, it's not accidental that mystery stories are drawn to tricky shufflings of viewpoint or chronology. A plotline built on a detective's present-time inquiry into past events helps us understand when the order of events is rearranged or character perspective changes. Knowledge of the genre facilitates accessibility, which in turn throws any new wrinkle into relief.

Genres often rely on story schemas familiar from folktales and fairy stories.[29] The road movie embodies the journey schema; the romantic comedy activates prototype stories of courtship. *Memento* is a variant of the quest, as is the "Gold Watch" episode of *Pulp Fiction*. Other sections of Tarantino's film incorporate the prototype of the raid (the hitmen's invasion), the rescue of the princess (Vincent's saving Mia's life), and the recourse to a wizard to solve a problem (help from Mr. Wolf in "The Bonnie Situation"). This is not to subscribe to the supreme power of an *Ur*-narrative or archetype, such as that of the Hero's Journey.[30] It's instead to propose, as the literary theorist Victor Shklovsky suggested, that storytellers grab schemas opportunistically, weaving them in or bolting them on to fill out their plots and provoke particular responses.[31]

Along with genre conventions and familiar action prototypes, a story's more distinctive design features can lead us to grasp the novelty. Repetition, emphasis, and other aspects of structure and style can make the unfamiliar aspects of a film or novel manageable. Because beginnings are privileged moments, Nolan christens *Memento* with a Polaroid photo decomposing from a clear image back into a blank surface. Our first encounter with the film announces a reversed time scheme. Nolan says he asked himself, "How can I help the audience watch this movie?"[32]

Pulp Fiction helps us in similar ways. At one point, the plot concludes the Butch story by showing him driving off with Fabienne. We are shifted back to an earlier story line, the one in which Jules and Vincent seize the briefcase from the fugitive preppies. At this point, we have to grasp the jump back as part of the film's narrational norm. How to firmly establish such a shift? Usually, through repetition.

Tarantino could simply have cut back to show the fourth preppy popping out of the bedroom and firing at Jules and Vincent. This is the crucial "miracle" that will lead to Jules's decision to give up gang life. Instead, before that assault Tarantino replays a stretch of the earlier scene in which Jules torments Rex and delivers his scriptural declaration of vengeance. Now, however, he's heard off-screen while the concealed preppy feverishly listens and decides whether to intervene (figs. 0.4 and 0.5).

0.4 During the interrogation of the preppies, Jules tells his target, "Yes, you did, Rex. You tried to fuck Marcellus Wallace."

0.5 At the beginning of the replay, that line and the rest of Jules's speech is repeated off-screen as the panicky hidden preppy listens and wonders what to do.

Genre factors surely govern this repetition. We can group what's going on because we know about gunplay in crime movies. But the replay fulfills local functions too. For one thing, it reminds us of Jules's reliance on his recitation as a rote vindication of his crime career. (That reminder will be fresh in our minds when, in the diner, he reinterprets the biblical passage as a sign to give up the criminal life.) In addition, there's suspense. Tarantino could have simply rerun the earlier scene in the main room and let us be surprised by the concealed preppy bursting in. Instead, the film gains tension by revealing that there's another man in the apartment, attaching us to his viewpoint, and letting us wonder if he'll dare to attack. Surprise has been discarded in favor of suspense.

The replay yields a more basic benefit. By repeating the earlier scene, Tarantino firmly links this moment to what we've already witnessed. We can master the jump back in time—showing us Vincent alive after we've just seen Butch kill him—because it provides continuity with the gunfire we've seen suspended before. Extending the replay reassures us that we are filling in a coherent line of action.

Repetitions like this help anchor us elsewhere in the film, as when in the diner climax we hear "*Garçon!*" somewhat before Pumpkin and Honey Bunny start their holdup. The more general principle is that genre conventions and specific choices about story and style, such as redundant cueing, can help us make sense of fresh revisions of storytelling schemas. The mass-audience storyteller balances the need for novelty with enough familiarity to ease comprehension. When many fictions in many media find ways to do this—when a variorum takes shape—audiences of any era can keep up. Apart from the difficulties of measuring human intelligence by IQ, the abilities it tries to track are probably less important than experience with the norms and forms of popular storytelling at different periods.

The urge to revise inherited devices is part of the tradition. What Hollywood screenwriters baptized as the "switcheroo" was the tweaking of a familiar device. In comedy, it was "a new different gag based on an old one."[33] More broadly, popular storytellers search for new ways to achieve established purposes. In lighting *Smash-Up: The Story of a Woman* (1947), the cinematographer Stanley Cortez sought to convey the heroine's disorientation without recourse to subjective imagery. "I didn't want to do the cliché thing and show her distorted impressions, but convey her thoughts with abstract play of lights alone."[34]

After innovations are assimilated, they can become familiar and can anchor fresh novelties. By 1994, Tarantino's time jumps were accessible to viewers because of the previous development of storytelling norms in film and other media. As novelists, playwrights, and filmmakers expand their powers of narrative experiment, audiences become more aware of the variorum. They can grasp tweaks and twists on what they've seen before.

Once we understand that chunks of story action can be rearranged, we can tolerate the absence of certain cues. For example, *Memento* could have tagged its episodes with titles emphasizing the reverse chronology, but it doesn't. Instead, Nolan resorts to the sort of repetition/redundancy that Tarantino applied. When we return to a previously suspended scene, Nolan activates our memory by replaying the tail end of the earlier fragment, with a bit of repeated sound. Without those overlaps to orient us, the film would have been far harder to grasp.

Similarly, Nolan complicates his task by incorporating a forward-moving story line as well. ABC scenes are sandwiched in between the 3-2-1 ones. To make the parallel structure more comprehensible, the forward-moving time line is in black-and-white, whereas the retrograde one is in full color. By withdrawing some cues but supplying fresh ones to compensate, the pleasurably difficult film teaches us how to watch it.

Intrinsic Norms: Teaching Us the Rules

This process extends across history. Johnson rightly indicates that we learn as readers and spectators. Once *Hill Street Blues* encouraged viewers to track multiple story lines, he suggests, later shows such as *The Sopranos* and *The Wire* could be more elliptical and fragmentary. Whether or not we got smarter, we did master new skills.

In fact, we've all been learning for a long while. Perhaps narrative complexity builds in waves across history and eddies out in different media at different rates. For example, although most Hollywood films of the 1930s had resolutely linear plots, a few films—*The Power and the Glory* (1933), *The Sin of Nora Moran* (1933), and *Dangerous Corner* (1934)—played with time more daringly.[35] By the 1940s, those films' innovations had become far more common, even deplored as routine. Their schemas could be further revised by overseas filmmakers such as Resnais and Godard.

If audiences learn, so do storytellers. After all, they're part of the audience. The dynamic give-and-take has been well described by Luis Buñuel's screenwriter Jean-Claude Carrière: "The makers of films, who are themselves viewers of films made by others, have a rough idea of whether or not they will be understood by their contemporaries. The latter, for their part, adapt (unwittingly, often unconsciously) to forms of expression which briefly seem daring but quickly become commonplace. . . . It was through the repetition of forms, through daily contact with all kinds of audiences, that the language took shape and branched out."[36] The storyteller's craft includes an awareness of the "how" cultivated by wide experience of reading, watching, and listening to narratives.

The process again highlights the similarity between exoteric and esoteric narratives. Popular storytellers, often driven by competition and an urge to display ingenuity and virtuosity, balance some formal innovations with familiar schemas. The story more or less explicitly teaches us how to read it through repetition, structural parallels, tagging, genre conventions, and broad background knowledge. The process creates what we might call "intrinsic norms," patterns we come to expect as typical of this particular story.[37] We learn to expect the retrograde movement of *Memento*, as well as forward-moving episodes sandwiched between the 3-2-1 scenes. We get accustomed to the chaptering of *Pulp Fiction*, so we're likely to be thrown off when a scrap from early in the film reappears untagged in the climax.

Meanwhile, avant-gardists also compete to show bold originality. How? They may digress, take description beyond the requisite sketching of weather and scenery, or try for greater ellipses. The results may demand of the audience a keener attention, greater patience, and more recondite knowledge (e.g., *Ulysses*'s recasting the plot of the *Odyssey*). Still, these strategies steer us toward comprehension. Like their exoteric counterparts, esoteric storytellers create intrinsic norms of plot structure, narration, and segmentation to guide us. But they reserve the right to violate those norms for the sake of creating the difficulty that Priestley deplores.

Like Nolan, modernists help us to understand the story, but after we get adjusted—after the texture has thinned out a bit—the narrative is likely to rethicken, to shift the norm and complicate our understanding. In writing *Ulysses*, Joyce explained the technical task he set himself as "writing a book from eighteen different points of view and in as many styles."[38] The polystylistic impulse was carried on by William Faulkner in *As I Lay Dying*, which not only let disparate voices pass the story to and fro but also refreshed the mix with new "rules": variations on applying italics, a numbered list, and a sketch of a coffin. The storyteller may not only transmit changing story events and situations but also modulate the manner of telling. Sometimes that means contrasting one mode of narration with another, as when a film shifts from color to black-and-white imagery. Other times the result can be more demanding, as when *Ulysses* destabilizes its intrinsic norm by unpredictable methods of presentation.

The dynamic of schema and revision, intrinsic norms established and played with, crosses media in part because some narrative techniques are available to filmmakers, novelists, and playwrights alike. It's apparent that moviemakers borrowed devices from literature and the stage; flashbacks and alternating viewpoints emerged in those media long before film was invented. Reciprocally, in the twentieth century, film techniques found their counterparts in other media. We often find playwrights and novelists mimicking crosscutting and voice-over commentary, and even trying for a cinematic style of narration in dialogue and descriptions of action. I don't want to push things too far, finding equivalents of "close-ups" in literary details or spotlighted faces on the stage. But my survey of norms will sometimes point up this two-way traffic between film and adjacent media. Ideas borrowed from filmmaking remain current in popular fiction: today's manuals for aspiring novelists explicitly adopt ideas of "story arc" and "three-act structure" that screenwriting gurus have popularized since the 1970s.[39]

Whatever the medium, the balance of innovation and convention, of schema and revision, of novelty and familiarity isn't simply a matter of formal games or one-off gimmicks. Manipulations of viewpoint, time lines, and segmentation make a difference in our experience. To see Honey Bunny and Pumpkin return to the story after a long absence creates a sense of formal neatness. To grope along Leonard's backward trajectory through *Memento* is to undergo an experience approximating the starts-and-stops of his amnesiac state. The embedded novel in *Cast Down the Laurel* is a satire on pretentious fiction, and the surrounding commentary unwittingly mocks the idea that art should faithfully reflect life. *All Star Cast*, with its play-within-a-novel, suggests the impossibility of squeezing down the magic of the theater, with all its incandescence of staging and performing, into a critic's few banal column inches. (And the glory is evanescent: a departing critic sneers, "I give it three weeks.") These themes aren't simply stated; they're enacted in the very tissue of the artworks and registered by the reader or viewer.

We shouldn't overrate larger significance, though. Often the theme of a work of popular narrative is pretty banal. A received opinion or a commonplace idea may serve as a pretext for a new wrinkle in viewpoint or style.[40] Indeed, the very familiarity of the work's "message" may keep us comfortable with formal twists and turns. In *Pulp Fiction*, Jules Winfield's conversion is a captivating touch, but the figure of a reformed bad man goes back at least to early cinema, to cowboy William S. Hart and crooks deciding to go straight. Tarantino's more original triumph is that *Ahhh!* I shared with others twenty-five years ago.

We won't fully understand mass storytelling if we don't grant the power of sheer, abrupt sensation. The storyteller is ruthlessly opportunistic, seizing on any pretext to vary a schema or, in the optimal case, produce a tour de force. Popular narrative aims to provide us with striking experiences; it often leaves deep meanings to the literati.

Which is not to say that the result is necessarily superficial. Many of the major issues of great literature are treated with intensity and intricacy in popular stories. The anxieties of family life are rendered with subtle power in Alfred Hitchcock's *Shadow of a Doubt* (1943), and the tensions of loyalty and betrayal are finely developed in the spy novels of John le Carré. Much of the mass-audience storytelling that endures stretches the imagination (*Alice in Wonderland*), enlarges the moral compass (*Uncle Tom's Cabin*), and demands complex judgment of motive (*Hamlet*). These qualities depend, nevertheless, on the writer's command of craft. That's my main concern in what follows.

The Poetics of Murder

What's all this got to do with murder? The second main contention of *Perplexing Plots* is that mystery-based storytelling has cultivated just the sort of innovations I'm tracking. Avant-garde works perplex us by being difficult; popular stories confound us with puzzles. What I call the "investigation plot" is one of the most common schemas in fiction and film. We're urged to follow a character who is asking what happened or who did what to whom or how a guilty party may be exposed. A more general pressure of mystery, the way a story makes us notice that something important is unknown, extends far beyond the investigation plot. Dickens, Balzac, Henry James, Fitzgerald, and other major writers invested their stories with enigmas.

Everybody has secrets, and storytellers can handle them in various ways. If we know all the secrets that the characters are keeping from others, we have classic melodrama. We wait for the wronged wife to learn of her husband's infidelity. Alternatively, we may not know that there's a secret, and it gets revealed by accident—the melodramatic reversal or recognition, such as when the hero discovers who his father is.

But sometimes we're nudged to realize that there are secrets but not told what they are. As Shklovsky suggested, we know there's something we don't know. If a character has the task of discovering the secret, we have a classic mystery. It might be a detective story or a thriller in which a person in danger must seek out the source of the threat. Sometimes the mystery involves following a character bent on committing a crime; in that case, the question is whether the effort will succeed. In most of these plots, murder is not far off.

Thrillers and detective tales, I maintain, were a major way in which popular culture allowed ambitious storytellers to experiment with narrative. They became a training ground for audiences' development of sophisticated skills in understanding and enjoying complex fictions. Readers and viewers learned to grasp unusual patterns of plotting, shifts of viewpoint, nonlinear time lines, and unusual ways of breaking up parts. From Edgar Allan Poe through Arthur Conan Doyle to Dashiell Hammett and beyond, writers of crime and detective fiction have created a rich body of conventions that audiences have mastered, and those have resurfaced in plays, films, and other media.

Why focus on mystery plots rather than on romances or westerns or tales of horror or fantasy? Those genres can harbor mysteries, but they don't have to do so. Their conventions bear chiefly on the story worlds they present. A prototypical romance, no matter how it's told, centers on the vicissitudes of a couple in love. A western presents life on a frontier, with all the hopes and dangers that affords. A fantasy or horror story may involve a mystery, but it need not. In many cases, straightforward quest tales or adventure scenarios will do the trick.

In contrast, a mystery story, because it's predicated on announcing that there's something we don't know, puts the act of storytelling at the center of its concerns. A mystery is defined not by its story world but by something structural: the presence of a "hidden story" that must be brought to light. Matters of form are fundamental to the genre; the how of storytelling is its central convention. Novelty and innovation will come through exploring that convention. Mystery novels are ingenious, Ben Hecht points out, "because they have to be."[41]

Often, the ingenuity is flaunted. Above or behind a mystery story's narration, we're often prompted to posit the figure of a duplicitous author. This sense is the basis of what the mystery novelist John Dickson Carr called "the Grandest Game," as conducted by "the old serpents, the gambit-devisers and trap-baiters." "It is a hoodwinking contest, a duel between author and reader. 'I dare you,' says the reader, 'to produce a solution which I can't anticipate.' 'Right!' says the author, chuckling over the consciousness of some new and legitimate dirty trick concealed up his sleeve. And then they are at it—pull-devil, pull-murderer— with the reader alert for every dropped clue, every betraying speech, every contradiction that may mean guilt."[42] The author becomes a genial but crafty puppeteer daring us to see the strings.

At the limit, there may be rewards for playing the game. Rereading the book or replaying the DVD may yield a surprise that rewards fan connoisseurship and celebrates the storyteller's virtuosity. How many first-time viewers noticed that *Pulp Fiction*'s climactic diner encounter was teased in the backgrounds of decentered shots (figs. 0.6 and 0.7)? The first can hardly be called a hint because a first-time viewer has no reason to pay attention to that white T-shirt; the foreshadowing could hardly be more inconspicuous. The later shot could have made the couple far more visible, but I suspect most viewers don't notice them.[43] Such all but undetectable details are the opposite of the redundancy that smooths our passage through the plot. As enticing fillips, they enable popular storytelling to deepen the bond between creator and public.

Does every mystery reader enter fully into this meta-game? Probably not. But the game premise shapes the very construction of the story. The demands of the genre push storytellers to be clever even if not every reader or viewer will appreciate all the flash and filigree. As one screenwriter put it, "It's not necessary that every viewer understand everything, only that everything *can* be understood."[44] Part of that understanding involves the awareness that the author is hovering over the text waiting for us to fail. This tension need not be part of the contract we sign with other genres.

Mysteries' emphasis on formal innovation suggests a larger argument about what's valuable in popular literature. Critical tradition tends to split character from plot and valorize works that explore personality, as we say, "in depth." To

0.6 During the prologue, while Honey Bunny questions Pumpkin, Vincent can be glimpsed in the background making his way to the toilet. At this point we have no idea who he is.

0.7 In the climactic diner scene, the couple is dimly visible in the lower left when Vincent leaves Jules. Spectators are probably concentrating on Vincent's gesture and are unlikely to notice the out-of-focus background figures. But Tarantino has "played fair," and viewers can check back to figure 0.6 to see what they missed.

treat characterization as being shaped by the pattern of incidents and the strategies of disclosure seems to do violence to what we prize about people. Yet plot, conceived as a dynamic process of guiding our attention and expectations, furnishes an experience of intrinsic power too. Ever since Aristotle argued for plot as the overarching dynamic of our engagement with narrative, we've realized that a well-wrought plot has its own artistic value. By studying the architecture of a story's action, its trajectory and its breakup into parts, and our gradual access to it through techniques of narration, such as point of view, we can better understand the enduring appeal of popular storytelling. Again, mystery plots offer a very convenient access point.

One more reason I've focused on the mechanics of this genre bears on influence. Mystery techniques have benevolently infected all other modes of storytelling, and at all levels. In the 1940s, Hollywood was especially prone to build plots around mystery. The biography *Citizen Kane* (1941) is framed as an investigation. A suburban novel about infidelity (*Letter to Five Wives*, 1948) became a movie whodunit, or rather a who-was-it-done-to.[45] The psychological drama *Sunset Boulevard* (1950) begins by showing a corpse floating in a swimming pool. These and hundreds of other fictions make the study of mystery-based storytelling one road to understanding the dynamics of popular narrative generally. Today, when prestigious novels unashamedly build their plots around crime and detection, the study of this tradition seems especially worthwhile. Tarantino borrows a lot from pulp fiction, but so, it turns out, does nearly everybody else.

It's for this reason that the bulk of this book provides a selective survey of conventions and innovations in mystery-based storytelling across the twentieth century. In the classic whodunit, the suspense thriller, and the hard-boiled detective story, we find ample evidence for the versatility of popular storytelling. These traditions foster skills that have enabled readers and viewers to understand and enjoy *Pulp Fiction* and other examples of the new narrative complexity and as well as scores of other stories. In addition, the three story types I concentrate on display family resemblances, the overlapping affinities that Wittgenstein picked out. The classic sleuth story, premised on an investigation, became the basis of a different sort of tale, the hard-boiled mystery. Likewise, the thriller often relied not only on mystery but on active investigation, especially when the viewpoint is focused on the killer's would-be victim. Critical tradition distinguished these three traditions through differences in historical period and national circumstances, but these genres, or subgenres if you like, have freely mingled with one another, which has boosted our ability to master their narrative techniques.

No two of us have read all the same novels, seen all the same plays, watched all the same movies. But thousands of films and books and plays have amassed a body of conventions that each of us has tapped into from our own points of entry. At certain points in history, those conventions have accumulated in a body of options and expectations, creating a critical mass available to lots of viewers. Through schema and revision, we all gain access to these conventions. The variorum lives in us. Whether youngsters first meet "multiple-draft" narratives in *Groundhog Day* (1993) or *Run Lola Run* (1998) or *Source Code* (2011) or *Happy Death Day 2U* (2018) or *Palm Springs* (2020), viewers are developing skills in understanding nonlinearity. An older fan might have encountered the same possibilities in *Dangerous Corner* (1932).

Someone might argue that still other genres have laid down storytelling innovations that have become central for our time. Science fiction and fantasy would seem to be just as important today as the mystery story. I agree, and studies of those popular traditions in this light would be very welcome. But I've excluded them from my survey because, as with the romance and the western, most challenges proffered by these mega-genres are based on world making. Science fiction tales motivate time travel or parallel realities by positing some speculative technology operative in the story world. Similarly, the breaches of causality or time in a fantasy are created by magic, the work of wizards, witches, or enchanted objects. In contrast, only mystery-based plotting takes as a sine qua non the fundamental manipulations of time, viewpoint, or cause and effect.

This isn't to say that duplicitous narration is ruled out of these other genres; the film *Arrival* (2016) and its source ("Story of Your Life," 1998) show some possibilities. But again, such maneuvers derive from the mystery tradition. On the whole, surprise in science fiction and fantasy depends centrally on imagination and awe; surprise in mystery-mongering relies on realizing that you've been had.

✳ ✳ ✳

This is an essayistic book. That term usually translates as "I haven't read all the literature," and it certainly holds good here. What follows is, first, an effort to chart some major principles of popular storytelling. Then I trace how the mystery-based plot and its variants have enlarged the techniques available to authors and the skills cultivated by audiences. I range across novels, plays, films, and radio drama because these media show important exchanges in forms and stylistic options.

My concern is less with interpreting the books, plays, and movies I encounter than in revealing their design. In an age that puts a premium on finding hidden meanings, especially cultural significance, my study of craft practices might seem plodding. For most academic critics, stories seem largely made of ideas, often objectionable ones. For me, they're made primarily of patterns—patterns of events, patterns of particles of the medium (words, shots). Ideas come along, of course, sometimes as materials that can provoke our interest. Throughout, however, subjects and themes are sculpted by the pressures of design choices. I treat storytellers as narrative engineers, subject to the constraints and compromises facing every artificer. I hope to show that analyzing technique is a useful way to understand how popular narrative wins the hearts and minds of its public.[46]

The book begins with three chapters that survey some major Anglo-American narrative strategies in the late nineteenth and early twentieth centuries. Initially, I trace how some prime techniques developed from prose fiction through the "proto-modernists" James and Conrad. My account can't do justice to the subtleties of these writers' work; I simply try to show how a schema/revision account sheds light on their contribution to the tradition I'm tracing. Alongside these canonical figures, chapter 1 traces the parallel development of idiosyncratic popular narrative forms, focusing on the "formalist" streak that emerged strongly in 1910s mass culture. D. W. Griffith's *Intolerance* (1916) is my principal example in film, but there are many others in adjacent media.

In chapter 2, I discuss assimilations and diffusion of some storytelling strategies identified with the "High Modernism" of Joyce, Wolfe, and Faulkner. Again, I can't do justice to the richness of these writers' achievements. I simply try to show some of their efforts to complicate easy understanding, and I point out ways narrative artists seeking a broader audience modified the innovations—call them "tactics of accessibility." At the same time, I propose that modernism owes a good deal to earlier traditions, and I try to show some concessions made by even the most demanding modernists to comprehensibility—an angle of analysis that's often neglected. I end by pointing out some ways that modernist aesthetics merged with popular genres during that period.

In chapter 3, I focus on the 1940s and argue that these years consolidated narrative conventions in ways that would drive innovation in later decades. Many strategies of plotting and narration, along with mystery-based storytelling, were now established as traditions that could be recast by a wide range of artists—and were, from the 1950s onward. Examples from novels, plays, and films (e.g., *Citizen Kane*) illustrate the lively exchange of nonlinear techniques across media. As before, my survey includes little-known works as well as milestone ones.

Throughout I use the fundamental categories of temporal linearity, point of view, and segmentation—all enduring concepts of narrative analysis that were brought to explicit awareness during this period. The second part of the book surveys these dimensions as they were mobilized in three major genres of mystery fiction during the interwar years.

Those genres are the "Golden Age" whodunit (chapter 4), the suspense thriller (chapter 5), and the hard-boiled detective story (chapter 6). I sketch each genre's narrative conventions before going on to show how innovations in technique have fulfilled and deepened them. My analysis of form and style reveals the achievements of Agatha Christie, Dorothy L. Sayers, Mary Roberts Rinehart, Alfred Hitchcock, Dashiell Hammett, Raymond Chandler, and other well-known figures. At the same time, I survey many lesser-known plays, novels, and films. As with "literary" novels such as *Seed on the Wind* and *All Star Cast*, we can find mysteries that offer intriguing experiments that reveal the versatility of popular storytelling.

Chapters 7 and 8 focus on the changes in the three major mystery genres during the 1940s, along with consideration of how their new versions consolidated premises for later storytellers. Both chapters consider mystery writers' efforts to merge conventions of the whodunit, the thriller, and the hard-boiled tale, resulting in crossovers similar to those that chapter 3 traces in popular storytelling generally.

The first two sections of the book run on parallel historical tracks. Writers and dramatists and filmmakers of the turn of the century crafted new storytelling norms and bolstered those with a stated "method" that defined best practices. Workers in the emerging genres of mystery fiction did the same thing. While modernist authors defined extremes of experimentation and declared new premises for advanced storytelling, writers of detective stories and suspense thrillers were likewise pushing for trickier but still ingratiating experiments in the poetics of murder. By the 1940s, High Modernism was on the wane, and the most prestigious authors and playwrights aimed at some degree of accessibility. Creators attuned to a wider audience cast about for novelty in a competitive mass culture. Accordingly, storytellers in the mystery genres put forth blends of many traditions that created a dizzyingly pluralistic storytelling ecosystem. That era, I argue, laid the foundations for the "crossover culture" we now inhabit.

Part 3 samples later developments in the mystery genre through a string of case studies. Most of these are acknowledged classics of the postwar period, and they demonstrate the formal richness of a tradition's variorum. A comparison of Erle Stanley Gardner and Rex Stout (chapter 9) sheds light on how verbal style can create experiments in narration. Setting Patricia Highsmith alongside Ed McBain (chapter 10) shows the powers of restricted and unrestricted viewpoint, the latter being illustrated in the development of the police procedural subgenre. Chapter 11, on the heist plot, allows us to appreciate the bold intricacy of the Parker novels by Richard Stark (né Donald E. Westlake), which play variations on geometrical plot structure.

Funded by the wealth of creative options on display in these case studies, chapter 12 returns to the complex narratives of the 1990s and after. Tarantino's work stands at the center of that inquiry because he explicitly borrows from canonical 1950s crime stories, but many other films from the last twenty-five years both invoke and reactivate the traditions I'm tracing.

The last case study considers yet another genre transformation, the changes in the domestic thriller in the late 2000s and since (chapter 13). In the churn of schema and revision, in the quick branching out that Carrière mentions, *Gone Girl* as both book and film is exemplary. It shows that the investigation plot can be merged with the woman-in-peril schema and subjected to the play of deceit and unreliability set in motion a hundred years earlier by the Golden Age detective story. Reciprocally, *Gone Girl* set off a burst of gynocentric thrillers that invited a reading public to play complex narrative games. The contemporary thriller shows that tricky strategies of playing with time and viewpoint and chopping the plot into bits are still thriving. This trend furnished mass storytelling with a variorum that continues to engage audiences in the sort of fan connoisseurship that has always sustained the mystery genre.

My tour of mystery fiction, drama, and films is far from comprehensive. It couldn't hope to compete with the classic in-depth histories of the genre offered by Howard Haycraft, Julian Symons, and most recently and comprehensively Martin Edwards.[47] Nor can my account of the mystery literature rival the many useful surveys of contemporary research.[48] My aims are tailored to other concerns. I want to delineate some core conventions of mystery-driven storytelling—its poetics or "principles of making"—and trace how those have drawn on some basic narrative methods and how, in certain times, that poetics has shaped adjacent genres.[49]

A brief conclusion points toward some current evidence of the enduring appeal of the techniques of popular storytelling while also indicating the continued vitality of the poetics of murder. I've been asked whether I think that classics of mystery fiction and film are "as good as" the masterpieces of James, Conrad, and their successors. I'd argue that the best works of popular storytelling are good of their kind. In turn, decisions about what kinds are superior to others will depend on weighing various criteria, such as thematic implication versus direct emotional appeal. In addition, we ought not to ignore the role of playful delight. In all the arts, our canons make room for wit, surprise, and sparkle: *Petrushka* as well as *Le sacre du printemps*, Rauschenberg as well as Anselm Kiefer, P. G. Wodehouse as well as Theodore Dreiser. If we welcome the thrill of artifice and the virtuosities of assured craft, the best of popular storytelling more than measures up.

PART I

CHAPTER 1

THE ART NOVEL MEETS
1910s FORMALISM

Blanche Warren has learned that Hugh Sainsbury, who's about to run off and marry Blanche's sister, is already married. She confronts Hugh in the forest; they quarrel; he's shot. Now Blanche is on the run and has taken refuge in the office of her sweetheart Harlan Day. Day, a lawyer, is determined to defend her and reveal the true murderer.

This is the premise of Ralph E. Dyar's 1919 play, *A Voice in the Dark*. Although it ran for half a year in New York, the script was never published and only a fragment of the film version survives.[1] Still, this forgotten potboiler can teach us a fair amount about the resourcefulness of popular storytelling at a particular point in history.

In Day's law office, three witnesses recount what they know, and flashbacks set off by blackouts reenact past scenes for the audience. First, Mrs. Maria Lydiard tells of the quarrel between Blanche and Hugh in the forest glade. Hugh is shot, and Blanche foolishly picks up the pistol before dropping it and running away. After Mrs. Lydiard leaves, Blanche tells Day her version of events, and that is replayed as well. Finally, the shabby Joe Crampton, who sells newspapers at the train station, tells of overhearing a brother and sister meeting there; the woman confesses to killing Hugh. Thanks to Joe's testimony, the real murderer is revealed.

Dyar saw his play as part of a trend employing "the 'cut-back' technique of the cinema."[2] He added a formal premise given in the play's original title: *Look and Listen*. The first witness, Mrs. Lydiard, is deaf. As a result, the flashback scene of Blanche and Hugh in the forest, ending with his death, is replayed without dialogue. The players' lips move, but the audience does not hear what they say.

The second replay, Blanche's testimony to Harland Day, is given as a full reenactment. After her quarrel with Hugh, he is shot down behind some rocks. Unfortunately, neither we nor Blanche can see the killer.

At the climax, the third flashback is recounted by Joe Crampton, the newspaper seller. Joe happens to be blind. The reenactment of his scene at the railway station is played out on a darkened stage. We in the audience can only hear the conversation between a man and his unnamed sister. Who is she? When we return to Day's office in the present, the killer is revealed as Amelia, Mrs. Lydiard's caregiver and Hugh's first wife. She's arrested, and Blanche and Day are united as a couple. The play ends with a chorus from the two witnesses who can't fully grasp the scene we're witnessing: "If I could only see!" "O, if I could only hear!"[3]

A Voice in the Dark displays strategies of storytelling that are central to the traditions I am considering. For one thing, it presents a nonlinear time, thanks to flashbacks from present-time occurrences, but that was not unique. The flashback that was common in film and prose fiction had been exploited on the stage in *Innocent* and *On Trial* (both 1914) and elaborated in *DeLuxe Annie* (1917) and *Yes or No* (1917). In 1919 alone, there was *Smilin' Through*; *For the Defence*, another trial play with reenactments, and *Moonlight and Honeysuckle*, in which a woman courted by three men tells each one a different story about her past. One critic was already complaining about "those modish second acts that take place before the first."[4]

The broken time line is motivated by another fundamental technique: patterning narration, or the flow of story information. Dyar conceives it as a matter of restricted point of view. The events in the present, the witnesses visiting Day's office, are observed objectively. But Dyar revises the emerging flashback schema by making the embedded testimony strongly subjective. Characters' dreams had been exhibited on the stage before, and characters had often reported what they witnessed. But *A Voice in the Dark* dramatizes sensory differences in the witnesses' accounts. Stagecraft makes palpable incidents as seen by a deaf woman and as heard by a blind man.

Dyar's play also shows the importance of overall organization. The play's basic structure is familiar to us: an investigation into past events, building to a crisis, and a revelatory climax. Many schemas fulfill this pattern: the police interrogation, trial testimony, examination of written records, and so on. The story arc, its internal structure of incident, might be packaged in various ways. The hidden story might be brought into the present in small bits, bigger chunks, or large-scale scenes. Internal divisions into scenes and episodes can be accentuated by external segments, such as an "exoskeleton" provided by parts or chapters in a book or large-scale acts in a play.

Dyar has tidily segmented his plot. *A Voice in the Dark* frames the replays as symmetrical blocks, each act designed for a specific response. The pantomime reenactment of the murder coaxes the audience to imagine what the characters might be saying. The central flashback, presenting both sight and sound, biases us toward assuming that Blanche is innocent. It gains further interest by confirming or disconfirming what we thought was said in the silent flashback.[5] The final reenactment presenting what Joe overheard in the station uses the darkness to delay revealing the killer's identity. The audience must listen keenly for any clue—most likely a voice we've heard in earlier scenes.

A Voice in the Dark is no masterpiece, but it shows that workers in popular media were prepared to self-consciously tinker with basic resources of narrative. Techniques of narration, time structure, and segmentation had been brought to the consciousness of all storytellers, not just the most ambitious or prestigious novelists and playwrights. For instance, Dyar's play embodies issues of point of view explored by Henry James and Joseph Conrad and articulated in 1910s literary criticism. Proscenium theater could not exactly render a single angle of vision as a painting or film shot could. It couldn't evoke a character's sensory awareness through rich prose. By making one witness deaf and another blind, and then subjecting the audience to those conditions, Dyar offers an approximation to a novel's restricted viewpoint. For all its obviousness, the play tries to present three Jamesian "centers of consciousness" on the stage.

In its willingness to experiment with basic storytelling techniques in a clear-cut, accessible manner, *A Voice in the Dark* reveals some prospects of popular narrative and is surprisingly typical of many such experiments at the time. And creaky though it looks today, *A Voice in the Dark* isn't wholly alien to us. Its play with point of view looks forward to a century of other popular experiments. Mrs. Lydiard's first, silent version of the crime anticipates *Rear Window* (1954) and *Blow-Up* (1966) in teasing us with ambivalent action viewed at a distance. The later blacked-out scene, with only dialogue guiding our understanding, has its descendants in the audiotaped replays of *The Conversation* (1974) and *Blow-Out* (1981). One could almost imagine a contemporary film adapting the play, using silent and blank-screen episodes. Popular storytelling is a tradition constantly revising familiar schemas and reviving even offbeat ones.

The Dangers of Baggy Monsters

The second half of the nineteenth century saw a huge growth in the reading public in the United States and the United Kingdom. Responding to this new audience, publishers produced vast amounts of fiction. Magazines and newspapers published not only short stories but serialized novels, which fostered long-form plotting.[6] Serialized stories as well as original ones could be printed in a two- or three-volume edition and sold to lending libraries and rented to eager readers. That edition might then be reissued in a single volume. By the turn of the century, many novels had sold hundreds of thousands of copies, with some reaching sales of a million.[7]

Henry James worried that the dominance of "the voluminous prose fable" was a danger to the novel as an artistic form.[8] The average novel was shapeless, offering "a vast formless featherbediness."[9] He was not evidently thinking of the wildness of *Moby-Dick* (1851), which constantly violates Ishmael's viewpoint and adds in travelogues, encyclopedic accounts of whaling technique, and scenes in playscript form. Far more sedate works attracted his censure. James attacked Hardy's *Far from the Madding Crowd* as "a simple 'tale,' pulled and stretched to make the conventional three volumes."[10] Eliot's *Middlemarch* was, despite arresting details, "an indifferent whole," and an Arnold Bennett novel displayed "a great dump of its material."[11] James famously placed *War and Peace* in the company of the "large loose baggy monsters."[12] If such venerated masters failed in organization, what would one say about the run-of-the-mill three-decker, with its seesaw plots, endless authorial interjections, and shameless padding? One author obliged her publisher by throwing in a train accident.[13]

It's a premise of popular narrative that form follows format. A TV network sitcom builds its plot within a fixed running time and plans peaks of action around commercial breaks. Similarly, a three-decker book might use the volumes to mark major segments; Pip's great expectations develop in three stages. Some authors imposed a local pattern on the narration. Dinah Maria Craik's *A Life for a Life* (1859) is throughout a "he said/she said" account, alternating extracts from a woman's diary with the laboratory journals of the man she loves. Dickens used a more daring alternation in *Bleak House* (1852), with chapters in first-person narration from Esther Summerson followed by chapters presenting a more omniscient account told in third person.

Much of this output consisted of variants of sentimental and Gothic fiction.[14] These strains fed into what was called sensation fiction, novels of secrets and suspense filled with looming threats to innocent, ordinary, bewildered people.[15] The prototypes were devised by Wilkie Collins, whose *The Woman in White* (1860) and *The Moonstone* (1868) were intricately plotted to fill out three volumes and end each volume on a strong cadence. Reviewers and readers were particularly engaged by Collins's disciplined handling of what we might call the dossier form.[16]

The epistolary novel as pioneered by Samuel Richardson in *Pamela; or, Virtue Rewarded* (1740) provided a robust schema that Craik and others exploited and revised. A story told through an exchange of letters became a common resource of the novelist. Collins went further in creating the "casebook," a novel presented as more or less sworn testimony, written out by a witness or participant. It offered opportunities for a virtuoso turn.

While devising distinctive voices for multiple narrators, the author could arrange the shifting viewpoints to intensify mystery. Clues could be dropped in minor characters' casual mentions, and incidents could be repeated from different viewpoints, growing in significance or uncertainty as they reappear. Collins's viewpoint characters have no privileged purchase; as a reviewer noted, the narrators are as befuddled as the readers.[17] The casebook format could also spring perspectival surprises. At a crucial point in *The Woman in White*, Marian Halcombe's diary is besmirched by a note from the villain, Count Fosco. We are startled to learn that he's been reading it "along with us."

Collins's two dossier masterpieces immensely influenced mystery fiction. For example, Bram Stoker's *Dracula* (1897) uses an array of documents to create suspense, with diary and letter extracts sometimes skipping back in time to delay certain revelations. The casebook model endured into the twentieth century in works by Dorothy Sayers, Vera Caspary, and many writers of domestic thrillers. The casebook provides both a superficial realism and a clear-cut exoskeleton, but its rigidity grated on some. Anthony Trollope famously deplored "the taste of the construction" in Collins's work.[18] But Collins understood that a taste *for* felt construction, for flagrant artifice, was something audiences enjoyed about mysteries. It is there, however ostentatiously, in Dyar's *A Voice in the Dark*. Treating a mystery as a playful experience of form would become central to popular storytelling.

James, although passionate about literary construction, was among the doubters. Although admitting Collins's ability to show terror in ordinary surroundings, he saw *The Woman in White*, with its "general ponderosity" as offering a modern version of the endless letters in Richardson's *Clarissa; or, The History of a Young Lady* (1748). Collins's novels were "monuments of mosaic work," not tightly designed compositions.[19] James admired Flaubert and Turgenev for the compact control of their stories. They showed that the novel could display the subtle rigor of a painting, James's reference point for exacting artistry.

Whether recounted in first or third person, whether split into documents or simply rendered in chapters, the great run of novels left James convinced that a more organic, less mechanical approach to form would lift prose fiction to a higher artistry. Every idea required its own expressive strategies. The artist-novelist needed a "method," a "ruling theory," a set of principles that guided handling of unique *données*, or story germs.[20] In his work and his critical writing, James proposed an explicit poetics of fiction. That includes some rich reflections on narration, particularly as it involves point of view and ideas about structure and segmentation. Storytellers had been using these techniques intuitively for centuries, but in the 1910s Anglophone writers became conscious of them to a new degree.

The "scenic picture," as James sometimes called it, demanded that the writer wring all the dramatic and emotional potential out of a situation. Both summaries of action and specific scenes, or "discriminated occasions," could gain point and purpose if treated with the concreteness of actions on the stage. "Dramatise, dramatise!" he urged.[21] And like a painting, the writer's scenic picture was inevitably rendered from a chosen viewpoint, a character who acts as a "center of consciousness," a perspectival stance on the action. The moment-by-moment intensity of a play could on the page become a drama of psychological pressure, giving access to character interiority denied to the theater. The choice of that center of consciousness could yield delicate effects not yet achieved by the fiction of the day.

James's 1898 novella, "In the Cage," from one angle is the story of a clandestine affair between Lady Bradeen and the out-of-pocket Captain Everard. Most novelists would have concentrated on the love triangle and its effects on the lovers, perhaps through a third-person moving-spotlight treatment shifting among the couple, the unsuspecting husband, and servants and other peripheral characters. Alternatively, because the couple communicates through telegrams to friends who help arrange their secret meetings, the dossier schema could give us shifting first-person accounts of action. James, however, focuses the action through the unnamed young telegraph clerk behind the counter in a caged corner of a grocery shop who prepares the messages that the lovers send to their enablers. She has her own life, populated by a helpless mother, an older female friend striving to serve high society, and Mr. Mudge (no first name given), a grocer who expects the heroine to marry him when his prospects improve.

The young woman becomes fascinated by the glimpses she gets of the affair. She enjoys helping it along, sharing a complicity with Everard, and comparing the affair judiciously with the romances in popular fiction. She comes from poverty and is sensitive to the couple's careless wealth, but she neither denounces them nor feels particularly envious. She haunts the street Everard lives on, and one evening he sees her there and they have their first conversation outside the shop. She blurts out, "I would do anything for you" before acknowledging that helping him expands her world. "All I get out of it is the harmless pleasure of knowing."

Whether the knowing is altogether harmless is for the reader to judge. The protagonist is admirable in her sensitivity, even in her rashness, but she fails to know certain things. It's a sort of mystery story, with her as the investigator working with tantalizing "clues" (James's word) that yield only vague outlines, even at the end. By then, marriage with Mr. Mudge looms.

It might seem that this character's restricted knowledge would be best rendered in a first-person account, like that of the barber in Ring Lardner's short story "Haircut." And James's method has often been taken as an urge to muffle the voice of an external, "authorial" narrator. In reaction to the chatty commentary of Fielding or Thackeray, some critics wanted the author to present things with great detachment. Stephen Dedalus declares his commitment to this emerging premise when he says that the author, like God, "remains within or behind or beyond or above his handiwork, invisible, refined out of existence, indifferent, paring his fingernails."[22] At the limit, the narration could become the "camera eye" that would be associated with Ernest Hemingway and the hard-boiled school.

James and his acolytes will not go so far. The third-person narration of "In the Cage" avoids moralizing, but it does widen our understanding by describing the minute fluctuations of the situation in ways the clerk couldn't. The encounter in the street, as tense as any playwright could wish, is saturated with emotional implication. When Everard promises to visit her cage every day, she remonstrates with him, "How can you?" James renders the moment in words that she couldn't summon up if she were telling the tale. "He had, too manifestly, only to look at it there, in the vulgarly animated gloom, to see that he couldn't; and at this point, by the mere action of his silence, everything they had so definitely not named, the whole presence round which they had been circling became a part of their reference, settled solidly between them."[23]

What that "whole presence" exactly is (obligation? the risk of exposing him? the temptation of love? a fantasy of conspiracy? her recognition of his fumbling gratitude?) remains unspecified. The emotional resonance is as mysterious as the causes and consequences of the couple's affair itself. Perhaps the woman can't grasp the unnamed presence; perhaps the narrator can't. But we know it's serious. She follows up with a trembling, "Your danger, your danger—!" No wonder Jacques Barzun called James a melodramatist. Yet Barzun recognized that James invested emotionally fraught situations with a haze of uncertainty quite different from the thumping contours of sensation fiction and the *coup de théâtre*.[24]

Narration and point of view require finesse. Once the telegraph clerk is picked as a focal point, the storyteller has to consider all the implications to be squeezed out of the blending of her life and job with her oblique inferences about the high-society lovers. "In the Cage" lays out that merger in marked parts, some twenty-seven numbered chapters, undergirded by a severe architecture. The street scene, composing chapters 15 through 17, sits, in page lengths, at the dead center of the tale. In the first block, the initial three chapters set the scene, building to the discriminated occasion that launches the plot. Lady Bradeen, then nameless, pushes a draft telegram across the counter. The second block ends the tale with three parallel chapters in which the young woman's friend, moving into society by marrying a manservant, fills in some, but not all, patches in the picture.

James's taste for niceties of construction is evident in this heightened awareness of segmentation. Neatness and symmetry called out to him. Under the pressure of serial publication, he worried about a book having unequal halves or a "makeshift middle."[25] *The Golden Bowl* (1904) is divided into two books, "The Prince" and "The Princess," of twenty-four and twenty-three chapters, respectively. *The Awkward Age* (1899) consists of a dozen "books," a layout modeled on a play's division into acts that give each segment "a divine distinction."[26] James planned the twelve parts as a ring of lamps lighting different aspects of the central situation. Long after the fashion for triple-deckers had waned, he divided *The Wings of the Dove* (1902) among three major characters. "There was the 'fun' . . . [of treating them as] sufficiently solid *blocks* of wrought material, squared to the sharp edge, as to have weight and mass and carrying power; to make for construction, that is, to conduce to effect and to provide for beauty."[27]

Does anybody but James put "fun" in quotation marks? His sensitivity to the fine-grained effects of every unit, from scenes and summaries to chapters and large parts ("books"), was captured in one critic's observation that James exemplified a broader pride in the "well-made" novel, in which balance, proportion, and tidy symmetries ran counter to the excesses of romanticism and realism alike.[28]

For all his originality, James relied on schemas circulating in his milieu. He contemplated writing an epistolary novel alternating letters between a mother and her daughter, "giving totally different accounts of the same situation."[29] Surprisingly, Collins's aesthetic wasn't completely out of tune with James's preferences. Collins anticipated James's "dramatic method" by modeling his scenes on stage dialogue and business, and he created "centers of consciousness" in a dossier, gathering many characters vying to understand the truth.[30] You could argue that the casebook schema made it thinkable for James to design *The Awkward Age* as a ring of strategically angled viewpoints. The dossier format also suppressed that voice of the all-knowing narrator that James wanted to hold in check.

The other canonized innovator of the period, Joseph Conrad, can be seen as revising schemas as well. Like James, Conrad wanted scenic vividness. His task, he wrote, "is . . . before all, to make you *see*. . . . to hold up unquestioningly, without choice and fear, the rescued fragment before all eyes in the light of a sincere mood."[31] To an unusual degree, Conrad created quick, intense visual impressions. The image of Heyst in *Victory* (1915) standing by a chair, his face and shoulders "lost in the gloom above the plane of light in which his feet were planted," might be a shot from a chiaroscuro film of the period (fig. 1.1).[32] A passage in *Chance* (1913) is devoted to one character's vision through a gap in a curtain as he watches fingertips slowly being revealed.[33]

Just as important, Conrad followed James in recasting plot structures. A long-standing narrative device is the story within the story, an account embedded in a situation of reading or listening. *Don Quixote* (1605, 1615) incorporated many substories into the knight's adventures. *Frankenstein* (1817),

1.1 *The Circus Man* (1914): David bends over Christine
in a bold chiaroscuro composition.

Wuthering Heights (1847), and many other novels absorbed letters, manuscripts, and oral reports within a larger frame. With characteristic nuance, James had revised the discovered-manuscript convention in "The Turn of the Screw" (1898). The bulk of the tale is told by the unnamed governess, but her account arrives at several removes. We enter the story via the first-person narration of a Christmas guest, who hears his host read aloud the governess's manuscript (itself written after the ghostly events she reports). The shock of the ending is magnified by James's refusal to return to the holiday framing situation, with the governess's final words providing harsh closure: "His little heart, dispossessed, had stopped."

Conrad multiplied narrators in *Lord Jim* (1900), but instead of laying them out in a row he let the fragmentation shuffle story chronology. The novel begins with an omniscient third-person voice recounting Jim's background, his thoughts while aboard the *Patna*, and the beginning of court testimony, as witnessed by Marlow. Why did Jim abandon ship in a momentary crisis? Then Marlow commandeers the narration. Over a long, unspecified evening at a much later point, speaking to an unidentified listener, he recounts the trial's progress. Marlow's account is interrupted by flashbacks to pretrial events, anticipations of later actions, and an embedded story involving another character.

The familiarity of the courtroom schema allows Conrad to try some risky revisions of the casebook principle. Once Marlow embarks on his own investigation, the novel presents not testimonies committed to paper but conversations prey to interruption and digression. Marlow has reunited with Jim at intervals and has run into other characters who provide information about Jim's past and his efforts to recover personal honor. The book's final section is a compressed dossier: a letter from Marlow to an unidentified correspondent, followed by a text in which Marlow reports a conversation tracing what led to Jim's death.

Like James's circle of lamps in *The Awkward Age*, Conrad's dispersal of observers creates a "prismatic" form as characters' varying judgments of Jim highlight facets of his personality. Marlow confesses the very opposite of authorial omniscience: "I don't pretend I understood him. The views he let me have of himself were like those gleams through the shifting rents in a thick fog—bits of vivid and vanishing detail."[34] In a gesture that would recur throughout twentieth-century fiction, the novel replaces the puzzle at the center of *The Moonstone*—how was the diamond stolen? who stole it?—with the mysteries of character.

Lord Jim interweaves incidents, shuttling us back and forth across Jim's life. *Chance* shows that a more modular, boxes-in-boxes organization can also complicate a time line. An unnamed "I" narrator encloses accounts that enclose other accounts, creating seven distinct time periods.[35] Chapter divisions provide a clear-cut exoskeleton, although the embedded conversations are sometimes interrupted by flashbacks or flash-forwards. Some moments are narrated more than once, from different viewpoints. A contemporary reviewer saw the prismatic possibilities: the characters of *Chance* are seen by "lights thrown on them from different angles."[36]

The tales of James and Conrad are not always easy reading, and critics of their day admitted as much. Some complained, but others found the result rewarding. Arthur Quiller-Couch preferred narration that was more straightforward but confessed a fascination with these writers' ability "to weave a situation round with emotions, scruples, doubts, hesitancies, misunderstandings, understandings, half-understandings; cutting the web sometimes with the fiercest of strokes; anon patiently spinning it again for another slice; and always moving with the calmness of men entirely sure of their methods, and confident that the end of the tale will justify them—as it always does."[37]

The qualities ticked off apply not only to the characters, with the hesitations and uncertainties of Lord Jim and Henry James's telegraph clerk, but to "half-understandings" that pervade the narration itself. Marlow knows Jim, he confesses, only through glimpses. The narration of "In the Cage" cannot pin down the mysterious "whole presence" sensed by the young woman and Everard. These authors not only rely on existing schemas but roughen them, retaining enough cues to keep us engaged but withdraw some and blur others. For the sake of psychological realism and nuanced readerly response, including a distinct brand of suspense, they turn the prototypical "easiest narrative" into something more perplexing.

In their fiction and their pronouncements on technique, James and Conrad built the major modern Anglo-American poetics of narrative. Over the same years, more obscure figures were widening the horizons of the storytelling craft. Dyar's *Voice in the Dark* is only one example of how popular writers introduced audiences to unorthodox strategies of narration, structure, and time shifting.

Some of these writers were doubtless influenced by the masters, but others seem to have arrived at an experimental attitude simply through the churn of schema and revision, the pressure of competition, and the urge to display ingenuity and virtuosity—all forces that characterize mass-market storytelling up to today.

Innovation Within Limits: Pushing the Variorum

Historians tracing the rise of modernism in the arts have taught us to look to the 1910s as an era of almost delirious ferment. The major compositions of Strauss, Mahler, Schoenberg, Berg, Webern, Ives, Stravinsky, Satie, and Debussy marked the dissolution of tonality and the development of new musical forms. Proust, Joyce, Eliot, Yeats, Gertrud Stein, Lawrence, Woolf, Dorothy Richardson, Wyndham Lewis, Ford Madox Ford, Paul Valéry, the Russian Cubo-Futurists, and many other authors began to create what would be identified as modernist literature. Picasso, Matisse, Gris, Kandinsky, the Italian Futurists, and the painters of the Armory Show were redefining pictorial representation. At a less avant-garde level, Willa Cather, Robert Frost, Katherine Mansfield, Edgar Arlington Robinson, Sherwood Anderson, and Sinclair Lewis found wide reading publics. World theater was in tumult thanks to the innovations of Stanislavsky, Meyerhold, Tairov, Reinhardt, Kaiser, Strindberg, Apollinaire, the Pitoeffs, and the Ballets Russes. Another measure of this turn toward formal awareness was seen in the rise of analytical criticism among the Russian Formalist literary scholars, Schenkerian music theory, and critics of painting such as Roger Fry.

Less remembered than my roll call of Great Names are the experiments in storytelling and style carried out before the eyes of millions. The 1910s saw a keen self-consciousness about form in the Anglo-American popular arts. G. K. Chesterton and H. G. Wells carried on their fascination with artifice throughout that decade and were joined by other talents, notably in the detective story. In music there was the aggressive pull of ragtime, cabaret and music-hall song, and Tin Pan Alley. In graphic narrative we had the triumph of George Herriman's zany Krazy Kat, along with Rube Goldberg's precariously engineered machines and Cliff Starrett's quasi-Surrealist *Polly and Her Pals*.

Mass-market experiments borrowed "modern" methods to some extent, but popular storytellers had their own traditions to draw on as well. Pressed to find gimmicks, stunts, twists, and new wrinkles, they probed narrative strategies in many directions. They made overt engagement with technique part of the entertainment package. That quest put on their agenda the narrative strategies made explicit by James, Conrad, and other more prestigious writers.

Novelists at all levels of appeal continued to explore fresh possibilities of viewpoint, time shifts, and plot structure. One Arnold Bennett book

(*Clayhanger*, 1910) presented a story from the viewpoint of the hero, followed by another book tracing the same incidents as experienced by the heroine (*Hilda Lessways*, 1911). Joseph Hergesheimer gained notoriety by block shifting perspectives among men of three generations in *Three Black Pennys* (1917), then among nine characters in *Java Head* (1919). In Clemence Dane's *Legend* (1919), the main character is dead when the story opens, and the action takes place in one room during one night. By decade's end, Somerset Maugham could win a large readership with *The Moon and Sixpence* (1919) in which the hero's story unfolds through an acquaintance who encounters him intermittently. Such novels domesticated the methods of James and Conrad while adjusting older traditions to modern tastes.

Academics and belletrists helped assimilate these techniques. In 1874, the critic George Lathrop had fielded ideas similar to James's strictures on organic unity and limited viewpoint.[38] Brander Matthews's Columbia University courses on modern literature widened interest in what was coming to be called story-telling "method."[39] Matthews's student Seldon Whitcomb surveyed a huge range of possibilities in the 1905 textbook *The Study of a Novel*. The exploding market in book publishing and the vast expansion of magazine circulation—the closest thing to a national medium in England and the United States—encouraged aspiring writers to try to break into print. There followed manuals with titles such as *Writing the Short-Story* (1909) and *The Art and Business of Story Writing* (1913). Writing tips and market trends could be found in periodicals such as *The Writer* ("A Monthly Magazine for Literary Workers") and other periodicals.

A consensus emerged about literary artistry. The modern novel would purge itself of the digressions of triple-decker plots. Characters could be narrators, and impersonal external commentary should be discreet. The author needed what Lathrop called "a unifying and creative view" that could create "the modern dramatically organized novel."[40] Likewise, short stories should follow the precepts of concentration laid down by Poe and exemplified by Maupassant, Kipling, and O. Henry.

Before the 1910s, critics had seldom discussed the implications of viewpoint, but now it was seen as a central creative decision. Manuals spelled out the differences between character viewpoint and authorial viewpoint, objective rendering and subjective coloring, limited view versus omniscience, single perspective versus multiple perspectives.[41] The "angle of narration," in the phrase of one manual, might be that of the protagonist or of a bystander or of someone at a great remove from the action.[42] Authors were urged not to vary viewpoint within a scene or chapter.[43]

All of these possibilities had been tacitly available long before James and Conrad, but the new methods and the public's growing appetite for fiction gave writers an incentive to chart their choices systematically. For example, the epistolary novel was a long-established form, but now authors were asked to weigh the advantages and drawbacks of building a book out of scraps of memoirs, journal jottings, even telegrams. Stunts like Brander Matthews's short story "The Documents in the Case," which consisted wholly of news clippings, IOUs, and court reports, were debated as valid models for literary narration.[44] Similarly, flashbacks were nothing new to literary construction, but now authors had to be aware that straight chronology had both advantages and drawbacks. A 1919 manual offers a rich array of options of what to skip over, how to fill gaps, and how to shift blocks of action to maximize curiosity.[45] It might almost be a recipe for *A Voice in the Dark*, which was mounted in the same year. Highbrow or lowbrow, writers faced a new self-consciousness about means and ends.

At the limit, writers eager for secrets of success could ransack *The Thirty-Six Dramatic Situations*, a 1916 translation of Georges Polti's 1895 French study. Like the folklore researchers of the era, Polti was trying to disclose universal units of narrative action. What he came up with was a catalog of basic "situations," each with characteristic agents, that was at once a recipe book and a Borgesian catalog. "The Avenging of a Slain Parent or Ancestor" (Third Situation, subset A1) counts as different from "Vengeance Taken for Kindred Upon Kindred" (Fourth Situation). "Enmity of Kinsman" (Thirteenth Situation) is somehow radically distinct from "Rivalry of Kinsman" (Fourteenth Situation). Long before Joseph Campbell's "hero's journey," Polti had offered an amateur anthropology of world narrative.

Americans of an entrepreneurial cast turned Polti's scheme into a literal machine. Wycliffe Hill, author of the surprisingly brief *Ten Million Photoplay Plots* (1919), manufactured the Plot Genie, a pinwheel of cardboard discs. Rotating them dialed up numbers that correlated with situations tabulated in a book. Now the author could generate new stories on demand. Some pulp writers claimed, perhaps shamefacedly, that the Polti compilation and the Genie's random ways could spark story ideas.[46]

Operating with more analytical delicacy was Clayton Hamilton, another Brander Matthews protégé. He made his name with the textbook *Materials and Methods of Fiction* (1908), followed by *The Manual of the Art of Fiction* (1918). As a lecturer and a critic of literature and drama for literary weeklies, Hamilton dissected both classics and commercial work.[47]

Hamilton became one of America's most prescient analysts of narrative conventions. He was sensitive to nuances of viewpoint, arguing in advance of Percy Lubbock that "the entire tone and tenor of the narrative" depended "directly on the answer to the question, Who shall tell the story?"[48] He noted the virtues of "limited omniscience," moving the spotlight from character to character for different scenes or chapters.[49] More than his peers, Hamilton understood that most fiction had nonlinear dimensions, as when a multistrand plot must skip back to supply exposition as a new character enters. At a broader level, Hamilton maintained that breaking chronology was justified if it showed the logical connection among events. As early as 1914, he proposed that a plot could arrange its incidents in reverse order, a strategy that would soon surface in various media.[50]

Hamilton probed the emerging innovations in theater as well. British dramatists had adapted the French well-made play to middle-class tastes for realism but retained many of its devices—the carefully prepared situation; the "obligatory scene" that brings the conflict to a head; and in between the misunderstandings, eavesdropping, secrets, discovered letters, and other devices that would persist throughout popular storytelling. After Ibsen, European drama underwent changes somewhat parallel to those seen in post-James fiction. The plots of Ibsen's social dramas relied on "well-made" principles but proposed a sharper organic development and greater psychological realism. British and American playwrights began to replace sensational melodrama with plays of character and "dramas of ideas."[51] The variety was sustained in the United States with a boom in production; throughout the 1910s, each Broadway season boasted between 87 and 162 new plays.[52]

Commentators strove to keep up. Hamilton's *Theory of the Theatre* (1910) and *Problems of the Playwright* (1917) were accompanied by William Archer's *Play-Making* (1912), George Pierce Baker's *Dramatic Technique* (1919), and other manuals. These treatises sorted out the new impulses in the post-Ibsen theater and suggested ways they could be made comprehensible to a broad audience.

An older model of dramaturgy was based in Gustav Freytag's "pyramid," in which a midpoint climax leads to a "falling action."[53] The turn-of-the-century writers jettisoned this schema and saw most modern plays as tracing a rising arc of conflict and tension.[54] The major turning point should come at the end of the penultimate act, one manual advises, following smaller climaxes that have ended earlier ones.[55]

This smoothly rising pattern gives a play something like the trajectory of modern novels and magazine stories. Hamilton had suggested that every plot should build to a culmination about three-quarters along, a rule that would govern both a play and a conventional novel.[56] Indeed, in an inversion of the Jamesian impulse, Hamilton suggested that the drama of the future would move closer to the compact intensity of fiction. It would also invest heavily in subjectivity, indulging in imaginary sequences and dream interludes. Hamilton was intrigued by *The Phantom Rival* (1915), in which the heroine's dream shows us her lover as being quite different from the man we see in the final act.

As critics outlined a poetics of the modern drama, they assigned a central role to segmentation. Tradition demanded that each act be a distinct block, set off by intervals. There were many conventional strategies for packing each act with incident, and commentators surveyed feather-duster exposition, piled on complications, turning points, stinging curtain lines, and the "quiet curtain."[57] Writers also considered varying the rhythm by breaking up the act, perhaps giving the plot a novelistic fluidity of time and space. During this period, European stagecraft was beginning to experiment with abstract sets and turntable staging, and soon the single drawing room set would emerge as merely one option among many.

The heightened awareness of technique promoted by critics, academics, and writing gurus reflected what was on the stage. As if in dialogue with the commentary, playwrights competed for ingenuity in structure, viewpoint, and time shifting. In *The Silent Voice* (1914), scenes are played out as registered by a lip reader. *Coat-Tales* (1914) shows the fate of a missing fur coat through flashbacks. Above the proscenium hangs a giant clock, its hands moving forward or back to specify the time period. Another flashback play, *The Unknown Purpose* (1918), presents a second act that takes place at the same time as the third act. Clayton Hamilton's request for a narrative run backward was fulfilled by Zoë Akins's *The Varying Shore* (1921). Alternative futures weren't ruled out either. Revising a schema Dickens used in *A Christmas Carol*, *Eyes of Youth* (1917) charts a woman's three possible fates as predicted by a fortuneteller, and a 1918 play adapted O. Henry's crossroads story "Roads of Destiny."

As for subjective point of view, Sophie Treadwell's *Eye of the Beholder* (1919) offers a "prismatic" play. Scenes reveal a woman as seen by her husband, her lover, the lover's mother, and her own mother. On each occasion, the protagonist's demeanor and costume change. *Overtones and Any House* (1916) goes further by showing characters accompanied by their alter egos.

The suppressive flashbacks and perceptual variations of *A Voice in the Dark* look less odd if we recognize the variorum flowering on the Anglo-American stage in the 1910s. Outré techniques could yield surprise and amusement. A famous example is George M. Cohan's perennially popular *Seven Keys to Baldpate* (1913). A successful author of sensational novels has bet that he can crank out a serious book in twenty-four hours. He settles down in an inn that is closed for the winter. Immediately Baldpate is invaded by gangsters, corrupt politicians, a femme fatale, a crooked sheriff, a hermit, and a young woman professing to be a reporter. The hero's literary efforts are disrupted by hugger-mugger, seductions, and a murder.

Last act, first twist: The hero's betting partner arrives and explains that he has staged the whole thing. The bet was a scheme for mocking the trash the hero usually writes. Curtain. Pause. Epilogue and second twist: At rise, the hero is finishing his novel, which is the entirety of everything we've seen, including the previous twist. He has won the bet, and he has contributed to serious literature by composing what we would now call a metafiction sending up his pet genre.

Subtitled "A Mysterious Melodramatic Farce," *Seven Keys to Baldpate* showcases an enduring feature of experiment in popular narrative: comedy can help the audience adjust. The same effect appears in *Stranger Than Fiction* (1917), in which a playwright concocts a story around people he has just met, and in

Pay-Day (1916), in which a melodrama is revealed to be the imaginary script of a film. The most knowing variant, however, comes from Clayton Hamilton himself, in collaboration with A. E. Thompson.

In *The Big Idea* (1914), Dick needs to save his father from financial ruin, so he starts to write a play. At the encouragement of Elaine, who thinks and talks faster than he can, he decides to write up his family crisis as it has developed. They start drafting Act I of his play. Elaine dictates: "The curtain rises," as the curtain comes down on our first act. In Act II, complications pile up, and Dick struggles to insert them into the script he's banging out. Because of the time pressure, Act II ends with Elaine dragging Dick off with their play unfinished, an action duly recorded in his manuscript.

At the office of a theatrical producer, Dick and Elaine offer him the script, but he balks when he sees that the third act is missing. They point out that the pitch they're presenting right now is the plot's resolution. Only if the producer buys the show can they include the happy end he demands. He relents, with the condition that he gets to play his role himself. He demands to appear at the beginning of the performance, explaining that everything the audience will see really happened. Of course that very prologue opened the performance we've seen.

The Big Idea satirizes "heart interest," the grim look of stage food, and other conventions. It occasionally jabs at the manuals. ("The essence of drama is struggle," Elaine insists.) Teasingly, the play shifts back and forth between the act of writing and the text being written. When Dick confesses he's falling in love with Elaine, she congratulates him on a nifty plot point. Needless to say, Hamilton and Thomas didn't miss a chance to game the system. In a newspaper interview, they reconstructed their quarrels during the composition of the play.[58]

Again, comedy proves to be one way to familiarize audiences with narrative innovations. To put it too simply, popular theater, at least in its light vein, was Pirandellian before Pirandello, and Brechtian well before Brecht. Of course, these masters added philosophy and politics, as well as certain complications. It fell to popular storytellers who drew on these writers to smooth out what they had roughened, while retaining cues that teased audiences with their manageable novelty. This is the way of the tactic of accessibility.

The Book Inside the Play Inside the Movie

How much popular storytellers were directly influenced by the elevated ideas of James or the more widely available ones of Hamilton and his peers is hard to say. And, of course, some of these creative options were available long before this time; the dossier novel provided an enduring model for shifting viewpoints. The important point is that storytellers of the 1910s had access to fresh ideas drawn from "advanced" literature and theater, tips promoted in writing manuals, and schemas lingering from the nineteenth century and before. This mix created a rich variorum. Guided by the need for a strong plot, external action, and quickly comprehensible narration, popular dramatists and fiction writers could make patterning more salient and create a new consciousness of form.

Dyar's acknowledgment of borrowing the flashback schema from movies points up another example of expanding narrative options at the period. As middle-class entertainment, cinema became the chief rival to theater, reducing the demand for touring companies and forcing many houses to convert to film projection.[59] How-to manuals, progenitors of Aronson's *21st Century Screenplay*, promised to help writers break into this booming market.[60]

As fiction films became feature-length stories running an hour or more, they absorbed techniques from adjacent arts. Filmmakers often modeled set design, performance, and scene construction on techniques of proscenium theater. Principles of perspective painting were also applied because the camera lens created a playing space very different from that of the stage (fig. 1.2).[61] When filmmakers began to break up scenes, they approached the flexibility of "novelistic" narration. Time could be adjusted through brief flashbacks, that "cut-back" that inspired *A Voice in the Dark*. Films could interrupt a present scene to remind the viewer of a bit of earlier action or to indicate the drift of a character's memory (figs. 1.3–1.4). More daringly, *The Gangster and the Girl* (1914) incorporates hypothetical alternatives (figs. 1.5–1.6). And by breaking the tableau into closer views from varying angles, filmmakers gained a great many ways to channel character knowledge (figs. 1.7–1.8). They found equivalents for literary shifts of viewpoint (figs. 1.9–1.14).

1.2 1910s "tableau" staging in film creates a perspectival space akin to that of classic painting (*Ready Money*, 1914). Because of varying sight lines in an auditorium, such a packed composition would not be feasible on stage.

1.3 In *Alias Jimmy Valentine* (1915), the reformed safe-cracker's old partner stirs his fond memories in hopes of coaxing him back to the gang.

1.4 The flashback inserts shots of Jimmy's elation during an old robbery.

1.5 *The Gangsters and the Girl* (1914): A young woman imagines informing the police . . .

1.6 . . . or trying to stop the gang herself.

1.7 *The Bargain* (1914): At a barroom roulette table, the gamblers gather and the croupier stretches his hand under the table.

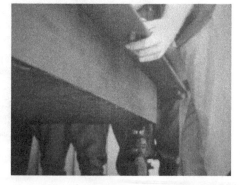

1.8 A cut to a close view shows the croupier pressing the button that controls the wheel. As in prose fiction, the narration reveals what the characters don't know.

1.9 *The Masked Heart* (1917): A mysterious masked woman peers through a curtain above the partyers.

1.10 Her viewpoint is approximated by a high angle and stressed by the iris masking.

1.11 A return to her reinforces our anchoring with her.

1.12 Reciprocally, a closer view of Philip shows him noticing the masked woman.

1.13 A new angle, carefully differentiated from 1.9 and 1.11, approximates his view.

1.14 Again, a return to the initiating shot of him confirms the interlocked viewpoints.

This wider range of knowledge might stretch beyond a single setting. Alternation of locales wasn't unknown on the stage, but it was far easier to create through film editing. Crosscutting, also known as parallel editing or the "switch-back," could carry the viewer to and fro among different lines of action, as omniscient narration did in a novel.[62] Identified largely with D. W. Griffith, crosscutting became a standard tool for building an exciting denouement. A crosscut chase or a rescue driven by a deadline could be amplified by making shots shorter as the tension rose. The technique could draw conceptual comparisons as well. In *A Corner in Wheat* (1909), Griffith alternates views of a rich man's banquet and his financial schemes with shots of desperate people waiting in line for bread.

Throughout Griffith's *The Birth of a Nation* (1915), crosscutting weaves the fates of two families into the social upheaval of the Civil War. Griffith pushes the technique to a paroxysm in the climax. Across nearly thirty minutes, the narration shifts among dozens of settings and four clusters of characters. The action culminates in two accelerating rescues: the Ku Klux Klan saves Elsie Stoneman from rape and then saves the Cameron family from the Black militia. These passages show that Griffith intuitively understood that crosscutting recasts time as well as space. All things being equal, alternating shots are assumed to be unfolding simultaneously, but the duration of a ride to the rescue is usually compressed while the dangerous situation runs on a slower clock (figs. 1.15–1.18). Rapid alternation of story lines would become a basic technique of world cinema, and many filmmakers exploited crosscutting's ability to stretch or squeeze duration.

Strategies of segmentation shaped films' plot structures. The first films were very short, less than a minute or two, so narrative action had to be brief and anecdotal. As films lengthened, form followed format. The single-reel film, lasting twelve to fifteen minutes, favored narratives akin to short stories or vaudeville "playlets."[63] When films ran to two, three, or more reels, plotting had to integrate more incidents, complex lines of action, and psychological exploration.[64] Some filmmakers took the reel to be a distinct "act" or "chapter" within the larger film. An ambitious film might be divided into still larger blocks. Across twelve reels, *The Birth of a Nation* presents a prologue, two epochs (war, then Reconstruction), and an epilogue.

Griffith mapped a comparable framework onto his mammoth production *Intolerance* (1916). A long prologue is allotted four reels, a first "act" takes four more, and the second act lasts five. As if following current playwriting advice, Griffith ends each segment with a powerful climax. Act II attaches an epilogue similar to that of *The Birth of a Nation*, a vision set in a phantasmic future in which "perfect love shall bring peace forevermore."

The eccentric innovations on display in this ramshackle masterpiece epitomize that formalist streak running through 1910s popular art. One critic

1.15 *The Birth of a Nation* (1915): While the southern families are besieged in the cabin . . .

1.16 . . . the Klan, miles away, rides to rescue them.

1.17 Cutting back to the cabin, Griffith shows the families in danger.

1.18 Suddenly the Klansmen arrive at the cabin, and the marauding soldiers flee. Crosscutting has stretched out the moments of the assault while compressing the ride.

declared *Intolerance* "the most incredible experiment in storytelling that has been tried."[65] It's not much of an exaggeration. No one in any medium had percussively alternated scenes from different eras for the sake of conceptual parallels. The film stands as a powerful instance of how much narrative audacity can be poured into popular forms. It also shows how extreme novelty calls forth extreme pressures toward comprehensibility.[66]

Intolerance presents four historical episodes illustrating its title theme. In ancient Babylon, Belshazzar's worship of the goddess Ishtar arouses the jealousy of the priests of Bel, who conspire with hostile forces to seize the city. Jesus, criticized by the Pharisees and condemned by Pilate, is shown in incidents leading up to the crucifixion. The massacre of the Huguenots ordered by Catherine de Medici illustrates state-initiated religious oppression. Today, reformers supported by industrial capitalism force workers to conform to pinched standards of morality. All four stories include a romance plot as well. It's minor in the Christ episode; he presides over the Wedding at Cana. In the modern and the French stories, seducers target the innocent, and in the Babylon story a lover betrays his beloved and the king she adores.

This "drama of comparisons," as the title calls it, invites block construction. Giving each period its own distinct chapter was the schema favored in later films such as Carl Dreyer's *Leaves from Satan's Book* (1920) and Buster Keaton's comedy *The Three Ages* (1923). While Griffith was preparing *Intolerance*, *'Twas Ever Thus* (1915) was released, a comedy that traced woman's roles through segments set in prehistory, the Civil War, and modern days.[67]

No one knows when or how Griffith decided on the more radical formal option of crosscutting the four periods. He saw that the technique he had used for creating conceptual parallels and building suspense within a single story world could be mapped onto epochs. The result would be an ever-shifting trans-historical grid of likenesses and contrasts. In addition, accelerating the cutting pace allowed Griffith to create a virtuoso climax, with rapid crosscutting both within stories and among them. Now wholly independent story lines would converge only on the screen.

The problem, particularly at this early period of film history, was comprehension. A stanza in Whitman's poem "A Passage to India" could glide across history and the globe, and a novel by Conrad could shift time frames in a paragraph. But a film that jumped among epochs, with no ghosts or time travelers to link them, risked incoherence. In addition, cinema poses a particular problem of comprehension. The reader of a book can pause and skim back to earlier pages to get oriented, but film viewers can't. As in theater, the spectacle sets the pace. Whisked from a factory strike to a Babylonian celebration and then to the French court, *Intolerance*'s viewer had to grasp action on the fly. To that end, Griffith used tactics of accessibility we've seen at work throughout popular narrative.

For one thing, the four episodes exemplify genres established in theater and historical fiction. Early filmmakers had produced dozens of passion plays, historical pageants, tenement dramas, and spectacles of antiquity including *Damon and Pythias* (1914), *The Sign of the Cross* (1914), and Griffith's own *Judith of Bethulia* (1913). Then the juxtaposition of these genres could be stressed in publicity. Advertisements for *Intolerance* reiterated both the basic premise—"four separate stories, each with its own set of characters"—and the method of construction. "Following the introduction of each period," the program explained, "there are subsequent interruptions as the different stories develop along similar lines, switching from one to the other."[68] A program for one roadshow presentation previewed the ending in purely formal terms: the four stories are "drawn swiftly close together and they go rushing on to the four smashing climaxes."[69] The film's formal audacity was proclaimed not only as a salable novelty but as a guide for comprehension.

The film's design features reinforce the differences. Of course, costume and setting identify each story, and distinct color tints help. So too do familiar plot patterns, not least the last-minute rescue, which Griffith incorporates into three episodes. (Only one rescue succeeds.) He goes further, though. He endows his film with a massive exoskeleton that relies on verbal tags, a hierarchy of intertitles that redundantly orient the viewer to the shifting action.[70]

Most obvious, opening titles announce the four stories and the method of shifting from one to another (fig. 1.19). In addition, Griffith provides the image of a book called *Intolerance*. It opens at the beginning of each story and remains open afterward. As an image, it moves the plot from epoch to epoch, and a superimposed title signals the transition (fig. 1.20). We might expect the book's text to introduce the historical action we'll be seeing in each sequence to come, but instead the paragraphs hammer home the film's form as the program notes had. Every shot of the book reveals identical facing pages, starting with "The book of this play is arranged in four parallel plot threads or lines of action," and ending with "How true it is that intolerance ever cloaks itself in the garb of righteousness that it may the more easily impose on the minds of men." For further clarity, when we move to a different era, an expository title reasserts time and place, not only in language but also in a background image keyed to the period (fig. 1.21).

Apart from all the verbal transitions, Griffith provides the celebrated figure of the woman at a cradle, with the Three Fates quietly sitting behind (fig. 1.22). As a mongrel-mythology emblem of eternal recurrence, the image is anchored by an intertitle citing, uncredited, Whitman's "Out of the cradle, endlessly rocking." In the prologue and Act I, the cradle and the book appear in tandem whenever the plot introduces an era. By the early stretches of Act II, either the book or the cradle suffices to signal the time switch. We're assumed to have learned the rule.

Griffith, a man of the theater, claimed that cinema as "the motion playhouse" would surpass "the speaking stage," but *Intolerance* doesn't so much turn away from theater as swallow it up.[71] It dubs itself "A Sun-Play for the Ages" and splits into segments not unlike the author's early play *War* (1906–7). Griffith found a more comfortable analogy in literature because cinema was "a novelizing, or storytelling form; it is epic rather than dramatic."[72] Acknowledging his debts to fiction, he attributed the switch-back to Dickens and hoped that a film could achieve a poetic quality reminiscent of Browning and Tennyson.[73] *Intolerance*'s persistent narrating voice provides commentary, adds footnotes, and takes the liberty of renaming some individuals as types ("The Boy," "The Friendless One").

1.19 *Intolerance* (1916): An opening title explains the film's structure.

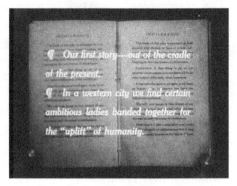

1.20 The Book of Intolerance: The two open pages are identical and reiterate that this image marks a pause and a shift to a new era.

1.21 Expository intertitles for each epoch reinforce the time shift by a graphic design behind the text.

1.22 The rocking cradle, the mother, and the Three Fates: the linking image signals a change of epoch and suggests eternal recurrence of situations. In some images, the cradle contains flowers.

Having locked in an intrinsic norm of language, graphic design, and moving images, the film can become more elliptical as it goes along. The novelistic discourse of the titles eventually drops away. Imagistic intertitles become rarer, and after the Boy of the modern story is given the Last Sacrament on his way to the gallows, the book device is discarded. Thereafter, only the cradle, an occasional expository title, or a simple propulsive cut (figs. 1.23–1.24) carries us from era to era. The climax presents film as the ultimate synthesis of storytelling resources. In its constantly changing viewpoint, its ability to skip to and fro in time, and its fracturing of blocks of history, the cinema draws from theater and literature but also exploits its own resources to create a turbulent rush of expressive images.

1.23 By the end of the film, Griffith can omit the transitions and cut directly from one era to another. Here the Babylonian story . . .

1.24 . . . gives way to the modern story.

The critic who called Griffith's film an incredible narrative experiment added: "He will never again tell a story in this manner. Nor will anyone else."[74] True, no surviving films of the period seem to have rivaled the ambitions of *Intolerance*. Filmmakers who wanted to achieve a historical panorama treated the epochs more simply, in block-by-block surveys such as Dreyer's and Keaton's films. Eventually, however, Graham Swift's *Waterland* (1983), Michael Cunningham's *The Hours* (1998), David Mitchell's *Cloud Atlas* (2002), Gregory Blake Smith's *The Maze at Windermere* (2018), and other novels would employ the strategy of intercutting distinct periods to create their own "dramas of comparisons," and these wouldn't resist the quasi-supernatural implications Griffith welcomed. Similar strategies would be activated in films based on some of these books. Griffith's idea that crosscutting could be a productive macro strategy was reinforced by Christopher Nolan, whose films toggle between stretches of time that overlap one another (*Dunkirk*, 2017) and interweave simultaneous dreams (*Inception*, 2010).[75]

Griffith's outlandish film did more. It made apparent a principle of construction going far back in the history of narrative. A story is predicated on chronological cause and effect, so we're inclined to map it as a line. But it can also be reconfigured as a grid, a form more spatial than temporal. Once story lines are brought together, even if you switch rapidly between them, they can be considered as columnar, a geometrical array of big blocks or smaller chunks. Four sealed-off eras, each with its own story world and cast of characters, nudge us to think in terms of what we now call a spreadsheet. This quasi-geometrical notion of narrative would emerge in modernist fiction but also in tales designed for mass audiences.

* * *

Some historians have seen in Griffith's achievement, and in early American cinema generally, a response to "modernity"—the bustle of the city, the compulsory rhythms of mass production, the fleeting sensations of the distracted window-shopper.[76] These "distal" factors, I've argued elsewhere, provide at best broad preconditions rather than delicate explanations.[77] If we consider the problem from the standpoint of the creator rather than the audience, we don't need to posit modernity as a brand new epoch in which people's sensory experiences were radically overhauled. We can see this as an era in which storytellers faced an expanding variorum and the pressures of mass production and large-scale competition.

Workers in the narrative arts cast about for fresh ways to exploit both emerging forms and those from earlier days that can be refreshed. The churn we talk about in modern media was evident then as well. Pressing himself to outshine *The Birth of a Nation*, Griffith created a more ambitious counterpart to *A Voice in the Dark*, a play that not only borrowed the "cut-back" from current cinema but also mapped traditional novelistic viewpoint shifts onto the apparatus of the playhouse. This sort of balancing, I think, is what storytellers tend toward. They adjust forms both old and new to their immediate purposes. In the process, they do not so much mimic the real world, modernizing or not, as create distinct story worlds.

The task, then, is to guide us through them. Critics who see *Intolerance* as akin to the experiments of Joyce and other modernists have a point, but it goes only so far.[78] *A Portrait of the Artist as a Young Man* (1916) doesn't resort to a redundant exoskeleton to help us grasp the formation of Stephen's consciousness. Stein's *Tender Buttons* (1914) simply declares, take it or leave it: "A sad side a size that is not sad is blue as every bit of blue is precocious." In the formalist 1910s, a great many popular storytellers believed that we needed explicit tagging, judicious redundancy, and a firm grip on conventions of genre and style if we were to enjoy a wild ride. Dyar, Griffith, and their peers obliged. Joyce, Stein, and a few other storytellers realized that they could snap off the trainer wheels and subject us to something more vertiginous.

CHAPTER 2

MAKING CONFUSION SATISFACTORY

Modernism and Other Mysteries

As we know now sixty years after the publication of Ulysses, the difficulties of experimental writing like that are not so great as they seem. . . . Joyce loves mysteries but does not like them to go on too long. . . . He is not always easy, but is never impossible.

—Anthony Burgess

Bill Sidney is a successful businessman deformed by his history with women. As a teenager he was initiated into sex by the good-natured Mrs. Davis. He had a brief affair with Millicent, a maid in his college dormitory. He enjoyed a sentimental, chaste romance with the aspiring singer Lucy. He has settled into a loveless marriage to the brittle socialite Erma, but he harbors a disturbing attraction to his sister Jane. These liaisons fuel his impulses and fantasies. A passive man easily dominated by Erma and his business partner Dick, Bill struggles to make a decisive change in his life. Now, threatened by a scandal that will wreck his career, he is poised to act. He will commit murder.

How Like a God, the novel recounting Bill's story, begins just before the climax. An unnamed man armed with a revolver is slowly walking up a staircase to a woman waiting in a third-floor apartment. His ascent is interrupted by chapters that review his life in a "limitless network of appeals, facts, memories that darted at him and through him."[1]

The result is a double-entry structure, two crosscutting story lines. One is simple, concrete, and brief: Bill's few minutes on the staircase. The other story line is more diffuse. Most of the sixteen backstory chapters present events in roughly chronological order, with an early group devoted to Bill's youth and the last to events leading immediately up to his visit. Other chapters alter chronology, gathering scenes showing Bill's relation to this or that woman and incorporating flashbacks and replayed scenes as well.

The novel revels in mild difficulty and somewhat eccentric technical choices. Instead of identifying the past segments with dated chapter tags, the book proposes an odd exoskeleton. Each moment on the staircase in the present is printed in italic type and assigned a title consisting of a letter of the alphabet. The segments run from A to Q, which becomes the final scene of the novel. These single-page bits are recounted in third-person narration and in the past tense. In contrast, the long chapters set in the past are printed in roman type and given Roman numerical titles from I to XVI. Instead of flatly informative dating, the typography and alphanumeric tags create a unique tabular layout.

Even more curious, the past blocks are recounted in the second person, as if Bill is addressing himself in an inner monologue: "You walked all the way home in the mild September night." This rare technique suggests a stage soliloquy (hence perhaps the title's reference to temporizing Hamlet) as well as a portrait of extreme solipsism. This man internalizes everything and upbraids himself for failure at every turn.

Steven Johnson might find this book an anticipation of the demanding storytelling so widely seen today. We often encounter a plot that introduces a moment of crisis and then breaks away to show flashbacks leading up to it. But the schema apparently posed no great problems for 1929 readers, in part because the novel's design features ease our access to it. The contrasts of typography and tagging in the two tracks redundantly mark out present and past, the immediate moment versus the flux of years. Within that framework, the narration helps us track the small cast of characters. We come to the book knowing the schemas of a man's career trajectory and of futile love story plots like that informing *Of Human Bondage* (1915). Scenes are invariably introduced with the usual specifiers, such as "Two days later" and "The months in New York, stretching to over a year." In all, a patient reader can construct a coherent time line, but the fact that we'd consider trying to do so is a measure of the moderate challenge the book offers.

The staircase segments contribute their own user-friendly effects. By beginning at the crisis, the plot creates both suspense and mystery. We have to wonder if Bill will actually kill the woman waiting for him. Moreover, the narration doesn't specify who the victim might be. As we continue through the book and meet the women in Bill's life, we are coaxed to ask, "Which of them will become Bill's target?" The narration frankly holds something back. Again, the suppression is motivated by the second-person monologue; Bill knows whom he intends to kill, so he has no need to mention her name.

The reader quickly masters the to-and-fro alternation, but the novel varies this intrinsic norm. As the narration goes along, it knits the moments on the stair more tightly to the chapters set in the past. A past episode ends with Bill saying, "For god's sake, Mil!" and the staircase follow-up starts with an echo of that phrase. As the climax approaches, the two time lines mingle, not unlike Griffith's crosscutting at the peak of *Intolerance.* In the present, Bill thinks, "You're just plain scared." Cut to the inner monologue track: "And not only because you're standing here on the stair." Thanks to the second-person address, past and present have converged. A refrain, "Go on in," bounces from the P track to chapter XVI, the last "you" chapter that brings us up to the moment of his entry to the room.

A second variation of pattern comes midway through the book. All of the previous chapter chunks have been devoted to Bill's past life, but in chapter VIII, provoked by the landlady's call to him on the staircase ("Are you going to answer her or not?"), Bill's inner monologue replies, "You might as well"— suggesting not just answering her but also killing the woman who waits. The chapter now skips ahead to the very recent past and then speculates about the future. Bill reviews his plan for the crime and imagines how the investigation might proceed. Anticipating police questioning, he starts to design an alibi. This effort provokes him to consider what clues to his presence he will need to destroy. After this hiatus, which introduces the possibility he'll commit suicide, the past-time chapters return to filling in the months leading up to the climax. Soon the identity of the waiting woman is revealed, and pure suspense takes over.

How Like a God was published in September 1929, a month before William Faulkner's *The Sound and the Fury.* It was declared brilliant, not only for its original technique but its probing of a respectable man's psychosexual dark side.[2] It was compared to Aldous Huxley's *Point Counter Point* (1928) and, somewhat later, to Faulkner's *Sanctuary* (1931).[3] One critic placed the author, Rex Stout, in the company of Faulkner, Virginia Woolf, and John Dos Passos.[4] No wonder: Stout had spent some years in Paris immersed in modernist writing and had met James Joyce and Gertrude Stein. The same critic saw the compression of an entire life into a few moments of tangled memory as the culmination of new experiments in stratified time in Virginia Woolf, Willa Cather, and Sherwood Anderson.[5]

Read today, the book seems not just modernist but modern. It could easily be turned into a film script, so familiar are we with nonlinear time schemes framed by an impending crime. It could also be said to anticipate a "micro narrative" such as Nicholson Baker's novel *The Mezzanine* (1986), a first-person account of a man's lunchtime saunter across a mall lobby and up an escalator. Fastidious descriptions of soda cans and knotted shoestrings give way to unwittingly revealing memories of childhood and office routine, all hectored by footnotes. A *nouveau roman* rewritten by an OCD nerd, *The Mezzanine* summons up schemas of action and mental life not so far from those in Stout's novel.

How Like a God, as unknown today as Ralph Dyar's play *A Voice in the Dark*, can also stand as an example of experimentation in more or less mainstream media. By 1929, complex storytelling had found a welcome in literary culture. The Jamesian principles of perspective and geometrical construction had reached a new explicitness, not to mention market visibility. Readers and critics, tutored by High Modernism, were smart now. They were attuned to nonlinearity, slippery viewpoint tactics, and eccentric segmentation. *How Like a God*, with its teasing narration and overt structure (even violations of its own norms are clear-cut), showed ways in which avant-garde experiments could be retooled for more accessible storytelling. Those ways often relied on the mechanics of mystery.

Onward to Ultraism

Percy Lubbock, who published editions of Henry James's letters and his two unfinished novels, presented a systematized version of 1910s poetics in *The Craft of Fiction* (1921). The book takes James's works, in particular *The Ambassadors*, as the prototype of the modern novel, a showcase for the "scenic" approach and of subtle modulations of point of view. In an unwitting echo of the Russian Formalists, Lubbock adds that the best case for any book is made by the critic who revealed "how the book was made."[6] Lubbock was not directly associated with the New Critics, but his attention to "method" marked a shift toward the "close reading" that would dominate criticism for the rest of the century.

Full awareness of craft options opened new vistas for the novel: "There are unheard-of experiments to be made."[7] We can be sure that Lubbock didn't include in that prospect the laconic objectivity of Ernest Hemingway's "The Killers" (1927) or Dashiell Hammett's *The Glass Key* (1931). He warned that too strict an adherence to the "dramatic method" eliminated the possibility of evocative atmosphere of the sort that James wrapped around the telegraph clerk of "In the Cage." We can be equally sure that Lubbock wouldn't consider Joyce's *Ulysses*, published a year after *The Craft of Fiction*, to fit the bill. This founding work of modernist literature seemed a repudiation of the trim, well-made novel of James, Conrad, Willa Cather, Ellen Glasgow, and others. *Ulysses* was followed by the canonical works of Dos Passos, Woolf, Hemingway, and Faulkner. Like their counterparts in other countries, these Anglophone writers seemed to be rejecting the new developments that had sought to enrich the heritage of nineteenth-century storytelling.

What caused the change? One explanation has predominated. Older modes of expression could not capture the convulsive changes in science and culture since 1900, or as Woolf famously specified, December 1910. "When human relations change there is at the same time a change in religion, conduct, politics, and literature."[8] New forms arise to capture the contemporary world more adequately. In the process, they attack the inherited forms. Stability of character, causal connections among events, linear time, the coherence of mental life—all these presuppositions of "realist" art, either Naturalist or Flaubertian/Jamesian, need to be overthrown. These premises might be subverted through breakup and dismantling or simply rejected. The result, however difficult it might seem in comparison with more transparent storytelling, strives to represent the shattering dislocations of modern life.

Yet this explanatory effort offers its own version of realism. Modernism is said to faithfully "reflect" the world we live in and our responding sensibility. The question I'm pursuing here—how we may understand the forms that emerge in popular storytelling across the twentieth century—suggests another angle of approach. That relies on the idea of schema and revision, reworking a received pattern to fulfill a particular function.

Nothing comes from nothing. Just as James, Conrad, playwrights, and filmmakers such as Griffith revised earlier storytelling techniques, their successors can be seen doing something similar. Modernist strategies of nonlinearity, ambivalent narration, subjective plunges, and puzzling segmentation don't utterly abandon inherited narrative schemas. To a large extent, they rely on them. Mr. Bloom, for all his errant psychic ways, satisfies many conditions of fictional personhood. He moves through the world as an individuated agent, and once we get used to the ways in which his thoughts are rendered, we can make some fair guesses at his motives and impulses. If a novel challenges received procedures, it must first invoke them.

Granted, the process poses difficulties for the reader. Just by dropping quotation marks, *Ulysses* creates a slight slippage between external action, inner monologue, and authorial commentary.[9] Yet we manage, thanks in part to precedents. Anthony Burgess has pointed out early versions of stream of consciousness in Dickens's *Little Dorritt*.[10] And Joyce does retain some cues from traditional schemas for reported thought.[11] For these reasons, I suggest we think not of rejection, or even subversion, but of creative transformation, a recasting of prior conventions so that both novelty and familiarity stand out clearly. Instead of Ezra Pound's "Make it new" we often find "Remake it new."

We're likely to conceive the process of schema and revision as conservative, operating within a stable tradition, managing minimal change. In contrast, we aren't used to thinking of "advanced" artistry as preserving some features of the past, except as citations or ironic jabs. We like our revolutions totalizing.

Yet "breakthrough" works often achieve striking effects through judicious reworking of what they surpass. Charles Rosen has traced how Haydn, Mozart, and Beethoven recast large-scale symphonic organization by incorporating patterns of thematic development from musical drama. The composers then mapped the symphonic schemas back onto opera, thereby endowing plot action with a more dynamic form.[12] Richard Taruskin has argued for a comparable process in the emergence of modern music, with Mahler's "maximalism" expanding the procedures of the classic symphony using several strategies, such as revising the extent and substance of the second theme of a movement.[13]

Something similar can be said about the visual arts. Ernst H. Gombrich suggests that the incompatible views in a Cubist still life rely on familiar forms (violins, bottles, fruit bowls) carefully juxtaposed according to classic principles of centering and balance.[14] More broadly, Kirk Varnedoe considers Western pictorial modernism as a process of drawing on "a fluid set of established conventions." He lays out the prospect that artists' works can be considered

> the product of individual decisions to reconsider the complex possibilities within the traditions available to them, to act on basic options that were, and remain, broadly available and unconcealed. This kind of art is conceivable only within a system that is in crucial senses unfixed, inefficient, and unpredictable—a cultural system whose work is done by the play within it, in all senses of the word, in a game where the rules themselves are what is constantly up for grabs.[15]

With respect to narrative, those basic options include the tools I invoke throughout this book: chronological sequence, narration and viewpoint, and segmentation. For popular narrative, those rules, although fairly firm, can be renegotiated if authors have ingenuity and pluck and are spurred on by competition with their peers.

What of modernism's engagement with the surrounding culture? Certainly subject matter and themes are prime materials for storytelling; current concerns can hook an audience. The most common innovations we find in popular storytelling likewise consist of absorbing new themes and subject matter into received forms, positing a fresh story world rather than a fresh way of presenting it. Often an unfamiliar *what* is given through a familiar *how*.[16]

If the tradition is in perpetual renewal, then we must allow some weighting to form and style as conditioning our responses. At the limit, perhaps the modernist narrative project serves less to reflect conditions in the outer world than to give us new experiences of story worlds. From this angle, social or political commitment, as well as memes and cultural flotsam, can motivate design features. For the modernists, themes of fragmentation and alienation could operate as alibis for formal innovation. Bill Sidney's disordered state of mind in *How Like a God* justifies jumbling temporal order. If in all dimensions—form, style, theme, subject—nothing comes from nothing, we can study how particular storytellers rework what they borrow from their predecessors when revising the rules for particular purposes.

The idea that literary modernists often took inherited devices as points of departure was broached by Joseph Warren Beach, a critic of the period. He suggested that James had reduced the range of story action very considerably before Joyce and Faulkner found deeper psychological currents in the "infinite expansion of the moment" and the "silent monologue."[17] More obviously, modernist plots rely on traditional devices such as adultery, private letters, accidental deaths, suicides, secrets, and coincidental moments in which someone witnesses a revelation. In Ford Madox Ford's *The Good Soldier* (1915), Leonora imagines belaboring Nancy with a riding whip in brisk melodramatic fury. Stream of consciousness, so strongly identified with modernism, was a nineteenth-century notion, articulated not only in *Les lauriers sont coupés* (1887) but by William James in his treatise *Psychology* of 1890.[18]

Needless to say, any debts to convention are often warped by structure, verbal style, and viewpoint refraction. A modernist storyteller can do what James and Conrad, as "proto-modernists," did: equivocate, skip over, or invert the importance of an action that the easiest narrative would put to the forefront. Most novels would play up the death of a major character, but *To the Lighthouse* (1927) reports it in a parenthetical shrug.[19] In such ways High Modernists roughed up the basic techniques that normally let us smoothly assimilate the plot action. To get a better sense of this more aggressive schema revision and the difficulties it triggers, let's look at a canonical Faulkner novel.

The Sound and the Fury consists of four blocks, narrated by three characters and then a noncharacter voice. Most baldly, the array is comprehensible as a version of the multiple-character accounts in Collins's dossier novels. The anonymous voice of the fourth part, readable as traditional third-person narration, recalls the omniscient chapters of Dickens's *Bleak House*. The second and third sections are flashbacks, not unlike the embedded flashback blocks in Conan Doyle's Holmes novels. And like the classic dossier, *The Sound and the Fury* helpfully labels its blocks with dates: April 7, 1928; June 10, 1910; April 6, 1928; April 8, 1928. Those days are shot through with recollections and references to earlier times, but the plot would be much more difficult to follow if the tags were omitted.

The narration we first encounter represents the thoughts of the mentally deficient Benjy Compson. Almost as disjunctive are the fraught musings of the second part, attributed to Quentin Compson in the lead-up to his suicide.

We're rewarded with a good deal more clarity in the third section, as Jason Compson takes up the story, and the fourth part, narrated objectively, anchors us firmly in the story world. Nonetheless, unlike Collins, Faulkner doesn't provide a framing situation for the blocks of narration. The characters aren't giving testimony or writing their memoirs. By this point in literary history, a first-person character narrator did not need to specify the overarching story-telling situation; *The Great Gatsby* (1925) and *A Farewell to Arms* (1929) were notable examples. Faulkner extended this convention to his multiple narrators and went further, suggesting that these sections were variously akin to soliloquies, stream of consciousness on the Joycean model, or what Dorrit Cohn calls "memory monologues."[20]

The narration of the first two parts is fragmentary and nonlinear, shifting among events that are sometimes barely indicated. Benjy's narration is in its own way utterly objective, forcing us to infer characters' motives and circumstances. It makes building up the story even more difficult. Yet the texture isn't impenetrable—again, thanks to Faulkner's selective schema revision. For example, in reporting speech, Benjy replaces commas with periods: "'Listen at you now.' Luster said."[21] This idiosyncratic choice becomes part of the intrinsic norm for Benjy's section, and although it has an expressive effect, creating a choppy rhythm, a reader quickly learns to "read over" it.

The time shifts in Benjy's account are rendered without tagging and in the most minimal way possible, through paragraph breaks. Many shifts to earlier events are presented in italics. On a single page, there might be three crosscut scenes drawn from different points in the story action, with one italicized and the others not. Having established an intrinsic norm of narration, Faulkner then strategically violates it, expanding its purview while refusing to let us feel that we have wholly mastered it.[22] This exemplifies the thinning and rethickening strategy I mentioned in the introduction. As we adapt to initial difficulties, new ones crop up.

Faulkner originally wanted the time fragments printed in color-coded inks, not so far removed from the varying tints Griffith assigned to different epochs in *Intolerance*.[23] This option indicates an urge to help us over the bumps (although the narration might have gone on to sabotage this pattern too). As the book stands, our sense of the ongoing action in different periods is our most reliable compass for navigating the time shifts, with paragraphing and italics serving as supplementary cues.

Quentin's first-person account in the second part bristles with new variations and obstacles. Quotations are punctuated in the standard way, but many passages have no punctuation, or even capitalization, and italics may roll out in a long block of text or erupt in bursts. The free flow of Quentin's narration flattens normal exposition, recalling Gertrude Stein's remark: "When I began writing the whole question of punctuation was a vital question. . . . The comma was just a nuisance."[24]

> "I adore Canada," Miss Dangerfield said. "I think it's marvellous."
>
> "Did you ever drink perfume?" Spode said. *with one hand he could lift her to his shoulder and run with her running Running*
>
> "No," Shreve said. *running the beast with two backs and she blurred in the winking oars running the swine of Euboeleus running coupled within how many Caddy*
>
> "Neither did I," Spode said. *I don't know too many there was something terrible in me terrible in me Father I have committed have you ever done that We didn't we didn't do that did we do that*
>
> "and Gerald's grandmother always picked his own mint before breakfast, while the dew was still on it. . . ."[25]

The italicized interjections suggest an earlier encounter crosscut with the current scene, but that quasi-flashback is distressed by a stream of consciousness ("beast with two backs") and fragments of classical education and halting, incestuous confession. Even here, however, a few standard cues survive: paragraphing, the consistent shift to italics, and commonplace action schemas for running and speaking with others. (Thanks, Quentin, for naming Caddy.)

Even so we hit some bumps, especially at moments when the intrinsic norms are violated and we have to consider why this or that passage is treated exceptionally. If nothing else, modernist writing demonstrates how massively redundant everyday storytelling is. As we struggle to grasp minimal cues, Faulkner reminds us of the prompts that steer us to understanding easier books such as *How Like a God*, which neatly segregates italic from roman type, third-person from second-person narration.

By subtracting some reliable cues—time tags, cogent transitions between scenes, sourced character commentary—and by setting up unusual intrinsic norms, Faulkner is typical of his modernist peers. He teaches us how to comprehend his book. The gaps and frustrations must themselves be patterned, as they are here: gathered in distinct sections, laid out in teasing bits, coaxing us to master a fluctuating process of structure and narration. The early chapters of *Ulysses* introduce us to stream-of-consciousness narration in gradual doses, but Faulkner's opening has confronted us with the book's most difficult stretches. Then he rewards us by making the third and fourth sections far easier to follow. After reading the last two parts of *The Sound and the Fury*, we're invited to return to the first two sections to discover what we missed.

Faulkner later helped his readers much more. When his reputation was rehabilitated in the mid-1940s, he wrote an appendix that supplied both a Compson genealogy and rich biographies of the characters (Of Benjy: "Gelded 1913."). Perversely, in some editions of the novel, this appendix served as a preface, a decision that helped readers navigate what followed.[26]

Well before then, however, Faulkner had counted on other aids. Modernists were aware that literary institutions could help readers appreciate difficult work. For one thing, publishers could guide reception. The jacket copy for *The Sound and the Fury* helpfully announced that the opening segment dramatized the mind of "the idiot son" and traced how he "reverts to his childhood routinely at a sound, a smell, a sight." There was also the expanding power of literary commentary. By 1929, Faulkner could count on press accounts easing readers into his book.

Again and again reviewers identified the major characters, explained that the book traced the decline of a family, laid out the four-column grid of narrators, and dwelled on the peculiarities of Benjy's and Quentin's styles.[27] One critic speculated that Quentin imagines himself responsible for Caddy's death.[28] Another suggested that he breaks his watch "to put himself outside time."[29] Even unsympathetic critics could set expectations, as when Clifton Fadiman deplored the book's demand for "puzzle-solving" and objected to "one hundred pages of an imbecile's simplified sense perceptions and monosyllabic gibberings."[30] Novelists could hope that gatekeepers and tastemakers would acquaint audiences with the most striking innovations on display. Today's media critics avoid spoilers, chiefly ones pertaining to the story's twists or ending, but they feel free to prepare viewers for unusual formal strategies.[31]

Eventually, academics would exhaustively plumb modernist classics in monographs, class lectures, and introductions to critical editions. The Faulkner revival brought forth *The Portable Faulkner* (1946) and the beginning of a vast analytical literature that would prepare generations of readers for *The Sound and the Fury*. (If you haven't read the book, I've done my part too.) When Joyce was asked to share the conceptual scheme undergirding *Ulysses*, he withheld it, arguing half-seriously, "I've put in so many enigmas and puzzles that it will keep the professors busy for centuries arguing over what I meant, and that's the only way of insuring one's immortality."[32]

The Sound and the Fury can stand as a convenient example of the sort of bold schema revision proposed by many modernist texts. It shows how innovation can arise from block construction, nonchronological plot arrangement, and gaps and frictions in voice and viewpoint. It also shows that the innovation relies on recasting, not simply rejecting or subverting, traditional schemas. From the audience's viewpoint, the partial presence of those schemas help us grasp the story action and appreciate the power unleashed by the innovation. The novelty stands out against a blurred background of familiarity, and the innovation is grasped by principles of pattern specific to the particular work— and sometimes by helpful critical commentary.

The High Modernist canon weaponized (as we might say today) virtually every technique of standard storytelling.[33] Many innovations are intelligible as more or less elaborate revisions of schemas inherited from more mainstream traditions. For example, the intersecting plots of the triple-decker found a new concentration in *Mrs. Dalloway*'s dual-track story lines riddled with dreams, memories, and hallucinations. The "city mysteries" of Dickens and Eugène Sue use crisscrossing intrigues to survey levels of society, and this formal strategy was recast in Dos Passos's *Manhattan Transfer* (1925), which also provides a variant of the alternation schema on display in Waldo Frank's *City Block* (1922). Dos Passos fully embraced a montage aesthetic in his USA trilogy (1930–1936). That effort built on *Manhattan Transfer* and Joyce's city epic by incorporating "Newsreel" and "Camera Eye" blocks and splintering the sort of quasi-fictional social reportage mapped out by Upton Sinclair.

More pervasively, the multiplying viewpoints and voices of modernist fiction rework the dossier tradition. Through conversational inquiry, Conrad "vocalized" witnesses' testimony that would have been written out in the epistolary and casebook formats. But the witnesses' accounts remain embedded in a frame story. Modernists could revise the schema by dropping the frame and turning characters' accounts into inner speech, as Woolf does in *The Waves* (1931), which dissolves the narration into six phantasmal voices. *As I Lay Dying* (1930), which Faulkner dubbed his "tour de force," provides a mosaic of monologues, including one issuing from a corpse, all complicated by tense shifts and stream-of-consciousness interruptions.[34] Seven interlaced narrators in *Absalom, Absalom!* (1936) fragment Conrad's collective storytelling schema, generating page-long sentences and untagged chapters embellished with new habits of punctuation and typeface. In the theater, Eugene O'Neill recast the traditional soliloquy as a polyphonic stream of consciousness in the nine-act *Strange Interlude* (1928).

Ulysses, the prototypical novel of English-language High Modernism, is at once a city novel, an impressionistic rendering of consciousness, a collage of perspectives, and a reworking of an ancient narrative schema, with the chapter blocks matching the books of the *Odyssey*. Any narrative can be laid out on a grid, but Joyce's monument teemed with leitmotifs (colors, arts, bodily organs) that he charted on a spreadsheet.[35] Made public by critics, the table became an emblem of the density of symbolic patterning sought by modernist ambitions.

When Joyce invoked the virtuosity and hard work demanded by writing in many points of view and styles, he added that these were "all apparently unknown or undiscovered by my fellow tradesmen."[36] In declaring that his peers have missed out on his discoveries, Joyce sums up the ambitions of what Harry Levin has called "Ultraism": "that reshaping spirit which must continually transpose its material and outdistance itself in a dazzling sequence of newer and newest manners."[37] Beginning *The Sound and the Fury* with Benjy's daunting narration exemplifies this effort to surpass prevailing norms. Joyce's table of motifs is in the same spirit, carrying Henry James's demand for rigor and density into the fine grain of each segment. The ultimate Ultraist work may have been *Finnegans Wake* (1939), which for all its urge to hurl itself out of the orbit of literature remains the story of a dream, a schema of ancient lineage.

I don't mean to minimize the shock of the new. All the priming of the critics can't fully domesticate the reader's unruly, moment-by-moment experience of *The Sound and the Fury.* Just as Webern will never be elevator music, it's extremely unlikely that a reissue of *Tender Buttons* or *The Waves* or *Absalom, Absalom!* will outsell the next Stephen King release. Booth Tarkington mocked Faulkner, but his description is apt: He, like other modernists, is "satisfactorily confusing in ways that demonstrate greatness"[38]

The shock of the new is sometimes still the shock of the very old. As the Russian Formalist critics put it, the son can resemble the grandfather.[39] Any storyteller draws judiciously on prior traditions, even marginal or unfashionable ones. Some schemas are preserved to facilitate pickup; some are reshaped through reconfiguring their patterns or infusing them with new implications. From the audience's standpoint, even radical innovations stand out against a background, however hazy, of recognizable landmarks. The experimental narrative needs some anchoring, however wobbly, in tradition.

Ghastly Italics and Friendly Exoskeletons

"The tactful part of boldness," Jean Cocteau remarked, "is knowing how far is going too far."[40] Perhaps the Ultraists were more bold than tactful, but other storytellers shared Cocteau's caution. They seized on techniques of modernism while aiming to create something accessible to wide audiences.

After all, the new techniques were detachable. Once Joyce had shown how to write stream of consciousness, others could try it. Virginia Woolf had contrasted the new methods to the "conventions" that had preceded them, but the novelties became conventions in their turn.[41] The rapid turnover of popular forms described by Jean-Claude Carrière required novelty from whatever source could be found. Modernist techniques were absorbed and assimilated by authors less committed to difficulty. The trick was to turn forbidding stories into enticing ones while keeping some tang of the difficult.

For instance, after we've been steadily restricted to a Somerset Maugham protagonist, if the third-person narration abruptly shifts to supply the background of a new character in a crisp, implausible depth, has Maugham slipped back to the old nineteenth-century omniscience? No, because the bulk of the story continues to take advantage of the protagonist's limited knowledge; no Tolstoyan panoramas here. Any lump of exposition we get is presented as a condensation of information the protagonist was given on this or several occasions. Gore Vidal has suggested that Maugham's one-off violations of restricted viewpoint aim at quick pickup. They are "a lot better than having someone sit down and tell you the story of his life, in quotation marks, page after page."[42] Maugham trims the bulkiness of Conrad's boxes-within-boxes structure, which does often yield birds' nests of single and double quotation marks, while still profiting from tantalizing Conradian time gaps and uncertainty about new situations.

In these ways, Anglo-American literature selectively absorbed the new methods. Exhibit A: Before writing *How Like a God*, Rex Stout steeped himself in Wilder, Dos Passos, Joyce, Proust, Gide, Faulkner, Huxley, Woolf, and D. H. Lawrence.[43] Like them, he exposed his plot's structural axis, a geometry not visible in the prototypical easy story. Louis Bromfield's *24 Hours* (1930) blended the day-in-the-life time span of *Ulysses* with the cross-sectional survey of *Manhattan Transfer*, but without the montage frictions: it became a popular play and film. Something similar happened with Vicki Baum's novel *Grand Hotel* (1929). Intersecting lives, and a geometrical blocking-out of them, were the basis of Thornton Wilder's *Bridge of San Luis Rey* (1927).

Faulkner's multiple-narrator method in *As I Lay Dying* became an influential model but was smoothed out in works such as William March's *Company K* (1933). Kenneth Fearing's *The Hospital* (1939) ushers in as narrators doctors, nurses, patients, switchboard operators, laundry attendants, even a tugboat. As Gide had revised the embedded manuscript schema for *The Counterfeiters* (1925), Arnold Gingrich could recast Gide's reflexivity for his satiric book-within-a-book *Cast Down the Laurel* (1935).

In some of these cases, we might want to accuse popular culture of preying on high culture. But the modernists had already appropriated many devices from popular sources and roughened them up. In response, assimilators had to repolish the schemas. They had to put back what was taken out, provide instructions for understanding, reiterate the patterns, and tag things less cryptically. To see these tactics of accessibility at work, consider italics once more.

By and large, Anglo-American texts reserved italic type for titles of artworks and phrases to be stressed. ("They all like me, *me*."[44]) But modernists recruited italics for more mysterious purposes. Italics distinguish the single-page "chapters" sandwiched between the stories of Hemingway's *In Our Time* (1925). *Manhattan Transfer*, *The Waves*, and Jean Toomer's story "Esther" (1923) employ italics in passages that open chapters, with the effect of marking parallel blocks.

Writers had tried various ways of quoting inner monologue, with most opting for no punctuation at all or for enclosing quotation marks.[45] Waldo Frank's *Rahab* (1922) goes a bit Joycean, using the "dialogue-dash" for thoughts and reserving quotation marks for uttered speech. In *Manhattan Transfer*, Dos Passos assigns italics to song lyrics that creep in as "sound effects" or bits of memory. "From the next room comes the wheezy doublebarreled snoring of her uncle and aunt. *Somebody loves we, I wonder who. . . .* The tune is all through her body, in the throb of her feet, in the tingling place on her back where he held her tight dancing with her."[46] Another 1925 novel moves toward a flat pile-up without markers. C. Kay Scott's *Siren* introduces us to its method early: "Belle went obediently from the room. They don't like me, I can't help kissing babies, they smell good, I could eat them up, she felt helpless."[47]

It doesn't take much imagination to see how to tidy this up. The more mainstream Christopher Morley provides an instruction kit in *Thunder on the Left* (1925).

> Her mind ran beside her, like a questing dog, while she tried to steer their talk into some channel of reality. Her thoughts kept crowding massively under her uneasy words, pushing them out before they were ready, cutting into her speech like italics in a page of swarthy Roman type.
>
> "We could all eat too much in hot weather, I dare say. *Oh, if I could only write him a letter I could make him understand. He's so sophisticated.*"[48]

Morley assures us that these are Sylvia's thoughts, not only through the typeface but also by shifting to the present tense and by having her call Martin "him" and "he" rather than "you," which might have implied speech. From this point on, Sylvia's dialogue alternates with passages in italics reliably indicating her thoughts.

Faulkner accepted the emerging convention of using italics to signal characters' inner lives. But the Benjy and Quentin sections of *The Sound and the Fury* delete Dos Passos's contextual cues and Morley's explicit guidance and, as we've seen, push toward much greater fragmentation. The italics allow Faulkner to create a jerky alternation of past and present less marked in *Rahab* and *Siren*. Faulkner continued his play with typography through the 1940s (even adding parentheses within parentheses), as if trying to outrun the emerging mainstream convention. He risked looking silly. Vladimir Nabokov complained about Faulkner's "absolutely ghastly italics."[49]

Meanwhile, some popular writers smoothed out the device, being careful to tag it and mark it off more plainly than Morley had. "*There,* thought Millicent, *is Joe and his family ten years from now. And I suppose he thinks he's going to turn me into that woman.* She shuddered delicately at the thought."[50] By the 1940s, the reader could presume that direct address in italics would not be voiced, and the "you" could be included without risk of misunderstanding. "Strangely enough, she had been the strong one then. Roger going all to pieces. *Remember that, Roger. Your wife was strong, stronger than you, stronger than Addie could ever have been.*"[51] Pulp stories picked up the convention.[52] When paperback publishers of the 1940s reprinted novels of earlier eras, they sometimes reformatted inner monologues as italicized passages.[53] This strict marking of objective action from subjective response coincides with the emergence of character voice-over as a common film and radio technique.[54]

"Roger going all to pieces" in the previous example indicates how popular storytelling repurposed stream-of-consciousness techniques as well. Although manuals and how-to articles seldom encouraged aspiring authors to push toward modernist disorientation, many handbooks were quite systematic in laying out viewpoint options. A 1934 guide discussed how contemporary writers had exposed the "subconscious" through free association. Techniques pioneered by Joyce, Faulkner, and Woolf were said to be embraced by "the popular new literature of today," like the best-selling *Anthony Adverse* (1936).[55] Ten years after Woolf's *Jacob's Room* (1922), a history of the English novel could remark that shifting stream of consciousness among characters posed little difficulty for average readers.[56]

The firm regulating of italics and roman type, of inner speech and dialogue, appears to have become one stylistic norm of popular literary narrative.[57] Comparable tactics emerged in American radio drama, which was coming into its own in the 1930s. A show's many vocal strands—an announcer, the characters, and increasingly a narrator—needed to be distinguished. As radio plays began incorporating flashbacks and inner monologues, the creators stratified auditory registers. A voice close to the microphone could suggest not only spatial proximity but also action in the present, as opposed to more distant reverberant action in the past.[58] Filters would signal dialogue over the telephone. Sound could cut in abruptly or fade in gradually, each difference signaling changes in locale or time periods. Orson Welles's 1937 adaptation of *Dracula* is a montage of texts—journal entries, news reports, telegrams, conversations, monologues, memories—delivered with widely varying pitch, pace, and volume, providing an auditory equivalent to the dossier structure of the original novel.

Writer-producer-director Arch Oboler became famous as the champion of stream of consciousness in radio. Oboler's technique relied mostly on inner monologue rather than Joycean fragmentation, but it still demanded scrupulous channeling to orient the listener. Just as Faulkner employs spacing and typeface to cue shifts in time and viewpoints, Oboler's auditory mix carries us into characters' heads. In "Baby," broadcast in 1939, the sounds are layered to present a woman walking in the present (traffic, footsteps on the sidewalk) while an inner voice, closely miked, meditates on her pregnancy and leads to crisply focused dialogue from past conversations with her husband. In England, a similar "novelistic" transformation of radio drama took place under the auspices of the BBC.[59]

Throughout popular media fairly daring techniques operate in a give-and-take with cues that provide accessibility. The popular storyteller, we might say, re-revises the modernist version of classic devices. This dynamic is apparent in the predictable alternation and signposting of *How Like a God*. It's there as well in Dalton Trumbo's novel *Johnny Got His Gun* (1938), which carries Jamesian restriction and internalization of viewpoint to a harsh extreme. A first-person narration recounts the waves of awareness engulfing a soldier surviving loss of arms, legs, and face. Joe Bonham, confined to a hospital bed, recalls his life in flashbacks and calculates how to make his sacrifice show the public the futility of war. As often happens, a theme circulating in cultural discourse is endowed with new vividness by a bold but accessible narrative strategy. Oboler turned Trumbo's book into a disturbing radio monologue in 1940.[60]

A more genteel example of crossover is the best-selling *The Late George Apley* (1937), whose subtitle declares it "A Novel in the Form of a Memoir." Mr. Willing has been asked to compile a posthumous biography of a pillar of Boston society. He draws upon letters, diaries, college essays, private lectures, and his own acquaintance with Apley—a classic dossier premise. In addition, in recruiting Willing for the task, Apley's son alludes to scandals and family secrets. A memoir, it seems, benefits from a novelistic whiff of mystery.

Willing's chronicle shuffles time periods in good modernist fashion. Early on, we jump from 1912 to 1902 to 1916 and then to 1883. The gears shift smoothly thanks to Willing's commentary, and there are explicit chapter tags ("Harvard Days"). But our compiler is no Walter Hartwright, trustworthy editor of the documents in *The Woman in White*. Mr. Willing is pompous and is satisfied offering anodyne praise of a secretly unhappy man. The chapters' blandly pretentious subtitles ("The Establishment of a Beloved and Challenging Institution") show that Willing is oblivious to Apley's descent into melancholy. The result gestures toward the "prismatic" possibilities of Conradian tales. A reviewer observed that Apley emerges as both "tender husband and father and the veriest snob."[61]

In a more mystical version of *Grand Hotel*, *The Dark Glass* (1935) by March Cost proposes multiple protagonists and several layers of time. The guests and servants in a genteel boarding house are living through All Souls' Eve and All Souls' Day 1929. They gather for meals and then disperse to their routines and appointments. In the course of twenty-four hours, some face crises and all recall episodes from their past, which are presented by third-person narration and out of chronological order. The faded actress remembers her glory days; the young novelist hopes his brother approves of his new manuscript. Occasionally there's a dream too. But Cost adds another dimension: some of the characters are transported ahead to the parallel day in 1930. What motivates the time travel is a mysterious new mirror installed in the hallway, as well as the belief that All Souls' Eve is the moment when the living confront the dead. One character discovers that in 1930 she will be a ghost.

With dozens of characters and decades of time to be traversed, *The Dark Glass* might have become a slurry of confusion. Woolf or Faulkner would have reveled in the chance to let character voices and scenes mingle indeterminately in this house. But Cost provides firm guardrails. *The Dark Glass*'s table of contents supplies an exoskeleton that lays out the structure of the book. The whole is doubly framed: a prologue and epilogue describe a massive flight of birds, and introductory and closing sections center on the woman who runs the boarding house. Within the double frame, six blocks of chapters are labeled by the day's clock, the viewpoint character, and the action played out. As with the intertitles in *Intolerance*, the time shifts are constantly signposted.

A tabular structure like this lies behind dossier novels such as *The Moonstone*; a more rigorous geometry was hinted at in James's *The Awkward Age* and was exposed by Conrad's chapter layout in *Chance*. Joyce used a more intricate grid for *Ulysses* but concealed it. *The Dark Glass*, laying bare its architecture to guide the reader, relies on the symmetrical blocks that we find in mystery fiction from Anthony Berkeley to Richard Stark. Such grids became central to domestic suspense in the 2000s, when novels label time, place, and character while, as we'll see, heightening the uncertainty by omitting a table of contents. Part of the suspense now depends on confronting unexpected tagging as we turn the page.

Can the mainstream novelist avoid such explicit signposting? With its cryptic alphanumeric tags, *How Like a God* tries to do so. So does George Cronyn's *Fortune and Men's Eyes* (1935), whose family saga stretches across thirty-five years. It is articulated in five parts consisting of fifty-five chapters tagged with teasing, uninformative titles such as "The Thousandth Man" and "Umbilical Digression." Relying on shifts of viewpoint, multiple narrators, and jumps across time, the text needs other ways of orienting us. It finds them by establishing a stable intrinsic norm of alternating voices, framed by a clinical situation.

After a prologue tells of a clergyman's sexual adventure in Manila, *Fortune and Men's Eyes* launches into a first-person report of Byron Peirce, the minister's son. Gradually we realize that he is recounting this to Dr. Bedell, a researcher into men's sexuality. Byron's account in the book's first part culminates in a flashback from the narrating situation to a recent disaster: his brother Max has committed suicide. This mystery teases us to ask what led up to it. Thereafter the book presents chronological third-person accounts of the careers of Byron, Max, and their brother Clyde, alternating with Byron's first-person recollections, which move a little more freely through time. First- and third-person chunks are carved into distinct chapters—not, as in *Absalom, Absalom!*, dissolved together. Passages from Dr. Bedell's journal interpreting the case are supplemented by other inquiries he has made into the family.

In all, we have a sleek update of the dossier format, in which the tags can be omitted because there are only two character narrators (plus an external voice expanding our access to other scenes). A reliable rhythm of alternation fits within the framing situation of the talking cure. Needless to say, the last word falls to the authoritative Dr. Bedell, and he is able to assure a happy ending to the surviving brothers and the women they love. Meanwhile, the reader has learned to read the book.

Even writers with modernist aspirations learned to adjust. Julian Shapiro had tried Joycean stream of consciousness in *The Water Wheel* (1933), but *Seventy Times Seven* (1939), published under the pseudonym John Sanford, judiciously guides readers through a fragmented story of two men's parallel lives in a rural town. The novel starts with objective, external narration presenting Aaron Platt finding a bum half-frozen in his barn. Platt takes up the story in first person, recounting events to an unidentified listener who interjects questions. Running alongside Platt's account is a soliloquy from the dying tramp Paulhan, in a first-person narration that hovers between lyrical inner monologue and speech. Both men's discourses contain flashbacks, often italicized. As the novel continues, the personal linkages between the men are revealed, and we gradually realize that Platt's account is his inquest testimony after Paulhan's death. By the end of *Seventy Times Seven*, the external narration returns to confirm the stability of the situation, and the classic trial schema has been revised but not rejected.

Compromises and blends like these offer a good reason to avoid "middle-brow" as the best blanket term for in-between cases. Granted, critics have posited characteristic middlebrow themes and subjects. Again and again we confront problems of individual consciousness, weakness of will, social identity, feeble political resistance, middle-class family life, and the passing of the old ways. *The Late George Apley* seems resolutely middlebrow in its fascination with the decline of an entitled patriarch, whereas the efficacy of psychological research in *Fortune and Men's Eyes* can be seen as promoting support for new sciences of mental health, not least the vogue for pseudo-Freudian psychoanalysis. *How Like a God* could be a case history of repressed incestuous desires: all the women Bill meets fail to measure up to his glorious sister Jane, who won his heart as a child when she gave him a cookie.

The themes and subjects of these books could have been treated in a much less zigzag fashion. Are the formal maneuvers simply clever bids for literary legitimacy? Not entirely. They govern our immediate uptake of the book. Although these stories don't radically call identity or social life into question, they aren't as complacent about motive and our understanding of it as they might be. Their construction nuances our experience in ways that a more straightforward rendering wouldn't. Their eventual reversion to the prototype of the easiest narrative retains the tang of transgression. So it isn't a waste of time to consider their tactics of accessibility. We can analyze how form and style are manipulated, thickened and thinned, in the overall architecture and in items as minute as typography and chapter titles.

Bringing the Children

The vast variorum of Anglo-American storytelling early in this century has forced scholars to expand the boundaries of modernist writing beyond the narrow canon of earlier times. A recent academic survey considers hard and soft modernism, high and low modernism, African American modernism, Imperialist modernism, Marxist modernism, reactionary modernism, transnational modernism, glamour modernism, queer modernism, feminist sublime modernism, and even podiatric modernism.[62]

Yet another zone, especially important for Anglo-American storytelling, seems worth charting. Henry James put "fun" in quotation marks, but other modernist works aimed for fun unadorned. Sometimes these less imposing works harbor more intricacy and imagination, not to mention delight, than we find in "difficult" but pedestrian avant-garde work. The shock of the new need not be a lightning bolt; it might be an aggressive tickle. Consider what happened on May 18, 1917, at the Théâtre du Chatelet.

That night bohemian Paris mingled with the well-off to witness *Parade*, a spectacle very much in the modern mood. On stage a barker offered previews of a carnival tent show. The attractions included a Chinese magician who spit fire, an American manager encased in a ten-foot-high skyscraper, a dancing horse, and a Little American Girl who pranced to ragtime while performing movie pantomime. Despite appearances, it was no amateur hour. It boasted sets by Picasso, choreography by Diaghilev's lead dancer, and exuberant music by Erik Satie. The whole spectacle was overseen by Jean Cocteau.[63]

As Cubist paintings had cut up newspaper ads, the "realist ballet" *Parade* gleefully flung together bits of circus, fairground, cabaret, movies, and jazz. The score offered, as Alex Ross puts it, "a new art of musical collage."[64] Today some would say it's all a mash-up, but we might as well call it light modernism.[65] Its motto might be what one distressed spectator confessed: "If I'd known it was so silly I'd have brought the children."[66]

Apart from Joyce, High Modernism isn't usually associated with comedy, but as we've seen, comedy can make formal innovation user-friendly. French examples from *Parade*'s era come easily to mind: Apollinaire's *Mamelles de Tiresias* (1917); Stravinsky's *L'Histoire du soldat* (1917) and the wrong-note Pergolesi of *Pulcinella* (1920); the paintings of Picabia and the films of René Clair; the music of Les Six, with Satie as innocently naïve inspiration. Light modernism became Cocteau's brand, from his opera *Oedipus Rex* (1925), with a narrator in evening clothes, to his late films such as *Le Testament d'Orphée* (1960). Parallels can be found in the Brecht/Weill collaborations, the stage productions of Meyerhold, and Shostakovich's opera *The Nose* (1928).[67] In the United States, the paintings of Stuart Davis give a lilt to Cubism and anticipate Pop Art, and Philip Furia has argued that rag-pulsed Tin Pan Alley songs of the interwar years produce staccato verse forms akin to those of William Carlos Williams and e. e. cummings.[68]

A comfortable home for light modernism is theater. Extroverted and exhibitionistic, stage comedy can sweeten offbeat experiments. Luigi Pirandello, for instance, insisted on calling his plays comedies, despite the ontological and epistemic problems they seemed to raise. From one angle, *Six Characters in Search of an Author* (1921) debates the philosophical implications of uncertain identity and false appearances. Characters the playwright has cut out of his script invade a rehearsal and demand to have their stories reintegrated. Once they become part of the text, they will live eternally. Hard luck for the actors, though; they will die. From another angle, *Six Characters* is self-parody. The play in rehearsal is written by one Luigi Pirandello, whose works, the Manager says, "require a 'highbrow' to understand them and never satisfy the actors, the critics, or the public."[69]

Six Characters won success around the world and led Pirandello to a Nobel Prize for Literature. He bequeathed modernism a trilogy of plays that laid bare paradoxes encompassing all the participants in the theater: the creator, the interpreter, the audience, and the critic.[70] Again, the schemas he activated weren't entirely new; they harkened back to *The Rehearsal* (1671), Sheridan's *The Critic* (1779), and other satires on stage life. But Pirandello's frame-breaking and fragmentation, his emphasis on indeterminacy of motive and consequence, were in the High Modernist spirit. So too was his view of theater as a bitter showcase of illusion. We deeply misunderstand ourselves, he maintained. We wear masks to hide our ignorance and unhappiness. "This is funny, if we stop to think of it."[71]

In the Anglo-American stage tradition, light modernism is perhaps most visible in the works of two authors forever branded as middlebrow. Both had successful novels in the 1920s but found their greatest fame as playwrights. J. B. Priestley was gripped by a very modernist concern with the mysteries of time. *Dangerous Corner* (1932) posits a forking-road, or butterfly-effect plot: change one detail, and an alternative future opens up. *Time and the Conways* (1937) reverses the chronological order of acts II and III without the alibi of a flashback, and *I Have Been Here Before* (1937) shows characters who know the future and are trying to avert it.

Wilder, believing that the theater had clung too long to novelistic conventions of realism, embraced Pirandello's efforts at serious fantasy.[72] In synchronization with a broader movement toward "Theatricalism," Wilder sought to return to the bare Elizabethan stage, with all its freedom to evoke an abstract time and space.[73] *The Long Christmas Dinner* (1931) shows a single meal stretching across ninety years, in which generations of family members replace one another at the table. *The Skin of Our Teeth* (1942) sets cave dwellers living in modern New Jersey.

Wilder modernized the return to the empty playing space through reflexivity: the inclusion of an impresario addressing the audience and steering the story back and forth in time. The stage manager of *Pullman Car Hiawatha* (1931) draws a plan of the train car, *Dogville* fashion, and presides over a chorale of inner monologues from the sleeping compartments. Yet Wilder's brand of Theatricalism also turned the stage more literary, with the stage manager offering the sort of omniscience and fluctuating viewpoints favored by narratives in prose and verse. In *Our Town* (1938), the narrator introduces the newsboy by explaining he'll die in the war to come, and the threnodies of the dead in the cemetery recall Edgar Lee Masters's monologues in *Spoon River Anthology* (1915).

Pirandello, Priestley, and Wilder, however playful, aimed at a degree of artistic gravity. Less prestigious entertainments explored novelty in ways reminiscent of 1910s formalism. Flashbacks were now common in Broadway's comedies, thrillers, and musicals. *Two Seconds* (1931; film, 1932) showed a man's life racing past him as he is electrocuted. Sometimes the flashbacks were not chronological; at the limit, the whole plot could be in reverse order (*The Varying Shore*, 1921; *Merrily We Roll Along*, 1934). *Three Waltzes* (1937) and other plays used blocks to parallel different couples in different eras, as the film spinoffs of *Intolerance* had. A West End vehicle by Ivor Novello, *Symphony in Two Flats* (1929), featured simultaneous action in two apartments. *Three Times the Hour* (1931) went further by presenting parallel action on three different floors of a mansion; the device of ending each act with a gunshot synchronizes them and anticipates Jim Jarmusch's film *Mystery Train* (1989).

Other innovations included subjectivity and reflexivity. *Made for Each Other: A Switchback Comedy* (1924) presented three versions of a bridegroom's reason for not appearing at the altar. *If Booth Had Missed* (1932) proposed alternative history. In an echo of *The Big Idea*, *The Last Warning* (1927) made the last act of this play furnish the first act of a fictitious one. A schema that was to prove durable in film and fiction was laid out in *These Few Ashes* (1928). After a man has died, three women visit the urn holding his remains, and flashbacks present each one's conflicting impressions of him.

The Pirandello vogue encouraged reflexive entertainments that replaced his bitterness and relativism with straight comedy and more explicit fantasy. *On Stage* (1935) shows an author dreaming that his characters refuse to be in his production; in *Knickerbocker Holiday* (1938) the author steps in as a deus ex machina. *The Schemers* (1924) assembles critics to discuss a play they've seen, a premise reworked in the novel *All Star Cast* (1936), mentioned in the introduction. There were plays within plays, including a comedy showing amateurs fumbling their production of *Hamlet*. Shakespeare himself appears, along with Francis Bacon, in *Good Theatre* (1926). As the authors loiter in the lobby during a performance of something called *Your Money or Your Life*, the doorman summarizes the plot in iambic pentameter. Did Tom Stoppard read this?

In the same vein, but more aggressive, was the manic *Hellzapoppin'* (1938). The Marx brothers had brought mayhem to *The Cocoanuts* (1925; film, 1929) and *Animal Crackers* (1928; film, 1930). In *Hellzapoppin'* comedians Ole Olson and Chic Johnson added to Marxian non sequiturs a fusillade of running gags, few funny in themselves but most wearing down resistance through escalation. As a punitive bonus, the action invaded the auditorium.

> Their stooges are clamoring the aisles and hanging out of the boxes and their audiences have to sustain a barrage of eggs (harmless), bananas (real) and spiders and snakes (simulated). The distractions are a fundamental part of the evening's brawl. During half the evening a sharp-voiced harpy wanders up and down the aisles calling "Oscar, Oscar" until she has to be shot. A desperate messenger tries to deliver a plant that grows alarmingly bigger every time he appears. Pity the ill-fated magician who not only fails to wriggle out of a strait-jacket in the five seconds allotted to his act but fails to wriggle out of it all evening.[74]

Audience members weren't spared during the intermission. Clowns harassed them.

A down-market counterpart to *Parade* and other Parisian spectacles, *Hellz-apoppin'* recycled virtually every gimmick of popular theater as Broadway-friendly burlesque. It played the huge Winter Garden Theatre for three years. It was made into a movie, which lost the interactivity of live theater but allowed film technique to take the goofiness in fresh directions (figs. 2.1–2.2).[75] Light modernism and its vaudevillian cousins suggest yet another overlap between severe, demanding narratives and something more accessible, sometimes charming and sometimes annoying. The shock of the new can be a poke in the ribs.

2.1 *Hellzapoppin'* (1941): A dust-up in the projection booth makes the film slip out of frame. The characters adjust.

2.2 *Hellzapoppin'*: Kane's sled turns up in a movie set. "I thought they burned that."

Crossing Over, from Both Sides

As Joyce, Woolf, Faulkner, and others strained to go further and "take the next step," they were competing with their prior work and each other's achievements. At the same time, all the melds, mergers, sports, and hopeful monsters in the 1920s may have goaded them on as well. The Ultraist impulse could outrun the Hergesheimers and Wilders, the "middlebrow" domesticators of High Modernist techniques. Faulkner, in particular, seems to have made each of his 1930s and 1940s novels a tour de force of fresh difficulty and hectic virtuosity.

The variety of all the in-between accomplishments flummoxes our best efforts to sort them into the three bins of high, low, and middle. The best I can offer is a current, conveniently vague label. Recognizing the High Modernist canon as the core of a blurred circle, or the looming tag in a cloud network, I'll just call all the middling cases *crossovers*. The term is usually used when two genres are combined (e.g., *Westworld*) or characters from one established fictional world visit another (Godzilla meeting King Kong). I'll use it to signal plots that blend techniques often associated with modernism with others associated with mainstream narrative. The term dodges a lot of questions, but at least it coaxes us to recognize that because many cultural levels blend and nourish one another we should examine specific strategies at work in each case.

We can find this crossover impulse in the proto-modernists Henry James and Joseph Conrad. Their mature periods coincided with the emergence of the detective story as a distinct novelistic genre. James's middle phase runs alongside Doyle's tales of Holmes and Watson, and Conrad's *Chance* (1913) was published the same year as E. C. Bentley's *Trent's Last Case*. Playing with time and viewpoint inclined James and Conrad to build plots around tantalizing secrets that attract bystanders. The half-hidden affair in "In the Cage" and the trail of clues in "The Turn of the Screw" lead the stories' protagonist on, as do the marital deceptions of *What Maisie Knew* (1897) and the puzzle of mismatched couples in *The Sacred Fount* (1901). *The Other House* (1896) revolves around a murder, and in "The Figure in the Carpet" (1896) James transposes the investigation plot into an inquiry into literary creativity. Conrad, one contemporary noted, "enjoys keeping you in doubt as much as any writer of detective stories."[76] *The Secret Agent* (1907) was inspired in part by a police officer's memoir and has the contours of a suspense thriller. In other books Marlow pursues investigations, aided in *Chance* by a co-narrator who reveals that the entire plot hinges on a double meaning of the word "Ferndale." These affinities shouldn't surprise us because many of the plot schemas and narration strategies James and Conrad revise were employed in Gothic and sensation fiction and the nineteenth-century "city mysteries."

Among the modernists proper we find a frank fascination with popular culture as a whole and tales of mystery in particular.[77] Jorge Luis Borges, another avatar of fantasy-skewed modernism, admired Doyle, Chesterton, and

American whodunits. T. S. Eliot compared Wilkie Collins favorably with Dickens and found the Collins test misleading: "We cannot afford to forget that the first—and not one of the least difficult—requirements of either prose or verse is that it should be interesting."[78] Eliot famously pilfered a passage from a Holmes story for a play that he gave a faintly pulpish title, *Murder in the Cathedral* (1935).

Perhaps the biggest fan was Gertrude Stein. What enticed her about mysteries wasn't the puzzle element: "I like somebody being dead and how it moves along."[79] She also liked the inevitable repetition arising from witnesses being questioned: "No matter how often the witnesses tell the same story the insistence is different."[80] When she visited the United States in 1942, she was keen to meet Dashiell Hammett because he had a proper appreciation of death. Stein avidly followed American murder cases, and during her stay in Chicago she rode with police patrols. In the following year, she wrote probably the most eccentric entry in the genre, *Blood on the Dining-Room Floor*. Characters are seldom identified, there seems to be no detective, the victim isn't named until the end, the murder apparently goes unsolved, and the narrators are as baffled as the reader. As the book is closing, we confront:

> Lizzie do you understand.
> Of course she does.
> Of course do you.[81]

Lizzie Borden isn't a character in the book (I think), but Stein occasionally dropped the name into her texts as an homage.

Stein's novel is a crossover from the avant-garde side, a phenomenon that goes back to Surrealist appropriations of Fantômas and Charlie Chaplin and to Soviet films' pillaging of imagery from Hollywood silent comedy. Traffic in the other direction, as we've seen, shows up when exoteric storytellers revamp modernist devices. We should remember, however, that if a particular technique has been made salient by modernism there's a good chance that it's a roughened revision of a device already available to popular storytellers. In turn, the venturesome popular storyteller will smooth out some of the bumps while retaining a sense of disruption.

A straightforward example is supplied by Horace McCoy. Known chiefly as a pulp writer, he found critical recognition with *They Shoot Horses, Don't They?* (1935). Fragments of a judge's pronouncement of sentence are crosscut with an inner monologue of the prisoner recalling a grueling dance marathon. The scenes in the past aren't tagged by chapter titles, but the chronology is signaled by the running total of the hours that couples spend hauling themselves across the floor. Italics, boldface type, and expanded fonts are used in staccato escalation until the finale: "may God have mercy on your soul." The suspense is driven less by mystery than inevitability; we expect that the protagonist will kill the woman he meets, and so the question is chiefly how that comes about.

Cora Jarrett had more genteel literary ambitions than McCoy, so she declared *Night Over Fitch's Pond* her "psychological and emotional novel of married life."[82] But it opens with a death in questionable circumstances. Despite Jarrett's claim that it was not a "guessing game," the plot of love among academics did have detective-story overtones.[83] The title is sinister, the narrator invokes "a sense of riddles unsolved," Poe's "Oblong Box" is referenced, and the action has a classic investigative arc.[84] It's almost as if *The Great Gatsby* began with Nick bending over Gatsby's corpse floating in the pool.

A professor has drowned during a summer holiday, and his colleague Walter sits vigil over the body. In first-person narration, he broods on what led to this . . . accident? suicide? murder? "Through the brain-chamber of my heavy head, pictures flickered and melted into one another, like a cinema."[85] Flashbacks as recounted by Walter, the deeply invested but limited onlooker, reveal tensions and infidelities among couples in the lakeside cabins. A second death is discovered, and Walter gradually comes to realize what has happened behind the scenes.

Along the way the narration refreshes the intrinsic norm through parallel couples, flash-forwards, and a stretch of hypothetical action in playscript format. As in *How Like a God*, present and past moments increasingly mingle in the protagonist's mind as his narration moves toward the climax. Again, a reader could map out a coherent time line quite easily. Jarrett doesn't use chapter titles to signpost the shifts, but the flashbacks within chapters are marked off by triple spaces and the usual specifiers of time and place.

Reviewers treated *Night Over Fitch's Pond* as a blend of mystery and serious fiction. There were complaints that the solution did not play fair, an indication that critics were applying the rules of the whodunit in spite of the novel's aspirations.[86] The book's crossover potential was exploited by its publisher, who took out an advertisement insisting that the book was more than a mystery but still ripe with suspense, "a tense psychological novel."[87] Jarrett's next novel was an unabashed mystery story.

C. H. B. Kitchin enjoyed the literary laurels Jarrett sought; his detective stories were published by Hogarth Press, owned by Leonard and Virginia Woolf. Kitchin's crossover fame rests on *Birthday Party* (1938), a round-robin quadruple-narrator account revisiting an apparent suicide within a wealthy family. The eight chapters create a four-by-two grid enclosing scrambled flashbacks that are conveyed through diary entries and inner monologues. The climax arrives when the family meet to celebrate the heir's birthday. The reader is guided by an initial notice—"The name at the head of each chapter is that of the narrator"— and by transitional tags that introduce the flashbacks. The book's affiliations are marked when one character tells another she seems destined "to live in a detective story"—a gesture of reflexivity conventional in the mystery genre.[88]

Some would say that mystery crossover reached a limit with Cameron McCabe's *The Face on the Cutting-Room Floor* (1937). The narrator purports to be the author himself, as well as a prime suspect in the murder of a movie actress. The book begins with a parody of legalese warning against libelous attacks on the author, and it ends with a fake critical essay summarizing the reviews that the novel received and meditating on the conventions of murder fiction. The story is told by McCabe across nineteen chapters, then told again by another character, and then retold by McCabe in a new version. Eventually there are nine versions of the action, a situation that the essayist interprets, with the zeal of a modernist critic, in good reflectionist fashion. "Nothing is firmly fixed, nothing steadfast, nothing solidly established. Everything is in the process of change, demolition, decay: an exact picture of the man and his age."[89] The multiplicity of story versions perversely becomes the book's intrinsic norm.

Something of a novelistic equivalent of Pirandello, with a movie studio standing in for a stage milieu, *The Face on the Cutting-Room Floor* employs reflexive comedy with affinities to *Hellzapoppin'* as well. Recent editions carry an afterword in which the author, émigré Ernest Borneman, admits that the book was written under the influence of Proust, Joyce, Dos Passos, and other modernist masters. It's not too much to see parody of them alongside mockery of mystery conventions.[90]

My opening example for this chapter constitutes another crossover case study. In 1919 *A Voice in the Dark* had dramatized a criminal investigation through modular "cut-backs" and stage techniques mimicking sensory deprivation. Ten years later in *How Like a God*, Rex Stout embeds a story of erotic frustration and a quasi-modernist play with time and viewpoint within a thriller framework. "The suspense in which the reader is held as he tries to guess which of the five women 'you' are to murder is of the detective-story order," noted an unsympathetic reviewer.[91] In a few years, Stout would forsake literary prestige and turn to writing mysteries. He would soon show that detective fiction could harbor verbal and narrative pirouettes reminiscent of modernist ones.

✳ ✳ ✳

There is a self-congratulatory side to avant-garde innovation not far removed from the cleverness we savor in genre storytelling. We call one genius, the other ingenuity. One yields discomfiting engagement, the other ingratiating audacity. Which is another way of saying that modernist storytelling is itself a tradition, wide-ranging and exploratory but still pledged to its own conventions of viewpoint, segmentation, and the patterning of time. That tradition is open to raids from many storytellers with other purposes, just as modernists seized and transformed resources of popular tradition, mystery chief among them. By the 1940s, the modernist tradition of satisfactory confusion had largely been superseded by something more accessible that would become the basis of our era of perpetual crossover.

CHAPTER 3

━━━

CHURN AND CONSOLIDATION

The 1940s and After

T he British film *The Woman in Question* (1950) begins when Agnes
Houston, a blowsy fortune-teller and gold digger, is found strangled in her down-market London flat. Superintendant Lodge
immediately questions several suspects. Each interrogation frames a batch of
flashbacks, and these are presented in eighteen chunks (more like the to-and-
fro movement of *How Like a God* rather than the three long blocks in *A Voice in
the Dark*). Often a single brief flashback is interrupted by an abrupt cut back to
Lodge pressing for more information.

The time frame is further complicated. Within each character's account, the
flashbacks are chronological, but because each character has interacted with
Agnes at varying points over the last ten months, we encounter the past scenes
out of chronological order. For example, the first flashbacks, rendered by the
landlady Mrs. Finch, start in the previous winter and proceed to the night of
the murder. The flashbacks later presented by the out-of-work magician Bob
Baker start earlier, in September. Those reported by the sailor Michael Murphy
start even earlier in the summer. The result is a mosaic of episodes, a "spatial
form" that could be laid out on a grid.

We're oriented to the overall focus of the action through scenes repeated in
whole or in part in different characters' testimony. This replay strategy had been
used in *A Voice in the Dark* and other popular narratives. The novelty of *The
Woman in Question* on this front is twofold.

First, to a degree unusual in popular filmmaking, the narration strictly confines itself to what the reporting character knows. The most striking example

is an apparently damning incident on the night of the murder. Agnes's sister Caroline and her fiancé Bob have been embroiled in an explosive quarrel with Agnes. On the staircase, Caroline and Bob threaten her: Bob calls Agnes rotten, Caroline says only killing Agnes would stop her, and Bob agrees he'd enjoy doing that. Three versions of this exchange are presented in the film, first in Mrs. Finch's flashback, then in Bob's, and finally by Mr. Pollard, the owner of the bird shop across the street The first and third versions, confined to Mrs. Finch and Mr. Pollard, don't reveal what the quarrel is about because these characters see only the aftermath on the stairs. Only Bob's version reports on what triggered the threats. This restriction of character knowledge is carried down into stylistic patterning, as director Anthony Asquith provides approximations of characters' optical viewpoints. (figs. 3.1–3.4.)

The disparities in characters' positions in the illustrations hint at the second novelty in the film's narration. The replays disagree about what happened in

3.1 *The Woman in Question* (1950): In Mrs. Finch's testimony, she and Mr. Pollard . . .

3.2 . . . see a dignified Agnes threatened by Catherine and Bob.

3.3 The replay of the quarrel, as narrated by Catherine, presents a shrieking Agnes . . .

3.4 . . . and a provoked Bob bridling at her threat to destroy the couple.

a scene. Some anomalies are outright lies; Mr. Pollard's testimony, for reasons that will become clear, is partially false. (In this same year Hitchcock released *Stage Fright*, with its famous "lying flashback," and the Japanese film *Rashomon* gained fame on similar grounds.) Other anomalies are justified, in retrospect, as faulty memory. No two versions of what Agnes, Catherine, and Bob say on the stairs are exactly the same. Lodge himself excuses this, mentioning at one point that he can't quite recall what words a particular witness used. But more significant disparities stand out in the film's effort to disclose what type of person Agnes was.

For decades storytellers had dreamed of the "prismatic" narrative, the one revealing contrasting or conflicting sides of a character through various viewpoints. Conrad's portrayal of *Lord Jim* was considered a model, and Sophie Treadwell's play *Eye of the Beholder* (1919), though little known at the time, came to be another example. The title of *The Woman in Question* suggests that the central mystery hovers around Agnes, and the varying testimonies aim to make her contradictory facets vivid.

To Mrs. Finch, Agnes is a dignified lady who resists the efforts of Bob to seduce her. To Catherine, her sister is a drunken slattern, disloyal to her husband who is dying in hospital. Bob presents Agnes as a woman bent on seducing him, who then becomes vindictive when he and Catherine plan to marry. (The staircase quarrel is the result of Agnes's threat to ruin Bob's impending divorce.) To Mr. Pollard, Agnes is the sweet, soft-spoken woman he wants to marry. Michael Murray's Agnes is treacherous and unfaithful, refusing to give up her promiscuous ways. The accounts crystallize at the climax when Lodge's questions about the real Agnes are sharpened in a flurry of single-shot flashbacks of four versions we've seen.

If this were simply a meditation on the ultimate mystery of human personality, we could leave it at that. But the genre demands greater certainty. Lodge assures us that ruling out inaccurate versions of Agnes will help solve the mystery.

That solution is aided in part by the overall organization of the action. However rosy Mrs. Finch's view of Agnes is, and however strong the "primacy effect" of presenting that view as our introduction to the character, it is soon enough challenged. Lodge warns us not to take Mrs. Finch's account as wholly reliable. From the start she is shown as a preening busybody, and subsequent flashbacks undercut her portrayal of Agnes.[1] These scenes consistently show a predatory woman providing her intimates with ample motives for murder. Moreover, although Catherine is presented as a shrew in Mrs. Finch's account, during Lodge's questioning, she is kindly and soft-spoken, willing to admit her own mistakes. Her frankness is suggested by a sudden frontal close-up when she addresses the camera (fig. 3.5). Likewise, the Bob of Mrs. Finch's story is a hard-edged grifter, not the hesitant ne'er-do-well we meet in Lodge's questioning.

3.5 Learning that Mrs. Finch accused her of being in love with Agnes's dying husband, Catherine pivots sharply to Lodge and to the viewer: "Well, let me tell you the truth!"

Bob and Catherine are far more sympathetic outside Mrs. Finch's flashbacks than within them, and we are invited to assume that her elevation of Agnes has led her to caricature the couple.

A comparable deflation occurs in Mr. Pollard's account. In his flashbacks, Agnes is utterly sweet and demure. But he is in love with her. His portrait, Lodge points out, "is entirely unlike any of the others. . . . He has built an ideal world around a woman." Coming after we have seen Agnes as lustful and vindictive, it's easy to grasp his account as utterly romanticized. In Michael's account, we'll learn that Agnes has played up to Pollard to extract favors and money. Watching Pollard's flashbacks, we're required to imagine that the scenes he reports did probably take place but that her gentle demeanor in them is a projection of his imagination.

The smaller disparities among the accounts offered by Catherine, Bob, and Michael are explainable as something else: Agnes's cunning role-playing. Alone with Catherine, having no need to pretend, she lets her sour cynicism out fully. With Michael, who promises money and excitement, she can play someone more acquiescent, although there might be a degree of his projection in the flashbacks showing her demurely willing to remain chaste during his time on the sea. It's Bob's version that shows most clearly how Agnes plays roles. She can seem ladylike at one moment and turn virago in another. Taken together, the accounts offered by Catherine, Bob, and Michael present a character driven by the urge for money, sex, and control over those who come into her ken.

The "prismatic" effect has been a pretext for sustaining the mystery, not a fully achieved result. Although Agnes's character turns out not to be multifaceted, the disparate versions of her help solve the murder. Lodge takes over the filmic narration in the denouement by visiting Pollard and proposing that the sailor, Michael, killed Agnes. Now we get the detective's hypothetical flashback to that scene, with his voice-over explicating how Michael might be guilty. As if in a trance, Pollard agrees.

But then the flashback resumes with Lodge's voice-over putting Pollard in Michael's place. The old man finally sees Agnes as she is. Her grande dame graciousness is gone, and she sneers, "Well, what do you want?" After she mocks Pollard's marriage proposal, he lumbers forward to kill her. The detective's multiple-draft replay has been a trap, consistent with the way that his role as *raisonneur* has recast the off-key flashbacks as the projections of the parvenu Mrs. Finch and the yearning Mr. Pollard.

By 1950, a mass-audience movie could present a fairly fragmented plot as recounted by five witnesses, using methods associated with "advanced" literary traditions.[2] The mildly experimental slant of the film is confirmed by split decisions in its reception. One U.S. reviewer worried that it would be too difficult for some American audiences, but another thought that it would "gratify the clever customer."[3] Other critics in both England and the United States claimed that it was too obvious and repetitive.[4]

Although *Rashomon* leaves its search for truth suspended in uncertainty, and *Stage Fright* counts on viewers forgetting exactly how they were misled, *The Woman in Question* mobilizes explicit cues for reliability that counterbalance its tug toward relativism. Thanks to the familiar contours of the investigation plot and some redundant design features (characterization of the witnesses, Agnes's consistent behavior in the most trustworthy flashbacks), the multiple-viewpoint schema could be revised to yield a final clarity—the accessibility typical of popular narrative.

The Case of the Missing Modernists

The opportunities open to Anglo-American fictional storytelling, both eso-teric and exoteric, widened considerably across the first half of the twentieth century. The year 1910 was the peak in U.S. book publishing in sheer number of titles and editions. Output dipped during the Depression, but by the 1940s the American market was flourishing again, and the British one, although less robust, was facing strong customer demand. Despite wartime restrictions on paper supplies, the book trade benefited from a new interest in reading.[5] If fewer titles appeared, many more copies were sold—more than 400 million in the United States in 1945.[6] American publishers benefited from practices established in the 1930s, such as book clubs, heavy promotion of top sellers, and particularly the new possibilities opened by paperback publishing.[7]

Cheap paperback editions had been issued in earlier eras, but the Penguin imprint in Britain in 1935 and Pocket Books in the United States in 1939 began to revolutionize the literary market. Most of the paperback houses that sprang up in their wake relied on reprints of hardback editions released by established presses. The many paperback originals also supported expansion of mystery, romance, western, and other popular genres. Paperbacks benefited from distribution outside the relatively small number of bookstores; they could be bought in drugstores, on newsstands, and at railway and bus terminals. By 1948, Pocket Books alone was producing 180 million units a year, and a first paperback printing of a novel would routinely run to 150,000 copies.[8]

Magazines boomed as well. "Pulps," printed on cheap woodpress, continued to favor the genres of crime, horror, fantasy, science fiction, and romance. "Slick" magazines catered to family and women's audiences, mixing journalism, essays, advice, and reportage with fiction. As in earlier decades, the *Saturday Evening Post, Collier's, Liberty*, and the *American Magazine* were hospitable to short stories, novellas, and novels that could be serialized. The expanding circulation of magazines, especially in the postwar years, gave writers new incentives.

At the same time, comic books were pervading popular culture. In Britain most such books were reprints of newspaper strips, but American companies developed long-form stories based around children such as Little Lulu, funny animals such as the Disney characters, and most prominently superheroes. Superman, created in 1938, was by 1941 joined by Batman, the Flash, Captain America, Captain Marvel, Aquaman, and Wonder Woman. Soon there were hundreds of comic book titles of all types. The market reached its peak between 1947 and 1952.[9]

Anglo-American performing arts enjoyed similar success. Although London's West End suffered under the blitzkrieg, Broadway did well. The 1944–45 season was the most financially successful in years, with eighty-three new plays and a quarter of those considered hits. American films triumphed even more spectacularly. From 1944 to 1947, more than eighty million people went to the movies every week, a record that has never been equaled. British movie going hit its own peak at the same time. Although Broadway, Hollywood, and UK filmmaking went into a slump in the late 1940s, as did most leisure industries, dozens of plays and films of the decade remain landmarks. *The Glass Menagerie, Death of a Salesman, Oklahoma!, South Pacific*, and the operas of Benjamin Britten were as powerfully influential as were *Citizen Kane, Casablanca, Rebecca, The Red Shoes, A Matter of Life and Death, Henry V*, and the crime thrillers called film noir.[10]

Radio, the most pervasive performing arts medium of the period, revealed that narrative could attract huge audiences.[11] Emerging in the 1930s, radio drama had initially favored popular genres such as crime and domestic melodrama ("soap operas"). It soon became more ambitious. The British Broadcasting Corporation invested in scripts written by major literary figures, and American networks embraced "highbrow" projects such as the Columbia Workshop.[12] Work by Val Gielgud, Orson Welles, Arch Oboler, Norman Corwin, Lucille Fletcher, and other major figures demanded a concentrated attention quite different from the casual overhearing of a news or music program. Attentive listening in turn encouraged radio writers to create more complex narrative effects. By 1940, radio was a mature vehicle of popular storytelling.[13]

The general widening awareness of creative options about plotting, viewpoint, linearity, and segmentation is evident in the advice given to novices. The two major magazines aimed at aspiring authors, *The Writer* and *Writer's Digest*, broadened their purview to discuss how to prepare salable material to all the modern media. Screenwriting manuals, which had flourished in the 1910s and 1920s, had died off as the Hollywood studio system consolidated in the sound era. Now, however, two major book-length guides to writing films appeared, and screenwriter John Howard Lawson updated his earlier treatise on playwriting to include motion pictures.[14] In the same period, Lajos Egri's *How to Write a Play* (1942), republished in 1948 as *The Art of Dramatic Writing*, became the standard work on plotting for the stage.

How to Write a Novel (1950), by the midlist author Manuel Komroff, offers a synthesis of major tendencies in literary composition since the nineteenth century. Komroff's wide range dwarfs the skimpy manuals of the 1910s and 1920s. He borrows ideas of dramatic compactness from James, and he goes beyond Lubbock in developing no fewer than eight creative choices of viewpoint, complete with a diagram.[15] Komroff reviews stream-of-consciousness techniques and gives advice about shuffling time sequence (make flashbacks chronological to ease comprehension).[16] He draws dozens of examples from classic fiction (*Tristram Shandy, Madame Bovary*), proto-modernism (*Lord Jim*), modernism (Joyce, Kafka), and what many would consider middlebrow or lowbrow work (*Of Mice and Men, Rebecca, The Bridge of San Luis Rey*). The massive industrialization of literary narrative in the 1940s finds its most complete user's manual in this work.

Meanwhile, modernism in its most demanding forms waned, and writers associated with it had already retreated considerably from its peak purity. Eliot embraced verse drama, Picasso returned to figurative painting, and Stravinsky declared himself a neoclassicist. For all the admirable qualities of *The Years* (1937) and *Between the Acts* (1941), *The Waves* remains the bold pinnacle of Woolf's work. *Finnegans Wake* (1938) was an extreme that no one was prepared to go beyond. Joyce and Woolf died in 1941, and it was easy to assume that Ultraism, that urge to create one formal breakthrough after another, died with them. Faulkner stopped writing novels for six years after *The Town* (1940); by then, only the sensational *Sanctuary* was in print. His shorter pieces shifted into a somewhat more user-friendly register; "The Bear" first saw publication in the *Saturday Evening Post*.

What replaced the classics of high modernism seemed less challenging. In France, the *rappel à l'ordre*, the call to curb avant-garde excesses, had already begun in the 1920s. George Orwell observed that the English and American writers of the 1930s were far more concerned with politics than with form; their focus was subject matter, not technique.[17] A central example was André Malraux's *Man's Fate* (1933).

America's "Popular Front Modernism," as identified by Michael Denning, employed some experimental devices to promote labor issues and social justice.[18] Roosevelt's Works Progress Administration drew on techniques of montage in shows such as *Triple-A Plowed Under* (1936). *Waiting for Lefty* (1935), played on a bare stage, presented a debate about a taxi strike, with the production pulling in participants from the audience. In contrast with proletarian realism, these works were daring, but they weren't radically disruptive. For example, *Lefty*'s integration of the audience had been anticipated by murder plays such as *Eye-Witnessed* (1926), which planted actors among the spectators. In radio, "epic" works such as Archibald MacLeish's *Fall of the City* (1937) owed a good deal to oratorio and cantata forms.

Later researchers would seek traces of a "postmodernist" or "late modernist" turn in prose fiction in the 1930s and 1940s, but writers of the time seem to have been more inclined to see the end of an era.[19] In *Enemies of Promise* (1938), Cyril Connolly posed the problem facing a young writer. Caught between the now-fading New Mandarins (Joyce, Woolf, Proust) and the "Vernacular Realists" (Hemingway, Maugham), the writer had to choose between leftist advocacy and mere journalism aimed at "the middle-class best-seller-making public."[20]

The latter option was arguably fulfilled in those books that did become contemporary classics: *The Grapes of Wrath* (1939), *Native Son* (1940), *The Power and the Glory* (1940), *For Whom the Bell Tolls* (1940), *Dangling Man* (1944), *Other Voices, Other Rooms* (1948), and *The Naked and the Dead* (1948). Commentators worried that ambition was waning and that the novel might be dying.[21] Similar worries appeared in the world of the theater where entertainment seemed to have swamped artistry. "Today," wrote one critic in 1945, "it is almost inconceivable that any drama could satisfy the canons of the most exigent criticism and also be popular."[22]

You could argue that Anglo-American intellectuals didn't realize that the modernist impulse in fiction was simply in a holding pattern. Avant-garde work was resurging in Abstract Expressionist painting, serial music, and experimental film. Quite soon avant-garde movements emerged elsewhere as the *Nouveau Roman*, Brechtian theater, and the Theatre of the Absurd. An austere "neo-modernism" would be revealed in the work of Beckett, and a playful one in the writings of Nabokov and the Oulipo circle. However, the relative accessibility of most Anglo-American storytelling exposed an embarrassing possibility: that the reign of implacable narrative difficulty, the Ultraist aspiration, was a brief episode, running from around 1920 to 1935 or so. Thereafter storytellers were unlikely to experiment with narrative as radically as the edgiest High Modernists had. There was a reversion to the mean, and the mean was controlled heterogeneity, shrewd appropriation—in other words, crossover in all media and at all levels of taste.

A Wider Variorum

The variorum in popular narrative expanded along the lines indicated by Jean-Claude Carrière. Audiences learned new wrinkles, storytellers (who were part of the audience) strove to replicate or revise innovations that emerged, and competition for innovations (aka switcheroos) intensified. Techniques of segmentation, viewpoint, and plotting time frames diversified swiftly, sometimes deliriously.

The explosion in mass media encouraged adaptations. Novels were turned into plays, films, and radio shows; films became radio plays; and a perennially popular radio play became a major film (*Sorry, Wrong Number*, 1948). This cross-fertilization encouraged storytellers to swap techniques. Egri's handbook on play construction resists Aristotelian models and favors a post-Jamesian conception of structure, in which the plot traces the psychological evolution of a character. A manual on radio writing urges beginners to study the parallel stories in Wilder's *Bridge of San Luis Rey*, the film *Tales of Manhattan* (1942), and Priestley's play *Dangerous Corner* (1932).[23] The freewheeling time jumping of Christopher Morley's novel *Kitty Foyle* (1939) yielded a 1940 film version that experiments with flashbacks and a doppelgänger who, living in a mirror, interrogates the protagonist.[24]

Film provided models of narration (crosscutting, montages) that could be imported into fiction, radio drama, and even plays, such as the early dramas of Tennessee Williams. In turn, first-person literary subjectivity could be conveyed on radio through voice-overs, music, and auditory effects such as echo and distortion. Orson Welles, Arch Oboler, and other radio artists had been a bit ahead of moviemakers in injecting subjectivity into objective scenes by layering dialogue, inner monologue, music, and effects. Soon, however, Hollywood caught up and created richly subjective sound mixes.

In general, if 1930s films were largely "theatrical" in their reliance on external behavior and stage technique, 1940s Hollywood became more "novelistic" in trying to present characters' inner lives. *The Woman in Question* inherits the same impulse. It's not hard to imagine each witness's flashback as a chapter in a detective novel, with first-person accounts framed by Superintendant Lodge's running commentary.

By now certain formal options seen in the 1920s and 1930s were solidly established and ripe for revision. Flashbacks were common in the novel, but writers tried to give them new vividness. Harking back to Virginia Woolf, Rumer Godden's *Take Three Tenses: A Fugue in Time* (1947) interweaves past, present, and future events pulled out of chronological order, assigning a different verb tense to each zone. Robert Penn Warren does something less clearly marked in *All the King's Men* (1946), varying the past segments not only through changes of tense but by the narrator's descriptions of himself in the third person during certain scenes.

Flashbacks were now often seen on stage, with major plays such as *I Remember Mama* (1944), *Home of the Brave* (1945), and *Death of a Salesman* (1949) giving them a cinematic fluidity through area lighting, rotating sets, and other staging techniques. Williams initially wrote *The Glass Menagerie* (1944) as a movie script. Radio made extensive use of the flashback, often starting the plot at a point of crisis and then skipping back to show what led up to the present.[25] Comic books could develop distinctive forms of nonlinearity thanks to the "splash panel" at the beginning of the story. It might show the story's opening scene or serve as a characterizing bit or present a summary tableau presenting hero and villain facing off in an abstract graphic space. The splash panel could also skip forward to a point of tension or combine several time frames into one (fig. 3.6).

Hollywood filmmakers caught up with their peers and eagerly embraced nonlinearity. Before the 1940s, flashback construction was looked down on as being too difficult for audiences to follow. Influential films such as *Wuthering Heights* (1939), *Citizen Kane* (1941), and *How Green Was My Valley* (1941) convinced filmmakers otherwise, and so the decade filled up with time jumping movies. In *The Big Clock* (1948), *Madame Bovary* (1949), and *The Great Gatsby* (1949), linear novels became films built around flashbacks. After just a few years, the convoluted chronologies of *Beyond Glory* (1948) and *Backfire* (1950) had exhibitors worrying that audiences would be baffled. *The Woman in Question* makes its own contribution to this developing menu of options. Like the wilder variants on display in American film noir, it looks ahead to nonlinear stratagems explored by Tarantino's generation.[26]

Sharply differentiated multiple viewpoints were now a primary novelistic technique. Meyer Levin's proletarian novel *Citizens* (1940), for example, lets untagged chapters carry the general story but intersperses those with flashback biographies of the ten men killed in a strikers' demonstration. The strategy was expanded across books by Joyce Cary, whose trilogy (*Herself Surprised*, 1941; *To Be a Pilgrim*, 1942; *The Horse's Mouth*, 1944) gives each of three characters a chance to tell the story that involves them all.

3.6 This page from a *Spirit* adventure, "Visitor" (February 13, 1949), presents a stream of events three times, both vertically (in text and in two sets of images) and horizontally. The different graphic styles on display in the snapshots and the changing "camera angles" on the investigation provide an occasion for Eisner to display his virtuosity, not that he needed one. *Source:* Copyright 2021 Will Eisner Studios, Inc. THE SPIRIT and WILL EISNER are trademarks owned by Will Eisner Studios, Inc., and both are registered in the U.S. Patent and Trademark Office.

Multiple-viewpoint construction migrated to radio and to cinema, most notably in *Citizen Kane*, but also in comedies such as *The Affairs of Susan* (1945) and in dramas such as *In Which We Serve* (1942), *Three Strangers* (1946), and *Three Secrets* (1950). In these instances, our attachment to one character for part of the plot may be accompanied by a voice-over reflection that makes the viewpoint character a subsidiary narrator. Shifting viewpoints were more difficult to convey on stage, although Tennessee Williams and Arthur Miller tried. One of the strangest of these efforts was Philip Barry's play *Foolish Notion* (1945). Each character was assigned an imaginary scene, which was to be signaled when the actor came onstage walking backward.

The Woman in Question's flirtation with a "prismatic" presentation of its murder victim wasn't unique. An American film, *Pilot No. 5* (1943), applied the same approach as friends of a pilot off on a mission compare their disparate judgments of him. The technique was more common in the novel, for example, when Wright Morris's *The Man Who Was There* (1945) provided constantly shifting appraisals of a man never shown independently to the reader. The most elaborate literary effort may have been Ben Ames Williams's *The Strange Woman* (1941), which provided seven viewpoints of men who knew Jenny Hager, who is dead at the beginning of the book. As with other efforts in this quasi-Conradian vein, the reader has no unfiltered access to the central figure. When a faceted tale spans many years, as here, we can ask whether the angles we're given capture genuine contradictions in the main character or instead sample moments in a process of character change.

Innovation in popular narrative typically centers on fresh subjects or themes rather than on experiments with form. Unusual settings and characters are treated through familiar plot patterns and stylistic techniques. The process was sharply in evidence as storytellers in all media drew on World War II as material to engage audiences. It's not surprising to find battlefield stories working with crossover forms that had been cultivated in earlier decades.

Segmentation by time is a common strategy in war novels. Howard Hunt's *Limit of Darkness* (1944) shows a single cycle of a bombing platoon's routine across twenty-four chapters, each covering a single hour and tagged with a picture of a clock face. The first block of *The Cross and the Arrow* (1944), Albert Maltz's account of a conscience-stricken Gestapo investigator, labels its chapters with times over a single night and day before flashing back to reveal prior action over several months; the third part resumes on the initial morning. More original is the verse novel *Beach Red* (1946), which traces the capture of a Japanese-held island by means of a strict formula. Each ten-word line measures a second, each sixty-line chapter covers a minute, and the whole book covers a single hour.

Although most war films were resolutely linear, *Passage to Marseille* (1944) offers one of the most complex Hollywood films of the era, with flashbacks within flashbacks and multiple narrators filling in story gaps. John Horne Burns's novel *The Gallery* (1947) yields a more space-based structure, in which a Neapolitan arcade frames "portraits"—third-person short stories built on the wartime experiences of citizens and soldiers. Several of these segments are linked by "promenades," first-person memoirs of an American recalling his stay in Naples. The result is something of a collage akin to that composed by Marc Blitzstein in his *Airborne Symphony* (1946). Guided by an omniscient narrator ("The Monitor"), the listener is given episodes from the history of aviation, culminating in experiences of aviators in modern war. The chorus takes on the role of bombing crews and of Nazi youths chanting phrases of hatred. Blitzstein exploits the opportunity to shift styles; one section gives the aviators a comic barbershop quartet.

The Naked and the Dead (1948), the best-selling war novel, epitomizes the pluralism of popular storytelling options of the period. Incorporating a great many characters, the narration unashamedly flits from mind to mind, between and within scenes. This reversion to nineteenth-century omniscience is counterweighted by inserts recalling Dos Passos's USA trilogy. "The Time Machine" segments provide capsule biographies of the men, complete with inner monologues. Blocks tagged as "Chorus," which assemble the platoon for chow or bull sessions, are treated as playscript exchanges with stage directions. These sections give the book an abstract geometry, breaking up the mostly linear account of taking a Pacific island. There is even a trace of comic book exuberance in the battle scenes: "A clod of dirt stung his neck. BAAROWWMM, BAA-ROWWMM."[27]

Almost anywhere we turn in the 1940s, we find storytellers consolidating and refining strategies from the 1910s on. In this context, *The Woman in Question* looks typical. By relying on multiple perspectives, dispersed but systematic sampling of different time periods, and expressive subjectivity (Agnes as each witness perceives her), the film samples the expanding menu of options. In addition, the film's suggestion of an underlying grid of alternatives lined up in blocks exemplifies another tendency, one we might call pattern plotting. It's not unique to the period, but it's a crossover technique that would persist into the 2020s.

Russian Dolls and Grids

A clear instance of pattern plotting is the "Russian doll" structure, the schema that sets one story within another. In verbal arts, that comes down to character A writing or speaking about events that character B has recounted. In books such as *The Decameron*, the embedded story pertains to characters not in the frame story, but many stories also used character testimony, letters, or other sources to fill out a unitary plot. In addition, the embedded story typically entailed a time shift, so it was likely to be a flashback. The flashbacks of *The Woman in Question* are simple instances of embedding.

Embedded stories with a unitary cast of characters were a common strategy of popular narrative in the nineteenth century, not least in epistolary and casebook novels. Conrad took the strategy to extremes. *Chance* (1913) is framed overall by a narrator ("I"), who learns the story from Powell and Marlow. But each of their accounts incorporates the narration of others, whose accounts frame still other voices. For example, Marlow reports the versions told to him by Powell, who bases his version on earlier accounts, presented successively from two other characters.

Complicated embedding of this sort was usually avoided in popular media, but novels might insert brief news clippings or diary entries. In the play *Joan of Lorraine* (1946), Maxwell Anderson presents a rehearsal session interrupted by long passages of the play to be performed. Other stage works, evidently under Pirandello's continuing influence, found ways to frame alternative versions of the action (e.g., *A Strange Play*, 1944; *A Story for a Sunday Evening*, 1950). Most ingeniously, Orson Welles moved toward more complex strata of embedding in his radio shows.

Welles's narrative techniques centered on manipulation of viewpoint, encapsulated in his slogan "First Person Singular." He replaced the role of radio announcer with a narrator who might be the character (and thus a vessel of inner monologue) or who might be a witty external voice commenting on the action. Welles's interest in point of view techniques made him a confirmed Conradian. He created a radio version of *Heart of Darkness* and planned a film version as his first Hollywood project. In it, the camera would have represented Marlowe's impressions, both visual and mental.[28]

On the radio, "first-person singular" often turned into something more plural. In 1938, Welles recreated the dossier format of *Dracula* through a barrage of news stories, telegrams, journal entries, and spectral voices drifting into earshot. More neatly segmented was the notorious "War of the Worlds" broadcast. It begins with Professor Pearson's narrating frame, explaining that Earth was a target for the Martians. We move to the past via a montage of news bulletins, snatches of music, and radio transmissions, culminating in the Martians' successful attack. The second part is centered on Professor Pearson, writing his notes of the event. These shift from present-tense descriptions of the devastation to the past tense in his concluding reflection on the elimination of the threat. Framing all this is the CBS announcement of the show, which concludes with Welles's saying that the whole project was merely Halloween fun.

Citizen Kane (1941), which harnessed flashbacks to an investigation plot, presents a startlingly symmetrical set of embedded modules. A prologue showing Kane's death is balanced by an epilogue taking us out of Kane's estate.

These sequences frame the entire film's action. The opening "News on the March" newsreel, as a survey of Kane's career, is matched at the end by the camera movement that recapitulates his life backward, as a single shot moving over his memorabilia to settle on his boyhood memento. The scene launching Thompson's mission, the assignment to track down "Rosebud," finds its enclosing mate in the scene among the rueful reporters who abandon the search. And within those frames are cradled five extensive flashbacks that enact phases of Kane's career, as recounted by his guardian Thatcher, his business manager Bernstein, his friend Jed Leland, his second wife Susan, and his butler Raymond. Each of those flashbacks is framed by the interview situation set up by Thompson.

Boxes within boxes, within boxes. Welles and screenwriter Herman Mankiewicz created the "News on the March" sequence as an overture that plants the action to come, not simply as backstory on Kane's career but also as a miniature model of the film's design. Like the film, the newsreel begins by showing Kane's death and the immensity of his estate. It proceeds to reveal background on his mother and his early newspaper career (covered in Thatcher's papers), his building of a journalistic empire (Bernstein's account), his first marriage and his disastrous political campaign (Leland's recollection), Susan's failed opera career and the couple's reclusive life in Xanadu (Susan's account), and Kane's last years (Raymond's curt report on his saying "Rosebud"). As a *mise-en-abyme*, the newsreel coils within itself both the substance and the form of the central modules. This media montage goes beyond "The War of the Worlds." It not only serves as exposition, presenting the public image that will be modified by the testimonies, but also helps teach us how to watch the film.[29]

These niceties of pattern plotting aren't always obvious, but they are, I think, sensed to some degree by the viewer. In particular, *Kane*'s segmentation, with strongly marked sequences and flashbacks emphasized as parallel to one another, inclines us to see the film as composed of weighty blocks, even a grid of alternatives (Susan's story versus Leland's, the initial entry to Xanadu as opposed to our final withdrawal).

Of course, with sufficient ingenuity, you can chart any narrative as a grid, but some stories call for it more than others. Grid layouts were implicit in nineteenth-century fiction, particularly in dossier novels. They became more explicit in High Modernism, with Joyce's infamous chart for *Ulysses* and the parallel chapters in Woolf's novels. We can easily grasp the grid underlying *Intolerance* as well: four time periods mapped across phases of the unfolding film, with the shifts between "columns" coming faster and faster.

In the 1940s, tendencies toward pattern plotting were enhanced when block construction created strong parallels of time period, location, or viewpoint. The most self-conscious example of this tendency I know comes in Philip Toynbee's short novel *Prothalamium* (1947). A woman has assembled seven guests at a tea party. The novel gives each one a solid, labeled block of first-person narration. The guest's narration is rendered in inner monologue, with running commentary on both the ongoing party and incidents in the past. Events and lines of dialogue are replayed from different viewpoints.

Toynbee could have presented the party through a linear, omniscient narration, a spotlight rapidly shifting among the characters' minds as each responds to unfolding events. Instead, encountering each character's experience of the party en bloc, we're obliged to construct the chronology of the party through back-and-fill reading. We must as well contrast character reactions by recalling orienting points, replayed bits of speech and action.

The geometry of this layout is brought to the reader's attention. Each narrator's segment is broken into two-page units, each bearing an alphanumeric tag reminiscent of the partitioning of Stout's *How Like a God*. The entire party consists of twelve units, but some guests leave early and so don't get the full ration. Tom Ford's section, for example, is labeled B1–B12 because he stays to the end, whereas Doug Tillett comes late (so his commentary starts at C2) and leaves early (at C7).

Only after modernism could a novel be published with this hermetic structure. Its self-conscious geometry was recognized as a bid for avant-garde credentials; one review compared Toynbee to Joyce and Woolf.[30] Toynbee diluted the novel's force, however, by prefacing it with a chart that mapped the narrator's episodes across time, enabling the reader to see how the characters' experiences overlapped. "Page A7 covers the same period as pages B7, C7 and so on, but each is the experience of a different person." We are instructed that passages in italics are "overheard by the narrator, but said neither by him nor to him."[31]

This apparatus offers the sort of reassuring skeleton key that Joyce and Woolf kept back. It would be as if excerpts from Stuart Gilbert's gloss on *Ulysses* were printed, complete with spreadsheet, as an introduction to Joyce's text. And because *Prothalamium*'s story is essentially simple, the chart reduces the book to an elaborate puzzle. The structure isn't hermetic after all, merely a clever variant on principles of viewpoint, segmentation, and temporal linearity familiar from the nineteenth century on.

The technique was seldom exposed as blatantly as *Prothalamium* does, but several of the novels I've mentioned depend on readers registering an abstract pattern cued by the book's exoskeleton. In the war novels, time or place is often supplied by chapter titles. A tabular structure can also be implied by tracing characters' fates across a narrow time frame. Gore Vidal's novel *In a Yellow Wood* (1947) follows a young Wall Street stockbroker across twenty-four hours, with the chapters split up geometrically. In a block tagged "Day," five chapters make Robert Holton our viewpoint figure, and the next four spread across people who have come in contact with him—a waitress, a secretary, an army acquaintance, an envious fellow broker. "Night" scenes portray a party and Robert's wanderings afterward. The cascade of events faces Robert with a choice about whether to change his life by marrying or becoming a sculptor. "In a Yellow Wood," set at the start of the next day, resolves the matter. Its two chapters condense the prior plot layout, with one focused on Robert going to work and the next assembling other characters' viewpoints as he returns to his routines.

The time frame and viewpoint shifts of *Shadows at Noon* (1943), by Martin Goldsmith, are even more strict. The book imagines a Nazi air raid on Manhattan. Divided into three blocks—tagged as 11:45, 12:00, and 12:15—it assigns one chapter per part to a character caught in the crisis, resulting in twelve segments. The four characters are remotely linked, but most never meet, although in the seventh chapter a chance encounter leads two of them to a bout of sex. A thirteenth chapter, surveying the damage done to the city, summarizes all their fates with a mixture of pathos, resignation, and hope.

Goldsmith's metropolitan network narrative has a suburban counterpart in John Klempner's *Letter to Five Wives*. Presented as a novella in the slick magazine *Cosmopolitan* in 1945, it was published at novel length in 1946. Both versions have a similar structure, but the book develops it more fully. The plot centers on five couples living in the same town. The action is presented through the viewpoints, in alternation, of the five women. All of their husbands have had some relation with the town flirt Addie Joss.

The first five chapters set up the couples through shifting viewpoints from woman to woman, each talking with her husband or a friend while recalling Addie's predations. In the sixth chapter, the women gather to draw up a report of their club's war effort. The meeting is disrupted by a letter from Addie declaring that she has run off with one husband. "Unfortunately I could take only one. Some day I may make the rounds. But which one this time? . . . Pretend that it couldn't possibly be yours, and know in your heart that it could."[32]

The rest of the plot shows each wife weighing the possibility that some episode in her marriage could have led to her husband's defection. Flashbacks reviewing each couple's history proceed, round-robin fashion, interrupted by the present-time business of the meeting. The suspense is accentuated by some women trying to call the men. Eventually the meeting ends, and the women, all putting up a brave front, go home. A final string of five chapters reveals the outcome.

The almost clinically neat structure can be laid out on a grid (table 3.1). Klempner has made his plot accessible partly through the predictability of the modular structure. The shift among characters is established as an intrinsic norm we quickly come to expect. The movement is impelled by a mystery, but without anyone being assigned the role of investigator. Instead, the flashback "testimonies" of the key "witnesses" spread suspicion among the husbands and invite the reader to look for clues.

TABLE 3.1 Grid outline of chapters and couples in John Klempner, *Letter to Five Wives* (1946)

	Rita & Josh	Gerry & Gil	Lora May & Porter	Martha & Roger	Deborah & Brad
The couples (chaps. 1–5)	1, 4	1, 3	2	3, 4	5
Wives gathering; letter arrives (chap. 6)					
Flashbacks (chaps. 7–11)	10	7	11	9	8
Wives' report (chap. 12)					
Flashbacks (chaps. 13–18)	14, 18	13	17	15	16
Wives' meeting ends (chap. 19)					
Fates of the couples (chaps. 20–24)	24	20	21	22	23

Our search is assisted by a bias within the imperfectly symmetrical structure. Rita benefits from being the first wife introduced in chapter 1. She gains our sympathy at the outset by being the only one in the circle, other than Addie, who has been divorced. She has struggled to build a new life as a writer and a wife to Josh, who is oblivious to her and easily flattered by Addie's coy attentions. Another likely candidate for the role of abandoned wife is Deborah, the socially awkward newcomer, and in the last array of flashbacks, she becomes a second figure of sympathy.

Rita gains further prominence by being assigned one extra flashback (chapter 18), breaking the book's intrinsic norm. There she realizes she's unhappy, she's not deeply in love with Josh, and she faces a drab future, even if her stories sell to those women's magazines that purvey "blissful romance . . . pure fiction." Rita recalls Josh's dismissive response when one of her stories earned a substantial check. This leads to a quarrel over money and his ominous remark: "My private life is run on a strictly cash basis."[33] So it's not a complete surprise when we learn in the penultimate chapter that Josh has run off with Addie. Rita is shattered.

Chapter 24's long italicized inner monologue ends with Rita returning home and contemplating the shame of confronting her friends. But Josh is there before her, brooding in his easy chair. He left Addie. Rita realizes that Addie had to gloat over her power and that this would wound Josh's manful pride. Now Rita has something to build on. After Josh said he's sorry, "she pulled her hand away gently, and went out into the kitchen."[34]

When we've stopped shuddering at this last line, we might recognize how Klempner has made his plot easy to assimilate. An arresting premise is turned into a mystery through manipulation of point of view, which allows him to chop the action into short stories, each endowed with extra tension based on its place in the macrostructure. Every husband's past behavior will be scanned for hints about his intentions with respect to Addie. This tactic exemplifies a wider tendency of the 1940s: to inject crime, enigmas, and thriller-level danger into nondetective genres, even "serious" fiction.[35]

It may be that the trend toward highly patterned plotting flows organically from composing novels with many characters, viewpoints, or time frames. Manuel Komroff recommended that the novelist prepare charts to help keep track of such matters.[36] In addition, perhaps earlier models, such as *As I Lay Dying* and heavily tagged 1930s novels such as *The Dark Mirror*, encouraged writers to neatly tabulate multiple story lines. This sense of abstract structure behind certain plots might also have shaped academics' emerging notion of "spatial form."[37] In any event, as mainstream storytellers consciously explored modular units that could be embedded in one another or laid out on grids, we can say that one modernist impulse lived on in crossover guise.

Close Reading and a Battle of the Brows

Modernism, high or not, lingered in other ways. For one thing, its canon became a central reference point for quality. The work of four men—Eliot, Joyce, Picasso, Stravinsky—was routinely treated as the apex of twentieth-century Western art. Moreover, and less obviously, the literary modernists opened paths in academic literary study. The "New Criticism," usually dated from the publication of I. A. Richards's *Principles of Literary Criticism* (1924), was emerging as a powerful force in universities and literary quarterlies. Like Shakespeare and the metaphysical poets, the masterpieces of proto-modernism and High Modernism demanded "close reading." The 1940s revival of interest in Henry James and Faulkner depended on recasting literary criticism as rigorous analysis of form and theme. After James, a serious novelist needed a "method." Now a serious critic needed one too.

The critic was no longer an elegant, gentlemanly essayist. The academic critic, as committed to precision as the scientist, dissected a text to display its ambiguities and ironies, its richness of allusion and implication. As American university departments grew after World War II, professors of English became less committed to teaching historical research methods and more focused on giving undergraduates a sensitive appreciation of style and meaning, and on training graduate students in the vocation of subtle interpretation.[38] "Technique as Discovery," the title of a 1948 essay by Mark Schorer, summed up the new focus. What technique "discovered" was an intricate play of meaning and an enduring value that belletristic writers did not dream of. "The writer capable of the most exacting technical scrutiny of his subject matter will produce works with the most satisfying content, works with thickness and resonance, works which reverberate, works with maximum meaning."[39]

Soon such "intrinsic" analysis was challenged by critics who asserted that the poem, play, or novel could not be easily split off from other realms. Inspired by Freud, Frazer, and Marx, some critics argued that the deepest meanings of the work could be plumbed by methods borrowed from the social sciences.[40] The ghosts in Henry James's tales can be considered projections of the author's Oedipus complex; Thomas Mann's Joseph novels are transpositions of virtually all myths known by modern anthropology.[41]

Just as High Modernism had encouraged close reading, it gave license to the emerging studies of literature as myth, ritual, and psychodrama. Eliot had invoked ancient ritual in *The Waste Land* and had disclosed the mythic foundations of *Ulysses*.[42] Joyce's and Woolf's plunges into the psyche had invited reflection on personal identity and inchoate desires. Faulkner had brought to regional literature a tangle of sexual neuroses, along with overt echoes of biblical legend. Many modernists, as heirs of Symbolism, encouraged critics to probe their texts for ever-wider implications.[43] In what observers were calling "the age of criticism," intellectual boldness was revealed less in new artworks than in dazzling explications.

The complexity and human significance laid bare by critics' patient scrutiny of the canon made the hollowness of mass culture all the more enraging. And that stuff was flooding every newsstand, movie theater, and radio network. As if in reply to Pound's "Make it New," Irving Howe poignantly described the 1940s situation as "the Decline of the New."[44] After the achievements of High Modernism, intellectuals strove to understand what had happened.

There ensued Americans' version of the "Battle of the Brows," which had emerged in interwar Britain.[45] Q. D. Leavis, aided by journalists, had made the highbrow/lowbrow/middlebrow triad prominent in cultural discourse, leading to Virginia Woolf's famous diatribe against middlebrow culture.[46] In contrast, in 1920s America, slightly before high modernist precepts had firmly taken hold of the intelligentsia, Gilbert Seldes had championed movies, comic strips, and other forms of popular art as a welcome alternative to genteel culture.[47] But the Joyce-Eliot cohort set a new standard for demanding artistry, and the explosion of mass media in the 1930s and 1940s provoked American intellectuals to take up the battle against vulgarization with punitive force. Writers who had initially admired Soviet communism came to believe that popular and middlebrow artworks were comparable to the banalities of Stalinist socialist realism.[48]

Critics of mass culture tailored the three categories to developments on the American scene.[49] High art demands training, concentration, and a willingness to be confounded, especially in its avant-garde manifestations. It is the province of museums, concert halls, and libraries of serious literature, but also of bohemian galleries, "little magazines," and shoestring theater troupes. It encompasses both revered classics and avant-garde experimentation. High culture obliges us to confront unpleasant truths in the hope that by doing so we are better equipped to live.

Popular culture, as opposed to folk culture, springs from modern urban society. It is better called mass culture because its producers conceive the audience as bonded by their desire for predictable experiences. Like other commodities, it's produced on an industrial model, with division of labor and systematic strategies of marketing. Mass culture flourishes in movie houses, Broadway theaters, Tin Pan Alley, radio, television, and bookstalls selling genre fiction. Perhaps in the days of Shakespeare or Dickens popular art was fresh and valuable, but by the twentieth century mass production has made it formulaic and regressive. It creates a synthetic substitute for folk art, addressed not to an organic community but to one unified by tastes imposed by modern capitalism. It aims to distract and reassure. It offers no problems it can't solve, and no solutions that don't gratify our preconceptions. It keeps its audience in diverted, comfortable passivity.

The high art/mass art duality is in effect a more detailed and accusatory version of the Collins test, the split between art and entertainment. But where does "middlebrow" art fit? Some cultural products in a mass society mimic high art but rest finally on appeals characteristic of mass culture. "Middlebrow" came to mean the art that appeals to the aspirational bourgeoisie, suburbanites who want to be thought sophisticated. By joining book clubs, subscribing to the right magazines, taking courses in art appreciation, and buying compilations of the world's greatest symphonies, the middlebrow struggles to achieve cultural capital. But in the end, declared Woolf, the middlebrow thrills to art that promises "money, fame, power, or prestige."[50] The media industry is happy to oblige. It produces prestige films (*The Best Years of Our Lives*, 1946; *Brief Encounter*, 1946), "serious" music (Gian Carlo Menotti, Rachmaninoff), and "important" theater (anything by Arthur Miller).

It's hard for us today to understand how deeply wounded the intelligentsia was by the barrage of popular and middlebrow art. Robert Warshow declared that the "mere existence" of mass culture "was a standing threat to one's personality, was in a sense a deep personal humiliation."[51] The fake artistry on display in middlebrow work was perhaps even more dangerous. A 1948 *Partisan Review* symposium skipped over the problem of mass culture in order to ask this: "Do you think that American middlebrow culture has grown more powerful in this decade? In what relation does this middlebrow tendency stand to serious writing—does it threaten or bolster it?"[52]

Where did the controversies leave popular storytelling? Most critics simply deplored it and considered it beneath scrutiny. Although the Jamesian poetics of the novel and comparable accounts of theater were widely known, and although the story gurus explicated craft conventions for the benefit of amateurs, the littérateurs did not apply these tools to mass or middlebrow culture. When cultural observers did study popular narrative, they usually wielded the "extrinsic" social science methods recently adopted by literary studies. Myth interpretation and psychoanalysis confirmed the assumption that the products of the culture industry reflected the audience's desperate need to evade contemporary life.

Film was a favored target for these interpretations.[53] For instance, two social psychologists sought to show how character types in Hollywood movies bore traces of cultural anxieties. A "good-bad girl" like Gilda in the 1946 movie of that name or Vivian Sternwood in *The Big Sleep* (1946) appears initially to be promiscuous but turns out to be virtuous. The character resolves the tension between the male need for a sexually attractive woman and society's conception of a respectable marriage partner.[54] Siegfried Kracauer undertook an examination of German mass culture in his book *From Caligari to Hitler: A Psychological History of the German Film* (1947), which argued that the society's unconscious urge to be ruled by a tyrant predated the Third Reich. "Germany thus carried out what had been anticipated by her cinema from its very beginning."[55] The Nazi example, like that of Stalin's Russia, showed that mass culture could be deeply dangerous.

A particularly clear-cut skirmish in the battles over mass culture focused on mystery and detective fiction. The genre's popularity and esteem made it a big target for anyone anxious about the decline of high art, but it also offered its defenders opportunities to show the powers of popular narrative. Perhaps surprisingly, the debate offered a path out of the mass culture impasse, and it's a path that has remained well-trodden ever since.

Murder for the Masses

By 1946, mystery stories made up one-quarter of all fiction published in the United States and a third of prime-time radio programs.[56] In Hollywood the B-level detectives Charlie Chan and Mr. Moto gave way to A-level productions featuring Sam Spade and Philip Marlowe. Prestigious thrillers won box office rewards and Oscar nominations. Weekly magazines teemed with serialized and abridged versions of novels by Rex Stout, Mignon G. Eberhart, and their peers. Dick Tracy, Rip Kirby, and The Shadow had their own comic strips, and comic books asserting that crime doesn't pay popped up on newsstands.

Murder made its way to Broadway in *Ladies in Retirement* (1940), *Arsenic and Old Lace* (1941), *Ten Little Indians* (1944), *An Inspector Calls* (1947), adaptations of *Rebecca* and *Laura*, and many lesser items. (*Meet a Body* of 1944 finds homicide in a funeral home.) *Angel Street*, as the play *Gas Light* (1938) was retitled, ran for almost 1,300 performances.

The war years gave Americans bigger incomes, and book and magazine publishers stoked readers' demands. Because best-sellers were not predictable, editors developed "category" publishing, a business plan devoted to acquiring massive numbers of romances, westerns, and mysteries. These could yield steady returns, especially from rental libraries. Mysteries proved to be the dominant category.[57] Publishers launched dedicated lines such as Doubleday's Crime Club and Simon & Schuster's Inner Sanctum Mysteries.

Mystery authors could be top sellers, as Ellery Queen, Erle Stanley Gardner, and Mickey Spillane proved. Each sold millions of copies. Agatha Christie, then on her way to international popularity, was offered $15,000 from *Good Housekeeping* for a novelette; that is $220,000 in 2021 currency.[58] A novelist today, who is lucky to sell 10,000 books, would be depressed to learn that a now-forgotten lightweight such as *See You at the Morgue* (1941) could sell 40,000 copies in hardcover alone.[59] When the paperback revolution arrived, the most numerous titles on top-selling lists were mysteries.[60] In 1941, *Ellery Queen's Mystery Magazine* was founded and soon began awarding prizes and mounting yearly anthologies. In 1945, authors founded the Mystery Writers of America (motto: "Crime does not pay—enough").

Mystery novelists would long labor under a sense of inferiority and strive to find ways to make their work more "literary." Yet their work already had a cerebral cachet missing in other genres. Whodunits were said to be the preferred leisure reading of professors and presidents. The *New York Times*, the *New York Herald Tribune*, the *Saturday Review of Literature*, *Harper's*, and other publications devoted regular columns to reviewing mystery novels. In 1941, a major New York publisher issued the first significant history of the genre: Howard Haycraft's *Murder for Pleasure*. This coincided with the Modern Library's publication of Ellery Queen's flagship collection of mystery short stories: *101 Years' Entertainment*. The press treated the more obsessive fans with bemused affection. As critics produced admiring surveys of Sherlock Holmes's career, *The Baker Street Journal*, a pseudoscholarly investigation of The Canon, began publication in 1946.

Dreiser's *An American Tragedy* (1925) was the rare instance of a major literary figure employing thriller and courtroom conventions. By the 1940s, other prestigious writers had been attracted to mystery techniques. Vladimir

Nabokov's *Real Life of Sebastian Knight* (1941) used an investigation plot to parody literary biography and riddled its text with references to classic detective fiction. The suspense genre held an attraction for well-regarded writers such as Robert Coates and Kenneth Fearing. Richard Wright produced two man-on-the-run novels transformed by assigning them Black protagonists. The best-selling *Native Son* (1940) details Bigger Thomas's unintended killing of a white woman and his attempt to flee. Wright's Dostoevskian *The Man Who Lived Underground*, unpublished until 2021 but written in 1941–42, follows an innocent Black handyman as he escapes the police who have tortured a murder confession out of him. Hiding in the city sewers, venturing out to rob basement offices and storage rooms, he discovers a wild sense of freedom, as well as a hallucinatory detachment from his identity and the everyday world.

Graham Greene gave the genre credibility in a more orthodox fashion. Accepting the Collins test, he distinguished his serious fiction from the harsh pursuit thrillers he called his "entertainments": *This Gun for Hire* (1936), *The Confidential Agent* (1939), and *The Ministry of Fear* (1943). Critics, impressed by the "straight" novels, declared that even these yarns had literary quality. Reciprocally, Greene invested his more prestigious works with crime and suspense. In *Brighton Rock* (1938), often considered his first significant exploration of Catholic guilt, the gangland setting allows signals of literary seriousness to sit alongside virtually pulp prose. "He trailed the clouds of his own glory after him: hell lay about him in his infancy. He was ready for more deaths."[61]

Greene had never been a hard-core modernist, but Faulkner had, and he too adjusted to the growing demand for whodunits. Always drawn to mystery situations, he made county attorney Gavin Stevens the investigator in six short stories, collected as *Knight's Gambit* (1949).[62] Stevens also played a role in what Faulkner called his "blood and thunder mystery novel," *Intruder in the Dust* (1948).[63] His plots had often been driven by the revelation of family secrets, but here his sprawling and sidewinding sentences and barely cued shifts across years delineate a conventional murder situation, tightly restricted to a sensitive boy's viewpoint. The puzzle relies on straightforward clues: bullets from different guns, bodies swapped in and out of a grave. More reader-friendly than most Faulkner novels, *Intruder in the Dust* boosted his public standing, thanks largely to paperback sales.[64] The film adaptation proved fairly prestigious as well.

Given the genre's growing respectability, intellectuals wondered why murder seemed so delectable. In 1944–45, in a series of polemics, the question gained a new intensity. Did the mystery story harbor artistic possibilities, or was it just another instance of mass or middlebrow culture? If something so beloved of literary tastemakers could be shown to be vacuous, then the rest of popular fiction was surely even more suspect.

Edmund Wilson's *New Yorker* essay, "Why Do People Read Detective Stories?" (October 14, 1944), became the best-remembered contribution to the debate. It was preceded by "The Time of the Assassins," in the *Nation* (April 22, 1944) by Louise Bogan, who was soon to become Library of Congress Poet Laureate. Wilson's critique was immediately countered by Jacques Barzun, Joseph Wood Krutch, and Bernard DeVoto in the pages of magazines identified with middlebrow tastes. In January of 1945, Wilson supplied further comments under the memorable title, "Who Cares Who Killed Roger Ackroyd?"[65]

These writers didn't explicitly invoke the categories of low or middlebrow art, probably because it's rather difficult to assign the mystery genre to one category or the other. Nonetheless, Wilson was clearly warning that this corner of publishing was vulgar and stupid, and his essays and the replies sketch out lines of attack and defense that would dominate thinking about popular narrative for years to come.

1. **Popular art is formulaic and predictable.** Wilson: Rex Stout's Nero Wolfe books are simply Doyle's Holmes stories in modern dress, but without Doyle's imaginative atmosphere of fog-encased London.

Counter 1: **High art has its own formulas.** Krutch: Classic storytellers have always worked within a tradition, and that furnishes formulas, better called conventions.

Counter 2: **Popular art's conventions vary across history.** DeVoto: Those who know their Doyle, and what came after, realize how much Rex Stout has transformed his heritage.

2. **Popular narrative is unrealistic in characterization, plot, and worldview.** Wilson: Lord Peter Wimsey is "a dreadful stock Englishman of the casual and debonair kind," and Ngaio Marsh fills her book with "a lot of faked-up English country people."[66]

Counter: **Popular genres adhere to other criteria than those of traditional literary realism.** Barzun: Detective fiction is comic make-believe, always aware of its stylized worlds. The outrageousness of some devices, like the locked-room murder, puts us firmly in the realm of artifice. In later years, Barzun would argue that the detective story is a modern incarnation of not the novel but the tale, both in folk literature and in the nineteenth-century work of Poe, Hawthorne, Stevenson, Twain, and others. It continues a respectable artistic genre not dependent on the realism of the novel after James (who also wrote tales).[67]

3. **Popular narratives are stylistically pedestrian, or worse.** Wilson: Agatha Christie has a "mawkish" style. A Margery Allingham book is "completely unreadable."[68]

Counter: **In all storytelling, style may be overridden by other components.** Krutch: The mystery story's characteristic force needs only a functional style. DeVoto: Wilson "would hardly require Theodore Dreiser to write gracefully. . . . Some first-rate mysteries are written in tolerably bad prose."[69]

4. **Popular genres constrain creativity.** Wilson: A mystery must subordinate all literary values to a puzzle, and the solution to that often turns out to be disappointing. The conventions of the genre prevent the writer from achieving artistic merit.

Counter: **Each genre opens up specific artistic possibilities of subject and form.** Krutch: "The acceptance of a tradition and with it of certain fixed themes and methods seems to release rather than stifle the effective working of the imagination."[70] Bogan: The detective story incorporates areas of experience forbidden to other genres, such as the struggle between logical reasoning and sensational violence. Barzun: The detective story's artistic strength lies in its focus on the mundane world around us. The interpretation of clues obliges us to recognize "all the little unregarded details of daily life."[71] Like a scientist, the detective subjects them to rigorous analysis and logical inference.

5. **Popular storytelling's predictability lets its audience sink into mindless, repetitive torpor.** Wilson: Mystery readers have "lax mental habits."[72] All the talk about literary values in the detective story is an excuse for an addiction.

Counter: **There are consumers, and there are connoisseurs.** Barzun: A true admirer of detective stories knows the tradition, spots mechanical recycling, and appreciates clever variants on standard ploys. As an outsider, Wilson can't recognize what's valuable about the classics he castigates.

6. **Popular art is a reflection of its times, or of universal concerns.** Wilson: Why do people read detective stories? The interwar years have inculcated a diffuse worldwide "fear of impending disaster."[73] Readers welcome a detective who can pin guilt to a particular source.

Counter: **All art reflects its moment and more widespread concerns. Like other literature, the detective story may reveal something about the collective mind.** So Bogan, probing for "archetypal subconscious themes," can find an underlying religiosity in the detective story, with a cult of investigation and Sherlock Holmes as a priest.[74]

One further line of defense mooted by these writers isn't a reply to Wilson so much as a larger reflection on literary history. **Popular narrative may satisfy appetites that more prestigious storytelling, in the wake of modernism, has ignored.** Earlier writers had used the mystery story as a cudgel to beat modernist writing. In 1926 E. M. Wrong declared that the "economy, tidiness, and completeness" of detective stories were "conspicuously lacking in some forms now much cried up." A 1929 article asserted that mysteries were in revolt against "sophomoric" psychological novels that withheld the appeals of plot. For its readers, the genre offers "escape not from life, but from literature."[75]

In the 1944 controversy, critics revisited this complaint. Krutch and Bogan note that mystery novels yield a clarity of plot and motive, a solid structure, and a finale promising poetic justice. These are time-honored literary values neglected by modernism and its followers. DeVoto asserts that the mystery novel is popular because "it is the only current form of fiction that is pure story."[76]

In his rejoinder, Wilson defends modernism as redefining what counts as a good story. Proust, Joyce, and Woolf tell tales, but they give us more. They have designed their books with an exceptional "intensity"—owing, presumably, to their Symbolist leanings—so their occasional *longueurs* are worth the cost. The art novel subordinates plot in the conventional sense to through-composed organic form, as James had advised.[77] Wilson might have added that the appeal of "pure story" dominates westerns and romance novels too, yet defenders of the detective story don't endow those genres with literary stature.

Wilson's strictures created terms for further debate. In 1946, as if pleading guilty to Wilson's accusations, W. H. Auden admitted that he was a detective story addict and that the genre had nothing to do with art. He presented it as a secular myth of the fall from Eden.[78] John Dickson Carr, a writer of classic mysteries, defended the genre as "the greatest game in the world," lifting the puzzle element to the level of an intellectual struggle: the battle of wits between criminal and detective is mirrored by that of author and reader.[79] Marshall McLuhan, eventually to become a guru of media studies, took to the pages of a literary quarterly to "provide the sleuth with a pedigree" stretching back to Renaissance drama.[80]

Wilson sharpened the battle lines by granting that psychological thrillers and stories of espionage had a better claim to literary status, so Graham Greene escapes his sanctions. He also largely exempted the hard-boiled tale, a gesture that left an opening for an unexpected entry in the discussion.

Reforming the Roughnecks

Raymond Chandler's reputation had been growing since publication of *The Big Sleep* (1939), and Knopf (publisher of not only Faulkner but also Dashiell Hammett, James M. Cain, and other hard-boiled writers) had promoted the novels strongly. The editor of the *Atlantic Monthly*, often considered a solid middlebrow monthly, was a Chandler admirer and invited Chandler to write an article on the detective story. "The Simple Art of Murder" appeared in December 1944 in the midst of the debate about mysteries that Wilson had touched off.[81] Although Chandler makes no reference to any of the disputants, he had read their entries.[82] His article amplifies Wilson's critique of the classic whodunit and offers the hard-boiled detective story as a form of detective fiction of genuine literary merit.

Through amusing demolition of several interwar whodunits, Chandler supports Wilson's objections. The classic puzzle is fatally unrealistic in characterization ("cardboard"), plot (riddled with implausibilities and contra-dictions), and worldview. "If the writers of this fiction . . . wrote about the kind of murders that happen, they would also have to write about the authentic flavor of life as it is lived. And since they cannot do that, they pretend that what they do is what should be done." The demands of the puzzle are a creative strait-jacket. "If [the story] started out to be about real people . . . they must very soon do unreal things in order to form the artificial pattern required by the plot."[83] The classic detective story comforts its readers rather than challenging them.

Chandler pledges himself to realism. In his 1946 revision of the essay, the version best known, he adds a defiant opening: "Fiction in any form has always intended to be realistic."[84] So are there realistic detective stories? There are, and Dashiell Hammett wrote them. Chandler devotes the last stretch of the essay to an appreciation of Hammett's version of the hard-boiled detective story. Hammett's novels display all the virtues that the whodunit lacks: plau-sibility, sharp character drawing, originality of form, vividness of style, and a commitment to portraying contemporary reality. Hammett depicts the world of crooked politicians and ruthless mobsters—the sordid city that the refined English writers refused to confront.[85] "It is not a fragrant world, but it is the world you live in."[86]

"The Simple Art of Murder" nowhere mentions Chandler's own novels, but in praising Hammett he is providing a rationale for his own aesthetic. This becomes especially clear in the article's final paragraphs, with the admission that hard-edged realism is not enough. There has to be hope. That's provided by the hero, a man of honor who is "neither tarnished nor afraid," who paces the "mean streets" in quest of righteous adventure.[87] He is, in short, private detective Philip Marlowe. This urban knight-errant is the one element of arti-fice Chandler seems to allow, but that is because, in all fiction, realism needs tempering by redemption.

Chandler later told a correspondent that his essay was merely a polemic. "I could have written a piece of propaganda in favor of the English detective story just as easily."[88] But by offering an ambitious alternative to the classic whodunit, the essay helped make Chandler a salient figure in literary culture. In early 1945, a month after the piece appeared, Edmund Wilson's second diatribe against mys-teries praised Chandler as the only writer in the genre who displayed the gift of storytelling. Knopf, quick to capitalize on notoriety, ran a full-page *New York Times* advertisement announcing that Chandler was now being recognized as "a truly great writer." Festooned with quotations from critics, the copy insisted that he was more than a mystery-monger. He was a novelist, "a part of contemporary American *literature*, along with . . . Hammett, Cain, O'Hara, Burnett."[89]

As if on cue, the *Atlantic Monthly* took up the cause. An article in early 1945 bestowed on Chandler "an artistry of craftsmanship and a realism that can rank him with many a famous novelist."[90] Later that year the *Times* carried a piece called "Raymond Chandler, and the Future of the Whodunits." In reviewing Knopf's well-timed release of an omnibus collection of Chandler's four novels, the critic declared that if these books hadn't been pigeonholed as detective stories they would have been best-sellers.[91] Thanks to such accolades, and the praise showered on *Double Indemnity* (1944) and other films indebted to his work, his career rose to new heights.

In the short term, "The Simple Art of Murder" did more for Chandler's reputation than that of the hard-boiled school. The pulpish Mike Hammer novels ruling the best-seller lists were difficult to defend as serious writing. Admirers of the classic puzzle form pointed out that hard-boiled fiction was no model of verisimilitude.[92] The tough detective is knocked unconscious several times per volume, voluptuous women crave him, and he miraculously recovers from frightful beatings, only to handily remember the one definite lie someone told that will give the game away.[93] Yet these conventions passed muster thanks to high art assumptions that grim drama is more realistic than the essentially comic rhythm governing the prim puzzle.

From the 1960s on, however, Chandler's rationale would be successfully applied to the entirety of hard-boiled literature and film noir. "The Simple Art of Murder" offered a path out of the 1940s impasse between elite art and mass culture. Yes, High Modernism was over. But there was a vernacular idiom of modern American writing, developed by Gertrude Stein, Sherwood Anderson, and Ernest Hemingway, that fed into Hammett's achievement.[94] This was the pedigree of the best of the hard-boiled school. Thematically, exposing the corruption of the capitalist city is one way to fulfill modern literature's effort to criticize what Josiah Strong calls the "storm-centers of civilization," where politics, class struggle, and sexual tensions erupt.[95]

At least one form of popular storytelling devoted itself not to peddling daydreams and distraction but to forcing its audience to face an uncomfortable reality. Wilson and Chandler conveniently ignored the elements of social criticism, particularly the emphasis on class inequities, to be found in many British whodunits. For defenders of the hard-boiled school, the artificial world of the English puzzle story simply reflects a realm of bourgeois comfort slightly knocked awry but put right by a figure of authority. The hard-boiled story, like proletarian fiction and the novel of social criticism, shows that popular narrative can knowingly reflect its moment. This bleak, confrontational worldview could never be confused with the consolations of mass culture.

James Naremore labels the leading hard-boiled writers "popular modernists" because they occupy a space between high art and mass art.[96] Eventually they proved to be a compelling crossover form not only for mass audiences but for generations of intellectuals.

Experiments Everywhere

In the 1940s, Anglo-American popular storytellers built the foundations for decades to come. Crossovers appeared in the 1920s and 1930s, but the waning of hard-core modernism left the field wide open. Now almost any innovative book, play, film, radio show, or comic book had to provide some degree of accessibility. Novelty of form and style tended to be the result of revising schemas from the classic tradition, from modernism, or from the blends and hybrids of recent years. The buffet was laid, and the menu could be expanded by judicious experimentation with inherited recipes.

Resistance to mass culture subsided, and nearly every intellectual found something to admire and enjoy. Detective fiction had already made forays into that audience, and soon science fiction, horror, and fantasy would count among their fans people who would have been called highbrows a generation before. Many of the mass-culture critics admitted they had been too pugilistic: their conception of the "mass" was undiscriminating.[97] By relegating everything that was not avant-garde to the category of mass culture, critics in effect swept into the same bucket *Our Town*, *His Girl Friday* (1940), and paintings of poker-playing dogs. And perhaps the consumers of popular art were not all being gulled. David Riesman pointed out that many pop music fans were discerning connoisseurs.[98]

Film was perhaps the mass medium easiest to grant some artistic potential. Many intellectuals were already hospitable to the idea; they had praised Chaplin, D. W. Griffith, Walt Disney, and German and Soviet directors of the silent era. The Hollywood studio cinema was a softer target and easily caricatured as an assembly line and a dream factory. But the most original American film critics of the 1940s, I've argued elsewhere, bypassed the mass-culture debates and showed that mainstream movies had their own realm of artistic achievement.[99]

With consolidation of the forms and techniques of popular narrative in the 1940s, the mystery gained new prominence, and many "literary" novelists turned to the genre. This trend persisted throughout the decades, as prestigious fiction writers and playwrights reworked mystery-based schemas. Norman Mailer, Joyce Carol Oates, Thomas Pynchon, Don DeLillo, Donna Tartt, Paul Auster, and many others found in the investigation plot and the suspense thriller fertile ground for artistry. In more oblique ways, the genre shaped prestige storytelling. Vladimir Nabokov claimed to detest mysteries, but *Lolita* (1958) is an amalgam of suspense plots. *Pale Fire* (1962), Nabokov declared in an interview, "is a combination of scholarly work, a poem, and a mystery thriller."[100]

This recognition of mystery-driven storytelling after the 1940s was part of the Anglo-American intelligentsia's wider acceptance of popular culture as a source of artistic vitality. In the 1960s, Pop Art burst onto the gallery and museum market as Pauline Kael was celebrating the rise of a "New Hollywood." Even the staunch *Partisan Review* had abandoned the barricades. It published Susan Sontag's sympathetic account of Camp and Richard Poirier's defense of the Beatles as "very great" artists, proof that "the arts really do not need to be boring."[101] Poirier's case echoed Gilbert Seldes's 1922 book, *The Seven Lively Arts*, which defended vaudeville, Tin Pan Alley, comic strips, and slapstick movies. Seldes had assaulted an age of genteel taste, but Poirier went further. However liberating the High Modernists had been, they and their academic enablers had suffocated pleasure. Poirier asked a basic question: "Is this any fun?"

Ever since then, esoteric storytelling has become, to one degree or another, exoteric. Choosing novels more or less at random: Wilkie Collins could recognize *Special Topics in Calamity Physics* (2008) as a variant of the dossier novel whose offspring, the *As I Lay Dying* model, had never gone out of style. *Ghostwritten* (1999) uses multiple narrators to reconstruct a terrorist attack, and *A Brief History of Seven Killings* (2014) does the same for an assassination attempt. *Lost Children Archive* (2020) offers documents and a novel-within-a-novel framed by a road trip.

Without daring to sum up decades of storytelling variants, let me end this survey with a final example. If I had to pick a figure who epitomizes the dazzling swirl of the crossover currents shaping Anglo-American popular narrative since World War II, that would be Stephen Sondheim. Beginning in the 1950s, he poured an astonishing range of cultural materials into music and movies that exemplify the vivacity of popular storytelling.

His work can be situated in the fondness for stage games found in "light modernism." One trend in British theater fused aspects of modernism (Pinter, Beckett, Ionesco) with the comedy of P. G. Wodehouse and *The Goon Show*. Tom Stoppard's *Rosencrantz and Guildenstern Are Dead* (1966) showed that what was "offstage" in one story could constitute the amusingly doom-laden plot of another.

Alan Ayckbourn dedicated his career to formal experimentation with space (three bedrooms as one in *Bedroom Farce*, 1975) and time (simultaneous action in *How the Other Half Loves*, 1969). *Intimate Exchanges* (1983) spreads forking-path plots across eight separate plays and sixteen possible endings. *House and Garden* (1999) consists of two plays performed simultaneously in two auditoriums, with actors dashing between them. Ayckbourn's most famous cycle of pattern plotting, *The Norman Conquests* (1973), displays a grid structure; each play gathers all the action taking place in one location, and the audience must reconstruct the order of story events.

Michael Frayn's virtuoso *Noises Off* (1982) probably owes something to Stoppard and Ayckbourn, but it offers its own switcheroo. The opening scene of a sex farce is rehearsed in the first act, comes off skillfully in the second, and collapses during the third. Crucially, the smooth show of the second act is presented to us in a backstage view displaying the intricate timing involved. Again, an abstract formal concept is mapped onto a conventional scenario, the comedy of a bungled stage production.

Not surprising, this trend had a nodding acquaintance with mystery genres. Ayckbourn plotted some plays as quasi-thrillers, and Stoppard's *The Real Inspector Hound* (1968) is a parody of the country house murder. Stoppard undercuts the mystery by a Pirandellian device: two critics down in front are commenting as the performance unfolds. This gives Stoppard a chance to mock pretentious reviewing language. The standard whodunit device of reenacting the murder transforms into a replay of the opening act, with the critics now taking the roles of detective and victim.

Also not surprising, both Ayckbourn and Stoppard declared themselves to be influenced by cinema, a reliable mark of crossover in modern media. Ayckbourn plays were adapted, with ingratiating wit, to film by Alain Resnais, and Stoppard wrote several scripts, most famously *Shakespeare in Love* (1998), which if the term means anything must count as defiantly middlebrow entertainment.

Sondheim was on the same frequency as these comic talents but had greater bandwidth. He plunged into cinephilia more deeply. His early musical influences were Hollywood scores, notably that for *Hangover Square* (1945); *Sweeney Todd, The Demon Barber of Fleet Street* (1979) was his tribute to Bernard Herrmann.[102] *A Little Night Music* (1973) and *Passion* (1994) were adapted from films. Many of his songs refer to movies, and he composed music for *Stavisky* (1974), *Dick Tracy* (1990), and other films. He was even a clapper boy for John Huston on *Beat the Devil* (1953).[103]

Instead of parodying mysteries, Sondheim was deeply committed to them. Detective fiction was his favorite reading, and as a puzzle addict he spent hours devising murder games. "I have always taken murder mysteries rather seriously."[104] Both *Company* (1970) and *Follies* (1971) were initially planned as mysteries, with the latter concerned not with "whodunit?" but with "who'll do it?"[105] *Sweeney Todd* is a paradigmatic revenge thriller; in planning the song plot, Sondheim consulted Peter Shaffer, author of *Sleuth* (1970). Asked by Herbert Ross to write a film, Sondheim and Anthony Perkins (another admirer of "the trick kind" of mystery practiced by John Dickson Carr) came up with *The Last of Sheila* (1973).[106] Directed by Ross, it is a blackly comic, cleverly structured whodunit—*And Then There Were None* as if redone by a Condé Nast gossip columnist. With George Furth, Sondheim wrote a thriller play, *Getting Away with Murder* (1996), and planned the unproduced *Chorus Girl Murder Case*, an homage to 1940s Bob Hope movies. The clues would be hidden in the songs.

Sondheim's zest for film and mystery fiction reflects a deep admiration for popular culture. It's one thing to enjoy it, as Ayckbourn and Stoppard clearly do, while also poking fun at its silliness. It's something else to appreciate its artistry in depth and try to master the conventions yourself. Despite learning "tautness" from the austere avant-garde composer Milton Babbitt, Sondheim took as his mentor Oscar Hammerstein II.[107] Tin Pan Alley, with its finger-snapping rhythms and suave wordplay, pushed him toward a brisk cleverness. The virtuoso rhymes in his bouncy "Comedy Tonight" (*A Funny Thing Happened on the Way to the Forum*, 1962) inevitably bring a grin: *Panderers! Philanderers! Cupidity! Timidity! . . . Tumblers, grumblers, bumblers, fumblers!*

While executing these pirouettes, the song provides a Cliffs Notes guide to Roman New Comedy. No tragedy tonight; weighty affairs will just have to wait. Sondheim similarly lays bare an inherited schema in the unproduced movie script *Singing Out Loud*, in which the couple gradually learn that it's okay to express emotion in song. "They have to learn to overcome the unreality of it and break into song in the conventional manner of all musicals."[108]

By taking fun seriously, by embracing the dynamic of schema and revision, Sondheim found in popular storytelling a vast arena for experimentation. He was crucially influenced by *Allegro* (1947), an ambitious Rodgers and Hammerstein musical he considered "startlingly experimental in form and style."[109] Hammerstein was "the great experimenter" who used the verse sections of songs to explore possibilities of structure, melody, and harmony.[110] *Allegro* also played daringly with overall structure and subjective viewpoint, techniques that Sondheim would take up. In his invaluable creative memoirs, *Finishing the Hat* (2010) and *Look, I Made a Hat* (2011), Sondheim shows how he sought out problems that could be solved through formal innovation that suited the subject and genre. Who else would decide to write all the songs for *A Little Night Music* in triple time, with each one in a different dance form?

His first major experiment was *Company* (1970), which consists of flashbacks framed by the protagonist Robert's thirty-fifth birthday party. Sondheim claimed it offered "a story without a plot."[111] The flashbacks don't supply a goal-directed character arc and instead sample Robert's bachelor lifestyle and its effects on his three girlfriends and the five married couples in his circle. The resulting compare-and-contrast pattern relies on principles of parallel construction going back to *Intolerance*. Complicating things further, bits of action are accompanied by a choruslike commentary from characters not in the scene. Still, there is a certain progression to the whole, indicated by Robert's disillusioned but hopeful final song, "Being Alive."

The nonlinearity of *Company* indicates how much Sondheim's innovations owe to the techniques I've been considering. Likewise, *Assassins* (1990) moves freely back and forth across a hundred years and shows off a Joycean "polystylism," integrating popular musical traditions from vaudeville to melodrama. (Sondheim strongly admired *Ulysses*.) In *Follies*, characters argue with their former selves. *Sunday in the Park with George* (1984), built on parallels between two painters, assigns inner monologues to both artist and model; characteristically, Sondheim expresses jumbled thoughts by avoiding the rhymes he normally strives to maintain.

Several plays utilize a narrator, who may take a role or converse with the characters. The Narrator of *Into the Woods* (1987) dies fairly early in the story he tells. The play's overall structure is a virtuoso braiding of classic folktales into a single plot. A different experiment in narration informs *Passion*, which Sondheim created as an epistolary musical. Characters writing or reading letters render the emotional climaxes as "read rather than acted."[112]

Sondheim's appetite for innovation drove him to revisit techniques accumulated over the century. Turning the 1934 Kaufman and Hart comedy *Merrily We Roll Along* into a musical in 1981, he happily tackled the problems of its 3-2-1 chronology. He signaled time shifts with recurring tunes sung by a chorus. Different productions experimented with ways of reinforcing these musical tags, such as a synoptic slide show reminiscent of the "News on the March" sequence of *Citizen Kane*. The inverted chronology also shaped the musical texture. In a linear plot, fully vocalized melodies are given reprises, shorter versions recalling the original number. Here, Sondheim had the reprises come first, as appetizers for songs yet to be fully heard, "undercurrents of memory" whose source would be revealed in later (that is, earlier) scenes. Similarly, one friend's leitmotif became accompaniment for another's main theme. Working in musical theater allowed Sondheim to infuse each moment with the density of allusion and recall sought by the modernist novel.[113] The puzzle addict tries to fit everything together.

Pacific Overtures (1976), a chronicle of Japan's engagements with the West, has the structure of a portmanteau film composed of distinct episodes. It too has a narrator, the Reciter, and its experiments include turning *renga* linked verse into a passed-along song. The most formally daring scene, "Someone in a Tree," stages the March 1854 signing of the treaty opening Japan to U.S. ships. We do not see the ceremony, which is held in a secure house. The Reciter questions an old man who claims that as a boy he watched the negotiations from a tree. During their dialogue, a boy clambers up the tree, and he and his older self collaborate in reporting the event he sees but cannot hear. Then the Reciter discovers a samurai guard hiding beneath the floorboards, and he reports what he hears but cannot see.

As the singers' accounts intertwine, history is assembled through partial perceptions, both in the moment and in recollection. In a Conradian gesture, the story, incomplete as it is, becomes accessible only through multiple viewpoints. "I'm a fragment of the day./ If I weren't, who's to say/ things would happen here the way/ that they're happening?" In adapting novelistic schemas of viewpoint to the stage, *Pacific Overtures* spontaneously revives and revises the sensory-deprivation experiment of *A Voice in the Dark*.

* * *

"The old avant-garde has passed," wrote Dwight Macdonald in 1960, "and left no successors." Midcult, middlebrow culture had bled high art dry. By this account, the storytellers we've encountered in this chapter are part of "the agreeable ooze" of midcult.[114] Sondheim had a fondness for the pastiche of popular forms, "Brechtian" songs, a willingness to pitch TV scripts while admiring Laurie Anderson and Marguerite Duras, and a shameless appropriation of Seurat and Japanese traditions—was this man not the ultimate middlebrow entertainer? What can you do with someone who declares no split between light and serious art? As Sondheim remarked, "I put Phyllis McGinley right up there with Keats and Shelley."[115]

Judged by the standards of High Modernism, much mass art will appear compromised. But I've argued that modernism can itself be considered a more or less demanding revision of schemas to be found in prior narrative traditions. I've also suggested that the purist peak of that effort, Ultraism, enjoyed a fairly brief moment.[116] What we have seen, in great plenitude, is Anglo-American narrative as largely a crossover phenomenon, a swirling blend of classic, proto-modernist, hard-core modernist, and modified-modernist schemas. And very often we find admirable skill, not to mention sheer enjoyment, in the crossovers. If Macdonald can, in all seriousness, favorably compare Fellini's "delightfully obvious masterpiece" *8 ½* (1963) to Mozart's *Magic Flute*, surely Sondheim deserves his day in court.[117]

In treating so many narratives, current and vintage, as revisions of inherited schemas, I might seem to be denying the notion of originality. Not entirely. I ask simply that we think of originality in exoteric media and in many esoteric works as a striking addition to tradition. We can see it as a play between freshness and familiarity, a confirmation that certain storytelling techniques that have come down to us are not absolutely rigid and can, when flexed or stretched, yield rewarding artistic experiences. Creative anachronism, skipping back to earlier works for inspiration, can be as artistically valid as "taking the next step" (which never seems obvious at the time). It's a conception of originality closer to some non-Western art making than to the Western bias toward upsets and breakthroughs. Forms can be gamelike and playful, as in Japanese court poetry. Virtuosity can discover unexpected possibilities within established schemas and rules. Tradition can be additive and constantly enriching itself through borrowings. Devices can be endlessly rediscovered.[118]

The qualities promoted by the New Critics—irony, symbolism, ripe ambiguities, the palpitations of consciousness—were characteristic of High Modernism as were the mythic/psychoanalytic resonances disclosed by cultural critics from the 1940s until today. But these perspectives may not be best adapted to appreciating the range and power of popular narrative.

I've sketched some rationales for this appreciation in summing up critics' responses to Edmund Wilson's attack on detective stories. Barzun, DeVoto, Krutch, and the others didn't need to assert that popular storytelling is ultimately "as good as" more rarefied forms. That judgment will depend on the criteria we apply across the board. If we demand that profound philosophical meditation on the human condition is necessary for greatness, much of mass art won't qualify (but then neither will much of prestigious art). Defenders of the mystery genre or other popular forms need only argue that these narratives fulfill worthwhile functions, and some of them will be very good of their kind. This line of defense remains in force today. An adroit thriller can, all things being equal, be a more worthy artistic endeavor than a muddled novel of psychological angst. In cinema particularly, many supreme achievements, from Hitchcock's suspense films to Ozu's domestic dramas, are "transcendent" genre pieces, wholly derived from mass storytelling traditions.[119]

The 1944 defenders of mystery proposed that innovative work can be found in all areas of culture. They suggested that we take seriously experts' and fans' efforts to gain intimate acquaintance with craft. They urged us to treat popular narrative as part of a history of forms and genres that have their own integrity.

We have the right tools available: awareness of craft norms, sometimes made explicit by practitioners themselves; historical information about institutions that produce and distribute mass culture; and not least, fundamental concepts of narration, viewpoint, segmentation, and temporal linearity. If we can reveal what Robert Hughes called "the spectacle of skill," we can enhance our understanding and enjoyment of popular narrative.[120]

The 1944 defenders of mystery stories were right to touch on some of narrative's basic human appeals, such as curiosity. The experimentalism on view in a play such as *A Voice in the Dark*, a novel such as *How Like a God*, and a film such as *The Woman in Question* will often pose questions about crimes completed or about to be committed. For a great deal of all popular storytelling, pleasure in story values is the reward, but the lure is mystery. That lure has inspired storytellers, and it has brought readers and viewers a bonus of enhanced skills in story comprehension. I'll try to convince you that the traditions of mystery storytelling helped audiences of all brows become more sensitized to the potential of narrative form and style. We learned to like the taste of the construction.

PART II

CHAPTER 4

THE GOLDEN AGE PUZZLE PLOT

The Taste of the Construction

In all media, popular storytellers from the 1910s onward found that mystery plotting encouraged tricky techniques. We confront a mystery, as critic Victor Shklovsky indicated, when the narrative announces that we don't know something.[1] If the action is focused on revealing that something, we can call the result an investigation plot. That plot must both track the inquiry and take us back to events leading up to the present.

As investigation plots became common, audiences grew adept at enjoying them. That engagement would, by the logic of the variorum, encourage innovation, even when the novelty seemed a little arbitrary. Anthony Trollope deplored "the taste of the construction" he felt after reading Wilkie Collins.[2] But that taste, actually a taste *for* felt construction, for flagrant artifice and sensed pattern, informs much of what audiences enjoyed about mysteries. Treating a mystery as a playful experience of form became central to popular storytelling.

It wasn't alien to more exalted writing either. "Psychological mystery stories" one critic called James's experiments in viewpoint, and Conrad's novels were compared to detective stories.[3] Ford Madox Ford's *The Good Soldier* becomes the written record of a husband's investigation of his wife, revealing a murder scheme and supplemented by cryptic questions to the reader about what characters might have been up to. (Ford, a fan of detective stories, went on to write the 1936 thriller *Vive le Roy*.) Most famously, William Faulkner's obsessive, circuitous inquiries into his characters' pasts, along with dark hints about their secrets, had obvious kinship with investigation plots. Faulkner's detective story *Intruder in the Dust* (1948) is the most obvious manifestation of an impulse that Conrad Aiken found in the very fibers of his style: "the whole elaborate method of deliberately withheld meaning, of progressive and partial and delayed disclosure, which so often gives the characteristic shape to the novels themselves."[4]

In this Faulkner was joining a popular tradition that crystallized in the 1910s and 1920s. Those years saw the emergence of three large-scale mystery genres, all developing in relation to one another. Each has a fairly distinct identity, yet they all have precedents. The storyteller aims to instill what we might call the mystery attitude, a perplexity that ignites curiosity, sustains suspense, and ends in surprise.[5]

The whodunit can be traced back to the Gothic novel and sensation fiction of the nineteenth century, but with the proviso that the mystery is solved by someone playing the role of detective. The puzzle is resolved, not through accident or quasi-supernatural means but by systematic inquiry and more or less logical analysis, often aided by intuition. The plot is driven by curiosity. We ask not just what comes next, a question basic to all narrative engagement, but what has already happened. In reconstructing those events and relationships, we are placed in suspense about how the solution of the mystery resolves the plot. That solution/resolution, if it's to pay off the perplexity, has to come as something of a surprise—a satisfying one, at that, showing how bits of information dovetail into a unitary pattern of causes and effects, accident and intention.

The psychological thriller, also an inheriter of the Gothic and sensation trends, emphasizes the roles of victim and perpetrator. The buildup to the crime, or series of crimes, forms the bulk of the action, and the protagonist may be the person under threat or the character plotting the crimes. The viewpoint may be restricted to one or the other, or it may alternate between them. Investigation may play a role, but it is likely to be offstage or taken up by the potential victim. In all, suspense is central to the thriller, which depends on a threat of future danger more intense than is usual in the whodunit. Narration thus plays a central role in distinguishing the genres and their dominant effects.

By putting an investigation plot in the foreground, the exploits of Sam Spade and Philip Marlowe and their peers offer a variant of the whodunit. The hard-boiled story restricts its narration to the investigator, usually a private eye, who may recount the story in first person. What sets the hard-boiled school apart, according to critical tradition, is the writers' resistance to the genteel milieu and manners of the classic British and American versions. Nearly all mystery stories involve some degree of adventure—patterns of risky quest and chase—but that quality dominates the hard-boiled mystery. It typically offers a conflict-filled, often violent urban adventure involving professional criminals and malfeasance at all levels of society. It has roots in Sir Walter Scott's historical romances and Fenimore Cooper's frontier stories of wilderness tracking and hunting. The hard-boiled plot balances our curiosity about the source of the mystery with suspense deriving from the dangerous urban setting: the investigator is likely to be in peril.

There's good reason to begin our exploration with the whodunit. Whatever their distant sources, the modern psychological thriller and the hard-boiled story have largely been defined by creators' efforts to distinguish their work from the so-called Golden Age detective story. The chief creators in that body of Anglo-American fiction were Agatha Christie, Dorothy L. Sayers, Anthony Berkeley Cox, S. S. Van Dine, Ellery Queen, and John Dickson Carr. Although most Golden Age authors are little read today, their contributions to popular storytelling shaped a good deal of what we encounter today, and not just in mystery genres.

From the Great Detective to the Golden Age

We tend to think of artistic movements, such as Symbolism or Surrealism, as being confined to the avant-garde. Literary historian LeRoy Lad Panek has shrewdly suggested that we can treat the Golden Age group as a literary movement too.[6] Most of its members knew one another. The most prominent English practitioners formed the Detection Club, which met in London restaurants to share ideas, collaborate on projects, and promote their work.[7] Many had prestigious literary agents; Cox's agent handled Hillaire Belloc, J. B. Priestley, and Evelyn Waugh. Through imitation and competition their novels gained a collective identity: the classic "whodunit." At the same time, these writers composed essays and reviews promulgating their ideas of the genre.

Detectives, amateur or professional, had appeared in fiction and drama throughout the nineteenth century.[8] Sensation novels such as Wilkie Collins's *The Woman in White* (1859) and *The Moonstone* (1868) took crime out of haunted castles and concentrated, as Henry James put it, on "the mysteries that are at our own doors." The plot set both professional investigators and interested parties to solving puzzles arising in "the cheerful country house and the busy London lodgings."[9] But Collins tended to spread the detective role among several characters. In contrast, Edgar Allan Poe's "The Murders in the Rue Morgue" (1841) made the detective the central figure, an introverted genius with immense powers of reasoning. Comparably charismatic investigators emerged in Emile Gaboriau's novels, and most powerfully in the stories of Arthur Conan Doyle. Sherlock Holmes, who made his bow in *A Study in Scarlet* (1887), remained a titanic literary force well beyond his last story, which was published in 1926.

By the 1910s, readers expected most mystery plots to revolve around a "Great Detective." Authors eagerly adopted the conventions Doyle had consolidated, not least because a striking figure could be the basis of a series of stories. A continuing hero could engage fans, aid world building, and not least highlight experiments. A familiar detective and milieu could serve as a comforting background against which the writer could introduce novelty. Late stories in which Sherlock Holmes narrates the case would be far less striking to a reader who didn't know the role of Dr. Watson in earlier entries. Agatha Christie's posthumous *Curtain* (1975) carries much more weight as the culmination of the Hercule Poirot saga than it would as a stand-alone.

The aspiring writer was urged to create a memorable detective through mannerisms, habits, dress, and tastes.[10] The "transcendent detective," as the hero came to be called, might be a forensic scientist (Dr. Thorndyke), a blind man (Max Carrados), a severe logician (the Thinking Machine), a pious Yankee (Uncle Abner), or a soft-spoken, surprisingly worldly priest (Father Brown). Like Holmes, transcendent detectives were given memorable eccentricities. The Old Man in the Corner solved mysteries from a tea shop booth while knotting and unknotting pieces of string.

Earlier traditions weren't wholly abandoned, as is shown by the work of Mary Roberts Rinehart. Although enormously popular, Rinehart's mysteries never earned respect from the Golden Age grandees.[11] She relied on coincidences, she put the romantic couple at the plot's center, and she bypassed the transcendent detective convention by assigning that role to an involved participant. *The Circular Staircase* (1908) followed the sensation novel in centering on threats to a familiar middle-class world. The intricate relations among the characters, most of them harboring secrets, recall Collins's plotting. Rinehart likewise revamped the Gothic convention of the heroine set loose in an ominous house. At the climax, the heroine is locked in a concealed room and at the mercy of the murderer. Rachel Innes became a model for the emperiled women in the domestic thrillers of Mignon G. Eberhart and later writers.[12]

Rachel is the driving force of an investigation plot. She must assemble evidence and work around the police. She opens *The Circular Staircase* with a sidelong challenge to the male supersleuth: "This is the story of how a middle-aged spinster lost her mind, deserted her domestic gods in the city, took a furnished house for the summer out of town, and found herself involved in one of those mysterious crimes that keep our newspapers and detective agencies happy and prosperous."[13] This sprightly heroine's personal stake in solving a murder gives her an energy quite different from the detachment of the "consulting detective" or observers such as Father Brown. If the series-based Great Detective came to define the genre, there was room for a minor line of threatened amateurs forced to take up the investigator role. These relatable, accidental detectives would propel suspense thrillers for years to come.

A remarkable body of commentary on the principles underlying the pure detective story grew up during the same period.[14] While followers of James and Ibsen were proposing new methods for fiction and drama, some literary essayists were doing the same for their favored genre. Most comprehensive and incisive was Carolyn Wells's *Technique of the Mystery Story* (1913), one of the most subtle writing manuals of the period.

Wells and her contemporaries noted that the investigation is launched when a crime has taken place. Therefore the plot must move forward, as the inquiry proceeds, and backward, as the causes of the crime are reconstructed through documents, testimony, and clues. Chronology may be manipulated through flashbacks that may both clarify and complicate our sense of the sources of the crime.

But not just any crime. Already the mark of the teasing whodunit was the baffling crime, the extraordinary one that challenges you to play with hypotheses, offer alternative solutions, and speculate about motive. What does this dying message mean? The more the crime flouts common sense, the better. Matters of whodunit could be clouded by matters of "howdunit," as Poe had already shown in the Rue Morgue case. How could someone be murdered in a room locked from the inside? The "impossible crime" offers many benefits to the investigation plot. It automatically puts the crime beyond plodding police routine, affords a chance for the Great Detective to show off, and has its own aesthetic interest—a what-if prospect that stirs the storytelling imagination.

The 1910s commenters agreed that the genre's primary appeal resides in intellectual curiosity. The story's resolution is the puzzle's solution, preferably with a surprise. As Poe had demanded of the short story, everything in the detective tale aims at a final startling effect. At the same time, the puzzle plot is also a game. Carolyn Wells suggests that the reader is playing against a "diabolically artful" author who will wrap the tale in deception.[15] Nevertheless, the game isn't rigged. The author is expected to play fair in supplying all relevant information to solve the mystery.

In addition, the story must display ingenuity in both the crime and the solution. Wells writes: "The reader is thus turned into an analytical observer who not only delights in the mental ingenuity exhibited by the detective, but actually joins him in working out the intricacies of a problem which, though at first seemingly insoluble, is at length mastered entirely. Thus his admiration for the 'investigator' is happily coupled with his own delight in unraveling the skein which the author has woven expressly for the purpose."[16] The Great Detective serves as a guiding figure. Most readers probably don't seriously try to solve the puzzle, but they enjoy following the hero's efforts. Typically the investigation is viewed by the detective's friend, and many writers followed Doyle's example in making that figure the source of first-person narration: a Watson.

No other popular genre attracted the serious critical reflection devoted to the detective story. But the growing awareness of craft principles raised a question: Could detective stories acquire literary value? Wells noted that the genre had ties to folktales, riddles, Greek myth, and other reputable precedents. The mystery's "fixed form," she suggested, had something of the stylized abstraction of heraldic devices and Middle Eastern embroidery. The best detective stories might be as worthy of respect as any "character studies, problem novels, society sketches or symbolic romances."[17] Many mystery writers accepted the Collins distinction between "great writer" and "storyteller," but some hoped to pass beyond the category of mere entertainment. The lure of literary respectability would tempt writers in all mystery traditions for the next century.

Many of the younger authors of the 1920s followed the Great Detective model and made their protagonists larger than life. Christie gave us Hercule Poirot, Carr the Chestertonian Dr. Gideon Fell, and Van Dine the languid aesthete Philo Vance. Other writers reacted against the towering eccentricity of Holmes by humanizing their protagonists. E. C. Bentley conceived the protagonist of *Trent's Last Case* (1913) as the untranscendent detective. Offended by fictional characters who are "ostentatiously unlike life," Bentley made Trent a lively young artist of good breeding and no peculiarities. "*Trent's Last Case* is not so much a detective story as an exposure of detective stories."[18]

Trent became the prototype of a new breed of masterminds; relaxed and bantering amateurs included Sayers's Lord Peter Wimsey, Margery Allingham's Albert Campion, and Berkeley's Roger Sheringham. At times indulging in the silly-ass babble of Bertie Wooster, they were akin to the Bright Young Things in the fictions of Michael Arlen and Evelyn Waugh. Sharply portrayed, they might also edge the mystery story toward the novel of manners, a genre of some literary repute.[19]

Golden Age writers were heir to many technical devices. Apart from the resources of Gothic fiction, sensation novels, and melodrama (disguise, secret passages, double identities), investigative plots around the turn of the century laid out a rich menu. There were alibis genuine and faked, dying messages, locked-room murders, blackmail as a primary motive, ciphers to be analyzed, false or misleading clues (footprints were a favorite), the least likely culprit, even the possibility that the detective is the guilty party. There was reflexivity as well, as we saw in *Seven Keys to Baldpate* (1913).

Golden Age writers inherited two particular problems from their 1910s predecessors. First, how much adventure should be included? In Poe's "The Mystery of Marie Rogêt" (1842), C. Auguste Dupin solves a murder wholly by reading news accounts, but his two other cases supplement the puzzle with scenes of the detective intervening in the action to expose the culprit. As usual, Doyle took Poe a step further. Any story titled "The Adventure of the . . ." suggested that Holmes's reasoning would lead to some exciting action. Doyle typically built his plots toward a chase, a hunt, or a suspenseful ambush as in "The Speckled Band": "The game is afoot!" An excursion into danger helped thaw the chilliness of a pure chess-game exercise.

The Great Detective writers who followed Doyle freely mixed ratiocination and adventure. But Golden Age writers were at pains, at least in their public rationales, to play down tendencies toward physical action. A book's title would proclaim itself a *Mystery* or a *Case* or a *Problem*. Disdaining the thriller, authors insisted that theirs was the only genre that could display the free play of the gifted mind, the excitement of logic wedded to imagination.

In practice, most writers weren't so austere. As Panek points out, few of them adhered to the idea of the pure puzzle.[20] Love interest, worrisome as a distraction from reasoning, could enter when suspects became romantically involved. The supernatural could be invoked, as Chesterton and Carr did, as long as it didn't prove to be the solution. Derring-do wasn't ruled out either. Sayers provided an airborne last-minute rescue to resolve *Clouds of Witness* (1926), and Ellery Queen, who billed each book as "a problem in deduction," turned the last stretch of *The Egyptian Cross Mystery* (1932) into a cross-country race against time.[21]

Patches of adventure-driven action could also help with a second problem writers inherited from sensation fiction and the Great Detective tradition. Poe and Doyle showed that the puzzle-based detective story was suited to the short story. The boom in magazine publishing at the turn of the century encouraged writers to showcase their Great Detective in the short format. But what to do about the novel? Collins developed intricate plots suitable to the three-decker novel, but even Doyle had problems sustaining interest in the non-Holmes stretches of *A Study in Scarlet* (1887), *The Sign of Four* (1890), and *The Valley of Fear* (1915).

In popular narrative, form often follows format. Carolyn Wells and others argued that a novel-length plot needed felicitous elaboration. Writers had to integrate more suspects, more crimes, more atmospheric descriptions of set-ting, and more twists to keep building to the ending. And great skill was needed to keep that ending vivacious; a chapter-long anticlimax was much harder on the reader than the brief windup of a short story.

Changes in publishing allowed Golden Age writers to create comparatively compact books, running 70,000 to 80,000 words.[22] Yet scaling up remained daunting, especially for those purists who disdained bursts of exciting action. In S. S. Van Dine's *The "Canary" Murder Case* (1927), a woman is found strangled in her apartment. Did her last guest, one of her lovers, kill her? She was heard screaming and talking in her apartment long after he left. But her lover did kill her. Before he left, he switched on a phonograph record of her voice he had prepared, and he recruited a witness to join him in listening to it in the hallway.

This is essentially a short-story idea, so it needs padding out. Van Dine, a believer in the purely logic-driven plot, fills the book with Q&A sessions featuring witnesses and suspects. There are seven potential culprits, each with motives to be exposed and alibis to be broken. Revelations spur more interviews. The police back the wrong solution, and the transcendent detective Philo Vance expounds on the psychology of crime to anyone who will listen. Van Dine adds to the cast a sneak thief who witnesses the murder while hiding in a closet. Said thief also devises a gadget that lets him leave the crime scene while locking the door behind him—a red herring that occupies several pages. The crucial clue, the phonograph record, is discovered at the climax during a fresh search of the apartment , thus flagrantly disobeying fair-play demands.

A more dramatic way to fill out the novel was tested by Bentley in *Trent's Last Case*. Halfway through, the hero's explanation is revealed as mistaken. The false solution, which had the benefit of making the protagonist attractively fallible (and here prey to romantic influence), became a convention of detective plotting. Another Queen novel, the virtuoso *Greek Coffin Mystery* (1932), proffers four false solutions, two of them engineered by the murderer himself. True Golden Age bravado on this front is displayed in the title of J. J. Connington's *Case with Nine Solutions* (1928). At the same time, a parade of imperfect solutions placed great weight, however unearned, on the last one. What came at the end was truth—by convention, if not fully by conviction.

One more strategy for expansion would prove to have a long legacy. Instead of starting the plot with the principal crime, typically the discovery of a murder victim, the investigation could be launched by a pretext crime. Raymond Chandler noted that "the most effective way to conceal a simple mystery is behind another mystery. This is literary legerdemain."[23] In *The Nine Tailors* (1934), for example, Sayers delays the central murder puzzle by teasing Wimsey and the reader with a tale of jewels stolen twenty years earlier. Hard-boiled writers would use pretext crimes as a bait and switch to draw the private detective and the reader into a complicated character network.

Puzzles, Rules, and Ingenuity

"Low-brow reading," fretted two British writers commenting on the interwar period, "was now dominated by the detective novel."[24] Whatever lowbrows thought, the genre was a favorite of the middle class as well. Across the interwar period, an estimated eight thousand mystery novels were published in the United States and the UK.[25] Juvenile readers were courted with the adventures of the young detectives Nancy Drew and the Hardy Boys.[26]

When the venerable Scribners publishing house sold hundreds of thousands of copies of S. S. Van Dine novels, it was an acknowledgment that detective fiction could be legitimate. Soon every major publisher had a stable of mystery writers, and some developed imprints devoted to the genre. Unlike romances and westerns, mystery novels were reviewed in the *London Times*, the *New York Times*, and other significant press outlets, as well as in magazines such as *Bookman* and the *Saturday Review*.

This broadening support encouraged Anglo-American mystery writers to coalesce as a self-conscious movement. They announced their goals and defended their creative choices. Their voluminous writings about the genre, built on the poetics articulated in the 1910s, served as manifestos for a distinct literary form. In both precept and practice, they tried to deepen and enrich a genre that was beginning to achieve respectability. Their strategies for doing so left a permanent legacy for popular narrative.

With a single-mindedness that would have done credit to a Jamesian, many of these writers wanted a new form of self-conscious artistry. Every book tried to be a tour de force. The plot should baffle, of course, but beyond that the division into chapters, the manner of narration, and details of style— even layout and typography—should tease and perplex. With a thoroughness a modernist might appreciate, writers weaponized all the resources of story-telling to enhance curiosity and surprise. Appreciation of ingenuity became the watchword of the genre. Techniques were bent toward creating an admirable artifice.

Central to that artifice was the puzzle aspect. Given an extraordinary crime, the rule makers insisted, mere physical action was a distraction. "Emotion, wonder, suspense, sentiment, and description" had no place here, according to Willard Huntington Wright (aka S. S. Van Dine), probably the most severe puzzle adherent. "These qualities are either subordinated to ineffectuality, or else eliminated entirely. The reader is immediately put to work, and kept busy in every chapter, in the task of solving the book's mystery."[27] The novel might have a bustling climax, but a long concluding chapter would trace the detective's reasoning blow by blow. Ellery Queen went so far as to accompany a 1932 book with a pamphlet, "How to Read the Queen Stories." He suggests that the novels have only two types of readers: those who don't use logic but merely guess the culprit, and those who seek "the intellectual stimulation which my analytical-deductive method provides."[28] For both sorts of readers, the puzzle is central and all other appeals are secondary.

Golden Age writers sought ways to intensify puzzle conventions. Clues— traces of the criminal's identity left at or near the scene—proliferated. Carr's *Arabian Nights Murder* (1934) furnished eleven enigmatic items—from coal dust to false beards—that needed explaining. Elaborate alibis needed to be broken by patience and careful routine, skills embodied in Freeman Wills Crofts's tireless Inspector French.

Clues didn't need to be purely physical. Poe had endowed his detective with psychological insight, as when Dupin reads the narrator's mind or realizes that the Minister in "The Purloined Letter" (1843) is the sort of man who would conceal something by putting it in the most obvious place. In solving one case,

Vance's reasoning rests on his belief that studying the "colossal, incommensurable concepts" of mathematics gave the murderer "an enormous contempt for human life."[29] Even psychoanalysis was flirted with. On the whole, however, physical clues and questions of motive and timing remained key to a solution. Any strong urge to probe characters' mental lives would steer writers away from pure detection and toward the psychological thriller.

Another convention was helpful in delaying the answer to the puzzle. Thanks to what Father Brown recognized as a "half-memory," the detective realizes that something seen or heard earlier would help at the moment, but he or she can't recall it.[30] The detective's half-memory is in effect a signal to us that fair play is in force. If we scan previous pages, we could in principle discover what the detective is struggling to remember.

The revelation of the answer comes in two phases: the detective solves the mystery, and then he or she explains this solution to others. When we're given access to the first phase, the plot provides the eureka moment. We're told that the detective grasps how a clue or a cluster of them solves the puzzle. We're not, however, given the actual solution until the final explanation; before that, the answer is hinted at cryptically.

Surprisingly, for a genre priding itself on ineluctable logic, the moment of insight is often triggered by accident—a casual remark by someone, or a glimpse of something that can be associated with the solution. Despite the emphasis on logic and reasoning in Golden Age dramaturgy, the unraveling may owe something to chance.

Not that the plot immediately explains the eureka moment. One advantage of a Watson was that the Great Detective could announce that he would not reveal his thinking until he had enough evidence to prove his conclusions. This delaying device could be stretched to book length by complications. The detective's tentative solution might be challenged by a contradictory clue or a fresh murder. Eventually, however, either through explanation or a foray into adventure, the detective provides a complete solution.

The Golden Age writers likewise outstripped their predecessors in pushing further the idea that the mystery was a game. Like the puzzle, the game analogy was often more rhetorical than real. The novel is already complete when we pick it up, and the author can't respond to our "moves." At best, reading the book would be like replaying a chess match that was already completed. Nevertheless, writers dramatized the process as a battle of wits. Carr declared it as "a hoodwinking contest, a duel between author and reader . . . with the reader alert for every dropped clue, every betraying speech, every contradiction that might mean guilt."[31] Not only do we weigh what characters say and do, but we try to read the mind of the cunning author.

By calling the story a game, defenders of the genre could suggest that rules could stimulate ingenuity. In the 1920s and 1930s, writers enunciated a body of doctrine as fierce in its Thou Shalt Nots as the demands of any literary avant-garde. No love interest for the detective, no homicidal butlers, "no Chinamen," no last-minute introduction of the guilty party, no clues withheld from the reader, no twins or doubles, no accidental or supernatural solution to the mystery—these were laid down as inviolable. There should be only one detective who solves the case and only one guilty party. For a novel, the most suitable crime is murder. If a professional criminal enters the plot, he or she cannot be the killer. There can be no poisons unknown to science, and no more than one secret passage per book.[32] Members of the Detection Club swore an oath to avoid "Divine Revelation, Feminine Intuition, Mumbo-Jumbo, Jiggery-Pokery, Coincidence, or Acts of God."[33] What had been guidelines in the 1910s became self-imposed restrictions that enabled writers to show their skill.

Similarly, Doyle had thought of fair play principally as a matter of avoiding accidents or coincidences that revealed the solution. "The detective ought really to depend for his successes on something in his own mind."[34] But by the 1920s, Golden Age authors conceived fair play as making all clues and hints discoverable in principle by the reader. The test: If you reread the book, you could find everything necessary to the solution there, buried or flaunted in the flow of the prose. This demand made detective novels more difficult to write than other sorts, but it also invited creative use of the constraints. "Once the evidence has been fairly presented," noted Carr, "there are very few things that are not permissible."[35]

The sheer artificiality of the puzzle and game components invited deeper reader involvement. Some novels were published with the last chapters sealed, daring buyers to resist curiosity and return the book for a refund. A novel such as *The Long Green Gaze* (1925) might tuck clues into crossword puzzles that the reader had to solve. The original editions of Sayers's *Five Red Herrings* (1931) generously left a page blank so the reader could jot down what Lord Peter must have asked the police to search for at the murder scene.[36] Books came packaged with jigsaw puzzles (*The Jig-Saw Puzzle Murder*, 1933; *Murder of the Only Witness*, 1934). "Murder dossiers" such as *File on Bolitho Blane* (1936) assembled facsimile documents accompanied by strands of hair, bloodstained scraps of fabric, and other physical clues. The party game of Murder, in which guests were assigned roles of victim, culprit, witnesses, and detectives, became a craze and was, naturally, incorporated into novels (*Hide in the Dark*, 1929).

Likewise, murder plays became more interactive than *A Voice in the Dark* had been. *The Last Warning* (1922) recruited spectators (played by actors) into a play-within-the-play. *Murder in the Astor Theatre* (1922) and *The Radio Murder* (1926) locked the audience in and hauled suspects onstage to be interrogated. *Eye-Witnessed* (1926) warned patrons of danger during the performance; sure enough, a spectator is murdered and police arrive to find the killer. A similar premise informs *Murder in Motley* (1934). Most famously, *The Spider* (1927) turns the auditorium into a vaudeville house in which newsreels, stage acts, and mind-reading stunts lead to a killing.

The demands of puzzle and game called forth that ingenuity that the 1910s critics had prized. Carr, a specialist in "impossible crimes," took pride in the cleverness that was needed. "Strokes of ingenuity make the game worth playing at all."[37] In a crowded field, with a new mystery novel rolling off the press nearly every day, pressures of the variorum mounted.

Exploring new settings was an obvious option. Murder could move out of the country house or apartment into a department store, a hospital, a museum, an advertising agency, an airline cabin, a movie studio. Rudolph Fisher's *The Conjure-Man Dies: A Mystery Tale of Dark Harlem* (1932) cast a whodunit wholly with Black characters and provided a backstory set in Africa. Each fresh locale presented challenges of technical detail, insider knowledge, and specialized routine that the writer would have to master. The schemas of the Great Detective period had to be upgraded too. Dying messages became more complex, or perhaps inauthentic, and impossible crimes proliferated. Murders in locked rooms were joined by murders in an empty street, trackless stretches of snow, and on a pristine tennis court.

The urge for ingenuity made fair play a pretext for self-congratulatory artifice. As if to help the reader solve the puzzle, the novel might include a list of characters, with identifying phrases for easy reference. There were maps, floorplans, and diagrams. One large-format novel includes pages with clue-filled photographs purportedly taken by the detective.[38] The mind-bendingly elaborate *Obelists Fly High* (1935) includes a cast list, a seating plan of an airplane cabin, two schedules (one of "reported movements," the other of "actual movements"), and a "Clue Finder" that guides the reader to the exact pages indicating "the murderer's mistake" and "the time of the victim's death." If you peek at the Clue Finder before finishing the story, you're reprimanded: "Isn't there enough cheating in the world without this sort of thing?"[39]

These ingratiating gestures toward fair play opened the way for further duplicity. The Great Detective tradition had introduced the ingenious criminal and the ingenious sleuth. The Golden Age novelists thrust forward a figure that had been somewhat more discreet in those days: the ingenious author. To the clues in the Great Detective plot were added flagrant hints in the narration.

Any feature of a physical book could create overt misdirection. The cast list might drop hints about suspicious characters. Indications of day and time at the beginning of chapters could be helpful, but they could also leave tell-tale gaps, so the reader would need to page dutifully through all of them to check.[40] Before the story begins, the table of contents could flaunt cleverness, as when the first letters of the chapter titles spell out the title of the book (*The Greek Coffin Mystery*), or when the chapter titles form part of the tease. Golden Age authors amplified the tantalizing section titles occasionally found in nineteenth-century novels.[41] One book's parts are headed: "Prologue: What Might Have Happened"; "The Old Bailey: What Seemed to Happen"; "Epilogue: What Really Happened."[42] Or an epigraph could drop a hint, as when a quotation from Chesterton tips the wary reader to recall a suspect's height.[43]

Once the story gets rolling, footnotes can certify that a piece of testimony is trustworthy. Joseph Shaw, magisterial editor of the hard-boiled magazine *Black Mask*, complained that notes were a feeble gesture toward realism.[44] Yet these marginalia might serve as feints and diversions. One Van Dine footnote, citing a book published by a suspect after the case was closed, appears to clear him. At the climax, we learn that the suspect is guilty and the book was published posthumously. John Dickson Carr excelled at using footnotes that seem frank and fair but only increase the mystery. One note-studded Carr novel is called *The Reader Is Warned* (1939).

Most detective stories in any era pause late in the plot, and the reader senses that the revelation is coming. It was typical of the Golden Age that Ellery Queen introduced an explicit Challenge to the Reader, an announcement by the narration that at this point the careful reader ought to be able to solve the puzzle. Pivoting the genre's canonical moment of discovery to aim at the reader, the Challenge invites us to plunge back into the labyrinth. Meanwhile the writer celebrates the rules of the game and flaunts his ability to create novelty within them.

Despite all this help, the reader's chances of solving the puzzle are slim. If you managed to guess the culprit, could you actually reconstruct the detective's reasoning? One member of the Queen collaboration admitted, "We are fair to the reader only if he is a genius."[45]

As with other devices, the main effect is to demonstrate the writer's cleverness and the plot's intricate design. Philip MacDonald's *The Rynox Mystery* (1930) takes a premise suitable for a not very unusual short story and smashes it to pieces. A mogul is killed, as in *Trent's Last Case*, but this crime novel lacks a detective, preferring to refract the effects of the murder through dozens of viewpoints and documents. The book begins with an epilogue and ends with a prologue set before the main action. That main action is in turn fragmented into short scenes, accompanied by brief pendants labeled "Comment." The circumstances of the crime are presented through a barrage of letters, police reports, floor plains, memoranda, parodic news stories, an inquest transcript, and minutes of corporate meetings. The last section consists of a letter written by the victim on the brink of death, and like a detective at a denouement he obligingly ties together everything, even providing a timetable. All the structural obfuscation makes *The Rynox Mystery* as showy a performance as anything produced in the period.

Ingenuity took subtler forms. Detective narration had long relied on vagueness of description (shadowy figures, hands clutching doorknobs) and elliptical presentation of crucial events (skipping over time, restricting viewpoint). Golden Age writers carried the urge to perplex and misdirect into the very texture of their prose. Consider two examples from a period in which Golden Age principles had fully ripened.

Many writers filled out their plots to novel length by incorporating the courtship of a romantic couple. John Dickson Carr frequently used the pair as viewpoint figures, as well as targets, witnesses, and allies of the Great Detective. But in "The House in Goblin Wood" (1946), Carr invokes the convention only to dismantle it.

Bill Sage and Eve Drayton execute a murder under the transcendent sleuth's very nose. Leading up to that revelation, Carr plays scrupulously fair. He never gives us access to the couple's minds. He keeps them offstage for most of the story and attaches us to detective Henry Merrivale. To maintain the surprise, however, Carr mustn't let us consider them as plausible suspects. Throughout "Goblin Wood," Carr steers our attention toward their intended victim, a teasing woman who has already pulled a disappearing act.

Most boldly, Carr's narration boldly aligns us with Bill and Eve from the start:

> In Pall Mall, that hot July afternoon three years before the war, an open saloon car was drawn up to the curb just opposite the Senior Conservatives' club.
> And in the car sat two conspirators.[46]

This opening locks in the romantic couple convention and will soon suggest that we are to take them as allies of H.M. The passage sets up a stylistic norm of chatty informality, a narrating voice that's a bit indulgent toward its characters. We take "conspirators" to be a light-hearted description of an attractive young couple planning to rope their cantankerous friend into a picnic. Only on rereading do we realize that the narration has been brutally frank: they really are conspiring, at homicide.

After Carr has presented this cheerfully disguised tipoff, he can sprinkle in further ones. "'Look here, Eve,' muttered the young man, and punched at the steering wheel. 'Do you think this is going to work?'"[47] In retrospect we can see Bill's nervousness and Eve's reassurance as hints of their scheme. As Carr noted: "Once we think an author is skylarking, a whole bandwagon of clues can go past unnoticed."[48] We can only imagine his glee at mentioning the "conspirators" again, rubbing our noses in his audacity.[49] With a single word choice, "The House in Goblin Wood" weaponizes Carr's jaunty style. As so often in Golden Age stories, genre connoisseurship demands that we scrutinize verbal texture.

Such fine-grained cleverness wasn't typical of earlier writers. In Melville Davisson Post's 1913 story, "The Act of God," Uncle Abner discovers that a letter purportedly written by a deaf mute has the wrong kind of misspellings for someone with that infirmity. But we are never shown the letter. Like many authors of the period, Post doesn't play fair. In contrast, Agatha Christie's *A Murder Is Announced* (1950) exposes a similar cluster of clues, but ensures that we probably won't notice them.

The crucial moments come casually. A scatterbrained neighbor seems to be misspeaking when she refers to Lotty rather than Letty. She's actually invoking a nickname we'll later learn belongs to a different character. The error, which might be registered merely as a misprint, is swallowed up in a story brimming with chiming character names and nicknames.[50] There is a Julian and two Julias, a Philip and a Philippa (but which is called Pip?). Given the plethora of proper nouns, it takes a while to sort out who's being referred to. (Cunningly, the book lacks a table of dramatis personae.) The elusiveness of identification is laid bare in dialogue: "Just a couple of names. . . . Nicknames at that! They mayn't exist."[51] The reader becomes accustomed to passages that seem a bit hazy about which character is being discussed.

To play fair (but also to be ingenious), Christie elsewhere warns us by slipping in the difference between "enquiries" and "inquiries." As with the names, a single letter of the alphabet becomes a clue. Christie stretches the formula without destroying it. More generally, the Golden Age writers put the rules and fair play in service of the puzzle. But those very constraints forced them to what French Structuralists would years later call textual duplicity, verbal feints that fans were invited to admire.

Weaponizing Watson

Choice of viewpoint might be routine in a romance story or a western, but it is critical in the mystery. While the James-Conrad-Lubbock strain of literary theory was defending a rigorous narration, the detective plot was moving toward a comparable self-consciousness.

Poe acknowledged the importance of restricted viewpoint in the first-person account in his 1844 story "'Thou Art the Man!'" At first the unnamed narrator seems to be a gullible eyewitness, and the naïve praise he lavishes on Charley Goodfellow leads us to suspect that Goodfellow could be the villain. At the climax, we realize that the narrator hasn't been taken in at all. He has suspected Goodfellow and rigs up a grisly trap for him. His account has shown how easily the townsfolk could be hoodwinked—and how ready we are to assume that we are a jump ahead of a narrator's understanding.

More orthodox are Poe's three Dupin stories, narrated by the detective's close friend. Doyle followed Poe in creating Watson as a hearty Jamesian center of consciousness. In the two cases in which Holmes acts as his own narrator, the detective grudgingly acknowledges what Watson had brought to their literary partnership. For one thing, Watson's external view could suppress Holmes's inferences. In "The Adventure of the Blanched Soldier," Holmes's narration feels obliged to tell us the odor of a telltale glove, whereas Watson could have reported only that Holmes sniffed it. "It was by concealing such links in the chain that Watson was enabled to produce his meretricious finales."[52]

Not least, the sidekick furnishes adoration. "I miss my Watson," Holmes confesses. "By cunning questions and ejaculations of wonder he could elevate my simple art, which is but systematized common sense, into a prodigy."[53] The false modesty shouldn't fool us; Holmes knows how Watson's rhetoric gave him heroic stature. The same reflected glory was evident in other Great Detective tales refracting the story through a trusting onlooker.

Ambitious Golden Age writers sought alternatives to Watson. Acknowledging the influence of Percy Lubbock, Dorothy Sayers outlined four possibilities:

1. "The detective's external actions only are seen by the reader."
2. The middle viewpoint: "We see what the detective sees, but are not told what he observes."
3. "Close intimacy with the detective, we see all he sees, and are at once told his conclusions."
4. "Complete mental identification with the detective." Presumably this involves interiority given through inner monologue, stream of consciousness, and the like.

Sayers illustrates how a single passage from *Trent's Last Case* jumps among the first three registers, from reporting Trent's behavior, to registering his perception, and finally to letting him announce his inferences.[54]

Poe and Doyle had shown that funneling narration through an observing character justifies limiting what we know about the sleuth's thinking. For this reason, Sayers calls the first option, the detached and objective one, "the Watson viewpoint." Later Watson figures might be barely characterized. The S. S. Van Dine novels presented a narrator who is virtually a phantom, almost never joining discussions or helping the investigation. At the other extreme is Rex Stout's Archie Goodwin, whose conversational gambits and asides to the reader make him no less a protagonist than transcendent detective Nero Wolfe.

Agatha Christie's debut, *The Mysterious Affair at Styles* (1920), had given Poirot a chatty, highly opinionated Watson in Captain Hastings. She went on to deviously exploit the device in *The Murder of Roger Ackroyd* (1926). Percy Lubbock noted in *The Craft of Fiction* that if you make the killer the narrator you would be obliged to divulge the character's thoughts.[55] Christie solves the problem in a shrewd way. At the beginning of the book, she establishes the Sheppard style—the narration's intrinsic norm—as bland and soporific. "Mrs. Ferrars died on the night of the 16th–17th September—a Thursday. I was sent for at eight o'clock on the morning of Friday the 17th. There was nothing to be done. She had been dead some hours."[56] Actually, this skates over the doctor's involvement in a blackmail scheme aimed at the dead woman. Sheppard isn't lying, but he is, as Poirot says in an understatement, reticent. "It's not unfair," Christie notes in her defense, "to leave things out."[57]

What she leaves in presents Sheppard as a reliable fellow. He admits things that put him in a bad light. Twice on the first page he writes the phrase "to tell the truth," and throughout the book he confesses to minor duplicities. When Poirot challenges him, Sheppard admits to holding back a piece of information, and Poirot seems satisfied. Indeed, Poirot explicitly turns Sheppard into a replacement for his trusted Captain Hastings.

After becoming accustomed to Sheppard's plodding style and acquiring a degree of trust in him, we are ready to be gulled by the most famous passage in Golden Age detective fiction.

> Now Ackroyd is essentially pigheaded. The more you urge him to do a thing, the more determined he is not to do it. All my arguments were in vain.
>
> The letter had been brought in at twenty minutes to nine. It was just on ten minutes to nine when I left him, the letter still unread. I hesitated with my hand on the door handle, looking back and wondering if there was anything I had left undone. I could think of nothing. With a shake of the head I passed out and closed the door behind me.[58]

This is Sheppard's report on killing Roger Ackroyd. Christie, in the spirit of leaving things out, might have simply stopped the paragraph with the sentence "It was just on ten minutes to nine when I left him, the letter still unread." Instead, she generously dwells on Sheppard's departure and even plants a hint that he has "done" something. We read right past it all.

Moreover, a diabolical use of tenses misleads us by blurring our sense of the time of Sheppard's telling. The default assumption behind a Watsonian account is that it has been written *after* the mystery has been solved. At various points, Sheppard suggests that this is the case here. "Miss Ganett is one of the chief of our newsmongers" implies that village life has continued into the time of writing.[59] But in the key passage when Sheppard asserts that "Ackroyd is essentially pigheaded," that's an anomaly. If Sheppard were writing after the case was closed, the accurate description would be "Ackroyd *was* essentially pigheaded."

Few readers will pause over a mere word. But much later Sheppard will casually mention that he has written his chronicle as events unfolded, more or less day by day. So in the crucial passage, presumably composed soon after Sheppard's departure on the fatal night, the use of the present tense hints that he left Ackroyd alive. We no longer have an innocent Sheppard writing

long afterward but a culprit engaged in covering his tracks. By later revealing Sheppard's actual method of composition, Christie is playing completely
fair. When we learn of it, it's up to the sporting reader to revisit the present-tense passages and entertain the possibility that they were composed in
the moment, to leave a false scent.

Sheppard's thudding, banal sentences aren't as breezy as Carr's skylarking
mention of "conspirators" in "Goblin Wood," but both stylistic stratagems glide
over a frank pointer to guilt. "The English," Chandler complained, "may not
always be the best writers in the world, but they are incomparably the best dull
writers."[60] *Roger Ackroyd*, like other Christie books, weaponizes the flat style for
which she was often criticized.

Spreading Suspicion

Apart from Watson figures such as Sheppard, side participants can become
focal points for narration. Writers could bring love interest smoothly into a
detective plot by making a young couple conduits for story information—the
strategy that enabled "The House in Goblin Wood" to fool us. In the standard
case, the lovers stand at a distance from the irascible detective, who can conceal
his thoughts from the couple, and from us.

But such restricted viewpoints are rare in both films and stage plays. Investigation plots in these media gravitate toward a broader narrational compass.
Even adaptations of Watson-centered stories became more wide-ranging.[61] This
strategy was identified by Lubbock as "panoramic" or omniscient. Older writers
shifted viewpoint within scenes, often many times, yielding a truly godlike range
of knowledge. In the modern era, omniscience was less overt and free-ranging.
The preferred option was a roaming-spotlight method, shifting our attachment
among characters scene by scene or chapter by chapter.

Typically the moving-spotlight strategy, whether in prose or in cinema,
relies on an objective, third-person baseline. Then the narration can pause
on a character and enrich the moment by optical or auditory subjectivity—
what she saw or heard—and by reports of impressions, feelings, and memories. This sense of subjectivity in a prose tale could be approximated on film.
Indeed, it's possible that the investigation plot pressured filmmakers to adopt
subjective techniques. In *The Sign of the Spade* (1916), a detective tailing a
gangster uses a hand mirror to spy on him (figs. 4.1–4.2), providing a technical flourish rare at the time.

Yet for detective stories, on paper or on the screen, subjective plunges run
a risk. Intimacy might reveal too much, so there had to be new rules. Ronald
Knox warned that the criminal "must not be anyone whose thoughts the reader
has been allowed to follow."[62] A Watson or the detective, as in Sayers's four

4.1 *The Sign of the Spade* (1916): The detective Harmon uses a mirror to get a view of his quarry.

4.2 An unusually exact close-up approximates his viewpoint.

registers of viewpoint, can be given a mental life, but the narration can never plumb a suspect's mind. Why not? Under the doctrine of fair play, as Lubbock had noted, access to characters' minds would force the writer to reveal who was the killer.

But Golden Age writers did more than obey the rules; they competed to bend them for the sake of a brazen literary performance such as Sheppard's duplicitous narration. Such audacity was prized by Golden Age writers as part of ingenuity. Thus Knox's viewpoint rule could be creatively bent. Sayers and Christie provide subtle examples—one plunging into characters' minds to open the puzzle plot to social commentary, and the other aiming, in typical Christie fashion, to let our assumptions about conventional narration mislead us.

Dorothy Sayers admired sensation fiction in the hands of Dickens and Collins. They achieved genuine literary quality with absorbing stories, vivid characters, and lively style—all the while embedding mystery in a sweeping social panorama. "The criticism of life was not relegated to incidental observations and character sketches, but was actually part of the plot, as it ought to be."[63] In *Murder Must Advertise* (1933), Sayers sought to enrich an investigation plot with portrayal of a milieu and its manners, to merge mystery with what Carolyn Wells had called the "problem novel" and the "social sketch."

Murder Must Advertise presents an advertising firm as not only a piquant setting for a crime but also an institution with unique rules and roles. The result is a much thicker description of a business than Ellery Queen's account of a Broadway theater, a department store, and a hospital in novels of the same period.[64] Sayers staffs Pym's Publicity with an astonishing three dozen named characters: managers, copywriters, illustrators, sales agents, stenographers, typists, custodians, and office boys. These are supplemented by another eighteen outsiders caught up in the investigation.

Pym's staff is presented in a perpetual bustle. Many scenes read as if scripted for a film, with brief descriptions, snappy overlapped conversations, and breezy transitions from room to room, with movement compressed into dialogue. In the era of *Grand Hotel*, Sayers lays out a chattering social network confined to a single space.

Putting so many characters in close quarters enables her to recast one of the core conventions of the mystery: the serial questioning of witnesses. Lord Peter Wimsey, pretending to be Pym's new hire, investigates the death of Victor Dean, who has fallen down a steep iron staircase. Instead of attaching ourselves to Bredon as he insinuates himself into the firm, the narration refracts his inquiry through the reactions of the staff. He becomes an object of gossip and speculation, and his offhand questioning is rendered from the standpoints of the witnesses he pumps. As a result, Sayers widens the social range of her story, indulges in some Dickensian caricature and, not incidentally, diverts us from a rather simple crime committed by what one chapter title admits is "an unskilled murderer."[65]

In a parallel story line, Wimsey as Bredon investigates Dean's involvement with a crew of brittle socialites who indulge in drink, drugs, and wild parties. Again, his probing of the group is rendered from the angle of a character reacting to him. Dean's former girlfriend, Dian de Momerie, is attracted by Bredon's masquerade as a mysterious Harlequin figure. The busy Pym chapters and party-going scenes are set alongside more sedate conversations in which Wimsey and his brother-in-law, Chief Inspector Charles Parker, review the evidence. They come up with the possibility that the agency and the Bright Young Things are linked by drug trafficking.

Bredon's shuttling between the two worlds contrasts the driven office workers with the idle rich, but there's an affinity as well. "As far as I can make out," Parker says near the end of the novel, "all advertisers are dope-merchants."[66] The theme is worked out at the level of imagery too. The dope gang wraps its cocaine in cigarette papers. This ploy finds an echo in Bredon's ad campaign for Whifflets cigarettes, which threatens to turn every Briton into a chain-smoker. ("We want to get women down to serious smoking. Too many of them play about with it."[67]) Hard drugs for the rich, gaspers for the working stiffs: the motifs run in tandem and yield the broader theme of advertising as a colossal cultural fantasy arousing perpetually unfulfilled dreams in the masses.

Sayers's panoramic survey is rendered in a narration that freely, sometimes sardonically, comments on character behavior and milieu. This voice coyly announces that Wimsey will be called Bredon during office hours, and it skips over Wimsey's visit to an unnamed woman because it "is in no way related to this story."[68]

We're introduced to this suavely confident narration early on. When the supervisor appears, the lounging employees scatter.

At Mr. Hankin's mildly sarcastic accents, the scene dislimned as if by magic. The door-post drapers and Miss Parton's bosom-friend melted out into the passage. Mr. Willis, rising hurriedly with the tray of carbons in his hand, picked a paper out at random and frowned furiously at it. Miss Parton's cigarette dropped unostentatiously to the floor. Mr. Garrett, unable to get rid of his coffee-cup, smiled vaguely and tried to look as though he had picked it up by accident and didn't know it was there. Miss Meteyard, with great presence of mind, put the sweep counterfoils on a chair and sat on them. Miss Rossiter, clutching Mr. Armstrong's carbons in her hand, was able to look businesslike, and did so. Mr. Ingleby alone, disdaining pretence, set down his cup with a slightly impudent smile and advanced to obey his chief's command.[69]

This narration sees everything at once, while the voice passes judgments on skillful or clumsy cover-ups. We cannot doubt that Mr. Willis chose a carbon at random, or that Ingleby is the sort of fellow who responds calmly to a crisis. The comedy is enhanced by the omniscience.

The big cast, the breezy and all-knowing narration, and the emphasis on the staff's reaction to Bredon pose Sayers with a new problem—that of concealing the killer. She believed, with Ronald Knox, that the gospel of fair play extended to detectives as well. "Once they are embarked upon an investigation, no episode must ever be described which does not come within their cognisance."[70] Yet *Murder Must Advertise* plunges us into the minds of no fewer than two dozen characters. Are they thereby eliminated from suspicion? Largely, yes. Based on opportunities and a timetable, Bredon arrives at two lists of main suspects. Few of them are rendered from inside, so they are solid Knoxian candidates. The inner lives of two other listed suspects are developed at some length, but fairly comically. A third suspect's mental life is sketched more briefly. He turns out to be the culprit.

Sayers justifies her breach of Knox's rule, I think, because she wants us to have some sympathy for this clumsy killer before he confesses to Wimsey. He explains that he has worked hard to support his wife and child but has been bled dry by Victor Dean's blackmail scheme. Our glimpses of his mind show a frustrated, pathetic figure struggling with his duties and his hatred of life at the agency.

Still, to keep him out of the spotlight and broaden the book's horizons, Sayers accesses the minds of many characters who don't turn out to be suspects. That stratagem fulfills Sayers's urge to embed a puzzle plot within a social milieu and push the genre toward the novel of manners. Here, as she recommended, "larger issues are at stake than the precise method by which the arsenic is administered, and the strings are pulled by a more awful puppet-master than a Chief Inspector of Scotland Yard."[71]

In *Murder Must Advertise*, the puppet master is commercial culture. Sayers chronicles the grinding routines of satisfying the corporate client Nutrax, whose managers inevitably spoil slogans and taglines with foolish alliterations. Still more broadly, the narration reveals Wimsey's new awareness of scrabbling consumerism, "a sphere of dim platonic archetypes. . . . the Thrifty Housewife, the Man of Discrimination, the Keen Buyer and the good Judge . . . perpetually spending to save and saving to spend."[72]

Moving beyond Wimsey's consciousness, the narration presents a cityscape crammed with pulsating signs (NUTRAX FOR NERVES—CRUNCHLETS ARE CRISPER), and in the book's final moments its "criticism of life" becomes a parody of consumer catchphrases.

> Tell England. Tell the world. Eat more Oats. Take Care of Your Complexion. No more War. Shine your Shoes with Shino. Ask your Grocer. Children Love Laxamalt. Prepare to meet thy God . . . Flush your Kidneys with Fizzlets. Flush your Drains with Sanfect. Wear Wool-fleece next the Skin. Popp's Pills Pep you Up. Whiffle your Way to Fortune. . . .
>
> Advertise, or go under.[73]

This declamatory montage, reminiscent of Dos Passos, ends a novel whose title suggests that even murder will go unremarked without a publicist.

If Sayers breaks Knox's rule about mental access gently, Agatha Christie casually neutralizes it. When Knox formulated it, he added that he had to be tentative "in view of some remarkable performances by Mrs. Christie."[74] He was probably thinking of *Roger Ackroyd*, but a neat later instance is *Death in the Air* (aka *Death in the Clouds*, 1935).

A woman is murdered during a flight from Paris to London. The narration is initially attached to Jane Grey, a beautician who has spent her modest lottery winnings on a getaway. During the flight and the investigation, Jane forms an attachment to Norman Gale, the young man she met at a roulette table. He will turn out to be the killer. Christie's task is to surprise us with this revelation, stretching a genre convention.

Norman is already an unlikely culprit. He's the love interest for Jane, our sympathetic and principal viewpoint character. Moreover, Hercule Poirot seems to trust him enough to recruit him to help the investigation. But Christie goes further by using narration to make Norman an exceptionally unlikely suspect. She bends Knox's precept by giving us some access to the thoughts of virtually *all* the characters—major and minor, suspects and investigators.

The dosing starts at take off. "As the plane roared above France on its way to the Channel the passengers in the rear compartment thought their various thoughts."[75] The spotlight moves from Jane to Norman, and then to other passengers. Any of them might turn out to be the killer. But none reveals any (obviously) murderous thoughts.

After probing the passengers' minds, the narration returns to Jane's consciousness and then Norman's, then Jane's and again Norman's. Apart from signaling their mutual attraction, the alternating access so early in the book sets them up as the plot's romantic couple. The pattern is reinforced in many chapters that follow, with the narration providing information about Jane's and Norman's thoughts. No other characters are given so much psychological depth. Like Carr in "Goblin Wood," Christie turns the convention of the love-interest subplot against the reader. But Carr did not dare, as she has, to break out of external, objective presentation.

Initially, Norman seems more sympathetic than other characters whose minds we plumb. As with Dr. Sheppard, though, once we know that Norman is guilty, we can turn back to his inner monologues and disclose the blandly equivocal hints they harbor. "I'm going to marry her . . . Yes, I am . . . But it's no good looking too far ahead. I've got to have some good excuse for seeing her often. This murder business will do as well as anything else." And later: "What a strange business murder is! . . . And I can't have her—yet . . . A damnable nuisance."[76] On the first pass, these thoughts are taken as his fear that his failing dental practice will make it impossible to marry Jane. In retrospect, we know that they represent his scheme to bring her into his murder plans.

By exposing every character's mind at least once, *Death in the Clouds* levels the playing field. Christie doesn't eliminate Norman as a suspect; if any of the others might be guilty, he might be too. Christie could have suppressed every character's inner life, but then we wouldn't have an experiment in narration that is at once "democratically" distributed and tacitly biased—in effect, an attempt at flexing the rules.

Broken Time Lines and Sharp-Edged Segments

Important as point-of-view modulations were, Golden Age writers elevated other formal possibilities too. In his preface to *The Second Shot* (1930), Anthony Berkeley cited an unnamed reviewer (perhaps himself?) noting that the mystery writer is now trying to "make experiments with the telling of his plot, tell it backwards, or sideways, or in bits."[77] We can't be sure exactly what the critic has in mind, but his phrasing seems at least to point to manipulations of time and strategies of segmenting the plot.

The classic investigation plot is inherently nonlinear. Even the most step-by-step investigation must skip back in time through testimony, traces at the crime scene, and speculation about motives and incidents buried in the past.

Nineteenth-century writers altered chronology in nonmystery plots, and by the time of Conrad and Ford, distinctly broken time lines were part of novelistic craft.

The formalist critics of the 1910s were sensitive to temporal manipulations. Recall that in 1914 Clayton Hamilton mused on the prospect of "building a play backward," arranging the acts in reverse order. Although strictly 3-2-1 plotting like this wouldn't emerge until a bit later, Hamilton's article inspired one playwright to adapt the idea to a mystery tale. After all, an investigation plot's raison d'être is to expose the past under the pressure of the present.

Elmer Rice read Hamilton's essay and decided to try the reverse chronology structure on stage, but he thought it would be anticlimactic unless some action also moved forward, toward a resolution.[78] Trained as an attorney, he settled on framing the central story by a trial. A man charged with murder refuses to plead innocent, and his testimony describing the crime is dramatized. Then a defense witness is called and testifies to action preceding the killing, yielding another flashback. A third witness tells of a scene that took place many years before, which provides a final flashback. Back in the present, the jury now understands what led up to the murder, and the defendant is acquitted.

This is a good example of schema revision tuned to accessibility. The fairly difficult narrative device of reverse chronology is rendered more comprehensible by being embedded in an ongoing present-time plot, and the reverse chronology is motivated by the characteristic mystery search for the "hidden story." Although Rice's investigation plot avoided the radical possibilities of pure reverse construction, Hamilton admired the way Rice had turned a trite story line into suspenseful drama.[79]

The success of *On Trial* (1914) led to a vogue for plays dramatizing courtroom conflict. The crucial innovation was the reliance on flashbacks for the plot's basic architecture. Critics claimed to see the influence of cinematic flashbacks in Rice's technique, but he denied it.[80] The premise had at least one precedent in Browning's *The Ring and the Book* (1868–69), but that exceptionally long verse novel included more than a dozen viewpoint characters.[81] *On Trial* had a simpler contour and a cogent central situation, which suited the demands of proscenium theater.[82]

Flashbacks framed by a Q&A situation became a common option for fiction, plays, and films. The schema was revised to allow the central crime to be reiterated from different viewpoints, as in the first two flashbacks of *A Voice in the Dark*.[83] In the trial film *The Woman Under Oath* (1919), the discovery of the crime is replayed, each time calibrated to the account offered by a witness (figs. 4.3–4.5). The replays in the film *The Witness Chair* (1936) create ellipses that conceal the identity of the culprit. Testimony during a police investigation could also be dramatized in flashbacks, as in the film *Affairs of a Gentleman* (1934) and the play *I Killed the Count* (1938). The interrogation leading to

4.3 *The Woman Under Oath* (1919): We're introduced to the clerk Jim O'Neill at the murder scene, looking guilty.

4.4 The hotel switchboard operator testifies that he found Jim standing over the corpse.

4.5 In a replay, Jim's testimony portrays him as entering the room and finding his employer's corpse.

flashbacks would become a common strategy in later films such as *Murder, My Sweet* (1944) and *Mildred Pierce* (1945). Films could also flash back to the crime to dramatize the detective's solution, as in *The Woman in Question* (1950). The film versions of *Trent's Last Case* (1929), *The Canary Murder Case* (1929), and *The Kennel Murder Case* (1933) are examples in early sound cinema.

Three of Doyle's Sherlock Holmes novels had used large-scale flashbacks to explain the circumstances leading up to the crimes Holmes had solved at the book's outset. These blocks were widely felt to be compromises, efforts to fill out the story to full length. Golden Age authors tried to integrate past and present more smoothly, so revelations of past events could build curiosity and suspense. For instance, in William Sutherland's *Death Rides the Air Line* (1934), an odious publisher is stabbed during a flight from Boston to New York. After some preliminary police inquiry in the first part, five parallel flashbacks provide the backstory of the principal suspects, tracing each from youth to the moments leading up to boarding the plane. These chapters fill in motives and establish connections to the victim and other passengers. Here the converging-fates structure of Wilder's *Bridge of San Luis Rey* (1927) is revised for an orthodox investigation plot. Sutherland's opening section is balanced by a concluding set of chapters showing how the police inquiry reveals the murderer.

Another murder-in-the-clouds novel seems more daring. C. Daly King begins *Obelists Fly High* with an epilogue, and ends it with a prologue. What comes between, however, is a fairly linear buildup to that opening situation. The prologue action is akin to the sort of "crisis" opening of many films today, a kind of flash-forward to an action peak that will be revisited after we learn what led up to it.

The ultimate challenge to linear order came with the curio *Cain's Jawbone: A Novel Problem* (1934). It's an almost avant-garde acknowledgment of the overlap between Golden Age mystery and puzzle pastimes. The novel's one hundred pages were printed out of order, and the reader was challenged to find the only true sequence. Although the scenes do move forward, the instructions warned that "the narrator's mind may flit occasionally backwards and forwards in the modern manner."[84]

The parallel sections of *Death Rides the Air Line* and the epilogue/prologue inversion of *Obelists Fly High* point to another distinctive feature of Golden Age mysteries. Many writers signaled their experiments with viewpoint and time shifting by highly patterned segmentation. The geometrical rigor proposed by James, Conrad, Woolf, and others and taken up by Hergesheimer, Stout, and other crossover writers found a popular counterpart in many investigation plots. The result was an explicit modular layout in the spirit of James's "solid blocks of wrought material, squared to the sharp edge, as to have weight and mass and carrying power."[85]

Act divisions in traditional stagecraft provide blocks automatically, a feature exploited to create the three parallel flashbacks of *On Trial* and *A Voice in the Dark*. A novel could likewise be divided into big chunks, as in Freeman Wills Crofts's *The Cask* (1920): "London," "Paris," and "London and Paris." Carr's *The Hollow Man* (1935) consists of "The First Coffin," "The Second Coffin," and "The Third Coffin."[86]

A block can constitute the bulk of the book. In Berkeley's *Second Shot*, a prologue consists of a newspaper account of a murder, followed by a preliminary report to a police commissioner. There follows a lengthy manuscript by one Cyrus Pinkerton recounting how a house party turned homicidal. The first half of Pinkerton's manuscript flashes back to the events presented in the police report. The second half picks up the police investigation and the intervention of amateur detective Roger Sherington. The murder is judged an accident, but in an epilogue, Pinkerton reveals what really happened.

Sometimes the blocks are presented as discrete chapters, markedly differing in source or texture. Bernard Capes's *Mystery of the Skeleton Key* (1919) daringly alternates chunks of a first-person manuscript account with third-person narration of a murder inquiry. A similar strategy is put to work in Agatha Christie's *Man in the Brown Suit* (1924). In both, we are led to suspect that the character's written record is withholding important information.

Testimony on the Page or on the Stand

Large or midsized tagged segments can create an exposed structure, an exoskeleton that guides reader uptake. This strategy can be regarded as a domestication of the macrostructures mobilized by Woolf (*To the Lighthouse*) and Faulkner (*The Sound and the Fury; As I Lay Dying*). But in many instances, it's also a revival of that dossier format that had been cultivated by Wilkie Collins, Bram Stoker, and others.

The document collection offers many storytelling advantages. The blocks, tagged with titles, ease comprehension. The format plausibly motivates shifting viewpoints, and it opens up gaps between them that can be creatively exploited. Absorption in one character's account can be broken when the frame shifts to a contradictory document, or to a sudden widening of the knowledge frame. For instance, Kay Cleaver Strahan's *Footprints* (1929) presents a block of letters that Judith Quirt receives from her sister Lucy, followed by another block from her brother Neal. These constitute the evidence that, in the frame story, the "crime analyst" Lynn MacDonald will use to study a horrendous death twenty-eight years earlier.

But Lynn is scarcely the protagonist. Her solution is announced indirectly, as an account that the family doctor passes along to Judith and then, in different form, to Neal. This quasi-Conradian refraction puts the emphasis on the doctor's coping strategy and on Neal's eventual reaction, which supplies a final piece of information that corrects Lynn's account. In this detective novel, the detective is pushed almost entirely offstage and is somewhat mistaken in the bargain.

Footprints doesn't distinguish much between Lucy's and Neal's idiolects, but Michael Innes's *Lament for a Maker* (1938) is boldly polystylistic. The first and last sections, the recollections of a shoemaker, are in a thick Scots style, and other blocks contrast a city slicker's glib mockery with dry lawyerly ruminations and the more poetic reflections of Inspector John Appleby. The novel's unabashed Gothic situation is rendered self-consciously literary through the clash of styles, which bear as much on class differences as on regional ones.

Lament for a Maker implies that the written narratives supplied by the characters are assembled for some official purpose, but Philip MacDonald's

The Maze (1932) is more explicitly in the "casebook" mold. This format compiles testimony, reports, and other documents, usually submitted for official consideration. MacDonald presents the complete transcript of a two-day inquest with no mediating narrator, no plunge into characters' minds, and no enclosing present-day frame. The preface justifies this as fair play carried to the limit: "The reader has had his information in exactly the same form as the detective—that is, the verbatim report of evidence and question. This is a *fair* story."[87] The book's final block, the detective's explanation in a private letter, balances the initial letter inviting him to review the dossier.

Just as indebted to Collins is Dorothy Sayers and Robert Eustace's *Documents in the Case* (1930).[88] Its dossier offers a more dense array of clues than *Footprints* and stronger social commentary than *The Maze*. The months leading up to George Harrison's death are introduced in letters from a woman living with him and his wife. Her correspondence goes on to alternate with letters and statements from John Munting, a young writer sharing an adjacent flat with the painter Lathon.

In the course of the book's first part ("Synthesis"), Munting's liking for his flatmate Lathon fades and his disdain for Harrison, apparently a perfect bourgeois fathead, gives way to respect for his dull decency. After Harrison's death, the second section ("Analysis") introduces his son Paul, who suspects that his father has been cuckolded, and eventually murdered, by Lathon. Paul takes up the role of investigator and shares narrating duties with Munting as the whodunit becomes a howdunit, a Sayers specialty.[89] Like *Murder Must Advertise*, *The Documents in the Case* aims at "criticism of life" through showing up the moral weakness of bohemian youth. These would-be artists who claim to know the human heart revel in snobbishness and remain oblivious to stolid virtues.

The dossier format took on performative dimensions when the Detection Club launched its eccentric collaborations. The British Broadcsting Corporation aired two radio series, "Behind the Screen" (1930) and "The Scoop" (1931), in which Sayers, Christie, Berkeley, and others read the installments they had composed. Hoping to earn enough money to establish a permanent meeting room, club members carried the idea into print with *The Floating Admiral* (1932).

This "round-robin novel" asked each author to add a chapter and pass the story along. Each author had to have a definite solution in mind, while taking into account all the problems left by the predecessors. By the time Berkeley got to the final chapter, he had a great many clues to reconcile and false solutions to demolish.[90] As in the radio installments, the need to differentiate each author's contribution to *The Floating Admiral* demanded explicit block construction. The book's appendix further spelled out the solution each author had in mind; Sayers's ran to twenty pages. Once more, the puzzle and the game became a pretext for displaying literary virtuosity.

The diversity of dossier novels of the period is impressive, but the spaciousness of the creative menu of the time is even more evident in the fortunes of the trial plot. A trial offers automatic opportunities for block construction, with the parade of witnesses and discrete days in session. The courtroom situation can play with time, manipulate viewpoint, and provide ongoing analytical commentary about the crime. There's also the challenge of building tension from a tightly circumscribed locale and duration. With considerable ingenuity, novelists, playwrights, and filmmakers turned investigations into courtroom confrontations.[91]

Rice's *On Trial* had shown the power of concentrating stage action in a court hearing supplemented by flashbacks. British and American playwrights explored the options further, offering *For the Defense* (1919), also with flashbacks, followed by a cycle of courtroom dramas: *The Woman on the Jury* (1923); *Accused*, *Appearances*, and *Chivalry* (all 1925); *Scarlet Pages* and *Ladies of the Jury* (both 1929); *Dishonored Lady* and *Room 349* (both 1930); and *Inquest* (1931). In *The Trial of Mary Dugan* (1927), Bayard Veiller turned the theater audience into courtroom spectators, and a character in *Nightstick* (1927) offered his attendance at Veiller's play as an alibi. Ayn Rand's *The Night of January 16th* (1934) selected the onstage jury from the audience.

Frances Noyes Hart adapted the theatrical premise to the novel in *The Bellamy Trial* (1927), which confines the action wholly to the courtroom. The viewpoint is focused on two nameless reporters registering the stream of sordid revelations. Mary Roberts Rinehart, characteristically putting romance at the plot's core, lets the defendant's lover narrate *The State vs. Elinor Norton* (1934). More starkly objective is *The Trial of Vivienne Ware* (1931), a dossier novel interleaving news clippings and the trial transcript, with no viewpoint character or editorial commentary. Similarly, Percival Wilde's *Inquest* (1940) frames sessions of questioning with embedded diary entries and trick testimony, such as that of a deaf witness. *The Brighton Murder Trial: X v. Rhodes* (1937) carries the transcript format into an alternative future. The "editor" Bruce Hamilton presents a 1940 trial set in "Soviet Europe" and creates a pastiche of the *Notable British Trials* records. The case, which involves a communist killing a fascist, is prosecuted as the first murder verdict based on political sympathies.

Filmmakers picked up on the trial premise; Hollywood adapted *On Trial* three times. Courtroom dramas were suited to early talkies, so there were screen versions of *The Bellamy Trial* (1929), *The Trial of Mary Dugan* (1929), and *The Trial of Vivienne Ware* (1932), the last boasting snappy flashbacks and voice-over radio commentary. *The Night of June 13* (1932) found clever ways for flashbacks to represent lying testimony: some are replays omitting key incidents, and others are revised on the fly (figs. 4.6–4.8). By the 1940s, the use of flashbacks for trial testimony had become so common that a review of *The Paradine Case* (1947) could praise Hitchcock for avoiding them.[92]

4.6 *The Night of June 13* (1932): In voice-over the prosecutor asks Morrow if, while leaving the train, he saw John Curry on the platform. We see Morrow alone as he hesitates in his testimony.

4.7 Through a dissolve, Curry appears on the platform.

4.8 "Yes," says Morrow, as we see the two men walk off. The dissolve has visualized Morrow's impulsive lie.

Once the full-length trial premise had been explored, novelists could vary it. One option was to embed the trial, either as drama or transcript, within a larger narrative frame. Carter Dickson's *The Judas Window* (1938) encloses the trial proceedings between a teasing opening and the master detective's explanation. A trial constitutes the first half of *The Dear Old Gentleman* (1935), and the second half traces a reporter's investigation of the crime filtered through the awareness of the newspaper publisher who discovers the reporter's notes. Less flagrantly, Erle Stanley Gardner incorporated lengthy trial episodes into his Perry Mason novels as a brand trademark. The television series based on the books commonly devoted extensive running time to solving the mystery through courtroom theatrics.

Alternatively, the trial could be chopped up and intercut with other action. This strategy was pursued in Richard Hull's novel *Excellent Intentions* (1938), which alternates trial testimony with flashbacks to the investigations of Scotland Yard detective Fenby. These, in turn, are filled out with further flashbacks presenting witness recollections. This complicated three-track structure sustains the whodunit puzzle in an original way: constantly switching time frames, the narration does not reveal who is standing trial until the summing up, which finally puts Fenby's evidence in order.

Novelists were far from exhausting the variorum possibilities of the trial premise, as they showed by turning attention to the jury. In the manner of the later *Twelve Angry Men*, Eden Phillpotts's *The Jury* (1927) lays out the case during jurors' lengthy deliberations. This schema was tweaked in *The Jury Disagree* (1934), in which jurors review the case systematically, with each one summarizing evidence around one point (motive, time factor, and so on). Although pledged to be neutral, the jurors begin to float alternative solutions and partisan defenses. The unity of time and place is broken by a surprise finale in which one juror discovers her hidden connection to the defendant. In effect, she becomes the investigator of last resort.

With that exception, the characters in *The Jury Disagree* are presented superficially; they're identified merely by profession, not by name. In contrast, Gerald Bullett's cross-sectional novel *The Jury* (1935) explores intimacies. In the first block, "The Twelve Converging," moving-spotlight narration introduces each juror in private life before he or she is summoned to court duty. "The Twelve Listening" presents, in transcript form, the court proceedings. Once the jury is sequestered ("The Twelve Debating"), the narration jumps from one juror to another, larding their conversation with flashbacks to incidents in their pasts.

In another approach to breaking time lines, Raymond Postgate's *Verdict of Twelve* (1940) displays a different form of omniscience. Each of twelve segments starts with the Clerk of the Assize administering the oath and passes quickly to a chunk of backstory concerning the juror. An ensuing block presents chapters moving back to dramatize the crime, the investigation, and the decision to charge a suspect. The trial is summarized, omitting some details we've encountered in the previous section, and the jury's meeting is covered very quickly. As in *The Jury Disagree*, a final twist reveals information that was not part of the court record.

The dossier novel and the trial plot show how smoothly Golden Age writers could use a realistic framework to integrate varying viewpoints presented in letters, written confessions, or legal testimony. That is exactly the sort of framework that the Ultraist phase of High Modernism jettisoned. No overarching situation encloses the monologues of Benjy, Quentin, and Jason Compson in *The Sound and the Fury* or the dissolving soliloquys of the characters in *The Waves*. Odd to say but Poe had pointed in this direction. The rantings of the "I" in "The Black Cat," like the friend's reports of Dupin's triumphs of reasoning, are not anchored as diary entries or speeches to a listener. In the mystery field, it was largely the hard-boiled school that reinvigorated Poe's strategy. The Continental

Op, Nick Charles, and Philip Marlowe need no pretext for passing their stories directly to us.

Golden Age reliance on framing situations might seem too beholden to nineteenth-century realist conventions, but embedded narration enhanced the books' efforts to magnify mystery. By turning their first-person accounts into testimony and documents, writers opened opportunites for ellipses, discordant replays, deception, and interrogation by other voices. Once first-person accounts become texts, they become as suspect as anything at the crime scene.

Comparative Detection and Combinatorial Explosions

If dossier novels and trial plots show the variorum in wide compass, one classic whodunit illustrates how kaleidoscopic multiplicity can arise from a very simple situation.

Sir Eustace Pennefather receives a box of chocolates at his club. Annoyed, he offers it to another member, Graham Bendix. Bendix takes it home to his wife. Bendix eats a couple of chocolates and falls violently ill. Mrs. Bendix eats several and dies. The candy has been poisoned. The police conclude that it's the random work of a madman.

Author Roger Sheringham has founded the Crime Circle, a group of amateur criminologists. They agree to tackle the case. After a week of investigations, they meet on six consecutive nights to hear each member's conclusions.

The Poisoned Chocolates Case (1929) might seem the ultimate in arid puzzle-mongering. The characters are superficial types, the descriptions minimal. There's no effort to invoke specifics of time or place; the conversations in the circle take place in a virtual vacuum. There's no adventure. Although the detectives are free to pursue leads offstage, we move almost completely in the realm of reasoning. The narration yields old-fashioned omniscience, shifting among characters' minds as if Sayers and Knox had never tut-tutted about confined viewpoint. But Anthony Berkeley's manipulation of Golden Age conventions makes a bare-bones premise an epitome of the self-conscious artifice of the Golden Age, as well as a witty critique of the genre itself.

The Poisoned Chocolates Case is an almost maniacal exercise in block construction. Each evening session consumes two chapters, with only a couple of detours into Roger's daytime inquiries. This stringent focus sets a rhythm that the reader comes to expect: every evening will replay the central convention of a detective denouement, the sleuth's explanation. But here the solution will be subject to objection, correction, and rejection. The false solutions, six in all, are not mere filler but the very spine of the book.

The last detective in the queue, Mr. Ambrose Chitterwick, arranges the prior solutions into a table (table 4.1). This "lesson in comparative detection," as

TABLE 4.1 Mr. Chitterwick's chart, *The Poisoned Chocolates Case* (1929)

Solver	Motive	Angle of View	Salient Feature	Method of Proof	Parallel Case	Criminal
Sir Charles Wildman	Gain	Cui bono	Notepaper	Inductive	Marie Lafarge	Lady Pennefather
Mrs. Fielder-Flemming	Elimination	Cherchez la femme	Hidden triangle	Intuitive and inductive	Molineux	Sir Charles Wildman
Bradley (1)	Experiment	Detective-novelist's	Nitrobenzene	Scientific deduction	Dr. Wilson	Bradley
Bradley (2)	Jealousy	Character of Sir Eustace	Criminological knowledge of murderer	Deductive	Christina Edmunds	Woman unnamed
Sheringham	Gain	Character of Mr. Bendix	Bet	Deductive and inductive	Carlyle Harris	Bendix
Miss Dammers	Elimination	Psychology of all participants	Criminal's character	Psychological deduction	Tawell	Sir Eustace Pennefather
Police	Conviction, or lust of killing	General	Material clues	Routine	Horwood	Unknown fanatic or lunatic

Source: Reprinted with permission of the Society of Authors as the Literary Representative of the Estate of Anthony Berkeley.

Mr. Chitterwick calls it, creates a clear-cut variorum within a single volume.[93] Turning blocks into a grid also neatly illustrates the thrust of Golden Age mysteries toward geometrical layouts akin to modernist notions of spatial form. It isn't far-fetched to recall the chart of times and motifs in *Ulysses* that Stuart Gilbert published a year after *The Poisoned Chocolates Case*. Unsurprisingly, Berkeley subtitled the book "An Academic Detective Story."

Focusing the plot around the nightly meetings seems to violate fair play because each investigator brings to the table new evidence discovered offstage. Yet there's a perverse sense of fair play across the whole. The evidence "unfairly" amassed by one detective is available "fairly" to the next one in line, and to the reader. The last solution must take into account earlier facts and inferences. In effect, the timid Mr. Chitterwick, who solves the problem, is in the position that Berkeley himself was in when he had to wrap up the round-robin novel *The Floating Admiral*.

There are puzzles aplenty. Obviously, we wonder who's the criminal. In the course of the evenings, several suspects are added to the initial trio. We're also asked to wonder "Who was the intended victim?" Presumably, Sir Eustace. But was perhaps Mrs. Bendix the target? And, as each night unfolds, another question emerges: Who's the best detective?

Roger's club consists of the barrister Sir Charles Wildman, the playwright Mrs. Fielder-Fleming, avant-garde novelist Alicia Dammers, mystery writer Morton Harrogate Bradley, and self-effacing hobbyist Mr. Chitterwick. Taking the *Trent's Last Case* device to the limit, Berkeley makes his series hero humiliatingly wrong, and unlike Trent Roger gets no redemption.

In effect, Roger's failure is dictated purely by structure. What comes at the end must be the truth, so his position on the fourth night dooms him. Putting Mr. Chitterwick at the end permits Berkeley to expose the arbitrary power of a finale. The plot exploits the device of the least-likely-suspect, and thanks to sheer patterning, Mr. Chitterwick, looked down upon by the other circle members, becomes the least likely detective.

This guying of the Great Detective as charismatic hero recurs throughout Golden Age stories. In Leo Bruce's *Case for Three Detectives* (1936), pastiche figures of Poirot, Lord Peter, and Father Brown compete to solve a grisly murder, only to be outdone by uncouth Sergeant Beef. *Ask a Policeman* (1933), the Detection Club's second round-robin novel, made fun of sacred cows by assigning authors to write about others' sleuths. Berkeley twitted Wimsey, and Sayers pushed the reliably fallible Roger Sheringham into new blind alleys.

The Poisoned Chocolates Case applies the same sort of satiric expansion to Golden Age plotting. Six armchair detectives are pitted against one another, and the action consists largely of their ability to persuade or pontificate. Although the book might be considered an inbred parody of the whodunit, it's much less heavy-handed than the spoofs with which Berkeley began his *Punch* career.[94] The poisoning gives him an opportunity to mock the harrumphing jurist, the brittle theater celebrity, the jumped-up non-U novelist, and the disdainful avant-garde author. Each nightly speaker preceding Mr. Chitterwick exhibits a self-regard soon punctured by the scornful skepticism of the others. Mastermind performance turns into cruel comedy.

The battle of wits is largely a battle of the books. Bookishness is central to the Golden Age novel. Someone is sure to compare the crime at hand with what usually happens in a mystery story, and the cast often includes one or more writers, often authors of detective stories. Wimsey's lover Harriet Vane writes thrillerish tales, and Ellery Queen signs the books in which he appears. Citation comes in too, as when the killer in *Five Red Herrings* has read a novel by a Sayers confrère and hides his copy from Wimsey.

More radically, a mystery story can be embedded in the book, as is the manuscript in *The Second Shot*. Barnaby Ross's *Tragedy of Y* (1932) depends on discovering a plot outline that uncannily matches the murder case at hand. At the limit, the book that's cited can be the very one we're reading. At the close of *The Egyptian Cross Mystery*, Ellery admits that his "sometimes impulsive erudition" led him to mistakenly believe there was an Egyptian motif in the case. Still, he gives the book a misleading title, just to fit the series brand and to cover his expensive road trip: "Let the public pay for it!"[95]

The Poisoned Chocolates Case doesn't have such a brazen address to the reader, nor does it wedge in other tales in dossier fashion. But it's bookish in its own way. Each detective's disquisition is in effect a short story, and the debates dwell on problems of mystery writing craft.

The circle's conversations touch on the rhetoric of the arrogant detective, the reliance on selective evidence, closed versus open sets of suspects, the most unlikely suspect, the parallel to real-life murders, and the appeal to material clues (risky) and to psychology (even riskier). Throughout, the participants muse on the detective's reliance on coincidence, not only in Sir Eustace's giving the chocolates to Bendix, but also in the lucky encounter that triggers Roger's eureka moment—dependent, no less, on a play called *The Avenging Chance*. The book's narration adds its own commentary on fictional conventions. "Miss Dammers was indeed to plume herself on the fact that she had no sense of construction, and that none of her books ever had a plot. . . . Stories, as Roger as a fellow-craftsman ought to have known, simply weren't done nowadays."[96]

Is Berkeley making Miss Dammers's taste an echo of Trollope's dislike of Collins's "unpalatable" construction? The passage anticipates Bernard DeVoto's riposte to Edmund Wilson: detective story craftsmanship is an antidote to the modernists' abandonment of appealing narrative.

This blatant acknowledgment of artifice is central to the Golden Age. It's seen at its most stark in the famous "Locked Room Lecture" in John Dickson Carr's *The Hollow Man* (aka *The Three Coffins*). There Dr. Fell reviews, again in outline form, all possible solutions to murder in a "hermetically sealed chamber." "We're in a detective story, and we don't fool the reader by pretending we're not. Let's not invent elaborate excuses to drag in a discussion of detective fiction. Let's candidly glory in the noblest pursuits possible to characters in a book."[97] Of course this transparency is only a gesture. The solution of the mystery must fall into one of the types Dr. Fell surveys, but Carr has arranged the categories to make that difficult to see. This frank layout of a mini-variorum serves as well to flaunt the author's prodigious invention, along with his virtuosity in hiding the correct answer from us.

Less overt but no less dazzling is the combinatorial explosion that follows from the false solutions in *The Poisoned Chocolates Case*. Mr Chitterwick points out that in detective fiction a clue is usually assumed to point in only one direction, but it's actually multivalent. The Crime Circle's proliferation of solutions stems from alternative interpretations of only three pieces of physical evidence. Psychological clues are just as unstable. Night after night, the debates rewrite the motives and reinterpret the characters' traits. Victim becomes villain, a loving wife becomes a cheat, a cheating husband an innocent.

To this collapse of certainty the detective novelist Bradley responds:

> "I'll write a book for you, Mr. Chitterwick. . . . in which the detective shall draw six contradictory deductions from each fact. He'll probably end up by arresting seventy-two different people for the murder and committing suicide because he finds afterwards that he must have done it himself. I'll dedicate the book to you."
>
> "Yes, do," beamed Mr. Chitterwick. "For really, it wouldn't be far from what we've had in this case."[98]

The indefinitely large number of solutions exposes an arbitrariness at the heart of the genre. As one explanation is mounted, heartily embraced, and then briskly demolished, Berkeley shows that the process could go on forever. (Two more solutions were published ninety years later.[99]) And for all the genre's claims of ineluctable logic, plot coherence is constantly threatened by chance (accident, half-memory, the eureka moment) and brute linearity (what comes last is true, regardless of plausibility). Even the murders in the Rue Morgue became a locked-room case by accident.

Arbitrariness and chance must be tamed by rules and best practices. The writer displays ingenuity by finding new and sporting ways to trim back the tangle of possibilities. For instance, in agreeing with Bradley's multiplication of deductions, Mr. Chitterwick casually prunes the possibilities with a hint about the solution he'll propose (a detective who is guilty). Many doors are opened, but most are quickly closed, more or less by fiat. How comforting is this? On the last page, Roger asks what they should do next: "Nobody enlightened him."[100]

This vision of indeterminate and ramifying interpretation, a value central to "literary" fiction from James to Kafka, is rarely made so explicit in Golden Age writing.[101] But it hovers over the very project of the investigation plot. The conventions of that plot, the rules of the game, exist to manage the indeterminacy. Fortunately, that can be done more or less ingeniously. The reader is invited to become a connoisseur who can admire how a fresh, formally tidy package can give contingency the illusion of necessity.

✳ ✳ ✳

Faulkner declared that he intended *As I Lay Dying* to be a tour de force.[102] The most ambitious writers of the Golden Age tried for the same thing. Mobilizing all the techniques available in fiction and theater, storytellers reworked the investigation plot in elaborate ways. They competed with one another in building a puzzle, playing the game (while finding weak spots in the rules), and above all flaunting ingenuity of structure and style. Endowed with a heritage of sensation fiction and Great Detective sagas, they brought the narrative subterfuges of 1910s formalism, modernist experiments, and traditional techniques of mystification to bear on the popular genre most hospitable to them.

Dorothy Sayers believed that a detective story that honored the tradition of Dickens and Collins could attain literary greatness.[103] Yet the Golden Age writers didn't achieve the prestige they sought. Their rarefied artifice, as playful as that on display in a Tudor masque or a Restoration comedy, was not welcomed by critical tastes favoring social statement, psychological realism, and thematic complexity. Today, with nonlinear narrative all around us, we can better recognize the value of weaponizing any technique at hand for the sake of mystification and displays of virtuosity. Caricatured as a reliquary of dusty devices—tranquil villages, courtroom shenanigans, corpses in private libraries—the Golden Age oeuvre today looks far more varied than we might expect.

The mechanics of classic detection are still available for retro recycling in Christie adaptations, Holmes pastiches, BBC series, and clockwork exercises suh as *Knives Out* (2019). But this tradition, which includes *A Voice in the Dark* and *The Woman in Question*, along with the casebook format and the trial premise, has had a wider impact. For one thing, the ingenuity of plot and narration yielded a glimpse of formal horizons beyond the demands of orthodox realism. To experimental artists, the investigation plot offered a rich menu of techniques for more or less avant-garde reworking. Alain Robbe-Grillet, Michel Butor, and other writers of the 1950s and 1960s nouveau roman school, as well as more accessible authors such as Umberto Eco and Donna Tartt, found in the rules of the game many expectations that could be fruitfully overturned. They realized that the sheer appeal of mystery could attract readers who might be disinclined to swallow rarefied approaches to technique. As with other crossover work, familiar elements threw into relief the more unusual aspects of form and style, but also made them seem less formidable.

There's an even more pervasive effect, though. The formal intricacies of the whodunit introduced a broad public to experiments—some mild, some more demanding—in narrative time, viewpoint, authorial address, and genre expectations. While inducing audiences to play the game, whodunits trained readers and spectators in a repertory of comprehension skills. These works' legacy lingers in our "puzzle films," "Complex TV," and more generally throughout today's mass-market crossover storytelling.

We always knew we couldn't always trust the characters. After James and Conrad, we learned not to trust the narrator. The investigation plots of the 1920s and 1930s taught us not to trust the author.

CHAPTER 5

<hr>

BEFORE THE FACT

The Psychological Thriller

I like a good detective story. . . . But, you know, they begin in the wrong place! They begin with the murder. But the murder is the end. The story begins long before that—years before sometimes—with all the causes and events that bring certain people to a certain place at a certain time on a certain day. . . . Even now . . . some drama—some murder to be—is in course of preparation.

—Agatha Christie

As Christmas approaches, Mr. and Mrs. Bunting sit brooding in minor-key despair. No longer able to find work as servants, they have bought a house and tried to rent out rooms. But the place is empty, and they're near starvation. Outside, boys hawk newspapers reporting the latest atrocity committed by "The Avenger," a stalker who dismembers women. The doorbell rings. The caller, a gaunt, nervous man, carries only a leather bag. He decides to rent a floor, but because he needs solitude and quiet for his "experiments," he pays extra to be the only guest. The Buntings are jubilant. He says his name is Mr. Sleuth.

The Lodger (1913) was published as a short story in 1911, then turned into a novel. Marie Belloc Lowndes was already a well-known author, but this became her most popular work. It was the basis for a play and five films. It's an exemplary piece of 1910s formalism, and it set a standard for a major genre in popular narrative for the next century.

A novel about a Jack-the-Ripper figure could have been a sensation-driven pursuit or a tale of rational detection. This one is a tale of suspicion seeping through a lower-middle-class household. Despite moments when Mrs. Bunting tries to discover what's in Mr. Sleuth's bag, *The Lodger* doesn't build its action around active investigation. There's a mystery, but all the detecting is done off-stage. During this period, story manuals were acknowledging that major action could be filtered through a bystander, and stories like James's "In the Cage" showed how it could be done. James had presented a furtive affair refracted through the limited awareness of the telegraph clerk who helps the lovers along. Belloc Lowndes traces a serial-killer investigation through a couple who in their willfully blind way safeguard him. *The Lodger* carries out principles of oblique viewpoint and spatial concentration—James's beloved "scenic method"—with a precision remarkable in mass-audience narrative.

Although the novel's narration briefly strays to the minds of others, it gains its force by concentrating on Mr. and Mrs. Bunting. The murders and the police investigation are presented through their reading of news accounts and the excited reports from Joe Chandler, an ambitious young cop and a friend of the family. The emphasis falls on the couple's growing suspicion that Mr. Sleuth is the Avenger, which puts them and their daughter Daisy in peril.

To the restriction of viewpoint, *The Lodger* adds other forms of confinement. The plot unfolds over a few weeks, with flashbacks yielding background on the Buntings' marriage. Spatially, nearly every scene takes place in the parlor, the kitchen, the couple's bedroom, or Mr. Sleuth's quarters. When the Buntings leave, we usually don't tag along. The few excursions we witness—to Scotland Yard's Black Museum, to the inquest, to Madame Tussaud's—stand out against a rhythm of household routines.

The confinement finds acute expression in the emphasis on hearing sounds. Every night the Buntings are assailed by a frenzy outside. "'The Avenger again!' 'Another horrible crime!' 'Extra speshul edition!'—such were the shouts, the exultant yells hurled through the clear, cold air. They fell, like bombs, into the quiet room."[1] Mrs. Bunting is alert to Mr. Sleuth's pacing above them, and more ominously to his footfall on the stairs as he slips out of the house after midnight. Alone in the kitchen, she becomes terrified at his approach. Soon she finds herself listening to what her husband and Daisy are saying in the next room. Mr. Bunting's ears become sensitive as well, as he starts to wonder what his wife is up to when she is furiously cleaning the staircase after one of their lodger's nightly excursions.

The result is the sort of psychological probing that some Golden Age writers had hoped to bring to their puzzle tales. Mr. Bunting, defeated in his search for work as a servant, has ceded control of the household to his wife. For most of the book, she becomes the center of consciousness, and her emotions are a turbulent mix.

At first she's relieved that they have a generous paying guest, but she becomes more apprehensive when she learns of his quirks, such as turning pictures of women to face the walls. Is he the Avenger? Should she confide her worries to Mr. Bunting? If the lodger is arrested, will the family be charged with harboring him? If he leaves, won't they slip back into destitution? If he learns of their suspicions, will he kill them? And Daisy is keen to meet Mr. Sleuth. Could she become his next victim? To Belloc Lowndes's credit, these questions aren't ever articulated so bluntly; they are implicit in Mrs. Bunting's fretful behavior. But such underlying uncertainties maintain our interest in a very different way than do questions about motive, method, and opportunity that propel the whodunit.

The pressure of the situation terrifies Mrs. Bunting, but she's oddly solicitous as well, transferring her concern for Daisy and Mr. Bunting to the lodger. It's as if by mothering him a little she can assure herself that he's innocent. Worse, during this ordeal she becomes as obsessed with the murders as her husband is, even longing for new ones that may rule out Sleuth as a suspect. Her feelings oscillate between fear and dismissal of fear. When Daisy is invited to spend a few days with her aunt, Mrs. Bunting is relieved.

> If anything horrible was going to happen in the next two or three days—it was just as well Daisy shouldn't be at home. Not that there was any real danger that anything would happen,—Mrs. Bunting felt sure of that.
>
> By this time she was out in the street again, and she began mentally counting up the number of murders The Avenger had committed. Nine, or was it ten? Surely by now The Avenger must be avenged?. . . .
>
> She began hurrying homewards; it wouldn't do for the lodger to ring before she had got back. Bunting would never know how to manage Mr. Sleuth, especially if Mr. Sleuth were in one of his queer moods.[2]

Mrs. Bunting's relations with her family start to crumble. She is driven to lie about her secret visit to an inquest, and she lets her long-standing resentment of Daisy surface, a reminder of her husband's first wife.

We're given access to Mr. Bunting's thoughts less often, and these brief reports provide another perspective on his wife's regression. She demands, almost hysterically, that they talk about the killings. "Bunting, staring across at his wife, felt sadly perplexed and disturbed. She really did seem ill; even her slight, spare figure looked shrunk. For the first time, so he told himself ruefully, Ellen was beginning to look her full age. Her slender hands—she had kept the pretty, soft white hands of the woman who has never done rough work—grasped the edge of the table with a convulsive movement."[3] This tale of terror is no less a portrait of a quietly collapsing marriage.

Because Mrs. Bunting tends to Sleuth while Bunting reads his newspapers, he comes to her realization late. In the early stretches of the book, his fascination with the murders matches the morbid excitement of the public. But on the day the newspaper publishes an image of the Avenger's footprint, Bunting finds Sleuth outside changing his shoes. As they go into the house together, Bunting sees blood smeared on Sleuth's coat.

Bunting becomes as worried as his wife, but they don't discuss their apprehensions. Eventually, when they accidentally leave Daisy alone with the lodger, the drama of divided knowledge reaches its proper pitch. "As they stared at each other in exasperated silence, each now knew that the other knew."[4] The revelation of their passive complicity is as powerful as the risk of exposing the Avenger's identity.

On the threshold of Madame Tussaud's Chamber of Horrors, the tension breaks. Believing that Mrs. Bunting has informed on him, Mr. Sleuth flees. He is never caught. The murders cease. Joe and Daisy marry. The central couple restabilizes, a situation rendered with a quietness characteristic of the whole book. At a few points, the narration has called Mrs. Bunting "the lodger's landlady," as if her relation to him had replaced her marital status. By the end, however, the narration tells us of "Mr. Bunting and his Ellen." We're told with ironic tact that they "are now in the service of an old lady, by whom they are feared as well as respected, and whom they make very comfortable."[5]

Like most mystery stories, *The Lodger* makes passing reference to the puzzle-based genre, thereby reasserting its own claim to "reality." There are mentions of Gaboriau and plots containing lots of clues. Mr. Bunting is fond of detective stories, and his wife reads them to help her sleep. When a serial killer names himself Mr. Sleuth, we might suspect that he's knowingly mocking the plots we encounter in Great Detective fiction.

Here, though, the obligatory citations aren't just inside jokes. Belloc Lowndes invites us to imagine another approach to mystery storytelling. *The Lodger* shows how formal rigor can render inchoate feelings and arouse sympathy for imperfect characters coping with moral quandaries—effects largely alien to the Golden Age. The suspense story could shape viewpoint and narration as skillfully as any detective story, but it could do something more. It could show what fear feels like.[6]

Hidden Histories of Murder

Today we'd call *The Lodger* a thriller, but the label was applied somewhat differently at the time. "Detective story" suggests a character and an activity, whereas "thriller" tells you that emotion is paramount. In the 1910s and 1920s, "thriller" often implied extravagant display. Scary carnival rides and parachute stunts were called thrillers; so were theatrical melodramas and adventure paperbacks aimed at boys.[7] By 1920, critics used the term to refer to novels by Sax Rohmer, E. Phillips Oppenheim, Edgar Wallace, and "Sapper," creator of freebooting Bulldog Drummond. A thriller boasted master criminals, hypnosis, hidden passages, sinister Asians, and other conventions of international intrigue. If mystery was invoked, the thriller plot tended to be based, according to one author, on "a vast amount of rushing to and fro of detectives or unofficial investigators in motor cars, aeroplanes, or motor boats, with a liberal display of revolver or automatic pistols and a succession of hair-raising adventures."[8]

For this reason, Golden Age writers vociferously denied that proper detective stories, tales of reasoning and fair play, should be considered thrillers.[9] Many of the rules posited by these writers were designed to purge sensational elements. The Detection Club's constitution demanded that the initiate could not qualify for entry with "adventure stories or 'thrillers' or stories in which detection is not the main interest."[10]

While Golden Age authors were building the tradition of the modern whodunit, other writers were creating tales of crime and mystery that lacked preposterous villains and dashing heroes. These came to be called *psychological* thrillers. The term appeared in the late 1920s and moved into general currency in the following decade. When Val Gielgud wrote to Patrick Hamilton requesting a new BBC radio drama, he suggested that "a psychological thriller along the lines of 'Rope' would be good."[11] Reviewers began using the term, and it was recruited to advertise novels, plays, and films. The label served to differentiate calmer works from the blood-and-thunder sensation of Wallace and the globe-trotting of John Buchan. If the "pursuit thriller" was based on an international chase, the psychological thriller was usually based in households, either middle-class or higher. This "domestic thriller" centered on homebound wives and white-collar husbands, professionals, artists, and students—neither adventurers nor professional crooks or investigators.

Narration and viewpoint were distinctive as well. Whereas the whodunit focused the action on the detective and associates, the psychological thriller favored the viewpoint of the criminal or victim. The Great Detective's exploits were likely to be filtered through a Watson or a bystander, but first-person accounts voiced by the target or culprit or both in alternation were more common in the thriller. The investigation plot was concerned with a buried story, but as Milward Kennedy described it, the new sort of thriller gives us the major crime as yet to happen, a lead-up to "the 'hidden history' of the murder itself."[12] If there is an investigation, it might be offstage, as in *The Lodger*, or it could be undertaken by the threatened victim.

Examples were being published while Golden Age whodunits were appearing. Isabel Ostrander's *Ashes to Ashes* (1919) tells of a business executive who murders his wife and then a college chum. We dwell almost wholly within the killer's mind as he alternates between panic and exultation. The plot of *The House by the River* (1920), by A. P. Herbert, might have come out of Patricia Highsmith. A writer strangles his maid during a sexual assault, then induces his weak friend to help him dump the body. He offhandedly allows the friend to be suspected of the crime.

Before C. S. Forester found success with novels of nautical adventure, he wrote two bleak psychological thrillers. *Payment Deferred* (1926) centers on a short-tempered bank clerk in genteel poverty who murders his nephew and then ruins his family through profligacy and alcoholism. In *Plain Murder* (1930), three advertising copywriters conceal a bribery scheme by killing their supervisor and then turning on one another. Forester uses the genre to reflect on the cruelties and delusions of the lower middle class.

Given the standard viewpoint options—perpetrator, victim—the bystander perspective of *The Lodger* stands out. This running side-story concentrates on the emotional effects of Mr. Sleuth's activities on those around him, some of whom might become victims. This unusual formal choice looks forward to Hitchcock's *Shadow of a Doubt* (1943).

As novelists explored possibilities of the psychological thriller, similar plots were creeping onto the English and American stage. The major vogue seems to have come in the late 1920s, as a *New York Times* correspondent put it, when London suffered "a theatrical crime wave . . . owing to a deluge of mystery plays and 'thrillers.'"[13] That wave included *Interference* (1927), *The Letter* (1927), *Spellbound* (1927; no relation to Hitchcock's film), *People Like Us* (1928), *Blackmail* (1928), and other "murder plays."[14] Hitchcock's film versions of *The Lodger* (1927) and *Blackmail* (1929) showed that the premises of the thriller—playing down investigation and playing up tension and guilt—were now part of popular storytelling in other media.

In these plots, critics realized, revealing the criminal's identity at the beginning doesn't slacken interest.[15] One wrote the following about A. A. Milne's play *The Fourth Wall* (1928):

> Though we saw the murder, we do not know what little slip Carter may have made in the arrangement of the room or the concoction of his own and Laverick's alibi. Thus while Susan continues her investigation we do not know what clue she will discover or how she will arrive at the truth; nor when she has a part of the information in her hands do we know how she will force Carter to reveal the rest.
>
> Here is scope for action enough, and not for action only but for as much drawing of character as is possible in the course of a narrative so full of events. The first act, which shows the murder, is admirable in its suspense and surprise.[16]

Similarly, in the *A Murder Has Been Arranged* (1928), the audience sees an heir kill his rival and then try to evade exposure. The first moments of Patrick Hamilton's *Rope* (1929), based on the Loeb-Leopold case, show two young men stuffing a body in a chest and then laying out a buffet on top.

By 1930, the Golden Age puzzle was at something of a crossroads. Writers who were becoming bored with convoluted deductions and mechanical clue planting were wondering how to deepen the emotional appeal of their stories. At the height of the puzzle story's prestige, Dorothy Sayers had argued that "it is better to err in the direction of too little feeling than too much."[17] The most famous statement to the contrary came from Anthony Berkeley in 1930: "There is a complication of emotion, drama, psychology, and adventure behind the most ordinary murder in real life, the possibilities of which for fictional purposes the conventional detective story misses completely."[18] Very soon Sayers was admitting that an emphasis on psychology and the circumstances leading up to the crime had created worthwhile "studies in murder." She realized that *Ashes to Ashes* and the Forester novels challenged detective writers to forge "a completely new technique."[19]

Well, this technique was not completely new. For one thing, Mary Roberts Rinehart had arrived at a method of blending detection with the domestic thriller. She showed that the action could move the protagonist, definitely not a Great Detective, from onlooker to investigator and then to target. This pattern of deepening involvement had proved very popular with the public, but the Golden Age adherents preferred fewer neo-Gothic trappings and more stress on the puzzle. "The interest of pure detection," wrote Berkeley, "will always hold its own."[20] Sayers wanted a formula that gave greater weight to serious psychology, creating "a puzzle of character rather than a puzzle of time, place, motive and opportunity." *The Documents in the Case* (1930) and *Gaudy Night* (1935) were among her efforts toward "a novel with a detective interest" rather than a "detective story pure and simple."[21] Ideally the Great Detective would still play a role.

One model of a hybrid had already been put forth by R. Austin Freeman's short-story collection *The Singing Bone* (1912). Freeman uses the first part of each tale to recount the commission of the crime, chiefly from the criminal's point of view. Part two traces the efforts of criminologist Dr. John Thorndyke to solve the mystery. Despite being far more linear than the back-and-fill plotting of the whodunit, Freeman's tales came to be called "inverted" stories.

With the killer's identity revealed at the outset, Freeman's narration must generate curiosity and suspense around Thorndyke's effort to discover the truth. Dr. Thorndyke's segment typically begins with him as a more or less pure reasoner, pondering anomalies in the case. Soon he questions witnesses and brings out his bag of instruments, his tweezers and reagents and portable microscope, to rake over the crime scene.

The scientific side of the plot demanded that Freeman not only exploit the conventions of motives, alibis, timetables, and the like but also supply the details of environment. He decided that an inverted arrangement could plant clues as firmly and unobtrusively as could the traditional format. "I calculated that the reader would be so occupied with the crime that he would overlook the evidence. And so it turned out. The second part, which described the investigation of the crime, had to most readers the effect of new matter. All the facts were known; but their evidential quality had not been recognized."[22] Freeman's formula provides the suspense and surprise that the critic found in Milne's *Fourth Wall*.

Most readers probably expect that a few particular traces of the crime will prove damning, but Freeman packs in so many details that Thorndyke's discoveries reconstruct the entire episode. In Freeman's founding story of the form, "The Case of Oscar Brodski," the giveaways include not only obvious ones such as blood smears and an iron bar but also cigarette papers, rare tobacco, shards of a wine glass, biscuit crumbs, string, fibers of a tablecloth, and a burned hat. Most of these are casually presented during the first part's fatal encounter. The second part patiently shows how each item contributes to the investigator's solution.

Thorndyke's inferences are corroborated by our memory of the tale's opening section; after all, we were witnesses. But once we're familiar with the inverted formula, we can be on our guard from the beginning. Freeman's unfolding crime scenes invite the sort of close reading promoted by the narration and dialogue of Christie, Carr, and their peers. Freeman's challenge to the reader is heightened because his perpetrators try to conceal their crimes. We must gauge how Dr. Thorndyke contends with the false scents and red herrings laid across the trail.

This three-way battle of wits becomes the basis of *Mr. Pottermack's Oversight* (1930). As is common in the genre, Freeman's problem is extending a short story premise to novelistic length. Mr. Pottermack is given an extensive past, dramatized in a prologue and fleshed out in an extended flashback. He is also in love with a local widow, who has her own past with the murdered blackmailer. Dr. Thorndyke is gradually brought into the case through scenes inserted between blocks of chapters devoted to Pottermack. Pottermack's strategy develops across the book as he manipulates faked footprints, then stolen banknotes, and eventually a substitute corpse. The title suggests a nontraditional source of mystery. What was the oversight we witnessed but did not grasp? As tradition dictates, the detective's summary scene yields a new revelation—not who did it, but how the crook bungled.

The inverted formula earned the respect of the Golden Age writers. Despite calling himself an "aged Victorian," Freeman was welcomed into the Detection Club and participated in collaborations.[23] *Rope* and other murder plays use his model, with the audience first viewing the crime and discovering the culprits. Much later, a strict adherence to the inverted format would become familiar in the television series *Columbo*.

Few Golden Age writers exploited the inverted plot in pure form, but some ingeniously inserted the "hidden history" of a crime into more intricate puzzle-driven patterns of plotting and narration. This is a neat instance of schema revision. The "pure" detective story was recast to assimilate features of the inverted tale, but in ways that preserved some elements of investigation, uncertainty, and surprise.

The simplest strategy was to present the criminal's viewpoint without identifying him or her. Mystery could arise from an unnamed first-person account, as in the diary excerpts of Philip MacDonald's *X v. Rex* (aka *Mystery of the Dead Police*, 1934). Here, as elsewhere, block construction proved especially useful in marking off the crime portions from the investigation sections. A more straightforward example was provided by Freeman Wills Crofts. Most of his novels were attached to Inspector French in his inquiries, but Crofts modified the *Pottermack* model in *The 12.30 from Croydon* (1934).

The novel begins with a poisoning during a plane trip and then flashes back to the origins of the crime, which is told in third person attached to the identified murderer. The early phases of Inspector French's inquiry are rendered from the killer's perspective as well, but they appear quite late in the novel. After the spotlight shifts to French, he provides a monologue wrapping things up. In the standard investigation plot, the "recovered story" is the crime; here the hidden story is the process of detection, which is kept from the reader's view.

In homage, Crofts makes his culprit well read in mystery fiction. He meditates in prison: "Somehow, alone there in the semi-darkness, the excellence of his own plans seemed less convincing than ever before. Stories he had read recurred to him in which the guilty had made perfect plans, but in all cases they had broken down. Those double tales of Austin Freeman's!"[24] Detective stories conventionally refer to other detective stories, apparently assuring us that the one we're reading is more "real" than its counterparts. Usually this gesture works to cite traditions that the reader enjoys recalling. *The 12.30 from Croydon* acknowledges that Freeman's formula made salient the possibility of a new mystery: How will the criminal err in committing and concealing the crime? Crofts exploited the inverted format further in *Antidote to Venom* (1938) and later novels.

A more light-hearted exercise in presenting a crime's hidden history was Richard Hull's *Murder Isn't Easy* (1937). In effect, it's a recasting of Forester's *Plain Murder*. Forester's murder scheme drew together three advertising agents, before one, fearing betrayal, tries to kill his mates. The story is told in compact, linear scenes. His narration is unashamedly omniscient, skipping among all the characters' thoughts within scenes and sometimes within paragraphs.

This traditional method yields a reliable, sometimes moralizing narration that lays bare the fluctuating emotions felt by the men, their employers, and their fellow employees.

In contrast, Hull's *Murder Isn't Easy* refracts its plot of ad-agency homicide through strictly constrained narration. Each of three partners has an urge to eliminate the other two, and each man is given a block of chapters in which to write up his scheme. But eventually we realize that the first account is untrustworthy, and the second one is incomplete. A third, no less misleading manuscript introduces the detective, one Inspector Hoopington. In a fourth block, the firm's secretary supplies an accurate wrap-up. After explaining Hoopington's solution, she follows his suggestion that publishing the documents could make up for losing her job.

> So that's how I came to take up a literary career, and while murder may not be easy, I must say I think writing is. You just go straight on.
> I'm beginning to simply adore it.[25]

Plain Murder had taken killing as a serious outgrowth of workplace bullying and shabby suburban routine. *Murder Isn't Easy* treats crime as an occasion for social satire. Male vanity is punctured, and as in *Murder Must Advertise*, the publicity game is relentlessly mocked. Three quarrelsome men stand revealed as being as inept in homicide as they are in business.

Hull's novel displays a self-conscious ingenuity quite alien to Forester's. The three manuscripts seed the buildup to the crime with outright lies, unobtrusive ellipses, and events replayed from different viewpoints. Meanwhile, the barely characterized Inspector Hoopington solves the case through old-fashioned clue spotting and intuition. The puerile written accounts have diverted us from what was evident to him. In its duplicitous structure and narration, *Murder Isn't Easy* offers an amusing synthesis of the psychological thriller and the virtuoso whodunit.

Here and in other hybrid plots, block construction facilitates both mystery and suspense because the segments can leave gaps in time or motive that will need filling later. Anne Meredith's *Portrait of a Murderer* (1934) is built of seven sections attached to various members of a rich, vastly unpleasant family. The first block reports the patriarch's death and the reactions of his kin. In the second, one son abruptly provides a first-person account of how he murdered the patriarch. Later sections employ third person, shifting-spotlight narration to show the killer's efforts to frame an odious in-law. Only after the crime is exposed do we learn the circumstances of the killer's confession. Another book would have maximized mystery and presented the confession as the solution, but here the emphasis falls, Crofts fashion, on whether the schemer's plan will succeed—and why his crime is presented to us in his own words.

"I am going to kill a man. I don't know his name. I don't know where he lives. I have no idea what he looks like. But I am going to find him and kill him." The first lines of Nicholas Blake's *The Beast Must Die* (1938) thrust us into the world of the psychological thriller. Yet the blunt confession gives way to a pirouette typical of Golden Age artifice. "You must pardon this melodramatic opening, gentle reader. It sounds just like a first sentence out of one of my own detective novels, doesn't it?"[26]

The keynote is set. The novel's first block consists of the diary of a man whose son has been killed in a hit-and-run accident. In emotionally wrenching detail, he tells of turning grief into a vendetta. He plays detective and discovers the driver's identity. Frankly confessing his qualms and self-loathing, he furthers his scheme by manipulating the killer's mistress and young son. The suspense of this section, however, is shot through with allusions to literature (notably *Hamlet* and *Macbeth*), as well as clever remarks on detective-story plotting. The writer, using his literary pseudonym Felix Lane, acknowledges genre conventions, mocks literary clichés, and considers that his story might suit John Dickson Carr or Anthony Berkeley. This is to be no less a literary performance than any other Golden Age novel.

In good thriller fashion, the second segment of *The Beast Must Die* dramatizes the naked confrontation between Felix Lane and Rafferty, the monstrously unredeemable killer. Lane has lured him out in a sailboat with the aim of drowning him, but Rafferty has a countervailing threat. This block is narrated in third person, shifting the viewpoint rapidly between the two men. Unlike Forester's transparent omniscience in *Plain Murder*, this novel displays the venerated literary technique as but one tool in the kit.

> The positions were now reversed. Felix was in a state of pitiable nerves, fidgeting no longer, but his whole body rigid with misery: George had regained his jocular tongue, his self-confident, supercilious, brutal attitude; or so it would have seemed to one of those ubiquitous, omniscient observers of Thomas Hardy, if such a one had been a third party in this bizarre voyage.[27]

Felix is defeated. Rafferty gloats and clambers onshore. The book is half over. What next?

Enter Blake's series detective Nigel Strangeways, the center of two more blocks and an epilogue. In the gap between parts two and three, Rafferty has swallowed poisoned medicine. Felix's diary is discovered, making him the prime suspect. Nigel attempts to defend Felix and find the real killer. His segments are dominated by his third-person perspective, but there are glimpses into the minds of Felix and Nigel's wife Georgia.[28]

Nigel is a model Golden Age figure, a genial snob given to quoting poetry and, like Philip Trent and Roger Sheringham, fallible. As the gifted amateur with upper-crust connections, he has license to tag along with Inspector Blount on rounds of questioning. He offers the obligatory allusion when he warns his wife Georgia that Rafferty's mother is behaving like "the sort of frightfully high red-herring that any detective-writer might draw across the trail," adding that if he were a detective in a book, he'd pick a different suspect than Felix.[29] Despite his belief that psychological analysis is his forte, Nigel relies on physical clues such as a medicine bottle, on intuitions about what certain people are like, and on serendipitous "half-memories" to jolt his inspirations. He duly produces a false solution, and Blount tops him with an equally wrong answer (one that the reader has probably considered). Eventually Nigel solves the case through a close reading of Felix's diary.

That solution accords with tradition by yielding the least likely culprit. But Blake invests that revelation with a sense of waste and sorrow that wouldn't be there without the thriller-driven intimacy of the first part. The diary at once supplies a cascade of unobtrusive clues and an emotional charge that propels the routines of ratiocination. In Claude Chabrol and Paul Gégauff's film adaptation (*Que la bête meure*, 1969), they dropped Strangeways altogether and produced a tighter, purer psychological thriller. They thereby eliminated the novel's effort to corrode the image of the breezy, pedantic Golden Age sleuth.[30] Nigel's whimsical insouciance at the beginning of part three is chastened by his discoveries, and at the close of part four, he has sunk into melancholy in response to what he calls in an epilogue "my most unhappy case."[31]

Whether satirical as in *Murder Isn't Easy*, puzzling as in *Portrait of a Murderer*, or somber as in *The Beast Must Die*, embedded first-person accounts show that the suspense of a thriller could merge with the curiosity and surprise propelling the straight investigation plot. Movie thrillers from the 1910s had often intercut crook and cop, a strategy taken to bold extremes in Fritz Lang's *Spione* (1928) and *M* (1931). But such films seldom harbored deep puzzles. In the 1930s, the juxtaposition of the crime's hidden history with the ongoing investigation became a live option for more or less pure whodunits.

From the 1940s onward, detective novelists grew comfortable with incorporating scenes from the criminal's side of things. Ed McBain, Charles Willeford, Laura Lippman, and many other writers would habitually alternate the viewpoints of police and culprit. Domestic thrillers of the 2010s would freely multiply women's voices, from both the present and the past. Usually these tales violate Knox's rule against entering the killer's consciousness, but writers realized that there were still opportunities for switcheroos. Although the novelist may widen the range of viewpoints, the disparate blocks harbor gaps, ambiguities, and deceptions that sustain a puzzle. The hybrid whodunits of the 1930s laid out a strategy that would pervade mystery storytelling in the decades to come.

Protagonist as Culprit and Victim

Apart from adapting Freeman's inverted strategy, the authors of hybrid stories were responding to a sophisticated revival of the pure psychological thriller, the plot concentrating on what Christie called a crime "in the course of preparation." Anthony Berkeley Cox, founder of the Detection Club and a devout believer in the puzzle form, had produced the bravura *Poisoned Chocolates Case*. But he also had felt the need for a deeper psychology in explaining literary homicide. Under the pseudonym Francis Iles, he published *Malice Aforethought: The Story of a Commonplace Crime* (1931) and *Before the Fact* (1932). They proved to be powerful models for tales of murder told completely from the inside.

Malice Aforethought traces how philandering Dr. Edmund Bickleigh poisons his domineering wife. In easy stages, he slips from the idea of murder to the careful weighing of lethal means and the painstaking execution of the scheme. Encouraged by his success, Bickleigh goes on to conceive of killing a would-be mistress, a threatening husband, and other people who annoy him. But his rational planning is accompanied by mood swings, as serene overconfidence is swept away by pangs of uncertainty. Bickleigh muses that perhaps he has turned to crime out of an inferiority complex, but soon he's chortling over the ease with which his superior intellect fools everyone.

The third-person narration restricts us almost completely to Dr. Bickleigh's mind, and we are nearly as surprised as he is when the police spring a trap. (Granted, the ironic narration makes us a bit more cautious than Bickleigh is.) The one major divergence from his range of knowledge comes at the book's midpoint, when an afternoon tea brings forth gossip that will lead to his second wave of homicidal enterprise. This skillful chapter recapitulates events of the year following his wife's death and structurally balances another expository node, the book's opening tennis party scene.

That party and the ladies' tea fully expose Iles's satiric take on suburbia. One guest's "solid flesh did look as if it was doing its best to melt." Miss Peavy is so upset that she blurts out something "mostly in italics." A mischievous young woman provokes Bickleigh to annoyance. "Quarnian hugged herself. She was far too much of an artist to overdo her effects."[32] Informationally the narration confines itself to Bickleigh, but judgmentally it offers sardonic observations on human nature and the byways of desire. The narration's ironic murmur primes us for the twists of fate that Bickleigh fails to foresee.

Like *Malice Aforethought*, Iles's companion novel, *Before the Fact*, traces a story that begins long before the investigation. Now, however, our perspective isn't that of an aspiring killer. "Some women give birth to murderers, some go to bed with them, and some marry them. Lina Aysgarth had lived with her husband for nearly eight years before she realized she was married to a murderer."[33]

At the time, this opening must have been doubly shocking—the prospect of a homicidal spouse and the offhand reference to copulation. Just as startling, the narration admits at the outset what Gothic romances only teased, the prospect that the bride's enigmatic partner is lethal. No puzzle here, the narration insists, only suspense. Will the bystander become a victim?

She will, but by small degrees. The plain but intelligent Lina is swept off her feet by the charming sociopath Johnnie Aysgarth. Trailing a bad-boy reputation, he showers her with the praise neither her family nor other men have offered. After their marriage, she learns little by little that he's a rotter. He lies, gambles, embezzles, steals from her and others, seduces women, fathers a child by a servant, and stages the death of Lina's father. All the while he convinces everyone that he's the most affable and generous man in town. Eventually Johnnie kills a dim, rich friend.

The book's debt to Golden Age mysteries shows up in the inclusion of a minor character, a mystery novelist whom Johnnie cultivates. Iles brazenly lets the novelist discover that forbidden whodunit cliché, the poison that leaves no trace. Johnnie learns about it, and he administers it to Lina.

Before the Fact traces Lina's anxieties with almost Jamesian finesse. As she learns little by little of Johnnie's crimes, she wavers between condemnation and acceptance, shock and rationalization. The recurring metaphor of the naughty schoolboy makes him "Johnnie, her child," the son she must protect. Without his knowing, she becomes an accomplice, destroying evidence and supporting his lies. She fears being alone and unloved, and she starts to share his conviction that the deaths he leaves in his wake aren't really murder. She catches a passive version of his psychopathology.

Only by such fastidious preparation could a novel convince the reader that a wife could let the scoundrel she adores serve her poisoned milk. Iles shrewdly gives Lina a chance to save her dignity through self-dramatization. When she realizes she's next on Johnnie's list, she takes up a literary role. "As tea went on, Lina had an odd sensation that she was living a play. It was the middle of the second act. The audience knew that at the end of the third act she was to be killed, to bring down the curtain; she did not know it. She was to sparkle gaily and nonchalantly right up to the end. Unconsciously she found herself acting up to this nonexistent audience."[34] This burst of Golden Age reflexivity echoes the book's opening and acknowledges our position as readers. For the first 250 pages, we have watched an unwitting Lina arrive at the fate we knew from the start. At last the enabler prepares to play the innocent victim.

To the end, she does sometimes consider choosing to live. After all, if she dies, who will cover Johnnie's further crimes? Yet when she realizes he is determined to poison her, she proceeds to smooth his path by feigning illness and faking a suicide note. She becomes an accessory before the fact to her own death. She even mentally thanks Johnnie for freeing her of the responsibility of protecting him. If murderers are made, she reflects at one point, so are victims.

Malice Aforethought and *Before the Fact* became prototypes of the domestic psychological thriller. They demonstrated how drama could grow out of festering motives, middle-class frustration, and the dawning realization that loved ones can't be trusted. The Golden Age detective story, with its least-likely-suspect convention, had relied on the idea that anyone could be a murderer, but the domestic thriller developed this idea in depth. The theme was doubtless accelerated by notorious murders committed by solid citizens such as Dr. H. H. Crippen, Loeb and Leopold, and baby-faced Sidney Fox. These fictions replaced the Napoleonic crimes of sensation thrillers with a sense that humdrum life harbored lethal passions.

Raskolnikov's Brothers

Iles's two books demonstrated the strength of rigorously restricted viewpoint, either that of the criminal or that of the victim to be. The first option had been traditionally fulfilled by male protagonists, as in James Hogg's *Private Memoirs and Confessions of a Justified Sinner* (1824), and Poe's short stories "The Pit and the Pendulum" (1842), "The Black Cat" (1843), "The Tell-Tale Heart (1843), and "The Cask of Amontillado" (1846). Although *Crime and Punishment* (1866) did not adhere to a single character's viewpoint, Dostoevksy considered the possibility: "Another plan: Narration from the author's point of view, as if by an invisible but omniscient being, but not leaving him [Raskolnikov] even for a minute."[35] Later, Roy Horniman's *Israel Rank: The Autobiography of a Criminal* (1907) presented a marginal heir trying to secure a legacy by purging his family rivals. (It became the 1949 film *Kind Hearts and Coronets*.) Ostrander's 1919 *Ashes to Ashes* continued in this vein of depicting the desperation of the aspiring gentleman.

Iles's witty social observation and the evocation of his protagonist's mixture of apprehension and bravado made *Malice Aforethought* distinctive. The book signaled a renaissance in English novels exploring the mind of a man bent on murder: Richard Hull's *The Murder of My Aunt* (1934), Henry Wade's *Heir Presumptive* (1935), Winifred Duke's *Skin for Skin* (1935), Bruce Hamilton's *Middle Class Murder* (1936), and James Ronald's *This Way Out* (1939). On the West End stage, *Rope* had shown how to sustain a drama of drawing room criminality. Theater pieces in this vein continued with the adaptation of *Payment Deferred* (1932), *Ten-Minute Alibi* (1933), *Without Witness* (1934), *Night Must Fall* (1935), *The Amazing Dr. Clitterhouse* (1936), *Poison Pen* (1937), *The Suspect* (1937), the *Rope*-derived *Trunk Crime* (aka *The Last Straw*, 1937), and a rare case of a female killer, *Ladies in Retirement* (1939). Some of these made their way to

Broadway, along with homegrown exercises such as *Riddle Me This!* (1932) and *Nine Pine Street* (1933), based on the Lizzie Borden case.

Murderous protagonists emerged in American fiction as well. Although James M. Cain's stories are stylistically affiliated with the hard-boiled school, in plot and narration they are brawny working-class counterparts of the genteel British thrillers. *The Postman Always Rings Twice* (1934), *Double Indemnity* (1936), and "The Embezzler" (aka "Money and the Woman," 1938) follow the thoughts of losers who launch impulsive murder schemes. The less well-known Don Tracy offered tales of men drawn into robbery and murder (*Criss-Cross*, 1934) or a lethal erotic triangle (*White Hell*, 1937). T. S. Matthews's *To the Gallows I Must Go* (1931) looked forward to Cain in presenting a woman enticing a man to kill her husband. Elisabeth Sanxay Holding's novel *Death Wish* (1934) focused, in a Patricia Highsmith vein, on a man who decides to kill his wife after realizing that a friend has dared to kill his.

In the criminal-centered psychological thriller, the protagonist is put under pressure by money troubles, overbearing bosses or colleagues, a disagreeable wife or blood relative, or lust for a woman. Murder arises as the most swift and effective way out. The bulk of the action consists of the character's plans, his execution of them, and his reactions to threatening situations. In most stories, the psychological development plays out as a series of anticipations and memories. The protagonist imagines best and worst outcomes, and he must react to new circumstances that put him in jeopardy.

The plot traces a conventional zigzag of emotions, from the heights of confidence to the pits of terror. That emotional swing between fear and elation, and the sense of superiority that comes with it, can be found in the prototypical murder tale *Crime and Punishment*. While justifying murder as the province of the superior mind, Raskolnikov is prey to the constant panic of being found out. Dr Bickleigh's elation at fooling his stupid neighbors, followed by his fear at having blundered, is a bourgeois successor to Raskolnikov's reactions.

In Elizabeth Sanxay Holding's *The Unfinished Crime* (1935), the protagonist is filled with "an immense exultation. . . . He could and he would escape from the bread-and-butter life." Suddenly, on the same page he learns that his scheme has faltered.

"This is the end," he said to himself.
   The end of all his plans, all his intelligence, the end of his one brief moment of life. Despair was on him, and he was mortally stricken.

Two pages later hope is rekindled: "He had been strong and resourceful before; he had met each danger as it came, and had triumphed. If he kept his head, perhaps he could triumph even now."[36] Suspense in the psychological thriller depends in part on the reader anticipating the protagonist's reaction to the inevitable mishaps that spoil his plan. The emotional ups and downs heighten the stakes of his next decision.

This inner oscillation is easier to present in prose than on stage, unless the playwright is ready to employ soliloquy. Patrick Hamilton found an ingenious solution in *Rope* by splitting his protagonist in two. The swaggering Brandon is supremely confident: having committed "immaculate murder," he tells his partner Granillo that he feels "truly and wonderfully alive."[37] But Granillo is fearful and apprehensive. He gets drunk in the course of their party and is at risk of exposing them. He externalizes the apprehensions that beset the divided protagonist of other thrillers.

Carrying out a murder may take on an aesthetic tint, and more refined killers may invoke de Quincy's "On Murder Considered as One of the Fine Arts." Israel Rank deplores the inartistic blunders that undo his schemes. *The Unfinished Crime*'s protagonist imagines himself a Renaissance prince, "a man who combined in himself a love of the arts, scholarship, and a capacity for swift ruthless action."[38] The husband of *The House by the River* chronicles his crime in an allegorical poem, and the culprit of *Portrait of a Murderer* immortalizes the deed in a painting. *Rope*'s Brandon is in this dandyish vein, with Nietzschean morality as another reference point. The narration makes the killer's moments of panic plausible responses to the tightening net, but we know that the visions of superiority are mere fantasies. Like Raskolnikov, the killer is bound to fail.[39] The interest lies in how.

The plot will center largely on the criminal's viewpoint, and in literary texts the writer must choose how to treat that restriction. Third-person narration offers the flexibility of straying occasionally to other viewpoints, a shift that can build suspense by playing off degrees of ignorance and knowledge. An external narrating voice also affords the chance for the dry comedy Iles, Hare, and others enjoy wringing out of provincialism and class friction. Duke's *Skin for Skin* develops a more poignant vein. The narration shifts the spotlight between the murdering husband and the neighbors who gossip about him. When he escapes justice and tries to resume his old life, they spurn him and make him regret his crime.

Alternatively, most first-person thrillers limit us to one narrating voice and justify that as coming from diaries, letters, or testimony. Cain believed that such motivation was necessary.[40] The ending of *The Postman Always Rings Twice* reveals that it's a prison confession, and *Double Indemnity* is motivated by a long suicide note. Not for some years would mystery writers emancipate their character-narrators and simply let them speak outside of a storytelling situation. An early example is Martin Goldsmith's *Detour* (1939), which centers on a hitchhiker on his way to meet his former girlfriend. He winds up faking his own death and killing a woman who threatens to expose him. First-person chapters from his viewpoint alternate with chapters recounted by his girlfriend, who is clawing her way to success in Hollywood, and neither narrator explains what has led them to tell their tales.

Detour, like the British thrillers, freely fills in the main characters' psychological reactions, but Cain suppresses them. The Postman Always Rings Twice is almost completely behavioral and objective in presenting Frank Chambers and Cora Papadakis's plot to kill her husband. Frank's narration dwells on externals of description and reported conversation. No inner debates about plans and executions, no signs of caution or remorse disturb his staccato prose. But when Frank finally senses the danger he's in, he intermittently reveals a mind. He has bad dreams, and he admits to suspicions that couldn't be expressed in behavior. "I was afraid if she got sore at me for something, she'd go off her nut and spill it like she had that other time, after the arraignment. I didn't trust her for a minute."[41] Cain's novels were called "doom stories," and here the protagonist seems to gain introspection only after his unthinking scheme has put him on the path to disaster.

The Road to Manderley

Most criminal-viewpoint plots relied on male protagonists, but victim plots were likely to center on women. Again there were distant precedents. The Mysteries of Udolpho (1794) and Jane Eyre (1847) were classics of romantic and sensation fiction, and Mary Roberts Rinehart revived some of those Gothic conventions while blending them with detection plots. The result, focused around a woman's viewpoint, carried more emotional punch than traditional puzzles. A mystery would still propel the action, but investigation becomes part of a larger dynamic of predator and prey. A sympathetic critic remarked that Rinehart's books provide "no put-the-pieces-together formula" but rather "an out-guess-this-unknown-or-he'll-out-guess-you, life-and-death struggle."[42]

That the heroine will come through it safely is usually taken for granted. Rinehart begins The Circular Staircase with her protagonist writing this: "When I look back over the months I spent at Sunnyside, I wonder that I survived at all."[43] This genre was sometimes mockingly called the "Had I But Known" (HIBK) school because that phrase seemed to justify the risks the heroine unwittingly takes: Had she known what awaited her, she wouldn't have crept up to the attic. Critics implied that these tales of inquisitive women have found their natural audience. Decades later the misogyny was still there. "These are the first crime stories which have the air of being written specifically for maiden aunts."[44]

But the HIBK label captures something else. It suggests that these novels, unlike most male-centered plots, have a retrospective air. The narration is often looking back on a harrowing adventure from a superior point of knowledge. When the protagonist isn't narrating in the first person, these passages present classic novelistic omniscience. "She did not know, then, that no power on earth could have prevented her own entanglement with the murders at 18 East Eden."[45]

What eventually became known as "romantic suspense" was the most lucrative mystery market in the United States. Slick magazines paid high fees for stories of women in jeopardy. Rinehart's chief rival, Mignon G. Eberhart, was paid $2,500 for a novelette she sold to *Redbook* and $7,500 for a serial novel for *Ladies' Home Journal*. By 1939, her serials were garnering $15,000 each (over a quarter of a million dollars in 2020 currency).[46] *Before the Fact* and other prestigious thrillers were in synchronization with this trend, but they—and, indeed, mysteries in other genres—did not reap these rewards.

That popularity may have provided envious critics and whodunit writers with additional reasons to dismiss the genre as HIBK frivolity. But the plot schema proved robust. Stage versions of the woman-in-peril premise appeared in London with *The Two Mrs. Carrolls* (1935), *Love from a Stranger* (1936), and another Patrick Hamilton triumph, *Gas Light* (aka *Angel Street*, 1938). Broadway didn't lag behind, importing such hits while adding *Double Door* (1933, an anticipation of *Rebecca*), *Invitation to a Murder* (1934), and *Kind Lady* (1935). Many of these plays were made into films.

A criminal-centered thriller often starts with the murderer already scheming, but the victim-centered plot may take some time to make the protagonist the target. Often she begins as a more or less innocent bystander. Lina Aysgarth in *Before the Fact* doesn't become Johnnie's target until late in the novel. The reader knows what she has yet to discover. Suspense arises from watching her suspicions crystallize slowly, and then from wondering whether she will accept the role of victim.

Alternatively, the protagonist's involvement in an initial mystery may draw her into jeopardy. Nan Bayne, the heroine of Eberhart's *The Pattern* (1937), is suspected of helping her former fiancé kill his wife. A police detective will eventually solve the mystery and exonerate them, but the narration is attached almost completely to Nan. She begins to receive mysterious phone calls. An intruder escapes with her purse. Poisonous spiders scuttle around her house. At the climax, the police wait in ambush elsewhere while she confronts the killer on the beach. Like Belloc Lowndes in *The Lodger*, Eberhart turns a murder puzzle into a suspense thriller by presenting an investigation from the standpoint of a vulnerable bystander.

The purest woman-in-peril plots relied on the threat in *Before the Fact*: a homicidal husband or lover. But most authors shrank from the harshness of Iles's climax and found ways to let the endangered wife escape. This was the option taken by two British plays. In Martin Vale's *The Two Mrs. Carrolls*, a woman learns that her husband has been poisoning her, and she is saved at the last minute by friends. Frank Vosper's *Love from a Stranger*, adapted from an

Agatha Christie story, provided a more violent denouement. A woman trapped with a murderous husband turns the tables by asserting that she is a murderess who is trying to kill *him*. He collapses from a heart attack, and her former fiancé arrives in time to console her. The rescuer is an underdeveloped version of what film historian Diane Waldman has called the "helper male," a figure who assists the threatened woman in escaping a dangerous husband and who can become a new romantic partner.[47]

The most famous example of a wife saved from a menacing husband came in the play *Gas Light*. Jack Manningham has killed an old woman for her rare rubies, but he has been unable to find them. Now, thanks to marrying well, he has moved into the house and spends his nights searching for the jewels. At the same time, he is systematically leading his wife Bella into believing she's delusional. Once he finds the rubies, he'll commit her to a madhouse. But Detective Rough has recognized Jack from years before and, with the help of a dazed Bella, finds the gems and arrests Jack.

Early portions of the play restrict our knowledge to Bella's, but she is off-stage at some key moments, such as when Rough confronts Jack. The peak of suspense arrives when her behavior makes us think that she has succumbed to Jack's plot. With Jack lashed to a chair and Rough allowing Bella to speak to Jack in private, she at first tries to help him escape—proof that, despite everything, she thinks he had her best interests at heart. But in fetching a razor to cut him free, she finds a missing grocery bill, one of many items he concealed to make her think she was losing her mind. She becomes bitter and taunting. "If I were not mad I could have helped you—if I were not mad, whatever you had done, I could have pitied and protected you! But because I am mad I have hated you, and because I am mad I am rejoicing in my heart—without a shred of pity—without a shred of regret—watching you go with glory in my heart!"[48] The scene is a tour de force, giving the performer a chance to play a woman on the edge of hysteria who can still grasp what her husband has done to her. *Gas Light*'s helper male, the avuncular Rough, will not become Bella's love interest, but that role was filled when the play became an MGM film in 1944.

As domestic thrillers proliferated, variations naturally appeared. The woman in peril might be presented from the viewpoint of her male partner, as in Eberhart's *The White Cockatoo* (1933). Authors began to explore unreliable narrators, finding ways to incorporate mystery elements that could generate twists. In Anita Boutell's *Death Has a Past* (1939), several women are gathered at a weeklong party. Their daily doings are intercut with blocks from a later, cryptic confession that starts with the killing of one guest—but which one? The confession's provenance and trustworthiness are put in question. It looks forward to the unsourced voices that ripple through domestic thrillers of the 2010s.

In film, thriller conventions were invoked in the peculiar Poverty Row production *The Sin of Nora Moran* (1933). But they were secondary to a hallucinatory shuffling of narrative perspectives. In the present, a district attorney is explaining to a friend's widow the circumstances of the affair she discovered in old love letters. Within his narrated flashbacks, we are taken first into the memory and dreams of Nora, on Death Row for murdering someone. (Who?) The film slides unpredictably between three time periods, with suspiciously neat visual linkages disguising disruptive switches of viewpoint. At one point, Nora wakes up just before her execution to find her old friend from circus days at her bedside, assuring her that she's still dreaming.

Once we leave Nora's mind, we learn of another letter, one written by her lover Richard. Those sequences plunge us into *his* memories and hallucinations, including a replay of their breakup, culminating in a posthumous visit from her (fig. 5.1). At various moments in both Nora's and Richard's scenes, there's the suggestion that everything we witness might consist of her imaginary rewritings of what really happened to the couple. The elemental situation of the wrongly accused woman barely holds together stock footage, overwrought montage sequences, and wandering voice-overs. *The Sin of Nora Moran* inadvertently proved that nonlinear narrative techniques had made a mark on American cinema.

At the other end of the prestige scale was Daphne du Maurier's carefully upholstered novel *Rebecca* (1938). Recounted by its unnamed protagonist, it offered a mournful revision of Gothic conventions. At the beginning of the book, Maxim de Winter and his second wife are quietly unhappy in a Mediterranean hotel, making the genre's retrospective view unusually rueful. They share a secret that the bulk of the book, in a long flashback, will expose. We know that the protagonist will survive, but what took the joy out of their marriage? The dead Rebecca, of course, whose memory is maintained with implacable determination by the housekeeper Mrs. Danvers. The early stretches of

5.1 *The Sin of Nora Moran* (1933): Although Nora has been executed, her apparition visits the man whose career she saved.

the book emphasize the anxiety of class embarrassment as the new wife fumbles her efforts to fit into the household.

Initially, the second Mrs. de Winter is frightened less by her moody husband Maxim than by Mrs. Danvers and all the neighbors and kin, for whom Rebecca was the epitome of "breeding, brains, and beauty."[49] Slowly the conventional pressures of an investigation plot build. The new wife questions servants and neighbors about Rebecca's life and the circumstances of her drowning. She learns of gossip surrounding Rebecca's relationship with her cousin Jack Favell. After tricking the protagonist into disgracing herself before Maxim, Mrs. Danvers urges her to suicide. What prevents this, and heals the breach in the couple, is the revelation that Rebecca's body has been found in her sunken boat. The last third of the novel is devoted to working out crime and punishment—a criminal-centered plot grafted onto a victim-centered one. As victims tend to do, the protagonist discovers the strength to survive.

"A Gothic is a story about a girl who gets a house."[50] Donald Westlake's observation holds good for many thrillers centered on vulnerable women, and *Rebecca* made the lush estate of Manderley practically a character. The novel, twice as long as the typical mystery, gained prestige in an era committed to doorstop volumes (*Anthony Adverse, The Citadel, Gone with the Wind*). Du Maurier fills her canvas with minute descriptions of the manor's grounds, routines, cuisine, and social chitchat, all filtered through the ill-at-ease new wife. The plot works out topographically, with Manderley radiating grimness but also harboring Happy Valley, where azaleas flourish and a path runs to the sea. The cottage where Rebecca entertained her lovers is left to fill with dust, mold, and rats. Maxim tries to start a new life in the house's east wing, but Mrs. Danvers preserves Rebecca's elegant west wing as a perpetual shrine.

The protagonist longs to bestow that timelessness on the best moments of her marriage. Her narration often fills in scenes with alternative futures, fantasies of the children she would like to have, or reconstructions of how Rebecca must have settled herself gracefully in the chairs that feel so awkward to a newcomer. She can even imagine Maxim's remembering the details of his wife's behavior. Like Lina in *Before the Fact*, she can envision herself as a character in a play, masking her inadequacies with rote lines. By quietly fleshing out every moment to suggest happiness or peril, echoes of earlier scenes and inferences about others' thoughts, the new wife's narration yields the psychological density sought by Golden Age writers.

For example, when the narrator curls up with Maxim under the chestnut tree, her satisfaction is undercut by a comparison to the family dog:

> I listened to them both, leaning against Maxim's arm, rubbing my chin on his sleeve. He stroked my hand absently, not thinking, talking to Beatrice.

"That's what I do to Jasper," I thought. "I'm being like Jasper now, leaning against him. He pats me now and again, when he remembers, and I'm pleased. I get closer to him for a moment. He likes me the way I like Jasper."[51]

Her hunger for Maxim's affection is mixed with her awareness that he feels himself her master. Is this not a man who, if goaded by a woman, would lose his temper and harm her? The menacing opacity of the powerful male, a premise of the domestic thriller, is treated in understated strokes that evoke our sympathy for the wife and our apprehensions about the husband.

The interiority of the HIBK school finds elaborate expression in the narrator's long inner monologues, with a dash of stream of consciousness. "He had followed me up from the hall. Why did dogs make one want to cry? There was something so quiet and hopeless about their sympathy. Jasper, knowing something was wrong as dogs always do. Trunks being packed. Cars being brought to the door. Dogs standing with drooping tails, dejected eyes. Wandering back to their baskets in the hall when the sound of the car dies away."[52] A conventional thriller would have simply reported Jasper's nuzzling the heroine's hand, neglecting the continuing parallel between her and Maxim's pet, but this book aims at the emotional breadth of serious literature. As a bonus, the passage prolongs the suspense.

No mystery novel since *The Hound of the Baskervilles* attained the cultural status accorded *Rebecca*. It was the best-selling mystery of its day, and the film version, despite drastic alterations, became a classic. Kept continuously in print, the book routinely turns up on lists of best novels of the twentieth century, and it has been scrutinized by academic critics for its gender politics and its debts to sensation fiction. In its moment and thereafter, it showed that the modern psychological thriller could, by recasting Gothic conventions, satisfy a broad public and attain enduring literary distinction.

Letters of the Film Alphabet

If the investigation plot depends principally on curiosity—about past events, about what clues mean, about motives and identities—the thriller depends heavily on suspense. Of course, even the pure whodunit generates some general suspense by virtue of asking what may happen next. But a puzzle plot lacks the element of danger that is usually associated with a thriller. An impending threat, sensed by either us or a character or both, shapes the fear that is central to suspense.

Perhaps for this reason the puzzle-centered plot seldom transferred well to film and theater. Alfred Hitchcock pointed out that a thriller summons up greater engagement from the audience than one finds in a whodunit. The viewer will "participate" strongly in the action, Hitchcock believed, when "some character who has the audience's sympathy is involved in danger."[53] A play-wright or filmmaker working in popular forms will often want the audience to be passionately absorbed in the unfolding action—something that thrillers are well-designed to trigger.

Another factor was hinted at by Dorothy Sayers. "In the thriller, our cry is 'What comes next?'—in the detective story, 'What came first?'"[54] The puzzle plot demands a good memory or a willingness to pause and reflect on the implications of the clues and testimony. A challenge to the reader or the detective's cryptic allusions to overlooked details could impel a search through earlier pages, even if few readers tried. But a play or a film doesn't allow the audience to stop or go back, so a pure puzzle on stage or screen would demand a level of concentration that was uncommon in audiences. Again, Hitchcock noticed this difference.[55] And in the 1920s and 1930s, filmgoers could drop in at a screening partway through, a practice that would ruin clue-dropping and clever misdirection.

The distinction between the genres isn't absolute. Detective stories can integrate the emotional appeals of sympathy or comedy, as we've seen. And often a thriller will proffer some mysteries, even one as trivial as the Hitchcock Mac-Guffin, a puzzling pretext that launches the plot. It's just that in the psychological thriller the suspense arising from an impending threat will dominate the plot development. "Curiosity, combined with emotional tension": this, proposed Val Gielgud, yields "a tremendous suspense quality."[56]

In 1930s Hollywood, a Great Detective was likely to have a film series: Charlie Chan, Mr. Moto, Sherlock Holmes, Philo Vance, Ellery Queen, and others. Yet the pure puzzle didn't find a comfortable niche in mainstream filmmaking. Most U.S. detective films of the period were B-level products, not top-budget features. Just as important, these films often introduced an element of danger into the investigation. The films created suspense by showing vaguely defined threats—groping hands, shadowy figures, infernal machines—that took the detective as a target (fig. 5.2). A puzzle resolved by exciting action, 1930s detective films often followed the hallowed tradition in which reasoning gave way to adventure.

Pure thrillers enjoyed a significantly higher status. Stage hits were adapted into films such as *Payment Deferred* (1932), *Guilty as Hell* (1932), *Kind Lady* (1935), *Night Must Fall* (1937), and *Love from a Stranger* (1937), and these films featured major stars such as Charles Laughton, Robert Montgomery, and Basil Rathbone. In the 1940s, the psychological thriller would become a major genre of American and British films, novels, theater, and radio.

The genre didn't acquire the rich theoretical literature lavished on the detective story, but some reflections on stage dramaturgy proved relevant. Writers on the theater had long recognized the power of the hierarchy of knowledge, the disparity between what the audience knows and what the various characters

5.2 *Mr. Moto's Gamble* (1938): Suspense within the investigation plot: the detective in danger.

know. This is a matter of restricted versus unrestricted narration. Long ago, the playwright Gotthold Ephriam Lessing had noted that a dramatist should not rely too much on surprise. "By means of secrecy a poet effects a short surprise, but in what enduring disquietude could he have maintained us if he had made no secret about it!" An artist can create a "short surprise" by concealing information, but a greater range of knowledge can become "the source of the most violent emotions."[57]

What Lessing calls enduring disquietude is usually called suspense. The distinction between surprise and suspense recurs throughout writings on the theater. In the 1910s, Brander Matthews, William Archer, George Pierce Baker, and other theorists emphasized the duality. Playwrights had already realized the relative power of each option, along with the possibilities of alternating swiftly between them. In 1881, Matthews praised Hugo's play *Cromwell*:

> There is the familiar use of moments of surprise and suspense, and of stage-effects appealing to the eye and the ear. In the first act Richard Cromwell drops into the midst of the conspirators against his father,—surprise; he accuses them of treachery in drinking without him,—suspense; suddenly a trumpet sounds, and a crier orders open the doors of the tavern where all are sitting,— suspense again; when the doors are flung wide, we see the populace and a company of soldiers, and the criers on horseback, who reads a proclamation of a general fast, and commands the closing of all taverns,—surprise again. A somewhat similar scene of succeeding suspense and surprise is to be found in the fourth act.[58]

The British theater doyen Henry Edwards applied the comparison to cinema. In a 1920 article, he argues that suspense depends on the dread that something awful will happen to the characters. "We must show the audience these dangers, and keep our characters ignorant of them until the proper moment; and it is the nearing of the danger to the blissfully ignorant character, making us long to cry out and warn him, that give suspense." Edwards's example is a man smoking in a shed and suddenly realizing that his match has ignited dynamite. Alternatively, imagine that we've seen workers set down a box of dynamite before he arrives. Now every gesture he makes prolongs the tension: Will he be blown up? Edwards concludes his piece: "The letters of the film alphabet are s-u-s-p-e-n-s-e."[59]

Hitchcock popularized the surprise/suspense distinction. A 1939 lecture recommended "letting the audience into the secret as early as possible. Lay all the facts out, as much as you can, unless you are dealing with a mystery element." He claimed to have recast the plot of *Jamaica Inn* (1939) so that "it became a suspense story instead of a surprise story."[60] He elaborated these ideas throughout his career. Very likely he knew Edwards's dynamite example; his own version was his famous parable of the bomb under the table. If you haven't told the viewer that the bomb is there, you will get short-term surprise. If you show the bomb, every gesture or line of dialogue builds tension. "The audience is longing to warn the characters on the screen: 'You shouldn't be talking about such trivial matters. There's a bomb beneath you and it's about to explode!'"[61]

Surprise is usually the result of restricting our knowledge to a single character. In literary thrillers, that can be achieved through first-person narration or third-person attachment. In other media, consistent attachment suffices. Anyone who thinks that Hitchcock abstained from surprise has forgotten one of the most striking shots in his work (fig. 5.3).[62] Tightly restricted narration can yield suspense as well, such as when a car ignition fails to start and

5.3 *The 39 Steps* (1935): The professor's incomplete pinky finger reveals that he's the man Hannay is searching for.

the character can't escape a murder scene. But suspense can just as easily be fostered by what I've called moving-spotlight narration. We might be tied to a character's knowledge for a scene or so, but if the narration shifts us to other characters, we're likely to learn things that the first character doesn't know. That can generate the sort of suspense that Edwards and Hitchcock consider central to engaging cinema.

Important as surprise is, most theorists assigned greater artistic power to suspense. In preferring the well-made play, commentators reacted against popular melodrama, with its episodic construction, wild coincidences, and unforeseeable plot twists. The preference for suspense acknowledges the playwright's adroit shaping of the plot, preparing the revelations carefully but also creating a steady arc of tension rather than a firecracker string of surprises. More broadly, the play is artistically satisfying if we gain what William Archer calls "the glory of omniscience. . . . The essential and abiding pleasure of the theatre lies in foreknowledge."[63] In treating suspense as superior to surprise, Hitchcock was in effect endorsing the artistically polished film.

In practice, few 1920s and 1930s plays and films presented tightly restricted narration. Moving-spotlight treatment was far more common, and the two media had different techniques for widening the viewpoint for the sake of suspense.

In proscenium theater, bound to fixed sets and traditional act segments, showing the audience that an unsuspecting character was in danger involved calculated entrances and exits. When the heroine of *Love from a Stranger* is offstage, we get hints that her husband is mentally disturbed. By the end of Act 2, he's alone and caresses a scarf before ripping it to pieces. Cinema, in contrast, offers the ability to shift locales instantly, so the film version of *Love from a Stranger* can follow the husband to the basement (never seen in the stage version) and crosscut his "experiments" with the unsuspecting wife's activities upstairs.

Even without crosscutting, cinema can create suspense through staging that transforms theater blocking. In the play *Kind Lady*, a sinister band of scofflaws gradually takes over the heroine's household, with the power dynamics played out in the parlor. At a crucial point, when she has ordered the invaders to leave, they ominously take up positions around her. In the staging instructions in the playscript, as the heroine realizes the invaders' intentions, she advances to the footlights with her back to the audience. The actors spread out across the set, and the leader strides steadily toward her along the central axis.[64] In the film version, the heroine stands in the center of the frame, more or less frontal. We see the characters entering the frame one by one, blocking her escape before she's aware of their purpose (figs. 5.4–5.8). On the stage, an array in depth like this wouldn't be readable from all sight lines, but because the camera is our surrogate eye, she becomes prey by a gradual tightening of the composition.

5.4 *Kind Lady* (1935): A hierarchy of knowledge is revealed through staging. Mrs. Herries is unaware of the scheme of her "guests."

5.5 We see her gradually surrounded, as she remains oblivious.

5.6 Mr. Edwards seats himself, opening an exit route for her. But in the background, the doctor descends.

5.7 The arrival of the gang's leader completes the encirclement.

5.8 Only when Mrs. Herries turns does she realize that she's in the gang's power.

These are moment-by-moment shifts, but the superior knowledge under-lying suspense can create a wider arc of interest. The retrospective viewpoint common in novels provides a general anticipation. At the beginning of *Before the Fact*, we know that Lina will, after eight years of marriage, discover that Johnnie is a murderer; but in the bulk of the book she is unaware of his cor-ruption, and we wonder how she will eventually discover it. Similarly, *Rebecca* begins with the couple's marriage already gone flat. In the opening of *To the Gallows I Must Go*, the narrator declares that he has committed murder, but in the early phases of the action he presents himself as not knowing where his illicit affair is leading. Very often, thriller suspense presses us to ask not what would happen but *how* it will happen—and what might happen after that.

Showing Us the Bomb, or Not

Hitchcock's interest in the principles of the thriller followed naturally from his practice. He made an old-dark-house thriller (*Number Seventeen*, 1932), a straight spy story (*Secret Agent*, 1936), chase thrillers from the standpoint of the pursued (*The 39 Steps*, 1935; *Young and Innocent*, 1937), and a chase thriller from the standpoint of the pursuers (*The Man Who Knew Too Much*, 1934). He directed two bystander thrillers (*The Lodger*, 1927; *The Lady Vanishes*, 1938). He could also tell a story largely from the standpoint of the guilty party (*Black-mail*, 1929). *Sabotage* (1936) starts as a criminal-centered plot and becomes a victim-centered one. *Jamaica Inn* (1939) is a historical thriller that incorporates some pursuit and women-in-peril elements.[65]

By the time Hitchcock left England for Hollywood, he was thoroughly iden-tified as a (if not yet *the*) "master of suspense."[66] An American critic observed soon after his arrival: "More than any other director in motion pictures, Alfred Hitchcock has staked his career on suspense. . . . Each of these British-made thrillers that built up his tremendous reputation was a separate and unique study in suspense."[67] In the United States, his debt to the British tradition yielded adaptations of two woman-in-peril milestones: *Rebecca* (1940) and *Sus-picion* (1941, drawn from *Before the Fact*). Later he would return to the English psychological thriller canon for *Rope* (1948).[68]

One-quarter of 1930s British features were crime stories, and many talented directors made them.[69] Yet Hitchcock's stood out, and they helped define what the film thriller would be in years to come. He accepted all the strategies of the genre: well-timed limitations on characters' knowledge and close attachment to them at moments of risk—all within a moving-spotlight narration that gave just enough information to indicate dangers that the characters didn't fully grasp.

One of Hitchcock's accomplishments was showing how techniques of view-point manipulation characteristic of the written psychological thriller could be manifested in the fine grain of the film medium. From moment to moment, he calibrated minute shifts among curiosity, suspense, and surprise. These strategies were treated with a cinematic élan seldom seen in his contemporaries.

The first step was to center the story on more or less ordinary protagonists. The people plunged into international intrigue aren't spies. Hitchcock's Richard Hannay in *The 39 Steps* isn't yet the professional he would become in the novels, and *Secret Agent*'s Ashenden, a reluctant recruit, quits after his first assignment. Adapting a convention of gynocentric thrillers, Hitchcock and his scenarists go on to develop a romantic couple, the better to increase audience sympathy. Hitchcock's version of *The Lodger* created a love interest that exonerated Mr. Sleuth and provided a happy ending. A plot of pursuit could throw a man and a woman together (e.g., *Young and Innocent*), and a couple's marriage might be reaffirmed by their plunge into danger (*The Man Who Knew Too Much*) or destroyed by it (*Sabotage*).

Similarly, Hitchcock believed that the thriller could engage audiences through a range of emotions, so he usually included comic interludes. Some were mere byplay, but some could be integrated into the action. In *Murder!* (1930), his one foray into a straight puzzle plot, he enlivened the standard interrogation scene by showing a policeman questioning actors waiting in the wings during a performance. Obeying the principles of fair play, this scene plants crucial information about the solution, but the actors' business helps it slip by (fig. 5.9).

Likewise, the epilogue of *Sabotage* might have been grim. Mrs. Verloc's little brother has been killed, and she has slain her husband. But the final line is a gag: a bemused police official can't recall the evidence that would solve the case. The last shot of *The 39 Steps* gives the conventional romantic reconciliation a witty twist (fig. 5.10). Hitchcock's tongue-in-cheek moments displayed the sardonic cheerfulness of *Malice Aforethought* and *The Murder of My Aunt*.

5.9 *Murder!* (1930): The testimony the actors supply is swamped by their bustling on and off stage and slipping into and out of their stage roles.

5.10 *The 39 Steps*: Hannay and Pamela clasp hands, but the handcuffs remind us of their comic conjoining during their adventure.

Hitchcock was able to develop fine-grained techniques of narration by borrowing schemas from the artistically ambitious silent cinema. Many filmmakers, notably the French Impressionists, had showed how to build scenes around subjective states. Hitchcock had no compunction about using optical point-of-view shots, distorted perceptions, and mental imagery. The famous transparent ceiling of *The Lodger*, aiming to convey the sound of Mr. Sleuth's steps above, is an outré example, but the later sound films still played with subjective states. In *Sabotage* (1936), the hesitant spy Verloc imagines the devastating results of his mission (fig. 5.11).

Just as important were passages of rapid or abstract cutting, a technique refined by French directors such as Abel Gance and brought to a pitch of

5.11 *Sabotage* (1936): Verloc glances at an aquarium, which he imagines as Piccadilly Circus collapsing under the bomb he must deliver.

intensity by 1920s Soviet filmmakers. This aggressive editing could create panoramic narration, such as the citywide montages opening *The Lodger* and *Sabotage*, or could plunge into subjectivity, as in *Sabotage*'s rapid shots of Verloc and his wife glancing at the carving knife. Hitchcock's debt to German cinema showed up less in Expressionistic touches (although *Number Seventeen* has them, and mocks them) than in the German "*entfesselte*" or "unchained" camera. Many Hitchcock films contain vigorous camera movements, with the most famous being the remarkable crane movement across a hotel restaurant in *Young and Innocent*. It carries us away from the characters looking for a man who blinks uncontrollably to an extreme close-up of the band's drummer, just as he starts spasmodically blinking. In effect, we have seen the bomb under the table, revealed with an impresario's pleasure in flaunting his skill.

Like other ambitious filmmakers, Hitchcock wanted to go beyond the theatrical dialogue of the "talkies" and create complex audiovisual effects. The "knife" refrain in *Blackmail*, another attempt to convey subjectivity, is the most famous example, but Hitchcock often relies on music and noise, without words. The Soviet filmmakers' call for "audio-visual counterpoint" is realized in scenes like that of *Secret Agent*'s alpine assassination, which is accompanied by the sound of the victim's dog whimpering back at the hotel, as if mourning his master. This is "pure cinema," achieving something possible in no other medium.

Oscillating between subjectivity and objectivity, the narration can narrow or expand our knowledge by small degrees. Early in the train trip of *The Lady Vanishes*, Miss Froy writes her name on the window (fig. 5.12). Later, after everyone has denied that Miss Froy was ever on the train, Iris and Gilbert sit at the same table and her name remains visible (fig. 5.13). It confirms Iris's story, but will she notice it? This, another bomb under the table, is a subtle variant on the use of the background figures in *Kind Lady*. The next few shots offer a lesson in the swift suspense/surprise alternation that Brander Matthews admired in *Cromwell* (figs. 5.14–5.18).

"Pure cinema," of both sound and image, encouraged Hitchcock to seek occasions to display technical virtuosity. The "knife" sound montage and the suspenseful camera movement across the restaurant provide good examples. The result was a cinema of flourishes and set pieces, detachable moments that could become as famous as Eisenstein's Odessa Steps sequence in *Potemkin* (1925). Hitchcock often conceived a film as a series of high points, pinnacles of emotion and cinematic technique. His virtuosity was akin to the ingenuity flaunted by Golden Age puzzle novels.

But how to weave one-off effects and set pieces into a smooth story? Hitchcock's scriptwriters were frustrated. Raymond Chandler complained: "He directs a film in his head before he knows what the story is. You find yourself trying to rationalize the shots he wants to make rather than the story. Every

5.12 *The Lady Vanishes* (1938): Mrs. Froy writes her name on the window.

5.13 After Gilbert lowers the window, "Froy" remains visible in frame center. He looks beyond it, and Iris doesn't notice.

5.14 Hitchcock sustains the suspense for two minutes as Iris and Gilbert chat and flirt. Then Iris glances at the window, stares a moment, and starts.

5.15 Hitchcock delays a point-of-view shot with an insert of Gilbert reacting to her.

5.16 We get her point-of-view shot as Iris urges him to look.

5.17 But the train goes into a tunnel . . .

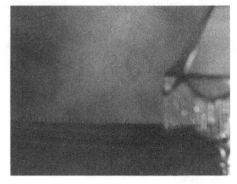

5.18 . . . and the smoke wipes away the name before Gilbert can see it.

time you get set he jabs you off balance by wanting to do a love scene on top of the Jefferson Memorial or something like that."[70]

Charles Bennett, who recalled that Hitchcock tended toward "a mosaic of vignettes," took on the role of "constructionist," the collaborator who faced the problem of "how the hell to get his ideas into the picture."[71] It's likely that Alma Reville Hitchcock and Joan Harrison, often uncredited decision-makers in the process, also helped find ways to stitch together the set pieces.[72]

Whoever was responsible, most of the films have an organic shape, often derived from simple itineraries. Adhering to the investigation plot, several of the films follow a quest pattern. A master clue or a string of clues carries the protagonists from one place to another. A mysterious message in *The Man Who Knew Too Much* provides an itinerary taking us to a dentist, the temple of the Rising Sun, and the Albert Hall. *Young and Innocent* has a clue sequence linking a raincoat, a hat, a belt, and a matchbook. Each way station offers a possible set piece: Hannay's political speech in *The 39 Steps*, the invasion of a little girl's birthday party in *Young and Innocent*, and the plan for the assassination in *Secret Agent*.

Something like this clue ladder is at work in the further development of the *Lady Vanishes* intrigue. During the first scene at the table, Miss Froy had demanded that the waiter make tea from her personal packet. In the sequence we've examined, Iris's recalling the lady's tea order primes her to glance at the window and see the FROY scrawl. Still later, Gilbert is glancing out the train window, and we swiftly alternate between his viewpoint and our superior knowledge (figs. 5.19–5.25). By now, a filmmaker can refine the point-of-view cutting schema developed in 1910s films such as *The Masked Heart* (see figs. 1.9–1.14).

The two major set pieces in *The Man Who Knew Too Much* depend on minute adjustments in the flow of information. When Jill goes to the Albert Hall,

5.19 *The Lady Vanishes*: Gilbert happens to be near a window.

5.20 Cut to the cook throwing out trash.

5.21 Cut to a shot of a train window, with the tea packet whirling up to stick on it. Does Gilbert see it?

5.22 Cut to Gilbert as he looks.

5.23 A quick point-of-view shot shows the brand name.

5.24 Then it whirls away in the wind.

5.25 Gilbert notices. This confirms Iris's story and puts Gilbert firmly on her side.

she knows very little. We know that Ramon the assassin is to wait for a dramatic pause in the score; it's followed by a shattering choral outburst that will muffle the pistol shot. We've been given a rehearsal of the passage in a gramophone record, but we don't hear the whole piece and can't predict exactly when the chorus will hit its peak. So we know more than Jill does, but not everything.

Hitchcock magnifies this uncertainty by letting the piece, Arthur Benjamin's *Storm Clouds Cantata*, play out in its entirety. It was composed for the film, and its combination of lyrical and dramatic passages blend into a stream of music that coincides with the emotional action on-screen. We have heard portions of the score earlier when the spies played a recording, so we have some sense of when the shot must be fired. Hitchcock goes on to structure the concert scene using nearly every technique in the silent cinema playbook. We get dynamically accentuated compositions, crisp point-of-view editing, subjective vision (even blurring as Jill drifts into a panicky reverie), and suspenseful crosscutting back to the gang holding Bob and Betty prisoner. All of these visual techniques are synchronized with the musical structure of the piece. Most obvious is the slow tracking shot back from Jill as the female soloist launches into "There came a whispered terror on the breeze. And the dark forest shook."

The techniques build to their own crescendo, with more and shorter shots of Jill, the orchestra players, and the curtain concealing Ramon. As the climax approaches, details of the players' performance pass in a flash. Then Jill notices the muzzle of Ramon's rifle, and she realizes that the diplomat is the target. She jumps to her feet and screams. A cut to the gang listening on the radio suppresses the result: Did Ramon's shot hit home? The narration postpones telling us for a time, dwelling instead on Jill's leading the police in their pursuit.

The same rapid shifts between suspense and surprise take place during the siege in the denouement. With Ramon edging out on the roof to grab Betty, the police sniper doesn't dare to fire. Hitchcock supplies a brisk set of interruptive cuts, culminating in Jill bringing Ramon down. It's no one-off flourish, because this moment gives her a second chance at the rifle competition she lost in the opening of the film (due, ironically, to Betty being distracting). The family is reunited in a symmetrical ending. The film's first line, "Are you all right?," is matched by the final moment of Jill reassuring Betty: "It's all right." The set pieces are smoothly integrated in a larger narrative arc.[73]

Through self-conscious style and clever plotting, Hitchcock's films became models of suspenseful film narration. In England he relied mostly on tales of pursuit and espionage, but he would soon provide prototypes of the domestic thriller with *Rebecca, Suspicion*, and *Shadow of a Doubt*. Eventually he would explore fine-grain fluctuations of rigorously restricted viewpoint in *Rear Window* (1954), a cinematic approximation of James's "In the Cage."

✳ ✳ ✳

Golden Age detective writers, at pains to elevate their genre, initially tended to minimize the vigor of the psychological thriller. But from *The Lodger* through *Before the Fact* to *Rebecca*, there was no denying the power and popularity of a genre that wed mystery to suspense, curiosity to apprehension and peril. In what Sayers called "studies in murder," ordinary men and women, victimizer or victim, faced danger and felt fear. All media welcomed these modern versions of Gothic and sensation fiction.

As investigation plots inspired Faulkner and other "literary authors" to cross over, psychological thrillers yielded access to wider audiences. Graham Greene's "entertainments" about paid killers and men on the run received serious attention. Nabokov, who had mocked the whodunit in *The Real Life of Sebastian Knight*, deployed schemas associated with the thriller in *Lolita* (1955). The first half parodies the murderous-husband plot, incorporating diary entries, courtroom theatrics, and hypothesized methods of murder (drowning, poisoning). Here, though, the reward isn't money or position but access to the wife's preteen daughter. When the treasure is attained, the tension doesn't slacken: the novel's second half summons up a couple-in-flight schema. Pursued by the ominously named Trapp, Humbert and Lolita traverse Highway America before a fateful showdown with a mastermind. The protagonist's confession, alternating between reckless boasts and mental crackup and prefaced by the obligatory clinical foreword, echoes Horniman's *Israel Rank*, Ostrander's *Ashes to Ashes*, and other books tracing a killer's tortuous path to doom. *American Psycho* (1991) would take it from there: an investment banker can be as terrifying as a pedophile.

By the end of the 1930s, the cerebral whodunit had a robust rival in the thriller. At the same time, another rival flourished: the "impure" whodunit that treated the investigation plot in a manner called hard-boiled.

CHAPTER 6

DARK AND FULL OF BLOOD

Hard-Boiled Detection

I t's risky to look for watershed years, but the temptation is hard to resist when considering Anglo-American writing in 1929. That year saw publication of *The Sound and the Fury, A Farewell to Arms, Dodsworth, Passing, The Blacker the Berry, Is Sex Necessary?, Flowering Judas, Look Homeward, Angel,* and the English translation of *All Quiet on the Western Front.*

Crime and mystery didn't lag behind. In 1929 the play *Rope* and several noteworthy novels appeared: Anthony Berkeley's *Poisoned Chocolates Case,* S. S. Van Dine's *Scarab Murder Case,* Ellery Queen's debut of *The Roman Hat Mystery,* and W. R. Burnett's *Little Caesar.* Count Rex Stout's crossover thriller *How Like a God* as well. Above all, there were *Red Harvest* and *The Dain Curse.* These two books, and the three that Dashiell Hammett completed in the few years that followed, would be as influential as anything signed by Faulkner or Hemingway. They changed popular storytelling in ways that we are still learning to appreciate.[1]

Realism and Other Alibis

From 1922 on, Dashiell Hammett was chiefly associated with *The Black Mask* (later just *Black Mask*). This American pulp magazine published western, romance, and adventure stories but emphasized "hard-boiled" crime fiction.[2] This version of the detective genre, editor Joseph Shaw explained, "embodies mental and physical conflict in man's most violent moods."[3] At a minimum, a hard-boiled crime story would show tough protagonists battling police and racketeers. Mystery might be played down. Carroll John Daly, initially the favorite author of the magazine's fans, made his hero Race Williams nominally a private investigator, but Race declares, "Guns are my business—action my meat."[4]

As a result, hard-boiled private-eye fiction defined itself against the Golden Age norms. Race Williams scorns "storybook detectives," "these intellectual, scientific detectives who catch their man with a microscope and dust pan."[5] Hammett wrote parodies of deduction-based mysteries. In one O. Henryish exercise, a murderer thinks he'll go free if he arranges evidence to make himself the obvious suspect. Unfortunately, the cop had never read a detective story.[6]

Hammett had been an investigator for the Pinkerton National Detective Agency, and his experience became a selling point for his work. When he wrote reviews of detective novels, he usually dismissed them as ignorant of real-world crime. He mocked the Great Detective as a showoff who more often than not obstructed solid police work. For Hammett, fiction's crimes should be solved by modern procedures: tailing and stakeouts, questioning, bluffing, negotiation, squeezing information from snitches, and relying on experience in judging suspects' behavior.

Two conceptions of realism circulated in the *Black Mask* milieu: realism as the portrayal of gritty contemporary life, the urban jungle that Race Williams swaggers through, and realism as a faithful rendering of modern methods of lawbreaking and law enforcement. In 1946, Shaw's introduction to an anthology of hard-boiled stories invested the *Black Mask* school with a third notion of realism, one that seemed out of the reach of puzzle plots.

Shaw claimed that as editor he had encouraged the portrayal of "character and the problems inherent in human behavior. . . . recognizable human character in three-dimensional form."[7] He was, I think, taking his cue from "The Simple Art of Murder," the 1944 Raymond Chandler essay that proposed a poetics of the hard-boiled private-eye story. Chandler mocks Golden Age conventions as dull and deeply implausible. The characters are mere puppets for the plot. "The gradual elucidation of character," he notes, "is all the detective story has any right to be about."[8]

Shaw and Chandler were rewriting *Black Mask* history. It's difficult to see rich characterization in a Daly serial that Shaw praised in 1927 as "the best Race Williams story he's ever written."

> Two hands reached for my throat—and my right hand came up. Thick lips snarled, great teeth parted—and his mouth opened for the shout of triumph as those hands felt for my neck. And I fired my last shot—not into that generous bulk that had tempted me before, but straight into that red, yawning mouth. We'd see how his digestive system worked. . . .

He died funny. Yep, I got a laugh out of it; a weird, gurgling sort of laugh. His mouth seemed to close upon the bullet, as if he tried the taste of it—his arms still stretched toward me.[9]

Shaw added a macabre note: "You'll fairly eat it up."[10] But he included no Race Williams story in his 1946 anthology. By then Daly had fallen out of favor and was eking out an existence in lower-grade pulps.[11]

For decades elite literary critics had demoted plot and elevated characterization, "a certain concern with the psychological basis of action."[12] An appeal to rich characterization in the mystery, launched when Hammett's reputation was strong and Chandler's was on the rise, sought to endow hard-boiled writing with artistic respectability. No less than the Golden Age writers, the most ambitious *Black Mask* boys yearned for the respectability of *belles lettres*.

The publishing milieu helped them. The prestigious Knopf firm brought out Hammett, Chandler, and other hard-boiled novelists. Hammett confided to Blanche Knopf that he wanted to write a novel in stream of consciousness.[13] Chandler declared that by quality of writing—not only characterization but also linguistic style and a coherent, realistic worldview—the hard-boiled novel could acquire literary value. Still later, Ross Macdonald would model his fiction on current conceptions of myth and depth psychology and declare that he was simply writing novels, not mystery stories.

In the long run, the hard-boiled school's search for legitimacy succeeded, and the puzzle makers never achieved the literary veneration bestowed on Hammett, Chandler, and Macdonald. Academics began to study them, and their work remained constantly in print. S. S. Van Dine and Ellery Queen did not become canonized in the Library of America alongside Henry James and Saul Bellow, but the "Big Three" did. Later writers in their tradition, from David Goodis to Elmore Leonard, were accorded comparable prestige.

This legitimacy isn't due only to the inherent quality of these books. Hard-boiled fiction adheres to canons of psychological realism typical of the mainstream novel. Told in homogeneous first or third person, playing few tricks with time or viewpoint, avoiding the bookish lacework of the Golden Age tale, these novels fit comfortably into the Hemingway or John O'Hara vein of laconic American writing. In addition, the hard-boiled school evokes themes of urban malaise and personal alienation long welcomed by the literati. Chandler reminded the Golden Age writers that they lived in a corrupt city to which they paid no notice. The hard-boiled dick confronts the grim America of Naturalism. He exposes the social rot on display in Steffens's *Shame of the Cities*, Sinclair's *The Jungle*, Dreiser's *American Tragedy*, and proletarian novels. He walks the mean streets consoled by the knowledge that, for all his vulnerabilities, he is true to a moral code in a corrupt world. With no Watson to prompt us to admire him, he must win our respect through that masculine version of sentimentality presented as righteous professionalism. Chandler, more ready to swagger than Hammett, sums it up in a title, "Trouble Is My Business."[14]

In the *Black Mask* world, trouble meant a high body count. Race Williams's delight in punches and pistol blasts was the most celebratory version of a bloodthirstiness at odds with Golden Age gentility. In Raoul Whitfield's *Green Ice* (1930), three people are shot dead in the first sixteen pages, five more by the end of the book. Hammett's "The Big Knock-Over" (1927) claims fifty-eight corpses. Violence became a marketing tool, as when Knopf's advertisement for *Red Harvest* asserted that its "constant gunplay and murder and sudden death" added "an element of reality so harsh that it reads like the latest news from Chicago."[15]

Daly's description of shooting a man in the mouth shows that a more visceral appeal to brutal realism was operating as well. Hard-boiled writers dwelt on the manner of death. The British preferred poison, throttling, or clean blade work, but the hard-boiled Americans didn't shrink from grisly damage.

> Doolin could no longer see Halloran's face. He watched the knife near Martinelli's chest, slowly.
>
> Martinelli, some way, made a high piercing sound in his throat as the knife went into him. And again as Halloran withdrew the knife, pressed it in again slowly. Halloran did not stab mercifully on the left side, but on the right, puncturing the lung again and again, slowly. . . .
>
> Halloran suddenly released Martinelli, stepped back a pace. Martinelli's knees buckled, he sank slowly down, sat on the floor with his back against the wall, his legs out straight. He sucked in air in great rattling gasps, held both hands tightly against his chest, tightly against the shaft of the knife.
>
> He lifted his head and there was blood on his mouth. He laughed.[16]

A Van Dine novel, Hammett complained, completely misdescribed what would happen to a man's head when a .45 bullet hit it.[17] Massacres and gore gained a new saliency in American popular culture; the hard-boiled school left its legacy in the free fire zones and blood geysers of *The Wild Bunch* (1969) and *Reservoir Dogs* (1992).

Which is to say that, despite their realistic alibi, the hard-boiled tales created their own conventions. The pro forma bloodbaths pull in corrupt plutocrats, suave hoods, brash and sexy women, apelike bruisers, and other members of the repertory company. Endless cigarettes are lit, gestured with, stared at thoughtfully, and stubbed out; cigars too. Gallons of alcohol are consumed. The Golden Age detective might stumble into a mystery by many routes, but the private dick typically gets into the case by (a) visiting the client or (b) being visited by a client. Corpses are lying behind every door he might open, although he usually manages to slip away before the police arrive. He is knocked cold at least once per story, and despite doses of drugs and a few beatings he can recuperate and survive the climactic gunfight. Hammett admitted that Sam Spade was a fantasy figure, and Chandler acknowledged that when he was at a loss to write a scene, he simply had a man with a gun walk in.[18]

One of the most striking conventions of the hard-boiled school is its mockery of the way movies portrayed detection and gangland. Holmes, Craig Kennedy, and other transcendent detectives stalked through 1910s cinema, as did inquiry agents such as Nick Pinkerton. There were gangland films too, notably *Musketeers of Pig Alley* (1912), *Alias Jimmy Valentine* (1915), and *Underworld* (1927).[19] Borrowing from Damon Runyon and O. Henry, moviemakers introduced a wide audience to con games and crook slang. But the *Black Mask* boys scoffed at these gestures. A 1926 Hammett story maintains that a man running a motion picture theater has a distorted view of what actual crime is like. As you'd expect, Race Williams pours contempt on movie stars who pretend to be tough but actually rely on doubles to fight. By 1933, a character in Paul Cain's *Fast One* (1933) is astonished that a gunfight looks just like the movies, and a tough woman warns a thug: "You've seen too many gangster pictures."[20]

For all their authors' disdain for the puzzle tradition, hard-boiled detective stories rely on most of the conventions of the investigation plot. There is still a mystery, usually several. Blackmail, theft, revenge, sexual jealousy, greed, and fear of betrayal are the typical motives. Like the Great Detective, the hard-boiled sleuth goes from place to place questioning suspects, although the trip may be enlivened by atmospheric descriptions of rundown neighborhoods or California rainstorms. There are faked deaths, misidentified corpses, false identities, dying messages, physical clues, red herrings, disguises, cryptic letters, and least likely culprits. The fallible detective of Golden Age novels has a brother in the private dick who loses the man he's tailing or succumbs to a femme fatale or trusts a treacherous friend. And despite the demands for realism, plenty of coincidences are convenient. In a novel abounding in lucky accidents, Chandler's narrator accepts Aristotle's precept of occasional implausibility: "I guess it's a genuine coincidence. They do happen."[21]

The author will likely play fair by Detection Club rules, supplying all the information necessary to solving the puzzle. There will be a eureka moment, goaded by intuition and perhaps the half-memory of a hint that slipped by us. But as ever the detective's reasoning will be suppressed, even in a first-person account. At the end, he will expose the perpetrators and reconstruct the crime. Usually justice will be done, perhaps outside the law, when a final shootout may spare the need for judge and jury.

The hard-boiled tradition justified its conventions as heightened realism. That effect was helped by the downbeat romanticism and a criminal milieu different from that of the Golden Age puzzle. (The professional crooks encountered by Peter Wimsey and Philo Vance came as walk-ons among upper-crust suspects.) In addition, the pervasive violence is motivated by the threatening city.

The hard-boiled hero is a good detective but he is not a Great Detective. Just ask him. Hammett characterized the Pinkerton ideal as not "an erudite solver of riddles in the Sherlock Holmes manner" but rather "a hard and shifty fellow, able to take care of himself in any situation."[22] As a result, he becomes less primly virtuous than the Golden Age amateur or upright policeman. Anyone pitting himself against the underworld is likely to be a bit rough-edged.

As with modern Robin Hoods such as Raffles and the Saint, hard-boiled authors created a sliding scale of rogues. A 1933 article advised would-be pulp writers to make the protagonist's adversaries deeply wicked. "If the black is black enough, the white can be soiled. . . . The narrative actors [heroes] need only be forgivable to be acceptable for a 'pulp' story. Here, as in life, the motive is what really counts."[23] The tough but temperate Continental Op, the cautious and shrewd Sam Spade, and the ironically disenchanted knight errant Philip Marlowe, for all their faults, are less aggressively amoral than the forces that threaten them.

Central to this characterization is sex. Couples live together out of marriage, young people are on the make, and the hero is likely to sleep around. Hammett once introduced the creators of Ellery Queen to an audience: "Mr Queen, will you be good enough to explain your famous character's sex life, if any?"[24] Sam Spade is having an affair with his partner's wife, and he beds his new client Brigid. In *The Thin Man*, after wrestling a woman suspect, Nick Charles admits to Nora that he got "a little" erection from it.[25] Publisher Alfred Knopf realized that the scene helped sell the book and so ran a piously winking advertisement denying that the scene had any impact on the book's sales. "Twenty thousand people don't buy a book within three weeks to read a five word question." Knopf obligingly supplied the page number.[26]

Sex, like violence, enhanced realism, but it too became a convention. It could be stylized through bantering dialogue, such as Nora's question about Nick's arousal. Mickey Spillane would in the postwar era be called semipornographic, but a vein of the pulps called "spicy detective" stories had already featured steamier situations than did the more respectable *Black Mask*. Novels of the late 1930s and early 1940s canonized the leering account of female anatomy. Some samples:

> There was something about the feel of her naked flesh that made my fingers tingle. She let the front of her negligee come open pretty far. I could see plenty of interesting things under the thin silk.
>
> When she went limp he slipped his arm around her waist to keep her from sliding to the floor; she hung there with her head back and eyes closed, her breasts taut against the thin knit jacket of her sports outfit.
>
> Her breasts were nippled sharply against a white middy blouse.
>
> From the way her buttocks looked under the black silk dress, I knew she'd be good in bed.[27]

With passages like these in the opening pages, the books promise something more stimulating than ratiocination. By the 1950s, private eyes were forever encountering women in lingerie, bikinis, and bubble baths, and hymns to pulchritude became as compulsory as quatrains in a sonnet.

The American lone-wolf private-eye tale is driven by mystery, but its main plot movement is that of an adventure. This premise was recognized by practitioners quite early. A 1932 manual advises writers to "apply the technique of a straight adventure story to the detective or mystery angle."[28] An adventure turns an investigation into a quest, a search for a missing person or precious object. Likewise, an adventure entails physical action—tailing, pursuit, combat, capture, escape, and the inevitable knockout. The adventurer-hero is perpetually in danger. Unlike the Golden Age sleuth, the hard-boiled detective confronts harm or death directly and often. The man who comes in with a gun may use it. This constant threat is another factor throwing sympathy to an imperfect hero's occasional transgressions.

Why are hard-boiled plots so hard to follow, let alone remember? In part because of all the lying, but we get that in whodunits too. More markedly, hard-boiled plots tend to abandon the Golden Age tidiness of physical clues, timetables, and a closed circle of suspects. Instead we must keep track of secrets shared among a vast cast spread across an urban milieu. Authors revamped the nineteenth-century "city mystery" novel and the modernists' montage version of it by presenting a network of characters who are entangled in crimes large and small. Cain's *Fast One* introduces more than fifty characters, most with names. Sometimes key players never come onstage; call it the Floyd Thursby gambit.

Most novels in any genre tie the characters into an array of relationships. But classic whodunits are likely to confine themselves to the groups around a village (*Roger Ackroyd*) or in a workplace (*Murder Must Advertise*) or in a country house. By and large the connections are those of friendship, work, class, and kinship. The hard-boiled plot makes the network more contingent, as befits the casual encounters of city life. The sprawling network allows for happy coincidences, accidental moments of sighting a suspicious character or overhearing a crucial conversation. When the whodunit expands its network, most of the minor characters serve as witnesses or Jamesian *ficelles* (such as the secretarial staff of Pym's Publicity). In the hard-boiled story, apparently minor or late-introduced characters may come to play central roles. Above all, whereas the classic whodunit favored a single culprit behind all the crimes, the hard-boiled network could multiply perpetrators. Unlike a Golden Age tale, the hard-boiled plot is more likely to show lawlessness as pervading all social relations. The formal principle of the diffuse network has a thematic payoff: the wealthy and powerful are as corrupt as the gangsters they are tied to, however remotely.

Without benefit of the city novel's omniscient narrator or moving spotlight, we enter this network narrowly alongside an investigator with incomplete knowledge. He inches from one thread or node to another, and the confined viewpoint allows enigmas to cascade. Initial problems turn out to be pretexts, bait-and-switch devices leading to a larger, more dangerous puzzle. Thanks to the network principle, side hustles distract from primary story lines, and apparently unconnected characters get hooked up at the denouement. All of these knotty affiliations must be picked apart by a man who is lied to at every turn.

Into this fog of mystification, moment-by-moment verbal texture injects clear air. The plot may be complicated, but the style can be high school simple. At its most spare, as in W. R. Burnett's *Little Caesar*, the narration is bare bones. In other hands, this objectivity yields flourishes in dialogue and description. Laconic eloquence, wisecracks, and showy metaphors decorate the hard-boiled page. Granted, such offhand filigree looks more artificial than ordinary language. Chandler admitted that even the laconic Hammett offered readers "the kind of lingo they imagined they spoke themselves. . . . When [language] develops to the point of becoming a literary medium it only looks like speech."[29] Yet Chandler was also right to suggest that the puzzle plot could be revitalized with new stylistic conventions.

Networks and the Great Tradition

Novelists, editors, and critics have long stressed the originality of the hard-boiled worldview, but this campaign seems to me to have obscured the books' debts to tradition. Granted, the Race Williams strain sneers at the Golden Age conventions: "There might be a hundred clues around and I'd miss them. I've got to have a target to shoot at."[30]

In contrast, Hammett's stories follow the Conan Doyle model: the detective's investigation of a mystery leads to exciting action. From 1923 to 1927, as Hammett develops his craft in short stories, that action becomes even more complex. He starts putting major action offstage and letting his sleuth fill in the reader and his colleagues at judicious moments. "The Big Knock-Over" elides key events and includes some reported flashbacks, the better to dramatize major carnage at the climax, when the hero must fight his way through a speakeasy.

Despite the dynamic action, Hammett is at pains to include bouts of reasoning. His protagonist, the nameless Continental Op, explains that he enjoys "catching crooks and solving riddles."[31] One Hammett story is called "The Tenth Clew," and an action-packed siege tale climaxes when the Op runs through eleven inferences that led him to crack the crooks' scheme. Nor did Hammett dismiss the Golden Age rules. In his book reviews, he objected when clues were suppressed and plotting went slack, and he appreciated *The Roman Hat*

Mystery as "a competent piece of work for those who like their detective stories straight."[32] In his own work, Hammett wanted to preserve the investigation plot within a new set of conventions, those roughly called realism.

Hammett's novels provided a range of models for doing that. In the space of a few years, he opened a treasure house of storytelling possibilities. Five diverse novels crystallized templates that would be revived and revised in hundreds of mysteries that followed.

The most spectacular of these templates is the cleaning-up-the-town premise of *Red Harvest* (1929). Summoned to Personville, nicknamed Poisonville, the Continental Op learns that the man who hired him has been murdered. The Op finds the city corrupt from top to bottom, and soon he vows to wipe out the gangs that have flourished under the oligarch Elihu Person. The Op solves the murder quickly enough, but in the rest of the book he sets mobster against mobster by shifting his loyalty and gathering evidence against them. Hammett had explored this scale of urban upheaval in some short stories, but as a *Black Mask* serial, *Red Harvest* seemed somewhat choppy. His editors at Knopf urged him to weave a more cohesive plot, so he tightened its structure by setting up the gang combats as tit-for-tat reprisals. At one point the Op assembles the adversaries in a fake peace conference, sowing suspicions that should, he estimates, yield "at least a dozen killings."

The Op's schemes pull in nearly fifty characters, most of them named and described. In gunfights, chases, bombings, and other bursts of wildly thrilling violence, about twenty of the major players are killed, along with innumerable walk-ons. The Op's provocations in turn create ancillary mysteries. These are clued in traditional ways: an ambiguous dying message, telltale bank checks and blackmail letters, and a victim's memo book full of secrets. As solutions are revealed, multiple perpetrators come to light.

Hammett realized the narrative resources of the heavily populated plot. News can travel along the network, so a detective can pick up information from press reports or informers. Clues that Golden Age authors would concentrate in a single crime scene can be scattered across the hidden network. Often the detective solves the mystery by concluding that X must be guilty because he or she has said or done something that's out of keeping with X's range of knowledge. The Golden Age reader needs to be alert for physical traces and alibis, whereas the hard-boiled plot demands that we keep track of who knows what, and how she or he could have learned it.

In addition, sprawling networks foster convenient coincidences. The decentralized plotting of many hard-boiled novels, with their expanding tendrils of secret allegiances and kinship, demands scenes that bring characters together fortuitously. In *Red Harvest*, when the Op isn't headed to meet someone, he hits the street or drops in at a pool hall and runs into someone who can advance his cause.

At the center of the Personville web is the young Dinah Brand, whom the plot gradually reveals as sexually involved with nearly all the men running the city. The Op induces her to help him clean up the town, but she too is killed. The Op finds himself the prime suspect in her death, and to expose the real killer he must force a final showdown between the two surviving mob leaders. In passing, the Op learns that his partner Dick Foley suspects he's guilty. It is a brief moment, but it initiates the theme of male trust that will become important throughout the following novels.

Hammett seems to have conceived the Op as the anti–Race Williams. He's chubby, forty years old, and a mere five foot six. He's tough and shoots straight, and he can punch, although sometimes clumsily. But he's not sadistic and prefers cunning to gunplay. Above all, he's got qualms. As the bodies pile up in *Red Harvest*, he confesses to Dinah that he's going "blood-simple." He could have reasoned with the gangs, but instead he has betrayed his professional ethos and set them to slaughtering each other. He's enjoying it. "It's easier to have them killed off, easier and surer, and now that I'm feeling this way, more satisfying. I don't know how I'm going to come out with the Agency. The Old Man will boil me in oil if he ever finds out what I've been doing. It's this damned town. Poisonville is right. It's poisoned me."[33] After this confession, he passes out on a mixture of gin and laudanum. He will wake up clutching an ice pick buried in Dinah's left breast.

As if Poisonville has purged him, the Op is comparatively chastened and cautious in *The Dain Curse* (1929). The theft of some diamonds brings him into contact with the Leggetts, whose daughter Gabrielle fears that she inherits a homicidal madness from her mother's bloodline. Everyone around her—father, mother, husband, servants, guru—winds up killed or damaged. The Op's urban adventure leads to two car crashes, a kidnapping, several homicides, a bombing, and a protracted cure for Gabrielle's morphine addiction. Harking back to sensation fiction, a spiritualist temple plays host to hypnosis and menacing ectoplasm.

Prefiguring Ross Macdonald's compassionate Lew Archer, the Op must play therapist. In a long scene, he tries to reassure Gabrielle that she's not cursed but rather the victim of a devious conspiracy. Ironically, there is indeed a sort of curse: the conspirator turns out to be another Dain, and insane to boot. But the book closes on a happy ending, with the suggestion that the Op's treatment has turned Gabrielle from a nearly feral girl into a woman ready for a mature marriage.

The Dain Curse exploits the network principle with a vengeance. More than sixty named characters generate multiple identities, delays, red herrings, concealed pasts, a fake suicide, collateral killings, and widespread suspicions. The network also permits several perpetrators to replace the single culprit, although here they are mostly cat's-paws. Again, Hammett's editor had asked that the sections of the *Black Mask* serialization be more smoothly integrated, and Hammett obliged by providing a recurring character who connects all the crimes and conceives most of them.[34]

As if to trim back the ramifying relationships, Hammett breaks the novel into three blocks. This device lets him impose a strict pattern of new crimes and false solutions as the Dain curse emerges in waves. Within each block of chapters, the Op and other characters float several alternative explanations, but answers seem to coalesce at the end of each block when the Op reviews the action with the novelist Owen Fitzstephan. Each session seems to clear up the mystery so far. It's a more relaxed, hard-boiled equivalent of the stacked explanations seen in *The Poisoned Chocolates Case*.[35]

Each of the three solutions turns out to be false. In the climactic chapter "Confessional," Gabrielle declares that she is the mastermind, putting her confession in parallel with the two earlier bursts of explanation. But the Op dismisses her fantasy and turns to Fitzstephan, now maimed by a bomb blast. Throughout the book, Fitzstephan has presented himself as the refined artist, a witty expositor and eager helper. As a victim, he seems ruled out as a suspect. But he's the puppeteer, manipulating everyone to get sexual access to Gabrielle. When the Op unmasks him in a fourth encompassing solution, Fitzstephan immediately announces that he'll plead insanity. The Op agrees that it's the right defense. The novelist is indignant: "It's no fun if I'm really cracked."[36]

Hammett's commitment to the formal rigor of the genre emerges in other ways. The exhumation of the Dains' perverse past recalls Doyle's lumps of backstory in *A Study in Scarlet* and *The Sign of Four*. By making the killer the Op's confidante, the nearest thing he has to a Watson, Hammett pays tribute to the least-likely-person convention. What adds the hard-boiled flavor is the personal betrayal: Fitzstephan has violated the code of male friendship.

Much more charismatic than the Op is Sam Spade, the "blond Satan." Spade, his author confesses, is a "dream-man," an ideal of the Pinkerton agents Hammett knew, and he has the profile of the cynical urban corsair.[37] If *Red Harvest* owes something to the classic scheming-servant plot, particularly Goldoni's *Servant of Two Masters* (1746), *The Maltese Falcon* (1930) shows the hard-boiled school's debt to primal quest stories. Ellery Queen pointed out that the search for the Black Bird is a tough-guy updating of a treasure hunt, "as romantic as *The Moonstone* or *The Rajah's Diamond*."[38] The murders that launch the plot are, like the murder at the beginning of *Red Harvest*, a call to adventure.

Spade's partner Archer is shot on assignment. At first Spade is in no hurry to investigate, but he falls under suspicion for the crime because he's been having an affair with Archer's wife Iva. Since the cops can't find Miles's killer, he must.

In addition, the man Archer was shadowing, Floyd Thursby, has been killed. After the client, Brigid O'Shaughnessy, spins a series of false stories, Spade discloses her actual mission: the recovery of the jewel-encrusted falcon statuette.

In the distant backstory, Brigid was part of a gang aiming to steal the falcon from its owner in Constantinople, but the gang split up and now her former partners are after her. She has made arrangements for the bird to be brought to San Francisco on a ship from Hong Kong, so she needs to stay safe until Captain Jacobi delivers it. He will be the third murder victim.

All of this is gradually revealed through Spade's encounters with Brigid and the gang: the jovial Casper Gutman, his daughter Rhea, Gutman's gunman Wilmer, and the dandy Joel Cairo. The searchers decide to cooperate and agree to cut Spade in if he can help them get the treasure. Spade's larger goal, because he finds Brigid attractive, is to meet her demand to "save me from—from it all."[39] So the quest includes a knightly effort to protect a fair lady—or rather, a tarnished one.

The *Maltese Falcon* network is rather limited (only eighteen characters), but Hammett keeps the action moving by shuttling between the investigation of Archer's death and the efforts to retrieve the statuette. This allows him to juggle multiple suspects. Did Iva kill Archer? Did Wilmer? Thursby? And who killed Thursby? Wilmer, Cairo, or someone else? The confinement to one viewpoint allows Hammett to dole out information sparingly; not for many chapters does Spade learn whether the same gun killed the two men. As if in deliberate contrast to the first two novels, virtually all the violence and many important scenes take place offstage. This puts the emphasis on Spade's resourceful reactions to changing situations, which include the possibilities that characters are lying. Indeed, every major character, including Spade, lies to others. Eventually, we learn that the two initial murders were committed by separate killers.

Again Hammett respects many rules of the game. A theater ticket and a shipping list torn from a newspaper become clues. The book is padded with a red herring, a gambler's revenge scenario tied to Thursby's past. Hammett revises another convention when Spade plans to cast a fall guy for the police to charge; in effect, the detective sets up the false solution.

Hammett also shows himself adept in hiding information in plain sight. In a page thick with descriptions of Spade searching Brigid's apartment, we get this: "He did not find the black bird. He found nothing that seemed to have any connection with a black bird. The only piece of writing he found was a week-old receipt for the month's apartment-rent Brigid O'Shaugnessy had paid. The only thing he found that interested him enough to delay his search while he looked at it was a double-handful of rather fine jewelry in a polychrome box in a locked dressing-table-drawer."[40] The jewelry, although emphasized, is actually not important, but the casually mentioned receipt is. Spade reveals at the climax that Brigid had secured the apartment five or six days before she told him she rented it. (Fair play at work: we have to remember the date she gave him.) That allowed her to prepare to frame Thursby for the killing of Archer—or of Spade, if he had been the partner who took her assignment.

Ultimately, the falcon quest proves futile, and the climax pivots on solving the initial murders. Thursby was killed by Wilmer, and Archer was killed by Brigid. Only one question remains: Will Sam turn Brigid over to the police? Yes. He itemizes the reasons with forensic clarity. First, he owes fidelity to his partner, if not out of liking then as a bond of professional conduct. Second, he can't trust her; she has lied to him ceaselessly. Third, he can live with losing her. Mr. Flitcraft, in the parable Spade recounted early in the book, radically changed his life but wound up adapting to new circumstances as mundane as the life he gave up. Spade too will adjust. Finally, Brigid has counted on being able to inveigle him, and others.

"I won't play the sap for you."[41] No more important scene has ever been played in the canon of detective fiction. Hammett's plot has built to a statement of an ethos grounded in professional duty and clear-eyed calculation of risk, framed by a pragmatic recognition of the need to survive. The Pinkertons' dream man is a cautious but principled hero. Spade's statement of hard-boiled morality rings through decades of private-eye sagas, and it would be elaborated, lyrically and philosophically, by Chandler, Macdonald, and many others.

The plot of *The Glass Key* (1931) inverts the dynamic of *Red Harvest*. There a murder triggered a gang war. Here the struggle for political power initially sidelines the mystery of who killed young Taylor Henry in China Street. In the Poisonville caper, an outsider turned a town upside down, but here an insider does. Central to that process is the ethos of masculine loyalty.

Against the advice of his friend and fixer Ned Beaumont, the political boss Paul Madvig seeks Senator Henry's support. He also hopes to marry the senator's daughter Janet. When Paul decides to attack his rivals just before the election, Ned apparently breaks with him. Ned seems ready to join Shad O'Rory's gang, but he refuses to betray Paul's plans. After some savage beatings that Ned barely survives, he continues to defend his friend by blocking Shad's efforts to influence the local press.

Ned's sacrifices seem in vain when Paul becomes the prime suspect in the murder. But Ned declares he will defend him "no matter who he killed."[42] His path becomes more difficult when Paul casually confesses to the murder. So great is Ned's trust that he refuses to believe him: If Paul had killed Taylor, he would have told Ned sooner. This is the sort of behavioral reasoning that hard-boiled authors hoped would replace traditional physical clues. "I'm only an amateur detective," Ned explains, but he insists that Paul must be protecting someone else out of loyalty, as Ned has been protecting Paul. With Janet, who has come to hate Paul, Ned investigates.[43]

The Glass Key's teeming political and gangland conflicts, stretching across more than fifty named characters, distract us from just how minimal the central mystery is. Hammett shamelessly pads the puzzle plot with a bookie, a mistress, and other ancillary suspects, as well as a string of poison-pen letters.

As in *The Maltese Falcon*, basic information is doled out slowly, with the central crime coming into focus only halfway through. Some eyewitnesses step onstage rather late, as does the least likely culprit. The mystery is solved thanks to the paraphernalia of traditional whodunits. Ned spots two clues missing from the crime scene, a hat and a walking stick, and he rouses a reliable half-memory ("It's been in the back of my head for a long time").[44]

The braided plotlines keep returning to the unspoken forces binding two men. Ned acknowledges his own corruption and solitude; Paul seems to be his only friend. In the final scene, their friendship comes undone, yielding the "novel of character" that many mystery writers hoped could transform the mystery story.

Hammett called *The Thin Man* (1934) "the nearest thing to a straight detective story I've done," and it's hard to disagree.[45] Through his social circle Nick Charles, retired detective, is drawn into a case of disappearance and murder. As narrator and reluctant investigator, Nick is fairly passive, drifting at several removes from the action. Only after being wounded by a gunshot and becoming a suspect does he take action. Once he gets involved, he circulates as comfortably as Wimsey or Poirot between suspects and police. He even has friends in the underworld.

After four novels, Hammett is able to map the network principle onto a traditional whodunit situation. Nick and Nora are swept into a froth of wealthy idlers and picturesque thugs. There are thirty-five named characters, seven never seen. (To add to the confusion, two are called Alice.) The multiplicity permits false identities and dead-ends to proliferate, as well as comic coincidences. Eventually the circle of likely suspects is as tight as in a Christie country weekend, with Nick as the link among a half-dozen candidates. As in *The Dain Curse*, Hammett exploits the tainted-family theme. The eccentric inventor Wynant is considered insane, and his son and daughter worry about whether their problems come from him. "They're all sex-crazy," Nick says.[46]

As a man of leisure, Nick is practically an armchair detective in the first half of the book. The plot is driven by offstage action, delivered to him via newspaper bulletins, policemen's reports, and an average of one phone call per chapter. There are physical clues, notably a bloody watch chain and a bullet-shattered phone receiver. There's the standard reference to Golden Age conventions when Nora asks how a detective solves a crime and Nick replies that the formula doesn't work in real life.

In obeisance to tradition, not only does Nick keep his conclusions to himself, but he conceals the culprit through shrewd narration. The killer is Herbert Macaulay, the attorney for the missing inventor Clyde Wynant. Nick introduces Macaulay as a helper and provides an appealing first impression of him. He is, Nick tells Nora, a pretty good guy, and the family dog Asta likes him. When Nora rules out Macaulay as a suspect, Nick doesn't correct her. Very late in the plot, Macaulay tells Nora that Nick saved his life in army combat. That seems to exempt him from suspicion but also provides a hint: Nick knows that Macaulay is a poor marksman and could have accidentally hit the phone receiver when he shot his confederate. The theme of the treacherous friend is made explicit in a long extract about cannibalism among men in a Colorado expedition, a literary tipoff as self-conscious as any classical citation in a British whodunit.

Nora calls Nick's solution pretty loose, and the relaxed plotting backs her up. But Hammett's emphasis is on the flow of witty banter. With *The Thin Man*, Hammett blends high-society mystery with sophisticated comedy. Interrogation and reasoning are replaced by repartee, some of it fairly naughty, with references to impotence, incest, and men chasing whatever is "hot and hollow." The crosstalk is blatantly theatrical, or rather cinematic. It's easy to visualize this taxicab trip in screenplay format.

> Nora said: "That booze." She put her head on my shoulder. "Your wife is drunk. Listen, you've got to tell me what happened—everything. Not now, tomorrow. I don't understand a thing that was said, or a thing that was done. They're marvelous."
>
> Dorothy said: "Listen, I can't go to Aunt Alice's like this. She'd have a fit."
>
> Nora said: "They oughtn't to have hit that fat man like that, though it must've been funny in a cruel way."
>
> Dorothy said: "I suppose I'd better go to Mamma's."
>
> Nora said: "Erysipelas hasn't got anything to do with ears. What's a lug, Nicky?"
>
> "An ear."
>
> Dorothy said: "Aunt Alice would have to see me because I forgot the key and I'd have to wake her up."
>
> Nora said: "I love you, Nicky, because you smell nice and know such fascinating people."[47]

Hammett worked in Hollywood in 1930–31, when filmmakers were striving to make snappy talking pictures. Inspired by the 1928 play *The Front Page*, screenwriters sought to build scenes out of rapid-fire wisecracks and non sequiturs. Hammett would surely have noticed the verbal fireworks on display in the adaptations of *The Front Page* (1931) and *Grand Hotel* (1932), along with such risqué films as *Rain* (1932) and *She Done Him Wrong* (1933). Plays such as *Holiday* (1928) and *The Greeks Had a Word for It* (1930) and films such as *No More Orchids* (1932) brought together heiresses, glamour girls, gamblers, and society gents in love affairs, sometimes complicated by gangland intrigue. Similarly, the racy socialites of Thorne Smith, Noël Coward, and other writers look forward to Hammett's tipsy couples.[48]

Hammett's talents suited him to the new trends, and his screenplay work gained a reputation for ingenious plots and witty dialogue.[49] He seems to have designed *The Thin Man* to suit the current tastes in screwball comedy. Several scenes, notably the fight in the Pigiron Club and the patter of the dumb cop Flint, supply pure movie moments. Some of the salty dialogue ("There's a woman with hair on her chest") was retained in the 1934 film version, and the book's description of Nick glancing at Nora over Dorothy's shoulder gained a comic topper (figs. 6.1–6.3).

Hammett's five novels opened new horizons for popular narrative. *Red Harvest* provided a schema for the city-under-siege plot that would be recast in novels such as Richard Stark's *Butcher's Moon* (1974) and films such as *Yojimbo* (1961) and *A Fistful of Dollars* (1964). *The Dain Curse* offered an initial prototype of the straight private-eye investigation and introduced the sort of tangled California families on which Ross Macdonald would build his fame. With *The Glass Key*, the mystery novel showed it could play host to the tensions between personal obligation and political calculation characteristic of the "social novels" of Upton Sinclair. *The Thin Man* yielded a model for dozens of stories in which amused couples breeze through mayhem.

6.1 *The Thin Man* (1934): "Nora, coming in to answer the telephone, looked questioningly at me."

6.2 "I made a face at her over the girl's head."

6.3 The camera pans back to catch Nora making a face too.

Most archetypal was *The Maltese Falcon*, which set in place enduring plot schemas: the mysterious gang, the treacherous woman, the thugs' invasion of the detective's office, the nocturnal visit to an alley or pier to find a corpse. A book's opening became as stylized as a minuet. Either an anxious client strolls into the private-eye's office (wry secretary optional) or, as in *The Dain Curse*, he arrives at a wealthy home to fence with an overbearing client. Either way, the detective is launched on an adventure far more dangerous than it initially seems.

More broadly, these books were bids for artistic legitimacy. After *Red Harvest* was accepted by Knopf, Hammett vowed that he would "take the detective story seriously. . . . Some day somebody's going to make 'literature' of it, . . . and I'm selfish enough to have my hopes."[50] Very soon those hopes would be realized. *The Maltese Falcon* was rapturously reviewed, with one critic asserting: "This is not only probably the best detective story we have ever read, it is an exceedingly well written novel."[51] In 1934 the book was welcomed to the ranks of the Modern Library series. André Malraux, visiting the United States, insisted on meeting Hammett, and he recommended the novels to Gide, who read them with admiration. At Malraux's urging, a French publisher brought out translations.[52]

Hammett was aware that mystery plotting wasn't off-limits for more elevated fiction. In the letter to Knopf he noted, "Ford's *Good Soldier* wouldn't have need [sic] much altering to have been a detective story."[53] But he also realized that artistically ambitious novels demanded a rethinking of the role of language and the very texture of narration.

First-Person Impersonal

By the late 1920s, Golden Age whodunits were paralleling mainstream fiction in fracturing time lines and shifting perspectives. But the hard-boiled school committed itself to linearity, the scenic method, and the singular viewpoint. In his 1946 reflections on the trend, Joseph Shaw was as strict as any post-Jamesian critic. *Black Mask* authors "gave the story over to their characters, and kept themselves off the stage, as every writer of fiction should."[54] Hammett displays the resourcefulness and ingenuity of tightly attached narration. In the process, he brought to detective fiction strategies of radical objectivity that were part of an austere strain in modern literature.

The pulp default option is, as ever, exemplified by Carroll John Daly's protagonists. "The False Burton Combs" (1922), sometimes taken to be the earliest instance of hard-boiled crime fiction, evokes Ring Lardner in its use of slang and vernacular tense shifts. Soon enough, though, Daly carries first-person prose to a nearly hysterical pitch. "As he turned the handle I give it to him right through the heart. I don't miss at that range—no—not me."[55] The Race Williams stories that followed inflate the hero's prowess while also letting us

In on his thinking, such as it is. Race's inner monologues capture the turmoil of his thoughts, with Daly's much-loved dashes punctuating interruptions and digressions.

Hammett had tried out many narrative strategies in his early stories for magazines, both pulp and otherwise, but he established his authorial signature with first-person accounts of the nameless Continental Op.[56] This pudgy, prudent, middle-aged bachelor talks a modest, conversational Americanese.

> I am neither young enough nor old enough to get feverish over every woman who doesn't make me think being blind isn't so bad. I'm at that middle point around forty where a man puts other feminine qualities—amiability, for one—above beauty on his list. This brown woman annoyed me. She was too sure of herself. Her work was rough. She was trying to handle me as if I were a farmer boy. But in spite of all this, I'm constructed mostly of human ingredients. This woman got more than a stand-off when faces and bodies were dealt. I didn't like her. I hoped to throw her in the can before I was through. But I'd be a liar if I didn't admit that she had me stirred up inside— between her cuddling against me, giving me the come-on, and the brandy I had drunk.[57]

The Op's nervous oscillation between temptation and suspicion is a polar opposite to Race Williams's braggadocio. The brandy is a bonus, in case he has to justify succumbing to her.

The Op's action scenes have a curiously bemused quality. He shoots a pistol out of a man's hand. Race would have celebrated his marksmanship, but the Op reports: "Looks like a great stunt . . . but it's a thing that happens now and then." He adds that he is only a fair shot, "no more, no less." Violence is presented in brisk, offhand glimpses. A man is blasted. "Dummy Uhl—all the middle of him gone—slid down to the floor and made more of a puddle than a pile there." During a stairway shootout, the Op flees. "The other of the big man-eaters caught me—caught my plunging hundred and eighty-some pounds as a boy would catch a rubber ball."[58]

The deflationary accounts of action match the Op's sardonic sense of humor.

> "The face she made at me was probably meant for a smile. Whatever it was, it beat me. I was afraid she'd do it again, so I surrendered."
> "Hsiu sat on the bottom step, her head over her shoulder, experimenting with different sorts of yells and screams."
> [Thrown from a horse:] I took my knees off my forehead and stood up.
> [Facing a Chinese gunman who demands the Op's pistols:]
> "You give 'em," he said politely.
> I gave 'em. He could have had my pants.

The Op has a meta-awareness that Race quite lacks. He can address his reader ("write the rest of it yourself"), and he admits that this yarn-spinning owes nothing to refined literature. "According to the best dramatic rules, these folks should have made sarcastic speeches to me before they left, but they didn't."[59]

In the *Black Mask* stories, the Op freely shares professional tips and lets us into his thinking, while still obeying the genre demand that he withhold the clue spotting and reasoning that enables him to crack the case. One late story, "The Gutting of Coffignal" (1925), looks ahead to Sam Spade's professional ethos. In this tale of a ransacked city, the Op confronts the woman who has engineered it all. She offers him money. He refuses to be bought. He likes being a detective, "and liking work makes you want to do it as well as you can." She offers him more. "You can have whatever you ask."

> That was out. I don't know where these women get their ideas.
>
> "You're still all twisted up," I said brusquely, standing now and adjusting my borrowed crutch. "You think I'm a man and you're a woman. That's wrong. I'm a manhunter and you're something that has been running in front of me. There's nothing human about it. You might just as well expect a hound to play tiddly-winks with the fox he's caught."[60]

He's right to be cautious. She has simply been stalling until her confederate arrives. Like Brigid O'Shaughnessy, she can't be trusted.

Having given us the detective as *l'homme moyen sensuel*, Hammett begins to pull us away from his mental states. In the novels, the Op hides his inner life in favor of neutrally describing the action around him. He keeps secrets from the other characters and the reader, and usually we learn of his plans only when he shares them in conversation. "A notion stirred in my noodle. To give it time to crawl around, I said: 'Sit down. This needs talking over.'"[61] The Op's confession of going blood simple in *Red Harvest* and his explanation of how Gabrielle Leggett could break her morphine addiction emerge as earnest announcement, not inner monologue.

Instead of psychological analysis, the Op expends his verbal skills on performance. Here are the wisecracks, the similes, and the sour descriptions that Raymond Chandler would expand in baroque directions. A man puts "a thumb as big as a heel on a tongue like a bath-mat." A doper is "laudanumed to the scalp." "I didn't think he was funny, though he may have been." The Op's ironic self-awareness emerges in both action and report at the climax of *The Dain Curse*. Mrs. Haldorn is taller than the Op, so he needs clever moves to disarm her.

> I tucked my head under her chin, turned my hip to her before her knee came up, brought her body hard against mine with one arm around her, and bent

her gun-hand behind her. She dropped the gun as we fell. I was on top. I stayed there until I had found the gun. I was getting up when MacMan arrived.

"Everything's eggs in the coffee," I told him, having trouble with my voice.[62]

The Op unblinkingly reports the maneuver's somewhat clumsy finish as a series of abrupt sentences. His wobbliness (fear? embarrassment?) is given not through a confession but through an aside on his vocal delivery.

In *Red Harvest*'s most virtuoso gun battle, concrete actions—"trotted," "third step"—become crucial.

I was the first man out, with my eye on a dark alley entrance.

Fat followed me to it. In my shelter, I turned on him and growled:

"Don't pile up on me. Pick your own hole. There's a cellarway that looks good."

He agreeably trotted off toward it, and was shot down at his third step.[63]

The Op lightning-sketches a car casually loading up with gunmen, plowing over a corpse, and hurtling toward an ambush.

The other machine slowed up for us to climb aboard. It was already full. We packed it in layers, with the overflow hanging on the running board.

We bumped over dead Hank O'Marra's legs and headed for home. We covered one block of the distance with safety if not comfort. After that we had neither.

A limousine turned into the street ahead of us, came half a block toward us, put its side to us, and stopped. Out of the side, gun-fire.

Another car came around the limousine and charged us. Out of it, gun-fire.

We did our best, but we were too damned amalgamated for good fighting. You can't shoot straight holding a man in your lap, another hanging on your shoulder, while a third does his shooting from an inch behind your ear.[64]

With no time to spare for verbs ("Out of the side, gun-fire"), action is chopped to bits. Precise syntactic parallels between events and paragraphs mark out the phases of the fight. That "we were too damned amalgamated" exposes the Op as one of the most brazen stylists of his century.

By draining first-person narration of psychological depth, by giving it laconic neutrality, Hammett eliminated the need for a Watson. At the moment when Sayers was advising writers to modulate external viewpoint to conceal the detective's thoughts, Hammett was showing that a detective could describe his own actions blankly and objectively, as if seen by a dispassionate observer. The bare fact that men jammed together can't fight effectively is floated not as an interesting idea but as a palpable tangle of laps, shoulders, and gun barrels squeezed against ears. Well before Sartre's Roquentin in *La Nausée* and Camus's Meursault in *The Stranger*, Hammett showed how first-person narration could be disturbingly impersonal.

The easygoing flow of Nick Charles's voice in *The Thin Man* has its own chilly detachment. A few times Nick shares his physical sensations, like the bump of getting hit by a bullet, but even more than the Op he's committed to being a recording machine. The taxicab fugue I've already mentioned is typical of Nick's deadpan reportage. Elsewhere, page after page consist of dialogue and snips of physical business, with characters' external expressions of emotions described with clinical brevity.

In a way, Nick is the Op grown more close-mouthed, reluctant to confide in us. Even his jokes depend on depersonalization. Nick carries his drunken friend Quinn home, where Alice is waiting. "Bring it in," she says wearily. Nick reports: "I took it in and spread it on a bed. It mumbled something I could not make out and moved one hand feebly back and forth, but its eyes stayed closed." This recycling of another character's word will be carried to flamboyant extremes by Archie Goodwin in the Nero Wolfe novels. But Archie would never characterize someone as flatly as Nick describes Quinn as a man: "He's all right."[65]

The noncommittal phrase reminds us that Nick's externalized narration functions in part to maintain suspicion. Nick's judgment of Quinn doesn't clear him as a suspect. His later affirmation that Macaulay is a good guy is more actively misleading. We may accept it, but that would entail forgetting that it doesn't come from the heart. It's just something Nick tells Nora.

Given the power of this opaque first-person technique, why did Hammett resort to third-person narration for what many regard as his two crowning achievements? *The Maltese Falcon* presents Spade resolutely from the outside, distancing the protagonist from us even more than the laconic reports of Nick Charles do. Description that would seem overwrought coming from a character narrator can form a quiet pattern of imagery. On the book's first page, the narration contrasts the eyes of Spade ("yellow-grey") with those of his secretary Effie ("brown and playful") and those of Brigid (blue, matching her outfit). Throughout, the narration is cautious, using "apparently" and "seemed" to relay ambivalent information, even about the hero. "Spade did not seem offended." When Spade grunts, we're told that it "probably meant yes."[66]

We're attached to Spade throughout, witnessing nothing he doesn't witness, but often we know less than he does. If the story were told in first person, Spade would pass along what he is hearing in a phone call, but this narration suppresses it. We are aligned with the protagonist spatially but not perceptually or psychologically. When Spade passes out from a drug in his drink, we remain resolutely outside his head; his dulled eyes and wobbly gait are the signs he's collapsing. Instead of the usual "blackness enveloped him," the narration reports: "Once more he tried to get up, could not, and went to sleep."[67] Hammett takes Captain Shaw's objectivity axiom to an extreme.

For all that, a *Maltese Falcon* scene is typically rendered with a density that we seldom find in the earlier books. Instead of writing "Spade rolled a cigarette," Hammett gives us more than a hundred words establishing Spade's meticulous concentration and smooth control over the act.[68] We expect precise description in a bout of physical action, but unlike the awkward maneuvers executed by the Continental Op, the punching of Joel Cairo is rendered as machine-tooled choreography, ending with a strong impression: "The pistol was small in Spade's hand."[69]

Perhaps most flamboyant is the adventure of Casper Gutman's envelope, which contains $10,000. Gutman tosses the envelope to Spade, who's sitting on the sofa. "Heavy enough to fly true," it strikes Spade in the chest and drops to his lap. Spade opens it and counts the bills. Gutman explains why there isn't a larger payment. "While Gutman talked Spade had tapped the edges of the ten bills into alignment and had returned them to their envelope, tucking the flap in over them. Now, with forearms on knees, he sat hunched forward, dangling the envelope from a corner held lightly by finger and thumb down between his legs."[70] Soon Spade will "put the envelope aside—on the sofa," ending this exercise in the biomechanics of deal making. No wonder that John Huston is said to have begun work on the film's script by transcribing the novel as a series of shots.[71]

The Glass Key is even more unforgiving in its impassivity. There are no extended descriptions of physical actions, as in Spade's cigarette-rolling or Gutman's byplay with the envelope. "He moved his shoulders a little," we're told, as if it would be going too far to say he shrugged. Instead of telling us he shook his head no, the narration reports "He moved his head slowly from side to side." Punched, Ned utters "something nobody could have understood."[72]

As in *Falcon*, we never directly access characters' mental states. Worse, their faces are often expressionless or projecting false feeling. Hammett's main, somewhat reliable hint at characters' thinking involves eyes. Ned is the central example.

His dark eyes glared fiercely into Madvig's blue ones.

A doubtful look had come into his eyes.

Ned Beaumont grunted derisively and blew cigar-smoke down at the declaration, but his eyes remained somber.

He seemed amused, though there was a suggestion of anger difficultly restrained in the glitter of his eyes.

His lean face, still bearing the marks of Jeff's and Rusty's fists, was tranquil except for the recklessness aglitter in his eyes.

His voice was light, but into his eyes, fixed on the log burning in the fireplace, came a brief evil glint. There was nothing in his eyes but mockery when he moved them to the left to focus on Mathews.[73]

Here is one gain Hammett derives from third-person narration: It would be perverse to have a first-person narrator interpreting the look in his own eyes.

Descriptions of eye behavior are commonplace in popular narrative, suggesting a folk belief that they reveal truth of the character. In *The Glass Key*, eyes yield both a teasing glimpse of character emotion and a motif associated with the watchful Beaumont, whose dark pearl in his shirt "was like a red eye winking."[74]

The Glass Key goes still further in skimming the surface of the moment. Ned's friend, the private detective Jack Rumsen, is introduced early but not by name. "The man was of medium height, young and dapper, with a sleek dark rather good-looking face." When Ned joins him, he says, " 'Lo, Jack." In effect, Jack gets his name when Ned hails him. This is a common fictional technique. But three chapters later, with Ned in the hospital, we encounter an almost hallucinatory replay.

> A man of medium size, young and dapper, with a sleek, dark, rather good-looking face came in.
> Ned Beaumont sat up in bed. " 'Lo, Jack."[75]

Did Hammett simply forget to revise or cut the repeated description?[76] I'm inclined to think that this passage betrays the narration's stinginess. There is simply nothing more to be said or known about Jack than this. The category "flat character" might have been invented for him.

The Jack problem expands across the book as a whole. Jack almost has no last name; it's mentioned just once, when Ned phones him. The thug Rusty gets no last name, and Jeff's last name, Gardner, is given only once. At the other extreme, in one of the most peculiar gestures in the book's narration, the protagonist is called Ned Beaumont, over and over.

Modernist writers occasionally played games with character names. Most famously, *The Sound and the Fury* features two characters with the same name, and one character with two names. And mystery novels commonly give characters false identities or present the same character in two guises. But every writer must decide how the narration will refer to the character. Calling a man Stephen implies intimacy; calling another Bloom suggests a certain distance. *The Glass Key*'s narration calls a Ned Beaumont pal Frank, and the welshing bookie is called Despain. But what if you want the flattest, most noncommittal choice? Neither Ned nor Beaumont, the hero's full name becomes an unmarked form, a mere slot-filler.

The problem expands after the senator's daughter enters the action. She's called "Janet" when Paul Madvig talks about her, but whenever she's onstage, she is Janet Henry. By a sort of contagion, the narration retreats to its low-affect distance from the woman with whom Ned will eventually leave the city. Perhaps this dry treatment tells us all we can expect from the future of their liaison.[77]

The withdrawal of the author's voice that Joseph Shaw found salutary takes on a severe, eccentric power in *The Glass Key*. Through these strategies Hammett forces us to suspend judgment, locking us into the immediate moment and presenting dialogue and action with very little guidance. Proposing the scenic method as one option for the novel, Percy Lubbock had considered Maupassant's narration as a model of the discreet author: "The story appears to tell itself."[78] Something like this goes on in *The Glass Key*, but Lubbock would surely have worried about the willful opacity of a drama relying so heavily on dialogue and minimal bits of behavior.

André Gide had contemplated writing a novel that offered "no surface interest—no handhold. Everything must be said in the flattest manner possible."[79] Hammett brought that strategy to the *roman policier*. You can argue that the investigation plot makes the genre a natural for suppressing the detective's inner life, but most hard-boiled writers share some thoughts with us. Hammett saw that the secretiveness demanded by mystery allows narration to push beyond the puzzle to deeper uncertainties about character motive and reaction. For much of *The Glass Key*, we aren't sure whether Ned's offer to work with O'Rory is a ploy or a genuine break with Paul. As Claude-Edmonde Magny notes in discussing Hammett as a member of the "behaviorist" school of American novelists, the result is an original kind of psychological fiction. "Hammett thus succeeded in creating a new type of hero—one whose innermost being was unfathomable."[80] Beaumont is akin to Faulkner's blank-slate Popeye, who lies smoking on his prison cot while a priest prays for him.

To its very last line, *The Glass Key* keeps its protagonist opaque, and now descriptions of eyes aren't any help. "Janet Henry looked at Ned Beaumont. He stared fixedly at the door."[81] Yet here as elsewhere the flatness gives the moment a cinematic sharpness. Much *Black Mask* writing displayed the nervous pulse associated with movies, but Hammett was exceptionally sensitive to the filmic dimensions of hard-boiled storytelling. Years before he joined the Hollywood studios, he reviewed Joseph Hergesheimer's novel *Balisand* (1924) as "a story that could be produced exactly as written. . . . *Balisand* is a moving picture."[82] In his stories, Hammett constantly prodded the reader's visual imagination, less through descriptions of setting than through gesture, as with Gutman's tossed envelope.

In fights, the Op's single-sentence paragraphs yield fragments that mimic cinematic shots.

> When he crouched close above me I let him have it.
>
> I patted his face with my gun as he tumbled down past me.
>
> A hand caught one of my ankles.
>
> Clinging to the railing, I drove my other foot back. Something stopped my foot. Nothing stopped me.[83]

The simplicity of the sentences, the unexpected word choice (was it really a pat?), the reversal of sequence (face patted before the victim's fall is reported), and the repetitions and parallels (stopped/stopped, something/nothing) render this as a fast-cut sequence. It recalls Joseph Shaw's suggestion that movies "educated the public to quick reading."[84]

Elsewhere, antiphonal dialogue could imply ongoing business.

> "Who's Reno?" I asked while she tied herself tighter in the apron by pulling the strings the wrong way.
>
> "Reno Starkey. You'll like him. He's a right guy. I promised him I'd show at his celebration and that's just what I'll do."
>
> "What's he celebrating?"
>
> "What the hell's the matter with this lousy apron? He was sprung this afternoon."
>
> "Turn around and I'll unwind you. What was he in for? Stand still."[85]

The Op supplies the soundtrack, we supply the pictures.

Hergesheimer's *Balisand*, however, is more than a movie. "Even as literature it is not terrible."[86] Despite the whiffs of cinema, Hammett made the detective novel a vessel of verbal artistry as that quality was understood by many in his time. The only road to his protagonists' mind is often a dream or embedded text, heavy with symbolism (most notably, a door with a glass key). He understands the post-Wagnerian, quasi-Joycean resources of verbal leitmotifs. Images of fog and a merry-go-round drift through *The Dain Curse*, and Flitcraft's being hit by "a piece of the sidewalk" looks forward to Spade's warning to Brigid that she might be hit by her scheme's "flying pieces." The lightweight *Thin Man* has a trim carpentry. In the first paragraph, Nick pronounces Dorothy Wynant's appearance "satisfactory." In the book's last paragraph, Nora complains that Nick's solution is far-fetched: "It's all pretty unsatisfactory."[87]

As a tagline, it could wrap up a stage comedy, but it also gives the connoisseur of literary craft something to appreciate. More radically, the writer who entertained the possibility of writing a mystery in stream-of-consciousness style went to the opposite extreme. Hammett showed how a ruthlessly objective viewpoint could bring an austere version of modern storytelling to a popular genre. It fell to another writer to do something that surprisingly few earlier writers had attempted: recount the investigation plot from deep inside the detective's head.

Lonely Men Always Talk Too Much

After Hammett, what was left for a writer to do? He provided several schemas that crystallized into a powerful prototype: the lone investigator probing urban crime and going up against crooks, police, tycoons, and politicians.

The variorum principle had governed the tales in *Black Mask*, and something like it began to shape the hard-boiled novels that were starting to be published in the late 1930s.

Hammett had benefited from good timing; he entered the pulp market at its peak. After the Depression, payment rates dropped, the number of magazines thinned out, and writers turned out serials and freestanding books. Authors struggled to differentiate themselves. The setting might be New York, Boston, Los Angeles, Las Vegas, or Miami. The detective would usually be a private eye, but he might be a news photographer, a Hollywood studio fixer, a newsman, a lawyer, a hotel snoop, a department store detective, or a fire marshal. He might not even be a he. Violet McDade was featured in pulp stories, Rex Stout introduced Doll Bonner, and Erle Stanley Gardner, writing as A. A. Fair, gave imposing Bertha Cool her own firm.

However varied these novels were, they locked into place many conventions that would linger for decades. The investigator is summoned to a mission, if not solving a murder then dealing with a family affair—blackmail, theft, disappearance, gambling debts, or kidnapping—that will bring murder in its wake. The ensuing adventure, played out in a treacherous city, features violence and sex, often more graphic than the pulps permitted. Following Spade's affair with Brigid, gumshoes take clients and suspects to bed. There are mocking allusions to the Great Detective and Golden Age puzzles. Crucially, whether the narration is in third person or first person, the viewpoint tends to be strictly limited to the hero's ken. Complex games with linearity or perspective are ruled out.

These conventions were coalescing as Raymond Chandler began his hard-boiled career. By 1937, the "hero story" for the pulp magazine market could be spelled out as a schema passed along to beginners.

> The story is told from the viewpoint of the hero out to solve the murder and capture the villain. A simple "who did it" puzzle is not enough. . . . To sell, you must create a hero who is sympathetic, you must make your readers want terribly for him to escape the dangers which threaten him and solve the case, and you must make it seem that the villain is so dangerously clever that the hero cannot win. Then, when your readers are ready to scream with suspense, the hero must pull the solution out of his clever mind and, through the proper interpretation of clues, back his proof with gunplay if necessary, and emerge victorious.[88]

Chandler's 1936 story "Goldfish" runs along these lines. Hired to recover stolen pearls hidden by the thief, the detective Marlowe discovers the thief's partner has been tortured to death. Other criminals are after the pearls, and when they find Marlowe they drug him. Following a lead, Marlowe gains an ally, but in a burst of gunfire, the ally and one of the criminals is killed. Marlowe pursues a clue that takes him to the original thief, who is quietly breeding goldfish in a small town.

In another gunfight, the pursuers and the thief are shot. The thief mutters a dying message that leads Marlowe to the pearls. They have been sewn into the bodies of the goldfish.

Throughout the first-person narration takes us into Marlowe's mind as he reacts to the situation: "She started to fall. Slowly, like a slow motion picture, she fell. There was something silly about it."[89] Terse descriptions of places and people interlock with crisp dialogue and action scenes. Scenes run only two or three pages, and Marlowe is constantly on the move, bluffing, striking deals, and facing down men and women, a good number of whom walk in with guns in their hands. If given a book-length format, the situation could be expanded with fuller descriptions, more characters, plot complications, and passages in which the protagonist reflects on his encounters. Chandler's biographer Frank MacShane rightly calls these stories "miniature novels."[90]

Between 1933 and 1939, Chandler published twenty stories in *Black Mask* and other pulps. In late 1938, a signed advertisement appeared on the cover of *Publishers' Weekly*.

In 1929   Dashiell Hammett
In 1934   James M. Cain
In 1939   Raymond Chandler

His first novel, *The Big Sleep*, will excite you as did *The Thin Man* and *The Postman Always Rings Twice*. Please read it. *Alfred A. Knopf*.[91]

While aiming for a new best-seller, Knopf was constructing a lineage that would endure to our day: Chandler is Hammett's successor. Perhaps too, given the publisher's prestige, this debut would launch a new phase in the genre's search for cultural legitimacy.

Knopf had reason to hope. In a letter echoing Hammett's ambitions of a decade earlier, Chandler explained to Knopf that he tried to create a plot "in which the mystery is solved by the exposition and understanding of a single character always well in evidence, rather than by the slow and sometimes long-winded concatenation of circumstances." The action would be filtered through the detective, not a Watson or a neutral authorial voice. Detection would be a matter of registering Philip Marlowe's thinking as he struggled to find the truth behind a series of dramatic, even melodramatic encounters. The emotional tone of the setting would be as important as the characters, and the action, still "sharp, swift and racy," would carry "a very vivid and pungent style, but not slangy or overly vernacular." The goal was "to acquire delicacy without losing power."[92]

Chandler declared that he would need at least three books to achieve this goal. In a parallel with Hammett's earlier pace of productivity, Chandler followed *The Big Sleep* with *Farewell, My Lovely* (1940), *The High Window* (1942), and *The Lady in the Lake* (1943). These novels secured his place as the most prominent practitioner of the hard-boiled school and as a major influence on later writers. They sought to differentiate him not only from the whodunit but also from the pulp writers who had just graduated to the book market.[93]

Chandler's education was in classical Greek and Latin, and he admired Flaubert, James, and Conrad.[94] Taking an academic path to the pulps, he had practiced rewriting Erle Stanley Gardner stories. Donald Westlake noted that with Chandler the private-eye novel moved to a phase of "ritual," in which the "raw material was not the truth but the first decade of the fiction."[95] Chandler revised Hammett's plot schemas, and at times he gave his detective the rueful self-deprecation of the Op. Like Hammett, he did not set out to leave the puzzle plot behind, at least initially, but rather to incorporate it in fictions that achieved literary value. Chandler rewrites the private-eye as an introspective, somewhat altruistic intellectual who happens to be a tough man of action.

This amounts to recalibrating the very idea of action. Years later Chandler explained that 1930s pulp editors were wrong to think that bursts of violence, nakedly stated, were all that readers wanted, or that the genre deserved.

> The things [readers] really cared about, and that I cared about, were the creation of emotion through dialogue and description; the things they remembered, that haunted them, were not for example that a man got killed, but that in the moment of his death he was trying to pick a paper clip off the polished surface of a desk, and it kept slipping away from him, so that there was a look of strain on his face and his mouth was half open in a kind of tormented grin, and the last thing in the world he thought about was death. He didn't even hear death knock on the door. That damn little paper clip kept slipping away from his finger and he just wouldn't push it to the edge of the desk and catch it as it fell.[96]

Here are several sides of Chandler's aesthetic: the dwelling on drab physical detail, the idea that the vivid part commands more attention than the blurry whole (scene, plot), and the sad shabbiness of death. We are in the realm of James's "discriminated occasion," the precise rendition of a unique moment. In the finished novel, the power and delicacy of such a scene would be filtered through the awareness of a man endowed with a sour wit, a crafty intelligence, and a stubborn commitment to honor.

Chandler's artistic self-consciousness made him one of the great theorists of the mystery writer's craft. In his correspondence and notebooks, we find a bounty of principles and, perhaps surprising, a clear-cut commitment to the whodunit tradition. His "Twelve Notes on the Mystery Story" are as strict as any of the Detection Club commandments. He insists strongly on fair play, careful construction, and avoidance of a love interest, unless it can be made an obstacle to the investigation.[97]

Chandler looked back beyond Hammett's austere version of modern prose to fuller-bodied literary traditions. By naming his hero Marlowe, Chandler evoked the Elizabethan playwright and Conrad's truth-seeking narrator. (He was originally named Mallory, referencing Arthurian legend.) Coming to maturity in the Edwardian era, Chandler took as a model the well-made novel of social observation and psychological insight. Therefore, the detective writer should try to sustain a puzzle without forcing characters to "do unreal things in order to form the artificial pattern required by the plot."[98] Milieu and atmosphere should be sharply observed. Most important was style, "all the virtuosities of the writing."[99] He found these virtuosities not in Faulkner or Hemingway but in Balzac, Maupassant, James, Conrad, and Max Beerbohm. He compared F. Scott Fitzgerald to Keats.[100] Stylistically, the detective story needed a richer texture than even Hammett had provided. "In his hands [the American language] had no overtones, left no echo, evoked no image beyond a distant hill."[101] Providing these overtones, echoes, and images would be Chandler's mission.

Chandler claimed realism of some sort as the basis of all storytelling, but he granted that every genre has an element of fantasy. This admission may owe something to Edwardian tastes. His work may be seen as accepting and recasting G. K. Chesterton's 1901 proposal that the detective story is ideal for presenting "the poetry of modern life . . . the realization of a great city as something wild and obvious." The hero, who protects us through "a successful knight-errantry," possesses "the loneliness and liberty of a prince in a tale of elfland."[102] But Chandler's wild modern city is dangerous and corrupt, not charming, and his knight is weary and disenchanted. Chesterton saw the police as the agents of virtue, but now justice must be brought by the solitary loner. Still, romanticism takes many guises, grim as well as fanciful. Los Angeles can be a malevolent fairy kingdom, and the anti-hero can be heroic in a modern way.

Compromise with actuality is demanded by genre convention as well. The urge for realism must adjust to the need for extreme emotions and improbably compressed chains of action. "Although such things happen," Chandler granted, "they do not happen so fast and in such a tight frame of logic to so closely knit a group of people."[103] If the writing could endow the characters' encounters with local color and plausibility, any problems of large-scale architecture would be overlooked, or at least forgiven.

Although Chandler didn't consider himself an adept plotter, he was fairly adroit in handling the network principle Hammett had worked with. His short stories are heavily populated, and when he built novels out of them, he found ways to interweave one cast of characters with another. *The Lady in the Lake* features twenty named characters, the other novels thirty or more. One way Chandler stretched stories to book length was by naming and characterizing even bit players. The opening chapter often alludes to people we won't meet for some time, suggesting phantom connections that will be confirmed or challenged in the plot to come.

A pretext crime based on theft or blackmail or disappearance brings Marlowe into a murder plot. His investigation reveals unexpected links among characters of different classes. Usually a disguised crime in the more distant past will come to light at the climax. The disappearance of Sean Regan in *The Big Sleep*, the defenestration in *The High Window*, and the murder of Dr. Almore's wife in *The Lady in the Lake* are examples. A variant is to link two distinct cases unexpectedly. In *Farewell, My Lovely*, one character's dual identity splices the Moose Malloy story line to a purported jade theft, both of which depend on antecedent crimes.

For a man who disliked *Trent's Last Case*, Chandler was remarkably dependent on a string of false solutions. At intervals, every book schedules sit-down scenes in which Marlowe and a confidant, usually a sympathetic cop, review the case so far. These conversations speculate on the shifting links among clues and crimes. Instead of clarifying the lines of inquiry, the play with alternatives can leave the reader fairly flummoxed. (The proliferation of names doesn't help. One novel includes both a Morny and a Morningstar.)

Chandler confessed that his love for captivating scenes and dueling conversations led him to squeeze in material "that insists on staying alive," but the early novels find smooth ways to integrate it.[104] The first chapters of *The High Window* dwell on a minor character, the skittish Merle Davis, in what seems to be a strained flirtation with Marlowe. But she will prove to be of pivotal importance when the past crime is revealed. In the end, Chandler's tangled plot schemes, as critic Leroy Lad Panek points out, enable the detective's solution to be as intuitively convincing as anything in a Golden Age puzzle.[105]

Multiplying characters and intrigues, a characteristic of adventure plotting in general, paid off in Chandler's quest for literary legitimacy. For one thing, his vast networks suggest the messiness of reality, the contingent connections among people in the modern city. Marlowe warns himself against solutions that have "the austere simplicity of fiction rather than the tangled woof of fact."[106] The presence of several murderers, acting independently and sometimes at cross-purposes, makes the whole tangle more weirdly plausible, if more difficult to comprehend, than the single mastermind of traditional detective villainy.

Just as important, network organization allows Chandler to suggest social critique. When a distinguished family or an executive or a movie star is revealed to be tied, however distantly or secretly, to gamblers, counterfeiters, and gangsters, you can't escape a sense of pervasive corruption. Marlowe reveals the handshake between the law and the lawless. Midway through *The Big Sleep*, he scans the network and decides that everything he has revealed about three murders will be covered up to protect the Sternwood family. A murderous woman binds the homicidal cop of *The Lady in the Lake* to a doctor peddling drugs, and the distinguished society wife of *Farewell, My Lovely* turns out to be a fugitive showgirl ready to betray anyone who crosses her. In *The High Window*, a family hanger-on kills two people, but his patrons, a wealthy widow and her son, are also murderers. Pettier crimes like pornography or counterfeiting are presented as side hustles for the decadent upper class. "To hell with the rich," says Marlowe. "They made me sick."[107]

Other, pulpier hard-boiled novelists of the period might reveal similar conspiracies, but Chandler's narration gives them a dense texture. His famous descriptions of places, for instance, go well beyond the bare-bones accounts we get from his contemporaries. What Hammett did not do for San Francisco, Marlowe did for Los Angeles—evoking its weather, its smells, its vegetation, and its neighborhoods. His Bunker Hill is as distinctly portrayed as *The Great Gatsby*'s West Egg.

Specific spots are given a Vermeer-like exactitude. Here for comparison is a casino from a 1940 novel by Brett Halliday.

> Shayne clicked the dice gently in his big fist and rolled them out on the green table. Under the soft diffused light they came to a stop showing a five and a four up.
>
> The houseman shoved them back to him with his ivory stick and Shayne clicked them again, then sevened out. He lifted his shoulders with negligent disapproval and relinquished the black-dotted cubes to the gambler on his left.
>
> The gambling hall was long, low-ceilinged, richly carpeted. Brilliant lights reflected on the tables from dark-shaded bulbs. Two crap layouts were deserted, and of the three roulette tables, only one was in operation this early in the evening.
>
> Against a background of ornate furnishings, men in evening clothes and women in backless gowns made no effort to dissemble feverish intentness as the ivory ball jumped erratically around the spinning wheel. Sharply indrawn breaths exhaled in an almost audible "ah-h-h" when the ball stopped in its niche.[108]

The writing is serviceable but vague ("richly carpeted," "ornate furnishings") and clumsy ("dissemble feverish intentness"). There also seem to be some respiratory problems; how are "sharply indrawn breaths" released in *almost* audible sounds? Still, the reader won't dwell on the style, because the purpose of the passage is just to sketch in the idle rich at play.

Chandler gives us not a sketch but a tableau, and he forces us to linger on it.

> The room had been a ballroom once and Eddie Mars had changed it only as much as his business compelled him. No chromium glitter, no indirect

lighting from behind angular cornices, no fused glass pictures, or chairs in violent leather and polished metal tubing, none of the pseudo-modernistic circus of the typical Hollywood night trap. The light was from heavy crystal chandeliers and the rose-damask panels of the wall were still the same rose damask, a little faded by time and darkened by dust, that had been matched long ago against the parquetry floor, of which only a small glass-smooth space in front of the little Mexican orchestra showed bare. The rest was covered by a heavy old-rose carpeting that must have cost plenty. The parquetry was made of a dozen kinds of hardwood, from Burma teak through half a dozen shades of oak and ruddy wood that looked like mahogany, and fading out to the hard pale wild lilac of the California hills, all laid in elaborate patterns, with the accuracy of a transit.

It was still a beautiful room and now there was roulette in it instead of measured, old-fashioned dancing. There were three tables close to the far wall. A low bronze railing joined them and made a fence around the croupiers. All three tables were working, but the crowd was at the middle one. I could see Vivian Regan's black head close to it, from across the room where I was leaning against the bar and turning a small glass of bacardi around on the mahogany.[109]

The description sets the room between two phantoms, one in the past and one in an alternative present: a mansion's ballroom haunted by ghostly dancers and a virtual high-tech casino (as if modern design, with its violent leather, had sadistic intent). The continuity of old money and new criminality is given through details of color, textures, and varieties of ripened wood. Such descriptions, fulfilling Conrad's charge to make the reader "see," are Chandler's efforts to evoke the "overtones and echoes" that Hammett's style lacked.

In addition, the room tells us about Eddie Mars, who's smart enough to realize that an ambience of faded elegance can give his game a veneer of class. Halliday, writing in the third person, simply reports Shayne shooting his black-dotted cubes (dice), whereas Chandler locks down the imagery as Marlowe's view from the bar. The paragraph caps its surprisingly static tableau with his glimpse of Vivian, who is central to the upcoming scene. This view is followed by a minute gesture, Marlowe calmly turning his glass on a surface that reminds us of the rich flooring. Mike Shayne circulates, but Marlowe stands off, reflecting on a moment of social history in which apparent respect for old California is merely the tribute modern vice pays to its forebears.

The description only seems to be objective; it is shot through with Marlowe's sensibility. In appraising him, commentators have probably paid too much attention to Chandler's figures of speech, which when they aren't clichés ("her eyes sparking fire," endless variations on ice cold) can be maudlin ("dead men are heavier than broken hearts," "old men with faces like lost battles") or borderline surrealist:

> The minutes went by on tiptoe, with their fingers to their lips.
> Her face fell apart like a bride's pie crust.
> It went into his pocket with a sound like caterpillars fighting.
> Suspicion climbed all over her face, like a kitten, but not so playfully.

These exaggerations don't hide their comic side, and they form the basis of some very funny passages, as when Moose Malloy becomes a lumbering creature out of a tall tale. There is quieter humor too, as with "a silvery ripple of laughter that held the unspoiled naturalness of a bubble dance." These bouts of sour wit put us strongly on Marlowe's side.[110]

Chandler descriptions, however colloquial, often carry moral judgments in the manner of Edwardian novelists such as Forster or Lawrence. Mars's gambling parlor is a "night trap," the "old rose" carpet reinforces the idea of decayed glory, and the parquet carpentry owes its beauty to the pillage of the California hills. Dead bodies can likewise exude visual and tactile associations.

> He lay smeared to the ground, on his back, at the base of a bush, in that bag-of-clothes position that always means the same thing. His face was a face I had never seen before. His hair was dark with blood, the beautiful blond ledges were tangled with blood and some thick grayish ooze, like primeval slime.
>
> The girl behind me breathed hard, but she didn't speak. I held the light on his face. He had been beaten to a pulp. One of his hands was flung out in a frozen gesture, the fingers curled. His overcoat was half twisted under him, as though he had rolled as he fell. His legs were crossed. There was a trickle as black as dirty oil at the corner of the mouth.[111]

Here the metaphors are buried. The image of a man "smeared" into the earth, rumpled like a laundry bag, his "ledges" of hair gooey with blood and brain, is capped, as often in Chandler, by an anticlimax. Until the last sentence, the victim has owned his parts, but at the paragraph's end, his mouth has been depersonalized, is now simply *the* mouth, and the oil is dirty, as if from a crankcase. Chandler's literary impressionism has traced how, in Marlowe's perception, a man has turned into a thing.

Dialogue is on the whole far more revelatory than in Hammett. Marlowe gives other characters' speech its due. "Man, that's liquor. . . . Man, this stuff dies painless with me." Above all, Marlowe can characterize himself just by telling us what he says. For all the wisecracks, many exchanges are close to the witty *repliques* of the London stage. Some lines could come from musical comedy or drawing-room farce.

"You're not drinking." "I'm doing what *I* call drinking."
"Money sharpens the memory." "So does liquor."
"That's really awfully kind of her." "Oh hell and fireflies," I said.
"For five I could start thinking." "I wouldn't want to make it that tough for you."
 "For ten I could sing like four canaries and a steel guitar." "I don't like those plushy orchestrations."[112]

Admitting that he couldn't handle group scenes well, Chandler stated his preference: "Give me two characters snotting each other across a desk and I am happy."[113]

Dialogue is also the prime vehicle of Marlowe's reasoning. He usually holds back his solutions from us until he can bring them out in conversation with cops or suspects. In approved hard-boiled manner, Marlowe marks his difference from the Golden Age, once giving his name as Philo Vance. When a character suggests mockingly that the butler would make a good suspect, he punctures the convention. "I inhaled some of my drink. 'It's not that kind of story,' I said. 'It's not lithe and clever. It's just dark and full of blood.'"[114] Yet Marlowe incarnates many lithe and clever Golden Age conventions himself. He plays chess and can quote Shakespeare with the assurance of Lord Peter. He mentions Proust and Pepys and Browning ("the poet, not the automatic") and nicknames a cop Hemingway because he keeps repeating himself.[115]

Marlowe is characterized no less by others' dialogue, and sometimes these passages tip into hero worship. Women call him big and strong. A doctor calls him a "shop-soiled Sir Galahad." But Marlowe is usually there to deflate his and others' pretensions. "What you see is nothing. I've got a Bali dancing girl tattooed on my right thigh." Pumped full of drugs, he talks to himself: " 'Let's see you do something really tough, like putting your pants on.' I lay down on the bed again."[116]

The deflation is intensified by Marlowe's awareness that he's often performing a literary role. Throughout the books, Marlowe displays typical *Black Mask* scorn for cheap crooks who imitate what they've seen on the screen. But he takes the convention up a notch by admitting that he's playing a role as well, and somewhat enjoying it. In one novel he grants he's "just like a detective in a book," and in another he remarks that the answer is "elementary."[117] It's tiresome to play a tough dick, but it can be fun.

I said: "Go ahead and be heroes."
I clicked the safety catch loudly.
Sometimes even a bad scene will rock the house.[118]

Naturally an awareness of performance leads to a reflection on the conventions of hard-boiled storytelling.

> "I've never liked this scene," I said. "Detective confronts murderer. Murderer produces gun, points same at detective. Murderer tells detective the whole sad story, with the idea of shooting him at the end of it. Thus wasting a lot of valuable time, even if in the end murderer did shoot detective. Only murderer never does. Something always happens to prevent it. The gods don't like this scene either. They always manage to spoil it."
>
> "But this time," she said softly and got up and moved towards me softly across the carpet, "suppose we make it a little different. Suppose I don't tell you anything and nothing happens and I do shoot you."
>
> "I still wouldn't like the scene," I said.[119]

Inoculating his text against the charge of conventionality, Chandler appeals to a high-literature criterion, reflexivity. We are not very far from John Dickson Carr's Dr. Fell, who introduces his locked-room lecture by admitting that he and his colleagues are characters in a book. The difference is that Marlowe momentarily undercuts the artifice with his final line, reestablishing his mortal danger should the conventions fail. Of course they do not. Marlowe escapes death. He is merely knocked out. Which is another convention.

Such self-consciousness depends on interiority, and Chandler pushed further inward. The action of *The Big Sleep* culminates in a florid passage of quasi-cinematic hallucination repeating, over and over, scenes that more or less resolve the case as they drift "through waves of false memory."[120] *Farewell, My Lovely* is saturated in subjectivity, and not only in the passages presenting Marlowe under the influence of drugs. He slices open a Russian cigarette on his desk. "I slit one down the middle. The mouthpiece part was pretty tough to slit. Okay, I was a tough guy, I slit it anyway. See can you stop me." Soon the scene turns a bit Bloomian, moving from inference to loose association.

> He must have forgotten it. It didn't make sense. Perhaps it hadn't belonged to him at all. Perhaps he had picked it up in a hotel lobby. Forgotten he had it on him. Forgotten to turn it in. Jules Amthor, Psychic Consultant.[121]

The fragmentation of sentences slips toward sheer impressionism, with the final sentence becoming a refrain taken from Amthor's business card. The eureka moment in *The High Window* becomes a staccato mental montage triggered by a photograph.

> Well, perhaps the guy liked the picture, so what? A man leaning out of a high window. A long time ago.

I looked at Vannier. He wouldn't help me at all. A man leaning out of a window, a long time ago.

The touch of the idea at first was so light that I almost missed it and passed on. A touch of a feather, hardly that. The touch of a snowflake. A high window, a man leaning out—a long time ago.

It snapped in place. It was so hot it sizzled. Out of a high window a long time ago—eight years ago—a man leaning—too far—a man falling—to his death.[122]

Hammett told Blanche Knopf he wanted to give the detective a stream of consciousness, but Chandler, in a few places at least, actually tried.[123]

There are, of course, limits. However deeply the narration moves inward, the detective story cannot yield a full-throated solution. Marlowe's window epiphany needs further explanation.

> Regardless of the candor of the first-person narrative there comes a time when the detective has made up his mind and yet does not communicate this to the reader. He holds some of his thinking out for the denouement or explanation. He tells the facts but not the reaction in his mind to those facts. Is this a permissible convention of deceit? It must be, otherwise the detective telling his own story could not have solved the problem in advance of the technical denouement.[124]

Sayers had tracked Bentley's shift of third-person emphasis in *Trent's Last Case*, and Hammett had, in vain, envisioned allowing the solution to strike the detective and the reader at the same moment. Chandler admits that the hard-boiled tale is bound to classic detective conventions. As ever, artifice triumphs over realism.

He struggled with these compromises, nowhere more visibly than in the essay "The Simple Art of Murder." He acknowledges that his ideal protagonist is an intensely romantic, idealized one.[125] However introspective and free of illusion the hero may be, he will adhere to the code of detective tradition. Chandler assures us that he will "protect the innocent, guard the helpless and destroy the wicked . . . while earning a meager living in a corrupt world."[126] "Down these mean streets a man must go who is not himself mean, who is neither tarnished nor afraid. . . . a man of honor, by instinct, by inevitability, without thought of it and certainly without saying it. He must be the best man in his world and a good enough man for any world."[127] He is a fantasy figure, Chandler admits, but at least he's closer to reality, and more admirable, than the eccentric fop who burbles about bodies in the bath.

This figure is elevated as much by the symbolic suggestions in the writing as by his mythic dimensions. *The Big Sleep*'s famous recurring motif of the knight errant isn't undercut by Marlowe's worry, as he shifts pieces on his chessboard, that this case "wasn't a game for knights."[128] He is as chivalric as he can be in this tarnished world. A bug in *Farewell My Lovely*, ashtrays in *The High Window*, dreams in *The Lady in the Lake* all project symbolic resonance and signify literary quality. Not for Chandler pulpish titles like *Murder in the Madhouse* or *Bullets for the Bridegroom*. More respectable for the literati is a metaphor (*The Big Sleep*) or an allusion (*The Lady in the Lake*).

Chandler believed that description, dialogue, character drawing, and atmosphere, filtered through an alert, introspective observer and rendered in an evocative style, could redeem a popular genre. His project, displayed in four novels of undoubted quality, was welcomed by a literary culture newly sensitive to the power of symbolism, social realism, and poetic imagery. Between 1939 and 1944, Chandler handed the detective story a dose of the cultural respectability it had longed for since the days of Collins and Gaboriau.

Hard-Boiled Into Noir

Chandler's 1944 essay "The Simple Art of Murder" endowed the hard-boiled mystery with a usable past. Chandler demanded that the detective story, without losing its identity as a mystery, be a realistic, character-driven, acutely written piece of social commentary. The genre could achieve significance by addressing its readers' world, one where the pervasive corruption threatened the common good and the guilty might defeat the innocent.[129] Chandler denounced Golden Age artifice while also criticizing most hard-boiled authors for mistaking brutality for strength and flippancy for wit.

Apart from fortifying Edmund Wilson's attack on the English whodunit, "The Simple Art of Murder" was a natural step in forging Chandler's literary identity. "Perhaps as a result of my business training I always knew that a writer had to follow a line with which the public would become familiar. He had to 'type' himself to the extent that the public would associate his name (if they remembered it) with a certain kind of writing."[130] As I suggested earlier, we can see this piece as justifying Chandler's first four novels. The venue, the *Atlantic* magazine, could define him for the literati as Hammett's heir.

"The Simple Art of Murder" voiced the prospect that the mystery story, focused on a detached contemplation of death, had no room for uplift. By the essay's end, however, Chandler suggested that his honorable detective provided just that: "In everything that can be called art there is a quality of redemption."[131] In offering a spark of light in a world shrouded in corruption, Philip Marlowe might not merely save his genre; he might save popular literature.

Chandler gave tastemakers and gatekeepers a strong rationale for admitting his books into the realm of serious art. J. B. Priestley and Somerset Maugham appreciated them.[132] W. H. Auden declared that "his powerful but depressing books should be read and judged, not as escape literature, but as works of art."[133] An early academic article on Chandler set an agenda for decades of discussion: his "taut sinewy prose" was said to present a dark world wholly appropriate to the postwar landscape.[134] Chandler's conception of storytelling suited a literary culture that favored the New Critics' emphasis on verbal texture, the reassessment of James and Conrad, and the modernists' awareness of narrative archetypes. "Philip Marlowe, private dick, is our myth," declared one critic.[135]

The essay benefited from good timing, and not just in responding to the East Coast debate about mysteries. Chandler had followed Hammett's path to Hollywood, and 1944 was his breakthrough year. *Double Indemnity*, written with Billy Wilder from a novel by James M. Cain, was released to great acclaim, and later that year *Farewell, My Lovely* enjoyed success as *Murder, My Sweet*. These became canonical instances of the new crime film.[136] In 1945 came *The Blue Dahlia*, from an original Chandler script, and another acerbic *Atlantic* essay, "Writers in Hollywood." In 1946 *The Big Sleep* arrived on-screen, and in the following year came film adaptations of *The High Window* (as *The Brasher Doubloon*) and *The Lady in the Lake*. Chandler's 1945 contract guaranteed him a $50,000 annual salary whether or not he delivered any scripts, and Universal gave him $100,000 for a script that was never produced.[137]

Although he published no new novel until 1949, Chandler's name was kept constantly before the reading public. The paperback boom fostered seven collections of his early short stories, which were also sold to syndicated newspapers nationwide. He figured prominently in the debates about the artistic legitimacy of the detective genre. Outside the United States his fame spread with Spanish and Nordic language translations. The Parisian *Série Noire* collection published three of his books in 1948.

Hammett had long since stopped writing novels, but Chandler had competition from others. While he labored in the Hollywood trenches and lobbied for the elevated possibilities of the private-eye novel, sensationalistic hard-boiled novels poured from publishers. He raged against the "violence and outright pornography" in Mickey Spillane, whose *I, the Jury* far outsold nearly any other mystery. "Pulp writing at its worst was never as bad as this stuff."[138] He wasn't much kinder to the more genteel Ross Macdonald. Radio programs featuring Sam Spade, Philip Marlowe, and other hard-boiled heroes filled the airwaves. The mean streets were crowded with wisecracking dicks, seductive dames, pistoleros, suave gamblers, and crooked businessmen.

Chandler responded with three novels that in various ways adjusted Marlowe to new circumstances. *The Little Sister* (1949), a bitter account of decadence in the film studios, set forth an equally blistering view of heartland America and its homegrown con artists. *The Long Goodbye* (1953) picked up the *Glass Key* theme of testing a friendship. Marlowe's loyalty to Terry Lennox complicates his effort to keep watch on the suicidal, alcoholic writer Roger

Wade, who might have killed Terry's wife. *Playback* (1958), a recasting of the aborted Universal film script, pulled an aged Marlowe into trailing a duplicitous woman on the run. In all of these books, Marlowe gets a sex life, and in the last one Chandler violates his own strictures against his detective moving toward marriage.

Some familiar strategies are back. Although *Playback* is rather sparsely populated, *The Little Sister* has a cast of more than thirty characters, *The Long Goodbye* more than forty. Each tangled plot demands four lengthy summaries before the final explanation. Energy is lavished on descriptions; in *The Long Goodbye*, a decadent restaurant gets four full pages, filled out by a disquisition on types of blonde women. Marlowe is now even more self-aware, confessing that he's a romantic and acknowledging "the tired cliché mannerisms of my trade."[139]

The word "tired" was common enough in the early books, but here it takes on a new weight. Eyeing his office, Marlowe dwells on the "tired, tired telephone." Symbols of exhaustion and lassitude (a fly and dead moths in *The Little Sister*, another drowsy moth in *The Long Goodbye*) lie alongside Marlowe's confession that his performance as hero is flagging: "I put the old tired grin on my face." He finds a doppelgänger in the writer Wade, who, uniquely in the novels, gives us first-person access to another mind. His drunken note drips with Marlovian self-laceration, brooding on similes and adjectives while admitting he too is burned out: "Does this sentence make sense? No. Okay. I'm not asking any money for it."[140]

Like Wade, Marlowe and the other fadeaway men in the late novels can summon energy for rants. We get tirades on democracy, bad sandwiches, theater chains, the historical novel, plutocracy, gamblers, God, and television ads. The condemnations that were implicit in the description of Mars's casino are spelled out at length. Despite flashes of the old humor and some rote deprecation of speechifying ("Lonely men always talk too much"), Marlowe's insistence on his noble solitude ("I just want to get off this frozen star") suggests that these books serve largely to hyperdramatize the program laid out in "The Simple Art of Murder."[141] Late Chandler can seem to be desperately reasserting his primacy in a tradition he helped found.[142]

By the end of the 1940s, that primacy had already changed the movies. The voice-over commentaries in *Double Indemnity* and *Murder, My Sweet* became models of auditory narration for hard-boiled film, radio, and television. The technique wasn't new to Hollywood, but it had tended to be used gently, for reminiscence (*Lydia, How Green Was My Valley, I Remember Mama*). Filmmakers were attracted by Chandler's approach of refracting imagery through a jaundiced, free-associating wit, as if the voice were riffing on the movie as we watched.[143]

Correspondingly, Chandler increased and expanded his novels' inner monologues. In a kind of fantasy sequence, Marlowe pictures Terry Lenox as a Rotarian in a train's club car. Without benefit of italics or quotation marks, Chandler runs an awkwardly polite imaginary dialogue. *The Little Sister* has a scene like the clinic nightmare in *Farewell, My Lovely*: Marlowe is drugged and his wooziness is expressed in disjointed phrases. Later, Chandler experiments with diaristic choppiness in an interlude beginning: "I ate dinner at a place near Thousand Oaks. Bad but quick. Feed 'em and throw 'em out. Lots of business." For three pages, Marlowe's mental flow mixes acid comments on California culture with fragments recalling clues and plot twists. "I trundle down to Bay City and the routine I go through is so tired I'm half-asleep on my feet. I meet nice people, with and without ice picks in their necks."[144] The screenwriter for *Murder, My Sweet* recast the early novel's commentary as what he called "syncopated narration."[145] *The Little Sister* created its own version of that rhythm in Marlowe's semi-Bloomian reverie. The title of the last novel, *Playback*, indicates the auditory shift Chandler registers: not only a rerun of a crime in the past but a rewound voice now fractured by its relays through many media.

On its side, Hollywood streamlined the hard-boiled conventions. In Chandler's first four novels, Marlowe was righteously celibate, but the film versions paired him off with women. Still, a lot of the distinctive qualities of hard-boiled fiction survived their transfer to the screen. A prescient article in a British film magazine saw the Chandler adaptations as opening a new phase in American cinema. Atmospheric shots caught the desolation of his cityscapes. The portrayal of Marlowe, for all the compromises of censorship, was closer to the "natural man" than other Hollywood heroes. These films and those that imitated them, the critic suggested, created a new genre that was as indigenously American as the western and the musical.[146] The French would call it *film noir*.

***

The creative choices made by Hammett and Chandler obliged audiences to grapple with sharply defined narrative strategies. These authors staked out the poles of restricted narration: the opacity of Hammett's objective view versus the Chandler protagonist's restless commentary on everything around him. The presentation of elaborate networks trained readers to recognize diffuse, sometimes misleading chains of affinity and action among characters. At the level of style, and aided by the presence of a mystery puzzle, the writers encouraged readers to go beyond the information given and speculate on character motivations and thematic implications—masculine loyalty in Hammett, Los Angeles's genealogy of corruption in Chandler. More generally, the clipped syntax, brief paragraphs, and in-depth dramatization of scenes made the stories more "cinematic" and the plot contortions easier to accept, or just ignore. Considered the closest thing in

6.4 *My Favorite Brunette* (1947): Bob Hope wants to be the assistant of tough dick Sam McCloud (Alan Ladd in a cameo).

6.5 *The Great Piggybank Robbery* (1946): The hard-boiled Duck Twacy intimidates the Great Detective: "Scram, Sherlock! I'm workin' this side of the street!"

the mystery realm to "popular modernism," the hard-boiled tradition became one vessel of mass culture acceptable to intellectuals.

Hammett, Chandler, and their counterparts discarded some schemas of the classic mystery, retained others, and revised still others. Thanks to the network principle drawn from the city-novel tradition, there could be many crimes and culprits, permitting greater density of plotting. The webs of relationships slowly revealed in *Pulp Fiction, The Usual Suspects, Miller's Crossing,* and *Memento* rely on viewers grasping intricate clusters of loyalty and deceit like those elaborated by the hard-boiled school.

All these strategies, both old and freshly minted, were recycled throughout mainstream media. The hard-boiled conventions became as familiar as those of the Golden Age whodunit, and as vulnerable to parody (figs. 6.4–6.5). In the process, those conventions underwent even more changes. During the 1940s, storytellers would subject the hard-boiled world to some of the outré formal strategies that had emerged in the puzzle plots and the thrillers. The three main strains of mystery merged and transmogrified, producing fresh tactics of nonlinearity, viewpoint, and segmentation. Under the pressure of mass production, the teeming variorum of popular narrative burst out in rousing, often delirious directions.

CHAPTER 7

THE 1940s

Mysteries in Crossover Culture

M ystery storytelling, central to popular culture for much of the twentieth century, saturated English-language media in the 1940s. The entertainments of that era supply our most vivid prototypes of crime and suspense. Consider the evocative magic of a few film titles: *The Maltese Falcon* (1941), *Double Indemnity* (1944), *Mildred Pierce* (1945), and *The Big Sleep* (1946). Hitchcock alone provides a panoply of examples, from *Foreign Correspondent* (1940) and *Shadow of a Doubt* (1943) to *Notorious* (1946) and *Rope* (1948).

When we want a model of the terrorized woman, we return to *Sorry, Wrong Number* (1948) or *Rebecca* (1940) or *Suspicion* (1941). When we imagine that a dead woman, especially captured in a portrait, can radiate a mesmerizing image, *Laura* (1944) as either novel or film becomes the ultimate example. When we want a term for a president who tries to blind us to the truth, we borrow the term "gaslighting" from a 1944 movie about sanity under siege. Although some of these classic sources predate the 1940s, the stories gained their cultural power by circulating endlessly through many media in the 1940s. These works represent the peaks, but if we dig deeper, we'll find scores of other mystery tales, many unjustifiably forgotten.

The sheer volume of production of mystery stories in every mass medium did more than challenge gatekeepers such as Edmund Wilson and invite distinguished writers to try their hand at the genre. The flood of mysteries created an immense pressure to innovate, to expand the variorum through assimilation of subjects and techniques from other media. Other innovations stemmed from cross-fertilization among the versions of the investigation plot I've been considering. Although all three subgenres retained distinctive identities, the powerful merging of story schemas and formal options was common in the 1940s. The hard-boiled model had an impact on the classic whodunit, as you'd expect. Even more important was the way formal strategies typical of Golden Age detection merged with story schemas in thriller and hard-boiled tales.

Many of these narrative strategies were circulating in "serious literature" as well, and by deploying them mystery storytellers probably gained some cultural cachet. By drawing on unusual techniques already found in crossover works adapted to a wide audience, storytellers could inject tales of mean streets and women in peril with fresh excitement. They sustained the impulse of Golden Age whodunits to make each work a tour de force, and along the way they taught audiences new comprehension skills.

Darkening the Puzzle

The success of mystery stories in all media and at all levels of taste enabled the variorum to flourish. Twists, thefts, borrowings, and switcheroos abounded. Storytellers competed to find new wrinkles. Why not make your protagonist a mystery writer? (Several books and movies did.[1]) Why not deny what you're doing? ("This is not a detective story," maintains the hero of the film *The Mask of Dimitrios*, 1944.) More broadly, why not expand the limits of mystery by inventing new strategies or renewing older ones?

You might, for instance, humanize the puzzle plot. Dorothy Sayers had sought to inject romance into her Peter Wimsey series, and some British hybrids brought the panic of the thriller into pure detection. American writers were pressed in this direction by the demands of the slick-magazine market. Likewise, married couples could introduce banter typical of light fiction. In novels, plays, films, and radio shows, Frances and Richard Lockridge created the amateur sleuths Mr. and Mrs. North, nearly as sophisticated and screwball as Nick and Nora Charles in the *Thin Man* films.

Magazine editors demanded less deduction, more characterization, and a story line that began well before the crime.[2] In the 1930s, Golden Age authors had already shifted the narrational weight from the detective to secondary players and had given the action a considerable buildup before the first killing. Rex Stout had shrewdly recast the Holmes/Watson pairing as a partnership of a mastermind and an insolent wisecracker, and the central crime might occur only after a web of character relations was established.

The late 1930s novels of Ellery Queen had introduced love-interest ingredients to satisfy the slick market, a tactic that often gave the nominal protagonist a secondary role (and a girlfriend of his own).[3] In a concession to the hard-boiled trend, *The Dragon's Teeth* (1939) impelled hyperintellectual Ellery to start an agency in partnership with a tough guy private eye. But in the 1940s, authors Frederic Dannay and Manfred B. Lee returned to playing with form. They imposed a gamelike geometry on a mystery situation, a mild, mass-market version of the "systems" Joyce used to structure *Ulysses*. *There Was an Old Woman* (1943) is based on a children's rhyme, *The Scarlet Letters* (1953) on the alphabet, *Ten Days' Wonder* (1948) on the Ten Commandments, and *The Origin of Evil* (1951) on stages of Darwinian evolution. This strategy echoed Christie's nursery rhyme plotting, but Queen took the device in pseudo-literary directions. Several of these conceit-books offered Chestertonian fantasy set in artificial worlds created by rich eccentrics.

In another vein, Queen came up with murder novels that probed small-town life: *Calamity Town* (1942), *The Murderer Is a Fox* (1945), *Ten Days' Wonder* (1948), and *Double, Double* (1950). In these novels, the detective is no longer a detached brain. Ellery becomes intimately, sometimes tragically, involved with the buildup to the crime, and this pushes him toward impulsive and often mistaken inferences. When the mystery is eventually cleared up, he must confront his own failure to save lives. The Wrightsville books and their successors force the Great Detective to realize that human passions can't be wholly understood through bloodless logic.

For example, *Calamity Town* thrusts a sordid drama of marital revenge into an apple-pie New England community. The depiction of Wrightsville evokes *Our Town*, not just in its folksy detail but also in its fluent mode of narration. The late 1930s Queen novels had abandoned the restricted viewpoint of the earlier books and now we're fully in the presence of Lubbock's panoramic technique. The narrating voice, a more urbane and ironic version of Wilder's Stage Manager, freely surveys the town's response to scandal. The moving spotlight catches a host of local characters, and the style plays with verb tense, stream of consciousness, and even proper names. (Three characters, including Ellery, have fake identities.) Here the superimposed pattern is that of holidays, from Halloween to Mother's Day, and the action, which culminates in the birth of a child, takes nine months.

The result, however exuberant in method, is a gradually darkening landscape. When Ellery arrives to write his novel, he sees only calendar-perfect Americana. Installed in a rented house in High Town, right next to the first family, he can also explore Low Town, a mix of zesty ethnic types out of William Saroyan. But when rough-edged Jim Haight returns to claim his bride Nora Wright, a third Wrightsville is revealed, one teeming with gossip, disloyalty, and hatred of the newcomer. Jim is accused of murder, and the town erupts. At the end of the book, Ellery reflects, "There are no secrets or delicacies, and there is much cruelty, in the Wrightsvilles of this world."[4] Ellery's disillusionment renders ironic the book's first chapter title, "Mr. Queen Discovers America." Frederic Dannay claimed that the inspiration for *Calamity Town* was Edgar Lee Masters's mordant *Spoon River Anthology*.[5]

From the beginning, the Queen canon posited that Ellery has turned his adventures into the fictions we consume. He is both author and protagonist, rendered in third-person narration. This conceit is undeveloped in the early books, but *Calamity Town* pursues its implications in ways recalling André Gide's *Counterfeiters*. We realize at the climax that the book we are reading is the book Ellery is writing (in Writesville?). The hero's disillusionment with the town is captured by the narration's shift from heartwarming appreciation to bitter critique.

Not that the author's account flatters him: despite knowing that a murder is imminent, Ellery fails to prevent it. He witnesses the crime and draws obvious but wrong conclusions. And he comes to realize that had he grasped one vital fact, three deaths could have been prevented. He divulges the solution to the mystery only by finishing his manuscript. "I've ended it, but it's always easy to change the last chapter—at least, certain elements not directly concerned with the mystery plot."[6] The remark invokes genre conventions: Ellery has cracked the case but he needs to wrap up the romantic story line. By confiding the truth to the book's central couple, he can help restore a shattered family.

Despite its dispiriting revelations about small-town life, *Calamity Town* ends on an affirmative note. This can't be said about the Queen books that follow, which chronicle Ellery's failures to prevent death or mete out justice. He had been wrong in his salad days, in the second-guessing manner of E. C. Bentley's Trent, but now his errors are more costly and agonizing. The showoffish brilliance of the young Ellery has turned into hubris. In another reflexive gesture, *Ten Days' Wonder* shows him taken in when a killer, a fan of his novels, frames a man by erecting the sort of farfetched pattern that Ellery loves to discover. The book was conceived by Dannay to be the protagonist's last case.[7] It wasn't that, but at the end of *Cat of Many Tails* (1949) Ellery remains haunted by guilt for all the preventable deaths, and he needs to be consoled by an old psychoanalyst: "You have failed before, you will fail again. This is the nature and the role of man."[8]

The classic Golden Age puzzle had an insouciant indifference to pain and mortality, but these Queen novels, along with their continuing use of outré structural strategies, gave mystery plotting some of the brooding self-consciousness and thematic ambitions of "serious" fiction. This impulse might also be attributed to the growing prominence of hard-boiled tales; Queen's late novels are contemporary with Raymond Chandler's sagas of California morbidity. More than is usually realized, 1940s Ellery Queen is another model for those later stories of sensitive private investigators devoted to saving innocent people but tormented by a failure to play God.

Hard-Boiled, Harsh or Sensitive

This hard-boiled stuff—it is a menace.

—Dashiell Hammett, 1950[9]

Some authors darkened the puzzle driven whodunit, and others expanded the horizons of private-eye plots. Chandler established his reputation in the early 1940s, and his novels showed younger authors that they could shift from the pulps to legitimate publishers. These writers had something their predecessors lacked: acute awareness of a literary form, with recognized conventions, acknowledged classics, and an emerging body of critical commentary. In 1946, Howard Haycraft assembled the anthology *The Art of the Mystery Story*, which showcased the most celebrated appreciations of the detective genre. In the same year, a top publisher released Joseph Shaw's *Hard-Boiled Omnibus.* The term "hard-boiled," once reserved for the writing of Hemingway and Cain, now became identified with pulp crime.

Up-and-coming writers confronted the perennial need to differentiate themselves from the competition. Ross Macdonald managed to do it through making the detective a prober of ancient family crimes. Lew Archer, quiet and introspective, lacks the detachment of Sam Spade and the disenchanted idealism of Marlowe. Modifying Chandler's subjective account of the investigator's reactions, Macdonald created a sensitive central consciousness that went well with a turn in academic literary taste.

Kenneth Millar, a PhD in English literature, found in Dashiell Hammett "deep understated poetic and symbolic overtones."[10] Writing as Ross Macdonald, Millar brought these qualities to the surface in a series centered on private investigator Lew Archer. Chandler could name his protagonist Marlowe in homage to the playwright and Conrad's narrator, but now the detective tradition could support an ingrown bookishness: Macdonald's detective is named after Sam Spade's partner. But Archer is no coarse flatfoot. In his debut, *The Moving Target* (1949), Archer recognizes a Kuniyoshi woodcut and compares a woman's body to an ancient terra-cotta sculpture. As Marlowe differentiated himself from the effete intellectual sleuths, Archer distinguishes himself from Marlowe. Asked if he wants a drink, he replies, "Not before lunch. I'm a new-style detective."[11] The killer is a match for him; he quotes Kierkegaard.

Macdonald's work bears the traces of 1940s literary criticism. His PhD dissertation, "The Inward Eye," traced Coleridge's conception of psychology, and his later essays on literature were committed to Romantic accounts of creativity. He thought his best books transmuted his childhood experiences into art.[12] While subscribing to New Critics' ideas of symbolism and organic unity, Macdonald drew ideas from other currents of modern criticism. Macdonald referred to Greek myth and revealed Freudian tensions shaping characters' fates. His novels developed Oedipal motifs, not least because he, too, "bore the mark of the paternal curse."[13] He wasn't immune to flights of interpretation, speculating that the Maltese Falcon might "stand for the Holy Ghost itself, or its absence."[14] Eventually he objected to being called a mystery writer at all.

As Chandler had sought to surpass Dashiell Hammett, Macdonald believed that he could go beyond Chandler (an "uncultivated and second-rate" mind).[15] Chandler had filled his pages with deflating descriptions of locale and caustic meditations on Los Angeles culture, but Macdonald, a lover of poetry and Santa Barbara, described settings with a pointed lyricism. Chandler argued that a vivid single episode was more important than the broader plot, a view suited to a writer who built novels out of short stories. Macdonald, who admired *The Great Gatsby* for its compact organization and resonant ending, was more committed to through-composed form.

Macdonald's plan for gentrifying the genre emphasized overall design. Unlike Hammett and Chandler, he didn't face the problem of moving from short stories to novels; he began as a long-form writer. A mystery novel's structure, he argued, "must be single and *intended*"—that is, organically developed from a single premise. Only then can it gain resonance so that the mystery's solution will "set up tragic vibrations that run backward through the entire structure."[16] At the center of this structure is Archer, a sensitive prober of motive. He "is less a doer than a questioner, a consciousness in which the meanings of other lives emerge." This conception of the hero as "the mind of the novel" was, Macdonald thought, his most original contribution to the genre.[17] The discipline of architecture, the unifying force of an observer's sensibility: Henry James is not far off.

The early Archer novels developed Macdonald's method, but *The Galton Case* (1959) affords an exceptionally clear example of his efforts to streamline and dignify detective fiction. The puzzle conventions remain intact, with clues, dual identities, false confessions, eureka moments, a big reversal, and a least-likely culprit. To these are added the trappings of the hard-boiled private-eye plot, not just a violent beatdown (Archer gets sprayed in the eyes with blue paint) but also an intricate web enmeshing more than thirty characters.

These conventions, Macdonald explained in an essay, let him manage the autobiographical material he poured into the book. Like other Archer stories, the novel plays down the role of career criminals and emphasizes the shameful secrets haunting families of the rich and the poor. Most of the action consists of Archer's patient exposure of the links between a missing heir and a lawyer's murdered servant. The network expands and shifts its weight. Who, finally, is most responsible for the cascade of crimes that fracture seven families?

Nominally, Archer is the protagonist, but he is almost a blank slate, seldom revealing his reasoning. He is less the wisecracker, more the pensive observer—closer to Conrad's Marlow than to Chandler's Marlowe. Macdonald explained that his "semitransparent" narrator "is not the main object of my interest, nor is he the character with whose fate I am most concerned."[18] As *The Galton Case* goes along, Archer becomes a facilitator staging encounters, a therapist coaxing out stories of betrayal and vengeance. One after another perpetrator confesses to him, and in the final pages he elicits the traumatic memory of a father holding a bloody axe over a baby's crib.

The Galton Case self-consciously endows detective story conventions with literary value through imagery and structure. A book about class mobility opens with Archer taking an elevator to an elegant office: "It gave the impression that after years of struggle you were rising effortlessly to your natural level, one of the chosen." A book about multiple impersonations includes a scene in which Archer studies a photo of the missing son: "I began to have some glimmering of the psychology that made him want to lose himself."[19] The plot depends on the fairy-tale motif of the abandoned prince seeking to recover his birthright, then adds in strains of classical myth. One son's symbolic killing of his father foreshadows what Macdonald's essay calls "the final catastrophe." "Like the repeated exile of Oedipus, the crucial events of my novel seem to happen at least twice."[20]

Macdonald's books are jammed with characters sharing secret identities and blood ties. A daughter may masquerade as her mother, or a young man's mother may turn out to be his wife. Apart from their mythic resonance, these tactics are a natural extension of hard-boiled fiction's revival of the conventions of nineteenth-century city novels that depended on concealed pasts and unexpected blood ties. However, this tradition of sprawl is in tension with Macdonald's urge for tight organic form. He thrusts the tangled networks of Chandler into a family's past, but then sorts them out by means of an empathic protagonist and thematic parallels among couples and offspring.

At times, Macdonald's erudition slides into archness, as when in *The Wycherly Woman* (1961) we have this airport exchange:

> She backed away from me with her fist at her chin. "What are *you* doing here?"
>
>   "Waiting for Godot."
>
>   "Is that supposed to be funny?"
>
>   "Tragicomic. Where do you want to go?"

When she tells him the person she's meeting is delayed, Archer replies: "Is Godot travelling by plane these days?" You have to agree with the woman's reply: "Har dee har."[21]

Dialogue like this can seem to confirm Chandler's early accusation that Macdonald is a shade too cute. In a letter, Chandler, ever alert to style, attacked some similes in the first Archer novel, seeing them as straining to show off. When you describe a car as "acned with rust," the reader's attention is directed to "the pose of the writer."[22] In a late essay on Chandler, Macdonald drew the distinction between them by restating his commitment to overall form. Chandler's "hallucinated brilliance of detail," he maintains, lacks the "tragic unity" of Hammett's work. Characteristically, he swerves from Chandler's commitment to vivid turns of phrase. "I'm not just interested in a simile for the sake of what it does in the sentence. I'm interested in what it does in terms of the whole book. . . . Imagery is a structural element."[23] The image of the eye is a commonplace in popular fiction, but one critic has argued that Macdonald uses it symbolically within single works and across his oeuvre.[24] As for the hero, Macdonald objects to Chandler's almost hero-worshipping commitment to Marlowe. He insists that a novel's redemptive quality inheres "in the whole work and is not the private property of one of the characters."[25]

The two writers float different conceptions of literary form, both well-suited to upper-tier postwar tastes: poetic precision of texture and organic unity of structure. Macdonald's academic training in English Romanticism and New Criticism kept him committed to a holistic aesthetic. By drawing on literary techniques from Henry James onward, he aimed to give the hard-boiled tale some up-to-date bona fides.[26]

That effort helped Macdonald achieve prestige, but very gradually. In the popular market, he was overshadowed by another newcomer. In contrast to the sensitive Archer, Mickey Spillane's Mike Hammer was as subtle as his name. Spillane reveled in blunt talk, sexual aggression, and the unflinching intimidation of suspects. Avoiding the complex plotting of Chandler and Macdonald, *I, the Jury* (1947) and the novels that followed reduced most scenes to a brutal confrontation between Hammer and anyone who stood in his way. Hammer reinvents Carroll John Daly's Race Williams for the postwar equivalent of pulp publishing, the paperback market. Other writers in the hard-boiled vein added humor (as Richard S. Prather did) or simply increased sex and gore.

The explosion of paperback originals encouraged writers to develop variations on the Spillane model. Chandler ruefully reflected in 1958: "I think the hardboiled dick is still the reigning hero, but there is getting to be rather too many of him. . . . They are too numerous, too violent, and too sexy in too blatant a way." Perhaps fortunately he did not live to see hard-boiled story schemas wildly amped up in subgenres such as "male action," identified with the vast and bloody *Executioner* series (1969–2017).[27]

The adventure-centered plots of hard-boiled novels made them natural for adaptation in other media. In particular, Chandler's widely praised books, along with his contribution to the screenplay of *Double Indemnity* (1944), helped push film toward greater expressiveness. Hollywood storytelling had long committed itself to a limited omniscience, a moving-spotlight narration that allowed us a wide range of knowledge. A film was seldom restricted to a single character's viewpoint. But *The Maltese Falcon* (1941) followed Hammett's third-person presentation by almost completely confining us to Sam Spade's range of knowledge. Even more restricted is *The Big Sleep* (1946), which doesn't retain Chandler's first-person commentary but does tie us tightly to Marlowe's experience.[28]

Radio adaptations such as the series *The Adventures of Philip Marlowe* (1947–1951) easily turned first-person prose into voice-over narration. The same strategy was used in *The Brasher Doubloon* (1947), a film based on Chandler's *High Window* (1942). Other films sought to render subjectivity more deeply. In *Murder, My Sweet* (1944), adapted from *Farewell My Lovely* (1940), Marlowe tells his tale to police questioners. In flashbacks, hallucinatory shots convey his mental states when he's drugged. At the extreme, *The Lady in the Lake* (1947), from the 1943 novel, presents Marlowe's investigation wholly in point-of-view shots, with the camera serving as his eyes. These flashback stretches are enclosed within scenes of Marlowe in his office telling the story to us. None of these first-person techniques was exclusive to crime films, but they came to be associated with mystery and detection.[29]

Reciprocally, the new movie and radio conventions fed into books. A striking early example is Steve Fisher's hard-boiled innocent-man thriller *I Wake Up Screaming* (1941). Told in first person by a novice screenwriter nicknamed Peg, the book is filled with references to Hollywood stars and business practices. A rapid-fire summary of a young secretary's transformation into a starlet invokes film technique explicitly. "In the movies they call it montage. Gaudy and noisy. Scenes and bits of music; snatches of dialogue and laughter; the flash of cameras, the clatter of typewriters. All of it building . . . building . . . building." Carefully signaled ("These are the things I remember"), a flurry of images and unsourced speech reminiscent of Dos Passos traces Vicky's rise. "Lunch at the Brown Derby with Robin. Vicky being pushed through dramatic school. Open your mouth wide. Now say Ah . . . Ah. . . . ah . . . ah. Put these stones in your mouth and talk. Scream, please. Cry, please, your heart is broken, cry. No, not that way!" One passage evokes the choral effect of radio through a barrage of voices, tagged only by name, that offer incompatible versions of Vicky's rise to stardom.

> *Hurd Evans:* "Yes, I discovered her. She was singing with a band in Glendale . . ."
> *Vicky:* "It was Mr. Evans who saw me first. It was a navy party in Coronado."
> *The flack:* "Hell, no she was never a secretary. Who ever said she was a secretary? She never saw a typewriter in her life."[30]

Later, when Peg finds Vicky murdered, fragmentary flashbacks burst into his consciousness. They're set off in parentheses, and italics give urgency to her sister's accusations in the present.

> I didn't say anything. I sat there not crying and my heart beating and my head hot and cheeks hot and I didn't say anything.

"You killed her!"

(We toasted her with champagne. We all stood there and toasted her, and Vicky was on the kitchenette table, and she said this was the happiest moment in all her life . . .)

"Peg, I'm going to kill you!"[31]

Throughout the 1940s, Cornell Woolrich and other novelists would strain to evoke in prose the staccato force of storytelling in film and radio.

The Aesthetics of Fear

After Daphne du Maurier's *Rebecca* (1938) became a best-seller, the domestic thriller, in which a woman is threatened by her husband, her lover, or a sinister outsider, entered the mainstream of popular storytelling.[32] Parallel to this development was a tendency that transferred the man-on-the-run plot from espionage tales to urban crime. The man in flight might be an innocent suspect, as in Graham Greene's *The Ministry of Fear* (1943), or a criminal stalking the city, as in Patrick Hamilton's *Hangover Square* (1941).

Many of these novels were turned into films, which made the thriller genre even more accessible to audiences. Movie audiences encountered murderous husbands (*Suspicion*, 1941), wives (*Leave Her to Heaven*, 1945), couples (*Double Indemnity*, 1944), and young ladies (*Guest in the House*, 1944). The figure on the run might be a woman (*Woman in Hiding*, 1950) or an innocent couple (*They Live by Night*, 1949).

Unlike the Golden Age puzzle, the thriller lacked an explicit poetics. Patricia Highsmith's remark that suspense is best understood as "a threat of impending violent action" was part of an emerging effort to articulate the genre's creative possibilities as they were opening up.[33] In 1947, novelist Mitchell Wilson laid out several precepts. Wilson noted that once the main character has secured our sympathy, the plot typically calls forth two stages of action. First, the target must suffer escalating threats, which the writer must describe in terrifying detail. At a certain point, the victim stops being passive and decides to fight back, a process that ratchets up our fear for his or her fate. The witticisms of the Great Detective and the wisecracks of the hard-boiled hero have no place here. Every scene, Wilson maintains, must be suffused with the main character's anxiety.[34] Wilson is thinking primarily of plots that make the protagonist the prey. In his book *None So Blind* (1945), a woman, married to a blind man, draws her lover into a murder scheme. (The novel became the film *The Woman on the Beach*, 1947.)

Our sympathies get more of a workout when the protagonist is the predator: the spouse bent on uxoricide, the serial killer who takes us along, or the adulterous couple preparing their escape. As we've seen, this situation had been developed in the British middle-class murder stories, and Cain intensified the premise with his sordid scheming couples.

The culprit-centered plot coaxes us to fear the detection and capture of an immoral figure we're perversely rooting for. The emblematic moment may well be that in Hitchcock's film *Rope* (1948), derived from the 1929 play, when a maid seems on the verge of discovering the victim's body in the trunk. Even if we find the two young killers loathsome, we suffer suspense in hoping that their crime won't be exposed—at least not quite yet.

As in the romantic thrillers of Mary Roberts Rinehart and Mignon Eberhart, fear doesn't abolish mystery. An innocent target is often unaware of who's on the prowl and why, as in *The Spiral Staircase* (1946), *The Ministry of Fear*, and *Sorry, Wrong Number*. The victim or a surrogate must turn detective to discover the source of the threat. *And Then There Were None* (1945) puzzles us about who might be the killer (and the final survivor). Merging the gynocentric thriller with the hard-boiled detective film, overseen by experiments in viewpoint and block construction, yielded *Laura* as book (1943) and film (1944).

In all, the aesthetics of suspense became central to popular storytelling of the 1940s. The paperback boom carried suspense fiction into households around the English-speaking world. Alfred Hitchcock's arrival in the United States helped the thriller become a major cinematic form, and the radio program *Suspense* (1940–1962) set off a wave of comparable shows.

In later years, the psychological thriller had greater literary cachet than the straight detective story. Edmund Wilson objected to puzzle stories, but perhaps because of the canonical status of Stevenson and James, and the growing recognition of Graham Greene's grim "entertainments," he did not find fault with "the murder story that exploits psychological horror."[35] Soon enough Robert Coates, Patricia Highsmith, and Meyer Levin attracted serious critical attention with their thrillers. By 1955, a critic could note that the thriller had merged with the mainstream novel: "If you're interested in serious fiction, you cannot overlook the literature published with the label of suspense."[36] The genre's growing legitimacy enabled writers of thrillers, along with those writing detective fiction both classic and hard-boiled, to train audiences in unusual narrative technique.

Time Recaptured

During this period, the formal strategies typical of Golden Age whodunits—casebook formats, block construction, unreliable narration, viewpoint subterfuge—reshaped story schemas in neighboring genres. Psychological thrillers became more flagrantly artificial, even delirious, and hard-boiled stories were subject to complex reworking. The classic *Black Mask* plots were chronological and single in viewpoint, but by the 1940s, private-eye adventures had some of the same architectural complexity to be found in Christie, Carr, and Sayers.

True, British hybrids of detection and thriller schemas had already emerged in inverted tales and in books such as *This Man Must Die*. But in the United States in the 1940s, and especially in Hollywood, the hard-boiled story underwent more radical surgery. Original stories that had been linear and single-perspective (*Double Indemnity, The Killers, Farewell My Lovely, Mildred Pierce*) became fragmentary, scrambled, multivocal movies. The result would be called film noir. The process is most evident in the way time is handled.

"I am sick of flashback narration and I can't forgive it even here."[37] The *Los Angeles Times* reviewer admired Billy Wilder's film *Double Indemnity* (1944), but his outburst was a response to Hollywood's flashback binge. Between 1940 and 1943, more than fifty American features employed the device—probably more than in the entire 1930s. Filmmakers had come to rely on it, and they would keep doing so for decades; but like other narrative strategies, it needed variation to keep audiences engaged. Once viewers had become familiar with the device, storytellers could push it in fresh directions. Arguably, the growing use of flashbacks in films pressed storytellers in other media to extend the device.

James M. Cain, author of *Double Indemnity*, declared that the film adaptation was refreshingly original. His novella presents Walter Neff's first-person account as a straightforward, linear monologue. The opening pages don't indicate a present-time narrating situation, only a paragraph referring teasingly to "this house of death that you've been reading about in the papers." The final pages reveal that Neff has been writing an extended suicide note. But the film begins by showing us the fatally wounded Neff recording his testimony on a Dictaphone. Cain admired this tactic: "I would have done it if I had thought of it."[38]

The film's opening sharply distinguishes present from past and frames those flashbacks that annoyed the *Times* reviewer. By announcing Neff's failed scheme at the outset, the film forgoes the surprise that closes the novella. As compensation, it gives the action a fatalistic arc—"I didn't get the money and I didn't get the woman"—in keeping with the doom motif of Cain's novels. *Double Indemnity*, cowritten by Wilder and Chandler, showed filmmakers that they could replace uncertainty about what will happen at the story's end with another question: How did this ending come about?

Decades of modernist and mainstream experiments had made nonlinear time schemes a standard narrative resource across all media. In film, flashbacks crept into every genre, even westerns and musicals, and proved, as in *Letter to Five/Three Wives*, to be a reliable way to imbue any drama with greater mystery. But flashbacks came to be strongly identified with crime stories, in part because two prototypical scenarios, the trial and the investigation, were already in place in Golden Age mysteries. Each situation could motivate returning to events that had taken place in the past.

Of the many films using the trial template, *A Woman's Face* (1941) early in the cycle treated it in a rather pure form. Like Rice's play *On Trial*, it arranges its flashbacks out of chronological order. Other trial-based stories would rely on such time shifting, with some variations, as when *Kiss Tomorrow Goodbye* (1950) presents one witness launching the flashback and then returns to the courtroom to show a different witness finishing the testimony.

Likewise, *Citizen Kane* (1941) made rich use of the investigation template, with the added complexity of the "News on the March" summary. In the same year, *I Wake Up Screaming* used seven flashbacks in its first twenty-five minutes to present witnesses' responses to police questioning. *Murder, My Sweet* (1944) found an equivalent for Chandler's first-person narration in Marlowe's recitation of scenes while in custody. In *Dead Reckoning* (1947), a veteran tracking down a killer tells his story to a priest. And, as if to grant the value of Cain's concern for anchoring voice-over in a specific situation, the main action of *The Postman Always Rings Twice* (1946) is revealed in an epilogue to be a flashback, when we see Frank Chambers on Death Row completing his confession to the prison chaplain.

Trials and investigations rely on flashbacks springing from recounting, the act of telling something that took place in the past. The alternative is recalling, presenting a character's spontaneous memory of an event not told to others. This technique had close affinities with literary time scrambling, as we've seen. During the 1940s, filmmakers relied heavily on memory flashbacks, both brief and extended. Often the longer ones are launched by a crisis situation. While driving an armored car, the protagonist of *Criss Cross* (1948) recalls incidents leading up to the robbery that will be taking place in a few moments. *The Big Clock* (1948) begins with the hero pursued through a skyscraper and thinking back on how he got into trouble.

Framed flashbacks, rare in the 1930s hard-boiled novels, became more common in postwar crime fiction. Geoffrey Holmes's *Build My Gallows High* (1946), which became the film *Out of the Past* (1947), alternates present-time scenes with a chronological backstory and shifting attachments to characters. The same shuttling between past and present governs another double-indemnity plot, Jim Thompson's novel *Nothing More Than Murder* (1949). A dimwit running a small-town movie house has let his wife entice him into an insurance scheme that will let him fake her death and marry the college girl he lusts for. In place of the relentlessly linear march to doom Cain assigns his losers, Thompson's first-person narration flashes back in alternating chapters and interrupts the action with dreams and hallucinations. Cain's protagonists don't reveal their inner states very often, but Joe Wilmot shares every passing thought, thanks to italics.

Things had been coming at me too fast. I didn't have anything left to fight with. I had to do something quick or I knew I'd be yelling the truth at her. *You're goddam right I'm afraid! You'd think I pulled you into this to get Elizabeth and me out of a hole! You think I'd sell anyone out! You—*
I got the cupboard door open and reached down the whisky bottle.[39]

In his fear that he's being made a chump, the hero of *Nothing More Than Murder* offers a hard-boiled equivalent to the panicky narration of thrillers devoted to apprehensive wives and sweethearts.

A stricter lineup of time shifts was laid out by Bill S. Ballinger in *Portrait in Smoke* (1950). Here a man pursuing a woman is allotted first-person narration, and other chapters render her past life in third-person scenes. Each trace of her that the man finds is explained in the flashback that follows. (Weirdly, the events of the past are labeled "Part II," and the present-time action is tagged as "Part I.") Ballinger employs the same sort of alternation in *The Tooth and the Nail* (1955), *The Longest Second* (1957), and *The Wife of the Red-Haired Man* (1957). The effect is to force the reader to imagine how the past line of action could yield the present-time consequences.

Screenwriters and directors also tried out more complex time schemes. *The Killers* (1946), *Behind Green Lights* (1946), *Backlash* (1946), and *Backfire* (1950) shuffle flashbacks very much out of chronological order. These elaborate time schemes recall the shifting blocks of Golden Age whodunits such as Hull's *Excellent Intentions* (1938) and domestic thrillers such as Boutell's *Death Has a Past* (1939).

The 1919 stage play *A Voice in the Dark* had replayed the crime from different viewpoints. The replay device was revived occasionally in the years that followed, but 1940s storytellers had a particular affinity for it.[40] Filmmakers that dared such repetitions usually made the plot hinge on contradictory testimony, as in the B-film *Thru Different Eyes* (1942) and *The Woman in Question* (1950). The "lying flashback" was better integrated into *Crossfire* (1947), which used conflicting accounts to illustrate social prejudice. More covertly, *Mildred Pierce* (1945) presents a misleading prologue that is corrected during the climax of the flashback.[41] Something similar goes on in Hitchcock's *Stage Fright* (1950).[42]

Reaching back to Conrad's embedded stories, a nested pattern appeared in the psychological thriller *The Locket* (1946). On his wedding day, a bridegroom is visited by a psychiatrist. The doctor explains that he married the bride-to-be Nancy some years before and discovered she was mentally unstable. His flashback includes a visit from a young painter who tells of his own troubled romance with Nancy. And that flashback includes yet another one, Nancy's own account of her childhood trauma. Boxes within boxes, each one posing the central mystery: Is Nancy really the sunny, unblemished woman she seems?

The Russian-doll structure suggests a geometrical symmetry, but Nancy's central flashback appears well before the middle of the film's running time. Most of what follows is devoted to elaborating the effects she has on her lovers. Restricting our knowledge to the men, the plot traces each one's growing awareness of Nancy's psychosis as it plays out in social settings. When we finally return to the present-day wedding, there's a new surprise: Nancy is marrying into the family that wronged her as a child. After being restricted to what the men see and say, brief flashbacks now probe Nancy's mind, yielding a swarm of bad memories as she totters down the aisle. *The Locket*'s structural finesse, unlike the leaky, misbegotten flashbacks in *The Sin of Nora Moran*, shows how highly 1940s storytelling prized clear-cut patterns of time shifting.[43]

Probably the most intricate use of flashbacks in a mystery play of the period was *Eight O'Clock Tuesday* (1941), by Robert Wallsten and Mignon G. Eberhart. Although its structural gimmickry recalls *A Voice in the Dark*, the production bore quasi-modernist trappings. Its source was an orthodox puzzle novel, Eberhart's *Fair Warning* (1936), but Wallsten claimed that it was transformed by adapting techniques from Priestley's *Dangerous Corner*, Wilder's *Our Town*, and the works of Pirandello.[44]

A rather unpleasant businessman has been murdered, and Inspector Wait investigates. He asks the suspects to reenact their doings before, during, and after the crime. Twelve flashbacks are presented out of order, with changes of lighting and actor position signaling breaks in chronology. Throughout *Eight O'Clock Tuesday*, Inspector Wait freely halts each reenactment to clarify a point, much as *Our Town*'s Stage Manager interrupts the action he sets in motion. Characters, one reviewer reported, are "speaking from their different pools of light and on their various levels of time."[45] Eberhart admitted the difficulties of making the fragmented action cohere, but once she had it sorted out, she declared, in an echo of Cain on *Double Indemnity*, "I'm so MAD because I didn't think of it to use ages ago for the book!"[46]

J. B. Priestley exercised a more adventurous conception of narrative time in the investigation play *An Inspector Calls* (1945). The prosperous industrialist Arthur Birling hosts a family dinner with his daughter Sheila's fiancé. Festivities are interrupted by Inspector Goole. He reveals that a young woman has committed suicide, and her diary leaves clues to her motive. Under questioning Birling admits sacking the woman two years before for organizing a strike. In the aftermath, she lost a job in a shop because of the daughter's vindictive treatment of her. Penniless and desperate, the woman became the mistress of the very man who now wants to marry Sheila. And just two weeks ago the woman, now pregnant, was refused aid from the Women's Charity overseen by Birling's wife. Who was the father? None other than Birling's thieving, alcoholic son Eric. After pointing out that the Birlings are to blame for this tragedy, Goole leaves.

There are coincidences and then there are outrageous coincidences. *An Inspector Calls* dares to make a single wealthy family apparently responsible for a young woman's death through a string of casual cruelties. At first glance, the pattern can be justified as sheer symbolism, Priestley's implausible but compact cross-section of social exploitation. Then comes the first twist. After the detective leaves, the Birlings face the prospect of scandal and disgrace. But a phone call to the police establishes there is no inspector named Goole. Have they been hoaxed? They recall that Goole showed the woman's picture to only one family member at a time. Perhaps the pictures were of different women? And the Birlings have only Goole's word that there was a suicide at all. Perhaps all the girls they harmed are still alive? A call to the infirmary reveals that there has been no suicide for months.

While the others relax into complacency, Sheila and her brother Eric are shamed by the stranger's visit. She points out that a tragedy was averted by sheer chance. And the story isn't over. In the play's final moments, there's a phone call from the police. A young woman has just died on her way to the infirmary. It is suicide. An inspector is on his way to question the Birlings. Slow curtain.

In its old-fashioned setup—six characters in a dining room, constant dialogue, no flashy effects—Priestley's play seems a staid piece. All the better to jostle us when the ground shifts under the characters' feet. He admits: "I have spent a good many of my writing hours devising means to conjure audiences away from the prevailing tradition, after persuading them, perhaps for the first half-hour of a play, that they were safely within its bounds."[47] Is Goole a traveler from the future, visiting the family of miscreants before the woman's suicide? Or did Goole's visit occur in a parallel universe, a virtual rehearsal for the investigation to come? Either way, instead of splitting time into two paths, as do *Dangerous Corner* and *Time and the Conways*, *An Inspector Calls* folds one time frame over another. Priestley injected his mildly experimental interest in "four-dimensional drama" into a standard mystery situation.

An Inspector Calls has enjoyed a long career in repertory and in other media, whereas Eberhart's *Eight O'Clock Tuesday* is forgotten. However, both indicate that by the 1940s authors and audiences were getting accustomed to broken time lines. Nonlinear ordering had to be carefully domesticated and varied within prudent limits, but it still led to fruitful, accessible experimentation.

Multiplying Visions and Voices

From the 1910s onward, mystery storytellers became as aware as their counterparts in mainstream fiction of the power of manipulating viewpoint. That recognition was displayed in the Golden Age whodunits, the psychological thrillers, and in the varying approach to hard-boiled narration pursued by Hammett, Chandler, and Macdonald. By the 1940s, with the expansion of these genres and increasing competition for new options, novelists, playwrights, and filmmakers became hypersensitive to Percy Lubbock's precept: "The whole intricate question of method, in the craft of fiction, I take to be governed by the question of the point of view."[48]

Sometimes the innovations were modest. In radio, for instance, the singular viewpoint became common in detective tales narrated by Joe Friday (*Dragnet*),

Philip Marlowe, and others. More rarely, we find radio plays recounted by the culprit, as in Norman Corwin's "The Moat Farm Murder" (1944), treated as a series of diary entries. Although Cain felt obliged to supply a narrating situation for his protagonist's first-person account, by the 1940s most storytellers simply let the writing or speaking point-of-view character address us straightforwardly, without any explanation for why he or she is talking. *The Great Gatsby*, *The Sound and the Fury*, and *As I Lay Dying* had avoided framing devices and simply let characters narrate freely. Likewise, radio drama popularized "choral" narration.

By the 1940s, readers of popular fiction could understand that a collection of first-person accounts no longer needed to be framed as documents or testimonies. An ambitious example is Kenneth Fearing's *The Big Clock* (1946). Fearing's *The Hospital* (1939) had experimented with fragmented viewpoints, but here he applies the technique to a mainstream mystery. *The Big Clock* plays out the man-on-the-run premise as a battle of wits between a philandering magazine editor and his publisher, who is determined to frame him for a murder. Echoing the Golden Age dossier format, major and minor characters supply first-person narration. The 1948 film version simplifies things by means of a crisis structure and an extended moving-spotlight flashback.

Fearing's cynical take on Manhattan intellectuals in *The Big Clock* was anticipated in his satire *Dagger of the Mind* (1941). A man is murdered in an artists' colony filled with backbiting writers, painters, sculptors, and musicians. Several guests, along with a police captain, take turns narrating the investigation. Their accounts are clouded by envy and drunken hallucinations. In addition, three of the narrators are killed in the course of the book, with two describing the moment of death. Although 1940s film, fiction, radio, and comics include dead narrators surprisingly often, including three in one story seemed to mock the conventions of first-person recounting. This tactic fits the book's parodies of highfaluting prose and gushing reviews in avant-garde magazines.

Splitting the story action among two or more first-person narrators became a significant storytelling option in the 1940s and beyond. Jim Thompson's *The Criminal* (1953) and *The Kill-Off* (1957) switches among many accounts, as does Fredric Brown's *The Lenient Beast* (1956). In Len Deighton's *Only When I Larf* (1968), three con artists provide alternating, comically incompatible accounts of their exploits. Variants of the *As I Lay Dying* technique would become a staple of mystery fiction, particularly domestic thrillers, well into the 2010s.

More subtly Agatha Christie continued her campaign of misdirection through style and character perspective. Building on her viewpoint stratagems in *Death in the Clouds* (1935), she explored intricate patterning of viewpoints in a psychological thriller, a whodunit recruiting three detectives, and a novel centered on Poirot. In *And Then There Were None* (1939), an unseen host assembles ten people, all guilty of homicide, on an island. Each one is mysteriously killed, in accordance with the nursery rhyme. They try to unite against the threat but fail to find the killer, and all perish. A confession turns up by accident that reveals how the series of murders was pulled off.

Christie's premise goes back at least to the novel *The Invisible Host* (1930) by Gwen Bristow and Bruce Manning, and the play based on it, *The Ninth Guest* (1930). (The ninth guest, as you might expect, is Death.) Variants include the plays *Halfway to Hell* (1934) and *Angel Island* (1939). Whether or not Christie knew of these earlier works, it was her version—thanks in part to superior craft and to her brand name—that became a perennially popular novel, a hugely successful 1943 play, and several film and radio versions.[49] Its influence lingered for decades and can be seen in Quentin Tarantino's shooting-gallery plot for *The Hateful Eight* (2015).[50]

And Then There Were None, said to be the best-selling mystery of all time, relies on an ingenious revision of the schema through a fractured point-of-view technique. Ninety-one chapters shuttle us among the thoughts of eight major characters. (The two servants don't rate.) In violation of the Detection Club creed, we are allowed to enter the murderer's mind; however, as in *Death in the Clouds*, those chapters don't reveal the plotter's identity. As an extra fillip, at the end we learn that the killer is the guest who has played the detective role, taking charge of the investigation and announcing, correctly, that the murderer must be one of their own.

With her typical resourcefulness, Christie prepared a stage version that allowed the romantic couple to escape. After all, one variant of the nursery rhyme mentioned survivors. The play became the source of René Clair's 1945 film. That version didn't respect the moving-spotlight precision of the novel (except in some abrupt to-camera addresses), but it did execute its own bit of sleight of hand, a sneaky ellipsis.

In *Remembered Death* (aka *Sparkling Cyanide*, 1945), Christie distributes third-person viewpoints in a more geometrical way. A year ago, Rosalind Barton died during a restaurant dinner. Now her husband George has received anonymous letters suggesting poisoning. In an initial chapter, Rosalind's sister Iris recalls this threat, as well as incidents in the weeks leading up to the death. Others' memories of Rosalind are activated in five more chapters, each restricted to one member of the dinner party. These chapters also expose secret affiliations among the dinner guests and interested outsiders. In an effort to find the killer, George invites the guests to the same restaurant to reenact the fateful evening. Another set of six chapters traces the effects of the invitation, with the difference that Colonel Race, a detective, is included. During the meal, George is killed.

Rex Stout once asked if one could undercut the conclusions of the primary detective by letting a subsidiary character come up with the correct solution. The climax would involve "exposing not only the real villain but the real hero."[51]

This stratagem governs the last section of *Remembered Death*. Brief, cross-cut chapters trace the inquiries of Colonel Race, another official, and a man romantically involved with a suspect. We're likely to expect that Colonel Race, Christie's series detective, will break the case, but the solution is found by the amateur (who had initially seemed to be a sinister force).

In *Remembered Death* Christie tidies up the splintered-viewpoint structure of *And Then There Were None* and applies it to a classic puzzle situation. Once more, she admits the reader into the minds of the suspects in a way that the Golden Age rules would discourage. That obliges her to find tricky ways of obscuring what the culprit is up to. She achieves this result by multiplying the sort of ellipses she exercised at one point in *Roger Ackroyd* and throughout *Death in the Clouds*.

And Then There Were None and *Remembered Death* use third-person narration throughout, but *Five Little Pigs* (aka *Murder in Retrospect*, 1942) incorporates a casebook block. It's also something of a grid book with a strict geometry, which is yet again built on a nursery rhyme. Many connoisseurs consider it Christie's supreme achievement.

Sixteen years ago Caroline Crale was found guilty of poisoning her husband. She offered no effective defense. Now her daughter asks Hercule Poirot to determine if Caroline was innocent. Poirot's investigation hinges wholly on testimony and recollection. After questioning five lawyers and police officials in five chapters, he then visits the five witnesses who were in the household on the fatal day. But Poirot needs more, so he induces the witnesses to write out their memories of the central couple and the day of the murder.

The five first-person memoirs do several things. They function as flashbacks, often replaying the same events from different points of view. (The gaps and disparities will provide Poirot with clues about what really happened.) In good Wilkie Collins fashion, the memoirs reveal more about the writers than they realize. A final five-chapter section reattaches us to Poirot as he asks his last questions (five, of course) and then assembles the suspects for the ultimate revelation.

Apart from its quintuple structures, *Five Little Pigs* offers Christie's version of the old novelistic dream, the prismatic narrative. The witnesses differ sharply in their appraisals of Caroline Crale. She is "a rotter," "a gentle creature," "very dangerous," and a victim, depending on who's talking and writing about her. The same multifaceted treatment is accorded the young woman Crale has taken as a mistress. The need to resolve the plot eventually forces Christie to establish who each woman truly is. Still, as Robert Barnard points out, the conflicting views that the witnesses express provide different parts of the solution.[52] As in Berkeley's grid geometry in *The Poisoned Chocolates Case*, the clues jostle and reconfigure themselves: there, depending on each detective's pet solution; here, based on each observer's incomplete knowledge of the central women.

A Frenzy of Recapitulation

All these devices—flashbacks, restricted knowledge, multiple viewpoints, first-person recounting—were often deployed in plots built out of large-scale sections. Several books and films, particularly those hinging on flashbacks such as *The Locket*, display block organization. The most thoroughgoing 1940s use of block construction proved to be a breakthrough novel by Vera Caspary.

Caspary was a Greenwich Village free-love practitioner, Communist Party fellow traveler, occasional screenwriter, boundlessly energetic purveyor of suspense fiction, passionate paramour of a married man, and advocate for women in prison. She became the queen of block construction in film and fiction. As a screenwriter, she turned the splintered viewpoints of *A Letter to Five Wives* into the neat episodes of *Letter to Three Wives*, and her screenplay for *Les Girls* (1957) resorted to the same pattern. Several of her novels (*Stranger Than Truth*, 1946; *Final Portrait*, 1971; *Elizabeth X*, 1978) were constructed in blocks presenting different first-person viewpoints.

In 1942 *Collier's* offered Caspary $10,000 for the serial rights to *Ring Twice for Laura*. The price tag indicates the health of the slick-magazine market, which could set an ambitious beginner on a path toward fame. Published as *Laura* in 1943, the book found acclaim, and the success of the 1944 film version was credited with confirming that a psychological thriller could be the basis of an A-level picture.[53]

The novel pivots on both a mystery story and a romance. A woman is found murdered in her apartment. Although a shotgun blast has disfigured her face, she's initially identified as advertising executive Laura Hunt. After the funeral, detective Lieutenant Mark McPherson is lingering in her apartment when Laura returns from a trip. The victim was actually Diane Redfern, a model. The misidentified-victim convention triggers an investigation into the usual sort of suppressed backstory: How did Diane wind up in Laura's place? Was she alone? Was she the target all along, or did the killer mistake her for Laura? Along the way, the cop—already half in love with Laura dead—begins to both woo and browbeat her.

At the same time, a cluster of suspects needs questioning: Laura's flighty Aunt Sue, her fiancé Shelby Carpenter, and her lordly patron, the columnist Waldo Lydecker. Laura isn't exonerated either because she has reason to hate Diane. The usual scatter of clues—the murder weapon, a bottle of cheap bourbon, and a cigarette case—tugs McPherson this way and that, although his final discovery of the killer depends as much on intuition about personality as it does on physical traces. The plot hole in the film (Why isn't the artist Jacoby, who painted Laura's haunting portrait, an obvious suspect?) is in the original novel as well, but few readers or viewers seem to notice it.

What is striking about the book is its point-of-view structure. Following Golden Age precedent, Caspary revives the casebook method of composition.[54] To take us through the nine days of the investigation, Caspary creates four first-person narrators, each assigned one or two blocks. There's a metafictional, anthological impulse too: each narrator's style has its own tenor, representing a particular subgenre of mystery fiction.

If you didn't know the *Laura* mystique already, you might suspect that the opening section, told from Waldo's perspective, would announce him as the brilliant amateur detective who will solve the case and surpass the plodding McPherson. Waldo is a celebrity columnist, a connoisseur of murder and lethal banter. Like 1920s detective Philo Vance, he collects art and lords it over others through intolerable erudition. Waldo writes in periodic sentences of eloquent self-congratulation: "My grief in her sudden and violent death found consolation in the thought that my friend, had she lived to a ripe old age, would have passed into oblivion, whereas the violence of her passing and the genius of her admirer gave her a fair chance at immortality."[55] There are even fake footnotes like those in S. S. Van Dine and Ellery Queen, attesting to the scholarly bona fides of this dandy.

Waldo's power over Laura, as her patron and guru, is expanded to a remarkable authority over the narrative in this first part. He recounts things he didn't witness, chiefly the early offstage phases of McPherson's investigation, and his explanation is that of the artist as god.

That is my omniscient role. As narrator and interpreter, I shall describe scenes which I never saw and record dialogues which I did not hear. For this impudence I offer no excuse. I am an artist, and it is my business to re-create movement precisely as I create mood. I know these people, their voices ring in my ears, and I need only close my eyes and see characteristic gestures. My written dialogue will have more clarity, compactness, and essence of character than their spoken lines, for I am able to edit while I write, whereas they carried on their conversation in a loose and pointless fashion with no sense of form or crisis in the building of their scenes.[56]

This is an extraordinary passage. At one level it evokes the tradition from Dupin to Nero Wolfe of the detective as Romantic artist, a demiurge who uses sympathetic imagination to solve the crime. At the same time, the reconstructions of scenes Waldo didn't witness opens the very 1940s possibility that what follows may be his fantasy. Only near the end of his text does Waldo assert that his knowledge of McPherson's investigation is derived from what Mark later told him one night at dinner. This all-seeing narrator actually doesn't know one incriminating fact. His omniscience is an illusion.

McPherson takes up the tale in the second segment. He has read Waldo's account and treats it as a piece of evidence. As McPherson swerves the action into the realm of professional detection, the verbal register shifts. If Waldo's style is showoffish, McPherson's is laconic. Waldo celebrates how his prose will immortalize Laura, but McPherson admits that his own version of things "won't have the smooth professional touch." Actually, though, it does. It reads hard-boiled. "As we stepped out of the restaurant, the heat hit us like a blast from a furnace. The air was dead. Not a shirt-tail moved on the washlines of McDougal Street. The town smelled like rotten eggs. A thunderstorm was rolling in." McPherson, channeling Chandler, gives us the voice of the tough but sensitive dick. There's an echo of James M. Cain when he signals that in retrospect he was wrong to trust this femme fatale: he sourly describes himself in the third person.

> She offered her hand.
> The sucker took it and believed her.

McPherson's eventual victory over Waldo is prefigured in the cop's reflections on writing up crime. When Waldo learned Laura was still alive, McPherson says, "The prose style was knocked right out of him." So much for a Wimseyish fop set down in a Manhattan murder.[57]

The hanger-on Shelby gets his voice in as well. A brief third section consists of a police transcript of McPherson's questioning. Aided by his attorney, Shelby withdraws some lies, dodges uncomfortable questions, and generally remains the most obvious suspect, as well as Mark's rival for Laura. At this point in the book, Caspary begins to play an intricate game of knowledge, in which we get bits of information that test the string of deceptions and evasions the suspects offer McPherson.

In the fourth block, Laura writes her testimony. Once more the circumstance of composition is explained to us. Laura confesses that she can't understand what she thinks and feels unless she sets it down. She has burned her old diaries, but now she has to start over. "It's always when I start on a long journey or meet an exciting man or take a new job that I must sit for hours in a frenzy of recapitulation."[58] Now the action is that of the inquiring woman in peril, the figure familiar from Eberhart and Rinehart. As a result, the stylistic register is "feminine," noting costume details and shades of color while tracking fluctuations of feeling. Laura's narration is also suspenseful and contemplative, dwelling on moments that seem to radiate danger: McPherson's trick questions, Waldo's sinister manipulations, and Shelby's pretense that he's protecting her rather than himself.

Laura carries the action to a pitch of emotion because she starts to realize that she has clung to two failed men. She will gradually accept that McPherson, despite his coldness, is the best match for her. Waldo is "an old lady" and Shelby is an overgrown baby. Caspary, the left-winger, gives these portraits the taint of class corruption. Waldo and Shelby are ghoulish creatures of the high life, and Aunt Susie is the faded, self-indulgent socialite Laura might become.

Laura's recognition of her unhappiness is rendered in a choppy, spasmodic fashion. Waldo's, McPherson's, and Shelby's accounts have all been chronological. Laura's is not. It skips around in time, replays scenes we've seen from other viewpoints, and incorporates dreams that, as in *The Sin of Nora Moran*, seem as well to be flashbacks. "This is no way to write the story. I should be simple and coherent, fact after fact, giving order to the chaos of my mind. . . . But tonight writing thickens the dust. Now that Shelby has turned against me and Mark has shown the nature of his trickery, I am afraid of facts in orderly sequence."[59] It's a story arc we find throughout 1940s in fiction and film: the strong career woman is thrown off balance and succumbs to confusion. The most notorious example is *Lady in the Dark*, the 1941 play that appeared on film in 1944, the same year as the film version of *Laura*.

The lady returned from the dead will need a real man to rescue her. That rescue is enacted, again, in prose texture when McPherson reassumes control of the narrative in a fifth block. In the first stretch of it, he provides a classic summing up of the case. It's rendered with a wide-ranging explanation that deflates Waldo's early, preening claim to artistic omniscience. There follows McPherson's account of rescuing Laura from Waldo's second attempt to kill her.

McPherson's hard-boiled diction has won out. As Waldo is taken away in the ambulance, however, he earns a degree of oratorical revenge. McPherson's narration quotes Waldo's mumbled phrases as, dying, he fills in plot points. In the process, Waldo's style is inserted, like an alien bacterium, into McPherson's curt passages.

McPherson, who can afford to be gallant, gives Waldo the last convoluted word. It comes in a quotation from a second manuscript found by McPherson at the climax, a passage that confirms Waldo's guilt. In Waldo's unfinished confession, Laura is the essence of womanhood, a modern Eve, but one who continually reminded him that he could never be Adam.

Laura anthologizes three traditions: whodunit, thriller, and hard-boiled investigation. Their stylistic registers would have been difficult to capture on film, but during production the filmmakers considered mimicking the novel's block construction. *Citizen Kane* had made multiple-viewpoint narration more thinkable in 1940s movies. Eventually, however, only Waldo's voice-over was retained, but at the cost of coherence. His voice initially frames the film, drops out as our attachment shifts to McPherson, and then mysteriously returns at the very end—suggesting that his declaration of love for Laura is uttered, somehow, after his death.[60]

Plotting the Twist

Caspary went on to other successes, but *Laura* remains her most memorable novel. It became a landmark romantic mystery and a prototype for the modern domestic thriller, which weaves together first-person accounts by many characters. It's also an enduring example of how a popular genre's innovations in viewpoint, time shifting, and block construction could engage a broad audience.

Still other crime stories yielded the same dynamic by pushing toward greater experimentation, applying mainstreamed modernist and Golden Age techniques to whodunits, thrillers, and hard-boiled tales. Josephine Tey's novel, *The Franchise Affair* (1948), filters the action through a secondary character while severely marginalizing Tey's series detective Alan Grant. (She makes him mistaken as well.) Tey's *Daughter of Time* (1951) is a Jamesian tour de force that turns the armchair detective into a bedridden one. Inspector Grant is confined to his hospital bed. Supported by helpers who bring him books and dig up documents, he discovers who really killed Richard III's cousins in 1483. Another novelist would have built the plot around the archival research, but confining us wholly to Grant's perspective enables Tey to track his thinking. She also dramatizes the play of hypotheses in conversations with his bedside visitors. The *Daughter of Time*, lauded upon publication, has long been considered one of the finest of all mystery novels.

Ingenuity flourished. There were stunts such as *It's My Own Funeral* (1944), narrated by a detective in a coffin, and *Dead to the World* (1947) in which the investigator's spirit travels back to the land of the living to find his murderer. Only a little more serious was Pat McGerr's *Pick Your Victim* (1946), which replaced the question *Whodunit?* with *To whom was it done?* Jamesian principles of limited viewpoint are playfully put into action when Marines in an Aleutian Islands outpost find a torn news story. They know who the murderer is but must figure out who was killed. A time jumping strategy dominates Richard Hull's *Last First* (1947), a mystery "dedicated," the book flap tells us, "to those who habitually read the last chapter first." But this is persiflage because the initial chapter is written so obliquely that it really doesn't give away the ending of the main action.

One celebrated debut novel encapsulates many of the prime formal options of the period. Ira Levin's *A Kiss Before Dying* (1953) shows how a book could gain a clockwork intricacy by exploiting a host of emergent storytelling strategies. It also looks forward to the "twist" aesthetic that would become important in later decades.

Classic puzzle stories create surprises through quietly deceptive narration, but in the 1940s more storytellers started creating surprise through flamboyantly unreliable narration. Agatha Christie could mislead us, but she would not indulge in demented narrators. Later, *Psycho* and *Fight Club*, both in novel and film form, would exploit the duplicitous narration that became a major option in mysteries in the 1940s and early 1950s.

The situation in *A Kiss Before Dying* has a folktale simplicity. Bud Corliss wants to marry money, and he targets Leo Kingship's three daughters. He seduces Dorothy, but when she gets pregnant, Bud realizes her father will dis-own her, so he fakes her suicide. His next plan, to marry Ellen, is spoiled when she discovers Dorothy's murder, so he kills Ellen as well. Now Bud targets Mar-ion. "Third time lucky . . . all the childhood fairy tales with the third try and the third wish and the third suitor."[61] But with the help of George Gant, a young man who knew Dorothy, Marion survives and Bud is killed.

Onto a three-block exoskeleton, labeled with the three daughters' names, Levin maps familiar plot schemas. The first part, "Dorothy," is largely restricted to Bud's viewpoint, as he tries to make her abort their child. His efforts are ren-dered in the manner of the stalking-killer plot. The second part shifts to Ellen's perspective as she investigates her sister's death. Through clever detective work she establishes that Dorothy was planning a wedding, and she tracks down two young men who took classes with her. Ellen's uneasy encounters with both suspects seem to make her a woman in peril. Part three puts Marion at risk of being killed by Bud. Now the moving-spotlight narration shifts from her to Bud to George in a classic passage of climactic crosscutting.

The firm tripartite geometry attests to the heritage of Golden Age mystery. In the same vein, Levin has resorted to letters and newspaper coverage of the murders. Ellen's letter laying out her suspicions is a swift exercise in classic detective clue-reading. There is also the genre's typical self-consciousness, with references to both Holmes and thrillers (notably *Rebecca*). Recycling a 1940s motif, Levin traces Bud's psychosis to the traumatic killing of a Japanese soldier.

But what sets the book apart, and provides a model for the twists that would drive later thrillers, is a simple weaponizing of a narrative option that usually passes unnoticed when we read. After the 1920s, perhaps picking up on Hem-ingway's cryptic pronouns in *In Our Time* (1925), crime novelists began teasing the reader by withholding a major character's name during a story's opening pages. The character is merely "he" or "she." It takes three pages for Howard Van Horn to be identified in Ellery Queen's *Ten Days' Wonder* and five pages for Dorothy B. Hughes to name Dix Steele in the first chapter of *In a Lonely Place* (1947). When the character's name is never given, as in Helen Eustis's *Horizontal Man* (1946), we get the book's first mystery: Who is the character doing all this? More experimentally, Hughes's *Dread Journey* (1946) switches viewpoints within scenes and often doesn't specify who's thinking what; a simple "he" or "she" leaves us to guess. At the limit, Faulkner's *Intruder in the Dust* doesn't divulge its protagonist's name for thirty pages, and almost never mentions it afterward.

Levin saw another possibility in the cryptic personal pronoun. He could use it as a structuring device across the novel's three blocks. Part one of *A Kiss Before Dying* presents Dorothy's murder from a third-person viewpoint restricted to the killer, but it never names the man, simply calling him "he" for more than sixty pages. At the beginning of part two, when Ellen explains her suspicions in a letter to Bud (who's purportedly back home), his being named discourages us from assuming that Bud could be the mysterious *he* of part one. We might expect Bud to eventually become the helper male of classic endangered-women thrillers.

To steer us away from Bud, Levin quickly provides two suspects on the campus, hinting that one or the other could be Dorothy's killer, the *he* of the opening block. The twist comes near the end of part two when Levin reveals that Bud is on the scene and he's the man whose thoughts we followed in the first part. Only then do we realize what my précis divulged: the two sisters were killed by Marion's fiancé Bud.

By the third part, we're fully informed and can participate in woman-in-peril suspense, as Bud cozies up to Marion and tries to get a job in her father's company. It's another local, George Gant, who becomes the helper male by discovering proof that Bud transferred from Dorothy's college to Ellen's. As often happens, George has to overcome the doubts of everyone in time to rescue Marion. In a sly echo of part one, George pretends to be a man named Dettweiler when he confronts Bud, and Levin's narration switches between his two names.

A Kiss Before Dying displays the sleek engineering that would make Ira Levin (only twenty-three when the novel was published) famous for *Rosemary's Baby*, *The Stepford Wives*, and *The Boys from Brazil*, along with the play *Deathtrap*. His tour de force demonstrates how traditional detective story strategies of misdirection and obfuscation could be applied to narration in the thriller as well. That sort of synthesis would continue for decades, up to Gillian Flynn's *Gone Girl* and beyond.

***

Across all media, storytellers reworked the strategies of mystery and suspense that came forward in glorious variety during the 1940s. The new hybrids of Golden Age whodunits, suspense thrillers, and hard-boiled detection became classics, many of them identified with film noir. The decade was an era of consolidation for Anglo-American popular narrative generally, and it laid the foundations for future developments of form and style in mysteries. That consolidation encompassed emerging genres such as the police procedural and the heist plot. Over the same years, in other wings of the variorum, we find some efforts that pushed subjective viewpoint to odd extremes, providing models that endure today.

CHAPTER 8

THE 1940s

The Problem of Other Minds, or Just One

An eloping couple picks up a hitchhiking tramp, and later the bridegroom is found murdered. Other murders follow, making the tramp the likeliest suspect. While the police comb the Connecticut hills, a neurosurgeon from New York is held as a witness. He begins to write about his experience as the chase unfolds. The problem is that his account—mixing his recollections, commentary, and imaginings—seems flagrantly unreliable. His free-associative meanderings and incantatory recitations of incidents suggest an obsessive fantasist, and perhaps a killer.

He tells us his name is Henry Riddle. Dr. Riddle's car broke down in the ideal spot for witnessing the tramp's carjacking, but he claims he did not see it. More curious, the tramp is seen wearing a hat that used to belong to Riddle, and the good doctor discovers in his pocket $2,500, the same sum that the dead bridegroom was carrying. In addition, for an eyewitness who seemed to have witnessed nothing, Dr. Riddle supplies descriptions of other murders—purportedly as he imagines them but displaying a disturbing degree of detail. One body is horribly mauled by what seem to be surgical instruments.

Denying us chapter breaks, presenting flashbacks out of chronological order, constantly replaying certain scenes, Joel Townsley Rogers's *The Red Right Hand* (1945) shows how pseudo-modernist literary techniques can becloud a mystery plot.[1] Episodes blur together, one crime interrupts another, and the whole thing becomes a phantasmagoria. We're teased by the remarkable similarities between Dr. Riddle and the killer: "I know the look of him as well as I know my own. Perhaps better." Does the tramp even exist? Is everything about the doctor a maniac's fantasy? The deep plunge into subjectivity and the refusal of external validation (the police seem politely skeptical of Riddle's account) yield a hazy collage of detective fiction motifs.

A contemporary reviewer found that *The Red Right Hand* provided "a perfectly logical" solution to its puzzles.[2] But the wrap-up, with its intricate coincidences and multiplied false identities (four characters turn out to be all one person), is outrageously forced. Calling it all "a bad dream without reality," our narrator seems to treat the solution as no more than a perfunctory end to a gory fantasia on 1940s mystery conventions.

One reason to consider the 1940s as a crucial phase in popular mystery storytelling is that both the hard-boiled novel and the psychological thriller enjoyed a new prominence in many media. The result was a burst of non-linear time schemes, strategic viewpoint shifts, block construction, and a general "cinematization" of literature and theater. These changes depend on a freewheeling crossover culture borrowing from 1910s experiments, modernism, modified modernism, and the flagrant artifice of Golden Age whodunits.

Experimenting with viewpoint, storytellers explored the powers of restricted narration to a new degree. Plunges into subjectivity became de rigueur in ordinary fiction and film, and representations of extreme mental states became pervasive, even hyperbolic. *The Red Right Hand* is only one of several works that pushed those techniques to delirious limits. Other novels made subjectivity unreliable, often under the aegis of psychoanalysis. In those, the tour de force impulse of the Golden Age remained in power. At least one novelist, who became emblematic of the edgy 1940s thriller, exploited these possibilities in unique, sometimes wacky directions.

Mind Games

Mainstream fiction and genre exercises had familiarized audiences with basic options for handling the Lubbock problems of narration: Who sees? Who knows? Who tells? Mystery writers and readers had learned that the restriction to a single viewpoint didn't require first-person prose. Literary narration can attach us to a character and still report action in objective third person, as Dashiell Hammett does in *The Glass Key*. A filmic parallel would be *The Big Sleep* (1946), which ties us firmly to Marlowe without any voice-over.

Third-person attachment more commonly yields some interiority, and 1940s writers were ready to explore it. Dorothy B. Hughes's *In a Lonely Place* (1947) closely follows serial killer Dix Steele, exposing his mind through inner monologues. Mystery writers occasionally employed stream-of-consciousness techniques as well. At the climax of *To Love and Be Wise* (1950), Superintendant Bryce asks Inspector Grant if the solution isn't simply death by drowning.

> As Grant did not answer immediately, he looked up and said sharply: "Isn't it?"
> Now you see it, now you don't.
> Something wrong in the set-up.
> Don't let your flair ride you, Grant.
> Something phoney somewhere.
> Now you see it, now you don't.
> Conjurer's patter.
> The trick of distracted attention.
> You could get away with anything if you distracted the attention.
> Something phoney somewhere. . . .
> "Grant!"
> He came back to the realization of his chief's surprise. What was he to say? . . . . With a detached regret he heard his own voice saying: "Have you ever seen a lady sawn in half, sir?"[3]

As if to underscore the eureka moment, this stretch of inner speech omits a front frame that would signal that Grant is lost in thought. Only his chief's words bracket the subjective passage.

Internal narration in mystery novels may feel a bit like a montage of cinematic voice-overs, a technique that rose to prominence in the 1940s. References to motion pictures pervade popular media of the period, and some novels and plays aimed for the cinematic fluidity Rodgers and Hammerstein sought in *Allegro* (1947). Sometimes the prose could be more "cinematic" than its film adaptation. The Hollywood version of David Goodis's 1946 novel *Dark Passage* starts solidly objective, showing us a metal drum in the bed of a truck leaving a prison. We see the drum tumble off and roll down a hill, and suddenly we're inside it (figs. 8.1–8.2). For a long stretch of what follows, we see most of the action through the eyes of the protagonist. But compare the opening transition in Goodis's original. The protagonist is standing before his cell bars when he decides to escape.

> Sleep was a blackboard and on the blackboard was a chalked plan of the yard. He kept tracing it over and over and when he got it straight he imagined a white X where he was going to be when the truck unloaded the barrels. The X moved when the empty barrels were place back on the truck. The X moved slowly and then disappeared into one of the barrels that was already in the truck.
> The blackboard was all black. It stayed black until a whistle blew. The motor started. The sound of it pierced the side of the barrel and pierced Parry's brain. There wasn't much air but there was enough to keep him alive for a while. A little while. The sound of the motor was louder now. Then the truck was moving.[4]

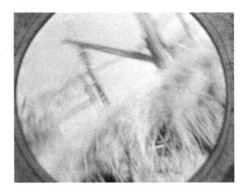

8.1 *Dark Passage* (1947): The escape in the oil drum.

8.2 *Dark Passage*: Parry's perceptual viewpoint. After this, we see the first part of the film through his eyes.

Now we are firmly in the scene, and Parry is actually escaping from prison.

It's a hallucinatory, quasi-filmic rendering, a pictorial transition from mental imagery (the planned escape) to a tangible sensory impression of Parry's successful escape. Through a kind of superimposition, Parry himself replaces the white X. The imagined blackboard becomes, perhaps through a fade-out, the darkness inside the barrel. A passage like this seems unlikely to appear in a novel written before 1940s motion pictures.

Cinematic techniques had shaped comic strips and comic books, but a peak was reached in Will Eisner's *The Spirit* (1940–1952). This series about a hardboiled private eye presumed dead who returns to solve crimes became an exercise in flamboyant pictorial display. The imagery carried film noir angles and chiaroscuro onto the page. Eisner freely employed flashbacks and fantasies, directly addressed the reader, and used "voice-over" texts and both optical and mental subjectivity.

Film references abound in that tour de force of mental collapse, Patrick Hamilton's novel *Hangover Square* (1941). The sad, aimless George Bone is a movie fan, and he eagerly attends *Tarzan Finds a Son, Goodbye Mr. Chips*, and other recent London releases. But the book goes further than mere citations. It begins with the schizophrenic Bone snapping into his alternative identity with a click he hears in his head. The change creates a "film" over his brain, and the word reminds him that "It was like the other sort of film, too—a 'talkie.' It was as though he had been watching a talking film, and all at once the sound-track had failed. The figures on the screen continue to move, to behave more or less logically, but they were figures in a new, silent, indescribably eerie world. Life, in fact, which had been for him a moment ago a 'talkie,' had all at once become a silent film. And there was no music."[5] Hamilton's book appeared just as the intelligentsia was becoming more sensitive to silent film as an art form.[6]

Throughout *Hangover Square*, the comparison of Bone's "dead mood" to movies reappears. When Bone leaves his silent cinema perception behind, the narration provides a rich sound array in a noisy pub or a crowded train. As Bone's condition deteriorates, the click and snap of his early disturbances turn into a violent crack inside his head. These devices become auditory enactments of the book's subtitle: "The Man with Two Minds."

Bone's fugue states provide an occasion for a pseudo-Joycean stream of consciousness. Planning to kill Netta, the woman who exploits him, Bone sees a woman with a hair-net.

> Netta. The tangled net of her hair—the dark net—brunette. The net in which he was caught—netted. Nettles. The wicked poison-nettles from which had been brewed the potion which was in his blood. Stinging nettles. She stung and wounded him with words from her red mouth. Nets. Fishing-nets. Mermaid's nets. Bewitchment. Syrens—the unearthly beauty of the sea. Nets. Nest. To nestle. To nestle against her. Rest. Breast. In her net. Netta. You could go on like that forever."[7]

Three hundred pages later, this punning reverie comes to maturity. After Bone has killed the woman, he carefully ties threads across her parlor furniture, securing her in his own net.

The subjectivity on flamboyant display in *Hangover Square* has a counterpart in a curious B-film, *Stranger on the Third Floor* (1940). Reporter Michael Ward gets his big break when he serves as the star witness in a murder trial and writes up the case. His fiancée Jane is happy that now they can afford to get married, but she harbors doubt about the young man who is convicted and sentenced to the electric chair. Michael recalls his own threats directed at the fussy old man in the apartment next to his. Eventually he's arrested on suspicion of murdering his neighbor. It falls to Jane to try to track down the real killer, a mysterious little man who prowls the neighborhood.

Over about sixty minutes, *Stranger on the Third Floor* anthologizes the subjective options that filmmakers would deepen in the years to come. As Michael passes the empty courtroom, an optical point-of-view shot puts us in his shoes. Quick flashbacks reveal incidents when Michael remembers threatening to kill his neighbor. When Michael falls asleep, a daringly stylized dream presents him standing trial for murder—anticipating his presumptive fate later in the film (figs. 8.3–8.4). His worries about his testimony are presented in several minutes of voice-over, along with auditory flashbacks to bits of dialogue earlier in the film.

None of these devices was new with this film, but *Stranger on the Third Floor* previews how filmmakers would weave them together in a thrust toward a "novelistic" interiority in mystery plots. Optical and auditory subjectivity, for

8.3 *Stranger on the Third Floor* (1940): The reporter whose testimony brought a death sentence on a young man dreams of standing trial himself. It plays out in looming Expressionistic imagery.

8.4 A similar stylization represents the reporter facing the death penalty.

example, would become common in 1940s films and later ones. Alfred Hitchcock had relied on these devices in his British work of the 1930s, and he probably influenced other filmmakers to take up the techniques. They were carried to extremes in *The Lady in the Lake* (1947), which like *Dark Passage* devoted long sequences limited to the protagonist's visual viewpoint. By 1952, a film could frankly launch a pure point-of-view sequence to begin the story action (fig. 8.5).

Deeper plunges into characters' minds were routine in mainstream fiction, and they were picked up in mysteries as well. Although dreams have been used as narrative devices for centuries, in the 1940s they became especially salient for

8.5 *Mr. Denning Drives North* (1940): In a condensation of familiar 1940s techniques, the opening scene provides both an optical viewpoint and a dream image.

novelists—a practice that continues to this day. Dreams can enhance character-ization and build on motifs. In mysteries, they can also trick us, as in the films *The Woman in the Window* (1944) and *Uncle Harry* (1945).

Indeed, deep subjectivity could structure an entire book. Chris Massie's novel *The Green Circle* (1943) brings together a man and a woman who offer competing accounts of a murder. At the climax, however, we learn that the stories are built out of fragments of the man's life, woven together in his fantasy. Margaret Millar's *Beast in View* (1955) looks forward to *Psycho*, both novel and film, in creating unreliable narration that suppresses crucial information about the protagonist's mental condition.

By the time filmmakers adapted *Hangover Square* for 1945 release, there was an expanded menu of subjective options available. In the screen version, George Bone is a gifted composer and not the drifter of the novel. The screen-play follows Hollywood tradition in creating a double plot: George has musical ambition, and he's also yearning for love. Barbara, daughter of an impresario, urges him to complete his flamboyant, slightly tortured piano concerto. The film's Netta figure is a music-hall singer who induces George to write songs for her. As in the book, she scorns him once she's gotten what she wants.

Unlike Hamilton's protagonist, the film's George is led to hair-trigger violence during his fugue states. He kills an old antiques dealer, then attacks Barbara, and finally strangles Netta and burns her body on a Guy Fawkes bonfire. Once he's dissociated from reality, the action he takes is usually to seek out a woman he thinks has wronged him. (We are never told why his first murder target is the shopkeeper.)

As we'd expect in a film, George's descents into madness are presented through distorted optical viewpoints and a stiffer performance style. More unusual is the use of music. As a composer, George undergoes bouts of amnesia triggered by discordant sounds. In Bernard Herrmann's experimental score, the noises that assail him (clanging metal pipes, tumbling violins) are followed by eerie chromatic passages for flute.

At the end, George performs his concerto while the police are closing in. The jagged, percussive keyboard work synchronizes uncannily with the swirl-ing tension of odd angles, rapid cutting, and sweeping camera movements. Playing his music provides George with a catharsis: abrupt flashbacks to his crimes reveal to him what he has done during his blackouts. As the salon burns, George dies playing the final passages of his composition. But it is the film's orchestral score that brings the piece to a resolution as the end credits appear. George's auditory imagination seeps into the very texture of the soundtrack—one evidence of how thoroughly 1940s cinema sought, sometimes in terms akin to that of prose, to make manifest the workings of characters' minds.

More generally, storytellers made subjectivity a major source of innovation in all media. A plunge into a character's dreams or memories could fruitfully complicate the unfolding of the plot and motivate formal experiment. For decades, novels, plays, films, and radio dramas and films would cross the border between objective action and subjective distortion.

All in the Mind

"Psychopaths sell like hotcakes," says the ambitious screenwriter Joe Gillis in *Sunset Boulevard*, and in the mid-to-late 1940s he was right. As an American version of Freudianism worked its way into popular narrative, it proved especially valuable in tales of crime and mystery. After all, deviant psychology is more interesting than plain old greed or jealousy. Psychoanalysis gave murder plots more gravitas. It also motivated the use of many pet 1940s techniques.

One of the first plays to treat psychopathology as a cause of crime was *Smoke Screen* (1935). A thug and his gang invade the home of a psychotherapist, who proceeds to analyze the crook's dreams. The doctor exposes the source of the thug's sociopathy as fear of his father, who died in a hail of police bullets. The play became a 1939 film as *Blind Alley*, which was remade as *The Dark Past* in 1949.

Storytellers realized that the talking cure could be treated as a detective story.[8] In what *Variety* called the "psycho film cycle," the therapist becomes an interrogator, the patient a witness or culprit. Flashbacks could dramatize the traumatic incident, and past events could be shot through with subjectivity. As in any mystery, the climax could tell us what really happened. These conventions appear in the grim schizophrenic drama *Bewitched* (1945), the paranoid thriller *Possessed* (1947), and *The Locket* (1946). In *Christmas Holiday* (1944), the ingratiating sociopath is diagnosed: "A psychoanalyst said Robert's relation with his mother was pathological."

More affirmative variants of the premise steer the subject toward mental health and a happy ending, as in *Spellbound* (1945) and *The High Wall* (1947). These add a romance to spice up the tension between analyst and patient. In *The Locket*, a lovely neurotic is responsible for two men's deaths. She manages to fool her lovers, one of whom is a psychiatrist, before she's overcome with a breakdown at her wedding. Even then, she is given a fair chance at recovery.

Psychiatric probing of crime appeared on stage during this period, including *The Walking Gentleman* (1942), in which a professor analyzes a serial killer. Lawrence Treat's novel *O As in Omen* (1943) makes its protagonist a psychiatrist who uses hypnosis and dream interpretation to solve the mystery. Robert M. Coates's *Wisteria Cottage* (1948) attaches us to a schizophrenic killer, with three psychiatry reports inserted to explain the action.

The domestic thriller was particularly prone to plots featuring women going mad. Patricia Highsmith's breakthrough short story, "The Heroine" (1945), suggests that its protagonist's pyromania is derived from her mother's neuroses. Patrick Hamilton's *Gas Light* (1938), a stage play that had two film adaptations, centered on a woman whose husband plots to make her think she's insane. Far more eccentric is Guy Endore's *Methinks the Lady . . .* (1945), which uses block construction and shifting viewpoints to explore, or rather exploit, Freudian theory.

Mrs. Spencer Gillian (her first name is never revealed) shoplifts a cheap pin from a department store. As the wife of a distinguished psychoanalyst, she is let off, but she is dogged by the store detective. When a woman is found murdered, stabbed with the mermaid pin that the heroine stole, she stands trial for murder and is found guilty. The next verdict to come will decide: Can she be considered insane?

All of this has happened before the novel opens. The first and longest block consists of Mrs. Gillian's memoir, composed in prison just before the second verdict. Through scrambled flashbacks, we learn of her childhood, her meeting her husband Spence, her bout of encephalitis, and above all her psychic turmoil. Her account is of a mind plagued by schizophrenia. She dreams that her sister Maggie, now a prostitute, visits her. Even after Maggie dies, the visits come to seem real. Mrs. Gillian splits into Maggie and imagines killing Mrs. Gillian (herself). The murder of the other woman convinces Mrs. Gillian and the police that her hallucinations had a real-life consequence.

The motif of the split psyche runs throughout her account. The heroine suffers from double vision, she asks Spence to explain doppelgängers, and she sees the store detective as the opposite of her husband. As if to confirm her schizophrenia, her memoir is constantly interrupted by passages of Q&A, with her assuming a second voice challenging her account or demanding that she stop digressing. Her long monologue, as is common in the "diary of a madman" genre, traces the dissolution of a personality.

Throughout the first part, Mrs. Gillian has reported her husband's technical disquisitions on neuroses and dreams. This married couple spends a remarkable amount of time reflecting on masturbation, infantile sexuality, and bodily functions. When the heroine grapples with her sister/herself, the fight turns into body horror. The heroine strips Maggie naked and scissors her legs around Maggie's shoulders. "I had her practically around the neck, her head was almost in my crotch. . . . Perhaps because of the wetness, perhaps because my mind had wandered, suddenly she had twisted in my grasp and brought her mouth over my pubis and she was biting down hard."[9]

During the struggle, the heroine senses Maggie as a dog, a cat, a horse, an elephant, a jellyfish, and a goat. Here and elsewhere we're reminded that the author was chiefly famous for the novel *The Werewolf of Paris* (1933). The shape-shifting creates a crucial ambiguity. Did the heroine really fantasize wrestling with an imaginary double? The title, *Methinks the Lady . . .* , hints that

Mrs. Gillian protests her madness too much. Could her entire confession be an effort to fake insanity? This possibility is broached in the book's second block, which shifts the viewpoint and the mode of writing.

Now three psychoanalysts discuss the text we've just read. Two are Freudians, one is anti-Freudian. Presented in playscript format, their conversations pick apart Mrs. Gillian's account. The analysts offer further interpretations of symbolism and analyze her husband. They also reflect on the judge in the case, who has mysteriously committed suicide before presiding over the insanity verdict. The skeptic argues that Dr. Gillian has coached his wife to fake her madness. Taking on the role of the detective, one analyst claims that the crucial question is "whodunit?"

But the real detective emerges in the next block, a return to Mrs. Gillian's account. She now submits a more objective document, the transcript of the hearing to determine her sanity. In Spence's testimony, he convinces judge and jury that his wife, although mentally disturbed (in part by her pregnancy), didn't commit the crime. When he names the real culprit, the classic conventions lock in. Physical clues (the mermaid pin again) and bits of behavior are reinterpreted to create a case against the least likely person. The book concludes with a card announcing the birth of a child to the Gillians and an epilogue in the name of the actual author, Guy Endore, writing to thank a certain Dr. B— McC—"for sharing details of his cases," while coyly apologizing for a title that mangles Shakespeare.

As in *The Red Right Hand*, the solution seems rushed and plagued by unanswered questions. But the crosstalk between the wife's digressive, free-associative confession and the clinicians' meanderings yields a playful dossier reminiscent of Philip MacDonald. Greeting the book as a "light-hearted" introduction to "Freudian or near-Freudian mysteries," "a danse macabre in boogie rhythm" that lets "the phallic symbols fall where they may," reviewers rightly sensed a game played not entirely in earnest.[10]

Perhaps the decade's extreme example of how psychoanalytic doctrines can motivate schizophrenic narration is John Franklin Bardin's *Devil Take the Blue-Tail Fly* (1948). It begins with harpsichord virtuoso Ellen Purcel leaving a mental hospital in the company of her husband Basil, a distinguished conductor. Around her departure hover disturbing dreams and flashbacks hinting at her guilt about her mother's death. Her journey back to their home is intercut with her first day there as she searches for a missing key—which turns out to be in plain sight. Her response: "She hated Basil, and she slapped his face hard." Are we in a *Gas Light* situation? Is he manipulating her environment, trapping her in madness?

Evidently not. Ellen is genuinely disturbed, and as she struggles toward normality the plot swirls together memories, hallucinations, and teasing glimpses of repressed items from the heroine's past. At the center of Ellen's adult problems is her college affair with a philandering folk singer, Jimmy Shad, who captivates her with the blue-tail fly song. Even this fairly definite episode is rendered in incantatory prose. Her memory of driving off with Shad is that of a swooping, dissociated aerial view:

> She opened her eyes and saw that she floated high in the air, that the moon was her neighbor and that small clouds raced playfully by her side. . . . So it was, by looking a little longer at this reckless car, by following it with her eyes and mind, by haunting it with her melody, that she discovered its occupants, the two of them: the lean, saddle-faced man who drove like a demon, eyes hard upon the black streak of road, arm thrown about the small form of the girl, the dreamy-eyed child nestled against his shoulder, the conservatory student who had fallen in love with a cabaret performer. . . . She realized that this was another of her selves that she was watching, another, more tangible Ellen.[11]

This image gives way to a more sordid one, another view from her floating vantage point, watching the couple sprawled on a bed. The evocation of man/child intimacy points back to the primal source of Ellen's troubles.

As with Woolf and Faulkner, the original experience is reshaped by the act of remembering, and the optics of Ellen watching herself points toward her growing schizophrenia. After leaving the hospital, her imaginary childhood friend Nelle ("Ellen" spelled backward) returns to trouble her. Eventually Ellen absorbs the now-grown, hard-bitten Nelle as an alternate personality. When Shad returns to New York, he seduces Ellen, but it's Nelle who kills him. By the end, with Basil perhaps also killed, Ellen retreats to her bed, haunted by memories of her father and mother struggling like two fairies over her crib. *"Don't you do it! I tell you, she is too young to touch that!" "If you touch a hair of her head, I'll murder you!"*[12]

The Red Right Hand warps and blurs the conventions of the detective story, and *Devil Take the Blue-Tail Fly* does much the same with the psychological thriller. The woman in peril suffers not from a creepy husband but from infantile abuse, and the murder she commits in a fugue state may never be discovered. There are no "objective" scenes assigned to official investigators, clinical observers, or family friends. The book locks us into Ellen's mental world, where the music that accompanies her both in life and in mind is torn by piercing screams.

Woolrich: The Overstrained Imagination

Cornell Woolrich is usually treated as an author with a uniquely haunting voice. Alcoholic and homosexual, he lived for decades in a hotel with his mother. After she died, he lost a leg to untreated gangrene. He pounded out pulp stories and thriller novels, the most famous of them published in the years 1940 to 1948. He dedicated one book to his typewriter.

His tales of suspense cultivated a hothouse morbidity. At his limit, Woolrich projects a paranoid vision of life without hope and death without dignity. But like all popular storytellers, he inherited situations, techniques, and themes. To present a bleak, aching world of precarious love and doomed lives, he carried detective and thriller conventions to a paroxysmic pitch. His faults and his virtues epitomize a great many of the distinctive narrative strategies of his time.

For him, one bout of amnesia isn't enough, so *The Black Curtain* (1941) doubles it: the hero, already having forgotten his previous identity, is clobbered by some falling bricks and now can't remember who he just was. The prototypical serial killer of the period is a man, but *The Bride Wore Black* (1940) lets a woman stalk her victims. Most thriller novelists are content to put one woman in jeopardy per book, but *Black Alibi* (1942) lines up six. Alternatively, when a woman tries to free her imprisoned husband by investigating four suspects, she's plunged into danger every time she meets one (*The Black Angel*, 1943).

Woolrich's plots bungle police procedure (his cops are exceptionally willing to help suspects), and the authorities often flounder. Suspense thrillers usually invoke the supernatural only to dispel it, but in *Night Has a Thousand Eyes* (1945), the authorities fail to save a life because one old man really can predict the future. Amateur sleuths do not fare much better. The unheroic hero of *The Black Path of Fear* (1945) could hardly be less effective; he has to be rescued by the Havana police.

Sometimes the straining for originality snaps. Critics have long pointed out improbabilities and contradictions in the plots. Woolrich's most devoted chronicler, Francis M. Nevins, warns of "chaotic ambiguities."[13] The chronology of *Rendezvous in Black* (1948) is impossible, and the climactic revelation of *I Married a Dead Man* (1948) is arguably incoherent. Characters are whisked from place to place without explanation, and convenient coincidences abound.

Add to all this a hypertrophied style that in every book slips into unabashed weirdness. "His face was an unbaked cruller of rage." "She sliced off a layer of air with her hand in my direction." "Her silhouette was that of a biped."[14] Woolrich probably offers more howlers than any other major thriller writer of his era.[15]

The plot problems and the vagaries of language can be attributed in part to the rush of Woolrich's production, his transport while hammering at his Remington portable. Pulp author Steve Fisher recalled, "Sitting in that hotel room he wrote at night—continuing through until morning, or whenever the story was finally completed. He did not revise, polish, and I suspect did not even read the story over once it was committed to paper."[16] Although Woolrich was grateful to editors who corrected his hundreds of errors in spelling and punctuation, he apparently resisted efforts to touch up his prose.[17] When an editor suggested a change to a single paragraph, he replied, "I knew you wouldn't like it," and broke with the publisher forever.[10]

Admiring readers excuse the faults by claiming that Woolrich's powers of evocation and the propulsion of suspense keep the pages turning. "Headlong suspense created by total, unrelieved anxiety," noted Jacques Barzun. "Breathless reading is the sole pleasure."[19] Raymond Chandler called him the "best idea man" among his peers, but admitted, "You have to read him fast and not analyze too much; he's too feverish."[20]

What keeps us reading? For one thing, the outré thriller situations. A couple hurrying to leave New York must clear the man of murder before the bus leaves (*Deadline at Dawn*, 1945). A killer stalks a city, but it's not a human: it's (apparently) a jaguar escaped from a sideshow (*Black Alibi*). A mail-order bride seems unacquainted with things she wrote in her letters (*Waltz Into Darkness*, 1947). And most famous, a man laid up in his apartment thinks he sees traces of a killing through a window across the courtyard ("Rear Window," 1942).

Outrages to plausibility carry their own allure. What, we ask, might come of these wild mishaps? A train crash kills a husband and his pregnant wife. In the melee an abandoned woman, also pregnant, is mistaken for the wife and welcomed by the husband's family (*I Married a Dead Man*). A man accused of murder has an alibi, to be provided by a woman he met in a bar. The trouble is, she's vanished, and all the witnesses deny she existed (*Phantom Lady*, 1942).

The development of the action also presents intriguing reversals. The lonely man gulled by the fake mail-order bride falls in love with her. People who claim not to have seen the phantom lady wind up dead. The woman trying to exonerate her husband falls in love with the guilty man and dreams about him even after he has killed himself.

There's another attraction, as Geoffrey O'Brien has pointed out. Woolrich's urban thrillers retain an air of brimstone and supernatural calamity. In his pulp days, he wrote horror stories, and his crime fiction was published in magazines offering "weird menace" tales. His overwrought style sometimes recalls fantasists such as Poe and Lovecraft.

With such strong hooks, it's no surprise that Woolrich has attracted filmmakers. Nearly all the novels were brought to the screen soon after publication, and by the 2010s his work had inspired more than a hundred movies and television shows. However faithful or unfaithful to the unfolding of the plot in the originals, the adaptations typically respected the intriguing premises and twists.[21]

Woolrich's novels tend to rely on two basic plot patterns, both derived from the hunt. Either amateurs try to solve a crime and move from suspect to suspect, or a serial killer stalks a string of victims. In the first option, our viewpoint is typically tied to the investigators, but in the second pattern, Woolrich is more innovative. Normally, the serial-killer plot either concentrates on the killer's viewpoint, as in the novels *Hangover Square* (1941) and *In a Lonely Place* (1947), or concentrates on the investigators, as in Ellery Queen's *Cat of Many Tails* (1949). A few bounce the spotlight among all the parties—killer, victims, and detectives—as in Fritz Lang's film *M* (1931) and Philip MacDonald's novel *X v. Rex* (1933).

In contrast, Woolrich emphasizes the viewpoints of the victims. The killer might appear only at the beginning and the end (*Rendezvous in Black*) or be introduced at intervals in brief, objective scenes (*The Bride Wore Black*). Less space is devoted to the investigators, although they may gain prominence as the crimes pile up. Woolrich puts his primary energies into building waves of suspense as one target after another confronts death.

The shooting-gallery structure enables Woolrich to copiously fulfill Mitchell Wilson's demand that the thriller show us what fear feels like.[22] The 1940s interest in intensely subjective narration helps out here, and Woolrich sustains it in detailed descriptions of victims' growing fright. In *Black Alibi*, Teresa is being stalked by an unseen figure:

> Something else now assailed her, again from without herself, but of a different sensory plane than hearing this time. A prickly sensation of being watched steadily from behind, of something coming stealthily but continuously after her, spread slowly like a contraction of the pores, first over the back of her neck, then up and down the entire length of her spine. She couldn't shake it off, quell it. She knew eyes were upon her, something was treading with measured intent in her wake.[23]

This passage comes as part of a ten-page account of the woman's wary progress through a night street, rendered wholly from her viewpoint.

Woolrich's other basic plot, the investigation of a murder, plays up the role of fear as well. His amateur detectives, lacking official firepower, are constantly facing danger from the suspects they track. "Fright was like an icy gush of water flooding over them, as from burst pipe or water-main; like a numbing tide rapidly welling up over them from below."[24]

In both of his favored plot schemes, these plunges into characters' minds and bodies help fill out a full-length novel. As we've seen, in popular narrative the scale of the format presents the storyteller with forced choices. Once Woolrich abbreviates some lines of action (professional police investigation, the killer's mental life), he needs to expand on the reactions of the victims or amateur detectives. But this very emphasis is one source of Woolrich's stylistic howlers. In stretching out his suspense scenes, he's tempted to pileups like this: "And the path that had led me to it through the night had been so black and so full of fear, and downgrade all the way, lower and lower, until at last it had arrived at this bottomless abyss, than which there was nothing lower."[25] Such rodomontade inflates the 1940s emphasis on subjectivity to staggering proportions.

He also recruits other techniques we've considered. They keep his action moving forward through time and hurtling into the unfolding scenes. And some tactics can help mask story problems. For example, by hinging his story around a search for a killer or a victim, Woolrich's plots tend to create a string of one-on-one encounters. Rather than disguising the episodic quality of these, he sharpens them by breaking the action into distinct blocks. Those blocks are presented as a checklist agenda, Woolrich's equivalent to the closed circle of suspects we find in the whodunit's weekend house party.

The *Black Angel* is a simple instance. After an initial cluster of five chapters presenting Kirk Murray sentenced to death, we follow Kirk's wife Alberta as she seeks the true killer among four suspects. Her efforts are given in four parallel chapters, each tagged with a telephone number. One that Alberta finds scratched out in an address book is presented just that way in the chapter title: "~~Crescent 6–4824~~." In a climactic fifth chapter, when she returns to one of the suspects, another title is recycled: "Butterfield 9–8019 Again (And Hurry, Operator, Hurry!)."

A more complicated example of modularity is *The Bride Wore Black*. It's broken into five parts, each titled with the name of a victim. Each part contains three sections. An initial one, "The Woman," shows the vengeful bride slipping into a new false identity. The part's second section, titled with the victim's name, shows how the murder is accomplished. A third section offering "Post-Mortem" on the victim consists of documents and conversations among police. Viewpoints are rigidly channeled as well. Each "Woman" section is handled in objective description, and each victim section presents the targeted man as the center of consciousness. As with other 1940s novels, the book seems to have been mapped out on a spreadsheet.

The modular layout and rigorous moving-spotlight narration risk choppiness, yielding something like a set of short stories. But the tidy exoskeleton helps mask problems of time and causality by making the plot seem rigorously organized. And the very arbitrariness of the pattern creates a sort of metacuriosity. Like the teasing tables of contents in 1920s and 1930s Golden Age fiction, a Wooolrich checklist of suspects or victims makes us aware of a larger rhythm. How will this pattern be filled out?

An overarching unity is provided as well by the demands of a deadline (another Hollywood-friendly feature). Thanks to this classic device, Woolrich can use time tags to trigger anticipation and yield a sense of shape. Long before the husband in *Phantom Lady* is accused of the crime, the first chapter bears the title, "The Hundred and Fiftieth Day Before the Execution," apparently dooming him from the start. *Deadline at Dawn* imposes a strict structure with illustrated clock faces.

Facing a ticking clock wedded to a clear-cut pattern, we become sensitive to variations among the modules. The victim-centered chapters of *The Bride Wore*

Black contrast the personalities and private lives of Julie's prey, along with her ever-more elaborate methods of murder, and the last chapter breaks the three-part format by inserted a flashback dramatizing the fatal wedding. *Rendezvous in Black* revives the shooting-gallery structure of *Black Angel* and *The Bride*, adding a schedule that sets each murder on May 31 of different years. Within this regularity ("The First Rendezvous," etc.), viewpoints multiply gradually, and the interplay of characters' range of knowledge becomes richer.

The modular structure shows up in milder ways. *Black Alibi* tags its chapters with victims' names and concentrates on one woman's terror at a time, with each chapter concluding with an exchange among investigators. *Deadline at Dawn* and *Phantom Lady* alternate scenes between two characters embarked on parallel investigations. *Night Has a Thousand Eyes*, in some ways the most ambitious of the books, embeds the checklist within the police investigation. As teams of cops trace parallel leads, their efforts are crosscut with the target under threat, waiting with his daughter and another cop.

A simpler, more poignant, rhyme-and-variations effect is supplied by a prologue and epilogue in *I Married a Dead Man*. The prologue's first-person narration, set off from the central chapters' third-person narration, finishes: "We've lost. That's all I know. We've lost, we've lost." An epilogue rewrites the prologue and yields closure: "We've lost. That's all I know. And now the game is through."

In his uncompleted autobiography, Woolrich reflected on his early efforts to compose scenes. A character takes a hotel elevator, and instead of writing, "He got in, the car started; the car stopped at the third and he got out again," the young Woolrich would pad the trip out to a page or more. This was amateurish, he thought at the end of his life.[26] This sort of expansion of minute activities is a hallmark of his 1940s novels. Episodes of terror and suspense are rendered in detail, as are the necessary touches of atmosphere. In *The Black Path of Fear*, the man on the run has told his story to Midnight.

> When I'd finished telling it to her the candle flame had wormed its way down inside the neck of the beer bottle, was feeding cannibalistically on its own drippings that had clogged the bottle neck. The bottle glass, rimming it now, gave a funny blue-green light, made the whole room seem like an undersea grotto.
>
> We'd hardly changed position. I was still on the edge of her dead love's cot, inertly clasped hands down low between my legs. She was sitting on the edge of the wooden chest now, legs dangling free.[27]

The behavior of light, the insistence on color, the items of setting, the description of the characters' postures and gestures—these are typical of Woolrich's scenes.

Much popular fiction peppers its dialogue exchanges with a few details of locale and demeanor, but in rendering even the most mundane action,

Woolrich employs Lubbock's "scenic method" to a disconcerting degree. To quote adequately would take pages, but some samples can suggest just how distended even perfunctory moments can be.

> I reached out for a little lamp he had there close beside the bed and clicked it on. Twin halos of light sprang out, one at each end of the shade, and showed up our faces and a little of the margin around them. The shade itself was opaque, to rest the eyes.
>
> Then I just sat back and waited for the shine to percolate through to him, sitting on the bias to him. It took some time. He was sleeping like a log.[28]

Any other writer would have retained just the first sentence and the last (but maybe not with the clichéd log simile). Who cares about the design of a light fixture, or whether the shade rests the eyes? Woolrich feels the need to show and tell as much as he has room for. Conrad's urge to "make you see . . . to hold up unquestioningly, without choice and fear, the rescued fragment" finds anxious expression in Woolrich's overripe descriptions.

Sights for Sore Eyes

Woolrich has Roderick Usher's "morbid acuteness of the senses." Scenes are thick with smells and sounds. One virtuoso section of *Rendezvous in Black* is all noises and speech because our center of consciousness is a blind woman.

Above all, Woolrich scenes revel in optical point of view. Sometimes the observer is imaginary, looking at things alongside the character. For example, Detective Wanger enters a murder scene:

> They seemed to be playing craps there in the room, the way they were all down on their haunches hovering over something in the middle of the floor. You couldn't see what it was, their broad backs blotted it out completely. It was awfully small, whatever it was. Occasionally one of their hands went up and scratched the back of its owner's rubber-tired neck in perplexity. The illusion was perfect. All that was missing was the click of bone, the lingo of the dicegame.[29]

Actually, the policemen are interrogating a boy whose father has been murdered. Surely Wanger, a hard-nosed cop, doesn't take the huddle for a craps game. We're given the mistaken impression of an innocent-eyed observer who's watching from a particular angle.

More often, it's the character who occupies a definite station point, determined by foreshortening and perspectival distortion. The supreme example is "Rear Window," whose original title was "Murder from a Fixed Viewpoint." Another tale tries, clumsily, for the same kind of positioning: "He turned and looked up, startled, ready to jump until he'd located the segment of her face far up the canal of opening between them."

Woolrich's interest in the geometry of looking, what can and can't be seen, finds a natural home in eyewitness plots, of which there were several in 1940s film and fiction (and even radio).[30] In "Rear Window," the protagonist Jeff tracks his neighbor's progress from window to window as if studying an Advent calendar. Woolrich strives to capture the exact angle of Jeff's field of view: "There was some sort of a widespread black V railing him off from the window. Whatever it was, there was just a sliver of it showing above the upward inclination to which the window sill deflected my line of vision. All it did was strike off the bottom of his undershirt, to the extent of a sixteenth of an inch maybe. But I hadn't seen it there at other times, and I couldn't tell what it was."[31]

Jeff's tightly focused attention contrasts with his neighbor Thorwald's casual surveys of the courtyard. The climax will come when Thorwald realizes he's been Jeff's target, and Jeff sees in the murderer's look "a bright spark of fixity" that "hit dead-center at my bay window."[32]

A similar effect occurs at the climax of "The Boy Cried Murder" (aka "Fire Escape") of 1947, the source of the film *The Window* (1949).[33] Buddy has been sleeping on a fire escape and is awakened by a murder. He watches through a slit in the window shade as the woman comes toward him. "She started to come over to where Buddy's eyes were staring in, and she got bigger and bigger every minute, the closer she got. Her head went way up high out of sight, and her waist blotted out the whole room. He couldn't move, he was like paralyzed. The little gap under the shade must have been awfully skinny for her not to see it, but he knew in another minute she was going to look right out on top of him, from higher up."[34] Again, there's a stylistic slip (of course she'll be higher up if she looks out on top of him), but it's a by-product of a struggle to vividly capture an optical viewpoint.

Sometimes Woolrich relies on typography.

I hurried down the street, and the intermittent sign back there behind me kept getting smaller each time it flashed on. Like this:

MIMI CLUB

Mimi Club

mimi club

I could tell because I kept looking back repeatedly, almost in synchronization with it each time it flashed on.[35]

The result points toward a peculiar kind of vividness—that of a film. The passage imitates alternating shots of the woman looking and the withdrawing club sign. If Woolrich's modular structure is indebted to strains in crossover fiction, the dense, overvisualized scenes inevitably suggest cinema.

Woolrich worked as a Hollywood screenwriter for a few years and had a lifelong affinity for movies. The books often use cinematic analogies and metaphors, and the characters are frequent moviegoers. (In a 1936 story, "Double Feature," a gangster takes a woman hostage in a projection booth.) Woolrich spent his last years holed up drinking and watching old films on TV. It is no surprise, then, that some passages echo the look and feel of Hollywood scenes.

Many writers, highbrow and lowbrow, were imitating cinema in Woolrich's day.[36] Some incorporated filmlike montage sequences to suggest dreams and stream of consciousness. In *Devil Take the Blue-Tail Fly*, the high-angle "crane shot" of Ellen's return to the past isn't a one-off visual effect. Earlier in the same passage we can easily imagine the filmic dissolve: "The closer she came to the quickly blackening glass, the fainter and more indistinct her own image became. Then, while she watched, the mirror seemed to dissolve, to lap away as tide recedes from a moonlit beach, revealing a depth, an emptiness, a greatly enlarged interior. . . . She found herself seated at a table in the midst of a darkened ballroom, her eyes fixed on a point in space not far from her where a spotlight stroked a silver circle on the floor."[37] In *Methinks the Lady . . .* , there is a sustained passage that "intercuts" Mrs. Gillian's vision of Maggie in her bedroom with her memory of a fairy tale told in her childhood, all the while (off-screen, so to speak) we hear her husband Spence counting off his morning exercises.[38]

But Woolrich goes further than nearly everyone. In the late novel *Fright* (1950), two paragraphs headed "Still Life" survey an empty room that shows signs of interrupted activity—a crumpled newspaper, a note, a burning cigarette, a swaying lamp chain. It mimics the sort of tracking shot over details we find in 1940s cinema, culminating a page later in a pan across a corpse jammed against the door.[39]

When a man realizes his beloved woman lies dead on the bed, a dash can imitate the abrupt effect of a cut:

> But her eyes were still blurry with slee—
> His hand stabbed suddenly downward toward the hairbrush, there before her.[40]

In *Night Has a Thousand Eyes*, a woman waits in her car while her father visits the fortuneteller over a period of weeks. Each brief scene starts with the same imagery and phrasing, creating a string of rhyming "shots" across three pages.

> I sat there waiting for him, cigarette in my hand, light-blue swagger coat loose over my shoulders. . . .
> I sat there waiting for him, rust-colored swagger coat loose over my shoulders. . . .

> I sat there waiting for him, plum swagger coat over my shoulders. . . .
> I sat there waiting for him, fawn swagger coat over my shoulders. . . .
> I sat there waiting for him, green swagger coat over my shoulders. . . .
> I sat there waiting for him, black swagger coat over my shoulders, as I'd
> already sat waiting so many times before.[41]

The modular approach ruling the book's overall architecture is carried down into the texture of scenes, here creating parallel miniblocks that convey the daughter's anxious acquiescence to her father's obsession.

Woolrich's literary optics aspire to the condition of movies. We get an effort to mimic a subjective tracking shot as a heroine circles a garden. "The little rock-pool in the center was polka-dotted with silver disks, and the wafers coalesced and separated again as if in motion, though they weren't, as her point of perspective continually shifted with her rotary stroll."[42] Likewise, a woman approaching a man slowly tapers into focus.

> She was up to him eye to eye before he could even take her in in any kind of decent perspective. His visualization of her had to spread outward in concentric, radiating circles for those eyes, staring into his at such close-range.
>   Brown eyes.
>   Bright brown eyes.
>   Tearfully bright brown eyes.
> Overflowingly tearful bright brown eyes.
> Suddenly a handkerchief had come up to shut them off from his for a moment, and he was able to steal a full-length snapshot of her. Not much more.[43]

This is just showboating, but it's uniquely *Woolrich* showboating.

The same goes for a passage struggling to describe people at a bar as if they were framed in the flattening view of a telephoto shot.

> There were eight people paid out along it. They broke into about three groups, each self-contained, oblivious of the others, but he had to look close to tell where the divisions came in. Physical distance had nothing to do with it; they all stretched away from him in an unbroken line. It was the turn of the shoulders that told him. The limits of each group were marked by a shoulder turned obliquely to those next in line beyond. They were like enclosing parentheses, those shoulders. In other words, the end men in each group were not postured straight forward, they turned inward toward their own clique. The groupings broke thus: first three, then a turned shoulder, then three again, then another turned shoulder, then finally two, standing vis-à-vis.[44]

Few writers would strive so hard to capture the positions of figures in space. It will take another page for the viewpoint character to realize that a left-handed drinker has stepped out: one beer mug isn't empty, and the handle is pointing in a different direction than the others.

It's not hard to imagine such scenes as Hitchcockian point-of-view shots. In *Waltz Into Darkness*, Durand notices a colonel and his lady in the reflection of the "thick, soapy greenish" window of a cafe. At first the view yields a blob sporting "three detached excrescences": a feather in a hat, a bustle, and "a small triangular wedge of skirt." Eventually this Kirchner-like monstrosity draws away "into perspective sufficient to separate into two persons."[45] Conrad's "impressionism," aiming to capture the limits of physical point of view, reaches a new height with Woolrich's account of straining, imperfect vision.

Many of Woolrich's verbal howlers result from the keyed-up emotion he tries to squeeze out of every scene. There's also sheer overwriting and padding, as well as his unwillingness to revise. But many errors stem from his urge to put every bit of action starkly before us. Straining for sensory vividness lures him into eccentricity and clumsiness ("triangular wedge," as if all wedges weren't triangular). When his narration falters, it's often the result of his dogged obedience to the narrative traditions he inherited. Henry James asserted that "a psychological reason is, to my imagination, an object adorably pictorial."[46] A Woolrich character puts it in a typically convoluted way: "Every time you think of anything, there's a picture comes before you of what you're thinking about."[47] Woolrich's excesses no less than his achievements stem from a period in which powerful conventions were crystallized and circulated in a dizzying host of variants.

✳ ✳ ✳

In the 1950s mysteries continued to proliferate on radio and film, moving into television and attracting stage audiences with *Dial M for Murder* (1952) and *Witness for the Prosecution* (1955). Although hardcover publishing contracted, the genre was sustained in magazines, book club editions, and paperbacks. Fairly soon, other genres gained wider fan followings. As horror titles, westerns, and erotic romances crowded best-seller lists, new subgenres of mystery—legal thrillers, techno-thrillers, and serial-killer investigations—joined them. Over the decades, James Patterson, Patricia Cornwell, Dan Brown, Janet Evanovich, Stieg Larsson, and Gillian Flynn dominated the charts and were translated around the world. One reviewer, exposed to a daily flood of such material, called mystery and suspense stories "the new mainstream of American popular fiction."[48]

By the beginning of the new century, mysteries shared the film and TV market with superhero sagas, fantasy franchises, and animated musicals, but they were much cheaper to produce and had an immense fan base. Print versions provided reliable midlist titles and an endless number of series detectives or miscreants (Hannibal Lecter, Dexter). Films, television shows, and other spinoff media assured crime stories a central place in mass culture, reinforced by true crime cable documentaries and podcasts.

In plot structure and narration, these proved the vitality of the variorum, confirming Jean-Claude Carrière's suggestion that in popular storytelling, as in cinema, "It was through the repetition of forms, through daily contact with all kinds of audiences, that the language took shape and branched out."[49] Ruth Rendell's manipulations of viewpoint in her stand-alone novels owe a great deal to thriller conventions consolidated in the 1940s. The modular plotting of Fredric Brown's novels, with blocks defined by character voice or time period, is in the Woolrich vein. An extreme instance is *Here Comes a Candle* (1950), with the ongoing action interrupted by renditions of scenes as if played out on stage, on radio, or in a film—an extension of the casebook format to adjacent media. Novelistic experiments with narration include *The Anderson Tapes* (1970), which renders a crime and investigation through wiretaps and official recordings, and Stanley Ellin's *Mirror, Mirror on the Wall* (1972) and Desmond Cory's *Bennett* (1977), both hallucinatory tales with echoes of Woolrich and *The Red Right Hand*. Throughout the years, the dossier format recurred as well, perhaps most flamboyantly in Barbara Vine's *The Child's Child* (2012) and Anthony Horowitz's *Magpie Murders* (2017), each embedding an entire novel within the one we're reading.

As the range of possibilities proliferated, the self-consciousness always present in the whodunit allowed for an updating of the comedy of murders that had emerged in the 1940s with *Arsenic and Old Lace* (1941) and the film *Murder, He Says* (1945). In an echo of *Seven Keys to Baldpate* and *Shadows on the Stairs* (1941), the comic play could take the writing of a mystery as its premise. Anthony Shaffer's *Sleuth* (1970), centering on a mystery novelist who aims to kill his wife's lover, gave its second act over to a baggy-pants pastiche of Priestley's *An Inspector Calls*. Ira Levin's *Deathtrap* (1978) went further, positing the play we're watching as an alternative version of the play being written. Like the 1920s productions that brought the audience in as jury, these had to spread their clues across the footlights. To conceal the fact that one character was another in disguise, *Sleuth*'s playbill listed a nonexistent actor in the second part. In *Deathtrap*, a scene description read out onstage corresponded exactly to the scene-setting boilerplate in the audience's program.[50] Such playfulness, wholly in the spirit of Golden Age artifice and the light modernism of Pirandello, confirmed the high degree of connoisseurship among mystery fans.

Among all these variants, authors continued to explore the ways verbal texture, the sheer laying of words on the page, could generate powerful effects of viewpoint and plot structure. At the same time, writers developed and refined genres minted in the 1940s—the police procedural, the heist plot—and these too trained generations of audiences in manipulations of time, viewpoint, and structure. The case studies in the following chapters sample some of the ripe formal and stylistic variety provided by this mode of storytelling.

PART III

CHAPTER 9

THE GREAT DETECTIVE REWRITTEN

Erle Stanley Gardner and Rex Stout

T he early hard-boiled tradition had shown how much could be achieved without the shuffled time schemes and booby-trapped viewpoints and baroque chapter divisions cultivated by the Golden Age experimenters. Dashiell Hammett and Raymond Chandler were committed to linear plotting and restricted point of view. But they too displayed the power of high artifice, showing how tightly confined viewpoint could yield Hammett's disquieting "detached attachment" or Chandler's fine-grained tracing of the detective's response to everything he encounters—qualities largely missing from the classic whodunit.

Two other writers provide some alternative options. Close contemporaries and veterans of pulp publishing, they found success when Hammett was abandoning novels and Chandler was serving his apprenticeship. Erle Stanley Gardner's first Perry Mason novel was published in 1933, and Rex Stout's first Nero Wolfe book appeared the following year. Hammett had been lucky to enter the pulps when they were booming; but the Depression devastated that market, and writers struggled.[1] Gardner and Stout realized that the future of detective stories lay in book-length fiction, ideally of a sort that could be serialized in slick-paper magazines aimed at the family or women's market. This decision gave the two men careers of great longevity, and both were still turning out novels in the 1970s.

Chandler scoffed at his rivals. He called Gardner "only by courtesy a writer at all" and declared Stout "one of the smooth and shallow operators" whose "words don't get up and walk. Mine do."[2] I'm inclined to put Chandler's rancor down to envy because Gardner and Stout were more prolific and more skilled at crafting work for the household magazines. Nevertheless, Chandler's disdain is shared by general opinion. Few historians have acknowledged the significance of Gardner and Stout in the tradition of perplexing plots. Because both men welcomed the Great Detective tradition more warmly than the hard-boiled writers did, they have been written off as formulaic, with Gardner marked a plodder and Stout dismissed as a charming lightweight.

These judgments aren't valid. Gardner was a thoughtful artisan, always on the lookout for fresh technical devices. He shows the extent to which a disciplined literary worker can create originality in a mass-market medium. More surprising, his work reveals how popular narrative can appeal to folktale archetypes and principles of oral storytelling.

Stout, a child of literary culture to an extent Hammett and Chandler never were, brought a refined aesthetic perspective to the detective story. He took some Great Detective conventions to new levels of intricacy, and his playful demotic draws unexpectedly on several traditions, not least that of "light modernism." Contrary to Chandler, Stout's words do get up and walk. Hell, they can dance.

Medium-Boiled

"Perry Mason, Criminal Lawyer" reads the scrawl on the jacket of *The Case of the Velvet Claws* (1933). "Remember that name. You'll meet him again. He is going to be famous." Thayer Hobson, president of the William Morrow publishing house, added that blurb because he had already purchased a sequel. In the wake of Christie, Van Dine, and Queen, Hobson expected that another series detective would enjoy a robust life.

He could hardly have known just how robust. Mysteries seldom achieved best-seller status in hardcover format, but once paperback publishing took off in the 1940s, the Mason titles became evergreens. In one month of 1946, Gardner novels sold more than thirteen million paperback copies.[3] By 1965, twenty-one of them had sold more than two million copies each.[4] The relentless, quick-witted criminal lawyer was featured in films, radio shows, and eventually in a top-rated television series.

Erle Stanley Gardner first published in *Black Mask* in 1923, only a year after Hammett's debut there. Calling himself the Fiction Factory, Gardner committed to pounding out a million words per year.[5] After mastering the electric typewriter, he quickly adopted dictation, passing Dictaphone recordings to several secretaries for transcription. *Velvet Claws* was his debut as a novelist and the first of eighty-two books centered on Mason. By 1979 he had written more than a hundred novels, and they had sold more than 310 million copies worldwide.[6]

Both fans and peers agreed that Gardner's readers were held by cunning plot construction. For him story stood above all. Gardner was a self-conscious literary craftsman, as obsessive as any follower of Flaubert or James in probing the principles underlying his narrative technique.

He was a creature of the 1910s and 1920s craze for manuals. Even while selling to the pulps, he scoured how-to books for tips. He toyed with *Plot Genie* and *Plotto*, and finding the plot wheels uninspiring, he devised his own discs that could randomly combine situations and settings to inspire a story. He absorbed the go-getting dynamics promoted in William Wallace Cook's *The Fiction Factory* (1912) and H. Bedford-Jones's *This Fiction Business* (1921). He became such a model pupil that Bedford-Jones invited him to write the preface to *The Graduate Fictioneer* (1932), a manual for early career authors.

Like Hammett and Chandler, Gardner wanted to preserve the investigation plot, with all its machinery of clues, misdirection, and surprises, as a mainspring for an urban adventure. But unlike Chandler, Gardner was convinced that a mystery pulled the reader along not by style but by the pattern and pacing of incidents. That led him to formulate guidelines for working out his plots.

The writer should plot the story, Gardner believed, from the murderer's viewpoint. He devised the Murderer's Ladder, a series of stages that begin with motivation and pass through temptation, planning, and first steps until culminating in the cover-up, the falsely accused suspect, and above all the need to manage "the little overlooked clues and loose threads."[7] Inevitably, the imperfections in the plan spur the killer to improvise, and the efforts to cover up errors yield "false alibis, false clues, misdirected suspicions."[8] By exposing these, the detective will solve the case.

Thinking structurally, Gardner sees those flaws in the execution of the crime as yielding incidental mysteries, and these can launch the plot proper. Instead of starting with the discovery of a dead body, let the novel unfold through an intriguing situation. A sleepless man calls on Mason to silence a howling dog. Or a client wants Mason to find the con man who's running a swindle as a beauty contest. Like the blackmail and missing-person pretexts in hard-boiled plotting, these legal contretemps delay the big crime—the murder—and ask the reader to imagine how they're related to it. They form part of what Gardner called a "clue sequence" that led to a continuous flow of unresolved situations that must eventually make sense.

Gardner was especially sensitive to the problem of maintaining reader interest during the detective's investigation. Questioning suspects one after another invites tedium, and there'll be plenty of grilling when the case gets to court. Golden Age authors had to pad out the investigation with detectives' eccentricities, colorful walk-ons, and more murders. Gardner solved the problem of the sagging middle by hurling his detective against adversaries whom he must bluff, bully, trick, or trap. Philo Vance and Hercule Poirot have the law on their side as they tag along with the authorities; the Continental Op and Philip Marlowe pursue private inquiries. Perry Mason is on a collision course with the police, the district attorney, and hostile attorneys with their own agendas.

As early as 1926, Gardner was imagining "a lawyer whose sense of justice is a lot stronger than his sense of legal ethics who habitually outsmarts the district attorney, with the action taken from court before a reader's eyes."[9] Mason would be no dilettante bantering with suspects and thick-headed police, but a hard-charging champion of the prime suspect. Mason strides into every scene with one purpose: outwitting the forces arrayed against his client. In the usual hard-boiled tale, conflict is surprisingly understated; stretches of quiet menace are broken by sudden violence. Gardner believed that blunt confrontations could sound a new note. "There hasn't been any real Jack London style of conflict developed by detective writers."[10]

The Continental Op and Sam Spade doggedly do their job without fanfare, and they sometimes reveal doubt about their dirty business. They're largely reactive. But Mason takes the initiative and radiates tireless, unquestioning strength.

> He was a fighter; a fighter who could, perhaps patiently, bide his time for delivering a knock-out blow, but who would, when the time came, remorselessly deliver that blow with the force of a mental battering ram.[11]
>
> "I'm representing my client, and when I represent a client, I fight for him—to the last ditch if necessary."[12]

In his struggle to protect his client, the hero will bend or break the law. He will hide his client from the cops and remove or destroy evidence. He will forge a document, send anonymous letters, bribe a witness, burglarize a crime scene, hire impersonators, or fabricate a confession.

The client is in jeopardy by mishap, but Mason embraces danger deliberately:

> "I'm gambling with everything I've got that he isn't guilty."
>
> "That's just the point, Chief," Della Street protested in hot indignation. "You're staking your professional reputation backing the play of an emotional kid about whom you know nothing."
>
> Perry Mason grinned at her, a grin which held no amusement, but was the savage grin of a fighter coming back into the ring to face a formidable adversary who has already inflicted terrific punishment. "Sure I am," he agreed. "I'm a gambler. . . . I play a no-limit game. When I back my judgment, I back it with everything I have."[13]

By casting the detective as an aggressor who takes big risks, the writer adds a layer of suspense that can carry the reader through the middle stretches of the book. To save his client and keep himself out of jail, Mason must unmask the killer.

Fortunately, his chance of winning is boosted by his gifts. Gardner believed that popular fiction had three essential archetypes: Cinderella, Robin Hood, and Sherlock Holmes.[14] In Mason he combined Holmes with Robin Hood. He's a smart detective, and his adroitness in squeezing out of tight spots makes him akin to suave rogues such as Raffles and the Saint. "I'm not a lawyer," he admits in one book, "except as a sideline. I'm an adventurer."[15]

Mason joins the hard-boiled tradition of making the mystery an urban adventure. The bait-and-switch premise that brings the detective into the case leads to something more perilous. Perry seldom faces immediate death, as the Op and Marlowe do, but the threat to the social order that Hammett and Chandler envision are class-based: the corruption of Poisonville, or the dependence of the rich upon the underworld. In Gardner, the danger is that of legal machinery that may crush an individual.

In classic hard-boiled tales, few people can be considered spotless, but Mason can take his client's innocence for granted. Typically, that client is a woman. She isn't above reproach; Mason's clients often lie, blunder, or hide evidence. But Gardner purifies the *Maltese Falcon* situation by making the woman in distress guiltless and not sexually alluring to Mason. His sympathy for her is unadulterated by suspicion or desire. She is in effect the Cinderella who must be rescued by magic. Gardner's recourse to courtroom showdowns shrewdly extends the 1920s and 1930s vogue for trial novels and plays, but these climaxes also display the knight in virtuous combat, defending his lady and shaming his opponents in a public tournament.

The Case of the Caretaker's Cat (1935) is an early example of Gardner's method. The plot is initiated through pretext mysteries: a questionable will, some missing diamonds, the hiding of a million dollars in cash, and a dispute over whether a family retainer can keep his cat after the master has died. In a whimsical moment, Mason takes the cat as his client, but he soon decides to represent a hard-working young woman cut out of the dead millionaire's will. Her purity is guaranteed by the fact that although she deserves a legacy she won't pursue it and prefers to run a waffle cafe. Soon the young man she loves is accused of murder, and Mason comes to his defense. At the same time, a shady attorney is bent on denying the woman any claim on the will, and Mason aims to bring down this predator.

For most cases, Mason hires detective Paul Drake to investigate witnesses and tap sources in the police force for inside information. Drake's role is to provide lumps of exposition about crime scenes and witness testimony, leaving Mason free to pursue his elaborate schemes. In *Caretaker's Cat* Mason rigs up a car-exchange trick that reveals the first murder victim is actually alive under a false identity. In court Mason clears the young man of the second murder, thanks to a slipup in one phase of the Murderer's Ladder: the culprit got scratches on his hands when trying to substitute a different cat for the caretaker's pet. All of the initial mysteries now fall into a coherent clue sequence.

As one of the *Black Mask* boys, Gardner saw Perry Mason as a two-fisted hero. But the initial drafts of the first two Mason novels worried Gardner's agent: the characters were "rather viciously hard-boiled."[16] Gardner's editor urged him to soften Mason, particularly with regard to his "hard-boiled paternalism" in the treatment of Della.[17] Gardner toned down Mason's aggressiveness by presenting him as being calmly confident about his powers.

Gardner further softened Mason's character in hopes of breaking into the slick-magazine market. One option was to give him a romantic side. Gardner's agent reminded him that both moviegoers and readers "like tenderness, heart interest."[18] Hopes for high-end serialization of the books pushed Gardner to toy with a Mason-Della liaison. In *Caretaker's Cat*, Mason recruits her for an elaborate charade in which they pretend to be honeymooners. One moment suggests that Della takes the ploy more seriously than he does.

> "I'm sorry," he said, "to wish this on you, Della, but you're the only one I know whom I can trust."
>
> "On a honeymoon?" she asked dryly.
>
> "On a honeymoon," he answered tonelessly.
>
> She snapped the wheel savagely, making the tires scream as the car slid around to the left and headed toward the Union Depot.
>
> "You don't necessarily need to collect any traffic tickets en route," he observed.
>
> "Shut up," she told him. "I want to collect my thoughts. To hell with the traffic tickets."[19]

Soon Della will halt the car to stare at Perry, ignoring the horns honking behind her. It's a scene easy to visualize on the movie screen, and it tantalizes the reader with the possibility that Della is frustrated with Mason's inability to grasp how his ploy might hurt her feelings. The book's last line has Perry remarking that they should keep the car they've bought "in case I should want to go on a honeymoon."

The tease continues in later books, for example, in *The Case of the Lame Canary* (1937), when Della and Perry plan a cruise to Asia together without Gardner ever specifying the sleeping arrangements. That book won serialization in the *Saturday Evening Post*, but Gardner wound up hating the compromise. He complained that he resorted to gimmicks ("silenced rifles and trick garages and substituted amnesia victims and what the hell have we"), but it's likely that he resented the infusion of love interest too.[20] His plots preferred to admit romance through the conventional secondary couple, as in *Caretaker's Cat*. For Gardner, Mason's softer side emerged not in passion for women but in his compassion for people threatened by the machinations of the law.

The demands of the magazine market recast Mason's professional ethics as well. Francis M. Nevins points out that the early Mason is willing to rig evidence to free a client he knows is guilty because Mason believes that the murder was justified. After signing up with the *Post*, Gardner straitlaced his hero more. "I never take a case unless I'm convinced my client was incapable of committing the crime charged."[21] The smoothing of Mason's edges continued in the last books and the popular television series. Gardner insisted that the program's writers rely on Mason's "sense of justice, his basic faith in human nature."[22]

Still, in the 1930s and 1940s books, Mason's pugilistic personal style marks him as a tough hombre. In one book he quotes Sam Spade:

Driscoll said with quivering lips, "I don't have to take this from you, you know."

"The hell you don't," Mason said easily. "You just think you don't. You'll take it and like it. Sit down!"[23]

Outselling the other *Black Mask* boys by orders of magnitude, Gardner mainstreamed the hard-boiled aesthetic while offering a more consoling vision of the urban adventurer. He saw Mason's strengths as "his mastery of dramatic courtroom technique, plus his fighting ability, his ingenuity, and his general hardboiled loyalty to his clients."[24]

As a man, Gardner lived his beliefs. While cranking out prose, he found time to defend penniless clients and form a Court of Last Resort to investigate wrongly convicted prisoners.[25] As an author, he gave readers not a lonely idealist walking mean streets but a ruthless white-collar professional who could skirt the law in the name of genuine justice. Perry Mason's flawed but idealistic successors fill the pages of our legal thrillers.

Writing Degree Zero

Gardner proves that a successful writer need not write well. His language is at best functional, at worst barbarous. In an early pulp story, within two pages we encounter:

And now the Lady of Death was smiling her incarnadined lips at me.

I confronted her with a questioning gaze which I did my best to maintain as a blank of unrecognition, yet filled with just that receptive leer which the character I impersonated would have used under such circumstances. . . .

And then her crimsoned lips sought my face, kissed me with sticky caresses, just as they had kissed the dying features of Al Kelaney and left telltale imprints on the clammy skin.

I saw a look of puzzled bewilderment.[26]

Gardner probably realized that a style like this wouldn't succeed in the book market, so the Mason novels retreat to a conservative strategy: cut the frills and pack the pages with plot complications and dialogue. Throughout, Gardner deploys a style so withdrawn and neutral, so dependent on speech, that he makes Hammett look florid. To lay a page of *The Maltese Falcon* alongside a Gardner page is to see the difference between musculature and skeleton.

Long before Elmore Leonard advised writers to "leave out the parts that readers tend to skip," Gardner was engineering his books for speed reading.[27] He avoids fine-grained description of settings or behavior. Those he does supply are sketchy or clumsy.

> The car purred smoothly up the Conejo Grade, ran past a rolling plateau country that was studded with huge live oaks. The wind had gone down now and the stars of early evening were resplendent in a sky that was clear as crystal.
> Mason took the small tin box, replaced the gum and studied it, tilting the box backwards and forwards so as to get a good view of both the top and bottom sides of the chewing gum.

The famous Gardner pace demands treating these descriptive bits as mere transitions. The scene-setting can be done in a phrase. In *Caretaker's Cat*, Mason gets a call from Paul Drake.

> "Okay," he said, "I'll come down."
> He switched out the lights, took a cab to the place Drake had indicated, and stared into the detective's pop-eyes. "You look as though you had something up your sleeve."[28]

Once on the scene, conversations start. Leonard again: "I bet you don't skip dialogue."[29]

The interchanges center on Perry confronting people or spitting out orders to Della and Drake.[30] "Make it snappy!" The conversations are sometimes maddeningly repetitive, with longer speeches broken up with filler such as "And then?" and "All right" and "Go on." (Pulp editors grudgingly admired Gardner's ability to pad out scenes to maximize wordage.) Some pages of *Caretaker's Cat* consist wholly of quoted dialogue, with no tags identifying speakers. The effect is like reading a screenplay or the script of a radio drama. There is little of Joseph Conrad's effort to "make you see": the Gardner pace makes you overhear.

This strategy is well suited to plots that culminate in courtroom testimony. By convention, these scenes consist of dozens of quick probes and clipped answers.

"Just one moment," Mason said. "Just one more question. You can recall other events which happened on that night with startling clarity, can you not, Mr. Archer?"

"I can recall them."

"You can recall having had Chilean wine for dinner?"

"Yes."

"You know that it was Chilean wine?"

"Yes, sir."

"A red wine?"

"Yes, sir."

"You recall that perfectly?"

"Yes."

"You recall asking for Chilean wine?"

"Yes, sir."

"You recall that you had a steak?"

"Yes, sir."

"You recall how it was cooked?"

"Yes, sir. Medium rare."

"You recall that is the way you ordered it?"

"Yes, sir."

"But you cannot recall whether or not immediately after the hold-up and before you telephoned the police you telephoned Villa Lavina?"

"No, sir?"

"Thank you," Mason said, "that's all."

"That's all," Fritch said wearily.[31]

Fritch isn't the only weary one. This passage concludes a stretch of back-and-forth that runs sixty pages.

Smothering scenes in dialogue helps Gardner suppress Mason's thinking. Sometimes we're told that Della Street is trying to figure out his plans, but the third-person narration is largely neutral and objective in the *Maltese Falcon* and *Glass Key* manner. (Gardner even adopts the Ned Beaumont tactic of giving us characters' full names again and again.) This is the Sayers principle of hiding the detective's reasoning: the narration trails Mason from situation to situation as he issues orders, but it seldom accesses his mind directly. In all, his opaque schemes add another layer of mystery to the plot.

The metronomic dialogue and narration bear the traces of oral composition. Years as a courtroom attorney turned Gardner into a talker. A 1946 profile noted that "the oratorical muscles of Erle's cheeks and neck have a herculean development from scores of millions of words barked in court and rattled off into a recording machine."[32] He had begun dictating his stories shortly before he launched the Mason franchise. Once he had outlined his plot on paper, he often took to the road in his motor home. Camping in wilderness solitude with his Dictaphone, he let his voice take over. No wonder the scenes read like plays; Gardner's desert recitations brought the rapid dialogue exchanges to life. His secretaries typed up the results and sent them to publishers with minimal revision.

For stage directions framing all the talk, he could tap into a store of fixed phrases that had served him well. Mason unlocks his office door, settles down with a pencil to scan a document, looks up when Della strides in. Gardner carries perfunctory scene-setting to almost parodic extremes. Consider these chapter openings from four 1930s books.

> Morning sun, streaming in through the windows of Perry Mason's private office, struck the calf-skin bindings on the shelved law books and made them seem less grimly foreboding.
> Late morning sun, streaming through the windows of Perry Mason's private office, fell across the big desk in splotches of golden light.
> Afternoon sun was slanting in through the windows of Perry Mason's office and casting reflections on the glass doors of the sectional bookcases as Perry Mason pushed through the office door and tossed a briefcase on the table.
> Morning sun streamed through the windows of Perry Mason's office. He sat at his desk, his eyes bloodshot from lack of sleep, looking across at Paul Drake.[33]

Later books open chapters in a no less ritualized way.

> It was Della Street, Perry Mason's confidential secretary, who first called the lawyer's attention to the glamorous ghost.
> Della Street, Perry Mason's confidential secretary, picked up the telephone and said, "Hello."
> Della Street, Perry Mason's confidential secretary, entered Mason's private office.
> Della Street, Perry Mason's confidential secretary, stood in the doorway between the lawyer's private office and the passage leading to the reception room.[34]

All of this has an archaic ring. Milman Parry and Albert Lord showed that Homer and other bards used epithets to fill out the metrical scheme of the tales they sang.[35] Their performances could plug in fixed phrases with astonishing fluency. In a perverse echo of antiquity, Gardner did the same for mass-media narrative. Performing his text out loud while "writing" it, he deployed his own stock of formulas. The phrase "Della Street, Perry Mason's confidential secretary" becomes a modern equivalent of a Homeric noun epithet such as "fleet-footed Achilles." Likewise, Gardner the fluent lawyer could draw on legal commonplaces to build interrogations and courtroom exchanges: "Court will recess until two o'clock." "I object on the grounds that it's incompetent, irrelevant, and immaterial." All of these set phrases facilitate rapid storytelling and speed reading.

It's sometimes said that in teaming up Nero Wolfe and Archie Goodwin, Rex Stout found a way to combine the brilliant-sleuth premise with hard-boiled dynamism. Stout's achievement is actually more complicated, but the judgment fits the Perry Mason stories fairly well. Insisting on a rigorous solution to a puzzle ("No thimblerigging!" he wrote to himself), Gardner shows that Mason is shrewd at spotting clues and drawing inferences. Although respecting the puzzle conventions, Gardner provides an alternative hard-boiled vision, one showing how a heroic protagonist spoiling for a fight and ready to protect an unfairly accused person will not succumb to Chandler's romantic melancholy. Gardner shows how the hard-boiled aesthetic could be adapted to classic mystery plotting and, undistracted by literary graces, give readers the satisfaction of watching a fighter win.

Gardner wouldn't have been as prodigal as he was without trying other styles. In 1939, the same year as *The Big Sleep*, Gardner launched another series under the pseudonym A. A. Fair. *The Bigger They Come* is told in first person by the short, clever lawyer turned private eye Donald Lam. Lam's narration displays Gardner's usual reliance on long dialogues, but it also shows that he had an urge to innovate. Rejecting the prototypical private dick, he made Lam incapable of defending himself against the bruisers who work him over. In the process, Gardner harks back to the old *Black Mask* days. He gives Lam's humiliation some of the bemused stoicism found in Hammett's Continental Op.

> His fingers hooked around the knot in my necktie, twisted it until it started choking me. He pulled on the necktie, and I came up out of the chair as though I hadn't weighed fifty pounds. His right hand swung up from his hips so that the heel of his palm pushed the tip of my nose back into my face and sent tears squirting out of my eyes. "Sit down," he said.
>
> Under the impact of that hand, I went down like a sack of meal. "Stand up," he said, and his hand on my necktie brought me up.
>
> I tried to get my hands up to block the heel of his hand as it came for my sore nose. He speeded up the punch just a little, and beat me to it. "Sit down," he said.
>
> I felt that the whole front of my face was coming off.[36]

Lam ultimately outwits the bullies he encounters, but his resignation to the inevitable beatdowns gives the series a comic flair. Just as important, Lam's boss is the tough, greedy, overweight Bertha Cool. In the prickly exchanges between them, Gardner taps into the vein that Rex Stout had opened up with the immortal pairing of Nero Wolfe and Archie Goodwin.

Holmes and Watson in Manhattan

Rex Stout began writing before Hammett, Chandler, and Gardner did. Between 1912 and 1917, he published more than thirty stories and four novels, most in pulp magazines. At age twenty-seven, Stout gave up writing to run a company that arranged for schoolchildren to set up savings accounts. The earnings from this business enabled him to move to Europe and launch a second writing career.[37]

The first fruits of that effort put him among authors who were adapting modernist techniques for a wider readership. *How Like a God* (1929) was called "an extraordinarily brilliant and fascinating piece of work," and *Seed on the Wind* (1930) made "the Lawrence excursion into sexual psychology seem pale and artificial."[38] Stout was compared favorably with Dostoevsky and Aldous Huxley.[39] In a contemporary survey of the novel, a distinguished academic had no hesitation including Stout in the company of Woolf, Dos Passos, and Faulkner.[40]

Stout mingled with the literati. He met G. K. Chesterton, Bernard Shaw, H. G. Wells, Ford Madox Ford, and Joseph Conrad. He got fan letters from Havelock Ellis and Mrs. Bertrand Russell. Manhattan tastemakers Mark Van Doren, Christopher Morley, and Alexander Woollcott became close friends.[41]

Yet soon Stout turned his back on experimentation. After the 1929 stock market crash, he needed to make money. *How Like a God* and *Seed on the Wind*, published by a firm he helped found, sold poorly. His next efforts were less formally adventurous but continued in a vein of erotic provocation. *Golden Remedy* (1931) traces the sexual frustrations of a philandering concert impresario. In *Forest Fire* (1933), a park ranger confronts his homosexual impulses. Both books garnered mixed reviews and few sales.

Stout took to heart the Collins test, the distinction between art and entertainment. Realizing that he was "a good storyteller but not a great novelist," he vowed, "To hell with sweating our another twenty novels when I'd have a lot of fun telling stories which I could do well and make some money on it."[42] His confession echoes a comment of several reviewers who had found that his first two novels, although technically a bit gimmicky, still managed to tell gripping stories.[43] More than one compared their effect to the suspense generated by detective fiction.[44]

In quick succession, Stout tried his hand at a political thriller (*The President Vanishes*, 1934), two comic romances, and detective novels. "There was no thought of 'compromise.' I was satisfied that I was a good storyteller; I enjoyed the special plotting problems of detective stories; and I felt that whatever comments I might want to make about people and their handling of life could be made in detective stories as well as in any other kind."[45] *Fer-de-Lance* (1934) launched a series centered on Nero Wolfe and Archie Goodwin, and after 1940, Stout would concentrate wholly on them. Their cases, chronicled more or less sequentially in thirty-three novels and forty short stories and novellas, ended in *A Family Affair* (1975), published shortly before Stout's death.[46]

When the author of *How Like a God* turned to mysteries, we might have expected him to produce a geometrically intricate block construction similar to *The Poisoned Chocolates Case*. After the reverse time scheme of *Seed on the Wind*, Stout might have launched something like *Obelists Fly High*, which begins with an epilogue and concludes with a prologue. Instead, Stout did something else. He carried a central convention of the detective story to a new, almost obsessive limit; he made that convention newly ingratiating; and in the process he revealed unexpected ways to experiment with style in a mass-market genre.

Nero Wolfe, weighing in at one-seventh of a ton, lives in a well-appointed brownstone on Thirty-Fifth Street. Here he breeds orchids, reads, drinks vast quantities of beer, and dines on meals of rare delicacy. To support his lifestyle, he works as a private investigator. But he is the ultimate armchair detective. His central rule of behavior, and the formal premise that founds the series, is that he leaves his home only under extreme necessity.

Wolfe's self-imposed isolation obliges him to employ an assistant, Archie Goodwin, who works as his secretary—typing correspondence, keeping plant records, dusting the office—and as an investigator. Archie fetches clients, witnesses, and suspects to meetings. Slender and strong, reasonably handsome, Archie is attractive to and attracted by women of many ages.[47]

Above all, Wolfe is committed to rationality—or at least as much as a detective in the intuitionist tradition can be. As a boy, Stout steeped himself in Doyle, Freeman, Collins, and other classics, and he admired Christie, Sayers, even Van Dine. He defended the orthodox detective story as a fairy tale "about man's best loved fairy": the belief in the power of reason to serve justice.[48] Wolfe, who grunts and purses his lips and closes his eyes, avoids displays of emotion, especially from women. He is the detached, arrogant, grumpy genius.

Archie Goodwin, as Wolfe describes him in an appreciative mood, is "inquisitive, impetuous, alert, skeptical, pertinacious, and resourceful."[49] He is good with weapons and his fists. He can bluff as well as Wolfe, but in an ingratiating, rapid-fire style. Although no less sensitive to money than Wolfe—he often has to goad his boss into taking a lucrative case—he has a streak of idealism and fair play, perhaps because he hasn't withdrawn from the world.

He has pals, including the heiress Lily Rowan and other lady friends, and he enjoys parties.

The contrast between Wolfe and Archie has inclined some commentators to see Stout's accomplishment as a teaming of two prototypical protagonists: the puzzle-solving genius and the hard-boiled man of action. It's true in part, but in the blend both components are changed.

Traditionally the armchair detective commands center stage. The prototype, Baron Orczy's Old Man in the Corner, is both protagonist and narrator. Prompted by a young woman, he recounts his cases in embedded flashbacks. Stout took the armchair detective premise as a formal problem. "Like the restrictions a sonnet writer is held to, Wolfe's chosen way of life offers a challenge that is fun to meet."[50] Stout's solution is to make the assistant participate fully in the action. Archie tells the story, and he is given plenty to do. In some books, Wolfe is offstage for many chapters.

Stout defended the use of a Watson as the best solution to the "purely technical problem" of fair play.[51] The writer must present all the information needed to solve the mystery, but the significance of crucial clues must be played down. A narrating sidekick not only justifies suppressing the detective's thinking, but it provides creative options. "A Watson keeps the reader at the viewpoint where he belongs—close to the hero—supplies a foil for the hero's transcendence and infallibility, and makes the postponement of the revelation vastly less difficult. Also, if your imagination is up to the task of making the stooge a man instead of a dummy, he will be handy to have around in many other ways."[52] Stout seized on the opportunities afforded by a restless, outgoing Watson who could contrast sharply with the great detective while complicating the plot and throwing his own mystifications into the mix. In effect, he turned the Poe-Doyle helper into a coequal protagonist.

Stout believed that what made Holmes attractive was not his reasoning power but his idiosyncrasies. He admired "the thousand shrewd touches in the portrait of the great detective. . . . It is stroked in quite casually, without effort or emphasis."[53] Archie is by turns frustrated and amused by Wolfe, and his reactions go beyond John Watson's gentlemanly tolerance. Recorded in Archie's respectful mockery, Wolfe's eccentricities and tantrums become diverting. "What makes Wolfe palatable," Donald Westlake notes, "is that Archie finds him palatable."[54]

Stout's major formal innovation is to make his Watson at least as interesting as his Holmes. The hard-boiled detective tends to be wary, weary, and withdrawn, but Archie the extravert is socially adroit. He's closer to the fast-talking newshound or salesman of 1930s movie comedies. And he has a conception of masculinity far more flexible than that of most hard-boiled heroes. He doesn't insult women or bully weak men. He can punch, but he also loves to dance in nightclubs and usually prefers milk to whisky. He almost never gets whacked unconscious. On the one occasion he is given knockout drugs, he wakes up weeping and takes a plausible stretch of time to recover.[55] Then there's his name: Who calls a tough guy Archie?

Stout admired Hammett enormously, ranking him above Hemingway, and it seems likely that Archie's patter owes something to the Continental Op's ironizing vernacular. But Stout detached himself from the "sex-and-gin marathon" on display in most hard-boiled novels.[56] In 1950, Stout parodies the Spillane style by having Archie impersonate a tough dick. He squeezes a target with phrases like "first-hand dope," "a nice juicy price," and references to "bitching up" a plan before he declares, in the noble Marlowe manner: "I have my weak spots, and one of them is my professional pride. . . . That's a fine goddamn mess for a good detective, and I was thinking I was one." Archie never normally talks this way. He walks away from the encounter grinning. "The game was on."[57]

Because Archie sees Wolfe through grudgingly admiring eyes, Stout can make their ongoing relations part of the plot. Stout turns the Watson/Holmes interplay into a battle of wits—not just a race to the crime's solution but a daily game of two men pushing against each other. Archie prods the lazy Wolfe to take cases, quarrels with him about tactics, teases him about his habits, and threatens to quit. (Archie claims to have resigned or been fired dozens of times.)

The petty friction of different temperaments working and living together makes every moment fraught with comedy. Both men bicker ingeniously. "You know me, I'm a man of action." "And I, of course, am super-sedentary." When Archie pushes too far, Wolfe will interrupt: "Shut up." They go through periods of sullen silence, usually broken by the need to cooperate on a case. Yet the interpersonal stratagems allow for a fundamental respect and affection. After Archie's boast about being a man of action, Wolfe reveals that he fetched the unconscious Archie home in a cab, with Wolfe cradling Archie's head in his lap.[58]

A stream of contrasts fills out the books. We have Archie's impudence versus Wolfe's stolidity, Archie's flood of words versus Wolfe's grunts and lapidary pronouncements, Archie crossing his legs and lifting his eyebrow and Wolfe closing his eyes and wiggling a finger. Literary analogies spring to mind: Quixote and Sancho Panza, the phlegmatic and sanguine characters of the Comedy of Humours. Whatever we settle on, it seems evident we are on archetypal terrain. "It is impossible," wrote cultural historian Jacques Barzun, "to say which is the more interesting and admirable of the two."[59]

Stout strengthens Wolfe and Archie's tie to the Great Detective tradition through Doyle's strategy of world building. Within an atmospheric London, the cozy bachelor redoubt at 221 B Baker Street was rendered with loving exactitude, from the *V.R.* bullet-holes on the wall to the shag tobacco kept in the

Persian slipper. Mrs. Hudson, Mycroft, Lestrade, and the Irregulars formed a repertory cast. Since Doyle almost no major writer of detective fiction had won readers through the sheer charm of the heroes' milieu.

Stout launched his series as critics were celebrating the richness of Holmes's world. By Doyle's death in 1930, an ardent fandom had sprung up among the Manhattan literary elite.[60] Entire books treated Holmes and Watson as actual figures, culminating in Vincent Starrett's *Private Life of Sherlock Holmes* (1933). In his influential introduction to the first collection of all the stories in 1930, Christopher Morley waxed eloquent about the "minor details of Holmesiana" and the "endless delicious minutiae to consider!"[61] There's the sitting room where clients call; Holmes stretched languidly on the sofa while he scrapes the violin; breakfasts on winter mornings; "The game is afoot!"—each scrap of information asks to be caressed and cherished. Morley founded the Baker Street Irregulars as an informal dining group. In 1934, the year *Fer-de-Lance* was published, Morley invited Stout to join the now habitually meeting Irregulars.

Stout's sardonic streak made him resist the cult's ponderous coyness. "The pretense that Holmes and Watson existed and Doyle was merely a literary agent can be fun and often is, but it is often abused and becomes silly."[62] He shocked an Irregulars dinner in 1941 with a remorseless paper asserting that Watson was a woman, probably the wife of Holmes and the mother of Lord Peter.[63] He was bemused by the efforts of the Wolfe Pack, a coterie of admirers who wanted to immortalize his creation through similar pseudoscholarship.

Who can blame them? All the trappings were there. This cantankerous genius had a Watson. Said Watson eventually confessed that the cases ("reports") were being published thanks to the ministrations of a literary agent named Rex Stout. Some characters had read the Wolfe books. As the series went on, sporadic revelations of Archie's Ohio childhood and Wolfe's youthful espionage work coaxed the faithful to ever-more patient rereading and ever wilder speculation. What fans today call head-canon proliferated. *Is Wolfe Mycroft Holmes's son? Or even Sherlock's, with Irene Adler? Is Archie Wolfe's son? Or just his cousin?* It was perhaps inevitable that the foremost Holmesian expert, W. S. Baring-Gould, would write a treatise on the Wolfe ménage.[64]

More than any other writer of the time, Stout gave detective eccentricity an obsessive-compulsive granularity. The brownstone on West 35th Street, however recognizably part of Manhattan, became an alternative world, ruled by routines capable of endless fine-tuning. Fritz Brenner cooks; Theodore Horstmann tends to the orchids. Wolfe's schedule is strict, from breakfast in his bedroom to the evening, when, if there are no meetings with clients, Wolfe reads and Archie is likely to go out on a date or to a poker game.

The geography of the brownstone is as sharply etched as its routines, and as the years go by, we learn more and more. Seven front steps lead to the door, which has a one-way glass and a chain bolt. Pressing the button activates a doorbell, which replaced the buzzer of the first book. The best chair in the office is red, with a small table positioned at a client's elbow for easy check-signing. At one end of the office is a big globe (first two feet, then three feet in diameter) that Wolfe likes to gently spin. On his desk is a thin gold strip that he uses as a bookmark. One drawer is reserved for the beer-bottle caps Wolfe occasionally counts. There's a safe, a cabinet for files, and built-in bookshelves holding hundreds of volumes. A painting conceals a peephole.[65]

In the last book of the series, after his most traumatic case, Wolfe contemplates ten days of peace. What will he do? "Loaf, drift. . . . Read books, drink beer, discuss food with Fritz, logomachize with Archie."[66] This is a world that tries to keep anything new from happening.[67]

Stout's casually stroked-in details pay homage to the master. Morley called the Holmes stories "this great encyclopedia of romance," but another detective novelist, Edmund Crispin, pointed out that the account of Wolfe's lair are "so encyclopedic and thoroughgoing that the Holmes-Watson ménage on Baker Street, in comparison, is reduced to the sketchiest of shadow-shows."[68]

Revising the Conventions

Apart from characterizing his Holmes and Watson in full array, Stout uses world making to fill out the novel's length. In the process, he enlivened central conventions of the classic puzzle mystery.

For instance, the armchair premise motivates not only Archie's excursions but the need to hire other investigators who become fixtures of Wolfe's world. These operatives become helpers, occasional obstacles, and Archie's comrades in arms. They also push offstage all the cycles of tailing and questioning that can make the action flag. Similarly, Wolfe's willful immobility recasts the convention of the bumbling police. Archie can be summoned to headquarters and even jailed as a material witness, but Wolfe can usually avoid that fate. The cops must come calling. Wolfe can subject Inspector Cramer and Sergeant Purley Stebbins to his schedule, and when he finally grants them an audience, he can intimidate, bargain, and dodge accusations in comfort.

The personal proclivities of the Great Detective have always helped flesh out the standard plot and build fan loyalty. Food is central to Stout's strategy. He delineates every exotic dish served in the household, every sandwich Archie gobbles in custody, even Cramer's stomach-turning snack of salami and buttermilk. Groceries, brought home by Fritz or picked up in flight from the police, are lovingly itemized. The Continental Op briefly notes his abalone soup and minute steak, and Marlowe typically just eats an unspecified lunch or dinner. Archie dwells on his dining options. "I had had it in mind to drop in at Rusterman's Restaurant for dinner and say hello to Marko that evening, but now

I didn't feel like sitting through all the motions, so I kept going to Eleventh Avenue, to Mart's Diner, and perched on a stool while I cleaned up a plate of beef strew, three ripe tomatoes sliced by me, and two pieces of blueberry pie."[69] Archie invokes another Wolfe domain, Rusterman's, only to head to the diner counter and indulge the Ohio boy's fondness for comfort food. The "sliced by me" defines Archie's insistence on taking charge, along with his appreciation of freshness. It's a touch nobody but Stout would include.

Building this unique world obliges Stout to alter the role of detecting as a profession. Philip Marlowe accepts what business he can scrape up, and Perry Mason can afford to take indigent clients, even a caretaker's cat. Wolfe and Archie rely on high-end customers. The clientele comes mostly from the plutocracy and the professions: lawyers, professors, media producers, company executives, and a surprising number of writers and publishers. Typically a financial or personal problem leads to a murder, and Wolfe and Archie are obliged to solve the crime in order to collect payment for the original assignment. In one book, Wolfe calls this "effecting a merger."[70]

More than most detectives, Wolfe takes on some clients in teams. He may be retained by a committee delegated to manage a crisis or representatives of a firm or professional association or a family of heirs or a band of old college classmates. The question-and-answer scenes of the classic mystery get recast as business meetings, or what Archie sometimes calls conferences. Wolfe summons a group of people with stakes in the matter. Refreshments are served—more detailing of beverages and preferences—and participants are free to examine Wolfe's library and furnishings. When Wolfe gets to work, the quizzing that is the mainstay of the classic puzzle is turned into an open-ended discussion. Jacques Barzun calls it Wolfe's seminar method.[71] "I doubt I'll have a single question to put to any of you, though of course an occasion for one may rise. I merely want to describe the situation as it now stands and invite your comment. You may have none."[72] Chandler, who had been an oil company executive, confessed he had trouble writing scenes with more than two people, but Stout, who founded a successful company, excelled in roundtable discussions.[73]

The mercantile tenor of the books reshapes the conventional denouement, the gathering of all the suspects. Archie, reflecting as usual on the artifice of detective conventions, calls these Wolfe's parties or charades. Theatrical they often are, but they don't have the inexorability of Ellery Queen's "exercises in deduction" or Perry Mason's annihilation of testimony. Wolfe's evidence is often flimsy, and he must provoke the guilty party to self-betrayal. Assembled in Wolfe's office, usually under the eyes of Cramer and Stebbins, the principals are lectured, hectored, bluffed, and misled. After the book's procession of meetings presided over by Wolfe, the climax seems less a blinding revelation than a boardroom power play.

Wolfe's conclusions are often risky intuitions, light on evidence that would convince a jury. Hence the frequent recourse to extralegal pressures that would give even Perry Mason pause. Wolfe will coolly order burglary, send out anonymous messages, and press the guilty party to commit suicide. Worse, later phases of the plot are likely to hide crucial information from Archie, and us. Stout may have taken comfort in the fact the best mystery mongers violated fair-play rules.[74] He claimed that Doyle ended his career by concocting "preposterous" mysteries, but that didn't lessen the magnetism of the Holmes/Watson relationship.[75] Stout never wanted to sacrifice character byplay to the Detection Club rulebook.

Wolfe's dodgy shortcuts, implausible as they sometimes are, create fine scenes. They generate suspense, offer Archie new challenges, allow Wolfe to earn his fee, prove his cunning, and provoke Cramer's wrath. Likewise, keeping Archie in the dark at the climax adds value, tightening household friction and giving him occasion for eloquent complaint.

Nearly all of the typical Stout dynamics are already on display in the first book, *Fer-de-Lance* (1934). The esoteric title distinguishes it from the run-of-the-mill detective novel of the moment.[76] Stout's trust in the reader's patience is apparent in the fact that the viper isn't mentioned for more than two hundred pages.

> I tried it again. "*Fair-du-lahnss?*"
> Wolfe nodded. "Somewhat better. Still too much *n* and not enough nose."[77]

Stout takes the opportunity to contrast heartland Archie and cosmopolitan Wolfe while letting smart readers enjoy linguistic play and instructing the rest of us in pronunciation. Of his next book, a reviewer would write: "Mr. Stout adorns his tale with lots of good writing adapted to highbrow and lowbrow alike."[78]

Fer-de-Lance, rather long for a mystery of its day, presents a cascade of coincidences and delays. The murder isn't revealed as such until the fourth chapter. Not until a hundred and fifty pages in do we learn that the victim was not the intended target. These plot zigzags are buried in the minutiae of Wolfe's world. The opening plunges us right in.

> There was no reason why I shouldn't have been sent for the beer that day, for the last ends of the Fairmont National Bank case had been gathered in the week before and there was nothing for me to do but errands, and Wolfe never hesitated about running me down to Murray Street for a can of shoe-polish if he happened to need one. But it was Fritz who was sent for the beer. Right after lunch the bell called him up from the kitchen.

Beer, Wolfe, Fritz, a successful case, an order issued by the employer, and household customs are all breezily taken for granted from the start. In an ordinary book, this would be a more typical middle chapter. The mystery isn't *Whodunit?* but *What's the big deal about the beer?* The scene centers on Wolfe (the "Nero" isn't supplied for three chapters). Archie hints at his bulk but concentrates on chronicling his eccentric thoroughness in sampling the entire array of legal 3.2 beer. "None shall lack opportunity."[79] He could have waited; prohibition is only a few months from ending.

We approach the main action at several removes. The operative Fred Durkin brings in Maria Maffei, whose brother Carlo is missing. Maria leads Archie to the key witness Anna Fiore, whom he brings back to the office. As Wolfe's involvement deepens, the first chapters provide demonstrations of personal styles. Archie's dogged but fruitless questioning of Anna in the boarding house is contrasted with Wolfe's patient conversations with her in the office. Archie takes two hours, a period Stout renders in a paragraph of summary, but Wolfe pursues her for five, with the crucial exchanges dramatized across several pages. "It was beautiful," Archie reports.[80] The questioning reveals that the missing brother is indirectly involved in the golfing death.

Next Stout gives Archie his own big scene. He delivers to the White Plains investigators Wolfe's $10,000 bet that the death was a murder and that poison will be found if the body is exhumed. This is the first display of Archie's gifts for politely annoying the hell out of authorities with a string of arguments, threats, and forced choices. Wolfe's confidence that he can turn the case to profit is amplified by Archie's grinning effrontery. Later we'll discover that they're also settling an old score with this district attorney, who among other transgressions has married money.

The first six chapters are occupied with these business maneuvers. A hardboiled novel would begin with the victim's daughter visiting the office, but here that comes eighty pages in. She's been lured by Wolfe's newspaper advertisement, itself the result of his accidental discovery of the murder. Once Wolfe is hired, Archie can rush toward the action he enjoys, and we get the characteristic cycle of his excursions, his reports to the boss, his tapping his newspaper sources, and the conferences with police and suspects. The hero-worshipping tone in the early chapters gives way to exasperation, as we're introduced to the rhythm of Wolfe's stubbornness and Archie's badgering that will pervade the series to come.

The opening stretches also display how Wolfe uses his supersedentary role to play puppeteer. He bends everyone to his agenda, with Archie summoning people to meals and interrogations while horning in on their private lives. The armchair premise, driven by Wolfe's self-centeredness, ultimately determines how he'll settle the case. By triggering the killer's murder/suicide, he will never have to bestir himself to testify in court.

Besides familiarizing us with the routines and introducing us to the protagonists' personal styles, this first book's opening portions set in place distinctive features of Stout's prose. Of course Archie's vulgar zest and Wolfe's pompous pronouncements dominate these sections, but *Fer-de-Lance* establishes a finer-grained pattern of echoes and refrains that show something just as distinctive in Stout's achievement. No less than Chandler, Stout brought novelistic finish to the detective story. He bent Archie's vernacular to verbal patterning that had become part of mainstream literary technique.

Early in *Fer-de-Lance* Wolfe says that Archie collects facts but has no "feeling for phenomena."[81] Wolfe tells Maria that Carlo's disappearance is only a fact. Apparently it doesn't become a bona fide phenomenon until physical clues let him grasp Carlo's role in the murder.

The phrase sounds good, but Archie, having looked up "phenomenon," suspects Wolfe is just parading. But Archie won't let it go. He will defend his hunches about one suspect as proving he too can pick up on "phenomena." When no suspect seems a prime candidate, Archie reflects that Wolfe may need to "develop a feeling for a new kind of phenomenon: murder by eeny-meany-miney-mo." Later, Archie confronts Wolfe and starts talking "just for practice": "The problem is to discover what the devil good it does you to use up a million dollars' worth of genius feeling the phenomenon of a poison needle in a man's belly if it turns out that nobody put it there?" In the closing lines, Wolfe says he's willing to take responsibility for the two deaths that conclude the action and keep him out of court. Archie replies:

> "Now, natural processes being what they are, and you having such a good feeling for phenomena, you can just sit and hold your responsibilities on your lap."
>   "Indeed," Wolfe murmured.[82]

More than Hammett and Chandler, Stout creates refrains that crisscross dialogue and the protagonist's commentary. He has precedents. Jane Austen, whom Stout considered "probably, technically," the greatest novelist, sends the word "likeness" chiming significantly through *Emma*.[83] After Wagner, artists in many media made more self-conscious use of motivic play, and it was a prominent strategy of modern literature and drama, as in Conrad and Bernard Shaw.[84] The most proximate source for Stout was perhaps *Ulysses*, with its refrains of "Met-em-pike-hoses," "agenbite of inwit," "Your head it simply swirls," and many more. Stout's first "art novel," *How Like a God*, introduces the rare word "vengeless" early and brings it back twice across the book to emphasize the protagonist's passivity.[85]

Too Many Cooks (1938) is a rich tissue of refrains, most set out in the first chapter and revived as needed. They're often traces of Archie's sarcasm, as when he always refers to the district attorney as his friend. After Wolfe declares that a guest is "a jewel on the cushion of hospitality," Archie fobs the phrase off on a dinner guest, who doesn't get it, and later, after seeing a Wolfe scheme foiled, grins and reflects on "how it probably felt at that moment to be a jewel on the cushion of hospitality."[86]

Stout relies on refrains across books as well as within them. For example, "satisfactory" is Wolfe's highest term of praise (and, interestingly, the framing motif of *The Thin Man*). In one book, Archie applies it to their guest: "That girl would have been a very satisfactory traveling companion." The word recurs at intervals and returns on the last page, where Archie works off his anger by punching an obstreperous guest whose "hundred and ninety pounds . . . made it really satisfactory."[87] Erle Stanley Gardner's repetitions from book to book are bland filler, whereas Stout's serve more literary ends of characterization and patterning, while quietly assisting world building.

Fer-de-Lance doesn't yet deploy "satisfactory" in the Wolfean sense, but it sprinkles in refrains such as "lethal toy," "genius," "artist," and "lovin' babe!" and pauses for a debate about the slang use of "ad" for "advertisement." Sometimes the iterations are closely packed, knitting together dialogue exchanges, but they can also recur at a distance. Archie reflects that somehow Wolfe could be called elegant, and when the obstinate witness Anna behaves with poise four pages later, he grants: "She was being elegant. She had caught it from Wolfe." Two hundred pages later, when Archie induces Anna to sign the decisive statement, he notices that their first client Maria has changed dramatically. "She looked elegant." Evidently she has caught it from Anna.[88] Compared with the "Goodbyes" that Chandler scatters through the last chapters of *The Long Goodbye* (1953), Stout's refrain is subtle and piquant.

Or take foreshadowing. The classic whodunit scatters clues deceptively, creating a sort of disguised foreshadowing. The gun hanging on the wall in act one might not be the murder weapon; something else is, but it will be barely mentioned or obliquely described. A more self-consciously literary novel can foreshadow action through imagery rather than clues and hints. For instance, the beer bottles brought in to Wolfe on the first page of *Fer-de-Lance* remain as props in later office scenes, as does the desk drawer in which Wolfe stores his opener and bottle caps. At the climax, that drawer is opened.

> "Look out!"
> Wolfe had a beer bottle in each hand, by the neck, and he brought one of them crashing on to the desk but missed the thing that had come out of the drawer. . . . I was ready to jump back and was grabbing Wolfe to pull him back with me when he came down with the second bottle right square on the ugly head and smashed it flat as a piece of tripe.

The beer and the drawer have been carefully planted, but most novelists, mystery mongers or not, wouldn't plant Archie's remark, two hundred pages earlier, long before we have heard anything about vipers and have met any suspects.

> I looked at Wolfe and back again at the pile on the floor. It was nothing but golf clubs. There must have been a hundred of them, enough I thought to kill a million snakes. For it had never seemed to me that they were much good for anything else.
> I said to Wolfe, "The exercise will do you good."[89]

Knowing that a snake will indeed pop up in the office and that Wolfe will dispatch it furiously, we can see Archie's imaginary serpent massacre and his teasing comment as classic instances of through-composed novelistic texture.

The Fortunes of *Pfui*

> *If you resent the vulgarity of Mr. Goodwin's jargon I don't blame you, but nothing can be done about it.*

—Nero Wolfe[90]

A vein of comedy runs through mysteries of the 1920s. Lord Peter warbling about a body in the bath is only the most obvious instance of the silly-ass characterization that crept into the puzzle form. London's Bright Young Things took up sleuthing in A. A. Milne's *Red House Mystery* (1922); and Margery Allingham's Albert Campion, with his sidekick former burglar Magersfontein Lugg, began as a parody of Wimsey. At a loftier level, Sayers, Anthony Berkeley, and others had thought that the detective story could legitimize itself by becoming a "novel of manners," with the mild comedy that the genre could sustain. A rougher, more sarcastic humor could be found in Hammett and other hard-boiled authors, at about the same time slick magazines were running folksy tales of comic detection.[91]

Film had offered some comic crime efforts as well. Howard Hawks turned *Trent's Last Case* (1929) into a Charley Chase farce, and *Seven Keys to Baldpate* (1930) revived that perennially popular stage mystery. But screwball comedy had the strongest influence. The film of *The Thin Man* (1934) showed the lively possibilities of socialites solving murders in the midst of high-end shopping, fine dining, and tipsy chatter. Even the hard-bitten Perry Mason of the novels became the louche drunk of *The Case of the Lucky Legs* (1935).

Stout had a funny side. He wrote humorous short stories in his pulp days, and after the second Wolfe novel he published some light romances. Occasionally the Wolfe books meld the conventions of the post-Doyle detective story with the prose equivalent of a screwball comedy. *Some Buried Caesar* (1939) begins with Archie crashing the sedan, as Wolfe jounces in the back seat. As they walk to a nearby farm, Wolfe notes that they're crossing a cow pasture. "Being a good detective, he produced his evidence by pointing to a brown circular heap near our feet." Soon, though, a bull charges them. ("He started the way an avalanche ends.") Archie runs to the fence and vaults clumsily over, to the amusement of two young women watching. Meanwhile Wolfe has somehow found a perch on a boulder in the field and is now standing as still as a statue, awaiting rescue.[92]

This slapstick episode launching *Some Buried Caesar* is, however, atypical. Stout's comedy is largely verbal, a torrent of wisecracks, teasing, mimicry, malapropisms, and barefaced silliness. Later in the book, a twenty-five-page interlude finds Archie jailed with a despondent con man named Basil and planning to organize the prisoners into a union. When Wolfe visits, it's not just to console Archie but to get ready cash. As Wolfe starts to recall his experience in a Bulgarian prison, Archie shuts him up by shouting through the bars, "Oh, Warden! I'm escaping!"[93] Lily Rowan, whom we first meet in the book, calls on Archie as well, using the nickname Escamillo, which will in later books recall the bull episode.

Doyle recalled, somewhat unfairly, that Watson never showed a gleam of humor, but Archie personifies fun. In nearly every story somebody accuses him of clowning, with good reason.

To Lily Rowan: "You're always right sometimes."

To Wolfe, after a stretch of inactivity: "I'm just breaking under the strain of trying to figure out a third way of crossing my legs."

To O'Hara, bearing a message from Wolfe: "He said to tell you you're a nincompoop, but I think it would be more tactful not to mention it, so I won't."

To a visitor who wants to see Wolfe: "You C A N apostrophe T, can't. Don't be childish."

To a suspect: "You're too careless with pronouns. Your hims. Your first him's opinion of your second him is about the same as yours."

A thug decides to lecture Archie about showing too much humor. "Someday something you think is funny will blow your goddamn head right off your shoulders." *Esprit de l'escalier* makes Archie ponder. "Only after he had gone did it occur to me that that wouldn't prove it wasn't funny."[94]

Archie's comment tops the topper, indicating that the smartass dialogue is set inside an even richer verbal texture. The Wolfe books are the only novels in which Stout employed first-person narration. "It's Archie who really carries the stories, as narrator," Stout noted. "Whether the readers know it or not, it's Archie they really enjoy."[95]

His performance calls on many tricks of yarn-spinning in the American grain. There's exaggeration, as when Archie declares of Wolfe's gift of a card case: "I might have traded it for New York City if you had thrown in a couple of good suburbs." There's Gracie Allen backchat: "I wanted to ask her what the difference was between asking her advice and wanting to see what she would say, just to see what she would say." Wolfe says he's glad Archie has come. Archie replies: "I was glad he was glad I had come, but I wasn't glad, if I make myself clear."[96] That Archie calls his books "reports" merely adds to the joke; nothing could be further from neutral description.

Above all, there's the mixture of spoken language and literary calculation. Chandler could tell us that a man has a face like a collapsed lung, but Stout gives us something more conversational. "He didn't look tough, he looked flabby, but of course that's no sign. The toughest guy I ever ran into had cheeks that needed a brassiere." As in this example, Archie's demotic can slam the gearwork between high and low, lofty and ingenuous. In one of the most brilliant passages Stout ever wrote, Archie is sharing a dinner with Wolfe and Cramer. "If you like Anglo-Saxon, I belched. If you fancy Latin, I eructed. No matter which, I had known that Wolfe and Inspector Cramer would have to put up with it that evening, because that is always part of my reaction to sauerkraut. I don't glory in it or go for a record, but neither do I fight it back. I want to be liked just for myself."[97] How to define the tone of this passage of mock defense—cast, inevitably, in terms of food and word choice? That last sentence is at once proud, self-deprecating, sincere, and a jab at the American conviction that one's individuality is precious, even during a burp.

This is the relaxed performance of a tall tale. Archie's vernacular makes him kin to Huck Finn, but there's as well the shuttling among registers we find in Twain's platform speeches and literary critiques. Instead of declaring the detective's noble creed (avenging a partner, fighting for a questionable client), Archie demonstrates he's a "trained investigator" by focusing on essential clues, like a woman's attractive mouth. "A habit of observation of minor details is an absolute must for a detective."[98] Philip Marlowe's ironic narration emphasizes his reluctant acceptance of the hard-boiled role, but Archie exploits the cliché for self-deprecating humor.

Throughout, the echoes that crisscross Archie's wordage enhance the comic texture. "Satisfactory" can work this way, but the most pervasive refrain is Wolfe's favorite exclamation.

"Pfui."
"Yes, sir. I agree."

Clearly, "pfui" is pronounced differently from Archie's equivalent.

> "What do you think of her?"
> "Pfui."
> "Go on and phooey."

As with everything he hears, Archie recycles it: "As Wolfe would say, pfui."[99]

Sometimes a refrain shows up as it would in a 1930s movie. In *Too Many Cooks*, a glass of spilled ginger ale in an early train scene is invoked in later dialogue and Goodwinian commentary. The gag pays off in the last chapter when back on the train Archie teaches his new "friend" the district attorney how to get a young woman's attention. The book ends with Archie quoting the DA's botched apology for spilled ginger ale from the first chapter: "It's rite all kite, it doodn't stain."[100]

More commonly, Wolfe enunciates a word or phrase, preferably something pedantic, and it returns to mocking effect in Archie's conversation and commentary. The title of *The Final Deduction* strikes the main chord, with "deduction" (as in an inference) chiming throughout the text. It will take on a new significance when we learn the tax-related motive for the murder scheme, but before that Archie rings a variant that once more punctures Wolfe's intellectual pretensions.

> At the dinner table, in between bites of deviled grilled lamb kidneys with a sauce he and Fritz had invented, he explained why it was that all you needed to know about any human society was what they ate. If you knew what they ate you could deduce everything else—culture, philosophy, morals, politics, everything. I enjoyed it because the kidneys were tender and tasty and that sauce of one of Fritz's best, but I wondered how you would make out if you tried to deduce everything about Wolfe by knowing what he had eaten in the past ten years. I decided you would deduce that he was dead.[101]

Even here, the "deduce" refrain is not a proper clue to solving the mystery. It's rather an invitation to enjoy your memory of early scenes, and of the whole Wolfe saga.

Stout's comic refrains are in the vein of P. G. Wodehouse. Like Archie, Bertie Wooster is fascinated by language. He's constantly picking up phrases from his butler Jeeves and then trying them out, usually in ill-fitting contexts.[102] Bertie's fumbling vocabulary lessons begin in earnest in *Right Ho, Jeeves*, which was published in 1934, the year of *Fer-de-Lance*. It seems likely that Stout borrowed the tactic and applied it to Archie's keener, more

flippant intellect. In exchange, Wodehouse praised Stout's books for bringing "excellent comedy into the type of narrative where comedy seldom bats
better than .100."[103]

The emergence of grimmer tints in Chandler and other hard-boiled novelists in the 1940s seems to have affected Stout's work. *The Silent Speaker* (1946),
the first postwar Wolfe novel, finds Archie much taken with Phoebe Gunther,
a plucky government assistant protecting her boss. She is murdered at Wolfe's
door. Archie is more distraught than we've ever seen him, telling Fritz to go to
hell and pressing Wolfe to investigate.

Deepening Archie's emotional investment in the case poses Stout with a
formal problem. How to absorb grim moments into the basically comedic register of these tales? The writer must steer a course between sentimentality and
coldness. In these cases, Archie's insouciant conceit is shaken by anger and a
sense of righteousness that goes beyond the cash matrix that both he and Wolfe
prize. Archie becomes something close to the one good man of the hard-boiled
tradition. The trick is how to tell it.

Stout solves the problem by regulating narrational depth. Normally
Archie shares with us his immediate perceptions. When he sees a person or
place, he files his report immediately. But in confronting Phoebe's violent
death, his narration shifts to externalities. Here what's neutrally described is
not Sayers's account of Trent finding a clue but a man responding naturally
to murder.

The technique is introduced brutally. Archie keeps from us the fact that
Phoebe is the crumpled shape he finds under the stoop. Instead we get pure
behavior. "Fritz had pulled the front door shut, and when I found myself
fumbling to get the key in the hole, I stood erect to take a deep breath and
that stopped the fumbling."[104] This behaviorist handling seems indebted to
Hemingway and Hammett. At the end of *A Farewell to Arms*, Frederic Henry's
stoic grief is given in single lines of dialogue ("You get out" to the nurse) and
a final line: "After a while I went out and left the hospital and walked back to
the hotel in the rain."[105] Leaving the reader to imagine Henry's devastation
adheres to Hemingway's "iceberg" principle, in which most of the meaning is
submerged.[106] Similarly, Hammett's detached narration in *The Glass Key* and
The Thin Man forces us to judge the protagonist's responses by the way he
acts. Borrowing this hard-boiled objectivity, Stout has dosed Archie's insouciant monologue with moments that evoke his emotions through flat accounts
of action.

Stout doesn't stay in the impersonal register. Once we've imagined the depth
of Archie's sense of guilt about Phoebe's death, he can open up a little. Sitting
with his milk in his bedroom, he briefly probes his reactions. "This seemed to
hit me in a new spot or something, and anyhow there I was, trying to arrange

my mind. Or maybe my feelings. All I knew was that something inside me needed a little arranging."[107]

Archie's emotional arranging condenses into a resolve to act. He is shaken but not shaking. "I had been sitting in my room twenty minutes when I noticed that I hadn't drunk any milk, but I hadn't spilled any from the glass."[108] Shock and recrimination turn Archie into the hard-boiled hero, but one bereft of self-pity. By this stoic standard, a Chandler ending such as "I felt tired and old and not much use to anybody" looks crybaby."[109]

The Silent Speaker supplies a template for three more cases that introduce Archie to emotional pain: *Murder by the Book* (1952), *Prisoner's Base* (1952), and *The Golden Spiders* (1953). Throughout these righteous-Archie books, Stout will suggest deep feeling through neutrally described behavior. The most laconic variant comes when Sergeant Stebbins visits with bad news about a boy killed in a hit-and-run.

> "His name was Drossos. Peter Drossos."
> I swallowed. "That's just fine. The sonofabitch."[110]

"That's just fine" is bitter sarcasm. "The sonofabitch" is pure rage. But Archie's swallow has already shown him recoiling from the blow.

The Silent Speaker has the most nuanced emotional arc of the righteous-Archie books. Here the recovery of the affirmative tone is more gradual. After Archie's recriminations ("the dirty deadly bastard . . . she had been utterly all right") and another display of callousness on Wolfe's part, the two men cooperate when they realize that Phoebe has hidden the telltale recording cylinder.

In the final pages, they reconcile. Archie realizes that Wolfe has avenged Phoebe's death by punishing the professional association that attacked her government agency. But was it ethical for Wolfe to collect a reward from the same association? Wolfe explains that in his own way he was moved by Phoebe's death.

> "She had displayed remarkable tenacity, audacity, and even imagination. . . . Surely she deserved not to have her murder wasted."
> I stared at him, "Then I've got a hypothesis too. If that was it, either primary or secondary, to hell with ethics."[111]

By now, we don't need access to Archie's thinking to appreciate his reaction. The partnership endures by asserting the worth of Phoebe's sacrifice in the light of each man's ethos. By injecting dashes of hard-boiled impassivity, Stout can mingle stoic resolve with a recognition of the good that Archie and Wolfe can do.

Logomachizing

Stout's effort to treat investigation plots with character-driven humor, carried by dialogue and narration, gives language a central role. As Wolfe puts it, "The success of any investigation depends mainly on talk, as of course you know."[112] Gardner embraced a nakedly functional style, propelled by a rapid plot. We read on to find out Mason's next move. Archie and Wolfe's verbal sallies are more dawdling, putting action on hold. We turn the pages to see what people will say next and how Archie will spin it. Gardner wants us to read past his stock epithets in order to follow his story, but Stout invites us to enjoy single words or phrases.

Gambit (1962) famously opens with Wolfe burning, page by page, the controversial third edition of *Webster's International Dictionary*. Its editors' crimes include finding "ain't" acceptable and permitting "infer" as a synonym for "imply." The client who comes calling wins Wolfe over, Archie reports, by "calling him a wizard and implying (not inferring) that he was the one and only." Naturally, the imply/infer couplet will become a refrain.

Language makes world building possible; it gives sap and savor to characterization; it creates sidelong humor. Not least, it permits a literary gamesmanship that makes the Wolfe tales deeply bookish. They're about the people who write and publish them, the people who read them, and the seductive power of prose. More than any of their mass-market counterparts, these detective stories preserve in their verbal maneuvers a fascination with the constitutive power of words.

Again and again Archie steers our attention to the sounds and sights of language. One book's central clue is a diphthong that links four names. Punctuation plays a big role too. Wolfe's long-standing contempt for "unquote" in lieu of "end of quote" becomes a refrain. As Wolfe dictates a letter, he stipulates punctuation marks, and when Archie reads it back, he signals every one. A cowhand writing to Archie asks about colons ("them two dots"). Archie's own discourse is perfectly punctuated, which warrants his criticism of Wolfe's typing: "I don't care for the semicolon after 'appointment.'"[113]

For Wolfe, words become weapons. He springs verbal traps and uses school-marm pugilism to browbeat the spoiled rich who treat him as a hireling. Asked if he plays Scrabble, Wolfe replies, "I like using words, not playing with them."[114]

Archie likes both. In both dialogue and his reports to us, Archie is ready to mobilize words for the attack. Challenged on a point, he waves a hand. "Persiflage. Chaff." In *The Red Box*, Archie tosses around *yclept* and *mise en scène*. He will accuse Wolfe of just spouting adjectives and rhetorical questions. He can seize the initiative when Wolfe lapses:

"Do you realize that that fool is going to let that fool make a fool of him again?"

I yawned. "Listen to you. If I did a sentence like that you'd send me from the room."[115]

But Archie also likes to hang around words and watch them fraternize. Listening to Wolfe and conning the lexicon have exposed Archie to some fancy footwork. The *belched/eructed* cadenza shows how good a pupil he has been. Archie is as skilled at persiflage and chaff as Wolfe is, but in a scatty, honky-tonk register. The next critic who suggests that he's a hard-boiled hero should consult this passage, his response to an invitation downtown from Lieutenant Rowcliff.

> I said, "Poop and poo. Both for you. You sound like a flatfoot catching kids playing wall ball. Maybe I wanted the glory of taking him to headquarters myself. Or maybe I wanted to help him escape from the country by putting him on a subway for Brooklyn, where I believe you live. You've got him, haven't you, with a handle I gave you to hold him by? Poops and poos for all of youse. It's past my bedtime."[116]

It's a domesticated Joycean farrago, a burlesque-house burst of 1930s double-talk, with phrases ("Poops and poos for all of youse") that might have been pulled from Stein's *Four Saints in Three Acts* ("With wed led said with led dead said"). No surprise that the Wolfe books were incessantly reread and quoted by critic William Empson, connoisseur of wayward verbal associations.[117] "A word in a speech which falls outside the expected vocabulary," he points out, "will cause an uneasy stir in all but the soundest sleepers."[118] By this standard, Edmund Wilson's dismissal of Stout showed him snoozing.

The speaking voice that pervades these books is altogether aware of being read. *The Counterfeiters* flaunted the conceit of a book about its own self-generation, but Twain had gotten there before, letting Huck Finn confess that making a book was "a trouble."[119] Stout, having reinvented himself in Bohemian Paris, came more and more to endow Archie's reports with a reader-friendly intimacy alien to Hammett's and James M. Cain's first-person fiction. The writer who in *How Like a God* identifies its protagonist as "you" is likely to be sensitive to address.

So Archie frets that his account of a case will be read by Wolfe or Cramer or the Internal Revenue Service. He wonders whether to include this or that detail, and he can acknowledge when he's hit a wall. "If you are inclined to quit because I seem to be getting nowhere, no wonder."[120] He may ask us to vote on whether he should proceed. Readers write to him, and some become clients.

In the Sherlockian tradition, these maneuvers reinforce the amiable pretense that Archie, Wolfe, and the whole ménage exist. But given the playful style, the outing of Archie as a literary creator comes off as one more effort—in a comic register, again—to create surprise at the level of the sentence. Stout's bookishness enables him to carry the reflexivity paraded in popular narrative and in detective exercises such as *The Poisoned Chocolates Case* and *The Three Coffins* down to the fine grain of the narration, with nods to literary modernism.

Consider the second Wolfe novel, *The League of Frightened Men*. Paul Chapin is lame because of a hazing prank at Harvard, and the men responsible have tried to atone by financing his literary career. When members of the group start to die mysteriously, the survivors receive mocking poems with the refrain, "Ye should have killed me."[121]

Wolfe investigates Chapin by reading his novels, tales of erotic obsession that echo Stout's early books. Wolfe concludes that Chapin took his revenge in his writing, not in the world. But Wolfe exposes Chapin's fixation on another man's wife, expressed through his fetishistic treasuring of her gloves and under-wear. Chapin vows to avenge himself by murdering a Wolfe surrogate in his next novel "in the most abhorrent manner conceivable."[122]

The League of Frightened Men is laced with conversations about fiction, poetry, plays, magazine articles, and literary devices. Archie and Wolfe argue about analogies and metaphors, and a client's visit is presented as a playlike dialogue transcript. There's an oblique reference to *Ulysses*'s current best-seller status in Wolfe's remark: "What good is an obscenity trial except to popularize literature?"[123] The refrains are notably arch: alongside Wolfe's "feeling for phe-nomena" we get references to Spenser, romanticism, the soul, and stigmata.

One self-conscious motif gets punned via Archie's vernacular. In the open-ing pages, alongside a news story covering Chapin's audacious obscenity case, there's a report Archie asks about. "Did you see the piece in the paper about a woman who has a pet monkey which sleeps at the head of her bed and wraps its tail around her wrist? And keeps it there all night?"[124] Since we'll later learn that Chapin forces his wife to steal the garments of the woman he worships, we're invited to wonder if the monkey story isn't a subterranean parallel.

The wondering ends when the woman whom Chapin desires asks Archie not to pity the betrayed wife: "A monkey might as well pity me because I haven't got a tail." She has no claim on Chapin, while his wife does. The motif gets its twist on the last page, when Archie reflects that he and Chapin have something in common, because both men were misled by Wolfe and Fritz. "They had made a monkey of *me* all right."[125] Stout's symbolic imagery is transmuted into slang by Archie's comic commentary.

Later books lure Wolfe into commercial publishing, a field ripe for Archie's satire. In *Murder by the Book* (1951), an investigation carries Archie through the process of moving a manuscript from author to professional typist to publisher. The usual play with language ensues, with refrains about virginity, powers of observation, ears, contrivances, and even a palm tree. There is a tour de force of Archie entertaining the secretarial staff of the law firm at Wolfe's dinner table, with each guest characterized by voice, as well as a visit to Chandler's California, where it is always raining.

In *Plot It Yourself* (1959), Wolfe must undertake what he calls "textual study" of five unpublished manuscripts. Unknown authors are accusing famous ones of plagiarism. Wolfe determines that all the manuscripts were written by the same hand, but not by any of the writers claiming damages. Throughout, characters quote each other, and Archie absorbs their idiolects into his narration. Special barbs are reserved for literary pretension, as when Archie recycles a vapid author's catchphrase "more felt than perceived" and reflects on a children's book: "She had written a book entitled *The Moth That Ate Peanuts*, which showed that she would stop at nothing."[126] That book becomes a running gag, which doesn't prevent its supplying Wolfe with a major clue.

Who but Stout the word lover would turn his detective to scrutinizing diction, syntax, and punctuation? Wolfe holds forth on tics of wording ("better than fingerprints"), but Archie's own style, in conversation and in narration, parodies his boss's inferences. Wolfe points out that weak writers substitute uncommon verbs for "said": "They have him declare, state, blurt, spout, cry, pronounce, avow, murmur, mutter, snap." A writer he suspects of plagiarism relies on "aver." A page later, Archie agrees: " 'I'm sold,' I averred."[127]

The metafictional machinery switches into high gear when Wolfe argues that habits of paragraphing are the most personal features of a writer's presentation. Wolfe goes to bed, leaving Archie to puzzle over the manuscripts. But that action is swallowed up in the longest paragraph in the book, launched by two sentences that cry out to be severed. "I put the stories in the safe and then considered the problem of the table-load of paper. The statuses and functions of the inhabitants of that old brownstone on West 35th Street are clearly understood." Archie tacks on 156 words of exposition about household routines, duties, and eating arrangements utterly irrelevant to the paperwork problem that headed the paragraph. He ends his inventory of "the castle" with this: "The next sentence is to be, 'but the table-load of paper, being in the office, was clearly up to me,'—and I have to decide whether to put it here or start a new paragraph with it. You see how subtle it is. Paragraph it yourself."[128] The command echoes the book's title, which is derived from a review Archie claims to have read in the *Times*.

These interactive high jinks appear early on, making us vigilant for all the wordplay and fussy distinctions to come. The climax of *Plot It Yourself* arrives when Wolfe discovers unexpected correspondences among the manuscripts and the published books. In the office showdown, the guilty party reveals the error. "I realized how stupid I had been not to write them in a different style, but you see I didn't really know I had a style. I thought only good writers had a style." Archie adds that hearing that reply "you might have thought Wolfe was conducting a class in the technique of writing."[129] A story that begins with Archie grading Wolfe's reading on a scale from A to D ends in patient close reading and a discussion of style. *Pace* Professor Barzun, the business conference has become a seminar.

* * *

It would be too glib to say that while Gardner softened Hammett's impersonal objectivity Stout put a comic spin on Chandler's presentation of the detective as filtering intelligence. The 1930s Wolfe novels were independent achievements, published while Chandler was learning his craft in the pulps. Archie Goodwin's voice seems to have been not a recasting of Chandler but a mixture of the Great Detective tradition with vernacular fiction—not just Hammett but breezy 1920s novelistic practice and Broadway patter.

Moreover, Stout's sensibility moved in a cosmopolitan direction. He echoed the "light modernism" of Cocteau and Pirandello, a playful fusion of old and new. Perhaps his stay in Paris acquainted him with that *rappel à l'ordre* sometimes called "neoclassicism" but better thought of as a romping willingness to bring suavity and faux naïveté to formal experiment. As *Parade* was openly eclectic, so are Stout's novels: Archie blends current slang with Twain, Hammett, Hemingway, Wodehouse, and even Gertrude Stein. Style in the Wolfe novels becomes like one of Fritz's sauces: the flavors of many literary traditions soak in and sharpen our appetites.

Accepting the framework of whodunit conventions, Stout delivered literary pleasure through old-fashioned appeals: agreeably eccentric characters, scenes of bluff and nerve, and a fully furnished world. He rendered it all in the brisk flow of American yarn-spinning, mixed with self-conscious motivic play and a willingness to let common words mingle with rare ones, *belch* cozying up to *eructed*. Of all detective writers of his day, he most fully realized the polyphonic possibilities—lexical montage, parody, ventriloquism—that Mikhail Bakhtin saw as the promise of the novel.[130] The intensity of verbal organization that Edmund Wilson praised in Woolf and Joyce but failed to find in mysteries is here, but in an unpretentious vein.

Stout abandoned the structural experiments of his "literary" novels, but his crossover achievement asked a question very much in keeping with the modernist sensibility. If detective fiction is a game of wits, why can't it also be a game of language?

CHAPTER 10

VIEWPOINTS, NARROW AND EXPANSIVE

Patricia Highsmith and Ed McBain

S ome of the narrative strategies I've surveyed might be dismissed as
desperate efforts at novelty. But two major writers who began in the
1950s remind us that the more traditional formal options mapped
out in the 1910s retained real power. Patricia Highsmith's reliance on classic
novelistic techniques of restricted viewpoint created subtle effects denied to
the hyperbolic subjectivity at large during the 1940s. At the other extreme,
Ed McBain showed how old-fashioned omniscient, chatty narration could
revise the multiple-protagonist plot. And both authors deployed their strategies
within genre frameworks. Highsmith's studies in morbid psychology relied on
thriller conventions, and McBain's revision of the cross-sectional "city novel"
found an ideal vehicle in a new genre, the police procedural.

Terror, Suspense, Justice, or Whatever

Should we even consider Patricia Highsmith in the tradition of popular
narrative? She seemed to be something more than a purveyor of thrills. The
books invoke myth (a labyrinth in *The Two Faces of January*, 1964) and flirt
with role playing and symbolic substitutions. Her games of male doubling
conjure up homoerotic associations, and a recurring emphasis on the obliter-
ation of identity—her characters often dream of being no one, free of any
marks of personhood—fits the ethos of many "serious" novels.

At the beginning of her career, Highsmith declared herself interested in aesthetic values. "The full force of a writer's energy and intellect must all his life be directed toward increasing his awareness of his art as an art." Feeling satisfaction in reading a story, she noted, "is to feel form."[1] Highsmith recognized that recurring themes added richness to a novelist's work, and she admitted her fondness for "the relationship between two men, usually quite different in make-up, sometimes an obvious contrast in good and evil, sometimes merely ill-matched friends."[2] She was, like the modernists, writing out of high ambition.[3]

Highsmith was committed to engaging readers. On the threshold of her first novel, she claimed to see no incompatibility between "professional" writing and "arty" writing.[4] She considered *Daisy Miller* "riveting entertainment."[5] Her mentors were Poe, with whom she shared a birthday, and Dostoevsky, whom she defended as a crime novelist. She leaned toward the extreme emotions of pulp. "The best writers' work has this indescribable, generally unisolable quality of satisfying one's sense of terror, suspense, justice or whatever."[6]

Highsmith declared, "I consider myself an entertainer. I like to tell a fascinating story."[7] In her youth, she worked along with Mickey Spillane writing scenarios for the comic book company that would become Marvel. She studied crime novels of the 1940s in preparation for "The Heroine" (1945), her breakthrough story of a quietly confident fantasist. Her first novel provided Hitchcock with his comeback film, *Strangers on a Train* (1951), and seemed to announce a splendid career in mass-market suspense fiction.

Nearly all of her twenty-one novels published between 1950 and 1991 embrace the conventions of the thriller. Like *Hangover Square* and *In a Lonely Place*, Highsmith's books tend to concentrate on mentally disturbed men on the run. The men have deliberately, or more often accidentally, killed someone; or they're the target of someone who wants to kill them. They're pursued by police or by someone who knows or suspects their secrets. To cover their tracks, the men may lie, forge documents, create fake identities, and assume disguises. Everything depends on suspense, which Highsmith defined as "a threat of impending violent action."[8]

Surely this ought to have been a winning formula. But the result didn't sustain a career on the level enjoyed by less gifted novelists. Most of her books sold fewer than 8,000 hardcover copies, about half what the top crime writers achieved. Her editors often demanded rewrites, and sometimes they simply turned down her manuscripts. Her only paperback original, and her most immediately lucrative book, was *The Price of Salt* (1952), a lesbian novel published under a pseudonym. Short stories aimed for *The New Yorker* wound up in *Ellery Queen's Mystery Magazine*. During some stretches she had no American publisher. Lionized in Europe, she was mostly ignored in the United States.

Unlike most women crime writers, Highsmith kept away from domestic suspense and the woman-in-peril plot, but she didn't accept the conventions of hard-boiled storytelling either. As if in defiance of Chandler, she took crime out of the shabby streets and away from the professional crooks. She thrust it back into the drawing room—or the American equivalent, the postwar split-level. Her men are engineers, architects, publishers, art dealers, and the idle rich. Others are painters, novelists, musicians, and all-purpose intellectuals. Tom Ripley, Highsmith's continuing series character, studies languages, savors wines and cigars, dabbles in drawing, and like Lord Peter Wimsey plays the harpsichord.

The action is likely to unfold in a big American city or in Rome, Paris, and other exotic locales. We're constantly told of business plans, dinner parties and country weekends, fine clothes and cars, where to shop and how much to tip. The people are cultivated. They know Bach and Vivaldi, Cocteau and Kafka, Malraux and Proust. In these books, murder invades the dream world of slick-paper fiction and *Holiday* photo spreads. The crime novel becomes the "novel of manners," but in a very different vein from that imagined by Dorothy Sayers and Anthony Berkeley.

Traditional whodunits had set crimes in the upper reaches of society, but Highsmith focuses her plots around the perpetrator, not a bringer of order such as Hercule Poirot or Philo Vance. Into bourgeois and bohemian life, her men inject radical disorder. They are outrageously reckless.

Vic, the cuckolded husband in *Deep Water* (1957), playfully encourages people to speculate that he killed his wife's old lover. When she takes up with a new man, Vic drowns him and savors the suspicions she can't confirm. In *A Suspension of Mercy* (1965), a writer wonders how to depict the disposal of a corpse. He experimentally buries a rolled-up carpet while his wife is on a trip. Of course he is seen burying it; and by the time the police investigate him, the wife has vanished, and he can't recall where he buried the carpet. No self-respecting hunted man in fiction would behave as suicidally as Highsmith's protagonists do.

The protagonist's recklessness shows up in capricious moments of weakness. Stricken by shame, Highsmith's characters are forever destroying evidence that would spare them future trouble. A novel may begin with a ridiculously unforced error. *The Cry of the Owl* (1962) is built around an aeronautical engineer, to all appearances normal, who has fallen into the habit of spying on a woman as she prepares her nighttime meals. The drama begins when she sees him and, contrary to common sense, doesn't call the police. Highsmith's admiration for Camus's *The Stranger* and the *acte gratuite* is revealed in protagonists who make fatal choices from obscure or arbitrary motives.[9]

The famous premise of *Strangers on a Train*—the exchange of murders—indicates the sheer contingency that rules these plots. In *The Blunderer* (1954), a man murders his wife; another man learns of the crime and imagines dispos-ing of his own partner. Then she is found dead. In *Ripley's Game* (1974), after Jonathan Trevanny slights Tom Ripley, Tom spreads the rumor that Jonathan's blood disease has worsened. As if to make amends, Tom sets up Jonathan as a contract killer; after all, his family will need money. Out of fear and weariness, Jonathan agrees.

Through careful modulation, Highsmith glides from a far-fetched premise into an outrageous result. "You cannot always create a good book by sheer logic. . . . Stretch the reader's credulity, his sense of logic, to the utmost—it's quite elastic."[10] We can understand why Ray Garrett, in *Those Who Walk Away* (1967), wants to explain his wife's suicide to her enraged father Coleman. But after Coleman tries to kill Ray (twice), anybody else would flee Venice or go to the police. Instead Ray skulks around the city hoping to calm down his stalker. Somewhere around the third chapter of every Highsmith book, Gra-ham Greene reckoned, the reader must simply accept the illogic of the hero's rash choices.[11]

From crime fiction of the 1930s and 1940s, Highsmith drew standard nar-rative techniques—hallucinations, inner monologues, dreams, even amnesia. We get newspaper bulletins and physical clues, such as rings and signatures. There's a lot of drinking, which often motivates characters' bursts of unreason. But she treats these devices without hyperbole, in unfussy prose.

In *The Glass Cell* (1983), an ex-convict's lawyer has been murdered. In a packed paragraph, banal routine sits calmly alongside ominous reflection.

> There was the usual Saturday shopping to do. Carter volunteered to do it, because Hazel obviously wanted to be near the telephone. She wouldn't rest, Carter thought, until she had found out who killed Sullivan, and until the murderer was properly punished—put behind bars or executed. What had he possibly thought he could achieve by killing Sullivan? He simply hadn't thought, of course. Carter started making up the shopping list on his own. No use asking Hazel what she wanted for the weekend. Hazel went into the living room to call the Laffertys. She had their number in her address book. While she was talking to them, Carter did the dishes. She talked a long while, and only finished as Carter was going out of the door with the wire shopping wagon.[12]

Today's author would split this into several short paragraphs, separating Carter's thoughts from his and Hazel's actions. By running them together, Highsmith flattens his memories of murder to the same level as household chores. The only concrete detail, the wire shopping wagon, gives the homey touch, and the superfluous "She had their number in her address book" seems to signal that Carter abruptly recalls his wife's habits from before he went to prison.

Violence that Woolrich or Jim Thompson would pump up is given in simple, brisk description in *Ripley Under Ground* (1970).

Then Tom was aware of being flung over by the shoulders, and of hands around his throat. Tom threshed his legs free of the covers. He was pulling ineffectually at Bernard's arms to get his hands from his throat, and at last Tom got his foot against Bernard's body and pushed. The hands left his throat. Bernard dropped with a thud to the floor, gasping. Tom turned on the lamp, nearly knocked it over, and did knock over a glass of water which spilt on the blue oriental rug.[13]

Highsmith deploys a Hammett-like minimalism, but it isn't quite the same thing as objectivity. Instead, a transparent use of language transmits a character's consciousness of his immediate surroundings. Again, the passage's only concrete detail comes at the end, when the house-proud Tom Ripley registers the water dripped on his precious rug. Soon enough we are seeing the damaged Bernard as Tom does, "on the floor, propped on one arm, in the position of The Dying Gaul."

As in Simenon, the flatness of the style helps create a neutral reportage that makes very unlikely events seem plausible. As Highsmith notes, "I am very fond of coincidences in plots and situations that are almost but not quite incredible."[14] In these books, people searching a city often just bump into their quarry. Throughout his adventures, Ripley miraculously avoids capture, largely because most people are trusting, docile, and afraid of making a gaffe.

Highsmith's cops are often as easily deceived as children. David Kelsey, in *This Sweet Sickness* (1960), can lead a double life, in a boarding house and in his upscale model home, and the police simply assume that there are two men. Working-class suspects would probably be more carefully scrutinized, but Highsmith's high achievers, however much they sweat under pressure, are usually handled lightly by the authorities. These professionals are surprised to learn that they can just brazen things through. Tell a lie, feign forgetfulness, be courteous, offer to cooperate, and you can usually get away with anything. The ease with which Tom Ripley can impersonate Dickie Greenleaf, the man he killed, elates him and the reader. Through misleading phone messages, forged letters, quick timing, and a touch of hair dye, Tom can fool, or at least puzzle, any cop he meets.

All of these deceptions exact a price, however. There is, for one thing, a fatal hesitation or blurriness of perception. The protagonists slip into a radical uncertainty about what they're doing and how they're judged. Highsmith mimics this in her style, yielding extraordinarily wavering accounts of action. "He put his hands over his eyes and yielded to the queasiness in his stomach, or his mind. He wanted to throw up and couldn't, or didn't." Even Tom Ripley, master of sangfroid, can lose his footing. "When they hung up, Tom felt stunned, and also angry, or irritated."[15]

During these intervals of unfocused response, the protagonists are at risk of dissolving their identity. Highsmith's men swing between fear of losing themselves and a bliss that comes from that freedom. They yearn to be corpses or ghosts or strangers wandering the landscape. Many are forced to admit that they have split themselves up. They may end up crushed—"Take me," says Guy in the last line of *Strangers on a Train*—or just possibly rescued by miraculous chance.[16] In *The Two Faces of January*, Rydal is saved by the deathbed confession of the man bent on killing him.

Men Alone, or in Pairs

Cornell Woolrich wraps his scenes in thick padding, but as early as 1947 Highsmith recorded in her notebook a commitment to short, swift presentation. "The point to be made in any given scene is the sole raison d'être of the scene, and must pull it through quickly." This vividness could be achieved through a rigorous control of viewpoint. "Give only the sensations of the main character. Or his sensations when upon mental speculation or observation two characters have acted upon him, or reacted."[17] The second sentence is a bit obscure, but it seems to open the possibility of a split perspective, involving a pair of characters. As it turns out, Highsmith's crime variorum exploits these two main formal options.

Some books are heavily restricted to one man's viewpoint. *Deep Water, This Sweet Sickness, The Glass Cell*, and nearly all of the Ripley books lock us to what the protagonist knows and thinks. If restriction magnifies mystery in the first-person tales of Raymond Chandler and Ross Macdonald, Highsmith's restrictive technique creates the standard thriller effects of suspense and surprise. We share the character's uncertainty about what others know about his transgressions.

The Tremor of Forgery (1969) illustrates the intensity Highsmith gains by riveting us to a single consciousness. Howard Ingham is staying in a cottage in Tunisia writing a novel. One night he senses a figure hovering at the door, and he hurls his typewriter into the darkness. He hears a body being dragged away. The entire scene is clouded in uncertainty. Was the man a burglar? Was he killed? Ingham learns little in the chapters that follow, which fill up with the familiar mix of self-recrimination, lies, and worries about how others will judge him. We never leave Ingham's mind. Everything is sifted through the hero's typical blurriness and hesitations.

The book's title, which Ingham intends to use for his novel, refers to the telltale trembling of the forger's hand. The story Ingham is creating seems pure

Tom Ripley: "a man with a double life, a man unaware of the amorality of the way he lived, and therefore he was mentally unbalanced." Soon Ingham realizes that the title won't work; his protagonist is an altruist, and he has no anxieties that would betray him. ("Dennison never trembled to any extent worth mentioning.") Instead, it's Ingham who is shaken, striving to bluff his way through the hazy morality of his crisis. In the last pages, saved by a wild Highsmithian coincidence, Ingham can with relief leave Tunisia to return to the woman he thought had abandoned him. "Even the typewriter in his hand weighed nothing at all now."[18]

Just as often, Highsmith relies on shifting viewpoint between the two principal characters. This pattern is established in *Strangers on a Train*'s oscillation between Bruno, who kills Guy's wife, and Guy, whom Bruno goads into killing his father. *The Blunderer* and *Those Who Walk Away* similarly switch our attention between protagonist and antagonist. Highsmith may add a third or fourth viewpoint occasionally, but the two-man seesawing remains central. "I prefer two points of view in a novel. . . . [They can] bring a very entertaining change of pace and mood."[19]

Highsmith's preternatural interest in alternating viewpoints led her to experiment with the very texture of scenes. By the time she began her career, writers of popular fiction were urged not to change viewpoint too often lest the bad habits of the omniscient author creep in. The James-Lubbock legacy promoted the idea that, as Edith Wharton put it, "sudden changes from one mind to another are fatiguing and disillusioning."[20] An entire novel could shift the spotlight among characters, chapter by chapter, but each scene ought to have no more than one center of consciousness.

Highsmith, instead, carefully plans moments that jump from mind to mind. Early scenes in *A Suspension of Mercy* and *A Dog's Ransom* (1972) oscillate viewpoints when characters encounter one another. In both books, the characters picked out will later have entire chapters devoted to them. They are the ones to watch.

More striking, in climactic passages, Highsmith mingles viewpoints that were earlier set apart. In *Strangers on a Train*, after Guy has killed Bruno's father, Bruno invades Guy's life more aggressively, as if the two murders have made them kin. The men meet for a restaurant lunch, and for the first time Highsmith's curt paragraphs rapidly switch between them.

Bruno wanted very much to put his hand over Guy's fist, that rested lightly on the edge of the table, just for a moment as a brother might, but he restrained himself. "Did she like you right away or did you have to know her a long time? Guy?"

Guy heard him repeat the question. It seemed ages old. "How can you ask me about time? It's a fact." He glanced at Bruno's narrow, plumpening face, at the cowlick that still gave his forehead a tentative expression, but Bruno's eyes were vastly more confident than when he had seen them first, and less sensitive. Because he had his money now, Guy thought.

"Yeah, I know what you mean." But Bruno didn't quite. Guy was happy with Anne even though the murder still haunted him. Guy would be happy with her even if he were broke. Bruno winced now for even having thought once that he might offer Guy money.[21]

And so on to the end of the scene. Each man reads the other's mind as tit-for-tat inner monologues stage the dance of dependency that occupied earlier, parallel chapters.

At the limit, Highsmith can let the minds merge. Many chapters of *Ripley's Game* feature quick shifts between Tom and Jonathan Trevanny in the Bruno/Guy manner. Now they have killed two Mafiosi in Tom's home. The narration initially attaches us to Tom, who's planning to dump the corpses.

> The Renault, he knew, had only slightly more than half a tankful, and the bodies were going to be in there. He and Jonathan hadn't had any dinner. That wasn't wise. Tom went back into the house and said:
>
> "We ought to eat something before this trip."
>
> Jonathan followed Tom into the kitchen, glad to escape for a few moments from the corpses in the living-room. He washed his hands and face in the kitchen sink. Tom smiled at him. Food, that was the answer—for the moment. He got the steak from the fridge and stuck it under the glowing bars. Then he found a plate, a couple of steak knives and two forks. They sat down finally, eating from the same plate, dipping morsels of steak into a saucer of salt and another of HP. It was excellent steak.[22]

We switch from Tom's thoughts (they need to eat something) to Jonathan's reaction (respite from the corpses). The report of Tom's smile is ambivalent: it's either Jonathan's observation or Tom's reclaiming control of the action. "Food, that was the answer—for the moment" dangles between the two men's minds. Although it echoes Tom's plan to calm the situation, it suggests that Jonathan welcomes a meal as well.

The men's shared awareness of their need emerges as concrete behavior when they split the steak and eat from the same plate. After this moment of ambivalent communion, the chapter alternates the two perspectives again as they go on to consummate their crime. Their complicity is given in the very flow of Highsmith's prose. And the judgment ("It was excellent steak"), like the wire shopping basket and the blue carpet, ends the murderers' meal with a domestic banality.

At first glance, Highsmith's narrative technique seems smoothly traditional. She avoids warping time, breaking the plot into blocks, misdirecting attention, and hiding crucial information. "I am not an inventor of puzzles, nor do I like secrets."[23] By concentrating on a few characters in a morally fraught situation, Highsmith exploits the classic resources of the post-James psychological novel.

In Highsmith's hands, linearity becomes a succession of fatal coincidences. Subjectivity becomes a swirl of passivity, hesitation, confusion, bursts of aggression, and resignation to doom. Alternating two viewpoints goes beyond differentiating characters and instead points to disturbing convergences and complicities. The conventions of modern crime fiction are rewritten by someone who, to use Sartre's phrase about Camus's achievement in *The Stranger*, is "very much at peace within disorder."[24]

Policeman's Lot

During the 1940s paperback boom, the most successful books were reprints of hardbound titles, but paperback originals became important as well. They ran between 55,000 and 80,000 words.[25] With books this brief, authors could churn out several a year and earn advances up to $2,000 per manuscript.[26] Paperback originals were the postwar equivalent of the pulp magazines, and their tawdry covers and suggestive taglines made them nearly as disreputable. But a great many of today's crime canon first saw publication in this format.[27]

Highsmith didn't benefit much from the rise of paperback originals, but others did. Even authors who had achieved hardcover publication, as Elmore Leonard had with his early westerns, shifted to the new market. One of these writers was Evan Hunter (né Salvatore Lombino). In the process, he redefined an emerging genre more extroverted than the severe intrigues of Highsmith. That genre would show that modern crime fiction had room for multiple protagonists, omniscient narration, and a swaggering mix of realism and artifice.

Hunter had found mainstream success with *The Blackboard Jungle* (1954), which portrayed high schools as nests of juvenile delinquency and, not least, included the word "fuck." Hunter recalled that in 1955 Pocket Books recruited him to start a paperback series of crime stories.[28] Writing as Ed McBain, he settled on the police procedural.[29]

The genre has roots in the nineteenth century "casebooks" purporting to be memoirs of police detectives, and some Golden Age books point forward to later developments.[30] A modern version crystallized in the late 1940s. There might be a mystery, with suspects and clues, but the brilliant intuitions and inferences of the master detective were largely replaced by a dogged pursuit of evidence. A mild example is *The Woman in Question* (1950), which lacks a Great Detective and is propelled by a dogged, quizzical Chief Inspector. His interrogations remain chiefly a justification for an experiment in prismatic narrative, not a demonstration of the rigors and boredom of the policeman's lot.

The procedural was celebrated as a turn toward realism. After all, in the modern world the gifted amateur didn't exist, and the private eye was someone you hired to track an errant spouse or a suspicious employee. Only the police could plausibly engage with major felonies.

The claims for realism were strengthened by the emphasis on mundane routine and scientific criminology. Lawrence Treat's novel *V as in Victim* (1945) is usually credited with providing a template for future writers. It's centered on two policemen, a detective and a lab technician, who collaborate to solve a murder. Another duo, a seasoned officer and a novice, crack the case in the film *Naked City* (1948). Even more than in *V as in Victim*, the plot stresses the tedium of the job and the overwhelming odds against finding a suspect or a piece of missing jewelry. As a result, chance takes on an important role in cracking a case— another appeal to a realism that would be out of place in the classic detective formula, which tried to conceal its lucky coincidences.

Naked City made use of a streetwise voice-over narrator identifying himself as producer and former newsman Mark Hellinger. Hellinger's Runyonesque wisecracks comment on the action, sometimes even providing dialogue for scenes we see. Voice-over narration, a technique borrowed from radio, returned to its home medium in the program *Dragnet* (1949–1955). Again, the protagonists are a pair of cops, one of whom, Joe Friday, crisply announces the time and place and purpose of each scene. Transferred to a feature film (*Dragnet*, 1954) and television (1951–1959, 1967–1970) and endlessly parodied and quoted ("Just the facts, ma'am"), Jack Webb's creation was the most widely known of all police procedurals.[31]

Friday is bereft of a personal history or a private life, becoming a relentless interrogator rapping out one-line questions and quips. At the opposite pole of Webb's spare objectivity was Mackinlay Kantor's novel *Signal Thirty-Two* (1950), an ambitious effort to probe the impact the job has on a pair of patrolmen. Through flashbacks, dreams, inner monologues, and the absence of a mystery through line, Kantor uses crossover techniques to portray crime fighters.

Like *Signal Thirty-Two*, Sidney Kingsley's play *Detective Story* (1949) is resolutely psychological. Why is McLeod, a good investigator, also self-righteous, merciless, and violent? When he learns that his wife once used the services of the abortionist whom he has sworn to imprison, his rigid morality collapses. He realizes that in reacting against his father's abusive ways he has become a brute himself. This really is a "detective story," the story of how a detective becomes morally unbalanced.

McLeod's line of action is at the center of the plot, but *Detective Story* showcased the convention of marginal cases that swarm into a copper's day. Over a few hours, the squad room fills up with petty criminals, victims, lawyers, and eccentrics. Each one has a story to tell. The minor cases may connect to the central story through sudden convergences (a burglar grabs a patrolman's pistol to threaten McLeod) or through parallels, as when a young couple embodies the possibility of a more solid marriage than McLeod has.[32]

Given the formal possibilities explored in all of these media products, the case for realism becomes harder to make. Granted, the procedural rests on research into how cops do their job, and the dialogue is full of police slang. The pressures of physical danger and stultifying routine are dramatized. The latest scientific techniques and gadgets are put on display. There will be descriptions of wounds, autopsies, and the effects of leaving a corpse in the water for weeks—gory naturalistic details not common even in hard-boiled fiction, let alone cozy Agatha Christie stories. The Scotland Yard novels of J. J. Marric and the Los Angeles series by Dell Shannon multiply the crimes we're tracking, skipping quickly from one to another, and they dare to leave some cases unsolved and some miscreants uncaptured—just as in life.

Yet Friday's rat-a-tat commentary is as stylized as *Naked City's* jaunty soliloquies. The character arcs in *Signal Thirty-Two* and *Detective Story* are as traditionally tidy as anything in straight fiction and theater. The two detectives in *V as in Victim* are carefully counterpointed, and the Marric books stress parallels between cops' off-duty lives and the crimes they investigate, all the while keeping CID Commander George Gideon central as a canny crime solver. And as often as not, the slice-of-life premise is undercut by the revelation that two or more cases are subtly connected.

Historically, the procedural owes something to the 1920s and 1930s puzzle stories, particularly in its reliance on interrogation and physical clues. But one advantage of the procedural format is its ability to absorb plot premises and dramatic situations from other crime genres. To build suspense, procedurals routinely shift the spotlight among the lives of cops, crooks, and civilians. While the detective is sweating over a report on the typewriter, the narration is likely to show witnesses being stalked and criminals pulling their jobs. These wide-ranging episodes put us in familiar thriller territory: the man on the run, the woman in jeopardy. One particular variant makes the policeman go undercover, so suspense is added when he becomes unaware that the gang members realize his identity.

The genre's use of moving-spotlight narration opens rich possibilities for experimentation. For example, Hillary Waugh's *Last Seen Wearing* (1952), another early milestone in the genre, offsets its documentary trappings (day and date tagging each chapter) with a wide-ranging narration moving between witnesses and cops. The investigation depends on a patient and lucky search for a missing purse. But the case ends with the protagonist, a small-town chief of police, ordering his men to arrest a perpetrator whom he and we have never seen. It's a flashy turn, flaunting a "limited omniscience" that keeps the killer permanently offstage.

He Do the Police in Different Voices

Once Ed McBain took up the genre, he pushed to extremes the poles of hard-edged realism and self-conscious artifice. No writer has insisted more on by-the-book accuracy. "The police routine," announces the opening page of every 87th Precinct novel, "is based on established investigatory technique." Yet no mystery writer was bolder in flaunting narrative form. Across fifty-two novels, McBain set out to find just how playfully artificial the police procedural could be. "I still try different tricks all the time."[33]

At the realism pole, McBain's novels go beyond their counterparts by including facsimiles of official reports, fingerprint cards, identification sketches, and other documents. It's as if the books are trying to replicate the close-ups supplied in cop films of the period. In addition, these items usually don't contain clues the way Golden Age floor plans and other visual material do. They're presented simply as guarantees of fidelity to (fictional) fact.

These drab bureaucratic records issue from a wholly imaginary space and time. McBain has affectionately furnished his city of Isola with named streets and distinct neighborhoods. Its detailed topography both is and is not a virtual New York. Similarly, despite scrupulous indication of season, days, and hours, the novels' calendars are warped. Across the series, some characters age a little, some quite a bit, and one, the long-suffering Meyer Meyer, remains perpetually thirty-seven—one of the many inside jokes aimed at devoted readers.[34]

By the time McBain began writing, the procedural was incorporating cops' personal lives in the drama. This enhanced the purported realism of the new subgenre; instead of hard-drinking solitary private eyes, we got family men, widowers, and policemen falling for suspects. Again, McBain pushes this convention to a limit. Detective Steve Carella and his colleagues are given fully rendered private lives, and in the late books their romantic and erotic impulses count for as much as the cases they crack. The wedding of Carella's sister is central to 'Til Death (1959), and the awkward ups and downs of Bert Kling's love life dominate later books. By now we're used to police stories dramatizing how work puts strains on a marriage, but McBain pushed cop soap opera to a high pitch. McBain freely takes us into the minds and hearts of all his characters, and he doesn't hesitate to exploit sheer schmaltz.

From *Naked City* and *Dragnet* onward, the building block of procedurals was the interrogation scene. *Dragnet* made stichomythia—the rapid-fire exchange of single lines—a trademark. McBain adopts it freely but again carries it to an extreme. As with Erle Stanley Gardner, we get pages and pages of such dialogue, with the rhythm of Q&A letting us keep track of the speakers.

Lieutenant Byrnes turns a father/son confrontation into "a cop questioning a suspect." After two pages of clipped exchanges, Byrnes realizes that Larry has become a junkie.

> "How bad is it?"
>> "Not too bad."
>> "Heroin?"
>> "Yes."
>> "How long?"
>> "I've been on for about four months now."
>> "Snorting?"
>> "No. No."
>> "Skin pops?"
>> "Dad, I . . ."
>> "Larry, Larry, are you mainlining?"
>> "Yes."
>> "How'd you start?"

And so on for another five pages full of white space.[35]

In these passages McBain takes Lubbock's "dramatic" method to a percussive limit. But these and the dry document facsimiles stand out against a jazzy commentary. McBain provides a modern version of the narrational judgments that Lubbock deplored. He translates the nineteenth-century novel's garrulous authorial voice, at once lyrical and philosophical, into a raffish demotic.

Warmer than Webb and zanier than Hellinger, this narration natters on about the weather, the city, the peculiar ways of men and women, and the ironies of fate. One book begins:

> She came in like a lady, that April.
>
> The poet may have been right, but there really wasn't a trace of cruelty about her this year. She was a delicate thing who walked into the city with the wide-eyed innocence of a maiden, and you wanted to hold her in your arms because she seemed alone and frightened in this geometric maze of strangers, intimidated by the streets and the buildings, shyly touching you with the pale-gray eyes of a lady who's materialized somehow from the cold marrow of March.

This murmured personification, with surprising citation of Eliot's *Waste Land*, rolls on for another three paragraphs before switching to something down market:

> For Detective Meyer Meyer, April was a Gentile.
>   Sue him; she was a Gentile. Perhaps for Detective Steve Carella April was a Jewess.
>   Which is to say that, for both of them, April was a strange and exotic creature.[36]

"Sue him," recalling *Guys and Dolls*, channels Meyer's argot. The omniscient voice shifts to Carella's consciousness and confidently presents his entrancement by April. The scene continues with the narration switching freely between the two men's minds as they work at their desks.

The reservation about Carella's fantasy woman ("Perhaps . . .") is uncharacteristic. By and large, the narration of these books knows everything—the characters' pasts, their inner longings and childhood frustrations, even how the action will turn out.

> But Hawes was already moving into the building, his gun drawn. He did not know that his conversation with the landlady had been viewed from a second-floor window. He did not know that his red hair had instantly identified him to his observer. He did not know until he was almost on the second-floor landing, and then he knew instantly.
>   The explosion thundered in the small, narrow corridor.[37]

Sometimes the narration interrupts itself and loses patience.

> They had planned to spend that Wednesday night in Sharyn's apartment, but because a cop had got shot downtown, and Sharyn was here in the city, anyway—
>   No matter where you lived in this city, Isola was still called The City. If you lived in Riverhead or Majesta or Calm's Point or even Bethtown, and you were taking the subway or a bus downtown, you were going into The City. That was it. Sharyn lived in Calm's Point, but Kling lived in The City, and since she was in the city anyways that day, they decided to sleep at his place, talk about lengthy exposition.[38]

Hunter, a college English major, was well aware that his debt to tradition violated post-Jamesian norms. "I know that in these books I frequently commit the unpardonable sin of author intrusion. Somebody will suddenly start talking or thinking or commenting and it won't be any of the cops or crooks, it'll just be this faceless, anonymous 'someone' sticking his nose into the proceedings. Sorry. That's me. Or rather, it's Ed McBain."[39]

So the clipped dialogue is counterweighted by a narration that won't shut up until the very end of the book, when it might discover tact, or a gag, or both. In a final exchange, Carella remarks of one culprit:

> "Maybe he's the rotten bastard in this kettle of fish."
>
>   "You mixed a metaphor," Hawes said.
>
>   The car went silent.
>
>   The men breathed the hot summer air. Slowly, the car threaded its way uptown to the precinct and the squad room.[40]

The self-conscious narration plays reflexive games. It makes mocking reference to *Dragnet, Detective Story*, and police procedurals in general. Such sideswipes are a convention of mystery fiction, as a way of claiming that this book isn't hokey like those commonplace ones. But with McBain, the constant refrain is part of his comic awareness of form. With *Romance* (1995), he offers a *mise-en-abyme*. The plot is built around a play called *Romance*, which itself includes another play of the same title ("where nobody gets to kiss the girl"). *Fat Ollie's Book* (2002) incorporates a short, inept novel that falls into the hands of a transvestite junkie. In treating the book as nonfiction, the crook follows preposterous clues but accidentally intervenes in a real case.

In another book, McBain's narration combines omniscience with omnipotence, pondering the possibility of replotting the characters' destinies. Then he shrugs off the idea.

> You are God and you can do it any way you want to. You can even get them married the next day before his ship sails. Anything you want to do. All the possibilities are there. And you're God, and there isn't anyone who's going to slap your wrist, no matter how you do it.
>
>   But God, man, that is the way it happened.[41]

All mass-market authors, and especially ones writing paperback originals, faced the problem of filling up a fixed format, the short novel. Writers of whodunits were able to build elaborate plots à la Agatha Christie or John Dickson Carr. But the procedural writers typically treated simpler crimes. That genre needed other ways to pad things out: dead-end clues, a long chain of evidence, a bevy of suspects, and questioning irrelevant but colorful witnesses.

Likewise, the bare bones of a typical McBain case could not sustain a classic puzzle intrigue, even to the 60,000-word minimum of a paperback original. He fattens his page count by incorporating, in the usual procedural manner, situations derived from suspense genres (killer's viewpoint, man on the run, woman in danger) alongside the extensive, often fruitless, police investigations.[42] But those choices wouldn't distinguish him from Marric and other writers. He also develops the unusual strategies I've mentioned: the richly furnished fake city, the cop soap opera, the pages stretched out with dialogue, the oversharing narration, and the reflexive asides. These forged a brand designed to work within the limits of a strict publishing format.

McBain's most famous formal gesture became an integral part of that brand. In planning the 87th Precinct series, McBain wanted to counter the heroic detective of the classic and hard-boiled traditions and also avoid the cop partners who were becoming standard in the procedural. His idea was the "conglomerate hero" that was formed by an entire squad. There would be "one cop stepping forward in one novel, another in the next novel, cops quitting, getting killed, and disappearing from the series, other cops coming up, all of them visible to varying extents in each of the books."[43]

The conglomerate plan didn't work out at first. McBain killed Carella's partner in the first book and planned to kill off Carella in the second, but the editor refused, believing that the series needed a strong single figure. McBain responded by creating an ensemble that emphasized Carella but still gave due attention to his colleagues. In one early book, Carella doesn't enter until the last chapter; in later books, other characters fill the role of protagonist. Many police procedurals try for this detectival democracy, but McBain succeeded more fully than most.

Once he had settled on multiple protagonists, McBain could pack his ramifying plotlines with incidents, pointed characterization, authorial commentary, and metaphorical values. He uses crosscutting, between chapters and within them, not only to juxtapose the progress of different investigations but also to attach us to victims, criminals, and bystanders. "Invention and imagination enter the books in the guise of the various people the cops meet along the way. I always give them center stage when they appear, relegating the cops to supporting roles at that time."[44]

The initial entry in the series sets the pattern. *Cop Hater* (1956) presents a serial killer preying on police detectives. In the course of the action, three cop marriages are compared, and scenes of domestic life are interspersed with the murders. The parallels serve to heighten the relative purity of Carella's love for his deaf-mute fiancée Teddy, and they provide important clues to the motive behind the killings. The husband/wife motif is given extra valence by a joking clue about a household misunderstanding that one victim-to-be doesn't get.

Alternating with these ingredients are the routines of the squad, the descriptions of the city in a summer heat wave, and a host of vivid minor figures, from the snitch Danny Gimp to the blowsy madam Mama Luz. In only 150 pages, we meet twenty-two interconnected characters, several of whom will reappear in later novels. *Cop Hater* also hints at the importance of thematic motifs in tying the action up; the cop hater doesn't hate all cops, just one. Thereafter, McBain will use titles as metaphors to link lines of action (*Killer's Wedge*, 1959; *Doll*, 1965; *Bread*, 1974; *Ice*, 1983; *Tricks*, 1987, and so on).

Most often, several squad members tackle one case from different angles, with personal plots running in tandem. Sometimes two cases converge, as they had in Kingsley's *Detective Story*. But McBain tried other variants. Chance may link the story lines. *Cop Hater's* subsidiary plot turns on a pure coincidence, an accidental barroom assault from a suspect who proves to be innocent of the major crimes.

Story lines proliferate. *Nocturne* (1997) has two fleshed-out plots running across two days, and *Tricks* presents three plots in an even shorter time span. *Widows* (1991) runs four plotlines in parallel. The limit is reached in *Hail, Hail, the Gang's All Here!* (1971). Here, across two shifts, fourteen cases—some major, some trivial—mobilize the entire squad. As usual, McBain parades his ingenuity. "This modest volume is dedicated to the Mystery Writers of America, who, if they do not award it the Edgar for the best *ten* mystery novels of the year, should have their collective mysterious heads examined."[45] Actual cops do work several cases at once, but again McBain subjects a realistic premise to an ambitious, flagrantly formal design.

Expanding the roster of cases responded as well to new publishing conditions. Successful authors of paperback originals made the move to hardcover just when editors began demanding longer books in most genres. From the 1970s onward, mystery novels of consequence were expected to run at least 80,000 words, and some could go to 100,000.[46] McBain accordingly filled out his books even more, adding cases and giving his cops more tangled romantic relationships.

McBain's invention didn't flag. On the surreal first page of *The Big Bad City* (1999), nine handcuffed basketball players are led into the squad room just as a perp in custody whips a knife out of his anus. By the end, two incompatible flashbacks will leave some doubt about a Florida murder. In *Candyland: A Novel in Two Parts* (2001), a descent into sordid sex in the first half, signed by Evan Hunter, is followed by a police investigation signed by Ed McBain.[47] It's another echo of Golden Age ingenuity, playing on the disparate styles of Hunter's erotic thrillers and McBain's procedurals.[48]

The posthumously published *Fiddlers* (2005) is a Balzacian tour de force incorporating more than ninety characters spread among all the classes and ethnic groups of Isola. Six murders lead the entire 87th team to a ramifying network of suspects, witnesses, friends, family, romantic partners, and casual hookups. Alongside the investigation are developments both happy and melancholy in the cops' personal lives. Meanwhile, *Fiddlers* trots out narrative tricks from earlier books, including a motivic title and neatly converging lines of inquiry. The narrating voice expounds on the fraught definition of a serial killer, and the regulars mull over the plot device governing *Cop Hater*. At the close of his career, McBain was still expanding his own variorum, a vast catalog of off-kilter riffs in a genre supposedly committed to solemn realism.

* * *

Highsmith's legacy is vast and deep. Apart from the many films based on her novels, she made the psychological thriller respectable for a literary audience. And Tom Ripley provided a prototype for the sympathetic sociopath so common now, from Hannibal Lecter to Lawrence Block's philatelist hitman Keller. McBain's impact is no less consequential. *Hill Street Blues* (1981–1987) made the squad room ensemble drama a television perennial.[49] With typical pugnacity, McBain wanted to sue. "If it hadn't been stolen from me I would have admired it greatly."[50]

CHAPTER 11

DONALD WESTLAKE AND THE RICHARD STARK MACHINE

D onald E. Westlake began publishing novels in 1959, a bit later than Evan Hunter. Both benefited from the postwar boom in mass-market fiction. Both writers started by working at a literary agency while sending out short stories. Both published first novels in hardcover before switching to paperback originals. Both worked in many genres, including science fiction. Hunter scotched rumors that he'd written erotic pulp at the beginning of his career, but Westlake cheerfully confessed he had, getting out of the business only because it didn't pay well.[1] Both writers produced dozens of books under plenty of pseudonyms, and both wrote notable screenplays.

And both writers used the series format to launch experiments in storytelling. Ed McBain's centrifugal energies multiplied plotlines and characters, whereas Westlake was a minimalist. He was celebrated as a master of clean prose, but he also had a unique formal project. He treated one crime genre with a Zen-like discipline. In the process, he unpretentiously engineered one of the great accomplishments in American popular fiction.

One Last Big Job

The police procedural is a streamlined revision of schemas familiar from literary anatomies of the city. In this genre, the random encounters and wayward fates of characters in Dickens's London, Sue's Paris, Bely's Petersburg,

Joyce's Dublin, Döblin's Berlin, and Dos Passos's Manhattan are given a more linear trajectory when a crime must be solved. The investigation provides a goal-directed plot, creating an ensemble of protagonists and ancillary figures. At the same time, a teeming city can enable chance events to derail or fulfill the investigation.

Much the same can be said of another genre of crime fiction that developed alongside the procedural: the heist or caper story. Here, too, the modern city is a landscape to be charted and mastered in pursuit of a goal, and a team of specialists assembles to do a job—but these working stiffs are crooks rather than cops. Here is the same patient attention to drudgery, the effort it takes to plan and execute a precise operation. There's a similar democratization of roles, so that the ensemble, rather than a single protagonist, may dominate the action. In some respects, both the procedural and the heist story can be considered versions of the military novel and film, which concentrates on teamwork focused around a well-defined mission.[2]

Stories of Robin Hood and gentlemen thieves such as Raffles aren't exactly heist tales, just as not all stories about police are procedurals. Donald Westlake defined the heist plot with his typical conciseness: "We follow the crooks before, during, and after a crime, usually a robbery."[3] This formulation points up two features. First, the viewpoint is typically organized around the criminals, not the detectives who might pursue them, as in a police procedural. Second, the plot is structured around the big caper, although lesser crimes might enable it, such as stealing weapons. The organizers recruit crooks with specific skills (safecracking, demolition, driving, and so on). Because the process matters so much, heist plots focus on details of time and physical circumstance, and they draw attention to impediments such as locks, alarms, and patrolling watchmen.

In this incarnation, the clear-cut heist plot is of relatively recent vintage. An early, rough example is Don Tracy's novel *Criss Cross* (1934). An armored-car driver is seduced by a thief's girlfriend and becomes the inside man in a robbery. In the aftermath, the hero is betrayed by the woman and nearly loses his life. In a more comic register, a 1941 play became the film *Larceny, Inc.* (1941), showing how a gang sets up a luggage shop in order to burrow into the bank vault next door. The twist is that their business starts booming and the crooks are distracted from their crime.

Two films helped crystallize the genre. The 1948 screen version of *Criss Cross*, in keeping with fashions of the time, begins at a point of crisis on the day of the robbery, with flashbacks that then lead up to the heist. *The Killers* (1946) applied the lesson of *Citizen Kane* (1941) by having an insurance investigator question witnesses, whose recollections are dramatized in out-of-order flashbacks. Both films looked forward to a key feature of heist books and films: a complex play with chronology.

Then came a novel that neatly laid out the heist plot. W. R. Burnett's *The Asphalt Jungle* (1949) provides the canonical sequence of actions that would govern the genre:[4]

> Circumstances lead one or more characters to decide to execute a heist (robbery, hijacking, kidnapping).
> The initiators recruit participants.
> As a group, they are briefed and prepare their plan. They study their target, rehearse their scheme, and take steps to make it easier.
> The heist begins and concludes.
> The aftermath of the heist, failed or successful, shows the fates of the participants.

Burnett's novel expands its cast to include the financier of the heist (and his cohorts), the specialists' families, the cops, and the press. As with the procedural, we enter a network of ancillary characters. Any of these could botch the job or betray the team.

The 1950 film version of *The Asphalt Jungle* somewhat simplified the novel's plot but gave the genre to the world. In good variorum fashion, moviemakers rang ingenious changes on the canon. *Rififi* (1954) sustains a thirty-minute robbery sequence without one line of dialogue, maximizing suspense and calling attention to minute noises. *Violent Saturday* (1955) intercuts the robbers' planning phase with townsfolk whose fates will eventually converge with the crime. The combat story overtones of the genre come to the fore in *The League of Gentlemen* (1960), which runs its heist, in the words of the leader, as "a full-scale military operation." The same analogy is treated more lightheartedly in *Ocean's 11* (1960).

Given the likelihood that slipups will spoil the heist, it's not surprising that comic caper films appeared too. The miscreants in *The Lady Killers* (1955) are undone by the kindly old lady who rents them their hideout. *Big Deal on Madonna Street* (1958) uses chapter titles to mock the canonical phases of the action. The blundering thieves of *Wrong Arm of the Law* (1963) scrutinize *Rififi* and other heist films for "education and training." *The Italian Job* (1964) became a cult favorite by recruiting zippy Mini Coopers as getaway cars.

The film version of *The Asphalt Jungle* offers a fairly pure instance of the basic structure. Events leading up to the heist—the circumstances, recruitment, and planning phases—consume the first forty-five minutes. The heist, lasting about eleven minutes, ends just before the film's midpoint. After that comes a gunfight initiated by a double-cross attempted by the financier and his henchman. That confrontation takes another seven minutes. The rest of the film runs another forty minutes or so. Although the balanced geometry puts the heist snugly at the center of the plot, the film devotes most of its time to showing many lives leading up to and away from the crime, and this enables more extensive characterizations of all involved.

This neat symmetry isn't the only possibility. Any phase of the action can be given great weight. The first half hour of *Bob le flambeur* (1956) is an episodic introduction to Bob's routines and associates. It's the circumstantial phase presented at low pressure, emphasizing the fascinating milieu Bob drifts through. Only when Roger points out a croupier at the Nantes casino does Bob formulate "the job of a lifetime." Then crew assembly and planning can begin. As the plot develops, characters and relationships presented casually in the exposition become crucial to the heist and its unraveling.

Other phases can also be stretched out. *Ocean's 11* (1960) dwells on the phase of gathering the talent. Before the start, Danny Ocean has already conceived the heist, but we aren't told the plan. Instead we watch his team members converge on Las Vegas. Not until the film's midpoint (at 53:00) is the plan revealed in a briefing. The dawdling exposition suits a film about cool ex-military guys hanging out.

The formation of the crew is exceptionally protracted in *Odds Against Tomorrow* (1959) because two members hesitate about participating. The racist Earl Slater, wracked by the shame of not providing for his wife, finally gets her to agree to let him join. Not until twenty-three minutes from the end does the African American musician Johnny Ingram finally accept a role in the heist, which immediately becomes the film's climax. The source novel for *Odds Against Tomorrow* handles the basic pattern very differently, putting the heist just before the midpoint and devoting the second half of the book to the increasingly hopeless getaway in which the interracial tensions play out at length.

The planning phase sometimes includes a rehearsal for the heist, and that may require a subsidiary crime, such as stealing keys or a vehicle. The film version of *The League of Gentlemen* (1960) has an unusually long planning phase, in which the gang masquerades as soldiers in order to seize weapons from a military post. This robbery, running nearly twenty minutes, takes longer than the central heist but serves to demonstrate the team's esprit de corps. The men's precision and resourcefulness, based on their wartime experience, lead us to expect a successful main event.

The heist can be the climax, as in *The Big Caper*, or it can be virtually the film's entire second half, as in *The Italian Job* (which arguably doesn't complete the heist and so never provides a proper aftermath). The flamboyant robbery in *Topkapi* (1964), involving elaborate subterfuges, dominates the film's later stretches, leading to a quick reversal in its epilogue. The heist is finished early on in *The Lady Killers*; the crucial action is the long aftermath in which, contradicting the title, the crooks dispose of one another. In contrast, the heist dominates nearly all of *Larceny, Inc.* Most of the film is devoted to the crooks' slowly deepening tunnel: the process is interrupted by breaks in the water main, a geyser of furnace oil, and their decision to abandon their plan in favor of going straight—before another crook comes along to continue the caper.

Given the pressure to fill out the variorum, it was probably inevitable that somebody would make a heist movie that keeps the heist off-screen and makes the action one long aftermath. In *Plunder Road* (1957), after the initial train robbery is completed, the rest of the film consists of chases and suspense sequences. The circumstances, recruitment, and planning phases are alluded to in dialogue, as suits a low-budget production. *Touchez pas au grisbi* (1954) starts the morning after the caper and shows thieves trying to protect their loot from a treacherous drug dealer.

The fact that *Topkapi* allowed Jules Dassin to parody his own *Rififi* was only one indication of the high artifice at work in the genre. As with the police procedural, a surface realism—serious crime, details of tradecraft, location shooting—is overbalanced by a frank acknowledgment of formal play. So clear-cut were the conventions that filmmakers could indulge in hypothetical sequences. *Bob le flambeur* includes a voice-over narrator who two-thirds of the way through announces, "Here's how Bob pictured the heist," and provides a scene of a successful robbery. Needless to say, that scenario isn't fulfilled. Similarly, a hypothetical sequence early in *Gambit* (1966) is countermanded by the actual progress of the heist.

Because the phases of a heist plot are so familiar, storytellers have felt free to rearrange them. Simon Kent's novel *The Lions at the Kill* (1959) begins long after the heist, when virtually all of the robbers are killed; we then flash back to the heist itself, which forms the bulk of the book, before returning to the present. The film *Seven Thieves* (1960) irons Kent's novel into a linear story, but a similar flashback structure is used in *The Lavender Hill Mob* (1951). More in the spirit of *The Killers* is *The Good Die Young* (1954). As four men drive to the target, each is given a flashback explaining what brought him into the gang (always a woman). When the backstories are complete, the robbery becomes the film's climax.

Just as some authors specialized in procedurals, others specialized in the heist plot. One was Lionel White. Most of his plots are straightforward linear accounts of recruitment, planning, execution, and aftermath. Because they shuttle viewpoints among characters, they often overlap time frames slightly. For example, by intercutting many characters carrying out a bank job, *Steal Big* (1960) jumps back in small bursts to replay events. *Coffin for a Hood* (1958) is more ambitious, involving a lengthy flashback from killers at a cafe to a survey of people whom they'll meet later.

White's most audacious and influential manipulation of time comes in *Clean Break* (1955).[5] A crook, his pal, a cashier, a bartender, and a crooked cop conspire to rob a racetrack. They will employ helpers to start a fistfight and shoot a racehorse. The early chapters devote short stretches to following each one, already recruited, through the circumstances phase of the heist template. The men assemble at their planning meeting, which is invaded by the snoopy wife of the weak cashier. She then tells her boyfriend about the heist, so another strand involving other characters is introduced.

On the day of the robbery, White's narration attaches itself sequentially to each man as he executes his role in the scheme. The early part of the book has a few mild jumps back in time to follow each heister, but on the day of the job extreme back-and-forth shifts occur. We follow the bartender going to the track on the fateful day, and the next subchapter skips back to the cashier waking up and then catching the same train. In a later section, we skip back to the previous day and attach ourselves to the sniper who will shoot the racehorse. Because of the overlapping lines of action, the shooting of the horse and the starting of the sham bar fight are presented twice. Everything eventually converges on Johnny Clay, the mastermind, who breaks into the money room and steals the day's revenue. These temporal overlaps emerge partly from the description of the action, but they're also marked either by characters looking at clocks or watches or by explicit mention, such as "It was exactly six forty-five when . . ."

In the film version, Stanley Kubrick's *The Killing* (1956), the staggered, overlapping time scheme is laid out by an impersonal voice-over narrator that could have come from a police procedural. Apart from lending an aura of authenticity, the voice-over exaggerates the time markers of the novel. The first five scenes are introduced with these tags:

"At exactly 3:45 . . ."
"About an hour earlier . . ."
"At seven PM that same day . . ."
"A half an hour earlier . . ."
"At 7:15 that same night . . ."

These lead-ins remind us of the ticking clock, set up parallels among the characters, and get us acclimated to the film's method of tracking one character, then jumping back in time to track another. This is moving-spotlight narration on markedly parallel tracks. The same method is applied during the heist, when ten consecutive scenes and several others are tagged in the same way.

It's not just the repetitions that play up White's jagged time scheme. When the sniper Nikki is shot after plugging the racehorse, the narrator reports drily: "Nikki was dead at 4:24." Cut to Johnny leaving a luggage store, and the voice-over announces: "At 2:15 that afternoon Johnny Clay was still in the city." In all, the time jumps more or less buried in White's prose are made dissonant in the film. Here the juxtaposition heightens the likelihood that Johnny's robbery won't go according to plan.

The replayed bits are also sharply profiled. As the blocks move from character to character and skip back in time, they include actions we've already seen.

The most persistent is the repetition of the track announcer calling the start of the crucial seventh race (which helps orient us), but we also see replays of the wrestler Maurice starting a fight, the downing of the horse, and glimpses of Johnny waiting to slip into the cash room.

Instead of lining up flashback blocks in the manner of *The Killers*, Kubrick's film offers brief parallel chunks of time stacked in a slightly overlapping array until they all square up in a single moment, the consummation of the robbery. This structure allows for the sort of character delineation we find in *The Asphalt Jungle* while also establishing early on that the robbery is doomed. In addition, there's a formal game for the viewer to enjoy. *The Killing* points in two directions—revising the flashback schema of many 1940s films but becoming a model for future filmmakers like Tarantino who want to make more unusual plays with time and viewpoint comprehensible.

Clean Break became a reference point in the genre. The robbers in the novel *The League of Gentlemen* (1958) take White's book as a *vade mecum* for their scheme. Perhaps in homage, the author presents their robbery with a staggered time scheme like White's. More generally, *The Killing* gave White's reputation a boost. Perhaps in a grateful spirit, his novel *Steal Big* included this scene.

> Donovan didn't look at the half-dozen worn, barely legible signs in the dingy lobby of the building. He went at once to the elevator and asked for the fifth floor. Getting out of the elevator, he turned left, took a dozen steps and knocked on a pebbled-glass door. The door bore the legend, KUBRIC NOVELTY COMPANY.[6]

Mr. Kubric, it turns out, supplies illegal guns and explosives.

Reverse-Engineering the Stark Machine

Why read Donald Westlake? His fans would say, for sheer fun. His motto was "I believe my subject is bewilderment. But I could be wrong." He made his name, or rather one of them, with comic intrigues such as *The Fugitive Pigeon* (1965) and *The Busy Body* (1966). Although *Dancing Aztecs* (1976) is probably his most virtuoso turn in this vein, *Help, I Am Being Held Prisoner* (1974) gets my vote as the funniest.

> Soon our food came, and so did the wine, but Eddie kept on telling me his reminiscences. Friends of his had fallen under tanks, walked into airplane propellers, inadvertently bumped their elbows against the firing mechanism of thousand-pound bombs, and walked backwards off the flight deck of an aircraft carrier while backing up to take a group photograph. Other friends had

misread the control directions on a robot tank and driven it through a Pennsylvania town's two hundredth anniversary celebration square dance, had fired a bazooka while it was facing the wrong way, had massacred a USO Gilbert and Sullivan troupe rehearsing *The Mikado* under the mistaken impression they were peaceful Vietnamese villagers, and had ordered a nearby enlisted man to look in that mortar and see why the shell hadn't come out.

It began after a while to seem as though Eddie's military career had been an endless red-black vista of explosions, fires, and crumpling destruction, all intermixed with hoarse cries, anonymous thuds, and terminal screams. Eddie recounted these disasters in his normal bloodless style, with touches of that dry avuncular humor he'd displayed during our hour at the bar. I managed to eat very little of my veal parmigiana—it kept looking like a body fragment—but became increasingly sober nonetheless.[7]

Few contemporary novelists could produce sentences as perfect, and hilarious, as these.

We also go to Westlake for his unique handling of crime fiction, a genre that was highly sensitive to tradition. He paid homage to McBain, Rex Stout, Lionel White, and many others in essays that show a keen critical mind. He also had an amused awareness of the broader conventions of popular narrative. Who else would take the trouble to puncture Arthur Hailey's oversized "institutional" novels *Hotel* and *Airport* with *Comfort Station* (1970), a parody set in a men's public toilet? He didn't spare his peers. Let Ross MacDonald write, "He had a long nose, slightly curved, which appeared both self-assertive and inquisitive," and Westlake will add, "I hope my nose is looking disbelieving."[8]

Possibly the strangest book Westlake wrote, *Adios, Scheherazade* (1970), offers a comic metafictional account of storytelling. Drawing on his experience writing sex novels to order, he gives us a first-person account by Ed Topliss. Ed has written twenty-eight dirty books on a monthly basis but just can't squeeze out another. Instead every day he types up his memories, fantasies, and free associations. Things get complicated when his wife discovers his manuscript and leaves him. Realizing that his fake confessions will lead him to jail, he goes on the run, compulsively batting out a new chapter on whatever typewriter he can find.

Into this farrago Ed tosses citations, in-jokes, and some of the precepts of mass-market writing I've considered in previous chapters. He explains how to pad a book to fit a format (for porn: fifty thousand words, ten chapters, a big sex scene in each). He mentions, and demonstrates, how to mount repetitious scenes and pile up short paragraphs. He outlines the four basic pornography plots: male protagonist, female protagonist, alternation between the two, and what he calls *La Ronde*, a daisy-chain of couplings. Stout's and McBain's novels were reflexive in bursts, and Westlake's could be as well, but here we have modernism fully burlesqued. In *Adios, Scheherazade*, Ed points out that it would be an avant-garde breakthrough to write a novel about writing a novel—or in this case, about failing to write one. As ever, comedy sells reflexivity, and André Gide's *Counterfeiters* is not far away.[9]

Adios, Scheherazade showed that Westlake not only played with structure but also enjoyed thinking about it. The book was written while Westlake was developing two self-consciously formal franchises of his own, both using the heist premise. In the comic one, John Dortmunder is a working-class thief whose ill-assorted gang typically fumbles every job they pull. From *The Hot Rock* (1970) to *Get Real* (2009), the Dortmunder series became a genial landmark in the genre.[10]

That series was born as an alternative to one Westlake had launched under the ominous signature of Richard Stark.[11] *The Hunter* (1963) introduced Parker, a hard-bitten professional thief whose look Westlake modeled on the young Jack Palance. Westlake later regretted not giving Parker a first name, and even the surname caused problems. "For 27 books I've had to find some other way to say, 'Parker parked the car.'"[12]

Between 1962 and 1969, Westlake pounded out twelve paperback Parkers. Under the Stark name he also signed a brief spinoff series featuring Alan Grofield, an extroverted actor who sometimes joins Parker's crew to finance a summer theater. The next four Parkers (1971–1974) shifted to hardcover publication. After pausing the series for more than two decades, Westlake composed eight new Parker adventures between 1997 and 2008, the year of his death. Novelist John Banville judged the series to be "among the most poised and polished fictions of their time and, in fact, of any time."[13]

The fourth book in the series sums up the protagonist's lifestyle. "Parker had lived the way he wanted, to a pattern he liked. He was a heavy gun, in on one or two institutional robberies a year—a bank, or a payroll, or an armored car—just often enough to keep the finances fat, and the rest of the time he lived in resort hotels on either coast, with a cover that would satisfy even the income-tax beagles."[14] The strict pattern of Parker's routine is paralleled by the rigorous way the novels recount his career.

Parker is not a romantic. Westlake decided that Parker has the values of a conscientious workman: precision, efficiency, tenacity. He prepares his heists meticulously and coldly calculates the odds. He never has sex when planning a job because that would distract him from his craft. He has no lust for violence, but he will kill if necessary. He will rabbit-punch a passerby to grab a car and will threaten the family of a policeman to get access to evidence. He will implacably pursue someone who has double-crossed him, which his associates do with foolish frequency.

Under normal circumstances Parker moves through the world without friction, stealing vehicles and picking locks with aplomb. But the genre demands that a heist be imperfect, so his abilities emerge most clearly when he has to think his way out of tight spots. To survive, he must often leave the loot behind.

Continuing characters are featured in any popular series, but Westlake restricted their number because his hero is a loner. Parker has no everyday friendships, only professional associates he calls on for a job. The sixteenth Parker novel, *Butcher's Moon* (1974), reunites several of them to carry out a spectacular raid to settle a matter that was left dangling two books earlier.[15]

As the series goes on, Parker gets a little less flinty. At one point he decides not to kill a drugged man because it would be like killing a child. (So he "broke three bones, all fairly important."[16]) His time with Grofield creates a bit of bonding. In the finale of *The Handle* (1966), instead of leaving Grofield for dead, he takes risks to rescue him. When Grofield thanks him, Parker is puzzled: "We were working together." In later books he leaves off vagabondage to join Claire (no last name) in a lakeside home that is both bolt-hole and bourgeois household.

Reflecting on the history of crime fiction, Westlake maintained that every genre springs from a source somewhat close to real life. It then becomes routinized into ritual. Dashiell Hammett knew the grimy world of crime, and Raymond Chandler, the cashiered executive, turned that realistic work into "a kind of narrative poetry." That ritual became "roughed up" after World War II, as writers were now more strongly emotional. The extreme instance is Mickey Spillane, but Westlake also mocks Chandler and Ross Macdonald for overwrought prose and sensational situations (homosexuality in Chandler, family secrets in Macdonald).[17] Westlake might well have included Jim Thompson's febrile plots and style as further evidence of the new excesses of crime fiction.

In contrast, Westlake made the Stark novels exercises in minimalist, objective narration. Chandler and other hard-boiled writers had let their protagonists tell the story, but Westlake wrote in the third person, and he strove to make it dry and detached. He tried "giving the character's emotion without stating what that emotion was. Not saying 'He was feeling tense,' instead saying, 'His hand squeezed harder on the chair arm,' as if staying outside the guy."[18] Westlake isn't completely outside; his novels follow the protagonist's train of thought to a degree that *The Glass Key* never does. But very seldom does Parker show or voice his emotions. He never rants as Spillane's characters do, nor babble like Thompson's traumatized losers.

Parker speaks as little as possible. When asked if his plane flight was good, he says yes. "Parker meant nothing by the word; it was simply a sound that ended that topic."[19] His reticence is contagious. Stark renders Parker's adventures in a far more laconic style than we find in Westlake's comic novels. In *The Mourner*, Parker and his sideman Handy have questioned a syndicate thug.

His fate ends a chapter: "They had him write the address down, and then they tied him and left him in a closet. They never did remember to go back."[20] Scenes of violence are presented in a clipped, almost offhand manner. Here Parker is moving quietly toward a man who's stalking him:

> There was a sudden scattering of leaves, and Negli was standing up in full sight, staring and staring the wrong way, his natty back to Parker and only five feet away.
> "Why don't you fight like a *man!*"
> Parker shot him in the back of the head.[21]

Compared to McBain's rodomontade, this prose is radically stripped down. Even "staring and staring" doesn't look wasteful because it emphasizes how stubbornly oblivious Negli is. The addition of "natty" to "back" heightens the contrast between Negli the showboater and the ruthlessly efficient Parker. Another chapter done.

More elegantly than Lionel White, Westlake rings variations on heist conventions. For one thing, Parker's targets are astonishingly varied. Parker knocks over the usual armored cars, but his field of action widens to a football game, a casino, a convention of coin collectors, an Air Force base, an African embassy, a rock concert, a revival meeting, a jewelry auction, and a rural racetrack. In one book, Parker and his team pillage an entire town.

Stark went on to twist the canonical plot structure in distinctive ways. In the first book, *The Hunter*, the heist has already taken place, and everything is aftermath. Following books treat smaller robberies rather than the One Big Caper. Not until the fifth book, aptly titled *The Score* (1964), do we get the full arc of action, from circumstances and planning to heist and aftermath. In other books, there might be aborted or abandoned heists (*Plunder Squad*, 1972) or miniheists carried out by lesser entrepreneurs (*The Outfit*, 1963).

For Westlake, building a whole book around a heist posed problems. Robberies, he said, "aren't *serial*. They happen and they're over with."[22] Burnett had overcome the problem by tracing out a network of characters affected by the crime, both before and after. White stretched out the heist with shifting viewpoints and time jumps. Westlake borrows from both writers, but he tries other solutions too.

One is to pack the setup and the aftermath with premises from other genres, as McBain had. Westlake provides confrontations out of hard-boiled detective novels, and one book, *The Jugger* (1965), has the contours of a traditional private-eye story.[23] Some books put Claire in a woman-in-peril situation. Most often, though, Stark novels fill themselves out with extended passages of pursuit.

When Parker isn't planning or executing a job, he's usually chasing someone or being chased. Again, *The Hunter* provides a template. Parker has been left for dead. He formulates two goals: to kill the man who double-crossed him, and to retrieve the money he's owed, even if that means challenging a crime syndicate. Later examples include *Slayground* (1971), in which the heist collapses at the beginning and the entire book consists of Parker's effort to survive a night trapped in a shuttered amusement park.

In expanding the heist plot through what Westlake called "the schnook on the run" premise, he updated an adventure prototype.[24] Leslie Charteris's urban bandit Simon Templar (aka the Saint) is suave and chatty, whereas Parker is blunt and hard-boiled. But both characters often go up against both cops and crooks, and their thefts can become secondary action to extended fight-or-flight maneuvers.

All of the Parker books take delight in describing the physical details of committing larceny. They fill out the genre template with loving descriptions of planning, raising funds, buying and disguising vehicles, assembling tools and weapons, and executing the job. When Westlake moved Parker from paperback originals to hardcover publication, the demand for a longer book pushed him toward more intricate descriptions. The first forty pages of *Deadly Edge* form a meticulous account of chopping a hole in an auditorium roof, slipping through it, subduing guards, and stealing the ticket money at a rock concert. (This is a print equivalent of *Rififi*'s virtuoso central sequence.) At the other end of the same book, Parker's stalking of the men who have invaded his home lasts nearly as long.

This painstaking specificity supplies a certain realism, but it's eventually in service to larger patterns. The title of *The Seventh* (1966) refers both to the division of spoils and to the book's position in the series. When Parker got a second wind in the 1990s, the first five titles created chain-link continuity: *Comeback, Backflash, Flashfire, Firebreak,* and *Breakout.* Branded titles are common enough in popular fiction (*A as in Alibi, The Cat Who . . .*), but Westlake's love of structure goes beyond whimsy. In the Stark books, he switches on a remorseless, almost frightening narrative machine.

Four-Way Split

With one exception, all the Parker novels display the same exoskeleton. A book is divided into four numbered parts, roughly equal. Within each part, the chapters tend to be rather short and modular. Each one presents a slice of the action as a single character experiences it in third-person narration.

All the chapters in the book's first part present the story action from Parker's viewpoint. The fourth part usually does the same. But at least one part in the middle will not adhere to him. Part two or part three may present another character's viewpoint across all its chapters, or more likely will shift viewpoints from chapter to chapter. As in much popular fiction, Westlake moves from mind to mind, but like Klempner in *Letter to Five Wives* he doesn't use tags. None of the chapters is labeled with time, place, or the viewpoint character's name.

Consider *The Score* (1964). In part one, Parker and the team assemble and plan to ransack Copper Canyon, North Dakota. In part two, we're still attached to Parker when he arranges for financing, gets guns, tests the road and hideout, and assembles the team for the heist. Part three traces the heist itself through ten chapters. Most are attached to a different thief or citizen as the pillage proceeds; two objective chapters provide more synoptic coverage.

Treating the heist from a series of perspectives builds suspense and explains details of execution not already previewed. It permits shrewd suppression of incidents because a lot can happen between viewpoint shifts. We also get some surprises about character motivation, as when the gutting of Copper Canyon is revealed as an act of revenge that Parker discovers too late. The part four chapters return our viewpoint to Parker as he deals with the new problems of the heist's aftermath.

In contrast, *The Green Eagle Score* (1967) makes the mobile-viewpoint block of chapters its second part. Again part one is attached to Parker, who sizes up the targeted Air Force base and starts making plans. Part two shifts among the other major characters: Parker's team members, the financier backing them, a woman who divulges their plans to her psychoanalyst, and the psychoanalyst himself who recruits two of his more unstable patients to help him rip off the gang's booty. In part three, the heist is rendered through Parker's perspective. As usual, part four sticks with Parker as he and the team pursue the stolen money.

Lawrence Block has compared the quadruple format to a symphonic structure, with each movement given a different tone and texture.[25] In modern terms, it's a spreadsheet layout. Of course heist novels often vary viewpoints on the action. *The Asphalt Jungle* and White's books freely mix perspectives within chapters and even single scenes. Westlake subjects this tendency to a principled rigor. His rules are odd, even obsessional: always start and end with Parker, shift viewpoints within only one middle part, typically restrict each chapter to only one character, even a minor walk-on. The books are a pop-culture cousin of Oulipo, the French literary school that required its members to embrace arbitrary constraints. Write a novel without using the letter "e," for instance, or describe the same action in sixty-six different ways. Through pattern plotting, Stark plays a suite of variations not only on types of heists but on possible ways of arranging viewpoint modules.

Stark's multipart, theme-and-variations format was recast for the first Dortmunder novel. It began as a Parker project. Suppose that Parker kept failing to steal a rare gem? The result veered into comedy, and Westlake put the manuscript aside for years before deciding to finish it. *The Hot Rock* varies the Stark geometry by dividing the action into six labeled phases, each recounting a heist attempt aiming at a different target. (The emerald migrates from a museum to a prison, to a police station, to an asylum, etc.) Each phase breaks the action into brief parallel modules: one chapter is devoted to casing the joint, another to gathering the gang, another to meeting at the O. J. Bar & Grill, and so on before culminating in another failed heist.[26] As with the Parker books, you can lay out the plot on a grid.

Westlake always claimed that he didn't outline his novels in advance. "I don't know what's going to happen next. The fun part is telling myself the story."[27] Perhaps this rigid, arbitrary template provided a framework that would regularize whatever he came up with, like pouring cement into molds. But it also constrained him in fruitful ways.

Westlake's task was to fill out 60,000 words or so. By always including one stretch that expands beyond Parker's perspective, he obliged himself to flesh out his story by probing the motives and goals of several characters. By packing in several characters and inventing business and backstory, he could make some figures central to the main action, some mere bystanders, and some who could create unhappy accidents to spoil the heist. Given slots, he had to fill them. Form follows (self-imposed) format.

Once he was committed to diverging systematically from Parker's range of knowledge, Westlake could try alternatives. The most common tactic is to let the off-Parker block sample several characters' viewpoints. *The Handle* (1966), in contrast, toggles between the viewpoints of just two, Grofield and the target of the heist, Baron. In *The Green Eagle Score*, the betraying woman's visits to her doctor alternate with scenes surveying other characters drawn into the scheme.

Given Westlake's skill in shifting stylistic registers—florid comedy for the Dortmunder novels, severity for the Parkers, something in between for the Grofields—we shouldn't be surprised that the chapters devoted to several characters are written to match their temperaments. In *Plunder Squad* (1972), Devers, the ladies' man, is given swaggering inner monologues, and the fussy Lou Sternberg resents lodging in a chain motel. "Ghastly. Drinking glasses in the bathroom were encased in little white paper bags imprinted with a message including the word 'sanitized.'"[28] Parker's mind is fastidious, but not along these lines.

A sly conversation in *The Mourner* lays bare Stark's signature four-block grid. Parker is explaining how a particular double-cross worked. Kapoor replies:

> "It sounds so complex. I have the feeling I've heard barely a quarter of the story."
> Parker shrugged. "You heard all of your parts."[29]

The four-part structure yields a trim economy, but it presents problems too. The block construction takes away one advantage of multiple viewpoints: rapid crosscutting among characters' perspectives. In a more normal novel, like one in McBain's 87th Precinct series, Parker's piecemeal activities would alternate with scenes featuring other characters acting at the same time. This moving-spotlight approach would build suspense as we learn more than Parker does. But the first part of a Stark book always ties us to him, as does the last and usually one in between. To cover what other characters are up to, within and between blocks, Westlake creates elaborate time jumps and realignments.

The simplest are flashbacks within a part. The novel usually opens with Parker in action—going to a meeting, fleeing a robbery gone wrong, dodging an ambush. Then the narration supplies the backstory we need. Then the action of the second or third part is likely to shift back to dramatize incidents mentioned in the Parker-centered chapters. Flashbacks across parts fill in gaps and replay events we understand better on the new pass. These time jumps are motivated by a character who provides a new perspective. As one critic puts it: "Stark loves to shift character points of view, not only to advance the story but to go back inside the action and examine it for further angles and riches. The result is noir that drives forward relentlessly while feeling kaleidoscopic and reflective."[30]

This ambitious strategy is on display in the first book, *The Hunter*. Here the alternative viewpoint is singular, that of the treacherous Mal.

Part one, Parker POV: Parker is on the lam after a heist. His wife Lynn, who betrayed him, has killed herself. He goes on to seek Mal, who double-crossed him.

In the part's final chapter, a flashback traces the heist, Lynn's attempt to kill Parker, and his escape.

Part two, Mal POV: Mal is fleeing Parker. He tries to gain status in the Outfit. Hiding out in a mob hotel, he sees Parker entering his bedroom window.

In the part's final chapter, a flashback takes us back to before the heist, when Mal set up Lynn to kill Parker. There is a replay of a scene in part one's flashback, when Mal and Lynn leave Parker for dead, this time rendered from Mal's perspective.

Part three, Parker POV: The first five chapters jump back in time. They return to Parker's search, which took place during part two, when we were restricted to Mal. The part culminates in a replay of Parker coming through the window (start of part two) and consummates it by dramatizing Parker's murder of Mal.

Part four, Parker POV: In straight chronology, Parker confronts the Outfit demanding the loot that Mal gave them.

The effect of this time shuffling is a constant pulse of curiosity (what's Parker doing when we're with Mal?), surprise (Parker's entry through the window), and suspense (Parker's window entry is cut off by a string of flashbacks tracing how he got there). By embracing block construction and grid patterning, Westlake guarantees himself the possibility of rearranging the time frame within parallel parts. In a sense, he carried to a new, stricter level the overlapping blocks that White had pioneered in *Clean Break*.

Stark novels happily explored a range of variations. Flashbacks can appear in any part, even the last, as a way of plugging gaps in earlier stretches. *The Mourner* has eight segments (flashbacks, replays) shifted across the parts. The simultaneity of parts laid out in *The Hunter* is treated for more intense suspense in *Deadly Edge*. During part two Parker is pursuing the man who double-crossed him; in part three, over the same days two thugs hunting Parker discover the home he shares with Claire. He calls her twice in part two, and the same calls are replayed from her viewpoint in the next part. These sync points encourage us to dread the outcome because the second call proves to Parker that she's under attack, and he's far enough away to make rescue unlikely.

Hand Westlake the most linear story imaginable and he will snap it into quarters, chop up the scenes, and shuffle them into back-and-fill patterns. *The Sour Lemon Score* (1969) is a basic chase plot. After the heist, which consumes the whole of part one, Parker must track down the treacherous Uhl. He will visit five possible contacts seriatim before finally confronting his quarry.

This simple string is knotted up in part three. Some of Parker's visits are presented out of order, and the contact characters' viewpoints replay and fill in stretches of parts one, two, and three. Part four, reattaching us to Parker, has the nerve to plug gaps in part two by adding more flashbacks, even a flashback within a flashback. Again, Stark bares a pet device:

> Parker grimaced. He and Uhl had been doing a long-distance dance up and down the eastern seaboard for three days. He'd gotten to Pearson before Uhl, but Uhl had caught up. And then Uhl had gotten to Barri Dane before Parker, but Parker didn't catch up. But that was all right, because Parker had gotten to Joyce Langer before Uhl, and that meant everything was caught up.
>
> But if only the timing had been a little different somewhere along the line.[31]

Surprisingly, Westlake's shameless formalism doesn't throw you out of the story world. Varied within strict lines from book to book, Westlake's design creates an almost hypnotic flow of engagement. The pages fly by. "The books," notes Luc Sante, "are machines that all but read themselves."[32]

The four-part structure is easy to follow, but what enables readers to grasp and enjoy the shuffled time schemes? The third-person narration is mobile but reliable, and flashbacks are clearly signaled. Westlake doesn't rely on the twists that arise from the concealment strategies of the thrillers I consider in chapter 13. We aren't misled through subjectively distorted flashbacks or unclaimed viewpoints. When we're surprised, it's usually because the four-part structure and the succession of scenes have skipped over a crucial incident that needs explaining in retrospect.

Moreover, the conventions of the heist genre help us break the action into phases (assembly, planning, execution, aftermath) and assign character roles (driver, gunman, explosives expert) on minimal cues. Characters adhere to a behavioral realism. The unity of mind, word, and deed is usually solid.

The modularity of chapters helps too. Each chapter is a discrete chunk of plot, so Westlake can set one scene into a block and then replay it in another block. We recognize a unit that we've already encountered, if only in part. And, of course, regular readers of the Stark saga come to the books expecting a fragmentary layout of events, so we're experts in sorting such things out.

There's evidence that readers of earlier eras could have handled Westlake's formal games. In 1922, the legendary pulp master H. Bedford-Jones revealed a new template for "the book-length," a novella to be run complete in a magazine issue. He suggested breaking the action into four distinct parts, with temporal displacements and viewpoint shifts. Part two should skip back to a period before part one but conclude later than that had ended. Part three should flash back to another stretch of part one, but now showing events from the villain's perspective. The final block could then return to the hero's viewpoint for an exciting climax.[33] It's possible that Westlake knew of Bedford-Smith's article or the novellas built along these lines, but it's just as likely that he came up with his more rigorous, time-looping modularity on his own, not least because of the tendency of heist plots to fall into sharply defined phases.

The last Stark novel of the first period is a sweeping anthology of earlier strategies. *Butcher's Moon* (1974) is twice the length of the paperback originals. Aiming to retrieve the loot that was lost in *Slayground*, Parker takes on the local mob, the political elite, and a police force. For help, he recruits eleven associates who have survived earlier jobs. Instead of a single heist, there are eleven, eight in a single night. The climax is an all-out assault on a gangster's mansion to rescue the wounded Grofield—another gesture showing that Parker isn't utterly amoral.

There are the usual grace notes, including bodyguards who while away their downtime playing Monopoly. At one point a go-between protests, "I'm only the messenger." Parker shoots him: "Now you're the message." The book's final lines expose Westlake's procedure. Grofield, unconscious for most of the action, whispers, "What the hell happened?" One of his team replies, "Well, that's a long story."[34]

In organizing this long story Westlake for once abandons the four-part structure. He builds the novel out of fifty-five chapters that switch viewpoints among two dozen characters, taken singly or in groups. The scenes are cross-cut, using the alternation technique that his parallel-block construction had avoided. Some bits of action, such as the shooting of Grofield, are rendered from three overlapping viewpoints. If you haven't read the earlier books, *Butcher's Moon* looks fairly conventional, but seen against the background of the previous novels, it's a departure.

Had *Butcher's Moon* exhausted his formal options? Westlake said that Stark's voice was suddenly "gone, erased clear out of my head."[35] He wrote no Parker novels for twenty-three years.

In the interim he agreed to adapt Jim Thompson's *The Grifters* for a 1990 film. The novel ties the action to Roy Dillon's viewpoint, but director Stephen Frears asked for more emphasis on Roy's mother. Westlake's screenplay creates an ensemble film by introducing the three main characters in a sequence that intercuts them executing their signature scams (fig. 11.1).[36] The balance may have reminded Westlake of his fondness for columnar patterns in the heist novels. In any event, after adapting *The Grifters*, he tells us that Stark's voice came back.[37]

The final eight Parker novels expand the template in ingenious ways. Westlake sets up more obstacles for Parker to overcome, both on the job and in his flights and pursuits. A plan for stealing paintings in *Firebreak* (2001) is put on hold when Parker has to find out who's stalking him. Eventually the two lines of action are connected. True to its title, *Breakout* (2002) sees Parker, consummate break-in artist, forced to escape from prison, find a way out of a sealed armory, and free his sideman's woman from jail. Westlake bares the book's device by having a crew member declare, "All we do is break outta things."[38]

11.1 *The Grifters* (1990): The plot's "level playing field" is solidified in a triptych split screen. This gesture toward abstraction reaffirms Westlake's inclination toward neat parallel structures.

Chapters multiply and scenes are stretched. The climax of *Comeback* (1997), a suspenseful confrontation among three men in a darkened house, takes sixty-nine pages. Minor characters are promoted. In *Flashfire* (2000), a realtor starts out as a neutral source of information, but she intervenes in Parker's pursuit several times, both as help and hindrance. The same book is filled out by a subplot when Parker becomes a witness to murder, and so a target himself.

In this second cycle, the chapters devoted to non-Parker characters become breezier, which allows for semicomic squabbles and in-jokes. In one book, a heister gets messages left for him in a library's copy of S. S. Van Dine's *Gracie Allen Murder Case*, a book so awful that it's never checked out. At times, Westlake goes full-bore Dortmunder. No first-period Stark book would have indulged in a passage in which Parker and a disgruntled employee move through an office at night.

> He had bumped into the wrong desk, causing the breakfast to flip over and hit the floor facedown. Lindahl stooped to pick up the plate, but the omelet stuck to the black linoleum, which was now a black ocean, and that omelet the sandy desert island, with the solitary strip of bacon sticking up from it, slightly slumped but brave, the perfect representation of the stranded sailor, alone and waiting for his cartoon caption. On the floor, it looked like what the Greeks call *acheiropoeietoi*, a pictorial image not made by a human hand.

When Lindahl suggests cleaning up the mess, Stark resets the style with a string of monosyllables. "'A mouse did it,' Parker told him. 'Drop the plate on it and let's go.'"[39]

In this period, the expanded story lines are still mapped out in four parts, but Westlake makes them very linear. The first five novels in the new cycle, from *Comeback* to *Breakout*, avoid elaborate time shifts. The same thing happens in the last three, which try something else: a single story line links them.

Butcher's Moon had picked up a situation left dangling in *Slayground*, and that book itself had been an experiment in oddly bifurcated narrative. In the opening scene of *The Blackbird* (1967), Grofield and Parker split up after a failed heist. The rest of the book follows Grofield into a government intrigue. What happened to Parker? The later *Slayground* begins with the same heist scene, slightly rewritten, and tracks Parker's escape into the Fun Island amusement park.

Elsewhere, story lines from earlier books are relaunched, usually when a character comes back from the past. The treacherous Uhl, for instance, wreaks his damage in *The Sour Lemon Score* and reappears three books later in *Plunder Squad*. Events that Uhl has set in motion pay off much later in *Firebreak*. Not until the final trilogy, though, does Stark bind successive novels together in a single tight sequence.

Nobody Runs Forever (2004) ends in suspension, with Parker fleeing into a forest. This was a jolt for the fans who read the book upon publication. Did the title suggest that Parker would be captured? *Ask the Parrot* (2006) picks up the story immediately and shows Parker rescued but forced to launch another caper. In *Dirty Money* (2008), Parker comes home to Claire but soon returns to the scene of *Nobody Runs Forever* to retrieve the spoils he left behind.

The three books add many new characters and bring back ones from earlier Parker adventures. There are nearly forty robbers, cops, bounty hunters, bystanders, and thugs wanting in on the action. There's also a parrot, with one chapter rendered from his point of view. To the very end, mishaps, lies, and double-crosses proliferate. In *Dirty Money*—in effect, our farewell to Parker—the fourth part is crammed with enough action and subterfuge to occupy an entire paperback original. Death prevented Westlake from writing another Stark novel, but this last entry fully rounds off the trilogy.

A man who writes *Adios, Scheherazade* is well aware of the refined pleasures of mass-market storytelling. For all their grimness, the Stark stories commit to a vision of form as play. McBain balances procedural accuracy with wild stylization, whereas Westlake seems to treat everything, including his hard-bitten hero, as part of a grand, rigorous artifice.

Here's a last piece of evidence. *Jimmy the Kid* (1974) shows one of Dortmunder's gang trying to pull off a kidnapping by following the scheme he finds in *Child Heist*, a nonexistent Parker novel. (Westlake was inspired by an actual case in which kidnappers mimicked a Lionel White novel.) Westlake ends the book with correspondence between Stark and his lawyer. They are contemplating legal action against a film based on the botched Dortmunder snatch. The paperback edition of *Jimmy the Kid*, presumably at Westlake's demand, bears a flyleaf headed, "STARK REALISM."[40] In other words, pop formalism.

✳ ✳ ✳

The heist genre encourages narrative complexity more than the western or musical does. It is not surprising that the tradition was revived in the 1990s and later, when caper plots attracted filmmakers who were keen to tell stories in fresh ways.

Among Americans it was Steven Soderbergh who returned to the caper film most devotedly. *The Underneath* (1995) is a remake of *Criss Cross*, with an extra layer of flashbacks. *Logan Lucky* (2017), with its lovable hillbilly desperados, joins the tradition of comic heist movies. *No False Move* (2021), exploring industrial espionage among automobile companies, starts with a failed robbery. The plot avoids flashbacks and reveals the crime's causes and consequences solely through dialogue and shifting viewpoints. In a genre disposed to time shifting, sticking to straight linearity creates novelty: the viewer must focus on characters' reactions to a gradually evolving situation.

More typical, and extreme, is the Ocean's series (2001–2018), which makes a fetish of the male camaraderie and playful plot tricks typical of the genre. The films pepper the action with voice-overs, cunning ellipses, and flashbacks within flashbacks. The plots hide key information about the plan. They fill the action with in-jokes, such as a star cameo by Bruce Willis commenting on box-office grosses. Piling up obstacles, reversals, bluffs, and double-bluffs, Soderbergh's franchise forms an anthology of the genre's tricks.

The most overstuffed entry is *Ocean's Thirteen* (2007), which gives short shrift to the early phases of the standard plot schema. The bulk of the film consists of a mind-bogglingly intricate heist, including planting bedbugs in a hotel room and manufacturing loaded dice in a Mexican factory under threat of strike. The network of rules and roles laid out in the 1950s—master mind, aged expert, financier, crooked helpers, allies and rivals and go-betweens and stooges—is given baroque elaboration and treated with a self-congratulatory panache.

If Soderbergh had adapted a Stark novel, we might have had something ambitiously nonlinear, along the lines of his Elmore Leonard adaptation *Out of Sight* (1998). Here events set in the past are distributed, in blocks and smaller chunks, within present-day scenes. By then, however, Westlake-style maneuvers had become common storytelling strategies in Hollywood. A new variorum emerged, with one filmmaker crystallizing its ambitions.

CHAPTER 12

TARANTINO, TWISTS, AND
THE PERSISTENCE OF PUZZLES

I guess what I'm always trying to do is use the structures that I see in novels and apply them to cinema.

—Quentin Tarantino

A udiences found a lot to like in *Pulp Fiction* (1994): the casually cool hitmen Jules and Vincent; the scandalous sight of sado-masochistic sex paraphernalia; and the shock of a hypodermic punched into a woman's heart. The looping, digressive dialogues about fast food ("Royale with cheese") and popular culture (the *Kung Fu* TV show) revealed a filmmaker willing to indulge his characters' obsessions and their narcissistic self-presentation.

Most startling of all was the unexpected play with time and viewpoint that released that *Ahhh* response I noted in the introduction. *Reservoir Dogs* had already made plain Quentin Tarantino's willingness to break up chronology, but we could expect that in a heist movie. The flashbacks to the planning of the holdup are carefully framed by the present-tense scenes in the warehouse. The structure isn't quite as simple as this, but *Pulp Fiction* did feel more disorienting than its predecessor, and perhaps for first-time viewers it still feels that way.

Tarantino emerged at a period when ambitious filmmakers were rediscovering the power of nonlinear techniques. Never shy about claiming cinema influences, Tarantino emphasized popular fiction as an important inspiration. "When you're reading a book, you're reading about Moe, Larry, and Curly doing something in chapters one, two, and three, and then chapter four is about Moe five years before. Then, when that chapter is over, you're back in the main thrust of the action again, but now you know a little bit more about this guy than you did before."[1] Along these lines, the section of *Pulp Fiction* called "The Gold Watch" flashes back to Butch's childhood, when he receives his father's wristwatch. This motivates his risky effort to retrieve it by returning to his apartment.

Tarantino's films imaginatively revise schemas circulating in popular cinema and crime fiction. His revisions would become influential over the next twenty years and beyond. With the expansion of narrative options from the 1990s to today—the varieties charted in screenplay manuals and film criticism—Tarantino's work offers a handy prototype of how popular narrative can innovate in ways that are at once challenging and manageable. The skills that viewers bring to bear on contemporary cinema are versions of the skills that made the works of Ed McBain and Donald Westlake and hundreds of other storytellers powerfully and pleasurably accessible.

Playing with Blocks

Tarantino began his film career in collaboration with Roger Avary, a coworker at a video store. Avary had written a screenplay called *The Open Road*, which Tarantino revised and expanded.[2] The result was a very long draft consisting of a story within a story. An outlaw couple is on the run, and during their flight the young man writes a screenplay about a couple on a cross-country murder spree. Eventually *The Open Road* was split into two screenplays: *True Romance* (which Tarantino finished writing in 1987) and *Natural Born Killers* (finished in 1990). After the success of Tarantino's directorial debut in *Reservoir Dogs* (1992), both scripts were made into features by other directors.[3] The screenplays show that Tarantino experimented with block construction and nonlinear time schemes from the start of his career.

The present-time action of the screenplay for *Natural Born Killers* is simple and straightforward. Police officer Jack Scagnetti is charged with transferring serial killers Mickey and Mallory Knox from prison to a mental facility. At the same time Wayne Gayle, a "commando journalist," approaches the couple for an interview to be broadcast on his series *American Maniacs*. Mickey agrees. But in the course of the interview a riot breaks out, and Mickey seizes the opportunity to kill his guards and take Gayle and others as hostages. He induces the officials to free Mallory, who kills Scagnetti. Using Gayle and his cameraman as human shields, the couple shoot their way out, take refuge in the forest, and murder Gayle before driving off.

Tarantino breaks his time line by opening with Mickey and Mallory shooting up a coffee shop. This prologue introduces us to their outrageous homicidal impulses and their mad love for each other. Early scenes with Scagnetti are interrupted by quick flashbacks illustrating their crimes, such as the killing of Mallory's parents. But the main time shift comes with a long block inserted after Gayle has gotten Mickey's permission for the interview.

"Mickey and Mallory's Reign of Terror" is an assemblage of Gayle's new *American Maniacs* episode, waiting only for the interview to be added. Like the "News on the March" segment of *Citizen Kane*, exposition is part of its purpose. But the details of the crime spree don't preview actions that will be filled out in the film to come, as in *Kane*. The main purpose of the "Reign of Terror" episode is to show how the couple's rampage intoxicated millions of fans.

Most outlaw couple films, from *They Live by Night* (1948) to *Bonnie and Clyde* (1967), strive to build some sympathy for their protagonists. Tarantino, steeped in VHS classics, probably also tapped *Gun Crazy* (1950), *Boxcar Bertha* (1972), and *Dirty Mary, Crazy Larry* (1974) to give his couple a more lunatic edge. Earlier films had considered the possibility of killers having a fan following; in *Bonnie and Clyde*, the couple are mailed an admiring poem. The idea is amplified in Tarantino's screenplay, which mocks the media's cult of celebrity. Gayle is presented as a smarmy hypocrite, tsk-tsking about bloodshed but eager to turn Mickey and Mallory into pop-culture heroes. Tarantino's rather heavy satire reveals them as admired for their rebellion and devotion to one another, but still monstrous.

The "Reign of Terror" episode begins with harsh juxtapositions. The couple's normal married life is captured in home-movie footage followed by photos of bloodied victims. Quick shots of Mallory as a little girl yield to rough TV footage of the couple's capture. Then, as in "News on the March," the presentation becomes chronological. After providing shocking accounts of several murders, the episode moves to cover the couple's trial and their growing fan following. Their popularity is confirmed by the insertion of another block: footage from *Thrill Killers*, an exploitation feature fictionalizing their story. The film's heroic death scene is fleshed out by a trailer and interviews with the stars and the director.

"Reign of Terror" reaches a climax in its coverage of the trial, at which Mickey acts as his own attorney and manages to stab a woman giving testimony on the witness stand. This atrocity obliges the judge to pass a sentence declaring that once imprisoned Mickey and Mallory can never meet again. The film's framing story presents their first reunion in many years—as they join forces to blast their way out of prison.

The *Natural Born Killers* script insists that the film is to be in 35mm color, but the *American Maniacs* episode has a different look and feel. Gayle's purring commentary scenes, shot on location and addressed to the camera, frame a polymorphous montage. We get 8mm and 16mm footage, still photos, post-cards, and video material, both from surveillance cameras and, in the court-room, from official recording devices. The result is both a parody of cable TV murder shows and a film geek's reveling in various capture devices. Yet there can be no doubt about what's at the top of the hierarchy. Gayle demands that the interview with Mickey be shot on black-and-white, high-contrast 16mm film. "Fuck video. This is just too damned important. This is for posterity. . . . Film . . . film . . . film!"[4]

Gayle's words eventually become ironic. At the climax, during the prison scenes, the narration cuts between orthodox 35mm color and the camera recording Mickey in black-and-white. Once he takes the cameraman hostage, the riot is captured in both formats.[5] After their escape, Mickey and Mallory have Gayle at their mercy. He reminds them that at every crime scene they have left one witness alive to tell of their exploits. They agree and kill Gayle while his 16mm camera watches.

The "Reign of Terror" block looks ahead to the movie-within-a-movie structure of *Grindhouse*, which also includes trailer footage. But in a sense, the entirety of *Natural Born Killers* is a block quarried out of the *Open Road* project. Another big chunk followed another outlaw couple. In making this his next proj-ect, Tarantino's place in the hard-boiled crime tradition became more evident.

In interviews Tarantino acknowledged debts to Jim Thompson, Cornell Woolrich, Fredric Brown, Charles Willeford, and other maestros of noir novels.[6] *Pulp Fiction*'s title would pay homage to mass-market crime writing. (The film was originally to be called *The Black Mask*.[7]) Tarantino's favorite author was Elmore Leonard, whose crime stories had by then attracted attention among the literati.[8] With *True Romance* "I was trying to write an Elmore Leonard novel as a movie."[9] Tarantino long imagined making a film from Leonard's *The Switch* (1978), and he would later adapt *Rum Punch* (1992) as *Jackie Brown* (1997).[10]

Leonard's plots throw together laconic peace officers, laid-back ex-military, third-rate con artists, frustrated wives, amiable psychopaths, reefer-buzzed bandits, and fumbling but still dangerous mob wannabes, all to lethal effect. This cast forms a fairly complex network, including a hierarchy of villains, some dangerous and others who only think they are.

Although praised for their easy momentum, Leonard's novels make some unusual choices about viewpoint. In *Killshot* (1989), a parking lot fight between an ironworker, a paid killer, and a hopped-up thief is presented in four ways. We're initially sharing the ironworker's viewpoint. Then, as he goes to work on his assailants with an iron bar, the perspective switches to that of his wife, watching from a window. That passage is followed by her later testimony to the police, which is rendered first as indirect summary and finally as extended quoted monologue.

Tarantino's love of protracted dialogue exchanges echoes another of Leonard's strategies. Leonard credits the conversation-heavy novels of George V. Higgins for confirming his own tendency "to move my plots with dialogue while keeping the voices relatively flat, understated."[11] In *Get Shorty* (1990), fifty pages are devoted to three characters talking around a kitchen table, with fluid shifts of viewpoint.[12]

Famed for a clipped style, Leonard also skillfully deploys the conventional novelistic technique of interrupting ongoing action with a chunk or chapter of backstory. The original script for *True Romance* experiments with a one-off expository block in the Leonard manner. Tarantino pulls a long early stretch of action—the couple meeting and sharing a night before Clarence kills Drexl and grabs the suitcase—out of chronological sequence. It's then inserted into a later phase of the action, triggered by Clarence telling Dick why they came to Los Angeles. The straightforward transposition of that block of action is typical of Leonard's back-and-fill inclinations, although he usually doesn't postpone expository material as long as Tarantino's screenplay does.

The *True Romance* screenplay displays explicit chaptering, another constructional feature that would become habitual with Tarantino. After a prologue showing Clarence meeting a woman in a bar, tags introduce "Motor City," "Hollywood," "Clarence and Alabama Hit LA," "Cass Quarter, Heart of Detroit," and "The Big Day." The chapters are minimally informative. They don't segregate characters by viewpoint, and they don't neatly demarcate time schemes. For example, the Cass Quarter section breaks up the block that shows Clarence killing Drexl. Chaptering became more strict in *Pulp Fiction* and the films that followed.

Although Tarantino's script structure wasn't retained in *True Romance* as produced, it shows how he applied a more novelistic model of block construction and time shifting than we find in the media collage of *Natural Born Killers*. His first directorial project would be further steeped in the crime tradition and abstract plot patterning.

Dogs in a Warehouse

Several aspects of *Reservoir Dogs* are indebted to Ringo Lam's Hong Kong gangland film *City on Fire*, as many have noted and Tarantino more or less acknowledged.[13] (When I asked Lam if he was offended, he smiled and said that Hong Kong films had been ripping off Hollywood for years.) But at the level of structure, there are other inspirations. One is Lionel White's novel *Clean Break* (1955) and Kubrick's adaptation of it, *The Killing* (1956). Both book and film present a racetrack heist in a staggered time scheme, following one character into the robbery before skipping back earlier to trace another.

A more pertinent pulp-literary inspiration is *The Hunter* (1963). This and other Richard Stark novels, Tarantino claimed, "were very influential to this film."[14] *Point Blank*, John Boorman's 1967 film adaptation of *The Hunter*, relied on fragmentary, often enigmatic flashbacks in the vein of other 1960s films (*The Pawnbroker*, 1964; *Petulia*, 1968). In contrast, Tarantino's heist story uses lengthy blocks to manipulate time in a way different from Leonard's work and more reminiscent of the Stark novels.

Reservoir Dogs treats a jewel store robbery through an alternation of past and present. Apart from a prologue showing the gang sharing a diner meal, the present-time scenes take place after the failed holdup. (The action of *The Hunter* likewise takes place in the robbery's aftermath.) One by one the surviving gang members gather in a warehouse and try to figure out how the cops knew about the heist. The past sequences trace the gathering of the team, culminating in the revelation of the mole among them and the robbery itself.

The film's structure is more complicated than I've suggested. There isn't an exoskeleton like the chaptering of *True Romance*'s screenplay; the inserted titles are localized and serve to introduce characters. But the film does have an underlying geometry that, as in the Parker novels, falls neatly into four parts.

The first part, coinciding with the classic act one of Hollywood construction, sets up the situation. After the diner session and the opening credits, the robbery is skipped over. Its aftermath begins with a shot of one robber, Mr. Orange, bloodied and shrieking in a car's back seat. When the team starts to gather after the holdup, Mr. White and Mr. Pink discuss the robbery, and a flashback shows Mr. Pink pursued by cops already near the scene. Mr. White concludes that there must have been an informer among the team. The question "Who's the mole?" drives the next part of the film.

In this second section, coinciding with what Kristin Thompson calls the "complicating action" of a classical Hollywood plot scheme, the mole is revealed.[15] That process begins with a flashback introducing Mr. White as Joe recruits him for the heist. Is he the mole? The narration returns to the warehouse in the present. Enter Mr. Blonde, with the policeman he has captured. A flashback shows Mr. Blonde being recruited to the team. Back in the present, after Mr. Blonde slices off the policeman's ear and prepares to burn him alive, the wounded Mr. Orange reveals that "I'm a cop" and shoots Mr. Blonde.

There follows a third stretch consisting wholly of flashbacks. Tagged "Mr. Orange," it explains how he slipped into the gang. Among scenes showing Mr. Orange meeting his plainclothes partner, there are embedded flashbacks to him rehearsing a fake story about a confrontation with cops in a men's room, which is eventually dramatized (figs. 12.1–12.2). Still more flashbacks trace stages of the heist: Mr. Orange and others driving to a meeting, Joe

12.1 *Reservoir Dogs* (1992): When Mr. Orange tells his fake story to Joe and others in a bar . . .

12.2 . . . the narration provides a lying flashback.

briefing the team, and Mr. Orange and Mr. White casing the jewelry store. This third section culminates in the failed robbery, shown briefly. Fleeing with Mr. White, Mr. Orange is shot by the driver of the car he tries to commandeer. He in turn shoots the driver.

As a distinct block, with flashbacks curled inside other flashbacks, this section resembles the "Reign of Terror" TV show of *Natural Born Killers*, and like that block, this makes points that go beyond sheer exposition. Thompson notes that the third part of a classical plot, which she calls the "development," often fills in prior events and character background. Here the backstory supplies a character arc. The "Mr. Orange" chapter, Tarantino has remarked, "is almost like another movie."[16]

Mr. Orange enters the undercover job confident, even cocky; he assures his plainclothes mentor that he's in solid with the gang. His main task is to project cool—a word that the gang members bandy back and forth. To a point

Mr. Orange succeeds; after hearing his commode story, Joe laughs approval. "You knew how to handle that situation. You shit your pants, and then you dive in and swim." But after Mr. Orange has killed an innocent woman and been seriously shot himself, he loses his cool, shrieking out on the car seat that he's dying. Like the repetition of Jules's biblical monologue in *Pulp Fiction*, this replay serves to remind us where the scene fits into the film's story action. But the replay also emphasizes the collapse of Mr. Orange's cockiness (figs. 12.3–12.4).

This comedown reminds us that Tarantino's films sometimes deflate the panache associated with cool. After Alabama sneaks Clarence an admiring note, "You're so cool," he's shot in the face. As for Mickey and Mallory, Tarantino notes: "You see them posturing and being cool and surly, and they're romantic and they're exciting. Then you see them killing people that don't

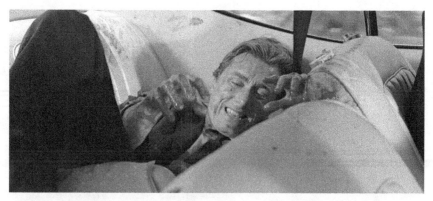

12.3 After an opening scene that buries Mr. Orange among several, more sharply delineated men at the diner table, this coda to the robbery picks him out as an important character. His "I'm sorry!" seems to be a self-recrimination for botching the job.

12.4 The replay of Mr. Orange's suffering. Because this is "his" chapter, the framing is closer. Now that we know he's the mole, "I'm sorry!" seems to beg his forgiveness for his betrayal—and his shooting of an innocent woman.

deserve to die. Hopefully, the audience will say, 'Wait a minute this isn't fun any more. Why aren't I having fun? And why was I having fun at the beginning?'"[17] The almost sentimental tenderness that Mr. White provides the dying Mr. Orange suggests that the bravado of cool masks a more fragile bond of feeling between men in action.

The male melodrama is rendered all the more painful in the finale. Joe and Eddie arrive at the warehouse and accuse Mr. Orange of being the informer. Mr. White defends him, and in a three-way standoff, all are shot. But then, cradled in Mr. White's arms, Mr. Orange confesses that he has betrayed their friendship. After the sorrowful Mr. White shoots him, the off-screen police finish off Mr. White. Mr. Pink has already run out with the loot.

The *True Romance* screenplay, with its five chapter titles, invites us to imagine a tabular structure in the Stark spirit. The four sections I've assigned to *Reservoir Dogs* lack tags, but given Tarantino's acknowledgment of *The Hunter* as inspiration, we can risk a chart. First, I offer a layout of the Stark novel (table 12.1; summarized in chapter 11). Comparing it with what we find in the film (table 12.2) shows some striking affinities.

TABLE 12.1 Richard Stark, *The Hunter* (1962)

Part One	Part Two	Part Three	Part Four
POV attached to Parker	*POV attached to Mal*	*POV attached to Parker*	*POV attached to Parker*
Parker on the lam after heist. He kills Lynn and seeks Mal.	Mal learns Parker is after him. He hides out, but Parker enters through hotel window.	**FB chaps. 1–5 simultaneous with Part Two: Parker's pursuit of Mal.**	Parker settles scores, with mixed success.
FB to heist and Lynn's attempt to kill Parker.	**FB to *before* Part One, when Mal sets up double-cross.**	**Chap. 6: Replay Parker's entry through window at start of Part Two.**	
Surviving the hit, he goes on the lam and pursues Lynn and Mal.	**FB to *within* FB in Part One: Mal sets up Lynn to kill Parker.**	Parker gets information about his money and kills Mal.	
	Replay of her attempt to kill Parker.		
	Mal gets job with the Outfit.		

Note: Chronological sequences are shown in roman type; flashbacks (FB) are shown in bold type.

TABLE 12.2 Quentin Tarantino, *Reservoir Dogs* (1992)

Part One	Part Two	Part Three	Part Four
Heist team meets in diner and strolls out.	Mr. White. **FB: Joe proposes heist to Mr. White.**	Mr. Orange. **Framing FB: Mr. Orange meets cop contact.**	Warehouse:
[Credits]	Warehouse: Mr. Blonde brings in cop he has captured.	**Embedded FB: Cop contact tells Mr. Orange the commode anecdote.**	Confrontation of survivors: Death of Joe, Eddie, Mr. White, and Mr. Orange. Mr. Pink escapes with loot.
[Ellipsis: Failed jewel robbery]	Mr. Blonde. **FB: Joe proposes heist to Mr. Blonde, with Nice Guy Eddie.**	**Embedded FBs: Mr. Orange rehearses at home; with partner.**	
Mr. Orange wounded, crying out in back seat as Mr. White drives.	Warehouse: The men rough up the cop. Mr. Blonde cuts his ear. Mr. Orange shoots Mr. Blonde. "I'm a cop."	**Embedded FB: Bar: Mr. Orange tells commode anecdote.**	
Warehouse: Mr. White brings Mr. Orange in, joined by Mr. Pink. They dispute whether there was a mole.		**Embedded Lying FB: Commode story.**	
FB: Mr. Pink flees robbery scene.		**Embedded FB: Bar: Joe approves of Mr. Orange.**	
Warehouse: Mr. White and Mr. Pink quarrel: "Who's the mole?"		**Framing FB: Mr. Orange and fellow cop conclude plan.**	
		FB: Mr. Orange prepares for heist.	
		FB: Heist team drives to meeting.	
		FB: Meeting: Joe briefs the team.	
		FB: Mr. Orange and Mr. White case the shop.	
		FB: The failed robbery.	
		FB: Replay of Mr. Orange crying out in back seat.	

Note: Chronological sequences are shown in roman type; flashbacks (FB) are shown in bold type.

In all, *Reservoir Dogs* is more structurally complex than the *True Romance* and *Natural Born Killers* screenplays. Tarantino thought its organization was a selling point for producers. Jane Hamsher mimicked his pitch: "He'd written this movie, see, about these guys and this heist gone bad, and it was told novel-istically, you know, with time folding back on itself, not linearly like most mov-ies, which he was really fascinated with."[18] The time scrambling in this movie is mild when compared with the fragments and whorls *Point Blank* created out of *The Hunter*. In his film's first half, Tarantino presents a traditional arc of mystery, with the question (whodunit?) answered at the end of the second part (whodunit), and more elaborately explained in the third (howdunit). Suspense then kicks in for the climax. A closer approximation to the Stark machine, eliminating the whodunit element, comes with *Pulp Fiction*.

Pulp Fiction as Pulp Fiction

True Romance, *Natural Born Killers*, and *Reservoir Dogs* display strategies Tarantino uses for mounting almost any plot he concocts. He usually relies on block construction, following Stark in attaching the block to a single character or group. Then the plot shifts to another block, another character, and a differ-ent, perhaps overlapping time sequence.

The simplest example is *Death Proof* (2007). The first half of the original the-atrical release presents four young women who are targeted by Stuntman Mike, a free-range master of vehicular homicide. All the women are killed, but in the second half Mike meets his match in a quartet of car-crazy film staffers, one of whom is a stuntwoman and another an expert driver. Mike is the only link between the film's episodes. More broadly, *Death Proof* constitutes one segment in a larger ensemble of blocks, the double-feature *Grindhouse*. That presents *Planet Terror* as another free-standing feature, the whole contraption padded out with fake trailers.

A more old-fashioned use of block construction appears in the Taranti-no-conceived *Four Rooms* (1995). He and three other American indie directors created four short films, which are strung together through the misadventures of a new bellboy at a classic hotel. The result revived the portmanteau film for-mat seen long before in *If I Had a Million* (1932) and *Flesh and Fantasy* (1943).

The blocks in *Four Rooms* are labeled with intertitles, a procedure Tarantino often relied on. Modeling his films on novels, he has often called his blocks "chapters," but they're so long that they approximate the parts that we find in the Stark books, not the more compact chapters of Elmore Leonard and other crime novelists.

A good example is the extended chronological blocks of *Inglourious Basterds* (2009). Here five tagged chapters show anti-Nazi forces at work in occupied

France. The first block shows Shosanna Dreyfus, harbored by a farm family, fleeing from Colonel Landa. The second chapter introduces us to the Basterds, the "Apache" force staffed by Jewish soldiers and Nazi turncoats. Brief flashbacks fill out the Basterds' history. Chapter 3 picks up Shosanna in 1944, now running a Parisian movie house under a false identity. Landa reappears when her theater is commandeered for the screening of Goebbels's latest propaganda effort. Shosanna decides to use the occasion to exact revenge.

Landa appears as well in the fourth chapter, which introduces a British espionage effort aided by a German actress. "Operation Kino" is to work with the Basterds in attacking the audience at the film premiere. Ironically, the Basterds and Shosanna are unaware of each other's mission. Chapter 5 shows the two forces converging at Shosanna's theater. The alternation between chapters before the climax is picked up within the final block, as crosscutting gives us a suspenseful, moving-spotlight view of the entire operation. An epilogue shows the Basterds' vengeance on Landa.

A simpler confluence of story lines occurs in *Once Upon a Time . . . in Hollywood* (2019). Three principal characters—fading cowboy star Rick Dalton, his loyal stunt double and amanuensis Cliff Booth, and rising star Sharon Tate—are followed across three days in 1969. These days constitute the film's chapters. The narration crosscuts among the trio until a climax brings members of Charles Manson's gang to Rick's driveway for a home invasion.[19] Like *Inglourious Basterds* and *Django Unchained* (2012), the film posits an alternative history, a strategy that leads Tarantino to more conventional time schemes than we find in the other films.

The Hateful 8 (2015) invokes the folk motif of converging fates, the intersection of disparate lives at a crossroads, on a vehicle, or in an inn. As in *Seven Keys to Baldpate*, hidden affinities come to light. The plot begins with two labeled chapters taking stagecoach passengers to Minnie's Haberdashery, a general store. Two longer chapters show their arrival and confrontation with several suspicious men already there. These chapters are chronological, except for some brief flashbacks in the third and a replay of a key moment, the poisoning of a coffee pot, in the fourth.

The fifth chapter is a block like those we find in the Stark novels. It skips back to show action simultaneous with the events of the first two chapters. While the travelers are on the road, the gang aiming to free Daisy Domergue takes over Minnie's place and kills the inhabitants. This block ends by replaying the visitors' arrival from the gang's point of view. The last block, "Final Chapter," runs chronologically, as in a Parker novel. Again, the structure is that of a mystery. Like the Mr. Orange section of *Reservoir Dogs*, chapter 5 of *The Hateful 8* functions as a climactic revelation of what really happened.

In *Jackie Brown* (1997) Tarantino mimics *Clean Break* and *The Killing*, but in miniature. He presents the shopping-mall money exchange three times, from different characters' attached viewpoints. The side-by-side replays make the whole money drop stand out as a block, as does the chapter title ("Money Exchange: For Real This Time") and the length (more than twenty minutes). A practice session for the exchange has already been presented as a parallel block, with its own introductory title ("Money Exchange: Trial Run"). As in a classic heist film, the multiple-viewpoint coverage keeps us aware of what each player contributes to the scam, and how he or she reacts to the others. During the replays, we watch for a glitch that will cause ruin down the line.

Kill Bill Volume 1 (2003) and *Kill Bill Volume 2* (2004) splinter time more extensively than other Tarantino films. The core story is quite linear. A young woman, known throughout as the Bride, is trained to join a team of elite killers. Sent to murder a rival, the Bride discovers she's pregnant and decides to quit the game. Her boss, Bill, learns she's getting married and sends a hit squad to the wedding rehearsal. But the Bride survives. Escaping from the hospital, she sets out to eliminate the hit team one by one and finally Bill himself, who has seized and raised her child.

Despite a shooting-gallery premise reminiscent of Woolrich's novels, *Kill Bill*'s plot skips around freely in time. The film begins by showing us the Bride's checklist of targets. The two films' ten chapters are arranged out of order and broken up by flashbacks—most notably, an animated chapter-within-a-chapter recounting the past of the Japanese assassin O-ren. In their use of parallel chaptering and shifting viewpoints, the films again recall the Parker template. But unlike Westlake, Tarantino inserts a tell-all flashback at the climax. Under the sway of truth serum, the Bride explains to Bill and to us that she defected because she was pregnant. Again, the denouement depends on solving a mystery.

In sum, the blocks in most Tarantino films achieve traditional effects. When they rearrange chronology, that tactic promotes suspense, compares characters and situations, and holds back a secret until the climax. These maneuvers don't inspire the intense response I encountered among others watching *Pulp Fiction*. Confronted with the revelations of *The Hateful 8* or *Kill Bill*, we might say "aha" but not *ahhh*. *Pulp Fiction* uses block construction not to create suspense but to create a surprise—a surprise not about the story world but about the manner of narration itself.[20]

Like a Stark novel, *Pulp Fiction* consists of four blocks, with three of them bearing chapter titles. The second block gathers all the characters who will dominate the film's plot: Vincent, Jules, Butch, Marcellus, and Mia. Along with secondary characters Fabienne, Zed, Maynard, Jimmy, and Mr. Wolf, this group constitutes the film's network. And somewhat as the novel *Laura* is a block-based anthology of mystery genres (effete sleuth, hard-boiled cop, woman in peril), *Pulp Fiction* juxtaposes plot schemas centering on contract killing, prize-fight corruption, and a clumsy heist.

As in the *True Romance* screenplay, one long block has been shifted out of order. That screenplay had skipped over the lovers' meet-cute and Clarence's killing of Drexl, reinserting those incidents when the couple explain past events to their LA friend. Similarly, the first section of *Reservoir Dogs* skips over the robbery that we will see more of in the third part. But in those cases the gaps are signaled more or less explicitly. *Pulp Fiction* instead plays down its ellipsis.

The first, untagged chapter ends with a fade-out as Jules and Vincent empty their pistols into the preppy. We might not sense that anything important that follows has been omitted, especially because we soon see the pair bring Marcellus the briefcase. At this point, some viewers might notice that the hitmen are now dressed like dorks. The same viewers might note that when the bartender mentions their clothes and asks how things are going they brush off the questions. For these viewers, there has been a minor but noteworthy gap that they could look forward to filling.

Other viewers probably don't dwell on these anomalies. The entry of Vincent and Jules is handled obliquely: they walk away from us, mutter their replies to the bartender, and become subsidiary elements in the scene. We've already been tasked with following the much more interesting monologue of a silky baritone threatening Butch from off-screen. Soon there's a new attention-grabbing moment at the bar, when Vincent calls Butch "Punchy" and foreshadows their clash in the third chapter.

Whether we notice the anomalies or not, the film's fourth chapter, "The Bonnie Situation," eventually fills the gap between the preppy slaughter and the hitmen's arrival in the bar. This chapter shows Vincent and Jules finishing off the preppies, grabbing the briefcase, accidentally killing Marvin, and cleaning the car with the help of Winston Wolf. (That's how the pair wound up wearing shorts and T-shirts when they reported to Marcellus.) Then they retire to the coffee shop, where they halt the robbery launched by Honey Bunny and Pumpkin. From there they set out to Marcellus's bar. Essentially one long block has been snipped out of the first chapter and pasted into the last. Table 12.3 illustrates the geometrical structure.

This is a pretty radical shift. In the third chapter, we've seen Butch win the fight, return to Fabienne, retrieve his father's watch, and kill Vincent. Then Butch and Marcellus are captured. Butch escapes, rescues Marcellus, and flees town with Fabienne. In the chronology of the story world, the last event to take place is the couple's departure.

Reservoir Dogs devotes its third section to a string of Mr. Orange flashbacks before returning to the warehouse confrontation, but *Pulp Fiction* dares something more unusual. It puts its flashbacks in the final chapter and never returns to the present-tense frame of the action.[21] If we think back while watching Vincent clean the car and defend the virtues of pork products, we would realize that he will be killed by Butch. Postponing the diner scene puts

TABLE 12.3 Quentin Tarantino, *Pulp Fiction* (1994)

Prologue: Honey Bunny and Pumpkin plan and launch robbery.			
Credits.			
Part One	"Vincent Vega and Marcellus Wallace's Wife"	"The Gold Watch"	"The Bonnie Situation":
			Flashbacks fill ellipsis at end of Part One.
POV attached to Jules and Vincent	*POV split between Butch and Vincent*	*POV attached to Butch*	*POV attached to Jules and Vincent*
Jules and Vincent kill double-crossing preppies.	Bar: Marcellus orders Butch to throw fight.	**FB: Butch as child receives father's watch.**	**FB: Jules and Vincent kill fourth preppy and Marvin.**
[Ellipsis suppressing "The Bonnie Situation" and the Prologue.]	Jules and Vincent bring Marcellus the briefcase.	Night: Butch wins prizefight and returns to Fabienne.	**FB: Mr. Wolf helps them clean up.**
	Next day: Vincent visits Lance to get heroin.	Morning: Butch retrieves watch from his apartment and kills Vincent. Leaving, he runs down Marcellus and crashes his car.	**FB: Diner: Jules declares he will leave criminal life. After off-screen replay of Prologue, Jules and Vincent confront Pumpkin and Honey Bunny. They swagger out of diner.**
	Night: Vincent takes Mia Wallace out for dinner.	Street: Butch and Marcellus are captured by Zed and Maynard. Butch rescues Marcellus, who forgives him.	
	Mia overdoses and Vincent saves her.	Butch flees town with Fabienne.	

Note: Story events are chronological within and between parts unless otherwise noted. Chronological sequences within chapters are shown in roman type; flashbacks (FB) are shown in boldface type.

climactic weight on Jules's decision to leave his life of crime—a decision that Vincent won't make, with fatal results. Once more, the self-assurance of cool is somewhat chastened.

But there's more to Jules's decision, and that involves his refusal to turn over the briefcase to the diner robbers. This gesture leads us to the film's other time shifting maneuver, placement of the Pumpkin-Honey Bunny dialogue at the beginning. Another variant of the miscreant couples in *Reservoir Dogs* and *Natural Born Killers*, this pair is quietly quarreling over the best target of armed robbery: liquor stores, banks, or maybe a coffee shop? We're initiated into the film by watching them spring to their feet to announce their heist (see fig. 0.3).

This prologue is replayed, partially off-screen, in the final chapter when Jules is eating breakfast and Vincent is in the toilet. Just as one long block of action from the beginning has been pushed to the end, now a triggering incident from that block has been previewed at the outset of the movie. In this respect, it's a more flamboyant equivalent of Mr. Pink's flashback to the robbery in the first portion of *Reservoir Dogs*, which also serves as a preview, pointing toward the heist glimpsed later. But the replay of Honey Bunny and Pumpkin calling the diner patrons to attention also helps us sort out story order, like the off-screen repetition of Jules's self-righteous scripture-quoting before the lurking preppy's assault.

The sudden return of this casually larcenous couple provokes the *ahhh* response because we've probably forgotten about the opening. After all, the scene ended more than two hours earlier. It was cut off by rousing credits and engaging action, and it was never referred to again. Reading is forgetting, Roland Barthes remarks in *S/Z*, but in many cases we might say that reading is forgetting until we're reminded.[22] As a bonus, the return of the first scene we encountered creates a satisfying rounding-off; the robbery launched at the beginning finds a conclusion in the film's last moments, which keeps the brief-case ready to be delivered to Marcellus.

The replayed prologue in *Pulp Fiction* is a step beyond Stark; the Parker books never yank a scene out of order and make it a forgettable prologue. The closest analogue I know is what Fredric Brown, one of the more eccentric crime novelists, offers in *The Far Cry* (1951). The book begins with a woman fleeing a knife-wielding attacker. Apparently unrelated scenes follow. Is this prologue a flashback to be explained as such, or is it a flash forward to an upcoming piece of action? Eventually, the plot leads to a final replay of this initial action, with the book closing itself in a circle as it exposes the identity of the attacker. But *A Far Cry* flaunts this device more vividly than does Tarantino's film. The prologue is given saliency by being printed in italics, and the whole scene is repeated about eighty pages in (as the narration asks: "Could he start the story there?"). The reader is teased to anticipate that the enigmatic opening will be explained.

By encouraging viewers to forget its first scene, *Pulp Fiction* gives us something rare and powerful. Simply pulling one scene from its normal sequence and putting it at the beginning, without fanfare, produces unexpectedly strong results. Here Tarantino uses block construction not to fill in a gap in the action but to nudge us to recognize how the story has been presented to us. After seeing the whole film, we might need some time to reconstruct the chronology, but in the moment the click effect of the coffee shop replay makes us aware of how we have been engaged, mostly unawares, by structure and narration. In this respect, Tarantino creates a prototype of what later will be celebrated as the "twist."

Tarantino and the Twist

Westlake's Parker novels pushed beyond 1940s plot schemas, and Tarantino pushed beyond Westlake. The worldwide success of *Pulp Fiction* shows that, once time shifting becomes familiar to audiences, storytellers in the popular tradition can continually extend the schemas in circulation.

A media archaeologist could find traces of many other films, plays, comic books, TV shows, and items of prose fiction in Tarantino's work. Merely hunting down Tarantino's specific citations has kept fans and scholars busy for years. More broadly, the violence unleashed within his story worlds builds on the escalation of cinematic gore that was especially pronounced from the 1960s onward. The characterization of his petty crooks and con artists relies on the hard-boiled tradition from Hammett to Leonard and beyond. Chaptered films have a long history, most notably in another object of Tarantino adoration, Jean-Luc Godard. But broad audiences were able to take *Pulp Fiction*'s tagged segments in stride because they had encountered the technique in resolutely mainstream films such as *The Sting* (1973) and the viewer-friendly *Hannah and Her Sisters* (1985).

As usual, familiarity balances innovation. The conventions of a crime-centered plot help the viewer understand *Pulp Fiction*'s narrative strategies (just as awareness of the undercover-cop and heist schemas anchor the time shuffling of *Reservoir Dogs*). We can grasp the emerging situations quickly because we recognize the daring daylight robbery, the stolen briefcase containing something precious, the hitmen on a mission, the thrown prizefight, and the figure of the all-powerful crime boss. The crime film has been a mainstay of American and British cinema at all budget levels, and before Tarantino's debut a host of detective and gangster films reiterated conventions that ambitious filmmakers could exploit: Francis Ford Coppola with *The Conversation* (1974), Brian De Palma with *Scarface* (1983), Abel Ferrara with *King of New York* (1990), and many others. In 1994, the year of *Pulp Fiction*, suspense thrillers *Disclosure* and *Speed* and the hired-killer movie *Leon the Professional* were released, along with Oliver Stone's version of *Natural Born Killers*.

Although Tarantino denied that he was indebted to the neo-noir trend of the 1970s and 1980s, there seems no doubt that viewers could see affinities with *Pulp Fiction*. From flat remakes such as *The Big Sleep* (1978) and earnest pastiches such as *Body Heat* (1981) to eccentric mockery (*The Long Goodbye*, 1973), American cinema had revised the hard-boiled tradition. The self-consciousness of this trend was epitomized in *Dead Men Don't Wear Plaid* (1982), a satiric collage of classic scenes linked by original scenes designed in 1940s style.

The retro sensibility was given its strongest insider cachet by a filmmaking duo widely seen as Tarantino's predecessors. Joel and Ethan Coen built their careers on grotesquely comic takes on familiar mystery genres. Well before *Pulp Fiction* they offered *Blood Simple* (1985), a suspense thriller reminiscent of *Double Indemnity*, and *Miller's Crossing* (1990), a blend of *Red Harvest* and *The Glass Key* (figs. 12.5–12.6). Bungled kidnap plots afforded the Coens opportunity to parody family comedies (*Raising Arizona*, 1987), mock police procedure in the hinterlands (*Fargo*, 1996), and satirize studio era Hollywood (*Hail, Caesar!*, 2016). They also filmed a doom-thriller in the James M. Cain mode (*The Man Who Wasn't There*, 2001), a comic heist film (*The Ladykillers*, 2004), a bloody police chase (*No Country for Old Men*, 2007), and a spy caper (*Burn After Reading*, 2008).

A good example of the Coens' absurdist revisionism is *The Big Lebowski* (1998), which brings a plot of Chandlerian intricacy into the Gulf War era. The detective is the hapless Dude, a stoned idler lured into a ransom scheme by a ferocious millionaire. Marlowe-fashion, he is repeatedly confronted by men coming in with guns. He is beaten senseless and plunged into surrealistic dreams. When the Dude meets a real private eye, a shabby shamus tailing him, he's told, "It's a wandering daughter job," a quotation from a Continental Op short story. These citations are exaggerated by the sheer grotesquerie on display: a nymphomaniac wife, a Katharine-Hepburnesque experimental artist, a raging philosemitic Vietnam vet, a gang of German nihilists, and a pedophile bowler named Jesus. The hard-boiled voice-over narration is supplied, bizarrely, by a drawling cowboy drinking at the bowling alley the Dude frequents.

The Coens' success indicates how firmly the crime film had settled into independent American cinema. After *Pulp Fiction* the impulse would attract many directors, most notably Bryan Singer with *The Usual Suspects* (1995) and Christopher Nolan with *Following* (1998) and *Memento* (2000).

Throughout all these films, the familiarity of mystery conventions throws new storytelling strategies into relief. For instance, the investigation plots of *Following* and *Memento* enable us to grasp their complicated flashback patterning. Nonlinear time schemes had long been made easy to grasp in courtroom dramas, police interrogations, and man-on-the-run memories. By the time *Pulp Fiction* arrived, *The Fugitive* (1993) had shown that audiences could handle a barrage of flashbacks that constantly interrupt present-day events with ever-changing glimpses of a murder in the past. Tarantino's films played out before audiences who were fairly well-versed in time shifting tactics and prepared to register fresh options.

12.5 *Miller's Crossing* (1990): Hammett's clue of Taylor Henry's lost hat in *The Glass Key* becomes a motif drifting through the protagonist's dream . . .

12.6 . . . and prefiguring a gesture in the final shot.

Likewise, the persistence of the anthology film in the off-Hollywood sphere invited filmmakers to find ingenious ways to link discrete story lines. Richard Linklater's *Slacker* (1991) offered a simple propinquity structure, with one story halting near a character who would launch the next one. Jim Jarmusch's *Night on Earth* (1991) consisted of three episodes taking place in the same evening in different countries. In *Mystery Train* (1989), Jarmusch bound the segments in a more laminated fashion: three blocks share the moment when a gun is fired.

Although *Pulp Fiction* was first planned as a portmanteau film, it became, as the screenplay calls it, "Three Stories . . . About One Story."[23]

Tarantino gave as much as he took. *Pulp Fiction* helped nonlinear patterning and block construction capture filmmakers' imaginations around the world. Whatever the degree of direct influence, the film became emblematic of a new narrative flexibility in Anglophone cinema, typified by *The Usual Suspects, Flirt* (1995), *Trainspotting* (1995), *Hard Eight* (1996), *L. A. Confidential* (1997), *Boogie Nights* (1997), *Lock, Stock, and Two Smoking Barrels* (1998), *Out of Sight* (1998), *Magnolia* (1999), and *Go* (1999). Many films both inside and outside the mystery genre would continue to juggle time, to shift viewpoints unpredictably, to present multiple drafts of certain incidents, to organize plots in solid blocks, and to expose connections among disparate story lines. Examples are *Me and You and Everyone We Know* (2005), *The Prestige* (2006), *A Perfect Getaway* (2009), *The Social Network* (2010), *Source Code* (2011), and *Moonrise Kingdom* (2012). More recently *La La Land* (2016), *Arrival* (2016), *Dunkirk* (2017), *Molly's Game* (2017), *Atomic Blonde* (2017), *Bad Times at the El Royale* (2018), *Rocketman* (2019), and *Wrath of Man* (2021) remind us that this dynamic of schema and revision is far from finished. It is this expanding variorum that manuals like Linda Aronson's *Twenty-First Century Screenplay* try to map.

"*Pulp Fiction* stuns with the glib twists of its plot," wrote a reviewer.[24] In the 1990s, with the rise of narrative self-consciousness and with "form as the new content," critics and viewers came to assign a new importance to sudden reveals, jarring reversals, and other forms of surprise. The term "plot twist," apparently seldom used before the 1960s, jumped in frequency during the 1990s and soared in the new century.[25] But what do we mean when we say that a narrative has a twist?

To some extent, current tastes have rehabilitated the role of narrative surprise. As we've seen, drama theorists after Lessing saw more artistic skill and deeper audience engagement in an intensifying suspense ("enduring disquietude") than in a sudden shock that soon wore off. Of course, surprise must play some role, especially in raising the stakes of suspense, as in Hugo's play *Cromwell*, which alternates between the two states, or as we saw in *The Lady Vanishes* (see chapter 5). Today, however, it seems that in place of what Lessing called "short surprises" audiences prefer big ones, major turns of action: twists.

As used by critics and audiences, the concept is broad enough to include almost anything that is surprising in a story. To capture one intuitive difference, we might distinguish between story world twists and narrational ones. A twist in the story world would consist of a discrete incident that violates our expectations. A pure case would be that of a sudden natural event, such as a tornado or an illness besetting a character. Many twists are one-off incidents occurring accidentally or having causes too remote or minor to be relevant, as when a coincidence reveals new information to a character. (Think of all the convenient moments when a character overhears a crucial plot point.)

A more drastic twist occurs when the narration violates an informational norm and suppresses basic premises about the story world. A tornado or illness or an overheard conversation wouldn't violate any fundamental premises of the story world; such things just happen, especially in stories. In contrast, a narrational twist tends to make us reappraise the status of what we've been told earlier. The story world twist tends to be one-off, the narrational twist reveals a hidden pattern.

The clichéd example of the narrational twist is the story that ends, "And then I woke up." This "ontological" twist recasts our understanding of the status of the whole fiction, admittedly in a throwaway manner. A comic example is the metafictional reframing of *Seven Keys to Baldpate* (1913), which overturns our assumptions about the existence of the action we've seen. More grimly, the film *The Sixth Sense* (1999) reveals that the protagonist, a pediatric psychologist studying a troubled boy who "sees dead people," is himself a ghost. In both cases, we have taken for granted premises that aren't operative, and the plot takes a very different shape. We're back to Christie's reminder: It's not unfair to leave things out.

In literary history, the narrational twist is often identified with the commercial development of the American short story, particularly in the hands of O. Henry.[26] The "sting in the tail" form can be traced back to Poe's edict that the short story, aiming at a single vivid impression, ought to build to it in its final pages. But in novels and films, twists can come rather early in the plot, or in the middle, as well as at the end. You can argue that the film *Psycho* (1960) has two narrational twists. One, arriving fairly early, kills off the protagonist. Posed at first as a mystery, it's later revealed as part of a pattern of narrational suppression. That hidden pattern comes to light in the second twist, when the finale reveals the true identity of Norman Bates's mother.[27]

All genres have exploited twists, but mystery plots and thrillers of the postwar era have been especially drawn toward them. As viewers became more familiar with the conventions, storytellers sought new ways to create surprise. *Psycho* as both book and film is a central example, but so is Ira Levin's novel *A Kiss Before Dying* (1953). Its narration incorporates a drastic twist at the end of the second part, when the identity of the "he" of the first two parts reveals a wholly different pattern of motive and identity than the earlier portions had suggested. The investigation plot of *The Conversation* (1974) coaxes us to assume that, although we're attached to surveillance expert Harry Caul, we are not registering his thoughts (except during his dream). We think we hear what his microphone picks up, but it's actually his interpretation of the fatal line of dialogue. The twist reveals that the narration has been subjective to an unexpected degree.[28]

As in the whodunit, the narration-driven twist depends on the viewer getting insufficient information, taking too much for granted, or failing to realize that certain incidents can be construed in nonobvious ways. With Christie's *Murder of Roger Ackroyd*, we're inclined to assume that the Watsonian narrator is trustworthy and that he isn't skipping over or misdescribing certain events. But once we know he's the killer, we can check back and discover that certain passages prepared for it but were designed to misdirect us.

Similarly, in *The Sixth Sense*, we take for granted that all the characters are on the same ontological plane. In most supernatural stories, if a ghost might be abroad, we are told. Having suppressed this information, the scenes of Dr. Crowe with other characters must allow for the possibility that the protagonist isn't apparent to them. Through stylistic choices about staging and shooting, the narration finds clever ways to justify the characters' failures to address him (figs. 12.7–12.8).

Such films show that for craft-conscious storytellers the twist aesthetic appeals to the fair-play tenet of the Golden Age mystery. Just as we ought to be able to page back and spot how a certain clue or description led us astray, so we should be able to notice hints and suggestions that, read properly, anticipated the twist. In *The Sting* we're informed of the plan to gull gambler Doyle Lonnegan, but we're not told of the backup system that sends fake FBI agents raiding the betting parlor. We take them as actual agents, so we're momentarily misled into thinking that the con has failed. But if we care to revisit earlier scenes, we can find a hint about the FBI sting to be pulled on Lonnegan, and us

12.7 *The Sixth Sense* (1999): A scene begins with Cole's mother and Dr. Crowe sitting in silence, as if there has been a pause in their conversation. The symmetrical framing also suggests that Crowe is as "present" as the mother.

12.8 In a restaurant, Crowe's wife is eating alone, but her apparent indifference to him is most easily construed as a sign of their troubled marriage.

(figs. 12.9–12.10). Determined viewers of *The Conversation* and *Psycho* should be able to go back to spots where they were misled.

The Sixth Sense offers a glaring hint that is striking only in retrospect. The boy Cole criticizes the efforts of Dr. Crowe to tell a bedtime story. "You have to add some twists and stuff." In classic whodunits, the detective would review the clues we misinterpreted. In this film, as in other twist movies, the narration

12.9 *The Sting* (1973): As part of the "big con," Johnny Hooker is apparently shot during the FBI raid, and a trickle of blood from his mouth seems to confirm his death.

12.10 When Hooker spruces up for the big con, we see him bite on something small and then slip it into his pocket. Later we'll realize it must have been a blood capsule to be released during the gunplay.

provides quick flashbacks reviewing the hints we missed. Our storytellers still adhere to Golden Age strictures about "fair play."

As we'd expect, storytellers compete to find surprising schema revisions. We are back to the process outlined by Jean-Claude Carrière whereby film-makers and viewers adapt "to forms of expression which briefly seem daring but quickly become commonplace."[29] The churn, as we now call it, demands ever-bolder twists. In *Obsession* (1976), *Vertigo* turns incestuous; the revelation in *Dressed to Kill* (1980) goes *Psycho* one better. After the investigating photographer in *Blowup* (1966) arranged and enlarged still pictures, the audio engineer in *The Conversation* cleaned up his "nice fat tape." In *Blow-Out* (1966), the sound recordist added still photographs to create his own stop-motion movie reconstruction. The variorum grows, switcheroos pile up, and fan connoisseurship follows.

What, then, about *Pulp Fiction*? The "glib twists" heralded by the reviewer include many surprises. Mia overdoses, Butch kills Vincent, Butch runs down Marcellus, the two men are captured by two predatory hillbillies, and Vincent accidentally shoots Marvin. But two twists bear less on the unexpected. Tarantino's big twists do something rare: they resettle the overall architecture of the film.

First, after Vincent is shot down and Butch has returned to Fabienne, we get a fourth block, "The Bonnie Situation," in which Vincent is alive again. The replay of the preppy massacre helps prepare us for the time shift, but it seems likely that for many viewers this flashback counts as a jolt. (A friend tells me that the packed theater he was in reacted with murmurs.) We took for granted that nothing important was skipped over at the end of the first shootout. Yet one can, as we've seen, scrub back through the film and find the giveaways during Vincent and Jules's visit to the bar in the first part.

Pulp Fiction's second twist comes with the *ahhh* reaction I signaled earlier: the realization that the prologue with Pumpkin and Honey Bunny is now being replayed. This doesn't require any elaborate checking back. We now more or less remember the scene, and we simply realize that it was a preview of action we'll see later.

* * *

Both of these twists tease us, during viewing or afterward, to assemble the film's chronology and thus appreciate the cleverness of the whole construction. We're pushed to ask: Why end the film with Jules's redemption and Vincent's moment of comradely triumph? Perhaps it's another puncturing of coolness. No longer snappy dressers, the hitmen now strut toward a parting of the ways, one toward death and the other, perhaps, to "wandering the Earth" like Caine in *Kung Fu*. Yet there's a residual coolness in the texture and form of the film itself, something that lets audiences congratulate themselves on understanding a puzzle of narrative structure that others won't get.

Media historian Jeff Sconce considers *Pulp Fiction* an example of "smart cinema," a group of 1990s films that celebrate "an aura of 'intelligence' that distinguishes them (and their audiences) from the perceived 'dross' (and 'rabble') of the mainstream multiplex."[30] Central to this smartness, Jason Mittell suggests, is the "operational aesthetic," in which admiring audiences "watch the gears at work marveling at the craft required to pull off such narrative pyrotechnics."[31] I'd add that the formal cleverness that the hip viewers savor is first cousin to the ingenuity that John Dickson Carr and Ben Hecht praised in Golden Age whodunits. We get the same "hoodwinking contest"—a display of virtuosity, a challenge to the reader (viewer), a conspiratorial invitation to share the logic of creative choices, and above all a spur to solve a mystery not of crime and punishment but of artistic form.

The domestic psychological thriller of recent years might not seem to have the same aura of cleverness, but it too invites the audience to join a self-conscious game of form. These connoisseurs, as demanding as fans of gunplay and neo-noir, want fresh twists.

CHAPTER 13

GONE GIRLS

The New Domestic Thriller

Thriller novels of all sorts were common before World War II, but they moved onto U.S. best-seller lists very gradually. Ian Fleming and John le Carré spy stories gained a wide audience in the 1960s and remained perennial. In the 1970s, horror exercises such as *The Exorcist* and *Jaws* set the keynote for comparable works by Stephen King, Anne Rice, and others. The 1990s saw legal thrillers by Scott Turow and John Grisham gain prominence, along with military thrillers by Tom Clancy, scientific thrillers by Michael Crichton, and forensic thrillers by Patricia Cornwell and Richard Patterson. Many were hybrids that mixed detection-driven investigation plots with parallel action attached to killers or targets.

Psychological thrillers by Mary Higgins Clark had been *New York Times* best-sellers, but *Gone Girl* was the first "domestic suspense" novel since the 1940s to crack the *Publisher's Weekly* top ten in annual sales. Published in June 2012, it sold nearly two million copies that year, and the 2014 film jolted the U.S. box office to life. Two years later the novel had accumulated sales of more than nine million copies in forty-one languages. And unlike most best-sellers, it was praised for making some serious social points.

Gillian Flynn had found middling success with two previous thrillers that showed a mind immersed in popular culture. As a shy child, she had been a keen reader and movie fan; her father, a film professor, shared *Jaws*, *Psycho*, *Alien*, and other modern classics with her. Flynn claims she was reading screenplays at age twelve. After trying straight journalism, she spent ten years reviewing movies and television for *Entertainment Weekly*. David Fincher, director of

Gone Girl, called Flynn "that popcorn-munching girl in the second row craning her neck to see the whole screen at Cinerama Dome."[1]

Many crime writers build their plots from actual cases, but Flynn tracks the conventions of fiction, movies, and TV. Inspired by Hitchcock's *Psycho* and Dennis Lehane's novel *Mystic River*, Flynn based *Gone Girl* on a primal genre situation: a man is suspected of killing his wife. Amy Elliott and Nick Dunne are hip writers hoping to rise in the Manhattan slick-magazine world. But both lose their jobs in the 2008 recession, and Nick's mother's cancer forces them to relocate to his Missouri home town. Their marriage frays. One day Amy disappears, leaving behind traces of a bloody struggle.

So far, so conventional. The controversy arose because Flynn turns the central situation into a grim diagnosis of the failures of love. Amy and Nick are striving urban sophisticates—smart, eloquent, sexy, and ironically self-aware. But their intelligence and social adroitness simply give them more weapons to use against each other.

One theme becomes the ultimate unknowability of one's partner. With so many images out there, we fashion identities that may not correspond with our uncertain, defensive selves. Flynn noted: "They each have a certain persona that they may have created and as that gets dismantled, what does that reveal?"[2] Suave Nick ultimately lacks ambition and a sense of responsibility, and witty Amy reveals herself as manipulative and deceptive on a colossal scale.

As Amy and Nick fight through their relationship, the very nature of marriage is put into question too. Amy starts with a trust fund established by her parents and based on their children's books starring a disgustingly perfect prodigy called Amazing Amy. Nick feels that Amy uses her money as a cudgel, but he forces her to move away from New York, plunging her into heartland purgatory. They argue about income, jobs, and having children. Worse than being unhappy, it seems, is being *conventionally* unhappy, becoming the standard issue surly husband and nagging wife. Because of their hyperintelligence, their marriage becomes a string of needling insinuations and sulking truces. Flynn's other main inspiration, she says, was *Who's Afraid of Virginia Woolf?*

Commenters eagerly took up the theme of unhappy overachievers. "*Gone Girl*'s Biggest Villain Is Marriage Itself," ran a typical headline, and one reviewer followed up Flynn's warning about the danger of "confusing persona with personality."[3] As a journalist who had interviewed filmmakers promoting new releases, Flynn knew the advantages of alerting the press to issues that could trigger think pieces. Quentin Tarantino and other directors had proven adept at angling press coverage. As director Claude Chabrol once explained, "You have to help the critics over their notices, right?"[4]

But catchy themes weren't enough to yield a massive best-seller. The book's force also depended on its form. *Gone Girl* is woven out of two voices. Nick's first-person account begins when Amy disappears. His daily updates initially alternate between excerpts from her diary stretching back to their courtship and Amy's first-person accounts after she's gone. The he said/she said architecture stretches back at least to Dinah Craik's *A Life for a Life* (1859). This device can lay bare characters' plans, reactions, and self-scrutiny, while prodding us to reflect on their faults and virtues. Our sense of the quiet fury of the Dunne marriage comes largely from these first-person ruminations. Amy's diary excerpts also recall the document-dossier format exploited by Wilkie Collins and other nineteenth-century writers and revamped in the alternating blocks of character viewpoint in the 1930s and 1940s.

But Flynn reworked these strategies in startling ways. One editor complained of other books' "tremendously soggy middles. This book's middle was an incredible, extraordinary hammer blow." Another editor gave *Gone Girl* to an author as "homework—to learn about plot structure."[5] Flynn's manner of telling yielded not only empathy and suspense but a shocking surprise. There was, in the jargon of the trade, a twist.

The twist was not merely a reversal of fortune or a surprise revelation of a past misdeed. It cast the Dunne marriage in a new and even more damaging light. To dissect a duplicitous couple, Flynn constructed a duplicitous narration. To present characters who deceive each other, she created narrators who mislead the reader. Tracing the fate of Nick and Amy became a game of wits between author and audience, just as in Golden Age mysteries. In the end, the cunning of *Gone Girl*'s storytelling would help ignite a cycle of popular fiction that shows little sign of flagging.

Deadlier Than the Male (Novelist)

The huge success of Daphne du Maurier's *Rebecca* (1938) and Patrick Hamilton's play *Gas Light* (1938) made the gynocentric thriller respectable. At a time when the "masculine" forms of police procedural and heist story were only beginning to emerge, publishers in England and the United States eagerly supported what was coming to be called "domestic suspense."

This development encouraged female authors. Some, most notably Patricia Highsmith, moved freely into the minds of male killers. But Margaret Millar, Elisabeth Sanxay Holding, Charlotte Armstrong, Dorothy Salisbury Davis, and many other women novelists gave the vulnerable-heroine premise new life. It slipped quickly into other media, as in the 1943 radio play *Sorry, Wrong Number* by Lucille Fletcher, and *Suspicion* (1941), Hitchcock's film version of *Before the Fact*. The premise flourished in Hollywood films of the 1940s and would prove to be a robust option for decades, notably in *Bunny Lake Is Missing* (1965), *Wait Until Dark* (1967), *Double Jeopardy* (1999), *What Lies Beneath* (2000), and *Safe Haven* (2013).

The central motif of the woman in peril was open to many variations. *Before the Fact*, *Rebecca*, and *Gas Light* restrict us to the wife's range of knowledge, but Sanxay Holding's *Lady Killer* (1945) presents the situation from a bystander's viewpoint. A woman caught in an unhappy marriage feels endangered on a Caribbean cruise, but she learns that she's not a target. Instead, a bigamous fellow passenger is attempting to kill his second wife, who responds by murdering the man's first wife, who's been posing as an innocent traveler. The homicidal couple leaves the ship, with each one likely to eliminate the other. The uncertain ending reminds us that the title cuts both ways: a man may be a lady-killer, but the lady can be a killer too.

The Gothic tradition often featured an innocent woman lured into a mansion teeming with dangers and overseen by a mysterious, often attractive master. This setting reappears in the somber Manderley of *Rebecca* and the overbearing household of *Gas Light*. But the modern thriller usually centers on suburbia and the city. The dashing husband or lover is now an apparently caring, sensitive executive or professor or artist. Yet in this genre of "domestic suspense," the cozy household turns threatening. The emotions of fear, dread, and uncertainty characteristic of the woman-in-peril genre are channeled into a recognition of the limited social options available to wives and daughters.

Just as the classic Gothic relied on dramatizing a forbidding house, for the modern Gothics, details of bed and board matter. The protagonist of Nedra Tyre's *The Death of an Intruder* (1953) is a meek woman who inherits a cottage. She comes to new life by furnishing and decorating it. But when her home is invaded by a guest who won't leave, she's forced to watch her beloved figurines and Matisse reproductions coldly taken away. The runaway wife of Nancy Price's *Sleeping with the Enemy* (1987) is characterized in part through food. While hiding in a small town, she's at first forced to live on oatmeal and catsup. Once she gets a job, she can return to cooking her favorite dishes. In the 1991 film version, groceries become a warning. Laura learns that her obsessive-compulsive husband has found her when she discovers that her canned goods have been neatly stacked in the way that he likes them. A woman's life can be menaced by a rearranged cupboard.

Within the routines of housekeeping, meeting friends, holding neighborhood parties, and ferrying the children to school and play dates, the wife finds herself facing peril. After an expectant mother exposes an abusive gynecologist in the film *The Hand That Rocks the Cradle* (1992), she becomes the target of his vengeful widow. Posing as a nanny, the widow tries to take over the family by planting suspicions of infidelity and mobilizing a battery of everyday items—baby monitor, breast pump, asthma inhalers—as weapons against the trusting wife.[6]

When the protagonist is more aware of her danger, the veneer cracks. She learns that the family around which she has built her life is threatened by an unfaithful husband, a blackmailer, or another woman. She's tempted to take the blame. Is she too cold or too warm? Is she spoiling her children or neglecting them? Should she accept her partner's bouts of drinking or try to make him shape up?

Celia Fremlin's *The Hours Before Dawn* (1958) exploits domestic guilt and inadequacy to the fullest. Louise is a lower-middle-class woman suffocating under the routines of raising obstreperous toddlers, pleasing an oblivious husband, quieting a baby who screams through the night, and fending off chattering neighbors. Everything from the jam stain on the carpet to Louise's drab coveralls accuses her of being a poor wife and mother. Half asleep every day, she can hardly meet the challenge of the poised, coldly pleasant roomer Miss Brandon, who seems to be seducing her husband. When Louise's baby goes missing, the waking dreams that haunt her are realized.

In *The Hand That Rocks the Cradle* and *The Hours Before Dawn*, the rival's hidden motives drive the plot. But the wife may have her own secrets. Consider Mary Higgins Clark's *Where Are the Children?* (1975). Nancy Eldridge is living in Provincetown with her husband Ray and her children Mike and Missy. Seven years earlier, during her first marriage, her children were murdered and she was convicted by circumstantial evidence and her own numb reluctance to fight. Only the disappearance of a key witness allowed her conviction to be overturned. Her husband Carl committed suicide. Nancy started over under a false identity and found happiness in her second marriage. But then her children Mike and Missy disappear on the same day that the local newspaper runs a story revealing her past.

Nancy retreats into shock and despair, and the local police are all too ready to charge her with the new abductions. Not until a local doctor administers sodium amytal does Nancy recall more of the old crime and the new one. In the meantime, Rob Legler, the missing witness from years ago, is roaming the town and becomes an alternative suspect.

The action unfolds in fewer than twenty-four hours, and the book's narration shifts rapidly among many characters in third-person mode. We get access to the thoughts of Nancy, husband Ray, Ray's assistant Dorothy, the good Dr. Miles, retired lawyer Knowles, police chief Coffin, and townspeople who notice incidents that bear on the kids' disappearance. Most teasingly, we're presented with the actions and thoughts of the mysterious man renting a vast house across the Bay and spying on Nancy's family with a telescope. Early on we learn that this giggling pedophile is the one who has kidnapped Mike and Missy. The suspense derives from the question of how he can be caught before he harms, and eventually kills, them. And by the way: Who is he?

Where Are the Children? interrupts the kidnap crisis with brief flashbacks to fill us in on the first crime. Bits of backstory reveal the tightly knit community of Provincetown. For the most part, the men are the active players, with Dr. Miles and the lawyer Knowles teaming with Ray to defend Nancy. The other women, Dorothy and assorted housewives, pick up on clues to the disappearance but are cowed by their husbands into dismissing their concerns. At the climax, the women come forward to report to the police, and Nancy realizes the importance of a dropped mitten and breaks away from male supervision. She rushes to the house to save Mike and Missy. There she learns that the kidnapper is her first husband, Carl. Seven years ago he killed their children, pinned the blame on her, and faked his suicide.

The faked death, a constant in crime fiction and especially common in the domestic thriller, is concealed from the reader by a narrational ploy. In the early chapters, as we follow the action and thoughts of the kidnapper, he's referred to only as "he." Halfway through, he gets a phone call from Dorothy, who addresses him as Mr. Parrish, the name he used to rent his hideout. When she brings a potential buyer to tour the house, she encounters him: "She looked up and gasped and stared into the searching eyes and perspiring face of the fourth-floor tenant, Courtney Parrish."[7] Because these chapters attach us to Dorothy's consciousness, the narration isn't lying. To her, he *is* Parrish. But thereafter, the novel's narration calls him Courtney or Parrish, even when we're sharing his thoughts. This simple slippage misleads us and creates the climactic twist.

Just as in the classic fair-play detective story, we should be able to turn back and find the hints we missed. For example, the "he" of the early chapters is well-acquainted with Nancy's past, and he recalls that he first saw her on campus. (Carl, we'll learn later, was a professor.) In our first pass through the book, we'll probably skim over such nudges, but the fan/connoisseur will keep an eye out for them, if only to be able to feel the pleasure of a game of wits like that promoted by Golden Age whodunits. Books such as Eustis's *Horizontal Man* and Levin's *A Kiss Before Dying* used the texture of prose to mislead us in ways akin to the maneuvers of Christie and Carr. Hitchcock, Tarantino, Shyamalan, and other filmmakers sought cinematic methods to suppress information for the sake of twists. It is no surprise, then, that Mary Higgins Clark and other writers applied the whodunits' formal and stylistic maneuvers to domestic thrillers as well.

Hopscotching Through the Past

Where Are the Children? is characteristic of the postwar domestic thriller in another way. It's fairly short; the thirty-one brief chapters, plus a prologue, add up to about 65,000 words. Today publishers and literary agents expect most popular novels to run 90,000 to 100,000 words or more. For this reason, as well as others, the domestic thriller became more complex. Its basic conventions, particularly those bearing on exhuming the past, were given expanded, intricate treatment.

A key figure in this change is Laura Lippman, a Baltimore-based novelist who began with a series centered on private detective Tess Monaghan. She edged into the suspense genre with *Every Secret Thing* (2003). Like a hybrid 1930s whodunit, it counterpoints an investigation plot with blocks devoted to the lead-up to the crime. Two young women recently out of prison for murdering a baby are accused in the death of another child. Across a number of months and several viewpoint characters, the original circumstances are revealed.

With *To the Power of Three* (2005), Lippman expanded on the double-entry plot structure, which would become her signature technique and a staple of the genre. Again, police take a significant role, but the emphasis falls on three girls involved in a shooting in a high school bathroom. The investigation is crosscut with chapters that trace the girls' friendship from third grade to their senior year. In the process, the girls' role in a student's death is exposed as the source of their violent confrontation.

The alternation of viewpoint from chapter to chapter, a schema we've encountered throughout popular narrative, is a shaping force in Lippman's plots. *What the Dead Know* (2007) alternates another police inquiry with clusters of chapters stretching back to 1975—again, showing how adolescent behavior shapes what people become. Another convention of the thriller, the enigmatic figure claiming to be a missing person, is put to good use.

From the angle of construction, Lippman can be seen as reviving R. Austin Freeman's "inverted tale." But Freeman starts with a block showing the crime planned and consummated, then follows that with another block tracing the investigation and solution. Lippman breaks the lead-up to the crime into short chapters, sometimes years apart, and intercuts those with the present-day investigation. The result is a two-column grid structure.

One police team recurs in these three books, although they are assigned increasingly minor roles. Lippman's later books abandon the procedural thread but retain an investigative premise. In *Life Sentences* (2009), the detective is a writer with personal stakes in the quest. Cassandra Fallows has written two tell-all memoirs, the first about her father and the second about her husbands. When her third book, a novel, fails, she decides to try to report on a crime committed by a schoolmate. Laying bare Lippman's zigzag forms, Cassandra explains her plan: "I'd weave the story of what happened to Callie as an adult with our lives as children together." She calls it "hopscotching through the past."[8]

Life Sentences uses Lippman's double-entry format to track present-day events in parallel with first-person passages from Cassandra's early memoir, *My Father's Daughter*. Both time lines are chronological, but the viewpoints fluctuate. The present-time chapters, rendered in the third person, are attached in turn to Cassandra, the African American murder suspect Callie, Teena the cop turned saleswoman, the flamboyant attorney Gloria, and a trio of grade school girls with a hold over Callie. All of these characters are given specific social circumstances, detailed routines, and pasts conjured up through flashbacks. The result is a book running to forty-six chapters and nearly 350 pages.

In each of these novels, Lippman keeps the reader oriented through an exoskeleton marked by segment tags. *Life Sentences* gathers its present-day chapters under dates and increasingly metaphorical titles, from "Banrock Station: February 20–23" to "Happy Wanderers: September 5–6." The portions from *My Father's Daughter* are set off by poetic titles and the absence of chapter numbers.

The double-entry structure has its precedents, such as in *Bleak House* and Bill S. Ballinger's postwar novels. But Lippman's later work rings more ingenious changes on the parallel-chronology layout. The first part of *I'd Know You Anywhere* (2010) intercuts the 1980s rampage of a rapist and murderer with the later life of the victim he spared; now a wife and mother, she learns of his possible release from prison. The remaining sections of the book intercut her reactions with that of other women connected to the case. *And When She Was Good* (2012) is simpler, alternating today's Heloise, who runs a high-end escort service (chronicled in the present tense), with her earlier life as Helen, a teenager fleeing into the arms of a drug dealer (past tense). The two time lines intersect when Helen decides to leave her lover, and the tense shifts wholly to the present.

The Most Dangerous Thing (2011) is a tour de force of pattern plotting, tracing the lives of several young grownups haunted by severe teenage mistakes. Strikingly, the sections ("Us," "Them," "Pity Them," "Pity Us All") are set off by different narrational marks. We get italics versus roman type; present tense for some sections, past for others; and stretches in which the actions of the friends are described by a collective narrator ("we").

With these books Lippman came to be considered a serious novelist, reviewed as such in the *New York Times*, the *Washington Post*, and elsewhere. She shows a surgically precise sensitivity to adolescent girls' friendships and betrayals, and her women are more ready to exercise agency than many heroines of earlier decades. Lippman would continue to create elaborate, absorbing variants on the dual time line exhumation of a past crime.

At the same time, the books are ingenious revisions of schemas already at work in the genre. It wouldn't be a stretch to rewrite Clark's *Where Are the Children?* along Lippman lines. We'd pull out the brief flashbacks dotting the present-time chapters and expand them into a parallel chronology. That would trace Nancy's student years and her too-early marriage to her professor Carl Harmon, who treats her as a pampered daughter. Later, through viewpoint shifts, we'd watch Carl plot and carry out the murder of their children. Perhaps all of this could be synchronized—"hopscotched"—with the abduction of Mike and Missy.

As for the present-time scenes, the mobile viewpoints could be expanded to supply more ample backstory on the secondary Provincetown characters. To mark the two time lines, we could put current action in the present tense and use dates and years to tag Nancy's early life with Carl. In a pinch, the major twist could be preserved by presenting Carl's infanticides in the "he" style, distinct from the characterization of him as Nancy's professor and husband—creating in the very style the split personality that inhabits him.

This wouldn't be just a matter of padding the book to 100,000 words or so. In our Lippman rewrite, a parallel time line could produce more fleshed-out characterizations, a contrasting ambience (California campus versus New England seaside), and a greater immersion in Nancy's first breakdown, which Clark's book is forced to render telegraphically through her drug-induced interrogation. The younger Nancy could be given friends who play a role in defending or condemning her. In addition, an extra layer of suspense could be mounted for everything that occurs in the past. (Will Nancy discover that her husband has framed her?)

I'm not suggesting that this reverse engineering would improve Clark's compact tale, only that the conventions she relies on could be expanded and thickened in the Lippman manner. As *Rebecca* gained cultural distinction by its length and psychological depth, I suspect that density of presentation played a part in many publishers avoiding labeling the modern thriller as "a novel of suspense" and simply calling it a novel. These books proudly signal the artistic prestige associated with a longer format, complex time lines, contrasting viewpoints, socially marked lifestyle details, and fuller characterization. Not as forbidding as "modernism" but not as bare bones as earlier thrillers, these works aim in their own way to cross over from genre fiction to literary fiction, aiming for the praise that crime novels have occasionally won across the decades—"as good as real literature." A *Washington Post* critic calls Lippman "one of the best novelists around, period."[9]

Amy, Amazing

Gillian Flynn was well aware of Lippman's work. "Every time Laura Lippman comes out with a new book, I get chills because I know I am back in the hands of the master. She is simply a brilliant novelist, an unflinching chronicler of life in America right now."[10]

For the most part, Lippman remained loyal to the detective-novel premise of solving a crime; her formal ingenuity lay in aligning the investigation with richly realized scenes from the past. Flynn followed a comparable model in her first two books. *Sharp Objects* (2006) centers on Camile Preaker, a reporter who returns to her small town to cover the murder of two girls. Through flashbacks she relives her own troubled past while she probes the crime.

Dark Places (2009) adopts a multiple-entry structure reminiscent of Lippman's early books. Libby Day has survived the massacre of her mother and two sisters. Her brother Ben has been sent to prison for the killings, and she has grown up living off her notoriety. Now, running out of money, she agrees to confirm Ben's guilt for a morbid true-crime club. The plot is split between Libby's investigation today (first person, past tense) and the eighteen hours leading up to the attack on Libby's family in 1985 (third person, past tense). That time line is further split between the viewpoints of Ben and Patty, their mother. At the climax, a third character's viewpoint is summoned to settle what really happened that night, and Ben's narrative line is brought into Libby's present.

Gone Girl (2012) constitutes Flynn's departure from the investigation plot and a shift into the pure domestic thriller. She outsources the detecting to the police, who are largely kept offstage. Her focus is the Dunne household and the disintegrating marriage, which is examined through the techniques of split viewpoint and parallel chronology developed in Lippman's work. During the book's first half, events after Amy's disappearance are confined to Nick's first-person account. Portions of that are intercut with entries from Amy's diary recounting incidents from the past.

The exoskeleton of the plot is exposed not only through the rocking-horse exchange of viewpoints but through tags. Nick's sections (always "Nick Dunne") are called "The Day of," "The Night of," "One Day Gone," and so on. The parallel sections are tagged "Amy Elliott Dunne, Diary Entry" and dated from January 8, 2005, to June 26, 2012. Nick gets the past tense, and Amy's diary, unexpectedly, is dominated by the present.

The novel's first half aims to throw suspicion on Nick. He has reason to resent Amy; he's failed at everything he's tried. Her diary excerpts trace the evolution of a selfish, abusive husband. His account—he seems to know we're reading this—contains evasions and lies. He conceals what he does for a couple of hours on the day of Amy's disappearance, and he admits:

> I have a mistress. Now is the part where I have to tell you I have a mistress and you stop liking me. If you liked me to begin with. I have a pretty, young, very young mistress, and her name is Andie.
>   I know, it's bad.[11]

If your plot centers on a murderous husband, you have a choice. You can let us in on his plans, as in Iles's *Malice Aforethought* and films such as *Dial M for Murder* (1954). But *Gone Girl* doesn't unequivocally show that Nick has killed Amy or even plotted to kill her.

The second alternative for handling a murderous-husband situation is to keep it uncertain, chiefly by confining us to the wife's range of knowledge. The premise is, "I think my husband is trying to kill me." This ploy was made famous in *Before the Fact* and in 1940s films such as *Secret Beyond the Door* (1948) and *Sleep, My Love* (1948).

The first half of *Gone Girl* uses Amy's diary entries, in alternation with Nick's account, to present the familiar arc of suspicion. The Dunnes' marriage weakens, and she becomes increasingly frightened. Just before their fifth anniversary she buys a gun for self-defense. In her last entry, she records her fear that he will kill her.

Nick looks guilty at first, but with the whiff of doubt, another convention kicks in: that of the "helper male."[12] If there's another man nearby able to rescue the wife and play the role of a future romantic partner, then the husband is likely to be exposed as villainous. Examples are the Hollywood version of *Gaslight* (1944) and *Sleep, My Love*. If no helper is visible, then we're likely to have a plot based on the wife's misjudgment of the husband, as in *Suspicion* and *Secret Beyond the Door*. In *Gone Girl's* first half, Amy seems to have no recourse to a helper male. This fact might dissolve some suspicion attached to Nick. Maybe, some readers might ask, Amy was indeed abducted by a third party?

So much for the convention of the killer husband. A second type of domestic thriller, rarer than the first, centers on a homicidal woman. She shows up in Vera Caspary's novel *Bedelia* (1945) and in films such as *Ivy* (1947), *A Woman's Vengeance* (1948), and *Too Late for Tears* (1949).

An especially shocking 1940s specimen of the killer wife is the poised, irresistible Ellen Berent in *Leave Her to Heaven* (novel 1944, film 1945). At first, Ellen wishes no harm to her husband Dick; she just wants to eliminate anybody with whom she'd have to share him. She lets his little brother drown, and fearing that her unborn child will come between them, she flings herself downstairs and induces a miscarriage. Eventually, though, she turns her wrath on Dick. As we'll see, Ellen's most extreme tactic looks forward to *Gone Girl*.

What is exceptionally clever about *Gone Girl* is that its central twist replaces the murderous-husband schema with a revelation of Amy as a spider woman. Nick discovers that his sister Go's shed is bursting with fancy consumer goods he never bought. He realizes he's been framed.

The diary extracts stop and Amy's voice reenters, in the present. "I'm so much happier now that I'm dead." An inner monologue begins, and she explains that she has faked her disappearance to get Nick convicted. This is the midway hammer blow that the editor found so compelling. Like other twists, it depends on suppressive narration, which in turn arises from a central convention of the new domestic suspense cycle: the unreliable narrator. True, the narration of *Where Are the Children?* is devious, but quietly so. In contrast, Amy's diary, filled with lies about Nick's misbehavior, is exposed as flagrantly untrustworthy.

The diary also lets Flynn shift the ground of the domestic thriller. The cheating husband, a classic threat to the wife, turns out to be a helpless victim. The wronged wife becomes an avenging fury. With icy calm, Amy explains her frustration with Nick's failure to be the man she tried to make him. She has tolerated playing Cool Girl to his masculine self-absorption, but now that he's taken a mistress she's decided he's not worth it. Her eloquent rant against the bad faith of modern courtship should stir discussion in book clubs around the world. Is she the new century's liberated woman, keen to send her husband to Death Row because he's become a bourgeois-bohemian cliché?

Amy's pride in her genius stems from not one but three trails she's laid for the police to follow. She leaves clues in the treasure hunt, a hyperclever game she obliges Nick to play every anniversary. This time, though, the hints point to Nick's infidelity and penchant for violence. A second array of clues—imperfectly cleaned bloodstains, obviously faked signs of abduction, big credit card purchases in his name—make Nick seem like a lying killer. Then there's Amy's diary, full of made-up abuses. She arranges for the diary to be discovered at just the moment that will harm Nick most. The diary entries initially coax us toward the before-the-fact situation, seeming to provide a record of a wife's growing apprehension of danger.

At first Amy intends to drown herself, so that when her body is discovered Nick will be executed. This vindictive-suicide motif is the extreme tactic Ellen Berent pursues in *Leave Her to Heaven*. Ellen poisons herself and sets up her sister Ruth, who's in love with Dick, as her murderer. Like Amy, she has left behind a damning testament, a letter that will lead the police to arrest Ruth.

The unreliability of Amy's diary shows how much Flynn owes to tradition. Since the 1930s, mystery fiction has long surprised us by questioning documents we'd initially trusted. *Murder Isn't Easy* sets up a string of more or less untrustworthy accounts of murders in an advertising agency. Likewise, *Death Has a Past* puts a confession's provenance and trustworthiness into question. Later authors in the woman-in-peril tradition would mostly avoid the misleading memoir in favor of a more prosaic realism. In one of her rare ventures into gynocentric suspense, *Edith's Diary* (1977), Patricia Highsmith presents a protagonist whose journal represents fantasies that compensate for her melancholy marriage and stifling household routine. Her husband leaves her and her son grows up a lout, but in her diary she has a happy, thriving family and becomes a grandmother. We're aware of her fantasies from the outset. Edith is an unreliable narrator, but Highsmith isn't. As ever, she's interested in tracing, in unshockable prose, the disintegration of a personality. There is no big twist, only Edith's reckless choices and clumsy efforts to hide her growing delusion.

Mary Higgins Clark saves the revelation of her killer's identity for the climax, but Flynn resists the temptation to make the diary revelation *Gone Girl*'s final twist. Apart from being a shock, the diary device works to reveal character.

Amy is even more Machiavellian than Nick suspects. Moreover, now that we know Amy's true nature, the novel can launch an ingenious new spiral of action. Having coupled two plot schemes across the first half of the book, the killer husband and the homicidal femme fatale, Flynn replays them in miniature.

On the run, Amy is robbed by the drifters Jeff and Greta. She calls her old lover, the rich Desi Collings, and convinces him that Nick represents a threat. In effect, Amy relaunches the lethal-husband scenario and recruits Desi as her helper male. Of course, in most such plots, the helper male rescues the woman from peril. Here she *is* the peril. Once Desi has given Amy luxurious refuge, she relaunches the lethal-woman schema. She scatters clues casting him as her abusive captor, framing him as she framed Nick, and then kills him.

No wonder *Gone Girl* is vastly longer than its counterparts, coming in at more than 145,000 words. It's plumped up not just by the ruminations on the lacerations of marriage but also by a section that enables Amy to abandon her suicide plan, recover her losses, and plot her return home, all the while reenacting the scenario of the first part. As a piece of pattern plotting, it's extraordinarily balanced, with alternating blocks lined up in parallel. It's a triumph of tagging as well; imagine a reader trying to assemble the plot without each chapter's labeling the time of the action (table 13.1).

Part One, "Boy Loses Girl," ends with Nick's discovery of the shed full of man-toys. Part Two, "Boy Meets Girl," signals Desi's being gulled by Amy. Here Flynn daringly throws her time schemes out of alignment. As Nick's proceeds day by day ("Seven Days Gone" and onward), the revived Amy's time line jumps back to "The Day of" and runs a bit out of sync with Nick's. Explicit tagging helps readers grasp the disjunction in time lines and look forward to their realignment. The convergence takes place when Amy sees Nick's contrition on a TV talk show, which spurs her to find a way to return home and regain control of him.

In Part Three, "Boy Gets Girl Back (or Vice Versa)," the alternating voices continue. What should have been a brief epilogue returns to marriage as combat. Amy comes home spattered in blood and bearing lies about Desi holding her prisoner. Nick tries to prove her perfidy, but she reveals herself to be a superior strategist. She becomes a heroic survivor, her parents' book series is relaunched, and she's writing a memoir herself (not, of course, from her texts we've been reading). For his part, Nick tries to write his own version (perhaps his texts we've been reading).

In the end, Amy blocks him again. She's pregnant by sperm she carefully preserved, and he can't bear leaving a child in her care. She vows to continue her program of shaping him up. "I don't have anything else to add. I just wanted to make sure I had the last word. I think I've earned that."[13] Whom is she addressing? Perhaps, like everything else she's done and said, it's a way of proving to herself that she's amazing.

TABLE 13.1 Gillian Flynn, *Gone Girl* (2012)

Part One: Boy Loses Girl		Part Two: Boy Meets Girl		Part Three: Boy Gets Girl Back (or Vice Versa)	
Nick Dunne: 15 chapters of recounting (first person, past tense) alternate with . . .	Amy Elliott Dunne: 14 diary entries (first person, present tense)	Nick: 11 chapters of recounting (first person, past tense) alternate with . . .	Amy: 12 chapters of recounting (first person, present tense)	Nick: 6 chapters as in Part Two alternate with . . .	Amy: 6 chapters as in Part Two
The Day of. . . .	*January 8, 2005*	*Seven Days Gone* (continued)	*The Day of . . .* (flashbacks to scheme)	*Forty Days Gone*: Amy returns	*The Night of the Return*
through	through	through:	*The Day of . . .*	through:	through:
Six Days Gone	*June 26, 2012*	*Thirty-Three Days Gone*	through:	*Twenty Weeks After the Return*	*Ten Months, Two Weeks, Six Days After the Return*
Seven Days Gone: Amy's frame-up exposed.			*Forty Days Gone:* Amy's second scheme achieved.		

A Blooming Ecosystem

Around the time of *Gone Girl*'s 2012 publication, other gynocentric thrillers offered shifting viewpoints and broken time lines: Lippman's work, S. J. Watson's *Before I Go to Sleep* (2008), and Alex Marwood's *The Wicked Girls* (2012). But like *Citizen Kane* and *Pulp Fiction*, Flynn's novel became a totemic work for a trend, a vivid prototype that could encourage a cycle of experimentation. After its success, publishers began to seek out the next *Gone Girl*.

The rising prestige of domestic thrillers was probably helped by the research of Sarah Weinman. She produced several essays celebrating the genre, edited a collection of classic short stories, and assembled a 2015 Library of America edition of eight domestic suspense novels from the 1940s and 1950s. Weinman played an important role in giving the new cycle a worthy past.[14]

Writers announced their allegiance to the emerging norms. Today's suspense novel, claims a manual for aspiring writers, favors nonchronological ordering, multiple points of view, parallel motifs, and flashbacks.[15] J. P. Delaney confessed a preference for "cutting between different narrators, jumping between time frames, creating contrasting viewpoints."[16] Delaney proves his point in *Believe Me* (2018), a bald-faced rewrite of his 2001 *The Decoy* (signed by Tony Strong). The books share the same plot premise and the same twists, but the new version employs shifting tenses, a clear exoskeleton, and the fancy device of occasionally describing scenes as if they were in a screenplay. (One chapter is called "Rewrites and Flashbacks.") The second book shows how much the genre had changed in just a few years.

Heidi Pitlor was equally explicit. For *The Daylight Marriage* (2015), "I wanted there to be two different storylines told at two different paces. One would cover a day, and one would cover months to a year."[17] The premises—when a wife goes missing, her husband tells of the investigation while she recounts what happened beforehand—led to the inevitable comparison. "Despite the acrid marriage, the his-and-hers narration, and the fact that Lovell quickly emerges as the primary suspect, this isn't really another *Gone Girl*."[18]

That reassurance reminds us that the market in popular narrative is driven by the search for novelty, even within narrow bounds. The search often proceeds according to the variorum principle, the pressure to saturate the ecological niche with fine differences that are recognized by fans. All genres court slight variation. What differentiates this cycle of domestic thrillers is the authors' and readers' awareness of nuances not just in setting and character but also in structure and narration.

Certainly the writer needs to create vivid characters. A tangible milieu of women's culture helps too, built out of granite countertops, running shoes, brand name cars and utensils, decorated baby rooms, iPads and iPhones, and Netflix subscriptions. But within this world are embedded traditional ingredients of mystery-based action. Again and again we encounter amnesia, mistaken or hidden identity, traffic accidents, tailing and stalking, fake deaths, impersonation, spying, children in danger, incriminating admissions. Often, then, a book's freshness depends on how the story is told.

At a basic level, mystery and suspense can be generated by multiple time lines, shifting viewpoints, unreliable narration, and the twists that emerge from suppressed information. For fans and connoisseurs working at another level, new wrinkles in any of these strategies will be a source of extra enjoyment. A 2017 review spells it out: "The use of a multi-viewpoint, chronologically complex narrative to create suspense by purposely misleading the reader is a really, really popular device. Two words: *Gone Girl*. While we are not the fools we once were and now assume immediately that we are being played, the question is whether we still take pleasure in the twists and revelations that follow."[19]

As in the classic detective story, the informed reader is invited to guess how the author will tweak storytelling norms. Fans of domestic suspense have acquired what Trollope deplored in Collins—the "taste of the construction."

Start with the most striking of the new norms: alternating parallel time lines. The simplest structure is on display in Mary Kubicka's *Every Last Lie* (2017). When a husband has a fatal car accident, the wife's search for the cause is interrupted by chapters tracing incidents leading up to the crash. Megan Goldin's *Escape Room* (2019) juxtaposes four executives trapped in an elevator with flashbacks from the viewpoint of a woman taking revenge on the team. A similar toggling between Now and Then shapes Peter Swanson's *All the Beautiful Lies* (2018). The murder of Harry Ackerson's father brings him back to his hometown, and alternating chapters survey the childhood and girlhood of Harry's stepmother, who may have arranged for the crime. In a second part, the alternation picks up other characters, one of whom is revealed as the killer. The structure allows Swanson to build suspense—how will the time lines converge?—while presenting rhyming situations of adults taking sexual advantage of the young people in their care.

The parallels of present and past become nakedly threatening in J. P. Delaney's *The Girl Before* (2017). Here the sinister Gothic mansion becomes a forbidding postmodern panopticon overseen by a suave, obsessive architect. Eighty-two chapters alternate to show startlingly similar events befalling Emma (who once lived in the house) and Jane (who's living there now). The parallel chapters suggest that the obsessive landlord has murdered Emma, and this heightens our concern for Jane's fate. Something similar happens in Amy Gentry's *Bad Habits* (2021), when the heroine, a hard-edged professor, encounters her college rival at a conference. Her steps toward murder alternate with chapters explaining the origins of her hatred.

The thriller's two time lines are usually chronological. This is an enormous aid to readers who must keep track of pretty complicated strings of events. But once that's established as an intrinsic norm, we can handle a dose of nonlinearity. Each parallel time line, for instance, will often include brief flashbacks and bits of backstory. And occasionally a writer will shift past-time scenes around. Marwood's *The Wicked Girls* shuffles crucial scenes out of order to delay key revelations. In one section of *All the Missing Girls* (2016), Megan Miranda puts chapters in reverse chronology to expose the pressures building toward a child's abduction.

Tagging, redundancy, and other design features enable the author to braid time lines in fairly complex ways. Heidi Pitlor's *Daylight Marriage* begins at night during a quarrel and then skips ahead by more than a day, when the wife goes missing. The aftermath of her disappearance unfolds in alternation with chronological flashbacks to events plucked from the thirty-hour gap. In Rebecca Fleet's *The House Swap* (2018), a 2012–13 chronology is intercut with two simultaneous lines of action from 2015. The simultaneity of the 2015 strands is only gradually revealed because one of them is untagged and attributed to an unknown narrator.

More elaborate is Lisa Scottoline's *After Anna* (2018). The bulk of the plot crosscuts the murder trial of Dr. Noah Alderman with the period when his wife Maggie brought home her daughter by her first husband. The days of Noah's trial are presented in reverse order, beginning with the moment the jury delivers its verdict. Scottoline works some past events into the trial phase through testimony and Noah's flashbacks. These often mesh with the adjacent episodes of Maggie's forward-moving chronology—less hopscotching than straddling. The tight cross-stitching of past and present exposes, virtually side by side, two characters' attitudes toward a single incident.

Another ambitious effort in pattern plotting is Paula Hawkins's *The Girl on the Train* (2015). It breaks an eighteen-month period into three strands attached to different women. The calendar governing the eyewitness Rachel and the anxious wife Anna keeps them in sync, but Megan's time line starts further in the past and never catches up with theirs. Needless to say, the fragments of time revealed in Megan's story furnish key revelations at the climax. As in *After Anna*, some events are replayed from different viewpoints, which help sharpen characterization and anchor chronology.

Multiplying Perspectives and Tagging Blocks

Whereas the domestic suspense stories of Mignon Eberhart and her rivals tended to limit us to what an endangered heroine or bystander knows, books such as *After Anna* and *The Girl on the Train* illustrate the extent to which the contemporary domestic thriller has made multiple perspectives a central convention. One way to avoid bogging down your plot, says Pitlor, "is to have alternating viewpoints. When you hit a wall with one, you switch to another. . . . There is energy just in the movement between characters."[20]

Multiple viewpoints were a staple of classic fiction and became a vehicle of experimentation early in the twentieth century. Nowadays any novel is likely to shift our attachment from character to character.[21] Ed McBain, Richard Stark, Elmore Leonard, and many other authors proved this to be a rewarding option for the hard-boiled urban adventure. When mystery novels use multiple viewpoints, the usual benefits include giving us access to a range of sympathetic or unsympathetic characters. This device also permits the author to omit key events, conceal motives, and deflect our attention, all of which can prepare the way for twists.[22]

A virtuoso example in the domestic thriller vein is Margaret Millar's 1957 novel *An Air That Kills*. A banal premise—a man is murdered by his wife and her lover—is treated in round-robin fashion, with the viewpoint shifting among friends, relations, bystanders, and (without acknowledgment) the guilty parties. Chapter by chapter, Millar charts a social network, with most of the major events occurring offstage, presented to us as people learn of them. Although she relies on third-person narration, she treats the central mystery with the sort of obliqueness we associate with Conrad's multiplying narrators.

Most of our recent domestic thrillers limit their viewpoints more severely. The titles I've already mentioned typically tie us to few characters per time line. The first part of Peter Swanson's *The Kind Worth Killing* (2015) alternates between Ted (present) and Lily (mostly past). After a major twist, all the action unfolds in the present, but a new dual viewpoint is established. Similarly, Mick Herron's *This Is What Happened* (2018) attaches us to only three characters, in blocks, before crosscutting all three at the climax.

More ambitious authors try shuttling among many viewpoints. *Big Little Lies* (2014) by Liane Moriarty reduces present-time episodes to fragments of gossipy dialogue, but its parallel story line roams among many characters' minds. Perhaps a limit is hit in Paula Hawkins's *Into the Water* (2017). The book has ten point-of-view characters, along with portions of a discovered manuscript, all deployed in a double-entry structure switching between 2015 and 1993. Readers registered their disappointment on the Amazon sales site. "The story is told through the visions of so many people that you lose what it is all about." "Quit halfway due to too many characters, no guide to who they are or who they're talking about. . . . It's a struggle to follow which timeframe each chapter is in."[23]

Those readers should have been grateful that Hawkins resisted the temptation to present the point-of-view characters as first-person narrators, as she had done with the central trio of *The Girl on the Train*. After all, I-centered storytelling is very much on the agenda for domestic thrillers. In the earliest European novels, it was motivated as a letter or journal or testimony, and that's still not out of bounds for today's writers, as the embedded journal in S. J. Watson's *Before I Go to Sleep* (2011) shows. But by the twentieth century, writers could simply present first-person narration as a monologue, with no listener or reader presumed.

First-person narrators hold a lot of advantages for domestic suspense. They can produce pointed characterizations; they can realistically justify limits on what we learn; and not least, they can help us keep time lines straight. In *Everything You Want Me to Be* (2017), three first-person accounts alternate within three overlapping periods. The varying voices distinguish the slightly out-of-sync chains of events. *He Said/She Said* (2017), a title inevitable in this genre, consists of two time lines. Within the 2015 one, the viewpoint bounces between Laura and Kit, both speaking in the first person and the present tense. For the period 2000 to 2005, however, the voice is mostly Laura's and in the past tense. And in each time line there's a crucial flashback at the end, narrated by one of the two centers of consciousness. The reliably recurring narrators underscore the larger rhythm of time shifts.

A domestic thriller can update the conventions of the document dossier by filtering a narrator's voice through contemporary media. Emails and text messages replace letters and telegrams, and websites do duty for library sources. *A Simple Favor* (2017) incorporates a character's blog into the alternating rhythm of first-person accounts. A podcast serves much the same function in Gilly Macmillan's *I Know You Know* (2018), and Snoop, a music-sharing app, lets us know that others are spying on characters in Ruth Ware's *One by One* (2020). In Macmillan's *The Perfect Girl* (2016), a Sunday night concert and its aftermath are intercut with Monday morning reactions, each time line anchored by a first-person narrator. Interspersed with these dueling voices are bits of a screenplay by another character, and eventually the aspiring filmmaker becomes a third narrator himself. In all, the polyphony that Mikhail Bakhtin found characteristic of the novel form is sustained in today's domestic thrillers (although the voices are more smoothly harmonized than he might prefer).

To succeed with a mass audience, the genre's play with these narrative strategies needs to present a clear-cut exoskeleton that relies on tagging. The barest segmentation (Chapter One, Chapter Two) couldn't easily alert us to parallel construction or point-of-view shifts. Instead, authors tend to split the novel into parts, titled or not, and then lay out the parallel time lines, often tagged as Now/Then or Before/After. Within the parts, the segments are likely to be labeled further with dates, locations, or character names. The character name is virtually demanded if the segment is narrated in the first person; if the narrator's identity isn't given, the wily reader will suspect something important is being suppressed. While helping us sort the story out, labels can perform the traditional function of teasing us. In retrospect, *Gone Girl*'s section title "Boy Gets Girl Back (or Vice Versa)" hints that both Desi and Nick will recover Amy, and she will "get back" both of them in different ways.

Despite their reliance on structural symmetries and labels, the books in this genre don't include tables of contents. Exposing the overall design so early might undercut some later surprises. In *After Anna*, where sections alternate "Noah, After" and "Maggie, Before," a table of contents would give away the epilogue, which is tagged "Maggie and Noah, After." The exoskeleton and tagging guide moment-by-moment uptake; the overall symmetry is felt, not paraded as in the tables of contents we find in 1930s mysteries or crossover novels such as March Cost's *Dark Glass* (1935).

As we've seen throughout, the very texture of the writing can help sharpen the differences between time frames and viewpoints. The contrast of past tense and present tense, or differences in typography (roman/italics, one typeface/ another), can help keep us oriented. Here again we see the diffused heritage of Woolf's and Faulkner's italics and Dos Passos's changing fonts, as well as crossover books setting up these cues as reliable orienting devices.

All of these strategies—the parallel time structures, the play of viewpoints, the use of the exoskeleton, and tagging both to stabilize the design and mislead the reader—are at the service of a convention celebrated by thriller writers and readers: the unreliable narrator. Across the twentieth century, it has become a convention of both esoteric and exoteric narrative.

"There are only so many ways a person can be unreliable," remarks an editor. "Either they're directly lying to you, or they have a problem."[24] Both options are common enough in domestic suspense. A first-person narrator may mislead us overtly with the sort of lies Amy plants in her diary in *Gone Girl*, or through omission as Nick does in his account of his actions on the fateful day. Or the narrator may hallucinate, sincerely reporting what isn't the case, as in A. J. Finn's *The Woman in the Window* (2018).

Unreliability can also arise from the overall structure of the book. In *Sometimes I Lie* (2017), Alice Feeney presents what appears at first to be a single first-person narrator acting in two time frames ("Now" and "Then") and declaring her thoughts in a diary (tagged "Before"). The "I" is deceptive, however, because it actually belongs to two different characters. Here each narrator is fairly reliable; it's the juxtaposition of voices that's misleading (as is the refusal to tag the speakers). The ensuing twist reshapes our understanding of the author of the diary.

To prepare for a twist, suppressive narration often extends the stratagems of duplicitous characters. For example, thriller characters commonly assume false identities, and the narration can conspire straight-facedly with the scheme. A single character in two time lines might have different names, as in *The Wife Between Us* (2017) and *Anatomy of a Scandal* (2017). The narration doesn't reveal the masquerade until it's ready. In many of the books I've already mentioned, there's a comparable shell game with the pronouns *I* and *he* and *she*— something we've already seen in Levin's *A Kiss Before Dying*.

Authors can exploit the reader's confidence that she has mastered the genre's conventions. The twist in *Sometimes I Lie* relies on the assumption that untagged "I" passages in parallel before-and-after segments are likely to belong to a single character. More drastically, *The Silent Patient* (2019) by Alex Michaelides plays on our assumption that the events in one time line are (again in the absence of tags) running chronologically. The twist comes when it's revealed that some of the "present," apparently chronological chapters are actually flashbacks to events in the second time line, albeit from a different character's viewpoint.

Readers of domestic thrillers embrace the gamelike nature of the plotting. They cultivate a high degree of connoisseurship, savoring not only new situations but also innovations in structure and narration. The back cover of one paperback edition slips easily between a "you" that indicates the protagonist to a "you" that refers to a knowing reader:

> When you think you're safe, YOU'RE NOT.
> When you think the past is over, IT ISN'T.
> When you think you know someone, YOU DON'T.
> When you think you've guessed this twist, YOU HAVEN'T.[25]

This marketing tactic might serve as a slogan for the entire genre.

As you'd expect, film adaptations of these novels largely respect their narrative strategies. *The Girl on the Train* (2016) uses parallel editing, a flurry of flashbacks, and some tagging to trace the three women's story lines. *A Simple Favor* (2018) turns one character's blog into a vlog and presents the time shifts through flashbacks. Setting the pace was the film version of *Gone Girl* (2014), which adheres to the main armature of the book and even retains the out-of-sync time lines after the midpoint revelation of Amy's fake diary.

Surely fans want some of the complexity and surprises of the books to be retained on the screen. But, again, novelty is needed. So for the movie, *The Girl on the Train* was given a bleak, deglamorized treatment suitable for a sordid story of alcoholism, anxiety, and female rivalry. In the hands of director Paul Feig, *A Simple Favor*, a straight novel of suspense, became an exercise in absurdity, with over-the-top costumes, sour humor, and preposterous but funny violence.

The film version of *Gone Girl* added another layer to the implications of the novel. Gillian Flynn's screenplay made a crucial alteration by starting with a close-up of Amy's alert face lying alongside the camera, accompanied by Nick's voice-over imagining opening up that skull to see what's inside. This prologue primes us to take Nick as a potential abuser, an impression reinforced in the plot's first half. At the end, however, Amy has been revealed as a monster and Nick is pinned down as her victim. In an epilogue repeating the first image of Amy staring dolefully out, we get Nick's voice-over again. "What have we done to each other? What will we do?" Perhaps more mayhem lies in the future? In any case, by providing this monologue, the film literally steals Amy's voice, deleting the novel's final line in which she claims the last word. Flynn has shrewdly given her fans another point of debate about gender power dynamics.

* * *

In the years after *Gone Girl*, the domestic suspense ecosystem teemed with offshoots and hybrids. There were some sports, nearly desperate pursuits of novelty. (One author showed false identities achieved through astral projection.)

Agents and editors were puzzled that the cycle was still in force.[26] With the explosive success of Finn's *The Woman in the Window*, it seemed clear that the market was not drying up. Said one editor, "This is women's fiction right now."[27]

In any variorum situation, competition grows keen. When Hitchcock came to Hollywood in the early 1940s, he made a string of successful thrillers. But soon he was being imitated left and right, so he had to surpass his imitators with something more offbeat. The results were the films *Lifeboat* (1944), *Spellbound* (1945), *Notorious* (1946), and *Rope* (1948). A comparable challenge faced Laura Lippman, who had done so much to establish the conventions of the new domestic thriller.

With *After I'm Gone* (2014), Lippman took on a family saga. This time the parallel story in the past isn't completely chronological. Three chapters are shifted out of order, the first as a tantalizing flash forward, and two others saved to fill a crucial gap. Accidents of teenage violence, always a lure for Lippman, recur in *Wilde Lake* (2016). Again, the chronology is slightly juggled before the past time line starts (and the heroine narrates *in utero*). With *Sunburn* (2018), Lippman moved away from domestic suspense and her double-entry time scheme, using a shifting viewpoint within a linear layout. This riff on a noir situation recasts the lethal femme fatale as a tough survivor of domestic violence and a mother plotting to protect her daughters. She followed with another effort at "repurposing the books that are beloved to me, trying to figure out how to further the conversations they began in my head."[28] *Lady in the Lake* (2019) paid homage to the hard-boiled tradition in its title but reverted to a multiple-viewpoint mystery structure and the possibility of a dead narrator—both tactics firmly in the 1940s tradition. *Dream Girl* (2021), a satiric tale of a bed-bound novelist, recast the situation of Stephen King's *Misery* (1987) but splintered it through scrambled flashbacks that yielded a satiric portrait of literary careerism.

Gillian Flynn pursued more diverse genre paths. She supplied a comic book script to Dave Gibbons, adapted a screenplay for a women's heist film (*Widows*, 2018), and prepared an American version of the British science-fiction television series *Utopia*. Always an aficionado of many media, and determined to create energetic female protagonists, she could afford to venture beyond a flourishing cycle she had helped create.

In that cycle, techniques I've tracked throughout this book are flagrantly on display. The dizzying matrix of formats shows how quickly one area of popular narrative can happily create its own variorum.

But those who decry popular culture, if there's anybody like that left, will argue that we see only formulaic recycling here. Like the crime novelists I examined in earlier chapters, writers of domestic suspense revise classic storytelling strategies. True, the skeptic might grant, there are some add-ons from literary modernism, such as unclaimed voices (eventually to be claimed) and stream of consciousness (but never disruptive to a Woolfian or Faulknerian degree). Still, the main lines—multiple narrators, time shifts, tagging and chaptering, twists, unreliable narration—can all be found in fiction a hundred years ago.

But this is in part my point. The history of popular narrative in the English-speaking world, and probably elsewhere, displays continuity and change, schema and revision. Difficulties must be balanced by clarity and redundancy. Teasing obscurities are usually illuminated. There is, however, room for refinement: new methods of clueing and misdirection, formal subterfuges playing on our presuppositions, stylistic innovations that turn common language multivalent. The case studies I've surveyed show that mass-culture storytellers have kept discovering fine-grained tactics that give us unfamiliar pleasures within a comfortably familiar frame. And those tactics aren't merely cosmetic; they fundamentally shape the experience we have of the story being told.

Another conclusion bears on the resourcefulness of audiences. They swiftly learn the rules of the game even while those rules are pushing into fresh territory. To understand the innovations, we need familiar landmarks. Just as important, many readers and viewers go beyond the minimal skills needed to keep up. They become connoisseurs sensitive to subtle alterations of well-worn forms. Once more, the "taste of the construction" that Trollope deplored in Collins's plots became a taste *for* construction, the trickier the better. Like audiences of earlier eras, who also encountered stories that posed pleasurably difficult challenges, fans have developed skills suited to the relentless, exhilarating churn of popular storytelling.

CONCLUSION

The Power of Limits

I had Following. *I had this movie that also had structural complexity that they could understand.*

—Christopher Nolan

W hen you have two or more stories to tell, *Intolerance* (1916) reminds us that you can arrange them in large blocks or alternate them. In this book, I took the block option, so it might be helpful to show how my two story lines could be crosscut.

In the early decades of the twentieth century, Anglo-American storytellers conducted experiments on both esoteric and exoteric platforms. Novelists, playwrights, and filmmakers became sensitive to techniques of plot patterning and narration. Nonlinear time schemes, variables of viewpoint, and strategic segmentation had all been utilized by earlier storytellers, but now there was a new self-consciousness and an urge to explore the capacity of these techniques. That awareness was spelled out in a poetics of fiction, articulated by critics and authors of manuals. Often the innovations were conducted under the aegis of comedy, as in *Seven Keys to Baldpate*, but not necessarily, as *Intolerance* shows.

At the same time, authors of mystery stories and plays became more self-conscious as well, conducting their own experiments and codifying best practices in their own guidebooks. How to perplex the reader while exposing the "hidden story"? How to assure both novelty and adherence to the rules that make the novelty stand out?

A sharper split between exoteric and esoteric storytelling appeared in the 1920s and 1930s. It was epitomized in High Modernism, which embraced the Ultraist idea of ceaseless revolution, maximal difficulty. These plots were perplexing at a different level than even Henry James and Joseph Conrad had dared. Now the perplexity lay as much in the how as in the what, the authorial "method" governing the very texture of the tale. What story is being told, and why is it told this way?

Meanwhile—to some extent under the influence of modernism but also relying on their genre tradition—authors of detective stories became a popular version of a modern literary movement. They raised their degree of artifice. The whodunit, always relying on a puzzle, ransacked the resources of viewpoint, linearity, and segmentation. Footnotes, diagrams, and tables of contents could be clues. Readers were invited to play behind the backs of the characters. What John Dickson Carr called the Greatest Game emphasized the "literariness" of mystery fiction. It was a new form of the reflexivity that had always been a tool of popular storytelling, but now it provided a mass-market parallel to the work of the avant-garde.

As Ultraism declined in the 1930s, "serious" writers and playwrights warmed to the idea of accessibility. There had long been crossover works—esoteric authors revising schemas from earlier literary traditions, popular storytellers revising and smoothing the difficult techniques on display in "high" literature. But with no modernist masterpieces emerging, the field was now clear for an explosion in popular storytelling fueled by wartime demands for entertainment and the rise of paperback publishing. During the 1940s, "prestige" fiction and drama developed models of crossover appeal comparable to ones already dominating cinema and radio. These efforts consolidated a vast variorum of strategies that future generations would revisit, revise, and refine.

In its own vein, mystery fiction did much the same. With principal subgenres well established, authors were able to update the menu of creative choices. There were blends (*Laura*'s anthologizing of whodunit, hard-boiled, and thriller), new stylistic refinements (Stout, Highsmith), and new plot options (the police procedural, the caper). Some authors pushed to delirious extremes, as in the examples of Cornell Woolrich and *The Red Right Hand*.

Perhaps most surprising, the classic whodunit also continued to provide creative options, and not just in the cozies that kept the English tradition alive. The whodunit's insistence on "the taste of the construction" could be imposed on private-eye adventures and woman-in-peril plots. Hard-boiled tales exploited time shuffling, viewpoint switches, and block construction. These strategies were especially evident in film noir, but they also appeared in novels, as in Richard Stark's Parker series. Domestic thrillers could recruit nonlinear story lines and multiple narrators (all potentially unreliable). The formal adroitness prized by the Golden Age authors became a hallmark of ambitious mysteries in adjacent genres for decades afterward. Christopher Nolan, who named the private yacht in *Dunkirk* after *The Moonstone*, remarks of his neo-noir: "I wrote *Memento* very much as a puzzle box. I was fascinated by the idea of structure."[1]

Narrational duplicity and misdirection—all the ellipses and grid layouts and unwarranted inferences—continue in the domestic thrillers and "puzzle films" of our day. Here the mystery may involve a crime, but it will also conjure up a metamystery about the way the story is told. The knowing reader or viewer should expect that the characters, the narrators, and the storyteller—that is, the plot structure and the filmic narration—may be willfully, playfully, misleading.

In my emphasis on recurring schemas, I don't mean to suggest an eternal return or simple recycling. We don't have to assume that 1940s viewers could fully understand *Inception* (2010). But, to recall Steven Johnson's point of departure, that doesn't make them dumb either. Today's viewers are heirs to a process of schema and revision through which Anglo-American popular storytellers constantly reinvigorated devices of viewpoint, time schemes, and segmentation. It would be possible to trace some larger tendencies—say, a tendency toward greater ellipsis, faster pace, more oblique presentation—that have governed the process. My point is that some principles have yielded arresting originality throughout the decades, and that testifies to the inexhaustible potential of basic choices of form and format.

None of us encountered all of these stories, but we each met enough of them to train us in their techniques. We tapped into the variorum at different points, but we all learned to cope with novelty in the hundreds of films and plays and novels on offer. Hence we could follow (to different degrees) films such as *Pulp Fiction* and appreciate how Tarantino's chaptering, viewpoint shifts, and looped time scheme created a fresh version of a tale of petty gangsters.

The glowing briefcase is the only mystery in *Pulp Fiction*, but through narrative artifice Tarantino creates a bigger one. The perplexity comes from asking how these stories connect, and the answer is very much in the spirit of ingenuity of Golden Age tales such as *And Then There Were None*. True, we have to do a bit more work than in Christie's case, but thanks to the variorum, we can manage. And the novices among us can learn. A generation of cinephiles and fanboys discovered complex storytelling by grappling with *Pulp Fiction*, possibly the coolest thing they'd ever seen.

Crossover Culture

When talking with friends about this book, I was often asked, "Where does postmodernism fit in?" The label has a specific meaning in certain arts, such as architecture, and for some purposes it's useful.[2] I'm less convinced by those macro-level accounts of the postmodern age as an era of late capitalism or as skepticism about grand narratives (while all too often presenting a grand narrative about . . . the emergence of postmodernism).

To answer my questions about narrative strategy and audience uptake, I think it's more fruitful to consider that works tagged as postmodernist offer idiosyncratic varieties of those amalgamations of classic, proto-modern, modern, and popular principles I've been trying to trace. Raymond Carver's minimalism builds on Stein, Hemingway, e. e. cummings, and others, while also providing cues to allow us to adjust to the story's idiosyncrasies. A PoMo narrative may have more recondite references than those provided as fan service by a superhero film, but it seems to me that the mixing and revising of inherited schemas remain. The postmodernist label may be useful in picking out conditions of production or reception, but in terms of form and style, we are usually best served by looking closely at the dynamic of perpetual, pluralistic recycling throughout the history of narrative. A great many works—*A Voice in the Dark, How Like a God,* and *The Woman in Question*—are quirky, offbeat, and largely forgotten. I think a more open, wide-ranging analytical approach does better justice to the churn of mass art.

That churn continues. No one needs convincing that popular storytelling pervades today's media landscape. Beyond plays, books, and films, thousands of stories are accessed through television, the internet, and streaming platforms. Radio dramas have been replaced by audiobooks and podcasts. Self-published novels, in print or digital forms, proliferate. So do fan fiction and websites such as Wattpad, which claims to have ninety million writers and readers. Beyond fiction, documentary books, films, and videos have been framed in narrative form. If "media literacy" means anything, it must include the deep grooves that repeated exposure to the variorum has carved into our minds.

The variorum of stories is now accompanied by a variorum offering craft advice and trade secrets. The self-consciousness about technique that emerged in writing manuals of the 1910s has persisted for a century and exploded with online writing and self-publishing. Amazon.com offers *How to Write a Novel That Will Sell Well and Satisfy Your Inner Artist, How to Write a Damn Good Novel, Write a Novel in a Year, The 24 Laws of Storytelling, Writing the Cozy Mystery, The 10-Day Screenplay, How to Write a Screenplay in 10 Weeks, How to Write a Screenplay That Doesn't Suck (and Will Actually Sell), How Not to Write a Novel,* and dozens more guides. The propulsion behind William Cook's Plotto and the Fiction Factory has not faded.

I've concentrated on Anglo-American traditions of mass storytelling because they're the ones I know best. I'm sure that a plunge into other national and cultural traditions would yield many differences. But from my exposure to Japanese, Chinese, and European popular culture, I'd expect that some principles would persist. We would find distinct versions of the variorum, of competition and churn, of scaling form to format, of ingenuity within limits, and of the basic techniques of segmentation, viewpoint, and chronology.[3] Narrative audacity and finesse have no boundaries.

Needless to say, this geyser of narrative has largely consisted of ordinary work. Raymond Chandler complained that the "average" detective story finds readers, whereas "you never see the average novel. It doesn't get published."[4] He was utterly wrong, as he could have discovered by scanning the paperbacks at the La Jolla bus terminal. Today any report of new publishing deals confirms the reassuring ordinariness of popular narrative. Here is one from May 2021: "A loosely autobiographical work of fiction about an American 20-something expat in London in a rollercoaster relationship with a charming, emotionally unavailable British man who cannot, will not love her back, and the dramatic repercussions on her mental health."[5]

Beyond the ordinary works are "literary fiction," prestige crossover items that draw on several of the traditions I've tried to illuminate. The he said/she said pattern of Dinah Craik's dossier novel *A Life for a Life* is transposed into two blocks in Carol Shield's *Happenstance: Two Novels in One About a Marriage in Transition* (1980). Like *Intolerance*, Barbara Kingsolver's *Unsheltered* (2018) alternates distinct historical epochs (but only two) in tracing lives lived in the same house. George Saunders's *Lincoln in the Bardo* (2017) splinters the cemetery-chorus schema of *Spoon River Anthology* and *Our Town* into scores of voices mourning the death of the president's son, the snippets quickened by horror and action-movie rescue attempts. Now that reverse chronology has become a minor option in the variorum, we can appreciate the different handling it receives in Pinter's *Betrayal* (1980), Sondheim's *Merrily We Roll Along* (1981), *Memento* (2000), and the film *Shimmer Lake* (2017). Given a network narrative, how can you stitch your characters together beyond the usual ties of friendship, kinship, crime, and convenient traffic accidents? How about binding their stories through their association with trees? You might even assign some narrative authority to trees and develop the whole through omniscient viewpoint, fragmentary segmentation, chapters tagged with character names, and (yes) judicious switches to italics. That is, Richard Powers's prizewinning novel *The Overstory* (2018).

The lure of mystery continues to shape popular storytelling, and most innovative creative choices induct us into fresh story worlds. The process is evident in the rise of regional mysteries; every town in the United States and in the United Kingdom seems to have its own local sleuth. Police procedure dominates the endless British television serials devoted to this or that remote village. Offbeat graphic novels have often relied on investigation plots, as in the work of Charles Burns and Daniel Clowes. Hard-boiled fiction, traditionally dominated by white male heroes, has proved amenable to other protagonists, such as women (Kinsey Millhone, V. I. Warshawski, and Tess Monaghan) and members of minorities (Easy Rawlins, Joe Leaphorn, Dave Brandstetter, and Lauren Lourano). Innovations in structure and style continue as revisions of long-standing schemas, which I've indicated in the tailpieces to some chapters. Schemas of hard-boiled fiction are recast in the episodic, telegraphic style of Lee Child's Jack Reacher novels and in the bebop narration and multiple story lines of James Ellroy. When a domestic thriller can be titled *It's Always the Husband* and one of the best crime writers can include, in a scene of high tension, the sentence "Let's take the back door, he suggested, in such a smooth undertone it barely required speech marks," the tradition of surprising ingenuity is in good shape.[6]

And mystery still provides a powerful menu of options for storytellers who want to make a more unusual work accessible. Colson Whitehead's social-network novel *Harlem Shuffle* (2021) unfolds as a heist, then an underworld revenge scheme, and finally a man-on-the-run situation. Each block corresponds to one influence that Whitehead acknowledged: Richard Stark, Elmore Leonard, and Patricia Highsmith.[7] The legacy of Golden Age artifice can be found in those current novels and plays that seek to turn any narrative into a game and a puzzle, as *Citizen Kane* and *Letter to Five Wives* did in the 1940s. Susanna Clarke's *Piranesi* (2020), for example, uses an investigation plot to move through parallel worlds, leading to the revelation of a crime. A Broadway producer mounting "avant-garde plays" is attracted to thrillers as experiments in narrative, dramas that "jump around in chronology or mess with point of view." The formal strategies fulfill, he says, "an appetite that has long existed" in independent film and Peak TV.[8] That appetite, as *A Voice in the Dark* reminds us, has been around longer than that.

Today we're unlikely to run into a pure instance of the easiest narrative: that linear, single-viewpoint, reliably recounted, neatly segmented story that I set up as a default in the introduction. Granted, extremely popular fiction sagas such as *The Lord of the Rings* and the Harry Potter series largely adhere to the norms of the nineteenth-century novel. Philip Pullman, author of the *His Dark Materials* trilogy (1995–2000), urges writers not to complicate their stories "by using a first-person stream of consciousness, or a number of differently situated narrators, . . . [or] . . . by making those narrators unreliable, their knowledge partial, their different agendas out there conflicting in the text. . . . So tempting. But *resist* it."[9]

Pullman's effort to defend classic technique suggests that what he's arguing against is all too common. The most banal paperback best-seller is likely to exhibit at least some of the roundabout strategies running through modern storytelling. If mystery stories were early adopters of unusual storytelling devices, now all genres use them. Stephen King's excursions into horror and fantasy are an anthology of experimental possibilities, not least the parallel-worlds novels *Desperation* (1996) and *The Regulators* (1996). Science fiction, rising to greater respectability after World War II, freely explored manipulations of viewpoint, linearity, and segmentation. The results can be pretty strange. The film *Source Code* (2011) posits technology that sends thoughts from one man to another, but it makes both characters identical on-screen, as if the sender has taken over the recipient's body as well as his mind. And both comedy and psychological subjectivity in any genre justify narrative innovations, as in *Groundhog Day* (1993) and *The Father* (2020).

Once these strategies saturate popular storytelling, our prior experience, aided by each work's design features, helps us grasp new stories we encounter. Our versatility with the variorum enables us to pick the right expectations to apply, while also appreciating what is fresh in this experience. Once we've adjusted to an intrinsic norm, the story's form and style can efface themselves and make "content" stand out. But if we're interested in the fine grain of craft, the "spectacle of skill," it's often worth pausing over technical choices and the adroitness with which they're managed.

It may be, in fact, that popular storytelling, taken in bulk, has left its most lasting legacy in training us in skills of comprehension. An astonishing number of the exoteric stories we encounter are easily forgotten, even those we quite enjoyed in the moment. I may not be the only fan who pauses before the paperback rack and wonders, "Have I read this one?" It's not just advancing age that makes me ask if I've seen that movie before. My ability to mistrust a narrator, note disparities of dates, pick up on cues of behavior, rush breathlessly through crosscut lines of action, and try to guess the twist is more enduring than the memory of this or that character or line of dialogue. The storytellers I've surveyed in part 3 are, for me, exceptions; they did more than sharpen my skills of pickup. I hope my little-known examples have shown that even mediocre work can give our story sense a decent workout, and that's no small thing. Once we've acquired the taste of the construction, a delight in language, stagecraft, or cinematic technique comes along as a bonus.

✳ ✳ ✳

Critics have long spoken of "experimental" writing, usually as a way of signaling that an avant-gardist has boldly pushed into unknown regions.[10] But throughout my argument I've followed more recent precedent in assuming that popular narrative can sponsor its own research projects. After all, a scientific experiment is an attempt to test specific hypotheses under constrained conditions. If you vary certain parameters, you can watch what happens. The results can suggest further adjustments in the constants and the variables, and perhaps a revision of the hypotheses.

Something like this seems to happen in innovative exoteric art. Genres, conditions of production and reception, and other traditions provide the constraints. Techniques of the sort I've considered can be held constant or varied, pressured by competition and the demand for novelty or virtuosity. Start with a standard whodunit but make the Watson figure the culprit. Start with a missing statuette and decline to describe any character's inner states. Start with a wife targeted for murder and follow her viewpoint as she comes to realize her peril. Start with casual encounters among petty criminals—hitmen, a prizefighter, a gang boss—and see what happens to the viewer's experience if you simply pull bits of action out of order. Start with a missing-person investigation plot and present it wholly through text messages, Google searches, news clips, and FaceTime sessions, as the film *Searching* (2018) does. Every decision triggers a cascade of problems of clarity and impact and implication, each demanding further adjustment.

As consumers of narrative, we ought to appreciate what these experiments reveal. Constraints can foster originality. Basic storytelling techniques seem at once recognizable and inexhaustible. Over more than a hundred years, fresh uses of familiar strategies can still captivate and move us. Not all stories are experiments, and not all satisfy us; but enough are and do to keep us marveling at how resourceful humans are in devising narrative experiences that we can't wholly predict.

When Sondheim described Oscar Hammerstein II as an experimenter, he wasn't exaggerating. Popular storytelling is, within self-imposed limits, an adventure in testing how artistic form and style can expand an art form and affect an audience. We often find that those limits are not so limiting.

NOTES

Introduction: Mass Art as Experimental Storytelling

1. On the "new complexity" in film narrative, see Allan Cameron, *Modular Narratives in Contemporary Cinema* (London: Palgrave Macmillan, 2008); Warren Buckland, ed., *Puzzle Films: Complex Storytelling in Contemporary Cinema* (London: Wiley-Blackwell, 2009); Warren Buckland, ed., *Hollywood Puzzle Films* (New York: Routledge, 2014); Miklós Kiss and Steven Willemsen, *Impossible Puzzle Films: A Cognitive Approach to Contemporary Complex Cinema* (Edinburgh: Edinburgh University Press, 2018). See also Jason Mittell, *Complex TV: The Poetics of Contemporary Television Storytelling* (New York: New York University Press, 2015).
2. Linda Aronson, *The 21st Century Screenplay: A Comprehensive Guide to Writing Tomorrow's Films* (Los Angeles: Silman-James, 2010).
3. David Bordwell, *The Way Hollywood Tells It: Story and Style in Modern Movies* (Berkeley: University of California Press, 2006), chaps. 2 and 3.
4. David Bordwell, *Reinventing Hollywood: How 1940s Filmmakers Changed Movie Storytelling* (Chicago: University of Chicago Press, 2017).
5. Noël Carroll, *A Philosophy of Mass Art* (Oxford: Clarendon, 1998), chap. 3.
6. J. B. Priestley as quoted in John Baxendale, "Priestley and the Highbrows," in *Middlebrow Literary Culture: The Battle of the Brows, 1920–1960*, ed. Erica Brown and Mary Grover (New York: Palgrave Macmillan, 2011), 77.
7. Unsigned review, *Saturday Review* (August 25, 1860) in *Wilkie Collins: The Critical Heritage*, ed. Norman Page (London: Routledge and Kegan Paul, 1974), 83.
8. Naomi Royde Smith, *All Star Cast* (New York: Macmillan, 1936), book jacket.
9. Lisa Jaillant notes: "The term middlebrow referred perhaps more clearly to mass-market venues and middle-class audiences than to formal characteristics of literary style." Lisa Jaillant, *Modernism, Middlebrow, and the Literary Canon: The Modern Library Series, 1917–1955* (Milton Park, UK: Routledge, 2016), 5.

10. Nicola Humble, *The Feminine Middlebrow Novel, 1920s to 1950s* (New York: Oxford University Press, 2004), 13–15.

11. See Jaillant, *Modernism, Middlebrow, and the Literary Canon*; Joan Shelley Rubin, *The Making of Middlebrow Culture* (Chapel Hill: University of North Carolina Press, 1992); Janice Radaway, *A Feeling for Books: The Book-of-the-Month Club, Literary Taste, and Middle-Class Desire*, rev. ed. (Chapel Hill: University of North Carolina Press, 1999); and essays gathered in Erica Brown and Mary Grover, eds., *Middlebrow Literary Culture: The Battle of the Brows, 1920–1960* (New York: Palgrave Macmillan, 2011).

12. Carroll, *Philosophy of Mass Art*, 47.

13. Ludwig Wittgenstein, *Philosophical Investigations*, 4th ed., ed. Joachim Schulte and P. M. S. Hacker (London: Wiley-Blackwell, 2009), section 66, 36e.

14. Meir Sternberg, *Expositional Modes and Temporal Ordering in Fiction* (Baltimore, MD: Johns Hopkins University Press, 1978), especially chaps. 4 and 5.

15. The history of popular narrative includes many forms that will seem ungainly to us alongside those recognizable as prototypes of our most common schemas. The literature on these is vast, so I will simply signal a few instances concerned just with the Western tradition: N. J. Lowe, *The Classical Plot and the Invention of Western Narrative* (Cambridge: Cambridge University Press, 2000); Margaret Anne Doody, *The True Story of the Novel* (New Brunswick, NJ: Rutgers, 1996); William W. Ryding, *Structure in Medieval Narrative* (The Hague: Mouton De Gruyter, 1971); Ian Watt, *The Rise of the Novel: Studies in Defoe, Richardson, and Fielding* (Berkeley: University of California Press, 2001). A broad global survey is Franco Moretti's two-volume compendium, Franco Moretti, *The Novel* (Princeton, NJ: Princeton University Press, 2006). Many of these studies indicate that choices about parameters of linearity, viewpoint, and segmentation remain pertinent to story-making across periods and cultures.

    More specifically, my ideal type is a good background norm for the period and the public I'm interested in here. See Jean Matter Mandler, *Stories, Scripts, and Scenes: Aspects of Schema Theory* (Hilldale, NJ: Erlbaum, 1984); and Alyssa McCabe and Carole Peterson, eds., *Developing Narrative Structure* (Hilldale, NJ: Erlbaum, 1991). See also Patrick Hogan, *The Mind and Its Stories: Narrative Universals and Human Emotions* (Cambridge: Cambridge University Press, 2003); and the *Literary Universals* website, https://literary-universals.uconn.edu.

16. Todd Berliner has suggested that most mainstream films pose at least mild cognitive challenges, ones that viewers enjoy overcoming. Todd Berliner, *Hollywood Aesthetic: Pleasure in American Cinema* (New York: Oxford University Press, 2017), chap. 1.

17. In what follows, I treat narration broadly as the patterned presentation of story information, concentrating on viewpoint techniques. For many theorists of narrative, narration also entails the voice of a narrator, a more or less personified agency recounting the tale. My own view is that novels, films, and other media do employ character narrators, such as Huckleberry Finn, as well as clearly delineated noncharacter narrators, such as the voice-over commentary in a documentary film. Otherwise, I treat narration as a general process in both verbal and nonverbal media, without assigning this or that passage to a distinct agent. I make a case for this position in David Bordwell, "Three Dimensions of Film Narrative," chap. 3 in *Poetics of Cinema* (New York: Routledge, 2008), 121–33.

18. Theorists of narrative have written extensively on manipulations of chronology and viewpoint, but matters of segmentation are often taken for granted. An exception is Sternberg, *Expositional Modes and Temporal Ordering*, 172–76. We notice how much we rely on paragraphing and other gaps on the page only when we encounter the unbroken

stretches in Faulkner's *Absalom, Absalom!* (1936) or the limit case of László Krasznahorkai's *Satantango* (1985), in which an entire chapter may consist of a single long sentence. Similarly, a film's division into scenes and sequences, like a play's division into scenes and acts, is crucial to our story comprehension.

19. See Robert Hughes, *Culture of Complaint: The Fraying of America* (New York: Oxford University Press, 1993), 110. A thorough account of the history of Pound's formulation is found in Michael North, "The Making of 'Make It New,'" *Guernica* August 15, 2013, https://www.guernicamag.com/the-making-of-making-it-new/. North proposes that Pound's conception of artistic innovation acknowledges "its debt, even as revolution, to the past, and the way in which new works are often just recombinations of traditional elements."

20. "An Exclusive Interview with Mary Higgins Clark: The 'Queen of Suspense' Talks About Her Life and Work," in *Loves Music, Loves to Dance*, by Mary Higgins Clark (New York: Pocket, 1991), n.p.

21. Steven Johnson, *Everything Bad Is Good for You: How Today's Popular Culture Is Actually Making Us Smarter* (New York: Riverhead, 2005).

22. Clayton Hamilton, "Building a Play Backward," *The Bookman* 38 (February 1914): 605–14.

23. See Carol Clover, *The Medieval Saga* (Ithaca, NY: Cornell University Press, 1982). Cf. Johnson, *Everything Bad*, 125–28. See also Richard C. West, "The Interlace Structure of *The Lord of the Rings*," in *A Tolkien Compass*, ed. Jared Lobdell, (LaSalle, IL: Open Court, 1975), 77–94.

24. Christopher Nolan as quoted in Tom Shone, *The Nolan Variations: The Movies, Mysteries, and Marvels of Christopher Nolan* (New York: Knopf, 2020), 76.

25. Charles Rosen, *The Classical Style: Haydn, Mozart, Beethoven* (New York: Norton, 1972), 71.

26. Ernst H. Gombrich, *Art and Illusion: A Study in the Psychology of Pictorial Representation* (Princeton, NJ: Princeton University Press, 1972), 168–74, 183–91.

27. On story schemas in scripture, see Robert Alter, *The Art of Biblical Narrative* (New York: Basic Books), 96–98. On folktale structures, see Axel Olrik, "Epic Laws of Folk Narrative," in *International Folkloristics: Classic Contributions by the Founders of Folklore*, ed. Alan Dundes (Lanham, MD: Rowman and Littlefield, 1999), 83–97.

28. For a more extensive discussion of schemas in the study of film history, see David Bordwell, *On the History of Film Style*, 2nd ed. (Madison, WI: Irvington Way, 2018), 151–54.

29. For a thorough consideration of basic story types, see Hogan, *The Mind and Its Stories*.

30. I consider the screenwriting vogue for Joseph Campbell's myth-oriented Hero's Journey in Bordwell, *The Way Hollywood Tells It*, 33–34.

31. For further discussion, see David Bordwell, "Pulverizing Plots: Into the Woods with Sondheim, Shklovsky, and David O. Russell," *David Bordwell's Website on Cinema* (blog), http://www.davidbordwell.net/blog/2014/03/03/pulverizing-plots-into-the-woods -with-sondheim-shklovsky-and-david-o-russell/.

32. Christopher Nolan as quoted in Shone, *Nolan Variations*, 120.

33. Harold Wentworth and Stuart Berg Flexner, *Dictionary of American Slang*, 2nd suppl. ed. (New York: Crowell, 1975), s.v. "switch," 534. See also H. T. Webster, "They Don't Speak Our Language," *Forum and Century* 90, no. 6 (December 1933): 372.

34. Stanley Cortez as quoted in Doug McClelland, *Forties Film Talk: Oral Histories of Hollywood* (Jefferson, NC: McFarland, 1992), 254.

35. Discussions of the first and last of these films can be found in David Bordwell, "Grandmaster Flashback," *David Bordwell's Website on Cinema* (blog), http://www.davidbordwell.net/blog/2009/01/27/grandmaster-flashback/; and David Bordwell, "What-If Movies: Forking Paths in the Drawing Room," *David Bordwell's Website on Cinema* (blog), http://www.davidbordwell.net/blog/2014/11/23/what-if-movies-forking-paths-in-the-drawing-room/.

36. Jean-Claude Carrière, *The Secret Language of Film*, trans. Jeremy Leggatt (New York: Pantheon, 1994), 15.

37. I develop the concept of intrinsic stylistic norms at greater length in David Bordwell, *Narration in the Fiction Film* (Madison: University of Wisconsin Press, 1985), chap. 4 and thereafter.

38. James Joyce letter of June 24, 1921, as quoted in Richard Ellmann, *James Joyce*, rev. ed. (New York: Oxford University Press, 1982), 512.

39. See Robert J. Ray, *The Weekend Novelist* (New York: Dell, 1994), 140–46; James Scott Dell, *Plot and Structure* (Cincinnati, OH: Writer's Digest, 2004), 23–34. I discuss this template in Bordwell, *The Way Hollywood Tells It*, 27–33.

40. Nöel Carroll suggests that many mainstream films aim to dramatize homilies, a process that becomes a significant way social and political ideologies are reinforced. Nöel Carroll, "Film, Rhetoric, and Ideology," chap. 18 in *Theorizing the Moving Image* (Cambridge: Cambridge University Press, 1996), 275–89.

41. Ben Hecht as quoted in Philip K. Scheuer, "A Town Called Hollywood," *Los Angeles Times*, June 30, 1940.

42. John Dickson Carr, "The Grandest Game in the World," in *The Door to Doom and Other Detections*, 2nd ed., ed. Douglas G. Greene (New York: International Polygonics, 1991), 310.

43. Dana Polan notes the opening's T-shirt hint in Dana Polan, *Pulp Fiction* (London: British Film Institute, 2000), 33.

44. Ted Elliott as quoted in Jeff Goldsmith, "The Craft of Writing the Tentpole Movie," *Creative Screenwriting* 11, no. 3 (May/June 2004): 53.

45. The original novel, minus two wives, became the 1948 film *Letter to Three Wives*, based on the same mystery premise.

46. Further explanation of my angle of approach is available in David Bordwell, *Poetics of Cinema* (New York: Routledge, 2008), chap. 1; and more informally in David Bordwell, "Zip, Zero, Zeitgeist," *David Bordwell's Website on Cinema* (blog), http://www.davidbordwell.net/blog/2014/08/24/zip-zero-zeitgeist/; and David Bordwell, "Hunting Deplorables, Gathering Themes," *David Bordwell's Website on Cinema* (blog), http://www.davidbordwell.net/blog/2020/04/09/hunting-deplorables-gathering-themes/.

47. Howard Haycraft, *Murder for Pleasure: The Life and Times of the Detective Story* (New York: Appleton-Century, 1941); Julian Symons, *Mortal Consequences: A History from the Detective Story to the Crime Novel* (New York: Harper and Row, 1972); Martin Edwards, *The Story of Classic Crime in 100 Books* (London: British Library, 2017); and Martin Edwards, *The Life of Crime: Detecting the History of Mysteries and Their Creators* (New York: HarperCollins, 2022). The many specialized monographs by LeRoy Lad Panek are also informative and original; a useful summary of his ideas can be found in LeRoy Lad Panek, *An Introduction to the Detective Story* (Bowling Green, OH: Bowling Green State University Popular Press, 1987).

48. Three useful critical surveys are Martin Priestman, ed., *The Cambridge Companion to Crime Fiction* (Cambridge: Cambridge University Press, 2003); Catherine Ross Nickerson, ed., *The Cambridge Companion to American Crime Fiction* (Cambridge:

Cambridge University Press, 2010); and Alfred Bendixon and Olivia Carr Edenfield, eds., *The Centrality of Crime Fiction in American Literary Culture* (New York: Routledge, 2017). The Palgrave Macmillan's series Crime Files offers in-depth monographs on many specific topics.

49. Mystery writers have not been shy about sharing their "practical poetics." The chapters that follow owe a good deal to Marie F. Rodell, *Mystery Fiction: Theory and Technique* (New York: Duell, Sloan and Pearce, 1943); A. S. Burack, ed., *Writing Detective and Mystery Fiction* (Boston: The Writer, 1945); Howard Haycraft, ed., *The Art of the Mystery Story* (New York: Simon & Schuster, 1946); Lawrence Treat, ed., *The Mystery Writer's Handbook* (New York: Harper, 1956); Herbert Brean, ed., *The Mystery Writer's Handbook*, rev. ed. (Cincinnati, OH: Writer's Digest, 1976); Martin Edwards, ed., *Howdunit: A Masterclass in Crime Writing by Members of the Detection Club* (London: Collins, 2020); and Lee Child (with Laurie R. King), ed., *How to Write a Mystery: A Handbook from Mystery Writers of America* (New York: Scribners, 2021). There are too many informative anthologies of critical writing on the genre to list here, but I should single out Francis M. Nevins, ed., *The Mystery Writer's Art* (Bowling Green, OH: Bowling Green State University Popular Press, 1970); and Bernard Benstock, ed., *Art in Crime Writing: Essays on Detective Fiction* (New York: St. Martin's, 1983). Works bearing on particular points are cited in later chapters.

1. The Art Novel Meets 1910s Formalism

1. For a review of the Goldwyn film, see "Stage Play Given Interesting Screen Presentation," *Wid's Daily*, June 12, 1921.
2. Ralph E. Dyar, "The Novelty in This Play," *A Voice in the Dark: A Play in Prologue and Three Acts*, Acting Version, unpublished manuscript, University of Oregon Special Collections, Collection no. Ax 255, n.p.
3. Ralph E. Dyar, *A Voice in the Dark: A Play in Prologue and Three Acts*, Acting Version, unpublished manuscript, University of Oregon Special Collections, Collection no. Ax 255, 3–22.
4. E. Clark, " 'Coat-Tales' Opens the New Season," *New York Times*, August 7, 1916.
5. "Novelty in Drama, 'Voice in the Dark,'" *New York Times*, July 29, 1919.
6. On American magazine serialization at this period, see Richard Ohmann, "Diverging Paths: Books and Magazines in the Transition to Corporate Capitalism," in *A History of the Book in America*, vol. 4, *Print in Motion: The Expansion of Publishing in the United States, 1880–1940*, ed. Carl F. Kaestle and Janice A. Radway (Chapel Hill: University of North Carolina Press, 2009), 102–15.
7. John Tebbel, *Between Covers: The Rise and Transformation of American Publishing* (New York: Oxford University Press, 1987), 179.
8. Henry James, "The Future of the Novel," in *Literary Criticism*, vol. 1, *Essays on Literature, American Writers, English Writers* (New York: Library of America, 1984), 100–101.
9. Henry James, *Selected Letters*, ed. Leon Edel (Cambridge, MA: Harvard University Press, 1987), 385.
10. Henry James, "*Far from the Madding Crowd*," in *Literary Criticism*, vol. 1, *Essays on Literature, American Writers, English Writers* (New York: Library of America, 1984), 1045. Hardy's book was originally published in two, not three volumes, but did run to some 900 pages, a common triple-decker length. See Guinevere L. Griest, *Mudie's Circulating Library and the Victorian Novel* (Bloomington: Indiana University Press, 1970), 118.

11. Henry James, "*Middlemarch: A Study of Provincial Life*," in *Literary Criticism*, vol. 1, *Essays on Literature, American Writers, English Writers* (New York: Library of America, 1984), 958; Henry James, "The New Novel," in *Literary Criticism*, vol. 1, *Essays on Literature, American Writers, English Writers* (New York: Library of America, 1984), 136.

12. Henry James, "The Tragic Muse," in *Literary Criticism*, vol. 2, *French Writers, Other European Writers, The Prefaces to the New York Edition* (New York: Library of America, 1984), 1107.

13. Greist, *Mudie's Circulating Library*, 108.

14. See Elizabeth MacAndrew, *The Gothic Tradition in Fiction* (New York: Columbia University Press, 1979).

15. For a wide-ranging survey, see Andrew Maugham, ed., *The Cambridge Companion to Sensation Fiction* (Cambridge: Cambridge University Press, 2013).

16. Collins revised schemas from many sources, including *Wuthering Heights* (1847) and a novella he wrote with Dickens and others, *The Wreck of the Golden Mary* (1856). See John Sutherland, introduction to *The Woman in White*, by Wilkie Collins (New York: Oxford, 2008), xv–xvi.

17. Anonymous review of "*The Woman in White*," *Saturday Review*, August 25, 1860, in *Wilkie Collins: The Critical Heritage*, ed. Norman Page (London: Routledge and Kegan Paul, 1974), 249–50.

18. Anthony Trollope, "The Unpalatable Taste of the Construction," (1883), in *Wilkie Collins: The Critical Heritage*, ed. Norman Page (London: Routledge and Kegan Paul, 1974), 223.

19. Henry James, "Mary Elizabeth Braddon," in *Literary Criticism*, vol. 1, *Essays on Literature, American Writers, English Writers* (New York: Library of America, 1984), 742, 743.

20. Henry James, "The Novels of George Eliot," in *Literary Criticism*, vol. 2, *French Writers, Other European Writers, The Prefaces to the New York Edition* (New York: Library of America, 1984), 912.

21. Henry James, "*Daisy Miller*" et al., in *Literary Criticism*, vol. 2, *French Writers, Other European Writers, The Prefaces to the New York Edition* (New York: Library of America, 1984), 1269.

22. James Joyce, *A Portrait of the Artist as a Young Man*, ed. John Paul Riqueline (New York: Norton, 2007), 189.

23. Henry James, "In the Cage," *The Complete Tales of Henry James. Vol. 10, From 1898 to1899*, ed. Leon Edel (New York: Lippincott, 1964), 198.

24. Jacques Barzun, "Henry James the Melodramatist," in *The Energies of Art: Studies of Authors Classic and Modern* (New York: Harper, 1956), 233.

25. Joseph Warren Beach, *The Method of Henry James* (1918), rev. ed. (Philadelphia: Saifer, 1954), 33–34; Henry James, "The Wings of the Dove," in *Literary Criticism*, Vol. 2, *French Writers, Other European Writers, The Prefaces to the New York Edition* (New York: Library of America, 1984), 1299.

26. Henry James, "*The Awkward Age*," in *Literary Criticism*, Vol. 2, *French Writers, Other European Writers, The Prefaces to the New York Edition* (New York: Library of America, 1984), 1131.

27. James, "*Wings of the Dove*," 1294.

28. Joseph Warren Beach, *The Twentieth Century Novel* (New York: Appleton Century Crofts, 1932), 8.

29. Henry James, *The Complete Notebooks of Henry James*, ed. Leon Edel and Lyall H. Powers (New York: Oxford University Press 1987), 11.

30. T. S. Eliot suggested that Collins was the principal influence on the "dramatic method" Dickens employed in his later novels. See Wilkie Collins, "Introduction to *The Moonstone*," In *The Complete Prose of T. S. Eliot: The Critical Edition: Literature, Politics, Belief, 1927–1929*, ed. Frances Dickey, Jennifer Formicelli, and Ronald Schuchard (Baltimore, MD: Johns Hopkins University Press, 2015), 357–60.

31. Joseph Conrad, "*The Nigger of the Narcissus*," preface to *Great Short Works of Joseph Conrad* (New York: Harper 1966), 23.

32. Joseph Conrad, *Victory* (New York: Doubleday, 1915), 204.

33. The passage is analyzed in Beach, *Twentieth-Century Novel*, 346–47.

34. Joseph Conrad, *Lord Jim*, ed. Thomas C. Moser (New York: Norton, 1968), 49.

35. A helpful summary of the temporal manipulations is offered in Robert N. Hudspeth, "Conrad's Use of Time in *Chance*," *Nineteenth-Century Fiction* 21, no. 3 (December 1966): 283–89.

36. C. E. Montagu, *Manchester Guardian* (review), January 11, 1914, in *Joseph Conrad: The Critical Heritage*, ed. Norman Sherry (London: Routledge, 1973), 274.

37. Arthur T. Quiller-Couch, "Four Tales by Mr. Conrad," *The Bookman* (June 1903), in *Joseph Conrad: The Critical Heritage*, ed. Norman Sherry (London: Routledge, 1973), 156.

38. George P. Lathrop, "Growth of the Novel," *Atlantic Monthly* 33 (June 1874): 684–97.

39. See Brander Matthews, *Aspects of Fiction and Other Ventures in Criticism* (New York: Harper, 1896). Beach's *The Method of Henry James* and Richard Curle's *Joseph Conrad: A Study* (Garden City, NY: Doubleday Page, 1914) are examples of emerging analysis of the novelists' characteristic technical choices.

40. George P. Lathrop, "The Novel and Its Future," *Atlantic Monthly* 34 (September 1874): 314.

41. See, for example, Clayton Hamilton, *Materials and Methods of Fiction* (New York: Doubleday Doran, 1908), 118–30.

42. Walter B. Pitkin, *The Art and Business of Story Writing* (New York: Macmillan, 1913), 176.

43. See Mary Eleanor Roberts, "The Single View-Point," *The Photoplay Author and Writer's Monthly* 5, no. 5 (May 1915): 140–41.

44. See Hamilton, *Materials and Methods*, 134–38; J. Berg Esenwein, *Writing the Short-Story: A Practical Handbook on the Rise, Structure, Writing, and Sale of the Modern Short Story* (New York: Hinds, Noble and Eldridge, 1909), 121–22.

45. Blanche Colton Williams, *A Handbook of Story Writing* (New York: Dodd, Mead, 1917), 98.

46. Polti provides continuous inspiration for filmmakers, as indicated by Mike Figgis, *The Thirty-Six Situations* (London: Faber, 2017).

47. An overview of Clayton Hamilton's career is provided in Frederick J. Hunter, "The Technical Criticism of Clayton Hamilton," *Educational Theatre Journal* 7, no. 4 (December 1955): 285–93.

48. Clayton Hamilton, *A Manual on the Art of Fiction, Prepared for the Use of Schools and Colleges* (Garden City, NY: Doubleday, Page, 1918), 120.

49. Hamilton, *Materials and Methods*, 127–29.

50. Clayton Hamilton, "Building a Play Backward," *The Bookman* (February 1914): 605–14.

51. This development in England is surveyed in John Russell Taylor, *The Rise and Fall of the Well-Made Play* (New York: Hill and Wang, 1967).

52. Jack Poggi, *Theater in America: The Impact of Economic Forces 1870–1967* (Ithaca, NY: Cornell University Press, 1968), 47–48.

53. Gustav Freytag, *Technique of the Drama: An Exposition of Dramatic Composition and Art*, 2nd ed., trans. Elias J. MacEwan (Chicago: Griggs, 1896), 114–40.

54. Elisabeth Woodbridge, *The Drama: Its Law and Its Technique* (Boston: Allyn and Bacon, 1898), v–x; Clayton Hamilton, *Studies in Stagecraft* (New York: Holt, 1914), 94–95.

55. Charlton Andrews, *The Technique of Play Writing* (Springfield, MA: Home Correspondence School, 1915), 106–9.

56. Hamilton, *Materials and Methods*, 66.

57. See George Pierce Baker, *Dramatic Technique* (Boston: Houghton Mifflin, 1919), 194, 211, 215; and Andrews, *The Technique of Play Writing*, 108.

58. "Collaborating on a Play Is a Ticklish Business," *New York Times*, November 22, 1914.

59. Poggi, *Theatre in America*, 30–31. For a compact overview of the American film industry's cultural role during the period, see Charlie Keil, "The Movies: The Transitional Era," in *American Literature in Transition 1910–1920*, ed. Mark W. Van Wienen (Cambridge: Cambridge University Press, 2018), 312–27.

60. Terry Bailey, "Normatizing the Silent Drama: Photoplay Manuals of the 1910s and Early 1920s," *Journal of Screenwriting* 5, no. 2 (June 2014): 209–24; Steven Maras, *Screenwriting: History, Theory, and Practice* (London: Wallflower, 2009); Stephen Curran, *Early Screenwriting Teachers 1910–1922: Origins, Contribution and Legacy* (London: AEC, 2019).

61. I review these developments in the online lecture, David Bordwell, "How Motion Pictures Became the Movies," *David Bordwell's Website on Cinema* (blog), http://www.davidbordwell.net/blog/2013/01/12/what-next-a-video-lecture-i-suppose-well-actually-yeah/. See also Charlie Keil, *Early American Cinema in Transition: Story, Style, and Filmmaking, 1907–1913* (Madison: University of Wisconsin Press, 2001); David Bordwell, *On the History of Film Style*, 2nd ed. (Madison, WI: Irvington Way Institute, 2018), chap. 6; and David Bordwell, *Figures Traced in Light: On Cinematic Staging* (Berkeley: University of California Press, 2005), chap. 2.

62. Crosscutting was also sometimes called "the switch-back" or, more confusingly, the "cut-back." Both could refer to a shift in either space or temporal order. See Edward Mott Woolley, "The Story of D. W. Griffith, the $100,000 Salary Man of the Movies," *McClure's*, September 1914, 116.

  Alternation of story lines was well-established in literature, from *The Odyssey* to the triple-decker, and historians of theater have disclosed "parallel editing" techniques in late nineteenth-century stage spectacles. See A. Nicolas Vardac, *Stage to Screen: Theatrical Method from Garrick to Griffith* (Cambridge, MA: Harvard University Press, 1949); and John L. Fell, *Film and the Narrative Tradition* (Norman: University of Oklahoma Press, 1974). For a broader analysis, see Ben Brewster and Lea Jacobs, *Theatre to Cinema: Stage Pictorialism and the Early Feature Film* (Oxford: Oxford University Press, 1997).

63. See Kristin Thompson "From Primitive to Classical," in *The Classical Hollywood Cinema: Film Style and Mode of Production to 1960*, by David Bordwell, Janet Staiger, and Kristin Thompson (London: Routledge, 1985), 160, 217.

64. See Kristin Thompson, "The International Exploration of Cinematic Expressivity," in *Film and the First World War*, ed. Karel Dibbets and Bert Hogenkamp (Amsterdam: Amsterdam University Press, 1995), 65–85.

65. Julian Johnson, "The Shadow Stage," *Photoplay Magazine* 2, no. 1 (December 1916): 77.

66. There are some variations among surviving copies of the film, and no one version contains all the footage found in others. I base my analysis on the circulating Museum of Modern Art 16mm print and video versions distributed on disc by Image, Kino Video, and Cohen Film Collection. I have focused on items common to these editions.

The intricate history of the film's versions is traced in Russell Merritt, "D. W. Grif fith's *Intolerance*: Reconstructing an Unattainable Text," *Film History* 4, no. 4 (1990): 337 75. Good overviews are available in William C. Drew, *D. W. Griffith's Intolerance: Its Genesis and Its Vision* (Jefferson, NC: McFarland, 1986), 81–90; and in essays under the rubric "*Intolerance*" in Paolo Cherchi Usai, ed., *The Griffith Project*, vol. 9, *Films Produced in 1916–18* (London: British Film Institute, 2005), 31–99.

67. '*Twas Ever Thus* has apparently not survived. Its release while Griffith was adding new epochs to *The Mother and the Law*, the germ of the modern story, may have spurred him to include four stories rather than three and to intercut them rather than set them side by side. See "Bosworth, Inc., Releases Fourth Elsie Janis Subject," *The Moving Picture World*, October 2, 1915, 97; and Lynde Denig, "'Twas Ever Thus," *The Moving Picture World*, October 9, 1915, 283. Thanks to Megan Boyd for telling me of '*Twas Ever Thus*.

68. A program quoted in "'Intolerance' Impressive," *New York Times*, September 6, 1916.

69. *Intolerance* program, Chestnut Street Opera House, Philadelphia, December 22, 1916.

70. Claire Dupré la Tour surveys the film's deployment of written language in Claire Dupré la Tour, "*Intolerance*: Intertitles," in *The Griffith Project*, vol. 9, *Films Produced in 1916–18*, ed. Paolo Cherchi Usai (London: British Film Institute, 2005), 81–88. See also Tony Liepa, "Figures of Silent Speech: Silent Film Dialogue and the American Vernacular, 1909–1916" (PhD diss., New York University, 2005), 418–33. I'm grateful to Charlie Keil for this last reference.

71. D. W. Griffith, "What I Demand of Movie Stars," *Motion Picture Classic* 3 (February 1917): 40.

72. Griffith, "What I Demand," 41.

73. Robert E. Welsh, "David W. Griffith Speaks" (1914), in *D. W. Griffith Interviews*, ed. Anthony Slide (Jackson: University Press of Mississippi, 2012), 9; Drew, *Griffith's Intolerance*, 81–90.

74. Johnson, "Shadow Stage," 81.

75. See David Bordwell and Kristin Thompson, *Christopher Nolan: A Labyrinth of Linkages*, 2nd ed. (Madison. WI: Irvington Way Institute, 2019), 19–24.

76. See Miriam Hansen, *Babel and Babylon: Spectatorship in American Silent Film* (Cambridge, MA: Harvard University Press, 1991); and Miriam Hansen, "The Mass Production of the Senses: Classical Cinema as Vernacular Modernism," *Modernism/Modernity* 6, no. 2 (April 1999): 59–77. See also Tom Gunning, "The Whole Town's Gawking: Early Cinema and the Visual Experience of Modernity," *Yale Journal of Criticism* 7, no. 2 (1994): 197–99; Tom Gunning, "An Aesthetic of Astonishment: Early Film and the (In) Credulous Spectator," in *Viewing Positions: Ways of Seeing Film*, ed. Linda Williams (New Brunswick, NJ: Rutgers , 1995), 128.

77. David Bordwell, *On the History of Film Style*, 2nd ed. (Madison, WI: Irvington Way Institute, 018), 129–39, 278–81. Other objections can be found in Malcolm Turvey, *The Filming of Modern Life: European Avant-Garde Film of the 1920s* (Cambridge, MA: MIT Press, 2011), chap. 6; Charlie Keil, "'To Here from Modernity': Style, Historiography, and Transitional Cinema," in *American Cinema's Transitional Era: Audiences, Institutions, Practices*, ed. Charlie Keil and Shelly Stamp (Berkeley: University of California Press, 2004), 51–65; and Charlie Keil, "Integrated Attractions: Style and Spectatorship in Transitional Cinema," in *The Cinema of Attractions Reloaded*, ed. Wanda Strauven (Amsterdam: Amsterdam University Press, 2006), 193–203.

78. See, for instance, Tom Gunning, "*Intolerance*: Narrative Structure," in *The Griffith Project*, vol. 9, *Films Produced in 1916–18*, ed. Paolo Cherchi Usai (London: British Film Institute, 2005), 47, 49.

2. Making Confusion Satisfactory: Modernism and Other Mysteries

The chapter epigraph is from Anthony Burgess, "Joyce as Centenarian," *Homage to Qwert Yuiop: Selected Journalism 1978–1985* (London; Abacus, 1986), 533.

1. Rex Stout, *How Like a God* (New York: Vanguard, 1929), 3.
2. David C. Tilden, "Exploring the Dark," *New York Herald Tribune*, September 8, 1929.
3. F. H., "Novel on the Stairs," *New Republic*, November 13, 1929, 357. The *Sanctuary* comparison was made by Peter Quennell, as quoted in John McAleer, *Rex Stout: A Biography* (New York: Little, Brown, 1977), 213.
4. Joseph Warren Beach, "The Novel from James to Joyce," *The Nation* 132 (June 10, 1931): 635.
5. Joseph Warren Beach, *The Twentieth Century Novel: Studies in Technique* (New York: Appleton Century Crofts, 1932), 274–75.
6. Percy Lubbock, *The Craft of Fiction* (1921; repr. New York: Viking, 1957), 274.
7. Lubbock, *Craft of Fiction*, 173.
8. Virginia Woolf, "Mr. Bennett and Mrs. Brown" (1923), *Collected Essays*, Vol. 1 (London: Hogarth Press, 1966), 319.
9. Peter de Voogd, "Joycean Typeface," in *Aspects of Modernism: Studies in Honour of Max Nänny* (Tübingen: Narr, 1997), 204–5; Bruce Arnold, *The Scandal of Ulysses: The Sensational Life of a Twentieth-Century Masterpiece* (New York: St. Martin's, 1991), 99, 159, 233.
10. Anthony Burgess, *Joysprick: An Introduction to the Language of James Joyce* (London: Deutch, 1973), 58–61.
11. Objective descriptions of behavior typically head the paragraph before we get the "stream of consciousness" passages, which tend to be sentence fragments. In addition, as Dorrit Cohn points out, Joyce uses the traditional distinction between tenses to keep us oriented. See Dorrit Cohn, *Transparent Minds: Narrative Modes for Presenting Consciousness in Fiction* (Princeton, NJ: Princeton University Press, 1978), 62–63.
12. Charles Rosen, *Sonata Forms*, rev. ed. (New York: Norton, 1986), 45.
13. Richard Taruskin, *The Oxford History of Western Music*. Vol. 4, *The Early Twentieth Century* (New York: Oxford University Press, 2005), 5–29.
14. Ernst H. Gombrich, *The Story of Art* (New York: Phaidon, 1950), 432–33.
15. Kirk Varnedoe, *A Fine Disregard: What Makes Modern Art Modern* (New York: Abrams, 1990), 22. For an in-depth account of how a modernist filmmaker can reactivate traditional schemas, see Malcolm Turvey, *Play Time: Jacques Tati and Comedic Modernism* (New York: Columbia University Press, 2019).
16. I've argued that a great deal of innovation in popular storytelling comes from applying received conventions to new subjects, themes, and story worlds. See Christopher Nolan, *A Labyrinth of Linkages* (Madison, WI: Irvington Way Institute, 2019), 5–6; and David Bordwell, "*Reinventing Hollywood* in Paperback: Welcome to the Variorum," *David Bordwell's Website on Cinema* (blog), http://www.davidbordwell.net/blog/2019/03/02/reinventing-hollywood-in-paperback-welcome-to-the-variorum/.
17. Beach, "The Novel from James to Joyce," 636.
18. See Leon Edel, *The Psychological Novel 1900–1950* (New York: Lippincott, 1955), 26–30. Apparently May Sinclair was the first to apply the term to literature in her essay. See May Sinclair, "The Novels of Dorothy Richardson," *The Little Review* 5, no. 12 (April 1918): 6.
19. Virginia Woolf, *To the Lighthouse* (1927), "Time Passes," part II, section 3.
20. Cohn, *Transparent Minds*, 247–49.

21. William Faulkner, *The Sound and the Fury: The Corrected Text* (New York: Vintage, 1990), 3.

22. I argue that a similar process of revising an intrinsic narration norm is at work in certain films as well. See David Bordwell, *Narration in the Fiction Film* (Madison: University of Wisconsin Press, 1985), 213–28.

23. See William Faulkner, *The Sound and the Fury: With Glossary and Commentary* (London: The Folio Society, 2016), vii.

24. Gertrude Stein, "How Writing Is Written," in *How Writing Is Written*, ed. Robert Bartlett Haas (Santa Barbara, CA: Black Sparrow, 1974), 153.

25. Faulkner, *Sound and the Fury: Corrected Text*, 148.

26. An example is "Appendix," *The Sound and the Fury*, in *The Sound and the Fury and As I Lay Dying* (New York: Modern Library, 1946), 3–22.

27. Reviews guiding prospective readers are summarized in Carl Rollyson, *The Life of William Faulkner*, vol. 1, *The Past Is Never Dead: 1897–1934* (Charlottesville: University of Virginia Press, 2021), 236–38.

28. Lyle Saxon, "A Family Breaks Up," *New York Herald Tribune*, October 13, 1929.

29. Basil Davenport, "Tragic Frustration," *Saturday Review of Literature*, December 28, 1929, 602.

30. Clifton Fadiman, "Hardly Worth While," *The Nation* 130 (January 15, 1930): 77.

31. See, for example, Todd McCarthy, "*Pulp Fiction*," *Variety*, May 23, 1994, https://variety .com/1994/film/reviews/pulp-fiction-1200437049/. In *Dunkirk*, Christopher Nolan "puts his stamp on the heroic rescue operation, offering a bravura virtual-eyewitness account from multiple perspectives—one that fragments and then craftily interweaves events as seen from land, sea and air." See Peter DeBruge, "*Dunkirk*," *Variety*, July 17, 2027, https:// variety.com/2017/film/reviews/dunkirk-review-christopher-nolan-1202495701/.

32. James Joyce as quoted in Richard Ellmann, *James Joyce*, rev. ed. (New York: Oxford University Press, 1982), 521.

33. Among the many discussions of narrative technique, a very useful overview is Stephen Kern, *The Modernist Novel: A Critical Introduction* (Cambridge: Cambridge University Press, 2011). An older but still informative collection is Malcolm Bradbury and James McFarlane, eds., *Modernism* (Harmondsworth, UK: Penguin, 1976). Accounts of theoretical debates about modernism may be found in Jean-Michel Rabaté, ed., *A Handbook of Modernist Studies* (Chichester, UK: Wiley, 2013).

34. William Faulkner, as quoted in Joseph Blotner, *Faulkner: A Biography* (Oxford: University Press of Mississippi, 2005), 248.

35. One version of Joyce's plan was published in Stuart Gilbert, *James Joyce's Ulysses: A Study* (1930; repr. New York: Vintage, 1961), 30. The schema is available online at https:// en.wikipedia.org/wiki/Gilbert_schema_for_Ulysses.

36. Letter of June 24, 1921, quoted in Ellmann, *James Joyce*, 512.

37. Harry Levin, "What Was Modernism?," *Massachusetts Review* 1, no. 4 (Summer 1960): 610.

38. Booth Tarkington as quoted in Kenneth Roberts, *I Wanted to Write* (Garden City, NY: Doubleday, 1949), 237.

39. Jurij Tynjanov as quoted in Katerina Clark and Michael Holquist, *Mikhail Bakhtin* (Cambridge, MA: Harvard/Belknap, 1984), 192.

40. Jean Cocteau, *Le Coq et l'arlequin* (Paris: Sirène, 1918), 11.

41. Virginia Woolf, "Modern Fiction," in *The Common Reader* (New York: Harcourt, 1925), 150.

42. Gore Vidal, "Maugham's Half and Half," in *United States: Essays 1952–1992* (New York: Random House, 1993), 244.

43. John McAleer, *Rex Stout: A Biography* (Boston: Little, Brown, 1977), 208–9.

44. Dorothy Richardson, *Pointed Roofs* (1915), chap. 1, section 3.

45. George Meredith's *Rhoda Fleming* (1865) puts thoughts in parentheses following lines of dialogue. Jean-Richard Bloch's *Nuit kurde* (1925) assigns a page to each character and runs three unbroken columns ("Dream," "Thought," and "Speech") as simultaneous discourse. Like Morley, Bloch is at pains to explain the technique. See *A Night in Kurdistand*, trans. Jean-Richard Bloch (London: Gollancz, 1930), 187–97.

46. John Dos Passos, *Manhattan Transfer* (1925), chap. 1, section 3.

47. C. Kay Scott, *Siren* (London: Faber and Gwyer, 1925), 9.

48. Christopher Morley, *Thunder on the Left* (New York: Penguin, 1946), 86–87.

49. Vladimir Nabokov, "Letter to Edmund Wilson," in *The Dixie Limited: Writers on William Faulkner and His Influence*, ed. M. Thomas Inge (Jackson: University Press of Mississippi, 2016), 95. Nabokov ascribed contemporary writers' "typographic broth" to the influence of *Ulysses*. See Fredson Bowers, ed., *Lectures on Literature* (New York: Harcourt Brace Jovanovich, 190), 363.

50. Joseph Harrington, "Subway Fire," *Saturday Evening Post*, January 21, 1939.

51. John Klempner, *Letter to Five Wives* (New York: Grosset & Dunlap, 1946), 53.

52. See Tom W. Blackburn, "Take with Soda" (1944), in *Pulpwood Days*, vol. 2, *Lives of the Pulp Writers* (Elkhorn, CA: Off-Trail, 2013), 139.

53. For example, compare the 1931 *Cosmopolitan* edition of Faith Baldwin's *Skyscraper* to the 1948 Dell reprint.

54. I consider this technique in David Bordwell, *Reinventing Hollywood: How 1940s Filmmakers Changed Movie Storytelling* (Chicago: University of Chicago Press, 2017), chap. 6.

55. Thomas H. Uzzell and Camelia Waite Uzzell, *Narrative Technique: A Practical Course in Literary Psychology*, 3rd ed. (New York: Harcourt, Brace, 1934), 462. On varieties of viewpoint manipulation, see Arthur Sullivant Hoffman, *Fundamentals of Fiction Writing* (Indianapolis: Bobbs-Merrill, 1922), 317–47; Carl H. Grabo, *The Technique of the Novel* (New York: Gordian, 1928), 33–66; and Van Meter Ames, *Aesthetics of the Novel* (Chicago: University of Chicago Press, 1928), 171–92. All betray the influence of James and Lubbock.

56. Robert Morss Lovett and Helen Sard Hughes, *History of the Novel in England* (Boston: Houghton Mifflin, 1932), 450.

57. This doesn't mean that more traditional techniques such as "He thought, 'I love her,'" went away. The new options coexisted with the older ones, sometimes within the same texts. See Melanie Conroy, "Before the 'Inward Turn': Tracing Represented Thought in the French Novel (1800–1929)," *Poetics Today* 35, no. 1-2 (Spring-Summer 2014): 166.

58. Neil Verma, *Theater of the Mind: Imagination, Aesthetics, and American Radio Drama* (Chicago: University of Chicago Press, 2012), 61–62.

59. See, for example, Mabel Constandoros and Howard Agg, "The Tunnel," in *Radio Theatre: Plays Specially Written for Broadcasting*, ed, Val Gielgud (London: Macdonald, 1946), 175–99; and Louis MacNiece, "The Dark Tower," in *The Dark Tower and Other Radio Plays* (London: Faber and Faber, 1947), 9–66.

60. *Variety*'s reviewer called it "appalling, horrible, heart-breaking, stomach-upsetting." Quoted in "80 percent Agreement," *Variety*, May 8, 1940.

61. John P. Marquand, *The Late George Apley* (New York: Little, Brown, 1937). For the reviewer's comment, see Percy Hutchison, "Mr. Marquand's Novel of the Boston Brahmin Tradition," *New York Times*, January 3, 1937.

62. These concepts are developed in the essays in Rabaté, *A Handbook of Modernism Studies*.

63. For detailed accounts of *Parade*, see Alan M. Gillmor, *Erik Satie* (Boston: Twayne, 1988), chap. 7; and Nancy Perloff, *Art and the Everyday: Popular Entertainment and the Circle of Erik Satie* (Oxford, UK: Clarendon Press, 1991), chaps. 3–5.

64. Alex Ross, *The Rest Is Noise: Listening to the Twentieth Century* (New York: Picador, 2008), 99.

65. It seems akin to what Robert Scholes, also resisting the duality of modernism/middlebrow, calls "durable fluff." See Robert Scholes, *Paradoxy of Modernism* (New Haven, CT: Yale University Press, 2006), chap. 5. A comparable account is in Turvey, *Play Time.*

66. Quoted in James Harding, *The Ox on the Roof: Scenes from Musical Life in Paris in the Twenties* (New York: St. Martin's, 1972), 38.

67. See the essays in Kirk Varnedoe and Adam Gopnik, eds., *Modern Art and Popular Culture: Readings in High and Low* (New York: Abrams, 1990).

68. Philip Furia, *The Poets of Tin Pan Alley: A History of America's Great Lyricists* (New York: Oxford University Press, 1990), 102–5.

69. Quoted in Walter Starkie, *Luigi Pirandello, 1867–1936* (Berkeley: University of California Press, 1965), 207.

70. Luigi Pirandello, "Premise: *Six Characters in Search of an Author*" (1933), in *Naked Masks: Five Plays by Luigi Pirandello*, ed. Eric Bentley (New York: Dutton, 1952), 209–10.

71. Luigi Pirandello, "On Humor," *Tulane Drama Review* 10, no. 3 (Spring 1966): 54; originally published in 1920.

72. Pirandello, preface to *Six Characters in Search of an Author* (1929)," in *Naked Masks*, 363.

73. On Theatricalism as a movement, see Mordecai Gorelik, *New Theatres for Old* (New York: Samuel French, 1940), chap. 7.

74. Brooks Atkinson, "On Light Fantastic Toes," *New York Times*, October 2, 1938.

75. In the absence of a published script, infeasible for obvious reasons, the press reports and the film are the best record we have of this farrago.

76. Robert Lynd, "*Chance*," *Daily News* (January 15, 1914), in Norman Sherry, *Conrad: The Critical Heritage* (Oxfordshire, UK: Routledge and Kegan Paul, 1973), 271.

77. An overwhelmingly wide-ranging account of popular culture's relation to modernist graphic art is Kirk Varnedoe and Adam Gopnik, *High and Low: Modern Art and Popular Culture* (New York: Museum of Modern Art, 1990).

78. T. S. Eliot, "Wilkie Collins and Dickens" (1927), in *The Complete Prose of T. S. Eliot: The Critical Edition: Literature, Politics, Belief, 1927–1929*, ed. Frances Dickey, Jennifer Formicelli, and Ronald Schuchard (Baltimore, MD: Johnsons Hopkins University Press, 2015), 171.

79. Gertrude Stein as quoted in Lawrence D. Stewart, "Gertrude Stein and the Vital Dead," in *The Mystery and Detection Annual*, ed. Donald K. Adams (Beverly Hills, CA: Donald Adams, 1970), 105. See also Stein, "Why I Like Detective Stories," 146–50.

80. Gertrud Stein, *Lectures in America* (Boston: Beacon, 1935), 167.

81. Gertrude Stein, *Blood on the Dining-Room Floor: A Murder Mystery* (New York: Dover, 1982), 71. I'm grateful to Tom Gunning for calling my attention to Stein's book.

82. Cora Jarrett as quoted in Will Cuppy, "Mystery and Adventure," *New York Herald Tribune*, September 16, 1934.

83. Cora Jarrett as quoted in "Book Notes," *New York Times*, October 27, 1933.

84. Cora Jarrett, *Night Over Fitch's Pond* (New York: Houghton Mifflin, 1933), chap. 16.

85. Jarrett, *Night Over Fitch's Pond*, chap. 18.

86. See Alvah C. Bessie, "Death Watch," *Saturday Review of Literature*, September 9, 1933, 93; "A Tragic Mystery," *New York Times Book Review*, September 10, 1933, 16.

87. Advertisement for *Night Over Fitch's Pond*, *New York Herald Tribune*, February 4, 1934.

88. C. H. B. Kitchin, *Birthday Party* (Richmond, VA: Valancourt, 1938), chap. 1.

89. "An Epilogue by A. B. C. Müller as Epitaph for Cameron McCabe," in *The Face on the Cutting-Room Floor*, by Cameron McCabe (New York: Penguin, 1982), 204.

90. "A Dossier on a Vanished Author and a Vanished Book by the Editors," in *The Face on the Cutting-Room Floor*, by Cameron McCabe (New York: Penguin, 1982), 270.

91. Clifton Fadiman, "Realism and Mannerism," *The Nation*, September 25, 1929, 329. Another reviewer praised the book's suspense; see Lewis Gannett, "A Man Talks to Himself," *New York Herald Tribune*, August 30, 1929.

3. Churn and Consolidation: The 1940s and After

1. The star image of Hermione Baddeley, who plays Mrs. Finch, may also make her account doubtful; she was known for brash, not overly bright characters.

2. Two of them are young women who together offer the same testimony, and they are minor characters. Hence the film's American title, "Five Angles on Murder."

3. "'The Woman in Question' with Jean Kent," *Harrison's Reports*, February 22, 1952; Bosley Crowther, "The Screen in Review," *New York Times*, February 19, 1952.

4. "'Woman in Question' Slow-Paced Drama," *Hollywood Reporter*, February 19, 1952; "New Films in London," *Times*, October 9, 1950; Otis L. Guernsey Jr., "On the Screen," *New York Herald Tribune*, February 19, 1952.

5. See Amy Flanders, "'Our Ambassadors': British Books, American Competition and the Great Book Export Drive, 1940–1960," *English Historical Review* 125, no. 515 (August 2020): 879; and James L. W. West III, "The Divergent Paths of British and American Publishing," *Sewanee Review* 120, no. 4 (Fall 2012): 508.

6. John Tebbel, *A History of Book Publishing in the United States*, vol. 3, *The Golden Age Between Two Wars* (New York: Bowker, 1978), 660, 680–81.

7. A detailed, wide-ranging survey of U.S. publishing after 1940 is provided in Beth Luey, "The Organization of the Book Publishing Industry," in *A History of the Book in America*, vol. 5, *The Enduring Book: Print Culture in Postwar America*, ed. David Paul Nord, Joan Shelley Rubin, and Michael Schudson (Chapel Hill: University of North Carolina Press, 2009), 29–54.

8. John Tebbel, *A History of Book Publishing in the United States*, vol. 4, *The Great Change 1940–1980* (New York: Bowker, 1981), 371; Kenneth C. Davis, *Two-Bit Culture: The Paperbacking of America* (New York: Houghton Mifflin, 1984), 125.

9. Ron Goulart, *Over 50 Years of American Comic Books* (Lincolnwood, IL: Mallard, 1991), 99.

10. On Hollywood films of the 1940s, see Thomas Schatz, *Boom and Bust: American Cinema in the 1940s* (New York: Scribners, 1997); and David Bordwell, *Reinventing Hollywood: How 1940s Filmmakers Changed Movie Storytelling* (Chicago: University of Chicago Press, 2019).

11. Douglas Gomery, *A History of Broadcasting in America* (Malden, MA: Blackwell, 2008), 77–78, 86–90. See also Michele Hilmes, *Only Connect: A Cultural History of Broadcasting in the United States* (Belmont, CA: Wadsworth, 2002).

12. Neil Verma, *Theater of the Mind: Imagination, Aesthetics, and American Radio Drama* (Chicago: University of Chicago Press, 2012), 20–22.

13. For a compact overview of the emergence of "experimental" broadcast programs, see Neil Verma, "Radio Drama," in *American Literature in Transition 1930–1940*, ed. Ichiro Takayoshi (Cambridge: Cambridge University Press, 2018), 267–84.

14. Eugene Vale, *The Technique of Screenplay Writing* (New York: Crown, 1944); Lewis Herman, *A Practical Manual of Screen Playwriting for Theater and Motion Pictures* (Cleveland, IL: World, 1952); John Howard Lawson, *Theory and Technique of Playwriting and Screenwriting* (New York: Putnam's, 1949).

15. Manuel Komroff, *How to Write a Novel* (Boston: The Writer, 1950), 62–95. Another nuanced and impressive overview is Thomas H. Uzzell, *The Technique of the Novel: A Handbook on the Craft of the Long Narrative* (New York: Lippincott, 1950). In revising his earlier manuals, Uzzell incorporates analyses of *Ulysses, Manhattan Transfer, Point Counter Point*, and *Sanctuary*.

16. Komroff, *How to Write a Novel*, 122–34.

17. George Orwell, "Inside the Whale," in *A Collection of Essays* (Garden City, NY: Doubleday Anchor, 1954), 231–37.

18. Michael Denning, *The Cultural Front: The Laboring of American Culture in the Twentieth Century* (London: Verso, 1998).

19. Tyrus Miller, *Late Modernism: Politics, Fiction and the Arts Between the World Wars* (Berkeley: University of California Press, 1999), 8–12; Robert Genter, *Late Modernism: Art, Culture and Politics in Cold War America* (Pittsburgh: University of Pennsylvania Press, 2010), 4–11. For an overview of these inquiries, see Douglas Mao and Rebecca L. Walkowitz, "The New Modernist Studies," *PMLA* 123, no. 3 (May 2008): 737–48.

20. Cyril Connolly, *Enemies of Promise* (1939; repr. Chicago: University of Chicago Press, 2008), 71.

21. Examples are Wallace Stegner, "Is the Novel Done For?," *Harper's Magazine*, December 1942, 76; Allen Tate, "The State of Letters," *Sewanee Review* 52 (Autumn 1944): 612–13; Diana Trilling, "What Has Happened to Our Novels?," *Harper's Magazine*, May 1944, 535; and Robert Coates, "The State of the Novel," *Yale Review*, 36 (Summer 1947): 610. See also the symposium, "The State of American Writing, 1948: Seven Questions," *Partisan Review* 15, no. 7 (July 1948): 855–94, which included this as the premise for one question: "It is the general opinion that, unlike the twenties, this is not a period of experiment in language and form." For a summary of this tendency, see Chester E. Eisinger, *Fiction of the Forties* (Chicago: University of Chicago Press, 1963), 13–20.

22. Eric Bentley, "The Drama at Ebb," *Kenyon Review* 7, no. 2 (Spring 1945): 174.

23. Josephina Niggli, *Pointers on Radio Writing* (Boston: The Writer, 1946), 76–79.

24. The way the film transforms the source novel is discussed in Bordwell, *Reinventing Hollywood*, 103–6.

25. See Niggli, *Pointers on Radio Writing*, 63–64; Luther Weaver, *The Technique of Radio Writing* (Englewood Cliffs, NJ: Prentice-Hall, 1948), 118–19.

26. Flashback strategies of American studio films of the 1940s are analyzed in chapter 2 of Bordwell, *Reinventing Hollywood*.

27. Norman Mailer, *The Naked and the Dead* (New York: Rinehart, 1948), 152.

28. James Naremore analyzes the *Heart of Darkness* script in detail in James Naremore, "Hearts of Darkness: Joseph Conrad and Orson Welles," in *True to the Spirit: Film Adaptation and the Question of Fidelity*, ed. Colin MacCabe, Kathleen Murray, and Rich Warner (New York: Oxford University Press, 2011), 59–73.

29. For a detailed comparison of the newsreel and the film's overall structure, see David Bordwell and Kristin Thompson, *Film Art: An Introduction* (New York: McGraw-Hill, 2019), 105–6.

30. Charles Poore, "Books of the Times," *New York Times*, August 7, 1947.

31. Philip Toynbee, "Notation of the Book," *Prothalamium: A Cycle of the Holy Graal* (New York: Doubleday, 1947), n.p.

32. John Klempner, *Letter to Five Wives* (New York: Dell, 1946), 27.

33. Klempner, *Letter to Five Wives*, 132, 135.

34. Klempner, *Letter to Five Wives*, 160.

35. *Letter to Three Wives* (1948), the excellent film adapted from Klempner's novel, shows another common alternative. Instead of the widely scattered flashbacks of the novel, Vera Caspary's screenplay offers something easier to assimilate on film. After the framing opening, each wife's story is treated as a block, and each is given a distinctive time frame: Deborah's first night in town after marrying Brad, the night of Rita and her husband's big quarrel, and Porter's long-running pursuit of Lora Mae. For a discussion of the film, see Bordwell, *Reinventing Hollywood*, 183–90.

36. Komroff, *How to Write a Novel*, 144–52.

37. See Joseph Frank, "Spatial Form in Modern Literature: An Essay in Two Parts," *Sewanee Review* 53, no. 2 (Spring 1945): 221–40; Joseph Frank, "Spatial Form in Modern Literature: An Essay in Two Parts," *Sewanee Review*, 53, no. 3 (Summer 1945): 433–56; and Joseph Frank, "Spatial Form in Modern Literature: An Essay in Three Parts," *Sewanee Review* 53, no. 4 (Autumn 1945): 643–63. Frank developed this idea in many directions, not all of them convincing to me, but it lingered in the critical literature. See also Joseph Frank, *The Idea of Spatial Form* (New Brunswick, NJ: Rutgers University Press, 1991).

38. This program is laid out in René Wellek and Austin Warren, "The Study of Literature in the Graduate School," in *Theory of Literature* (New York: Harcourt, Brace, 1949), chap. 20. Overall, the book is a judicious defense of the logical and methodological priority of the "intrinsic" approach.

39. Mark Schorer, "Technique as Discovery," *Hudson Review* 1, no. 1 (Spring 1948): 67.

40. The most polemical case for adding "extrinsic" approaches to the critic's toolkit can be found in this survey by Stanley Edgar Hyman, *The Armed Vision: A Study in the Methods of Modern Literary Criticism* (New York: Knopf, 1948).

41. Saul Rosenzweig, "The Ghost of Henry James," *Partisan Review* 11, no. 4 (1944): 436–55; William Troy, "Thomas Mann: Myth and Reason" (1938), in *Selected Essays*, ed. Stanley Edgar Hyman (New Brunswick NJ: Rutgers University Press, 1967), 241.

42. T. S. Eliot, "*Ulysses*, Order and Myth" (1923), in *The Complete Prose of T. S. Eliot: The Critical Edition: The Perfect Critic, 1919–1926* (Baltimore, MD: Johns Hopkins University Press, 2014), 476–81.

43. For an influential argument for modernism's development out of symbolism, see Edmund Wilson, "*Axel's Castle: A Study in the Imaginative Literature of 1870–1930*" (1933), in *Literary Essays and Reviews of the 1920s and 1930s* (New York: Library of America, 2007), 641–854.

44. Irving Howe, "The Culture of Modernism," in *Decline of the New* (New York: Harcourt, Brace, and World, 1978), 3–33.

45. For an overview, see Erica Brown and Mary Grover, "Introduction: Middlebrow Matters," in *Middlebrow Literary Culture: The Battle of the Brows, 1920–1960* (New York: Palgrave Macmillan, 2012), 1–21.

46. Virginia Woolf, "Middlebrow," *The Death of the Moth and Other Essays* (New York: Harcourt, Brace, 1974), 176–86.

47. Gilbert Seldes, *The Seven Lively Arts* (New York: Harper, 1924). See also Michael Kammen, *The Lively Arts: Gilbert Seldes and the Transformation of Cultural Criticism in the United States* (New York: Oxford University Press, 1996).

48. See Dwight Macdonald, "Soviet Cinema, 1930–1940, a History" (1939–40), in *Dwight Macdonald on Movies* (New York: Prentice-Hall, 1969), 218–44; Clement Greenberg,

"Avant-Garde and Kitsch" (1939), in *Collected Essays and Criticism*, vol. 1, *Perceptions and Judgments, 1939-1944*, ed. John O'Brian (Chicago: University of Chicago Press, 1986), 14–17.

49. For a careful discussion of these and related categories, see James Naremore and Patrick Brantlinger, "Introduction: Six Artistic Cultures," in *Modernity and Mass Culture* (Bloomington: Indiana University Press, 1991), 1–23.

50. Woolf, "Middlebrow," *Death of the Moth*, 180.

51. Robert Warshow, "American Popular Culture," *The Immediate Experience: Movies, Comics, Theatre, and Other Aspects of Popular Culture* (New York: Atheneum, 1971), 7.

52. "State of American Writing," 855.

53. I discuss this trend in David Bordwell, *Making Meaning: Inference and Rhetoric in the Interpretation of Cinema* (Cambridge, MA: Harvard University Press, 1988), 73–78; and in David Bordwell, *The Rhapsodes: How 1940s Critics Changed American Film Culture* (Chicago: University of Chicago Press, 2016), 20–31.

54. Martha Wolfenstein and Nathan Leites, *Movies: A Psychological Study* (1950; repr. New York: Atheneum, 1970), 25–41.

55. Siegfried Kracauer, *From Caligari to Hitler: A Psychological History of the German Film* (1947; repr. New York: Noonday, 1959), 272.

56. James Sandoe, "Dagger of the Mind," in *The Art of the Mystery Story*, ed. Howard Haycraft (New York: Simon & Schuster, 1946), 254; Neil Verma, *Theater of the Mind: Imagination, Aesthetics, and American, Radio Drama* (Chicago: University of Chicago Press, 2012), 171.

57. Janice Radway, *Reading the Romance: Woman, Patriarchy, and Popular Literature* (Chapel Hill: University of North Carolina Press, 1984), 30–31.

58. Janet Morgan, *Agatha Christie: A Biography* (London: Collins, 1984), 260.

59. Lawrence G. Blochman, "Plot and Background," in *The Mystery Writer's Handbook*, ed. Herbert Brean (New York: Harper, 1956), 95.

60. Radway, *Reading the Romance*, 245n28.

61. Graham Greene, *Brighton Rock* (London: William Heinemann, 1938), part 2, chap. 2. The skewed citation is to Wordsworth, "Ode: Intimations of Immorality from Recollections of Early Childhood," lines 65–67.

62. See Warren French, "William Faulkner and the Art of the Detective Story," in *The Thirties: Fiction: Poetry, Drama* (Deland, FL: Everett/Edwards, 1975), 55–62; and Annette Trefszer and Ann J. Abadie, eds., *Faulkner and Mystery* (Jackson: University of Mississippi Press, 2014).

63. William Faulkner as quoted in "Editors' Notes," *Intruder in the Dust* (New York: Vintage, 1994), 243.

64. Lawrence H. Schwartz, *Creating Faulkner's Reputation: The Politics of Modern Literary Criticism* (Knoxville: University of Tennessee Press, 1988), 70–71.

65. The following references to the debate draw on Louise Bogan, "The Time of the Assassins," *The Nation*, April 22, 1944, 475–78; Edmund Wilson, "Why Do People Read Detective Stories?," in *Literary Essays and Reviews of the 1930s and 1940s* (New York: Library of America, 2007), 657–61; Jacques Barzun: "Not 'Whodunit?' But 'How?': First Aid for Critics of the Detective Story," *Saturday Review of Literature*, November 4, 1944, 9–11; Joseph Wood Krutch, " 'Only a Detective Story,' " *The Nation*, November 25, 1944, 647–52; Bernard DeVoto, "The Easy Chair," *Harper's*, November 20, 1944, 34–37; Edmund Wilson, "Who Cares Who Killed Roger Ackroyd?," *Literary Essays and Reviews of the 1930s and 1940s* (New York: Library of America, 2007), 677–83.

66. Wilson, "Who Cares Who Killed Roger Ackroyd?," 672, 679.

67. Barzun develops this idea in detail in Jacques Barzun, "Detection and the Literary Art," in *The Delights of Detection*, ed. Jacques Barzun (New York: Criterion, 1961), 9–21; Jacques Barzun, "A Tale Is Not a Novel," *A Catalogue of Crime*, ed. Jacques Barzun and Wendell Taylor (New York: Harper, 1971), 7–9; and Jacques Barzun, "The Novel Turns Tale," in *New Views of the English and American Novel*, ed. R. G. Collins and Kenneth McRobbie (Winnipeg: University of Manitoba Press, 1971), 33–40.

68. Wilson, "Why Do People Read Detective Stories?," 657; Wilson, "Who Cares Who Killed Roger Ackroyd?," 679.

69. DeVoto, "Easy Chair," 36.

70. Krutch, " 'Only a Detective Story,' " 647.

71. Barzun, "Not 'Whodunit'?," 10.

72. Wilson, "Who Cares Who Killed Roger Ackroyd?," 682.

73. Wilson, "Why Do People Read Detective Stories?," 661.

74. Bogan, "Time of the Assassins," 476.

75. E. M. Wrong, "Crime and Detection," in *The Art of the Mystery Story*, ed. Howard Haycraft (New York: Simon & Schuster, 1946), 24; and Marjorie Nicolson, "The Professor and the Detective," in *Art of the Mystery Story*, ed. Howard Haycraft (New York: Simon & Schuster, 1946), 113.

76. DeVoto, "Easy Chair," 37.

77. Wilson's point in effect grants the DeVoto/Krutch argument that not all components of a literary work are of equal weight. DeVoto and Krutch could reply that the detective story executes its own balancing act by downplaying verbal texture to the benefit of plotting.

78. W. H. Auden, "The Guilty Vicarage," in *The Complete Words of W. H. Auden*, Prose vol. 2, *1939–1948*, ed. Edward Mendelson (Princeton, NJ: Princeton University Press, 2002), 261–70.

79. John Dickson Carr, "The Grandest Game in the World," in *The Door to Doom and Other Detections*, ed. Douglas G. Greene (New York: Harper, 1980), 308–25. This essay, originally published in 1963, was written in 1946.

80. Herbert Marshall McLuhan, "Footprints in the Sands of Crime," *Sewanee Review* 54, no. 4 (October-December 1946): 620.

81. Raymond Chandler, "The Simple Art of Murder," *Atlantic Monthly*, December 1944, 53–59.

82. Miranda B. Hickman, "The Complex History of a 'Simple Art,' " *Studies in the Novel* 35, no. 3 (Fall 2003): 294.

83. Raymond Chandler, "The Simple Art of Murder," *Atlantic Monthly*, December 1944, 56, 57.

84. Raymond Chandler, "The Simple Art of Murder," *Later Novels and Other Writings* (New York: Library of America, 1995), 977.

85. Chandler charged that the daintiness of the English mystery revealed writers unacquainted with the harsh side of life. This stirred John Dickson Carr to fury. When he reviewed a Chandler collection of stories, he noted with heavy sarcasm: "Of course these people know nothing of violence, especially those who lived in London and were on duty from 1940 to 1945." See John Dickson Carr, "With Colt and Luger," *New York Times Book Review*, September 24, 1950. Carr, an Anglophile American who lived through the German blitzkrieg, may have been casting shade on Chandler, an English expatriate who had a "good war" in California.

86. Chandler, "Simple Art of Murder," 991.

87. Chandler, "Simple Art of Murder," 991–92.

88. Letter to Howard Haycraft, December 9, 1946, in *Raymond Chandler Speaking*, ed. Dorothy Gardner and Kathrine Sorley Walker (Plainview, NY: Books for Libraries, 1962), 52.
89. "Once in a Blue Moon" (advertisement), *New York Times*, April 8, 1945.
90. D. C. Russell, "The Chandler Books," *Atlantic Monthly* 175, no. 3 (March 1945): 123.
91. D. C. Russell, "Raymond Chandler, and the Future of Whodunits," *New York Times Book Review*, June 17, 1945.
92. Particularly vehement were the remarks of the two cousins who wrote under the pseudonym Ellery Queen. See Joseph Goodrich, ed., *Blood Relations: The Selected Letters of Ellery Queen 1947-1950* (Lexington, KY: Perfect Crime, 2012), 81–84.
93. Jacques Barzun, "From 'Phèdre' to Sherlock Holmes," in *The Energies of Art: Studies of Authors Classic and Modern* (New York: Harper, 1956), 320–23; Jacques Barzun, "Detection in Extremis," in *Crime in Good Company*, ed. Michael Gilbert (London: Constable, 1959), 144; Robert Barnard, *A Talent to Deceive*, rev. ed. (New York: Mysterious Press, 1987), 110–13.
94. See Philip Weinstein, "Innovators II: Prose," in *American Literature in Transition 1920–1930*, ed. Ichiro Takayoshi (Cambridge: Cambridge University Press, 2018), 84–91.
95. Josiah Strong as quoted in Malcolm Bradbury, "The Cities of Modernism," in *Modernism*, ed. Malcolm Bradbury and James McFarlane (Harmondsworth, UK: Penguin, 1976), 98.
96. James Naremore, *More Than Night: Film Noir in Its Contexts, Updated and Expanded Edition* (Berkeley: University of California Press, 2008), 48, 220.
97. See Paul R. Gorman, *Left Intellectuals and Popular Culture in Twentieth-Century America* (Chapel Hill: University of North Carolina Press, 1996), 186–92.
98. See David Riesman, *The Lonely Crowd: A Study of the Changing American Character* (New Haven, CT: Yale University Press, 1950), 311–67; and David Riesman, "Our Country and Our Culture," *Partisan Review* 19, no. 3 (May-June 1952), 310–11.
99. Bordwell, *The Rhapsodes*, chap. 2.
100. "Unidentified Interview" (1962), in Vladimir Nabokov, *Think, Write, Speak: Uncollected Essays, Reviews, Interviews, and Letters to the Editor*, ed. Brian Boyd and Anastasia Tolstoy (New York: Vintage International, 2019), 313.
101. Susan Sontag, "Notes on 'Camp'," *Partisan Review* 31, no. 4 (Fall 1964): 515–30; Richard Poirier, "Learning from the Beatles," *Partisan Review* 34, no. 4 (Fall 1967): 528, 529.
102. Stephen Sondheim, *Finishing the Hat: Collected Lyrics (1954-1981) with Attendant Comments, Principles, Heresies, Grudges, Whines and Anecdotes* (New York: Knopf, 2010), 332.
103. Steve Swayne provides a thorough analysis of the role of cinema in his career; see Steve Swayne, *How Sondheim Found His Sound* (Ann Arbor: University of Michigan Press, 2005), 159–213.
104. Craig Zadan, *Sondheim & Co.*, 2nd ed. (New York: Harper and Row, 1986), 135.
105. Meryl Secrest, *Stephen Sondheim* (New York: Knopf, 1998), 185.
106. Secrest, *Stephen Sondheim*, 236.
107. Sondheim, *Finishing the Hat*, 303.
108. Stephen Sondheim, *Look, I Made a Hat: Collected Lyrics (1981—2011) with Attendant Comments, Amplifications, Dogmas, Harangues, Digressions, Anecdotes and Miscellany* (New York: Knopf, 2011), 363.
109. Sondheim, *Finishing the Hat*, 168.
110. Sondheim, *Finishing the Hat*, 379, 232.
111. Sondheim, *Finishing the Hat*, 166.

112. Sondheim, *Look, I Made a Hat*, 147, 177.
113. Sondheim, *Finishing the Hat*, 301.
114. Dwight Macdonald, "Masscult and Midcult," in *Against the American Grain: Essays on the Effects of Mass Culture* (New York: Random House, 1962), 56, 74. Cf. Dwight Macdonald, "A Theory of Popular Culture," *Politics* 1, no. 1 (February 1944): 20–33.
115. Sondheim, *Finishing the Hat*, xviii.
116. You can argue that the Ultraist impulse returned in music and the visual arts, but these largely nonnarrative modes aren't my concern here. The operas of Philip Glass, John Adams, and other "minimalists" are of course narrative, but musically they are crossover works in the sense I'm claiming.
117. Dwight Macdonald, "8 ½: Fellini's Obvious Masterpiece," in *Dwight Macdonald on Movies* (Englewood Cliffs, NJ: Prentice-Hall, 1969), 15–31.
118. See, for example, Earl Miner, *An Introduction to Japanese Court Poetry* (Stanford, CA: Stanford University Press, 1968), 31–33; Makoto Ueda, *Literary and Art Theories in Japan* (Cleveland, OH: Case Western Reserve University Press, 1967), 37–54; T. C. Lai, *Chinese Painting* (New York: Oxford University Press, 1992), 3–17.
119. I discuss Ozu's reliance on popular genres in David Bordwell, *Ozu and the Poetics of Cinema* (Princeton, NJ: Princeton University Press, 1988).
120. Robert Hughes, *The Spectacle of Skill: Selected Writings* (New York: Vintage, 2016).

4. The Golden Age Puzzle Plot: The Taste of the Construction

1. Viktor Shklovsky, "Sherlock Holmes and the Mystery Story," in *Theory of Prose*, trans. Benjamin Sher (Elmwood Park, IL: Dalkey Archive, 1990), 101.
2. Anthony Trollope, "The Unpalatable Taste of the Construction" (1883), in *Wilkie Collins: The Critical Heritage*, ed. Norman Page (London: Routledge and Kegan Paul, 1997), 223.
3. Joseph Warren Beach, *The Twentieth Century Novel* (New York: Appleton-Century-Crofts, 1932), 210; Robert Lynd, "Review of *Chance*" (January 15, 1914), in *Joseph Conrad: The Critical Heritage*, ed. Norman Sherry (London: Routledge, 2013), 271.
4. Conrad Aiken, "William Faulkner: The Novel as Form," in *The Dixie Limited: Writers on William Faulkner and His Influence*, ed. M. Thomas Inge (Oxford: University Press of Mississippi, 2016), 102.
5. See Meir Sternberg, *Expositional Modes and Temporal Ordering in Fiction* (Bloomington: Indiana University Press, 1978), 64–66, which treats these as basic appeals invoked by all narratives to one degree or another.
6. LeRoy Lad Panek, *An Introduction to the Detective Story* (Bowling Green, OH: Popular, 1987), 122–31.
7. A thorough history of the Detection Club is provided in Martin Edwards, *The Golden Age of Murder: The Mystery of the Writers Who Invented the Modern Detective Story* (London: Harper Collins, 2015).
8. For an excellent, wide-ranging survey, see Martin Edwards, *The Life of Crime: Detecting the History of Mysteries and Their Creators* (New York: HarperCollins, 2022), chaps. 1–5. Leroy Lad Panek has documented the early years of detective fiction in his admirable monographs: Leroy Lad Panek, *The Origins of the American Detective Story* (Jefferson, NC: McFarland, 2006); Leroy Lad Panek, *Before Sherlock Holmes: How Magazines and Newspapers Invented the Detective Story* (Jefferson, NC: McFarland, 2011); and Leroy Lad Panek (with Mary M. Bendel-Simso), *The Essential Elements of the Detective Story*,

1820–1891 (Jefferson, NC: McFarland, 2017). See also Nathaniel Williams, "Dreiser, Dey, and Dime Novel Crime: The Case of Nick Carter," in *The Centrality of Crime Fiction in American Literary Culture*, ed. Alfred Bendixen and Olivia Carr Edenfield (New York: Routledge, 2017), 53–73.

9. Henry James, "Mary Elizabeth Braddon" (1865), in Henry James, *Literary Criticism*, vol. 1, *Essays on Literature, American Writers, English Writers* (New York: Library of America, 1984), 743.

10. Van Wyck Mason, "Suggestions for the Character-Detective Story," *The Writer* 46, no. 6 (June 1934): 241.

11. Howard Haycraft calls her "one of the great story-tellers of the age" but also deplores the role of "happenstance" in her plotting and her reliance on romantic liaisons to forward the action. He considers her on the borderline between "mystery" and proper detective fiction, with her protagonist serving as both "participating (usually interfering!) Watson and detective-by-accident." Howard Haycraft, *Murder for Pleasure: The Life and Times of the Detective Story* (New York: Appleton-Century, 1941), 89.

12. For a subtle analysis of Rinehart's novels, see Jan Cohn, "Mary Roberts Rinehart," in *Ten Women of Mystery*, ed. Earl F. Bargainnier (Bowling Green, OH: Bowling Green State University Popular Press, 1981), 183–220.

13. Mary Roberts Rinehart, *The Circular Staircase* (New York: Pocket Books, 1943), 1.

14. For examples, see Arthur Bartlett Maurice, "The Detective in Fiction," *The Bookman* 15, no. 3 (May 1902): 231–34; Cecil Chesterton, "Art and the Detective," *The Living Age*, no. 251 (November 24, 1906): 505–15; Brander Matthews, "Poe and the Detective Story," *Scribner's Magazine* 42, no. 3 (September 1907): 287–93; Julian Hawthorne, "Riddle Stories," in *The Lock and Key Library: Classic Mystery and Detective Stories*, ed. Julian Hawthorne (New York: Review of Reviews, 1909), 9–19.

15. Carolyn Wells, *The Technique of the Mystery Story* (Springfield, MA: Home Correspondence School, 1913), 61.

16. Wells, *Technique of the Mystery Story*, 62.

17. Wells, *Technique of the Mystery Story*, 12.

18. E. C. Bentley, *Those Days* (London: Constable, 1940), 254.

19. The novel of manners, in which the individual achieves self-definition in relation to social structures, composes what many consider the "great tradition" of the British novel, from *Pride and Prejudice* to *Barchester Towers*. Joseph Wiesenfarth argues that it owes more to the Gothic novel than many suppose. See Joseph Wiesenfarth, *Gothic Manners and the Classic English Novel* (Madison: University of Wisconsin Press, 1988). This prospect makes Dorothy Sayers's dream of a merger with the detective tale somewhat plausible.

20. LeRoy Lad Panek, *Watteau's Shepherds: the Detective Novel in Britain, 1914–1940* (Bowling Green, OH: Bowling Green State University Popular Press, 1979), 22–28.

21. Panek deftly analyzes the role of adventure in Golden Age mysteries in Panek, *Watteau's Shepherds*, 9–16. See also John Cawelti, *Adventure, Mystery, and Romance: Formula Stories as Art and Popular Culture* (Chicago: University of Chicago Press, 1976), chaps.1 and 2.

22. Dorothy L. Sayers, introduction to *Great Short Stories of Detection, Mystery and Horror, Second Series*, ed. Dorothy L. Sayers (London: Gollancz, 1931), 16.

23. Raymond Chandler, "Twelve Notes on the Mystery Story" (1946), in *Later Novels and Other Writings* (New York: Library of America, 1995), 1007.

24. Robert Graves and Alan Hodge, *The Long Week-End: A Social History of Great Britain 1918–1939* (New York: Norton, 1931), 289.

25. David Welky, *Everything Was Better: Print Culture in the Great Depression* (Champaign-Urbana: University of Illinois Press, 2008), 178.

26. For a history, see Carol Billman, *The Secret of the Stratemeyer Syndicate: Nancy Drew, the Hardy Boys, and the Million Dollar Fiction Factory* (New York: Ungar, 1986).

27. Willard Huntington Wright, *The Great Detective Stories* (New York: Scribner's, 1928), 36–37.

28. Ellery Queen, *How to Read the Queen Stories: A Personal Message from Ellery Queen* (pamphlet) (New York: Stokes, 1933), 1–2.

29. S. S. Van Dine, *The Bishop Murder Case* (New York: Scribner's, 1929), 269.

30. G. K. Chesterton, "The Sins of Prince Saradine," in *The Annotated Innocence of Father Brown*, ed. Martin Gardner (New York: Oxford University Press), 167.

31. John Dickson Carr, "The Grandest Game in the World," in *The Door to Doom and Other Detections*, 2nd ed., ed. Douglas G. Greene (New York: International Polygonics, 1991), 310.

32. These precepts can be found in E. M. Wrong, "Crime and Detection" (1926), in *The Art of the Mystery Story*, ed. Howard Haycraft (New York: Simon & Schuster, 1946), 18–32; Willard Huntington Wright, "The Great Detective Stories" (1927), in *The Art of the Mystery Story*, ed. Howard Haycraft (New York: Simon & Schuster, 1946), 37–42; S. S. Van Dine, "Twenty Rules for Writing Detective Stories," in *The Art of the Mystery Story*, ed. Howard Haycraft (New York: Simon & Schuster, 1946), 101–89; Ronald Knox, "A Detective Story Decalogue," in *The Art of the Mystery Story*, ed. Howard Haycraft (New York: Simon & Schuster, 1946), 194–96.

33. "The Detection Club Oath," in *The Art of the Mystery Story*, ed. Howard Haycraft (New York: Simon & Schuster, 1946), 198.

34. Sir Arthur Conan Doyle, "A Gaudy Death," *Tit-Bits*, December 15, 1900, www.arthur-conan-doyle.com/index.php/A_Gaudy_Death:_Conan_Doyle_tells_the_True_Story_of_Sherlock_Holmes%27s_End.

35. Carr, "The Grandest Game in the World," 323.

36. Sayers was quite proud of "this little stunt" and floated the possibility of printing the missing passage in a sealed page at the end of the book. See Janet Hitchman, *Such a Strange Lady: A Biography of Dorothy L. Sayers* (New York: Avon, 1976), 88–89.

37. Carr, "The Grandest Game in the World," 310.

38. Van Wyck Mason, *The Castle Island Case* (New York: Reynal and Hitchcock, 1937). Mason, a widely read mystery-adventure novelist, explains his project in Van Wyck Mason, "The Camera as a Literary Element," *The Writer* 51, no. 11 (November 1938): 325–26. I discuss the book and its counterparts in more detail on *David Bordwell's Website on Cinema* (blog), http://www.davidbordwell.net/blog/2021/06/20/what-you-see-is-what-you-guess/.

39. C. Daly King, *Obelists Fly High* (New York: Dover, 1986), 277.

40. Philip MacDonald, *R.I.P.* (London: Collins, 1937). This novel, whose action runs in a single house from 6:00 p.m. on one day to 4:15 a.m. on the next, appears to be an experiment in rendering filmic continuity of action on the page.

41. Chapters of Wilkie Collins's *Hide and Seek* (1854) are grouped into "The Hiding" and "The Seeking," with these parts enclosed within a curtain-raiser and a tailpiece.

42. Carter Dickson, *The Judas Window* (Harmondsworth: Penguin, 1951), 3.

43. John Dickson Carr, *The Crooked Hinge* (New York: Collier, 1978), 235.

44. Joseph Shaw as quoted in Eugene Cunningham, "The Art and Success of Dashiell Hammett," *El Paso Times*, March 9, 1930.

45. Quoted in Francis M. Nevins, *Ellery Queen: The Art of Detection* (Perfect Crime Books, 2013), 15, Kindle.

46. John Dickson Carr, "The House in Goblin Wood," in *The Third Bullet and Other Stories* (Roslyn, NY: Black, 1954), 112.

47. Carr, "House in Goblin Wood," 112.

48. John Dickson Carr as quoted in Douglas G. Greene, *John Dickson Carr: The Man Who Explained Miracles* (New York: Otto Penzler, 1995), 304.

49. We're kept from dwelling on the conspirators by H.M.'s arrival on the scene, majestically slipping on a banana peel. "In placing a cryptic clue," Carr advised, "be sure that your reader never sees it at eye level. This can be done by using love scenes or comic scenes" (as quoted in Greene, *John Dickson Carr*, 106n). In an appendix to the first publication of the story, Ellery Queen discusses how the slapstick incident also foreshadows key elements in the plot. See "About the Story," *Ellery Queen's Mystery Magazine* 10, no. 48 (November 1947): 20–22. It is interesting that this analysis focuses on the clues in the story, not the hints in the enveloping narration.

50. Robert Barnard suggests that the prevalence of Christie novels in cheap paperbacks might nudge readers to see the Letty/Lotty stratagem as a typographical error, all the better to mystify the reader. See Robert Barnard, *A Talent to Deceive: An Appreciation of Agatha Christie*, 2nd ed. (New York: Mysterious, 1987), 94.

51. Agatha Christie, *A Murder Is Announced* in *Murder Preferred* (New York: Dodd, Mead, 1960), 196.

52. Sir Arthur Conan Doyle, "The Adventure of the Blanched Soldier," in *The Complete Sherlock Holmes* (New York: Garden City, 1960), 1188.

53. Doyle, "Adventure of the Blanched Soldier," 1192.

54. Dorothy L. Sayers, "The Omnibus of Crime" (1928–29), in *The Art of the Mystery Story*, ed. Howard Haycraft (New York: Simon & Schuster, 1946), 98–100.

55. Percy Lubbock, *The Craft of Fiction* (New York: Viking, 1957), 163. Daniel R. Barnes suggests that Lubbock's mention may have influenced Christie's book. See Daniel R. Barnes, "A Note on *The Murder of Roger Ackroyd*," in *Mystery and Detection Annual 1972*, ed. Donald Adams (Beverly Hills CA: Donald Adams, 1972), 254–55.

56. Agatha Christie, *The Murder of Roger Ackroyd* (New York: Pocket, 1975), 11.

57. Agatha Christie as quoted in Charles Osborne, *The Life and Crimes of Agatha Christie: A Biographical Companion to the Works of Agatha Christie* (New York: St. Martin's, 1982), 45.

58. Christie, *Murder of Roger Ackroyd*, 48.

59. Christie, *Murder of Roger Ackroyd*, 122. More felicities of Christie's stratagems in this and other novels are carefully charted in John Goddard, *Agatha Christie's Golden Age: An Analysis of Poirot's Golden Age Puzzles* (London: Stylish Eye, 2018), 89–110.

60. Raymond Chandler, "The Simple Art of Murder," in *Later Novels and Other Writings* (New York: Library of America, 1995), 985.

61. William Gillette's play *Sherlock Holmes* (1899) and the 1916 film adapted from it begin by revealing the villains' scheme, and Watson enters relatively late in the first act. Two German films of *The Hound of the Baskervilles* (1914 and 1929) move freely among the characters, while still keeping back essential information.

62. Knox, "A Detective Story Decalogue," 194.

63. Dorothy Sayers, "Gaudy Night," in *The Art of the Mystery Story*, ed. Howard Haycraft (New York: Simon & Schuster, 1946), 209. For a stimulating analysis of the book, see Dawson Gailard, *Dorothy L. Sayers* (New York: Ungar, 1981), 55.

64. The relevant novels are *The Roman Hat Mystery* (1929), *The French Powder Mystery* (1930), and *The Dutch Shoe Mystery* (1931).

65. Dorothy L. Sayers, *Murder Must Advertise* (New York: Avon, 1967), 274.

66. Sayers, *Murder Must Advertise*, 203.

67. Sayers, *Murder Must Advertise*, 228.

68. Sayers, *Murder Must Advertise*, 100.

69. Sayers, *Murder Must Advertise*, 12–13.

70. Sayers, "Omnibus of Crime," 101n. In introducing her play *Busman's Honeymoon*, she offered even more strict guidelines, claiming that fair play means "every clue must be shown at the same time to the public and the detective." "Author's Note," Dorothy L. Sayers and M. St. Clare Byrne, *Busman's Honeymoon* (New York: Samuel French, 1939), 5.

71. Dorothy Sayers, "Grand Manner in Crime Stories" (1933), in *Taking Detective Stories Seriously: The Collected Crime Reviews of Dorothy Sayers*, ed. Martin Edwards (Perth, Scotland: Tippermuir, 2017), 80.

72. Sayers, *Murder Must Advertise*, 153.

73. Sayers, *Murder Must Advertise*, 79, 288.

74. Knox, "A Detective Story Decalogue," 194.

75. Agatha Christie, *Death in the Air* (New York: Berkeley, 1984), 3.

76. Christie, *Death in the Air*, 49, 130–31.

77. Anthony Berkeley, "To A. D. Peters," *The Second Shot* (London: Langtail, 2010), n.p.

78. Elmer Rice, *Minority Report: An Autobiography* (New York: Simon & Schuster, 1964), 103.

79. Clayton Hamilton, "Building a Play Backward," in *Problems of the Playwright* (New York: Holt, 1917), 23–24.

80. Rice, *Minority Report*, 104.

81. Early on G. K. Chesterton considered *The Ring and the Book* a detective story. See G. K. Chesterton, *Robert Browning* (New York: Macmillan, 1904), 160–76.

82. When *The Ring and the Book* was adapted for the stage as *Caponsacchi* (1926), the play radically condensed the original by focusing on one major character.

83. As Clayton Hamilton's speculations about time shifting had inspired *On Trial*'s flashbacks, Dyar claimed that Hamilton's writing on point of view led him to a dramaturgy emphasizing sensory differences among witnesses' accounts. See Rebecca Drucker, "A New Playwright Comes Out of the West," *New York Herald Tribune*, September 21, 1919.

84. Torquemada [Edward Powys Mathers], "Can You Solve Torquemada's Murder Mystery?" *Cain's Jawbone: A Novel Problem* (London: Unbound, 2020), n.p.

85. Henry James, "The Wings of the Dove," in *Literary Criticism*, vol. 2, *French Writers, Other European Writers, and Prefaces to the New York Edition* (New York: Library of America, 1984), 1294.

86. Anna Katherine Green anticipates this tagging strategy in *The Leavenworth Case* (1878), which bookends its chapters under the rubrics of "The Problem," "Henry Clavering," "Hannah," and "The Problem Solved." She appears not to have used this device in other books.

87. Philip MacDonald, introduction to *The Maze* (London: Collins, 1980), 2.

88. For some years Sayers worked on a book on Collins. For background on this project and Collins's influence on her novels, see E. R. Gregory, introduction to *Wilkie Collins: A Critical and Biographical Study* by Dorothy L. Sayers (Toledo, OH: Friends of the University of Toledo Libraries, 1977), 7–15.

89. On Sayers's fondness for the howdunit, see Hitchman, *Such a Strange Lady*, 94.
90. On the round-robin novel as support for the club, see Edwards, *Golden Age of Murder*, 246–55.
91. Jon L. Breen offers a comprehensive view of trial fiction; see Jon L. Breen, *Novel Verdicts: A Guide to Courtroom Fiction*, 2nd ed. (Lanham, MD: Scarecrow, 1999).
92. Brog, "The Paradine Case," *Variety*, December 31, 1947. A discussion of flashbacks in trial films of the 1940s can be found in David Bordwell, *Reinventing Hollywood: How 1940s Filmmakers Changed Movie Storytelling* (Chicago: University of Chicago Press, 2017), 79–82.
93. Anthony Berkeley, *The Poisoned Chocolates Case* (London: British Library 2016), 226.
94. See A. B. Cox, "The Detective Story" and "The Mystery Story," in *Jugged Journalism* (London: Jenkins, 1925), 33–57.
95. Ellery Queen, *The Egyptian Cross Mystery*, in *The Ellery Queen Omnibus* (New York: Grosset and Dunlap, 1932), 334.
96. Berkeley, *Poisoned Chocolates Case*, 173–74.
97. John Dickson Carr, *The Hollow Man* (New York: Orion, 2013), 152.
98. Berkeley, *Poisoned Chocolates Case*, 227–28.
99. See Christianna Brand, "A New Denouement" and Martin Edwards, "Epilogue (Second Part)," in Berkeley, *Poisoned Chocolates Case*, 249–67. Edwards's contribution is a brilliant fantasia on Golden Age motifs, wholly in the spirit of the novel's gesture toward endlessly proliferating solutions.
100. Berkeley, *Poisoned Chocolates Case*, 247.
101. Linda Schlossberg suggests that the several false solutions in *Trent's Last Case*, along with Trent's eventual repudiation of pure logic as a means of understanding human affairs, puts the book closer to the modernist novels that depict an ambiguous and unreliable reality. See Linda Schlossberg, "Trent's Last Case: Murder, Modernism, Meaning," in *Formal Investigations: Aesthetic Style in Late Victorian and Edwardian Detective Fiction*, rev. ed., *Studies in English Literatures*, Vol. 4, ed. Paul Fox and Koray Melikoglu (Stuttgart: Ibidem, 2014), 247–65.
102. Rob Spillman, "On William Faulkner's *As I Lay Dying*," *Pen America*, October 15, 2012, https://pen.org/on-william-faulkners-as-i-lay-dying/.
103. Dorothy Sayers, "The Present Status of the Mystery Story," *London Mercury* 23 (November 1930): 52.

5. Before the Fact: The Psychological Thriller

The chapter epigraph is from Agatha Christie's *Towards Zero* (New York: Harper, 2011), 4.
1. Marie Belloc Lowndes, *The Lodger* (New York: Dell, 1964), 193.
2. Lowndes, *Lodger*, 102.
3. Lowndes, *Lodger*, 58.
4. Lowndes, *Lodger*, 209.
5. Lowndes, *Lodger*, 224.
6. Useful accounts of the thriller can be found in Ralph Harper, *The World of the Thriller* (1969; repr. Baltimore, MD: Johns Hopkins University Press, 1974); Charles Derry, *The Suspense Thriller: Films in the Shadow of Alfred Hitchcock* (Jefferson, NC: McFarland, 1988); Martin Rubin, *Thrillers* (Cambridge: Cambridge University Press, 1999); and Patrick Anderson, *The Triumph of the Thriller: How Cops, Crooks, and Cannibals*

Captured Popular Fiction (New York: Random House, 2007). Most of these authors include detective stories in the category of the thriller, but they also provide analyses of the narrower genre I'm considering here. I examine emerging ideas of the thriller during the 1930s and 1940s in chapter 10 of David Bordwell, *Reinventing Hollywood: How 1940s Filmmakers Changed Movie Storytelling* (Chicago: University of Chicago Press, 2017).

7. Examples are W. W. Wister, "Why Photoplays Have Killed Melodramas," *Nickelodeon*, March 18, 1911, 299–300; Franklin K. Mathiews, "Books as Merchandise and Something More," *Publishers' Weekly*, May 11, 1915, 1487–91; and Henry Alton, "Some Dangerous New Grafts on the Old Tree of Nickel Thrillers," *McBride's Magazine Advertiser*, December 1915, 17.

8. R. Austin Freeman, "The Art of the Detective Story" (1924), in *The Art of the Mystery Story*, ed. Howard Haycraft (New York: Simon & Schuster, 1941), 10.

9. Basil Hogarth argues for a broader conception of the genre and treats detective stories as one type of thriller. See Basil Hogarth, *Writing Thrillers for Profit: A Practical Guide* (London: Black's Writers and Artists Library, 1936). Hogarth devotes the bulk of his book to detective stories, which need smooth carpentry, but the chapter on "the thriller of sensation" advises the novice to pile up action-driven episodes in which "intrigue and coincidence can be stretched as far as you please" (138). Hogarth doesn't acknowledge the psychological thriller as a creative option.

10. Detection Club constitution as quoted in Martin Edwards, *The Golden Age of Murder* (London: Collins, 2017), 92.

11. Patrick Hamilton as quoted in Sean French, *Patrick Hamilton: A Life* (London: Faber and Faber, 1993), 139.

12. Milward Kennedy, *Death to the Rescue: A Detective Story* (London: Gollancz, 1931), 6.

13. "Chaplin in 'Circus' a London Sensation," *New York Times*, March 16, 1928.

14. Beatrix Hesse has estimated that two-thirds of all crime plays written before 1930 were staged between 1926 and 1929. See Beatrix Hesse, *The English Crime Play in the Twentieth Century* (New York: Palgrave Macmillan, 2015), 1.

15. Many writers believed that a pure whodunit plot was ineffective in a play. Collins gave away the mystery in his stage version of *The Moonstone*, as did A. E. W. Mason when adapting *At the Villa Rose*. See Hesse, *English Crime Play*, 23–24.

16. Charles Morgan, "Mr. Milne Tries a New Trick with a Mystery Play," *New York Times*, March 25, 1928.

17. Dorothy L. Sayers, "The Omnibus of Crime" (1928–29), in *The Art of the Mystery Story*, ed. Howard Haycraft (New York: Simon & Schuster, 1941), 102.

18. Anthony Berkeley, dedication to A. D. Peters, in *The Second Shot* (Garden City, NY: Crime Club, 1931).

19. Dorothy L. Sayers, introduction to *Great Short Stories of Detection, Mystery and Horror, Second Series* (London: Gollancz, 1931), 17.

20. Berkeley, *Second Shot*.

21. Sayers, *Great Short Stories*, 17.

22. Freeman, "Art of the Detective Story," 13.

23. Quoted in Edwards, *Golden Age of Murder*, 184.

24. Freeman Wills Crofts, *The 12.30 from Croydon* (London: Poison Pen, 2016), chap. 18, e-book.

25. Richard Hull, *Murder Isn't Easy* (New York: Putnam, 1936), 248.

26. Nicholas Blake, *The Beast Must Die* (New York: Dell, 1958), 7.

27. Blake, *Beast Must Die*, 98.

28. As in the second part, Blake "bares the device" of the moving-spotlight narration in a string of three sentences that juxtapose the thinking of Nigel, Georgia, and Felix. Blake, *Beast Must Die*, 180.

29. Blake, *Beast Must Die*, 156.

30. In the same spirit, Raymond Chandler objected that the intrusion of "the amateur gentleman" Nigel had "a devastating effect" on a "damn good and extremely well written story." See Raymond Chandler, *Selected Letters of Raymond Chandler*, ed. Frank MacShane (New York: Columbia University Press, 1981), 246. As indicated, I think Blake designed the clash between the narrative modes as a way to criticize the limits of Golden Age detection.

31. Blake, *Beast Must Die*, 222.

32. Francis Iles, *Malice Aforethought: The Story of a Commonplace Crime* (New York: Dover, 2018), 14, 111, 108.

33. Francis Iles, *Before the Fact* (New York: Pocket, 197), 1.

34. Iles, *Before the Fact*, 259.

35. "From Dostoevsky's Notebooks," "Backgrounds and Sources," in *Crime and Punishment*, trans. Jessie Coulson, ed. George Gibian (New York: Norton, 1964), 534.

36. Elizabeth Sanxay Holding, *The Unfinished Crime and the Girl Who Had to Die* (New York: Stark House, 2020), 105, 107.

37. Patrick Hamilton, *Rope* (New York: Samuel French, n.d.), 4.

38. Holding, *Unfinished Crime*, 65.

39. Until Highsmith's Tom Ripley, that is.

40. Cain was delighted with the use of the tape recorder to chronicle Walter Neff's voice-over account in the film version of *Double Indemnity* (1944). See Peter Brunette and Gerald Peary, "James M. Cain: Tough Guy," in *Backstory: Interviews with Screenwriters of Hollywood's Golden Age* (Los Angeles: University of California Press, 1986), 115, 127.

41. James M. Cain, "*The Postman Always Rings Twice*," in *The Postman Always Rings Twice, Double Indemnity, Mildred Pierce and Selected Stories* (London: Everyman's Library, 2003), 121.

42. Quoted in Howard Haycraft, *Murder for Pleasure: The Life and Times of the Detective Story* (New York: Appleton-Century, 1941), 90.

43. Mary Roberts Rinehart, *The Circular Staircase* (New York: Pocket, 1943), 1.

44. Julian Symons, *Mortal Consequences: A History—From the Detective Story to the Crime Novel* (New York: Harper and Row, 1972), 97.

45. Mignon G. Eberhart, *The House on the Roof* (Lincoln: University of Nebraska Press, 1996), 246.

46. Carl D. Brandt, introduction to Eberhart, *House on the Roof* (Lincoln: University of Nebraska Press, 1996), vi.

47. Diane Waldman, "Horror and Domesticity: The Modern Gothic Romance Film of the 1940s" (PhD diss., University of Wisconsin–Madison, 1981), 5–56.

48. Patrick Hamilton, *Angel Street* (New York: Samuel French, n.d.), 107.

49. Daphne du Maurier, *Rebecca* (Harmondsworth, UK: Penguin, 1962), 264.

50. Donald Westlake as quoted in Bill Pronzini, *Gun in Cheek: A Study of "Alternative" Crime Fiction* (New York: Coward, McCann, and Geoghegan, 1982), 199.

51. du Maurier, *Rebecca*, 100.

52. du Maurier, *Rebecca*, 308.

53. Alfred Hitchcock, "Why 'Thrillers' Thrive" (1936), in *Hitchcock on Hitchcock: Selected Writings and Interviews*, ed. Sidney Gottlieb (Berkeley: University of California Press, 1995), 110.

54. Dorothy L. Sayers, "Detective Stories and a Thriller" (1934), in *Taking Detective Stories Seriously: The Collected Crime Reviews of Dorothy L. Sayers* (Perth, Scotland: Tippermuir, 2017), 116.

55. Alfred Hitchcock, "Hitchcock on Stories" (1937), in *Hitchcock on Hitchcock 2: Selected Writings and Interviews*, ed. Sidney Gottlieb (Berkeley: University of California Press, 2015), 29. Sayers's 1937 play *Busman's Honeymoon* tried to adapt the puzzle plot for the stage by presenting some visual clues that are available to the audience but ignored by the characters. The result, she claimed, was "a perfect dramatic formula" for a detective play. Few other authors seem to have pursued this "contrapuntal" technique. See "Authors' Note," in *Busman's Honeymoon*, by Dorothy Sayers and M. St. Clare Byrne (New York: Samuel French, 1939), 6.

56. Val Gielgud, foreword to *Money with Menaces and To the Public Danger: Two Radio Plays*, by Patrick Hamilton (London: Constable, 1939), v–vi.

57. "Dramatic Notes," in *Selected Prose Works of G. E. Lessing*, ed. Edward Bell (London: George Bell, 1889), 377–78.

58. J. Brander Matthews, "Victor Hugo," in *French Dramatists of the Nineteenth Century* (New York: Scribners, 1881), 20–21.

59. Henry Edwards, "The Language of Action," *The Bioscope*, suppl., (July 1, 1920): iv. I'm grateful to Charles Barr and Michaela Mikalauski for calling this piece to my attention.

60. Alfred Hitchcock, "Lecture at Columbia University" (1939), in *Hitchcock on Hitchcock: Selected Writings and Interviews*, ed. Sidney Gottlieb (Berkeley: University of California Press, 1995), 273–74.

61. François Truffaut, *Hitchcock*, rev. ed. (New York: Simon & Schuster, 1983), 73.

62. Maria Belodubrovskaya thoroughly explores the role of surprise in Hitchcock's work in "The Master of Surprise: Alfred Hitchcock, the Surprise Plot, and Cataphoric Pleasures," forthcoming.

63. William Archer, *Play-Making: A Manual of Craftsmanship* (Boston: Small, Maynard, 1912), 172.

64. Edward Chodorov, *Kind Lady* (New York: Samuel French, 1936), 71–74.

65. Charles Barr offers a revealing discussion of *Jamaica Inn*'s mixed handling of narration. See Charles Barr, *Jamaica Inn* in *English Hitchcock* (Moffat, Scotland: Cameron & Hollis, 1999), 202–6.

66. "New Films in London: 'Blackmail,'" *Times* (London), May 25, 1936; "Films of 1938," *Times* (London), January 2, 1939; "Gaumont Cinema: 'Rebecca,'" *Times* (London), June 27, 1940. Hitchcock's early strategies for maintaining his distinctive profile are detailed in Janet Staiger, "Creating the Brand: The Hitchcock Touch," in *The Cambridge Companion to Alfred Hitchcock*, ed. Jonathan Freedman (New York: Cambridge University Press, 2015), 40–50. See also Robert E. Kapsis, *Hitchcock: The Making of a Reputation* (Chicago: University of Chicago Press, 1992), chap. 2.

67. Lupton A. Wilkinson, "He Makes the Movies Move," *Los Angeles Times*, January 5, 1941.

68. Illuminating discussions of Hitchcock's debts to literary and theatrical traditions can be found in R. Barton Palmer and David Boyd, eds., *Hitchcock at the Source: The Auteur as Adapter* (Albany: SUNY Press, 2011), especially Thomas Leitch, "Hitchcock from Stage to Page," 11–32; and Mark Glancy, "*The Man Who Knew Too Much* (1934): Alfred Hitchcock, John Buchan, and the Thrill of the Chase," 77–88.

69. Tom Ryall, *Alfred Hitchcock and British Cinema* (London: Croom Helm, 1986), 75–76.

70. Raymond Chandler, "Letter to Hamish Hamilton" (September 4, 1950), in *Raymond Chandler Speaking*, ed. Dorothy Gardiner and Kathrine Sorley Walker (New York: Houghton Mifflin, 1962), 132.

71. Charles Bennett, *Hitchcock's Partner in Suspense: The Life of Screenwriter Charles Bennett* (Lexington: University of Kentucky Press, 2014), 67.

72. See Pat Hitchcock O'Connell and Laurent Bouzereau, *Alma Hitchcock: The Woman Behind the Man* (New York: Berkley, 2003), 31–91; and Christina Lane, *Phantom Lady: Hollywood Producer Joan Harrison, The Forgotten Woman Behind Hitchcock* (Chicago: Chicago Review, 2020), 35–125.

73. I offer more detailed analyses of the film in David Bordwell, "*The Man Who Knew Too Much*," http://www.davidbordwell.net/filmart/ManWhoKnewTooMuch_FilmArt_2nd _1988_292.pdf; and David Bordwell, "Sir Alfred Simply Must Have His Set Pieces: *The Man Who Knew Too Much*," *David Bordwell's Website on Cinema* (blog), http://www .davidbordwell.net/blog/2013/02/14/sir-alfred-simply-must-have-his-set-pieces-the -man-who-knew-too-much-1934/.

6. Dark and Full of Blood: Hard-Boiled Detection

1. This chapter is especially indebted to the suggestive account of "popular modernism" in James Naremore, *More Than Night: Film Noir and Its Contexts*, 2nd ed. (Berkeley: University of California Press, 2008); and his wide-ranging essay, James Naremore, "Dashiell Hammett and the Poetics of Hard-Boiled Detection," in *Art in Crime Writing: Essays on Detective Fiction*, ed. Bernard Benstock (New York: St. Martin's, 1983), 49–72; as well as to Geoffrey O'Brien's nuanced discussion of hard-boiled style in Geoffrey O'Brien, *Hardboiled America: Lurid Paperbacks and the Masters of Noir*, expanded ed. (New York: Da Capo, 1997). Chapter 6 of John G. Cawelti, *Adventure, Mystery and Romance: Formula Stories as Art and Popular Culture* (Chicago: University of Chicago Press, 1976), is also incisive and informative.

2. For a compact history, see Brooks E. Hefner, "Pulp Magazines," in *American Literature in Transition 1920–1930*, ed. Ichiro Takayoshi (Cambridge: Cambridge University Press, 2018), 434–48. On *Black Mask*, see William F. Nolan, *The Black Mask Boys: Masters in the Hard-Boiled School of Detective Fiction* (New York: Morrow, 1985). David M. Earle links the pulps to quasi-modernist magazines and to the paperback revolution in David M. Earle, *Re-Covering Modernism: Pulps, Paperbacks, and the Prejudice of Form* (Burlington VT: Ashgate, 2009).

     John Locke has edited two invaluable collections on publishing practices: John Locke, *Pulpwood Days*. Vol. 1, *Editors You Want to Know* (Castroville, CA: Off-Trail, 2007); and John Locke, *Pulpwood Days*. Vol. 2, *Lives of the Pulp Writers* (Castroville, CA: Off-Trail, 2013). The autobiographical accounts in the latter are matched by the vivid memoir by Frank Gruber, *The Pulp Jungle* (Los Angeles: Sherbourne, 1967). Another good collection of original articles on pulp practices is Ed Hulse, ed., *The Penny-a-Word Brigade: Pulp Fictioneers Discuss Their Craft* (Dover, NJ: Murania, 2017).

3. Joseph T. Shaw, "The Aim of *Black Mask*," *Black Mask*, June 1927, iii.

4. Carroll John Daly, "*The Snarl of the Beast*" (1927), in *The Snarl of the Beast: The Collected Hard-Boiled Stories of Race Williams*, vol. 2 (Boston: Altus, 2016), 79.

5. Carroll John Daly, "The Hidden Hand" (1928), in *The Snarl of the Beast: The Collected Hard-Boiled Stories of Race Williams*, vol. 2 (Boston: Altus, 2016), 301.

6. Dashiell Hammett, "Another Perfect Crime" (1925), in *Hardboiled Mystery Writers: Raymond Chandler, Dashiell Hammett, Ross Macdonald: A Literary Reference*, ed. Matthew J. Bruccoli and Richard Layman (New York: Carroll and Graff, 2002), 207–10.

7. Joseph T. Shaw, ed., introduction to *The Hard-Boiled Omnibus: Early Stories from Black Mask* (New York: Simon &Schuster, 1946), vi–vii.

8. Raymond Chandler, "The Simple Art of Murder," *Later Novels and Other Writings* (New York: Library of America, 1995), 991.

9. Daly, "*Snarl of the Beast*," 129.

10. Joseph T. Shaw, "We're On Our Way!!" *Black Mask*, May 1927, vi.

11. Brooks E. Hefner surveys Daly's career in Brooks E. Hefner, introduction to *Them That Lives by Their Guns: The Collected Hard-Boiled Stories of Race Williams*, vol. 1, by Carroll John Daly (Boston: Altus, 2015), xi–xviii. See also G. A. Finch, "A Fatal Attraction," *The Armchair Detective* 13, no. 2 (Spring 1980): 112–24; and Michael S. Barson, "'There's No Sex in Crime': The Two-Fisted Homilies of Race Williams," *Clues* 2, no. 2 (Fall/Winter 1981): 103–12.

12. Cleanth Brooks Jr. and Robert Penn Warren, *Understanding Fiction* (New York: Appleton-Century-Crofts, 1943), viii. This textbook, which exemplifies the extent to which New Criticism was being integrated into college curricula, warns instructors that their students are likely to prefer "the crudest story of violent action." (viii). Brooks and Warren may have had pulp fiction in mind.

13. Dashiell Hammett, *Selected Letters of Dashiell Hammett 1921–1960*, ed. Richard Layman and Julie M. Rivett (Washington, DC: Counterpoint, 2001), 46.

14. Raymond Chandler, "Trouble Is My Business," in *Collected Stories* (New York: Knopf, 2002), 989.

15. Advertisement for *Red Harvest*, *New York Times Book Review*, February 17, 1929, as quoted in Lisa Jaillant, "New Publishers," in *American Literature in Transition: 1920–1930*, ed. Ichiro Takayoshi (Cambridge: Cambridge University Press, 2018), 404.

16. Paul Cain, "Gundown" (1933), in William F. Nolan, *The Black Mask Boys: Masters in the Hard-Boiled School of Detective Fiction* (New York: Morrow, 1985), 220.

17. Dashiell Hammett, "Poor Scotland Yard!," in Matthew Bruccoli and Richard Layman, eds., *Hardboiled Mystery Writers: Raymond Chandler, Dashiell Hammett, Ross Macdonald: A Literary Reference* (New York: Carroll and Graff, 2002), 105.

18. Dashiell Hammett, "Introduction to *The Maltese Falcon*," in *Hardboiled Mystery Writers: Raymond Chandler, Dashiell Hammett, Ross Macdonald: A Literary Reference*, ed. Matthew Bruccoli and Richard Layman (New York: Carroll and Graff, 2002), 117; Raymond Chandler, introduction to "The Simple Art of Murder," in *Later Novels and Other Writings* (New York: Library of America, 1995), 1017.

19. For more on crime films of the 1910s, see David Bordwell, "Film Noir a Hundred Years Ago," *David Bordwell's Website on Cinema* (blog), http://www.davidbordwell.net/blog/2017/04/18/film-noir-a-hundred-years-ago/.

20. Dashiell Hammett, "The Creeping Siamese," in *The Black Lizard Big Book of Pulps*, ed. Otto Penzler (New York, Vintage, 2007), 15–24; Carroll John Daly, *Snarl of the Beast: The Collected Hard-Boiled Stories of Race Williams*, vol. 2 (Boston: Altus, 2016), 43; Paul Cain, *Fast One* (Monroe, IL: Gutter, 2013), 173, 191.

21. Raymond Chandler, *The Lady in the Lake* (London: Pan, 1979), 150. Aristotle notes that in plots "it is likely that some things should occur contrary to likelihood." Stephen Halliwell, *The Poetics of Aristotle: Translation and Commentary* (Chapel Hill: University of North Carolina Press, 1987), 63.

22. Hammett, "Introduction to *The Maltese Falcon*," 117.

23. John Gallishaw, "What the Men's 'Pulp-Paper' Magazines Are Buying," *The Writer* 45, no. 5 (May 1933): 133.

24. Dashiell Hammett as quoted in Ellery Queen, "The Sex Life of a Gentleman Detective," *In the Queens' Parlor and Other Leaves from the Editors' Notebook* (New York: Biblio and Tannen, 1969), 47.

25. Dashiell Hammett, *The Thin Man* (Boston: G. K. Hall, 2001), 205.

26. As quoted in Richard Layman, *Shadow Man: The Life of Dashiell Hammett* (New York: Harcourt Brace Jovanovich, 1981), 145.

27. Robert Leslie Bellem, *Blue Murder* (Miami: Dennis McMillan, 1987), 10; Brett Halliday, *Dividend on Death* (New York: Mysterious, 2015), chap. 1; Steve Fisher, *I Wake Up Screaming* (New York: Popular Library, 1941), 4; Jonathan Latimer, *Solomon's Vineyard* (London: Planet Monk, 2014), chap. 1.

28. H. Bedford-Jones, *The Graduate Fictioneer* (Denver, CO: Author and Journalist, 1932), 74.

29. Chandler, "Simple Art of Murder," 989.

30. Daly, "*Snarl of the Beast*," 104.

31. Dashiell Hammett, "The Gutting of Coffignal," in *The Big Book of the Continental Op*, ed. Richard Layman and Julie M. Rivett (New York: Vintage, 2017), 347.

32. Dashiell Hammett, "*The Roman Hat Mystery*," *Saturday Review of Literature*, October 12, 1929, 262. Ellery Queen's 1958 novel *The Finishing Stroke*, set in 1929, shows the young Ellery chafing under this review, which calls him a "philovancish bookworm." Ellery Queen, *The Finishing Stroke* (New York: Pocket, 1963), 23.

33. Dashiell Hammett, *Red Harvest* (New York: Vintage, 1972), 152.

34. Editor Harry Block, worried that the book "falls too definitively into three sections," asked for a "connecting thread." Harry Block as quoted in Dashiell Hammett, *The Big Book of the Continental Op*, ed. Richard Layman and Julie M. Rivett (New York: Vintage, 2017), 629. Fitzstephan's role was expanded in the novel.

35. James Sandoe and Martin Edwards make this point. See Martin Edwards, *The Story of Classic Crime in 100 Books* (London: British Library, 2017), 241.

36. Dashiell Hammett, *The Dain Curse* (New York: Vintage, 1972), 217.

37. Hammett, "Introduction to *The Maltese Falcon*," 117.

38. "A Man Called Hammett," *Times Literary Supplement*, November 17, 1950, in *Hardboiled Mystery Writers: Raymond Chandler, Dashiell Hammett, Ross Macdonald: A Literary Reference*, ed. Matthew Bruccoli and Richard Layman (New York: Carroll and Graff, 2002), 195.

39. Dashiell Hammett, *The Maltese Falcon* (New York: Knopf, 1930), 53.

40. Hammett, *Maltese Falcon*, 122.

41. Hammett, *Maltese Falcon*, 274.

42. Dashiell Hammett, *The Glass Key* (New York: Vintage, 1972), 156.

43. Hammett, *Glass Key*, 177.

44. Hammett, *Glass Key*, 210.

45. Hammett, *Selected Letters*, 71.

46. Hammett, *Thin Man*, 217.

47. Hammett, *Thin Man*, 155, 173.

48. Lea Jacobs traces the emergence of the sophisticated comedy; see Lea Jacobs, *The Decline of Sentiment: American Film in the 1920s* (Berkeley: University of California Press, 2008), chap. 3.

49. Richard Layman, introduction to *Return of the Thin Man*, by Dashiell Hammett, ed. Richard Layman and Julie M. Rivett (New York: Mysterious, 2012), 2.

50. Hammett, *Selected Letters*, 47.

51. "Behind the Blurbs," *The Outlook and Independent*, February 26, 1930, 350.

52. Axel Madsen, *Malraux: A Biography* (New York: Morrow, 1976), 114–15.

53. Hammett, *Selected Letters*, 47.

54. Shaw, introduction to *Hard-Boiled Omnibus*, viii.

55. Carroll John Daly, "The False Burton Combs" (1922), in *Them That Lives by Their Guns: The Collected Hard-Boiled Stories of Race Williams*, vol. 1, by Carroll John Daly (Boston: Altus, 2015), 635.

56. Sensitive analyses of Hammett's 1920s writing are offered by LeRoy Lad Panek, *Reading Early Hammett: A Critical Study of the Fiction Prior to The Maltese Falcon* (Jefferson, NC: McFarland, 2004).

57. Dashiell Hammett, "The Whosis Kid," in *Big Book of the Continental Op*, ed. Richard Layman and Julie M. Rivett (New York: Vintage, 2017), 232.

58. Dashiell Hammett, "Zigzags of Treachery," in *Big Book of the Continental Op*, ed. Richard Layman and Julie M. Rivett (New York: Vintage, 2017), 99; Dashiell Hammett, "Dead Yellow Women," in *Big Book of the Continental Op*, ed. Richard Layman and Julie M. Rivett (New York: Vintage, 2017), 311, 329.

59. Dashiell Hammett, "The Golden Horseshoe," in *Big Book of the Continental Op*, ed. Richard Layman and Julie M. Rivett (New York: Vintage, 2017), 183; Hammett, "Dead Yellow Women, 329; Dashiell Hammett, "Corkscrew" (1925), *Big Book of the Continental Op*, ed. Richard Layman and Julie M. Rivett (New York: Vintage, 2017), 276; Hammett, "Dead Yellow Women," 311; Dashiell Hammett, "The House in Turk Street," *Big Book of the Continental Op*, ed. Richard Layman and Julie M. Rivett (New York: Vintage, 2017), 129.

60. Hammett, "The Gutting of Coffignal," 347.

61. Hammett, *Red Harvest*, 171.

62. Hammett, *Dain Curse*, 35; Hammett, *Red Harvest*, 87; Hammett, *Dain Curse*, 203, 206.

63. Hammett, *Red Harvest*, 193.

64. Hammett, *Red Harvest*, 192.

65. Hammett, *Thin Man*, 154, 104.

66. Hammett, *Maltese Falcon*, 15, 229, 152.

67. Hammett, *Maltese Falcon*, 169.

68. This passage is dissected with great subtlety in Naremore, "Dashiell Hammett and the Poetics of Hard-Boiled Detection," 60–62.

69. Hammett, *Maltese Falcon*, 68.

70. Hammett, *Maltese Falcon*, 224.

71. Rudy Behlmer, "'The Stuff That Dreams Are Made Of': *The Maltese Falcon*," in *The Maltese Falcon*, ed. William Luhr (New Brunswick, NJ: Rutgers University Press, 1995), 112–13; Don Hartman, "Two Heads Are Worse Than One (Especially if They're on You)," in *Hello, Hollywood!: The Story of the Movies by the People Who Make Them*, ed. Allen Rivkin and Laura Kerr (New York: Doubleday, 1962), 155–56.

72. Hammett, *Glass Key*, 60, 156, 42.

73. Hammett, *Glass Key*, 116.

74. Hammett, *Glass Key*, 145.

75. Hammett, *Glass Key*, 40, 106.

76. The repetition is in the original *Black Mask* serial. Perhaps Hammett repeated the passage in the third installment to reintroduce Jack, a minor character, to readers who had forgotten his role in the second installment. No other character is reintroduced this way, however, and the passage would normally be modified or eliminated when an author was recasting it for book publication. See "Dagger Point," *Black Mask* 13, no. 4

(May 1933): 53. Perhaps Hammett also wanted to try a comma-filled variant on the first Gertrude Steinian description?

77. Without referring to Hammett, Walter Nash discusses the use of full names in contemporary adventure novels; see Walter Nash, *Language in Popular Fiction* (London: Routledge, 1990), 57–63.

78. Percy Lubbock, *The Craft of Fiction* (New York: Viking, 1957), 113.

79. André Gide, "Journal of *The Counterfeiters*," in *The Counterfeiters*, trans. Dorothy Bussy and Justin O'Brien (New York: Modern Library, 1955), 442.

80. Claude-Edmonde Magny, *The Age of the American Novel: The Film Aesthetic of Fiction Between the Two Wars*, trans. Eleanor Hochman (New York: Ungar, 1972), 43.

81. Hammett, *Glass Key*, 214.

82. Dashiell Hammett, "Mr. Hergesheimer's Scenario," *The Forum*, November 1924, 720.

83. Hammett, "Dead Yellow Women," 329.

84. Joseph Shaw as quoted in Francis L. Fugate and Roberta Fugate, eds., *Secrets of the World's Best-Selling Writer: The Storytelling Techniques of Erle Stanley Gardner* (New York: Morrow, 1980), 76.

85. Hammett, *Red Harvest*, 134.

86. Hammett, "Mr. Hergesheimer's Scenario," 720.

87. Hammett, *Maltese Falcon*, 89, 117; Hammett, *Thin Man*, 11, 272.

88. Lutton Blassingame, "The Detective Fiction Market," in *Penny-a-Word Brigade: Pulp Fictioneers Discuss Their Craft*, ed. Ed Hulse (Dover, NJ: Murania, 2017), 116; originally published in *Writer's Digest*, January 1937.

89. Raymond Chandler, "Goldfish," in *Collected Stories* (New York: Knopf, 2002), 515.

90. Frank MacShane, *The Life of Raymond Chandler* (New York: Dutton, 1976), 55.

91. *Publishers' Weekly*, December 24, 1938, cover advertisement.

92. Raymond Chandler, *Selected Letters of Raymond Chandler*, ed. Frank MacShane (New York: Columbia University Press, 1981), 4.

93. Illuminating discussions of Chandler can be found in Philip Durham, *Down These Mean Streets a Man Must Go: Raymond Chandler's Knight* (Chapel Hill: University of North Carolina Press, 1963); MacShane, *Life of Raymond Chandler*; Miriam Gross, ed., *The World of Raymond Chandler* (New York: A & W, 1977); William Luhr, *Raymond Chandler and Film* (New York: Ungar, 1982); and Owen Hill, Pamela Jackson, and Anthony Dean Pizzuto, eds., *The Annotated The Big Sleep* (New York: Vintage, 2018). A bracingly skeptical take is Julian Symons, "Raymond Chandler," in *Criminal Practices: Symons on Crime Writing, 60s to 90s* (London: Macmillan, 1994), 143–57.

94. On Chandler's training, see Kathleen Riley, "Latin Woostered and Hard-Boiled: The Classical Style of P. G. Wodehouse and Raymond Chandler," *Arion* 26, no. 2 (Fall 2018): 17–32.

95. Donald E. Westlake, "The Hardboiled Dicks," in *The Getaway Car: A Donald Westlake Nonfiction Miscellany*, ed. Levi Stahl (Chicago: University of Chicago Press, 2014), 41.

96. Chandler, *Selected Letters*, 115.

97. Raymond Chandler, "Casual Notes on the Mystery Novel" (1949), in *Raymond Chandler Speaking*, ed. Dorothy Gardiner and Kathrine Sorley Walker (Plainview, NY: Books for Libraries, 1971), 69.

98. Chandler, "Simple Art of Murder," 987.

99. Raymond Chandler, "Twelve Notes on the Mystery Story," in *Later Novels and Other Writings* (New York: Library of America, 1995), 1010.

100. Chandler, *Selected Letters*, 152, 239. The fact that the suicidal writer in *The Long Goodbye* (1953) signs himself "Roger (F. Scott Fitzgerald) Wade" has inclined one critic to see the

book as Chandler's rewriting of *The Great Gatsby*. See Leon Howard, "Raymond Chandler's Not-So-Great Gatsby," in *The Mystery and Detection Annual*, ed. Donald Adams (Beverly Hills, CA: Mystery and Detection Annual, 1973), 1–15.

101. Chandler, "Simple Art of Murder," 989.

102. G. K. Chesterton, "A Defence of Detective Stories," in Howard Haycraft, ed., *Art of the Mystery Story* (New York: Simon & Schuster, 1941), 4, 6.

103. Chandler, *Selected Letters*, 151.

104. Chandler, *Selected Letters*, 129–30.

105. LeRoy Lad Panek, *An Introduction to the Detective Story* (Bowling Green, OH: Bowling Green University Popular Press, 1987), 153.

106. Raymond Chandler, *The Big Sleep* (New York: Ballantine, 1972), 166.

107. Chandler, *Big Sleep*, 67.

108. Brett Halliday, *The Private Practice of Michael Shayne* (New York: Dell, 1965), 15.

109. Chandler, *Big Sleep*, 135.

110. Chandler, *Big Sleep*, 24, 45; Raymond Chandler, *The High Window* (New York: Vintage, 1976), 57; Chandler, *Lady in the Lake*, 70; Chandler, *Big Sleep*, 55; Chandler, *Lady in the Lake*, 70; Chandler, *Farewell, My Lovely* (New York: Vintage, 1988), 8; Chandler, *High Window*, 38.

111. Chandler, *Farewell, My Lovely*, 51.

112. Chandler, *Farewell, My Lovely*, 91, 107, 8; Chandler, *High Window*, 205, 34.

113. Chandler, *Selected Letters*, 187.

114. Chandler, *Farewell, My Lovely*, 264.

115. Raymond Chandler, *The Little Sister* (London: Hamilton, 1969), 80; Chandler, *Farewell, My Lovely*, 140.

116. Chandler, *High Window*, 165; Chandler, *Big Sleep*, 90; Chandler, *Farewell, My Lovely*, 241.

117. Chandler, *High Window*, 190; Chandler, *Lady in the Lake*, 185.

118. Chandler, *Farewell, My Lovely*, 241.

119. Chandler, *Lady in the Lake*, 152.

120. Chandler, *Big Sleep*, 201.

121. Chandler, *Farewell, My Lovely*, 80–81.

122. Chandler, *High Window*, 170.

123. "I want to try adapting this stream-of-consciousness method, conveniently modified, to a detective story, carrying the reader along with the detective, showing him everything as it is found, giving him the detective's conclusions as they are reached, letting the solution break on both of them together." Hammett, *Selected Letters*, 46.

124. Chandler, "Twelve Notes," 1009.

125. For a detailed comparison of the two versions, see Miranda B. Hickman, "Introduction: The Complex History of 'A Simple Art,'" *Studies in the Novel* 35, no. 3 (Fall 2003): 292–98.

126. Raymond Chandler as quoted in MacShane, *Life of Chandler*, 70.

127. Chandler, "Simple Art of Murder," 992.

128. Chandler, *Big Sleep*, 154.

129. Although Chandler doesn't mention it, Hammett was a member of the Communist Party. "The Simple Art of Murder" tacitly encouraged later critics to find in Hammett's work traces of proletarian literature's denunciation of American capitalism and international fascism. See Michael Denning, *The Cultural Front: The Laboring of American Culture in the Twentieth Century* (London: Verso, 1997), 255–58.

130. Chandler, *Selected Letters*, 448.

131. Chandler, "Simple Art of Murder," 991.

132. MacShane, *Life of Chandler*, 148.

133. R. W. Flint, "A Cato of the Cruelties," *Partisan Review* 14, no. 3 (May-June 1947): 328; W. H. Auden, "The Guilty Vicarage: Notes on the Detective Story, by an Addict" (1948), in *Prose. Vol. 2, 1939-1948, The Complete Works of W. H. Auden*, ed. Edward Mendelson (Princeton, NJ: Princeton University Press, 2002), 265.

134. Graham McInnes, "Elementary, My Dear Watson," *University of Toronto Quarterly* 16, no. 4 (July 1947): 411-12.

135. Flint, "Cato of the Cruelties," 328.

136. Stephen Pendo provides detailed comparisons of the films with their sources; see Stephen Pendo, *Raymond Chandler on Screen: His Novels Into Film* (Metuchen, NJ: Scarecrow, 1976).

137. Matthew J. Bruccoli, "Afterword: Chandler and Hollywood," in *The Blue Dahlia: A Screenplay*, ed. Matthew J. Bruccoli (Carbondale: Southern Illinois University Press, 1976), 131.

138. Chandler, *Selected Letters*, 310-11.

139. Chandler, *Little Sister*, 70.

140. Chandler, *Little Sister*, 237; Raymond Chandler, *The Long Goodbye* (New York: Vintage, 1988), 32, 210.

141. Chandler, *Little Sister*, 14, 188.

142. If, as some speculate, Raymond Chandler's 1957 short story "English Summer" was an effort to establish himself as a writer of "straight" fiction, that would suggest he was still anchored in the 1910s. The narration suggests at once the influence of James (the protagonist is an American abroad) and of Ford Maddox Ford.

143. I discuss the use of flashback narration in David Bordwell, *Reinventing Hollywood: How 1940s Filmmakers Changed Movie Storytelling* (Chicago: University of Chicago Press, 2017), 67-124, 237-60.

144. Chandler, *Little Sister*, 86, 187.

145. Luhr, *Raymond Chandler and Film*, 11.

146. Harry Wilson, "The Dark Mirror," *Sequence* 7 (Spring 1949): 19-22.

7. The 1940s: Mysteries in Crossover Culture

1. Films in which the protagonist is a mystery writer include *Footsteps in the Dark* (1940), *Whistling in the Dark* (1941), *Dangerous Blondes* (1943), *The Mask of Dimitrios* (1944), *Home Sweet Homicide* (1946), *The Unsuspected* (1947), and *Seven Keys to Baldpate* (1947).

2. Frederick C. Davis, "Mysteries Plus," in *Writing Detective and Mystery Fiction*, ed. A. S. Burack (Boston: The Writer, 1945), 210-12; Frederick C. Davis, "What Makes a Post Serial?," *The Writer* 60, no. 7 (July 1947): 289.

3. The publishing dynamics governing the Queen stories are explored in Matthew Levay, "Preservation and Promotion: Ellery Queen, Magazine Publishing, and the Marketing of Detective Fiction," in *The Centrality of Crime Fiction in American Literary Culture*, ed. Alfred Endixen and Olivia Carr Edenfield (New York: Routledge, 2017), 101-22.

4. Ellery Queen, *Calamity Town*, in *The Wrightsville Murders* (Boston: Little Brown, 1948), 197.

5. Frederic Dannay as quoted in Francis M. Nevins, *Ellery Queen: The Art of Detection* (Lexington KY: Perfect Crime, 2013), 109.

6. Queen, *Calamity Town*, 186.

7. *Ten Days' Wonder* was to be, Dannay wrote in a letter to Lee, "an exposure of detective novels and of fictional detectives." See Frederic Dannay, "Letter of October 24, 1947," in *Blood Relations: The Selected Letters of Ellery Queen, 1947–1950*, ed. Joseph Goodrich (Lexington, KY: Perfect Crime, 2012), 19.

8. Ellery Queen, *Cat of Many Tails* (Boston: Little, Brown, 1949), 241.

9. The epigraph is from "Dashiell Hammett Has Hard Words for Tough Stuff He Used to Write," *Los Angeles Times*, June 7, 1950, A3.

10. Kenneth Millar as quoted in Matthew J. Bruccoli, *Ross Macdonald* (New York: Harcourt Brace Jovanovich, 1984), 19.

11. Ross Macdonald, *The Moving Target* (Boston: Gregg, 1979), 9.

12. In a 1977 essay, Macdonald refers obliquely to Edmund Wilson's 1941 book of biographical criticism, *The Wound and the Bow*. See Ross Macdonald, "Down These Streets a Mean Man Must Go," in *Four Novels of the 1950s*, ed. Tom Nolan (New York: Library of America, 2015), 893.

13. Ross Macdonald, "Archer at Large," in *Self-Portrait: Ceaselessly Into the Past*, ed. Ralph B. Sipper (Santa Barbara, CA: Capra, 1981), 31.

14. Ross Macdonald, "The Writer as Detective Hero," *Four Novels of the 1950s*, ed. Tom Nolan (New York: Library of America, 2015), 870.

15. Ross Macdonald, "Letter to Alfred A. Knopf," in *Four Novels of the 1950s*, ed. Tom Nolan (New York: Library of America, 2015), 862.

16. Macdonald, "Writer as Detective Hero," 873.

17. Macdonald, "Writer as Detective Hero," 874.

18. Ross Macdonald, "Writing *The Galton Case*," in *Four Novels of the 1950s*, ed. Tom Nolan (New York: Library of America, 2015), 887.

19. Ross Macdonald, *The Galton Case*, in *Four Novels of the 1950s*, ed. Tom Nolan (New York: Library of America, 2015), 653, 676.

20. Macdonald, "Writing *The Galton Case*," 889.

21. Ross Macdonald, *The Wycherly Woman* (New York: Vintage, 1989), 175–76.

22. Raymond Chandler, "Letter to James Sandoe" (April 14,1949), in *Selected Letters of Raymond Chandler*, ed. Frank MacShane (New York: Columbia University Press, 1981), 164.

23. Ross Macdonald as quoted in Ralph Burns Sipper, "An Interview with Ross Macdonald," in *The Mystery and Detection Annual 1973*, ed. Donald K. Adams (Beverly Hills, CA: Donald Adams, 1975), 52–82.

24. Daniel R. Barnes, "'I'm the Eye': Archer as Narrator in the Novels of Ross Macdonald," in *Mystery and Detection Annual 1972*, ed. Donald K. Adams (Beverly Hills, CA: Donald Adams, 1972), 181–88.

25. Macdonald, "Writer as Detective Hero," 870.

26. Outstanding studies of Macdonald's work include Matthew J. Bruccoli, *Ross Macdonald* (San Diego, CA: Harcourt Brace Jovanovich, 1984); Bernard A. Schopen, *Ross Macdonald* (Boston: G. K. Hall, 1990); and Tom Nolan, *Ross Macdonald: A Biography* (New York: Scribner's, 1999).

27. Will Murray, "The Executioner Phenomenon," in *Murder Off the Rack: Critical Studies of Ten Paperback Masters*, ed. Jon L. Breen and Martin Harry Greenberg (Pulp Hero Press, 2018), 111–18.

28. An analysis is in David Bordwell, *Narration in the Fiction Film* (Madison: University of Wisconsin Press, 1985), chap. 5.

29. For a survey of narrative strategies in American films beyond the mystery genre, see David Bordwell, *Reinventing Hollywood: How 1940s Filmmakers Changed Movie Storytelling* (Chicago: University of Chicago Press, 2017).

30. Steve Fisher, *I Wake Up Screaming* (New York: Popular Library, 1941), 29–30.

31. Fisher, *I Wake Up*, 34.

32. On Eberhart's writing income, see Rick Cypert, *America's Agatha Christie: Mignon Good Eberhart, Her Life and Works* (Selinsgrove, PA: Susquehanna University Press, 2005). In 1936 alone, she earned $50,000, the equivalent in 2017 of nearly a million dollars. As with most successful authors, the largest revenues came from the sale of movie rights.

33. Patricia Highsmith, "Suspense in Fiction," *The Writer* 67, no. 13 (December 1954): 406.

34. Mitchell Wilson, "The Suspense Story," *The Writer* 60, no. 1 (January 1947): 15–16.

35. Edmund Wilson, "Why Do People Read Detective Stories?," in *Literary Essays and Reviews of the 1930s and 1940s* (New York: Library of America, 2007), 660–61.

36. Anthony Boucher, "A Matter of Crime," *New York Times*, December 4, 1955.

37. Philip K. Scheuer, "*Double Indemnity*, Study of Murder Without Bunk," *Los Angeles Times*, August 11, 1944.

38. James M. Cain as quoted in Peter Brunette and Gerald Peary, "James M. Cain: Tough Guy," in *Backstory: Interviews with Screenwriters of Hollywood's Golden Age*, ed. Pat McGilligan (Berkeley: University of California Press, 1986), 125.

39. Jim Thompson, *Nothing More Than Murder* (New York: Vintage, 1990), 147.

40. George Cukor wanted the trial testimony in *A Woman's Face* to include witnesses' contrasting versions of scenes, and Joseph Mankiewicz wanted the recollections of two characters in *All About Eve* (1950) to involve a replay, but neither aspiration made it into the final film. Cukor judged that a replay would have been "too complicated for audiences." See Philip K. Scheuer, "A Town Called Hollywood," *Los Angeles Times*, May 11, 1941.

41. For a discussion see David Bordwell, "Twice-Told Tales: *Mildred Pierce*," *David Bordwell's Website on Cinema* (blog), http://www.davidbordwell.net/blog/2013/06/26/twice-told-tales-mildred-pierce/.

42. See Kristin Thompson, "Duplicitous Narration and *Stage Fright*," in *Breaking the Glass Armor: Neoformalist Film Analysis* (Princeton, NJ: Princeton University Press, 1988), 135–61.

43. I discuss *The Locket* in more detail in Bordwell, *Reinventing Hollywood*, 117–23.

44. Robert Wallsten as quoted in Cypert, *America's Agatha Christie*, 97.

45. Wolcott Gibbs, "Flatbush Idyll," *The New Yorker*, January 18, 1941, 36.

46. Eberhart as quoted in Cypert, *America's Agatha Christie*, 98.

47. John B. Priestley, introduction to *The Plays of J. B. Priestley*, vol. I (London: Heinemann, 1948), vii–viii.

48. Percy Lubbock, *The Craft of Fiction* (New York: Viking, 1957), 251.

49. Apparently without being aware of the earlier versions, Ellery Queen was planning a similar plot but abandoned it when the authors saw Christie's novel serialized in the *Saturday Evening Post*; see Nevins, *Ellery Queen*, 58–59.

50. Justin Chang offers a detailed analysis of Tarantino's debt; see Justin Chang, "*The Hateful Eight*: How Agatha Christie Is It? (An Investigation)," *Variety*, December 28, 2015, https://variety.com/2015/film/columns/the-hateful-eight-agatha-christie-quentin-tarantino-1201667948/.

51. Rex Stout, "The Mystery Story," in *The Writer's Book*, ed. Helen Hull (1950; repr. New York: Barnes & Noble, 1956), 64.

52. Robert Barnard, *A Talent to Deceive: An Appreciation of Agatha Christie* (New York: Mysterious, 1979), 83–85. Barnard, himself a distinguished crime novelist, has created in this book a superb study in the craft of mystery fiction. For a detailed consideration of plotting and clueing in *Five Little Pigs*, see John Goddard, *Agatha Christie's Golden Age: An Analysis of Poirot's Golden Age Puzzles* (London: Stylish Eye, 2018), 461–83.

53. Henry Klinger, "The Story That Sells to the Movies," in *The Mystery Writer's Handbook*, ed. Herbert Brean (New York: Harper, 1956), 187.

54. See A. B. Emrys, *Wilkie Collins, Vera Caspary, and the Evolution of the Casebook Novel* (Jefferson, NC: McFarland, 2011), 111–39.

55. Vera Caspary, *Laura* (New York: Vintage, 2012), 7.

56. Caspary, *Laura*, 20.

57. Caspary, *Laura*, 65, 66, 75, 65.

58. Caspary, *Laura*, 123.

59. Caspary, *Laura*, 145.

60. For a discussion of the film's play with narration see Bordwell, *Reinventing Hollywood*, 256–58.

61. Ira Levin, *A Kiss Before Dying* (New York: New American Library, 1954), 128.

8. The 1940s: The Problem of Other Minds, or Just One

1. Joel Townsley Rogers, *The Red Right Hand* (New York: Carroll & Graf, 1997).

2. Isaac Anderson, "Among the New Mystery Novels," *New York Times*, May 13, 1945.

3. Josephine Tey, *To Love and Be Wise* (New York: Dell, 1950), 188.

4. David Goodis, *Dark Passage* in *Four Novels* (London: Zomba, 1983), 252.

5. Patrick Hamilton, *Hangover Square: A Story of Darkest Earl's Court* (London: Penguin, 1974), 11.

6. See David Bordwell, *Reinventing Hollywood: How 1940s Filmmakers Changed Movie Storytelling* (Chicago: University of Chicago Press, 2017), chap. 11.

7. Hamilton, *Hangover Square*, 23.

8. Freud noted that the hidden information in the patient's case inevitably reappears: "It cannot rest until the mystery has been solved." See Sigmund Freud, "Analysis of a Phobia in a Five-Year-Old Boy" (1909), in *The Standard Edition of the Complete Psychological Works of Sigmund Freud*. Vol. 10, *(1909): Two Case Histories*, trans. James Strachey et al. (London: Hogarth Press, 1964), 122.

9. Guy Endore, *Methinks the Lady . . .* (New York: Duell, Sloan and Pearce, 1945), 176.

10. Iris Barry, "New Fiction: *Methinks the Lady . . .*," *New York Herald Tribune Weekly Book Review*, November 4, 1945, 11; James MacBride, "Schizoid," *New York Times*, November 4, 1945.

11. John Franklin Bardin, *Devil Take the Blue-Tail Fly* (London: Victor Gollancz, 1948), 111.

12. Bardin, *Devil Take the Blue-Tail Fly*, 179.

13. Francis M. Nevins Jr. *Cornell Woolrich: First You Dream, Then You Die* (New York: Mysterious, 1988), 336.

14. Cornell Woolrich, *The Black Curtain* (New York: Ballantine, 1982), 35; Cornell Woolrich, *The Black Path of Fear* (New York: Ace, n.d.), 50; William Irish [Cornell Woolrich, pseud.], *Waltz Into Darkness* (Philadelphia: Lippincott, 1947), 158.

15. For astute comments on Woolrichian prose, see Geoffrey O'Brien, *Hardboiled America: Lurid Paperbacks and the Masters of Noir*, 2nd ed. (New York: Da Capo, 1997), 97–100; and Thomas C. Renzi, *Cornell Woolrich from Pulp Noir to Film Noir* (Jefferson, NC:

McFarland, 2006), 17–18. Surprisingly, Woolrich isn't represented in Bill Pronzini's compilations of bad crime writing; see Bill Pronzini, *Gun in Cheek: A Study of "Alternative" Crime Fiction* (New York: Coward, McCann, 1982); and Bill Pronzini, *Son of Gun in Cheek* (New York: Mysterious, 1987).

16. Steve Fisher, "I Had Nobody," *The Armchair Detective* 3, no. 3 (1970): 164.

17. Mark T. Bassett, introduction to *Blues of a Lifetime: The Autobiography of Cornell Woolrich* (Bowling Green, OH: Bowling Green University Popular Press, 1991), xii.

18. Lee Wright as quoted in Nevins, *Cornell Woolrich*, 257.

19. Jacques Barzun and Wendell Hertig Taylor, *A Catalogue of Crime*, rev. ed. (New York: Harper & Row, 1989), 561.

20. Raymond Chandler, "Letter to Alex Barris" (1949), in *Raymond Chandler Speaking*, ed. Dorothy Gardner and Kathrine Sorley Walker (Plainview, NY: Books for Libraries, 1971), 55.

21. For comparison of the works with the media adaptations, see Nevins, *Cornell Woolrich*, 453–524; and the book-length study by Renzi, *Cornell Woolrich from Pulp Noir to Film Noir*. On the film adaptation of *The Black Path of Fear*, see Bordwell, *Reinventing Hollywood*, 331–35; and David Bordwell, "Back on the Trail of *The Chase*," *David Bordwell's Website on Cinema* (blog), http://www.davidbordwell.net/blog/2016/11/01/back-on-the-trail-of-the-chase/. For a comprehensive introduction to the Woolrich oeuvre, both in print and on the screen, see James Naremore, "An Aftertaste of Dread: Cornell Woolrich in Noir Fiction and Film," http://jamesnaremore.net/wp-content/uploads/2019/04/Woolrich-and-Dread.pdf.

22. Mitchell Wilson, "The Suspense Story," *The Writer* 60, no. 1 (January 1947): 15–16.

23. Cornell Woolrich, *Black Alibi* (New York; Ballantine, 1982), 33.

24. William Irish [Cornell Wooolrich. pseud.], "Deadline at Dawn," in *The Best of William Irish* (Philadelphia: Lippincott, 1944), 419.

25. Woolrich, *Black Path of Fear*, 136.

26. Bassett, introduction to *Blues of a Lifetime*, 11.

27. Woolrich, *Black Path of Fear*, 85.

28. Woolrich, *Black Path of Fear*, 175.

29. Cornell Woolrich, *The Bride Wore Black* (New York: Ace, n.d.), 88.

30. Eyewitness plots are discussed in David Bordwell, "The Eyewitness Plot and the Drama of Doubt," *David Bordwell's Website on Cinema* (blog), http://www.davidbordwell.net/blog/2018/07/23/the-eyewitness-plot-and-the-drama-of-doubt/.

31. William Irish [Cornell Wooolrich, pseud.], "Rear Window," in *The Best of William Irish* (Philadelphia: Lippincott, 1944), 273.

32. Irish, "Rear Window," 288.

33. For a discussion of the film, see Bordwell, "The Eyewitness Plot and the Drama of Doubt."

34. William Irish [Cornell Wooolrich, pseud.], "Fire Escape ," in *Dead Man Blues* (Philadelphia: Lippincott, 1948), 112–13.

35. Cornell Woolrich, *The Black Angel* (New York: Avon, 1946), 147.

36. I point out some examples in Bordwell, *Reinventing Hollywood*, 52–54, 276–85.

37. Bardin, *Devil Take the Blue-Tail Fly*, 105.

38. Endore, *Methinks the Lady . . .* , 102–3.

39. Cornell Woolrich, *Fright* (New York: Hard Case, 2007), 80–82.

40. Cornell Woolrich, *Rendezvous in Black* (New York: Modern Library, 2004), 94.

41. George Hopley [Cornell Woolrich, pseud.], *Night Has a Thousand Eyes* (New York: Farrar and Rinehart, 1945), 112–14.

42. Cornell Woolrich, *I Married a Dead Man* (New York: Ballantine, 1983), 94.

43. Woolrich, *Black Curtain*, 62.

44. Irish, *Deadline at Dawn*, 408.

45. Irish, *Waltz Into Darkness*, 119.

46. Henry James, "The Art of Fiction," in *Literary Criticism*, vol. 1, *Essays on Literature, American Writers, English Writers*, by Henry James, ed. Leon Edel (New York: Library of America, 1984), 61.

47. Hopley, *Night Has a Thousand Eyes*, 89.

48. Patrick Anderson, *The Triumph of the Thriller: How Cops, Crooks, and Cannibals Captured Popular Culture* (New York: Random House, 2007), 6.

49. Jean-Claude Carrière, *The Secret Language of Film*, trans. Jeremy Leggatt (New York: Pantheon, 1994), 15.

50. Rupert Holmes's campy *Accomplice* (1990) builds on schemas exploited in *Sleuth, Deathtrap*, and other murder plays, not least the duplicitous cast list and an announcement before the performance that a new player has been substituted for one that is indisposed.

9. The Great Detective Rewritten: Erle Stanley Gardner and Rex Stout

1. Several accounts of the decline of the pulp market in the 1930s can be found in John Locke, ed., *Pulp Fictioneers: Adventures in the Storytelling Business* (Silver Spring, MD: Adventure House, 2004).

2. Frank MacShane, ed., *Selected Letters of Raymond Chandler* (New York: Columbia University Press, 1981), 152, 174.

3. Alva Johnston, *The Case of Erle Stanley Gardner* (New York: Morrow, 1947). 9.

4. J. Kenneth Van Dover, *Murder in the Millions: Erle Stanley Gardner, Mickey Spillane, Ian Fleming* (New York: Ungar, 1984), 15.

5. A penetrating analysis of Gardner's career, including appreciations of his non-Mason stories, is Francis M. Nevins, "Erle Stanley Gardner," in *Cornucopia of Crime: Memories and Summations* (Lexington, KY: Ramble House, 2010), 23–52.

6. Van Dover, *Murder in the Millions*, 15–19; Francis L. Fugate and Roberta B. Fugate, *Secrets of the World's Best-Selling Writer: The Storytelling Techniques of Erle Stanley Gardner* (New York: Morrow, 1980), 193n.

7. Erle Stanley Gardner as quoted in Fugate and Fugate, *Secrets of the World's Best-Selling Writer*, 214.

8. Gardner as quoted in Fugate and Fugate, *Secrets of the World's Best-Selling Writer*, 215.

9. Gardner as quoted in Fugate and Fugate, *Secrets of the World's Best-Selling Writer*, 65.

10. Gardner as quoted in Dorothy B. Hughes, *Erle Stanley Gardner: The Case of the Real Perry Mason* (New York: Morrow, 1978), 102.

11. Erle Stanley Gardner, *The Case of the Sulky Girl* (New York: Ballantine, 1961), 2.

12. Erle Stanley Gardner, *The Case of the Howling Dog* (Della Street Press, 2012), chap. 3, Kindle.

13. Erle Stanley Gardner, *The Case of the Caretaker's Cat* (New York: Garden City, 1963), 1022.

14. Fugate and Fugate, *Secrets of the World's Best-Selling Writer*, 89–99.

15. Gardner, *Case of the Caretaker's Cat*, 88.

16. Fugate and Fugate, *Secrets of the World's Best-Selling Writer*, 96.

17. Fugate and Fugate, *Secrets of the World's Best-Selling Writer*, 101.

18. Fugate and Fugate, *Secrets of the World's Best-Selling Writer*, 174.
19. Gardner, *Case of the Caretaker's Cat*, 126.
20. Gardner as quoted in Hughes, *Erle Stanley Gardner*, 131.
21. Erle Stanley Gardner, *The Case of the Perjured Parrot* (Mattituck, NY: Aeonian, 1976), 17.
22. Erle Stanley Gardner as quoted in Nevins, "Erle Stanley Gardner," 49. A thorough consideration of the television series can be found in Thomas Leitch, *Perry Mason* (Detroit, MI: Wayne State University Press, 2005).
23. Erle Stanley Gardner, *The Case of the Lame Canary* (Della Street Press, 2013), chap. 7, Kindle.
24. Gardner as quoted in Hughes, *Erle Stanley Gardner*, 25.
25. See Erle Stanley Gardner, *The Court of Last Resort*, rev. ed. (New York: Pocket, 1954); and Hughes, *Erle Stanley Gardner*, 255–69.
26. Erle Stanley Gardner, "Hell's Kettle" (1930), in *The Black Mask Boys: Masters in the Hard-Boiled School of Detective Fiction*, by William F. Nolan (New York: Morrow, 1985), 114–15.
27. Elmore Leonard, "Writers on Writing: Easy on the Adverbs, Exclamation Points and Especially Hooptedoodle," *New York Times*, July 16, 2001.
28. Erle Stanley Gardner, *The Case of the Crooked Candle* (London: Arcturus, 2012), 56; Erle Stanley Gardner, *The Case of the Terrified Typist* (London: Heinemann, 1955), 41; Gardner, *Case of the Caretaker's Cat*, 24.
29. Leonard, "Writers on Writing."
30. See Van Dover, *Murder in the Millions*, 39–45, for a good analysis of the repetitions and interjections in these conversations.
31. Erle Stanley Gardner, *The Case of the Hesitant Hostess* (New York: Pocket, 1959), 204–5.
32. Johnston, *The Case of Erle Stanley Gardner*, 12.
33. Gardner, *Case of the Caretaker's Cat*, 14; Erle Stanley Gardner, *The Case of the Curious Bride* (New York: Pocket, 1953), 205; Erle Stanley Gardner, *The Case of the Lucky Legs* (Thorndike, ME: Hall, 1999), 39; Erle Stanley Gardner, *The Case of the Velvet Claws* (New York: Pocket, 1970), 219.
34. Quotations come from the first chapters of *The Case of the Glamorous Ghost* (1955), *The Case of the Lucky Loser* (1957), and *The Case of the Screaming Woman* (1957), in *Seven Complete Novels*, by Erle Stanley Gardner (New York: Avenel, 1979), 1, 261, 367; and Erle Stanley Gardner, *The Case of the Singing Skirt* (New York: Pocket, 1961), 5.
35. See Milman Parry, "Studies in the Epic Technique of Oral Verse-Making: 1. Homer and Homeric Style," *Harvard Studies in Classical Philology* 41 (1930): 73–146; Milman Parry, "Studies in the Epic Technique of Oral Verse-Making: 2. The Homeric Language as the Language of an Oral Poetry," *Harvard Studies in Classical Philology* 43 (1932): 1–50; Albert B. Lord, *The Singer of Tales*, 2nd ed. (Cambridge, MA: Harvard University Press, 2000), 30–67. Thanks to John Belton for his advice on the poetics of oral narrative.
36. A. A. Fair [Erle Stanley Gardner, pseud.], *The Bigger They Come* (New York: Pocket, 1943), 92–93.
37. For a longer version of what follows, with more gags, see David Bordwell, "Rex Stout: Logomachizing," *David Bordwell's Website on Cinema* (blog), http://www.davidbordwell.net/essays/stout.php.
38. David C. Tilden, "Exploring the Dark," *New York Herald Tribune*, September 8, 1929; William Soskin, *New York Evening Post*, quoted in advertisement for *Seed on the Wind*, *New York Times Book Review*, September 28, 1930, 16.
39. Clifton Fadiman, "Realism and Mannerism," *The Nation*, September 25, 1929, 329; Francis Hackett, "Novel on the Stairs," *New Republic*, November 13, 1929, 357.

40. Joseph Warren Beach, "The Novel from James to Joyce," *The Nation*, June 10, 1931, 35.

41. John McAleer, *Rex Stout: A Biography* (Boston: Little, Brown, 1977), 223–28.

42. Rex Stout as quoted in John McAleer, *Royal Decree: Conversations with Rex Stout* (Ashton, MD: Pontes, 1983), 3.

43. See, for example, Fred T. Marsh, "*Seed on the Wind*," *The Bookman*, November 1930, 305.

44. Fadiman, "Realism and Mannerism"; Hackett, "Novel on the Stairs"; Ernest Sutherland Hayes, "A Modern Hamlet," *Saturday Review of Literature*, October 26, 1929, 312.

45. Rex Stout as quoted in McAleer, *Rex Stout*, 243.

46. For a comprehensive list of Stout's publications, see Guy M. Townsend, *Rex Stout: An Annotated Primary and Secondary Bibliography* (New York: Garland, 1980). For a solid critical study of themes of politics and family in the Wolfe books, see David R. Anderson, *Rex Stout* (New York: Ungar, 1984). An early, still useful study is Mia I. Gerhardt, "Homicide West; Some Observations on the Nero Wolfe Stories of Rex Stout," *English Studies* 49, no. 2 (Summer 1968): 107–27.

47. The fullest published description of the protagonists is given in Rex Stout, "Fourth of July Picnic," in *And Four to Go* (New York: Viking, 1958), 130–31. In a 1948 memo sent to a radio producer, Stout prepared physical descriptions of Wolfe and Archie; these are reproduced in McAleer, *Rex Stout*, 383.

48. Rex Stout, "Grim Fairy Tales," *Saturday Review of Literature*, April 2, 1949, 34.

49. Rex Stout, "Blood Will Tell," in *Trio for Blunt Instruments* (New York: Crimeline, 1997), 197.

50. Rex Stout as quoted in McAleer, *Royal Decree*, 43.

51. Rex Stout, "What to Do About a Watson," in *The Mystery Writer's Handbook*, ed. Herbert Brean (New York: Harper's, 1956), 162.

52. Stout, "Grim Fairy Tales," 34.

53. Rex Stout, introduction to *Introducing Mr. Sherlock Holmes*, ed. Edgar W. Smith (Morristown, NJ: The Baker Street Irregulars, 1959).

54. Donald E. Westlake, introduction to *The Father Hunt* (New York: Bantam, 1993), vii.

55. See the extraordinary in-depth handling of Archie's poisoning in Rex Stout, *The League of Frightened Men* (New York: Farrar & Rinehart, 1935), chaps. 18–19.

56. Stout, "What to Do About a Watson," 162.

57. Rex Stout, *In the Best Families* (New York: Bantam, 1995), 192–93.

58. Rex Stout, *The League of Frightened Men* (1935; repr. New York: Pyramid, 1974), 185.

59. Jacques Barzun and Wendell Hertig Taylor, "Rex Stout: *Too Many Cooks*," in *A Book of Prefaces to Fifty Classics of Crime Fiction 1900–1950* (New York: Garland, 1976), 101.

60. The process is traced in Mattias Boström, *From Holmes to Sherlock: The Story of the Men and Women Who Created an Icon* (New York: Mysterious, 2017), 201–2.

61. Christopher Morley, "In Memoriam Sherlock Holmes," in *The Complete Sherlock Holmes*, by Sir Arthur Conan Doyle (New York: Garden City, 1960), ix.

62. Rex Stout as quoted in McAleer, *Royal Decree*, 43.

63. Rex Stout, "Watson Was a Woman," in *The Art of the Mystery Story: A Collection of Critical Essays*, ed. Howarad Haycraft (New York: Simon & Schuster, 1946), 311–18.

64. W. S. Baring-Gould, *Nero Wolfe of West Thirty-Fifth Street: The Life and Times of America's Largest Detective* (New York: Viking, 1969).

65. The fullest inventory, chronology, and cast list I know is to be found in O. E. McBride, *Stout Fellow: A Guide Through Nero Wolfe's World* (Lincoln, NE: iUniverse, 2003).

66. Rex Stout, *A Family Affair* (New York: Bantam, 1976), 169.

67. Stout himself was a creature of routines, at least in his later decades: to bed at eleven, up at eight, breakfast followed by gardening, an afternoon snack, dinner at 6:30. See McAleer, *Rex Stout*, 349.

68. Morley, "In Memoriam," viii; Edmund Crispin, "Archie, Your Notebook," *Sunday Times*, June 4, 1967.

69. Stout, *In the Best Families*, 193.

70. Rex Stout, *The Rubber Band* (New York: Jove, 1979), 65.

71. Jacques Barzun, "About Rex Stout," in *A Birthday Tribute to Rex Stout* (New York: Viking, 1965), 7. He adds that Wolfe's "are the only seminars in which truth of any kind has been found." Elsewhere Barzun describes Stout as having "acclimatised the Business Conference to the uses of detection." See also Jacques Barzun, "Detection in Extremis," in *Crime in Good Company: Essays on Criminals and Crime Writing*, ed. Michael Gilbert (London: Constable, 1959), 144–45.

72. Rex Stout, "When a Man Murders . . . ," in *Three Witnesses* (New York: Viking, 1956), 117.

73. Raymond Chandler, *Selected Letters of Raymond Chandler*, ed. Frank MacShane (New York: Columbia University Press, 1981), 187.

74. Rex Stout, "The Mystery Novel," in *The Writer's Book*, ed. Helen Hull (New York: Harper, 1950), 64.

75. Stout, introduction to *Introducing Mr. Sherlock Holmes*.

76. A search on Google N-gram yields no mention of the fer-de-lance in any books published between 1922 and 1934, the year Stout's novel appeared.

77. Rex Stout, *Fer-de-Lance* (New York: Bantam, 1992), 238.

78. Will Cuppy, "Mystery and Adventure: *The League of Frightened Men*," *New York Herald Tribune*, August 8, 1935.

79. Stout, *Fer-de-Lance*, 1–2.

80. Stout, *Fer-de-Lance*, 17.

81. Stout, *Fer-de-Lance*, 58.

82. Stout, *Fer-de-Lance*, 134, 163, 164, 285.

83. Rex Stout as quoted in McAleer, *Royal Decree*, 22. I'm grateful to Joseph Wiesenfarth for alerting me to the "likeness" refrain in *Emma*, a book that Stout was rereading shortly before his death.

84. Shaw discusses leitmotifs in Bernard Shaw, *The Perfect Wagnerite: A Commentary on the Niblung's Ring* (New York: Brentano's, 1916), 119–28. An example in Shaw's own work is the boa constrictor slithering through *Man and Superman*.

85. Rex Stout, *How Like a God* (New York: Vanguard, 1929), 4, 41, 237.

86. Rex Stout, *Too Many Cooks* (New York: Pyramid, 1963), 88, 104, 163.

87. Rex Stout, *Prisoner's Base* (New York: Bantam, 1979), 44, 221.

88. Stout, *Fer-de-Lance*, 69, 74, 268.

89. Stout, *Fer-de-Lance*, 236, 37.

90. The epigraph comes from Stout, *Some Buried Caesar*, chap 9.

91. The most famous example would be Octavius Roy Cohen's caricatured portrayal of Black detective Florian Slappey in *Saturday Evening Post* stories.

92. Rex Stout, *Some Buried Caesar* (New York: Bantam, 2008), 7.

93. Stout, *Some Buried Caesar*, 223.

94. Rex Stout, *Death of a Dude* (New York: Bantam, 1994), 7; Stout, *League of Frightened Men*, 9; Rex Stout, *And Be a Villain* (New York: Bantam, 1961), 148; Rex Stout, *The Red Box* (New York: Bantam, 1982), 73; Stout, *A Family Affair*, 67; Stout, *In the Best Families*, 195.

95. Rex Stout as quoted in McAleer, *Rex Stout*, 282.

96. Stout, *League of Frightened Men*, 97; Stout, *A Family Affair*, 46; Rex Stout, *If Death Ever Slept*, in *Seven Complete Nero Wolfe Novels* (New York: Avenel, 1983), 318.

97. Raymond Chandler, *The Long Goodbye* (New York: Vintage, 1988), 186; Stout, *If Death Ever Slept*, 252; Rex Stout, *Murder by the Book* (New York: Bantam, 1992), 15.

98. Rex Stout, *Might As Well Be Dead*, in *Seven Complete Nero Wolfe Novels* (New York: Avenel Books, 1983), 234.

99. Rex Stout, *Too Many Clients* (New York: Viking, 1960), 88; Stout, *Some Buried Caesar*, 154; Stout, *If Death Ever Slept*, 352.

100. The packed first chapter of *Too Many Cooks* is a scale model of Archie's literary method, from refrains and ventriloquizing to literary parody; the latter consists of puzzling how to describe helping Wolfe undress in the confines of a Pullman car: "Dear Reader. . . ."

101. Rex Stout, *The Final Deduction* (Thorndike, ME: Thorndike, 1999), 96.

102. On the linguistic playfulness of the Jeeves novels, see Kristin Thompson, *Wooster Proposes, Jeeves Disposes; or, Le Mot Juste* (London: Heineman, 1992), 282–90. She also discusses the parallels between the Jeeves/Wooster stories and the Holmes/Watson partnership (105–9).

103. P. G. Wodehouse, foreword to *Rex Stout: A Biography*, by John McAleer (Boston: Little, Brown, 1977), xv–xvi. Not incidentally, Wodehouse had already written a book called *The Indiscretions of Archie* (1928).

104. Rex Stout, *The Silent Speaker* (Harmondsworth, UK: Penguin, 1977), 96.

105. Ernest Hemingway, *A Farewell to Arms* (1929; repr. New York: Scribners, 2014), 284. The several alternate endings Hemingway considered are appended (303–22).

106. Ernest Hemingway as quoted in George Plimpton, "An Interview with Ernest Hemingway," in *Ernest Hemingway's The Sun Also Rises: A Casebook*, ed. Linda Wagner-Martin (New York: Oxford University Press, 2002), 29.

107. Stout, *Silent Speaker*, 98. Exceptional in the novels, this is a two-page chapter devoted wholly to Archie's reaction to death.

108. Stout, *Silent Speaker*, 99.

109. Raymond Chandler, "Killer in the Rain" (1935), in *Collected Stories* (New York: Knopf, 2002), 215.

110. Rex Stout, *The Golden Spiders* (New York: Bantam, 1979), 13.

111. Stout, *Silent Speaker*, 207.

112. Rex Stout, *Gambit* (New York: Chivers, 1996), 134.

113. Rex Stout, *A Right to Die* (New York: Bantam, 1965), 60; Rex Stout, "The Rodeo Murder," in *Three at Wolfe's Door* (New York: Bantam, 1974), 186; Rex Stout, "Disguise for Murder," in *Full House: A Nero Wolfe Omnibus* (New York: Viking, 1955), 516.

114. Stout, *Death of a Dude*, 72.

115. Stout, *Too Many Cooks*, 140.

116. Stout, *Red Box*, 143.

117. "His main joy was Rex Stout, whose books he would read again and again, until Nero Wolfe assumed near-reality and figured as a quotable authority in his conversation." See John Henry Jones, "The Empsons," *London Review of Books*, August 12, 1989.

118. William Empson, *Seven Types of Ambiguity: A Study of Its Effects in English Verse* (New York: Meridian, 1955), 7.

119. Mark Twain, *The Adventures of Huckleberry Finn* (New York: Airmont, 1962), 318.

120. Rex Stout, *Please Pass the Guilt*, in *Seven Complete Nero Wolfe Novels* (New York: Avenel, 1983), 169.

121. Stout, *League of Frightened Men*, 24.

122. Stout, *League of Frightened Men*, 210.
123. Stout, *League of Frightened Men*, 10.
124. Stout, *League of Frightened Men*, 8.
125. Stout, *League of Frightened Men*, 159, 210.
126. Rex Stout, *Plot It Yourself* (New York: Bantam, 1986), 34.
127. Stout, *Plot It Yourself*, 39–40.
128. Stout, *Plot It Yourself*, 32.
129. Stout, *Plot It Yourself*, 177.
130. Mikhail Bakhtin, *Problems of Dostoevsky's Poetics*, ed. and trans. Caryl Emerson (Minneapolis: University of Minnesota Press, 1984), 5–46.

10. Viewpoints, Narrow and Expansive: Patricia Highsmith and Ed McBain

1. Patricia Highsmith, "The Sense of Form," *The Writer* 61, no. 1 (January 1948): 12–13.
2. Patricia Highsmith, *Plotting and Writing Suspense Fiction*, 2nd ed. (Boston: The Writer, 1981), 138.
3. Several essays in an anthology by Wieland Schwanebeck and Douglas McFarland, *Patricia Highsmith on Screen* (London: Palgrave, 2018), explore thematic affinities between Highsmith and modernist literature. See also Tom Perrin, "On Patricia Highsmith" http://post45.research.yale.edu/2012/12/cluster-introduction-patricia-highsmith/.
4. Highsmith, "Sense of Form," 11.
5. Highsmith, *Plotting and Writing Suspense Fiction*, 140.
6. Highsmith, "Sense of Form," 14.
7. Patricia Highsmith as quoted in Andrew Wilson, *Beautiful Shadow: A Life of Patricia Highsmith* (London: Bloomsbury, 2003), 2.
8. Patricia Highsmith, "Suspense in Fiction," *The Writer* 67, no. 12 (December 1954): 403.
9. Highsmith's admiration for *The Stranger* is examined in Wilson, *Beautiful Shadow*, 121–22.
10. Highsmith, *Plotting and Writing Suspense Fiction*, 38, 60.
11. Graham Greene, foreword to *Eleven*, by Patricia Highsmith (Harmondsworth: Penguin, 1989), ix.
12. Patricia Highsmith, *The Glass Cell* (Harmondsworth: Penguin, 1983), 165.
13. Patricia Highsmith, *Ripley Under Ground* (New York: Penguin, 1970), 164.
14. Highsmith, *Plotting and Writing Suspense Fiction*, 56.
15. Patricia Highsmith, *The Two Faces of January* (London: Sphere, 2014), 172; Highsmith, *Ripley Under Ground*, 219.
16. Patricia Highsmith, *Strangers on a Train* (London: Vintage, 1999), 268.
17. Patricia Highsmith, entry in Cahier 16 (dated 11/22/47), A-05/16, Archives littéraires Suisse. Thanks to Stéphanie Cudré-Mauroux for helping me gain access to this text. It is not reprinted in Anna von Planta, ed., *Patricia Highsmith: Her Diaries and Notebooks* (New York: Liveright, 2021).
18. Patricia Highsmith, *The Tremor of Forgery* (Harmondsworth: Penguin, 1987), 18, 154, 256.
19. Highsmith, *Plotting and Writing Suspense Fiction*, 90.
20. Edith Wharton, *The Writing of Fiction* (1925; repr. New York: Simon & Schuster, 1997), 69.
21. Highsmith, *Strangers on a Train*, 195.

22. Patricia Highsmith, *Ripley's Game* (New York: Vintage, 1993), 232.

23. Highsmith, *Plotting and Writing Suspense Fiction*, 140.

24. Jean-Paul Sartre, "Camus' 'The Outsider,'" in *Literary Essays*, trans. Annette Michelson (New York: Philosophical Library, 1957), 35.

25. "The Pocket Book Market," in *The Writer's Market*, ed. Ruth A. Jones and Aron M. Mathieu, 14th ed. (Cincinnati, OH: The Writer's Digest, 1956), 125, 221–22. See also Thomas L. Bonn, "Elements of Success," *Paperback Quarterly* 4, no. 4 (Winter 1981): 35–47.

26. See "The Book Market: Paper-Bound Editions," *The Writer* 66, no. 7 (July 1953): 2245–46.

27. See Geoffrey O'Brien, *Hard-Boiled America: Lurid Years of Paperbacks* (New York: Van Nostrand Reinhold, 1983); Jon L. Breen and Martin Harry Greenberg, *Murder Off the Rack: Critical Studies of Ten Paperback Masters* (Jefferson, NC: McFarland, 1989); and Brian Ritt, *Paperback Confidential: Crime Writers of the Paperback Era* (Eureka, CA: Stark House, 2013).

28. Ed McBain, introduction to *Cop Hater* (New York: Signet, 1973), vi.

29. My discussion of McBain's work has benefited from the very thorough survey provided by Erin E. MacDonald, *Ed McBain/Evan Hunter: A Literary Companion* (Jefferson, NC: McFarland, 2012).

30. For an overview, see Mike Grost, "Casebook Fiction," *A Guide to Classic Mystery and Detection*, http://mikegrost.com/casebook.htm. Philip Macdonald's serial-killer novel *Murder Gone Mad* (1931) can be considered a forerunner of this genre as well.

31. Webb's contribution to the genre is discussed in detail in Jason Mittell, *Genre and Television: From Cop Show to Cartoons in American Culture* (New York: Routledge, 2004), chap. 5.

32. Bartlett Cormack's 1927 play, *The Racket*, anticipates *Detective Story* in setting its action wholly in a police station, but nearly all the crimes passing through are connected to the central situation of the struggle between police captain McQuigg and mob boss Nick Scarsi.

33. Ed McBain as quoted in Tom Callahan, "In the Shadow of Ed McBain," *Writer's Digest* 76, no. 9 (September 1996): 29.

34. George N. Dove furnishes a visitor's guide to Isola and a careful reconstruction of the books' antichronology in his fine study. See George N. Dove, *The Boys from Grover Avenue: Ed McBain's 87th Precinct Novels* (Bowling Green, OH: Bowling Green Popular Press, 1985), chap. 2 and 3.

35. Ed McBain, *The Pusher* (New York: New American Library, 1987), 61.

36. Ed McBain, *The Heckler* (New York: Pocket, 2003), 13.

37. Ed McBain, *Lady Killer* (New York: Otto Penzler, 1994), 110.

38. Ed McBain, *Fat Ollie's Book* (New York: Simon & Schuster 2002), 108.

39. McBain, introduction to *Cop Hater*, viii.

40. Ed McBain, *Killer's Choice* (New York: Ballantine, 1975), 158.

41. Ed McBain, *See Them Die* (New York: Signet, 1976), 146.

42. McBain had written many short stories exploiting these conventional premises. "By the time I wrote the first of the 87th Precinct novels, all of the elements were already in place. Here were the kids in trouble and the women in jeopardy, here were the private eyes and the gangs. Here were the loose cannons and the innocent bystanders. And here too were the cops and robbers." Ed McBain, introduction to *Learning to Kill: Stories* (Orlando, FL: Harcourt, 2006), xv.

43. McBain, introduction to *Learning to Kill*, vii.

44. Evan Hunter, "An Interview with Ed McBain," *The Writer* 82, no. 4 (April 1969): 11.

45. Ed McBain, "*Hail, Hail, the Gang's All Here!*," in *Three from the 87th* (New York: Doubleday, 1971), 3.

46. See "Book Publishing," in *Writer's Market '74*, ed. Jane Koester and Rose Adkins (Cincinnati, OH: Writer's Digest, 1974), 585–667.

47. A sensitive discussion of *Candyland*, along with a tribute to McBain's work as a whole, is offered in Thomas Leitch, "The Importance of Ed McBain," *Mystery Scene* no. 70 (2001): 30–33.

48. John Dickson Carr considered "collaborating" with his pseudonym Carter Dickson: "There is a fourth dimensional quality about it that I like." See Douglas J. Greene, *John Dickson Carr: The Man Who Explained Miracles* (New York: Otto Penzler, 1995), 212.

49. On *Hill Street Blues*, the standard source is Todd Gitlin, *Inside Prime Time* (New York: Pantheon, 1983), 264–324. A more updated survey of later programming is provided in Jonathan Nichols-Pethick, *TV Cops: The Contemporary American Television Police Drama* (New York: Routledge, 2012). Erin MacDonald traces McBain's overall influence on the genre; see MacDonald, *Ed McBain/Evan Hunter*, 283–87.

50. Ed McBain as quoted in Bill Slocum, "If It's Murder, It's McBain," *New York Times*, April 30, 1995.

11. Donald Westlake and the Richard Stark Machine

1. Samples of Westlake's tongue-in-cheek erotic writing can be found in Lawrence Block and Donald E. Westlake, *Hellcats and Honeygirls* (Burton MI: Subterranean, 2010).

2. In contrast, John G. Cawelti sees the caper film as an offshoot of the "new mythology of crime" that develops out of the gangster genre. See John G. Cawelti, *Adventure, Mystery, and Romance: Formula Stories as Art and Popular Culture* (Chicago: University of Chicago Press, 1976), 68–76. Cawelti discusses Westlake's work on pages 68–69.

3. Donald E. Westlake, "Introduction to *Murderous Schemes*," in *The Getaway Car: A Donald Westlake Nonfiction Miscellany*, ed. Levi Stahl (Chicago: University of Chicago Press, 2014), 53.

4. For a fuller discussion of the genre, see Stuart Kaminsky, "The Big Caper Film," in *American Film Genres: Approaches to a Critical Theory of Popular Film* (New York: Pflaum, 1974), 79–99; and Daryl Lee, *The Heist Film: Stealing with Style* (London: Wallflower, 2014).

5. Lionel White, *Clean Break* (New York: Dutton, 1955).

6. Lionel White, *Steal Big* (New York: Fawcett, 1960), 47.

7. Donald E. Westlake, *Help, I Am Being Held Prisoner* (New York: Mysterious, 1974), 94–95.

8. Donald E. Westlake, "The Hardboiled Dicks," in *The Getaway Car: A Donald Westlake Nonfiction Miscellany*, ed. Levi Stahl (Chicago: University of Chicago Press, 2014), 50.

9. For a detailed discussion of the reflexive strategies of *Adios, Scheherazade*, see Fred Fitch, "Review: Adios Scheherazade," *Westlake Review*, https://thewestlakereview.wordpress.com/2015/04/01/review-adios-scheherazade-chapter-2/.

10. Largely on the strength of these novels, conservative pundit William Kristol claimed that he nominated Westlake for the Nobel Prize in Literature. See William Kristol, "Donald E. Westlake, 1933–2008," *Weekly Standard*, January 19, 2009, https://www.weeklystandard.com/william-kristol/donald-e-westlake-1933-2008.

11. Westlake claimed he took the "Richard" from Richard Widmark's characterization in *Kiss of Death* (1947) and the last name from the style he aimed at: "crisp and lean, no fat,

trimmed down . . . *stark.*" Richard Stark [Donald Westlake pseud.], "Richard Stark introduced by Donald E. Westlake," in *Payback* (New York: Warner, 1999), viii.

12. Donald Westlake as quoted in Christopher Bahn, "Interview: Donald Westlake," *AV Club*, November 16, 2006, https://www.avclub.com/donald-westlake-1798210202.

13. John Banville, "Criminal Odes," *Bookforum* 14, no. 4 (December 2007/January 2008), https://www.bookforum.com/print/1404/the-tumultuous-decades-between-the-wars -saw-the-birth-and-development-of-a-new-genre-pulp-fiction-that-sought-in-the -gritty-seams-of-american-life-a-fresh-moral-code-one-that-made-sense-for-hard -times-and-harder-people-1376.

14. Richard Stark, *The Mourner* (Chicago: University of Chicago Press, 2009), 34.

15. There are, however, a great many recurring partners in crime, along with numerous walk-ons. A list is at https://parkerseries.uchicago.edu/character_guide/.

16. Richard Stark, *The Sour Lemon Score* (Chicago: University of Chicago Press, 2010), 147.

17. Westlake, "Hardboiled Dicks," 33–52.

18. Bahn, "Interview: Donald Westlake."

19. Richard Stark, *Plunder Squad* (Chicago: University of Chicago Press, 2010), 167.

20. Stark, *The Mourner*, 64.

21. Richard Stark, *The Seventh* (Chicago: University of Chicago Press, 2009), 144.

22. Donald E. Westlake, "Tangled Webs for Sale: Best Offers," in *The Getaway Car: A Donald Westlake Nonfiction Miscellany*, ed. Levi Stahl (Chicago: University of Chicago Press, 2014), 92.

23. Jean-Luc Godard freely adapted the investigation plot for his *Made in USA* (1967), a film that Westlake managed to keep out of distribution for years. See Albert Nussbaun, "An Inside Look at Donald E. Westlake," in *The Getaway Car: A Donald Westlake Nonfiction Miscellany*, ed. Levi Stahl (Chicago: University of Chicago Press, 2014), 157–58.

24. Donald Westlake, "Introduction to *Levine*," *The Getaway Car: A Donald Westlake Nonfiction Miscellany*, ed. Levi Stahl (Chicago: University of Chicago Press, 2014), 83.

25. Lawrence Block, "Trust Me on This: Stealing Time with Richard Stark," *Los Angeles Times*, December 23, 1990. The pattern may also owe something to Lester Dent's advice in Lester Dent, "The Pulp Master Fiction Plot" (1936), in *The Mystery Writer's Handbook*, ed. Herbert Brean (New York: Harper, 1956), 45–56.

26. For the sake of variety, not every stage in every heist is shown, but most are; and some are presented out of chronological order, a strategy that Westlake had begun in the Parker series.

27. Donald Westlake, as quoted in Stuart Kaminsky, *Behind the Mystery: Top Mystery Writers Interviewed* (Cohasset, MA: Hot House, 2005), 41.

28. Stark, *Plunder Squad*, 102.

29. Stark, *The Mourner*, 190.

30. Richard Rayner, "At the Speed of Pulp," *Los Angeles Times*, September 14, 2008, https://www.latimes.com/entertainment/la-caw-paperback-writers14-2008sep14 -story.html.

31. Stark, *Sour Lemon Score*, 144.

32. Luc Sante, foreword to *The Handle*, by Richard Stark (Chicago: University of Chicago Press, 2009), ix.

33. H. Bedford-Jones, "Something New About the Book-Length," *Writer's Monthly* 19, no. 6 (June 1922): 483–86.

34. Richard Stark, *Butcher's Moon* (Chicago: University of Chicago Press, 2011), 169, 306.

35. Donald E. Westlake, "Writers on Writing: A Pseudonym Returns from an Alter-Ego Trip, with New Tales to Tell," in *The Getaway Car: A Donald Westlake Nonfiction Miscellany*, ed. Levi Stahl (Chicago: University of Chicago Press, 2014), 28.

36. In the DVD commentary for the film, Westlake explains how he came up with the opening, and Frears expresses his satisfaction with the solution (*The Grifters*, Miramax DVD ed. no. 27184, 3:06–5:08).

37. Westlake, "Writers on Writing," 28–29.

38. Richard Stark, *Breakout* (Chicago: University of Chicago Press, 2017), 231.

39. Richard Stark, *Ask the Parrot* (Chicago: University of Chicago Press, 2017), 99.

40. Donald E. Westlake, *Jimmy the Kid* (New York: Mysterious, 1974), inside flyleaf.

12. Tarantino, Twists, and the Persistence of Puzzles

The epigraph is from Graham Fuller, "Answers First, Questions Later," in *Quentin Tarantino: Interviews*, rev. ed., ed. Gerald Peary (Jackson: University of Mississippi Press, 2013), 37.

1. Quentin Tarantino as quoted in Graham Fuller, "Answers First, Questions Later," in *Quentin Tarantino: Interviews*, rev. ed., ed. Gerald Peary (Jackson: University of Mississippi Press, 2013), 38.

2. Tarantino discusses the *Open Road* screenplay in Erik Bauer, "Method Writing: An Interview with Quentin Tarantino," *Creative Screenwriting* 5, no. 1 (1998): 39.

3. Tom Shone, *Tarantino: A Retrospective* (San Rafael, CA: Insight, 2017), 42–53. For a detailed comparison of the two versions of *True Romance*, see Robert Arnett, "*True Romance*: Quentin Tarantino as Screenwriting Auteur," *Creative Screenwriting* 5, no. 1 (1998): 50–55.

4. Quentin Tarantino, *Natural Born Killers: The Original Screenplay* (New York: Grove, 1995), 27.

5. Tarantino's script confines the mixed-media technique to the "Reign of Terror" episode and the footage from Gayle's camera, but Oliver Stone's adaptation of *Natural Born Killers* (1994) combines formats from the beginning. Stone constantly cuts between color and black-and-white shots of the same scene, and he inserts footage shot in different media—usually without any realistic justification. He had already experimented with mixing formats in *JFK* (1991), which might have influenced Tarantino's treatment of Gayle's project. Stone continued his hybrid technique in *U-Turn* (1997) and later films.

6. Paul A. Woods, *King Pulp: The Wild World of Quentin Tarantino* (New York: Thunder's Mouth, 1996), 102–4. See also Geoffrey O'Brien, "Pulp Fantastic," in *Filmmaker*, June 8, 2019, https://filmmakermagazine.com/107629-pulp-fantastic-geoffrey-obrien-on-quentin -tarantinos-pulp-fiction/#.X-Ov2C2ZOys.

7. Jason Bailey, *Pulp Fiction: The Complete Story of Quentin Tarantino's Masterpiece* (Minneapolis, MN: Voyageur, 2013), 33.

8. In 1985, Leonard's *Glitz* landed on the *New York Times* best-seller list, and he appeared on the cover of *Newsweek*. The same year saw appreciative comments by George F. Will, introduction to *Dutch Treat: Three Novels* (New York: Arbor House, 1985), ix–xiv. Later appreciations include Martin Amis, "Maintaining on Elmore Leonard" (1999), in *The War Against Cliché: Essays and Reviews 1971–2000* (New York: Vintage, 2002), 225–28.

9. Tarantino as quoted in Fuller, "Answers First," 36–37.

10. Tarantino as quoted in Erik Bauer, "The Mouth and the Method," in *Quentin Tarantino: Interviews*, rev. ed., ed. Gerald Peary (Jackson: University of Mississippi Press, 2013), 114. Leonard later repaid the compliment by mentioning *Pulp Fiction* approvingly in *Out of Sight*. See Elmore Leonard, *Four Later Novels: Get Shorty, Rum Punch, Out of Sight, Tishomingo Blues* (New York: Library of America, 2016), 618.

11. Elmore Leonard, introduction to *The Friends of Eddie Coyle*, by George V. Higgins (New York: Holt, 2000), vi.

12. When I asked Leonard about this in 1990, he said he was unaware that this was a tour de force. "I just thought it had to be that long." He also confirmed that in the novel Shorty is a surrogate for Dustin Hoffman.

13. See Mike White, *Who Do You Think You're Fooling? (The Story of a Robbery)* (1994), https://www.youtube.com/watch?v=7HgbSAL8OKY. In a 1995 interview Tarantino noted, "It's a really cool movie. It influenced me a lot. I got some stuff from it." See Stephen Hunter, "Before 'Reservoir Dogs,' There Was 'City on Fire,'" *Baltimore Sun*, April 14, 1995, https://www.baltimoresun.com/news/bs-xpm-1995-04-14-1995104053 -story.html.

14. Quentin Tarantino as quoted in Michel Ciment and Hubert Niogret, "Interview at Cannes," in *Quentin Tarantino: Interviews*, rev. ed., ed. Gerald Peary (Jackson: University of Mississippi Press, 2013), 9.

15. Kristin Thompson, *Storytelling in the New Hollywood: Understanding Classical Narrative Technique* (Cambridge, MA: Harvard University Press, 1999), 28–29.

16. Quentin Tarantino as quoted in Ciment and Niogret, "Interview at Cannes," 11.

17. Quentin Tarantino as quoted in Fuller, "Answers First," 44.

18. Jane Hamsher, *Killer Instinct: How Two Young Producers Took on Hollywood and Made the Most Controversial Film of the Decade* (New York: Broadway, 1998), 5–6.

19. Jeff Smith analyzes the film as both a network narrative and a counterfactual-history plot; see Jeff Smith, "When Worlds Collide: Mixing the Show-Biz Tale with True Crime in *Once Upon a Time . . . in Hollywood*," *David Bordwell's Website on Cinema* (blog), http://www.davidbordwell.net/blog/2019/08/09/when-worlds-collide-mixing-the -show-biz-tale-with-true-crime-in-once-upon-a-time-in-hollywood/.

20. Something similar but milder takes place in Tarantino's novelization *Once Upon a Time in Hollywood* (2021). The climax of the original film, a bloody home invasion, is alluded to early in the book and never dramatized or mentioned again. This invites the reader who has seen the movie to consider the possibility that the book's version of the story will have a new, unpredictable ending, which it does. I discuss the effects of this displacement in David Bordwell, "Once Upon a Time in Hollywood, Again: Tarantino Revises His Fairy Tale," *David Bordwell's Website on Cinema* (blog), http://www.david bordwell.net/blog/2021/07/10/once-upon-a-time-in-hollywood-again-tarantino-revises -his-fairy-tale/.

21. An earlier example of this rather rare strategy is *How Green Was My Valley* (1941), which ends with a reprise of family memories and never returns to the grim present.

22. Roland Barthes, *S/Z: An Essay*, trans. Richard Howard (New York: Hill and Wang, 1974), 10.

23. *Pulp Fiction: A Quentin Tarantino Screenplay* (New York: Hyperion, 1994), n.p.; see Bailey, *Pulp Fiction*, 30–37.

24. Stephen Hunter, "Tarantino's Twisted 'Pulp Fiction,'" *Baltimore Sun*, October 14, 1994, https://www.baltimoresun.com/news/bs-xpm-1994-10-14-1994287163-story.html.

25. See "plot twist," Google Books Ngram Viewer, https://books.google.com/ngrams.

26. Charles E. May, "A Summary of Short Story Criticism in America," in *Short Story Theories*, ed. Charles E. May (Athens: Ohio University Press, 1976), 5–9.

27. In keeping with the theory I set forward in "Three Dimensions of Film Narrative," story world twists should ultimately be seen as originating in narration as well because I believe that all story world information stems from the process of narration. See David Bordwell, "Three Dimensions of Film Narrative," in *Poetics of Cinema* (New York: Routledge, 2008), 96–100, 110. Strictly speaking, when the tornado strikes the character's home, the narration is likely to suppress background information about sources of the bad weather. But that is information that wouldn't normally be supplied unless it was somehow relevant to the character's immediate circumstances. In a science-fiction story, it might turn out that a supervillain opposed to the character has found a way to control the weather; in that case, the eventual revelation of the scheme would be a narrational twist. Here the distinction between story world twists and narrational ones is pragmatic, of use in distinguishing cases for the purpose of critical analysis.

28. For a philosophical analysis of subjective twists, see George Wilson, "Transparency and Twist in Narrative Fiction Film," *Journal of Aesthetics and Art Criticism* 64, no. 1 (Winter 2006): 81–95.

29. Jean-Claude Carrière, *The Secret Language of Film*, trans. Jeremy Leggatt (New York: Pantheon, 1994), 15.

30. Jeffrey Sconce, "Irony, Nihilism and the New American 'Smart' Film," *Screen* 34 (Winter 2002): 351.

31. Jason Mittell, *Complex TV: The Poetics of Contemporary Television Storytelling* (New York: New York University Press, 2015), 43.

13. Gone Girls: The New Domestic Thriller

1. David Fincher as quoted in Gina McIntyre, "Thrills, Chills for Gillian Flynn in Adapting 'Gone Girl,'" *Los Angeles Times*, September 5, 2014, https://www.latimes.com/entertainment/la-et-mn-ca-sneaks-gone-girl-20140907-story.html.

2. NPR Staff, "The Marriage Is the Real Mystery in *Gone Girl*," *NPR Morning Edition*, June 5, 2012, https://www.npr.org/2012/06/05/154288241/the-marriage-is-the-real-mystery-in-gone-girl.

3. Amy Gutman, "A Marriage Gone Missing," *Chicago Tribune*, July 28, 2012, https://www.chicagotribune.com/entertainment/books/ct-prj-0603-gone-girl-20120728-story.html.

4. Claude Chabrol, "Chabrol Talks to Rui Noguera and Nicoletta Zalaffi," *Sight and Sound* 40, no. 1 (Winter 1970–71): 6.

5. Juliet Annan and Maxine Hitchcock as quoted in Sarah Rainey, "*Gone Girl*—The Female Noir That Puts *Fifty Shades of Gray* in the Shade," *Telegraph*, March 27, 2013, https://www.telegraph.co.uk/culture/books/9956996/Gone-Girl-the-female-noir-that-puts-Fifty-Shades-of-Grey-in-the-shade.html.

6. I discuss this film's narration in David Bordwell, "Learning to Watch a Film, While Watching a Film," *David Bordwell's Website on Cinema* (blog), http://www.davidbordwell.net/blog/2021/07/02/learning-to-watch-a-film-while-watching-a-film/.

7. Mary Higgins Clark, *Where Are the Children?* (New York: Pocket, 2005), 143.

8. Laura Lippman, *Life Sentences* (New York: HarperCollins, 2009), 29, 12.

9. Quoted in Megan Labrise, "Laura Lippman," *Kirkus Reviews*, February 21, 2018, https://www.kirkusreviews.com/features/laura-lippman/.

10. Gillian Flynn blurb for *Sunburn*, https://www.faber.co.uk/9780571335664-sunburn.html.

11. Gillian Flynn, *Gone Girl* (New York: Broadway, 2014), 142.

12. Diane Waldman, "Horror and Domesticity: The Modern Gothic Romance Film of the 1940s" (PhD diss., University of Wisconsin–Madison, 1981), 5–56.

13. Flynn, *Gone Girl*, 415.

14. Sarah Weinman, ed., *Troubled Daughters, Twisted Wives: Stories from the Trailblazers of Domestic Suspense* (New York: Penguin, 2013); Sarah Weinman, ed., *Women Crime Writers: Eight Suspense Novels of the 1940s and 50s* (New York: Library of America, 2015). Several of Weinman's essays can be found on the *Women Crime Writers of the 1940s and 50s* website, http://womencrime.loa.org; and on the *CrimeReads* website, https://crimereads.com/author/sarahmweinman. See also Cullen Gallagher, "Women and Crime: An Interview with Sarah Weinman," *The Paris Review* (blog), October 19, 2015, https://www.theparisreview.org/blog/2015/10/19/women-in-crime-an-interview-with-sarah-weinman/.

15. Jane K, Cleland, *Mastering Suspense, Structure, and Plot: How to Write Gripping Stories That Keep Readers on the Edge of Their Seats* (New York: Writer's Digest, 2016), 21–31.

16. J. P. Delaney, "Pacing the Thriller: Believe Me," *Writing.ie*, July 30, 2018, https://www.writing.ie/resources/pacing-the-thriller-believe-me-by-jp-delaney/.

17. Heidi Pitlor as quoted in Nicki Porter, "Page Turner," *The Writer* 129, no. 8 (August 2016): 23.

18. Tina Jordan, "*The Daylight Marriage* by Heidi Pitlor," *Entertainment Weekly*, May 11, 2015, https://ew.com/article/2015/05/11/the-daylight-marriage-heidi-pitlor-review/.

19. Anonymous, "*The Wife Between Us*," *Kirkus Reviews*, September 28, 2017, https://www.kirkusreviews.com/book-reviews/greer-hendricks/the-wife-between-us/.

20. Heidi Pitlor as quoted in Porter, "Page Turner," 23.

21. On contemporary practitioners' recognition of the importance of multiple viewpoints, see Steven James, "Mapping the POV Minefield," *Writer's Digest* 96, no. 5 (July/August 2016): 44–47.

22. Len Deighton's *Only When I Larf* (1968) and Charles Willeford's *The Shark-Infested Custard* (1993) each alternates three first-person narrators. Jim Thompson's *The Kill-Off* (1957) presents an astonishing twelve.

23. Comments are at https://www.amazon.com/Into-Water-Novel-Paula-Hawkins/dp/0735211205/ref=sr_1_1?keywords=hawkins+into+the+water&qid=1554218346&s=books&sr=1-1.

24. Carrie Feron as quoted in Rachel Deahl, "Vying to Be the Next *Gone Girl*," *Publishers Weekly*, October 7, 2016, https://www.publishersweekly.com/pw/by-topic/international/Frankfurt-Book-Fair/article/71714-vying-to-be-the-next-gone-girl.html.

25. Sarah Pinborough, *Cross Her Heart* (London: HarperCollins, 2019), back cover.

26. Says editor Tess Calero: "I've read several articles examining the 'woman' and 'girl' trend. No matter how overdone, this seems to be working." See Cris Freese, "Seeking Thrills," *Writer's Digest* 98, no. 1 (October 2018): 35.

27. Allison Callahan as quoted in Deahl, "Vying to Be the Next *Gone Girl*."

28. Laura Lippman, *Dream Girl* (New York: HarperCollins, 2021), 401–2.

Conclusion: The Power of Limits

1. Christopher Nolan as quoted in Jeff Goldsmith, "The Architect of Dreams," *Creative Screenwriting* (July-August 2010): 21.

2. For studies of narrative, the most persuasive account I know remains Brian McHale, *Postmodernist Fiction* (New York: Methuen, 1987).

3. I discuss some of those traditions in David Bordwell, *Ozu and the Poetics of Cinema* (Princeton, NJ: Princeton University Press, 1988); and David Bordwell, *Planet Hong Kong: Popular Cinema and the Art of Entertainment*, 2nd ed. (Madison, WI: Irvington Way Institute, 2011).

4. Raymond Chandler, "The Simple Art of Fiction" (1946), in *Later Novels & Other Writings* (New York: Library of America, 1995), 979.

5. Announced in "Dealmaker: St. Martins," *Publishers Marketplace*, https://www.publishers marketplace.com/dealmakers/detail.cgi?id=2561.

6. Michele Campbell, *It's Always the Husband* (New York: St. Martin's, 2017); Mick Herron, *Slough House* (New York: Soho, 2020), 158.

7. Alexandra Alter, "Colson Whitehead Reinvents Himself, Yet Again," *New York Times*, September 8, 2021. See also David Bordwell, "Crime in the Streets and on the Page," *David Bordwell's Website on Cinema* (blog), http://www.davidbordwell.net/blog/2021/10/10/crime-in-the-streets-and-on-the-page/.

8. Jesse Green, "How Radical! How Broadway?," *New York Times*, September 8, 2021.

9. Philip Pullman, *Daemon Voices: On Stories and Storytelling* (New York: Vintage), 144.

10. Zola's essay "The Experimental Novel" follows this line, although for him the avant-garde pathway is toward Naturalism. See Emile Zola, *The Experimental Novel and Other Essays*, trans. Belle M. Sherman (New York: Cassells, 1893), 43–44.

INDEX

Page numbers in *italics* refer to images or captions.

FILM AND CULTURE

A series of Columbia University Press

Edited by John Belton

CPSIA information can be obtained
at www.ICGtesting.com
Printed in the USA
JSHW081452130223
PP12321400002B/2